# "JUDGE" McLANE
*His Life and Times*

*Circa 1960, Summer Outing at the Graf's.* Judge McLane surrounded by some of his law partners and spouses. From left: Stan Brown, John McLane, Jr., Ruthanne Raulerson, Judge, Harriet Mansfield, Ken Graf, and Bob Raulerson (on porch), Mary Graf (back). Foreground, Elisabeth McLane and Ann Middleton.

# "JUDGE" McLANE
## *His Life and Times*

and

## THE McLANE LAW FIRM
### *The First Fifty Years, 1919–1969*

John R. McLane, Jr.

PETER E. RANDALL PUBLISHER
Portsmouth, New Hampshire
1996

Design by Tom Allen

Peter E. Randall Publisher
Box 4726
Portsmouth, NH 03802

ISBN 0-914-339-58-3

# CONTENTS

APPENDICES

The Appendices include anecdotes, stories, and biographies that were not particularly germane to the text but that will enrich the reader's view of Judge, his family, and the firm.

# FOREWORD

Two world wars, extraordinary prosperity, unprecedented depression, unrivaled expansion of government power transformed the first half of the twentieth century. Histories of the era chart the course of these changes. John McLane's account of his father's life and times, 1886–1969, humanizes those changes. John uses "Judge's" diary, his own memories of his father, family and friends' recollections of Judge, records of the McLane law firm, and historical research to chronicle Judge's life as both witness and actor in this era. We see important public events in the period from a personal and family point of view.

Judge was present at the Russo-Japanese peace conference in Portsmouth, hosted in 1905 by his father, Governor John R. McLane. In 1914, stirred by social conscience to help the disadvantaged, Judge helped found the New Hampshire Children's Aid Society (now Child & Family Services of New Hampshire). He championed the cause of the Progressive Party to expand the role of government in ensuring fairness and social welfare. Judge's dedication to these ideals, influenced by his father and Teddy Roosevelt, shaped his role as a leader in the moderate wing of the Republican Party. John McLane's history is sprinkled with stories of his father's political friends such as Huntley Spaulding, Ernest Martin Hopkins, Frank Knox, Robert and John Bass, Louis Wyman, and especially John Gilbert Winant. This history provides a perspective on politics in New Hampshire, in particular the conflict between Progressives and Conservatives, not available in other sources.

Judge's professional and civic lives were intertwined. He began his legal practice in 1912 in the firm of Taggart, Burroughs & Wyman in Manchester. In 1919 he founded the McLane law firm, which became one of the leading firms in the state. An important contribution of this history is the rise of the McLane firm to prominence. Judge's legal career spanned Manchester's ascendance in textile manufacturing, the collapse of the Amoskeag Company in 1935, and the city's recovery before and after the Second World War. Judge was deeply involved with the life of his community as a political activist, trustee of the Manchester Savings Bank, founder of Amoskeag Industries, and as counsel to local businessmen such as Abraham Machinist, Sam Shaer, Frank Carpenter, and Norwin Bean. Through Judge's legal career we gain a new perspective of central events and leading individuals whose names are synonymous with that period of Manchester's history.

Besides being a public figure, civic leader, and prominent lawyer, we learn about Judge the man. We read about tennis, skiing, hiking, gatherings of family, such as the Bancrofts, and friends like law partner Ken Graf. John McLane's history portrays an era that was both innocent and exuberant. Judge's diary, John's memories, and the recollections of family create personalities where biographers might only describe people. Like an oral history, readers will get a feeling for the lives of Judge, his family, friends, and colleagues.

John McLane's account helps to fill a gap in the histories of the first half of this century. More than that, its stories and insights provide a unique perspective of that period. They are intimate, personal, based on Judge's diary, the memories of many people, and careful research. A labor of love, affectionately told, there is much to be gained from reading John McLane's history of his father's life and time.

*John Resch, Associate Professor of History,*
*University of New Hampshire at Manchester*

*Judge John R. McLane*, about 1940. Credit: Dartmouth College Library.

# Introduction

My primary purpose in writing the history of the McLane law firm is to provide its past, present, and future employees with the story of its founding and growth. As I wrote, however, a more compelling reason emerged—namely, to describe the interplay between the firm and its founder, "Judge" McLane, and the political, economic, and social life of the period 1919–1969. The "First Fifty Years" covers the period from the founding of the firm in 1919 by "Judge" John R. McLane and includes the years following his stroke in 1961, after which he was no longer active in the firm, until his death on April 21, 1969. "Judge" was a nickname conferred by his father, who, upon coming home from work, inquired of his wife, "How is the little judge today?" His father called him that because his son was so sober. This is the name by which John was known through elementary and secondary school, college, and graduate school. In adult life, he was known as "Judge" by his friends and by others who considered the name a title. The name conveyed his serious and proper demeanor.

"Judge" (the quotation marks will be omitted hereafter), who was born in Milford, New Hampshire, in 1886, founded the firm in February 1919 after returning from service with the War Department in Washington. He dominated the firm until the 1960s, when he no longer practiced law. He generated most of the business and made all the important decisions regarding the hiring of attorneys, their salaries, and the percentage the partners received. He was always generous to others, and everyone was happy to let his opinion stand. There were no written partnership agreements—just a spoken word and a handshake.

Writing this account serves two of my deepest interests—law and history. At Dartmouth, history was my major. One of the requirements was original historical research and a thesis. I selected the Social and Economic Development of Manchester from 1838 to 1858 as my topic and scrounged around the Manchester Historical Society, the city library, and the Baker Library in Hanover searching for source material. Writing about the firm now supplements this earlier attempt at Manchester's history, albeit fifty years later.[1]

I am aware that if I don't write about the firm, probably nobody will. I had talked with my law partner Harriet E. Mansfield at her retirement home about my proposed project, which she approved, and in which she indicated a great willingness to cooperate with me. She was a wealth of information about past clients and all of the firm's personnel and could have provided me with much valuable information because she was connected with the firm as secretary, law associate, and partner from 1925 to the 1980s. Unfortunately, I procrastinated too long, and she passed away before I got started. There are fewer and fewer people left who have any recollection of the early years. Another of my seniors, Ken Graf, was helpful in reading some of the manuscript and in recollecting events, cases, and people I did not know. However, there were a number of questions I never asked him before his death in 1991.

For source material, I am fortunate to have my father's diaries, which he started on January 1, 1898, when he was not quite twelve. In those early years, there were gaps, but starting on January 1, 1905, he used a five-year diary with five lines for each day and religiously kept up the entries until November 1, 1961, when he suffered a stroke. His right arm was paralyzed and he lost his power of speech. His wife, Elisabeth, kept up the diaries herself on trips and spent many evenings reading aloud from them recalling many happy memories of family, friends, places, and events in their rich life. After Judge's death in 1969, Elisabeth (affectionately known to the family as "Ibus") kept the journals close to her, sharing with family and friends reminiscences of the past. After Ibus' death in 1983, her children gave the diaries to the Dartmouth College Library, where they could be available for research. The college made bound photocopies for each of the children. The diaries contain entries of a personal nature—about family, friends, athletics, and weekend, holiday, and vacation events—as well as significant professional and political activity.

When I was growing up, my father always assumed that I would go, as he did, to St. Paul's School in Concord, New Hampshire, Dartmouth College, and Harvard Law School and then return to Manchester to practice law with him. He communicated his expectations in such a nondirective way that it really never occurred to me that there was any alternative. I always assumed that his choice had actually been my decision.

I acquired a considerable amount of knowledge about the "office" even before I was ten years old. On summer evenings sitting on the porch at Newfound Lake, or around a picnic campfire, or on trips to and from the White Mountains to go hiking or skiing,[2] my father would tell stories of clients and cases, which I found fascinating. In Manchester, I was permitted to sit quietly in the living room and listen to the adult conversation when my father and mother were entertaining. My memory of some of the details of those people and events augments the diary entries.

I have talked with present and past attorneys connected with the firm seeking their recollections of people and events. There are a number of histories of New Hampshire and Manchester from which I have gleaned information about the Amoskeag Manufacturing Company, other corporations, and the city. Published biographical reference works have helped in writing about clients and other principals. The filmed records of the Manchester newspapers have also been a valuable resource. William Rotch, former editor of the *Milford Cabinet,* and Elizabeth Lessard, librarian of the Manchester Historical Society, performed yeoman's service in my research for this book.

Yet there are large gaps in the history, particularly relating to the activities of the older partners, because many of them have passed away and because most of the old files and records of the firm were disposed of years ago.

Because much of the work of a law firm is routine, personal, and essentially uninteresting to others, I have attempted to select items that are interesting or have some historic significance. (And I have limited the history of the firm almost entirely to Judge's lifetime, because he influenced so much of the history of the firm and created the record in his diaries.)

I am greatly indebted to my late sister-in-law, Virginia S. Deane; my wife, Betsy; and our daughter Katie for critically reading and editing much of my material. Their input, comments, and suggestions were an invaluable aid to me. Elaine Snider and Margot Bergeron, my secretaries at different times, were very patient with me in correcting, printing, and assembling the many drafts of the manuscript. Two historians, the late Elting E. Morison, formerly a professor at the Massachusetts Institute of Technology, and John Frisbee, director of the New Hampshire Historical Society, after reading my initial work offered many helpful suggestions with respect to format, content, and style and encouraged me "to let loose" in writing to make the material more interesting and readable. I shall always be grateful to Professor Jack Resch of the University of New Hampshire at Manchester, who was infinitely patient in reading several versions of chapters and communicating his thoughts on how to improve the text. The McLane law firm made my time available to write this history and underwrote the publication cost.

A brief synopsis of Judge's law business and the growth of the McLane law firm follows by decade.

## 1910–1919

Judge finished his legal education and started the practice of law in Manchester with the Taggart firm, where he learned lawyering skills. He served in the War Department during World War I on labor negotiations. After the war, he returned to Manchester; unable to make a satisfactory arrangement with his old firm, he hung out his shingle as a solo practitioner. Thus in February 1919 in the Amoskeag Bank building the McLane law firm began.

## 1920–1929

Between 1920 and 1929 future partners joined the firm: Ralph Davis (1920), John Carleton (1925), as associates, and Harriet Mansfield (1925) as office manager. John Carleton also served as assistant attorney general and Ralph Davis as attorney general. The firm was very successful in handling much plaintiff litigation, and developed a reputation as top trial attorneys. During this period Judge was heavily involved with Progressive Republicans, particularly Governor Gil Winant and his business interest, Coyle Concord Oil Company, which was extremely active in Texas.

## 1930–1939

In this decade Ken Graf started as an associate. The depression was evident, leading to the bankruptcy of the Amoskeag Manufacturing Company and the sale of all its assets to the newly formed Amoskeag Industries, Inc., which Judge joined as clerk and general counsel. The firm represented a large number of newly arrived manufacturing concerns, frequently incorporating them in New Hampshire. Late in the decade, business recovered fast as the country moved out of the depression and closer to World War II. The firm bought 40 Stark Street, a four-apartment house that had been occupied by Amoskeag Mills foremen and renovated them into attractive offices. The bankruptcy of the Merrimack River Savings Bank and the criminal charges brought against its CEO, Arthur Hale, kept the office busy. Judge was the liquidating agent for the bank, and Ralph Davis, as attorney general, was the prosecuting officer in Hale's trial, which resulted in guilty verdicts on all charges. Judge was elected president of the Manchester Savings Bank, which became an increasingly important client. The firm's probate practice expanded with the settlement of a number of estates and the administration of many trusts.

## 1940–1949

Manchester's economic activity expanded because of the war in Europe and the growing U.S. defense buildup. Grenier Field, a U.S. Air Force base, was completed. The war slowed most courts to a crawl as law firms and the courts operated with reduced staffs, but after the peace in 1945 the pent-up demand of the depression and war years stimulated manufacturing and business picked up. Housing construction and mortgage banking thrived. Returning servicemen married and started families. The newly organized

*New Hampshire Sunday News*, through some excellent investigative reporting, uncovered irregularities in the office of state controller Stephen Story, which implicated Manchester contractor Donat Cote. After further investigation by the attorney general and professional consultants, indictments were returned against both men. Kenneth F. Graf was appointed special prosecutor and, with Arthur Greene and Stanley Brown, obtained convictions in a long criminal trial in Concord during the summer of 1949.

## 1950–1959

Judge spent more time on his directorships of the Boston & Maine Railroad, National Life of Vermont, Dartmouth College, and St. Paul's School. The Manchester Savings Bank was planning for its future with a new building and the retirement of Mr. Bean as CEO. The textile industry in the North, which tottered during the depression and was given a reprieve by World War II, came to an end. Many companies moved or were sold or liquidated, and the vacant plants, many functionally obsolete, became available for a new variety of smaller businesses. The same thing was happening to the New England shoe industry, in which Ken Graf was involved. The interstate highway system was inaugurated. Industrial parks, with large amounts of land for one-story manufacturing facilities and adequate parking, were built on Brown Avenue and at the airport.

## 1960–1969

Judge suffered a severe stroke in November 1961 that left him partially paralyzed and unable to speak. This terminated his active legal career. Nevertheless, he and Elisabeth traveled around the United States and Europe, including Greece, Italy, and France. They continued entertaining friends, particularly the partners of the firm for dinners and occasional parties for the whole firm at apple blossom time in May. Elisabeth read aloud to Judge from his diaries, enabling them to reminisce about their many enjoyable trips and friends. Judge died in November 1969. The office continued its steady growth for the next twenty-five years, becoming more specialized and organized into departments.

## Notes

1. My daughter Virginia, while working on a writing project at Central High School that involved the history of Manchester, perused the index of the Manchester Historical Society for material. That evening at home she reported that there was indexed a manuscript written by a "J. McLane" on the

early history of the Amoskeag Mills and Manchester. She asked me if I knew about it—was it any good and was the author a relative. She believed that, since the history was about the 1830s, it must have been written then, and was pleasantly surprised to discover she was addressing the author.

2. I suspect that telling stories was also a way to keep himself awake on those three-hour drives to and from Pinkham Notch in the White Mountains.

# ONE

# John R. McLane
1886–1918

The McLane law firm began in February 1919 when thirty-three-year-old Judge[1] McLane hung out his shingle as a single practitioner in his fourth-floor office at 875 Elm Street, the Amoskeag bank building at the corner of Elm and Hanover Streets, Manchester, New Hampshire.

Judge McLane's father, John McLane, was a successful self-made manufacturer who owned a cabinet shop in Milford. He was the proprietor from 1876 until the business was incorporated in 1907 as the McLane Manufacturing Company, of which he was the sole owner until his death in 1911. (See Chapter Six, Governor McLane and the McLane Manufacturing Company.) The company's principal product was post office equipment, which was sold throughout rural America. John McLane was a popular businessman and active in the community. He was president of the Souhegan National Bank from 1892 to 1911, a director of the Fitchburg and Milford Railroad, the Milford Building and Loan Association, and the New Hampshire Fire Insurance Company in Manchester. He became involved in politics as a Republican, serving two terms in the state legislature, from 1885 to 1887, and two terms in the senate, from 1891 to 1893, as president both terms (unprecedented). He was a delegate to the 1896 Republican National Convention,[2] which nominated McKinley and Roosevelt for president and vice president. In 1904 he was elected governor for a two-year term.

Judge was born on January 7, 1886, in Milford, the third of four children of John and Ellen McLane. He grew up in a household that bustled with business and politics. Judge went to the Milford elementary schools, a year of high school, and then St. Paul's School in Concord, New Hampshire, following in the footsteps of his older brother, Clinton. Judge was a scholar and an athlete. He achieved high academic honors and played football, baseball, and tennis. At Dartmouth, Judge was a top student, Phi Beta Kappa; he was manager of the football team and played on the baseball team and tennis squad. He was elected a Rhodes scholar, and after graduating in 1907 he spent two postgraduate years (1908–1909) at

*John McLane family*, in 1898. Seated, from left: Ellen Tuck McLane, Charles Malcolm McLane, John McLane. Standing, from left: Clinton Averill McLane, Hazel Ellen McLane, John R. McLane.

Magdalen College, Oxford University, studying European history, particularly the French Revolution. He entered Harvard Law School in the fall of 1909 and graduated three years later, having served as an editor on the *Harvard Law Review*, the highest honor possible.

Judge started his law practice with a number of pluses: top academic credentials; a prominent family background, which provided good name recognition; and a wide knowledge of and acquaintanceship with important people in the state through his father's political prominence.

Judge McLane was sworn in before the New Hampshire Supreme Court on June 28, 1912, and started practice with the Manchester law firm of Taggart, Burroughs & Wyman on August 1 with a "stipend" of fifty dollars a month. He did just about what any starting lawyer does today, namely, investigated accident cases, prepared a tenant eviction, drew declarations for writs, drafted a store lease, searched titles in the Registry of Deeds, et cetera. He spent one evening "arresting three Greeks about to skip town." One of his early clients in 1912 was Hudson Water Company, which later retained Judge when he started his own firm in 1919. Hudson's successor, Southern New Hampshire Water Company, remains a client of the firm in 1996. Judge notes in his diary many usual "firsts": deposition and "tried first case."

While working with the firm in Manchester, Judge lived with his mother in Milford to keep her company after his father's death in 1911. He commuted to work by the Manchester and Milford Railroad. (I remember him telling me that he rode the first and last train of that short-lived little railroad.) Judge was fond of Milford. During his years at Harvard Law School, he frequently took the train to Milford on Saturdays to "take" (conduct) the service in the Episcopal church, which had too small a congregation to afford even a regular part-time minister. He continued to do this during the period he lived with his mother. So far as I know, his parents were not Episcopalians and were not particularly religious. Judge's exposure to the Episcopal teachings at St. Paul's School made a lasting impression on him. He remained active in church affairs throughout his life.

Besides his practice Judge had an active athletic, social, and political life. He played semipro baseball in Nashua and other communities.[3] He continued his tennis playing in many tournaments in New Hampshire. He took up golf and even cricket and joined the YMCA to use the gym for exercise in the fall and winter. As a Boy Scout commissioner, he went on a Scout camping trip to Lake Massabesic and attended meetings of scoutmasters. Judge was active in the Progressive Party, formed by Teddy Roosevelt after splitting with the Republicans under William Howard Taft in 1912. Judge gave his first political speech in November of that year. At the end of the year he started to court his future wife. On December 30, 1912, he attended a leap-year cotillion in Concord with "Elizabeth" Bancroft, then a sophomore at Smith College, and her sister, Jennette, a Vassar graduate, who was with her fiancé, Asa Shiverick. Although the Bancroft and McLane families knew each other, this appears to have been Judge's first "date" with Elisabeth (the correct spelling of her name; he did not know how to spell her name correctly). However, his future mother-in-law misspelled Judge's family name. When the McLane family visited the Bancrofts at their summer place "Pasquaney" on Newfound Lake three years before, on October 10, 1909, she wrote "McLean" instead of "McLane" in the guest book.[4] Elisabeth does not appear to have been present on that occasion; she was probably attending school at Dana Hall in Massachusetts.[5]

A busy man, Judge continued to build his practice. In 1913 he wrote: "Tried my first case for defendant in assault, no time to prepare, did a poor job." This was followed by his first divorce case. He became involved in a variety of professional activities. With Mr. Louis Wyman, Judge had a hearing before the Public Utilities Commission on Hudson Water Company. On another occasion he went to Concord to have a talk with the

Streeter, Demond, Woodworth and Sulloway firm, at their request, about joining them; he turned them down. Attorney Ashton Thorpe in Manchester suggested that he and Judge join forces, but Judge declined. As a measure of his growing success, Judge's salary doubled to one hundred dollars a month.

Other opportunities came his way. Professor Colby of Dartmouth approached him about taking a position on the Dartmouth faculty. Although intrigued with the intellectual life and security of a college professorship, Judge felt that his new and growing career in law offered greater long-term opportunities, so he turned Colby down.

Judge's social life continued to grow. Obviously, the New Year's cotillion with "Elizabeth" had made a big impression. His diary records his courtship of "the Bancroft girl": January 28, 1913, "called on Elizabeth Bancroft"; February 3, "To Concord to masquerade, went as a Scottish Highlander"; February 21, "Concord, Snowshoe Club for supper with the Bancroft wedding party. Fine lot of girls, Elizabeth, Speck Flad" (Betsy Deane McLane's mother);[6] February 22, "Jennette and Asa Shiverick married"; March 29, "Concord, Elisabeth [notice the correct spelling now] Speck, Stuart Rand [cousin of Elisabeth] and I walked around Long Pond damming brooks, swinging from birches, musical evening"; June 18, "We became engaged + or - 2 a.m."; June 19, "Saw Dr. Bancroft and got his consent." Judge was twenty-seven and Elisabeth twenty-two when they decided to marry.

The young attorney continued to learn his trade by engaging in more facets of the law. He noted in his diary: January 2, 1914, "Wrote first will"; February 6, "1st Jury case, lost it"; October 14, "Argued my first Supreme Court case"; November 16, "First appearance in Federal Court, before Judge Aldrich." Judge also became interested in putting into practice some of the Progressive Party causes, specifically child protection. Judge, along with a statewide group of people interested in the condition of children, organized the New Hampshire Children's Protective and Placing Society (later New Hampshire Children's Aid Society, now Child & Family Services of New Hampshire). The new organization elected Judge's senior law partner, Sherman Burroughs, president. Judge became treasurer, a position he held for forty-four years. He participated in a State Conference of Charities and Corrections and a Child Welfare Conference and was named secretary of the Progressive Party Convention, which met in May, and the Progressive Party Caucus and Convention, which met in October. He was so imbued with the principles of the Progressive Party that he ran for representative on its ticket in Milford. He was defeated, which ended his career in elective political office. In the spring Judge started a naturalization class for about twenty immigrants, which continued into the fall. Despite his busy schedule, he accompanied Dr. and Mrs. Bancroft to Northampton,

Massachusetts, to attend the graduation of their daughter Elisabeth from Smith College in June 1914. At the end of the year, as a further example of his social involvement, he worked for the Belgian War Relief Fund, raising money for the victims of the German invasion of their country.

Judge was appointed probation officer to the Manchester municipal court, a part-time position, which brought in some welcome extra cash. He notes there were a lot of chicken thieves: "Met my chicken stealing boys; visited the parents, Rowell and Shea"; "had a hearing." The diary fails to disclose the disposition. There must have been spring fever, for in late March, seven little Polish boys were before the court for stealing from freight cars. The next day a "lot of little boys were in for playing around a new house, defacing it."[7] Apparently that complaint was discharged. During the year, Judge was admitted to the U.S. District Court, argued cases before the state supreme court, and was involved in a number of trials.

In December 1914, Dr. Bancroft was removed as superintendent of the New Hampshire State Hospital, a position he had held for more than twenty-five years. I don't know the details but believe it was political, since he was exonerated, and unanimously reinstated in April 1915. Judge notes that in January he was busy moving furniture from the superintendent's quarters at the hospital to the house across Pleasant Street, which Dr. Bancroft's father, Jesse, had purchased when he retired as superintendent of the hospital in the 1880s.

In the spring, Judge writes that he and Elisabeth went to the new Palace Theater on Hanover Street, which had been completed the preceding fall. They attended performances one or two times a month.[8] June was a big month. Wedding presents started coming in May and the wedding party arrived in early June. On the eleventh, there was a picnic supper at the Smiths' Hillside Inn at Newfound Lake, followed by dancing and singing. On the twelfth, Judge and Elisabeth were married on the porch of Pasquaney Lodge overlooking the lake. After a honeymoon of hiking and camping in the White Mountains around Waterville Valley, they assembled their possessions and moved into a rented house at 62 Monroe Street in Manchester.

As of January 1, 1916, Judge's financial arrangement was changed from a flat salary of one hundred dollars a month to a 12 1/2 percent share of the net profits. Judge tried a number of railway and electric streetcar accident cases with one or another of his senior partners, Mr. Burroughs or Mr. Wyman. In one crossing case, they obtained a verdict of $1,900 and in the other, $7,167. Judge was probably involved with the McLane Manufacturing Company,[9] which was having problems. Because the postal business was dropping off, the company was exploring other lines, such as phonograph cabinets. During this time the law firm moved "into the bank

*Pasquaney Lodge at Newfound Lake.* Purchased by Dr. Bancroft in 1908, and added to many times. Used extensively by the Shiverick and McLane families in the summers.

building" on the seventh floor of the new Merchants Bank building, 839 Elm Street, at the corner of Elm and Manchester Streets. The structure had been built following the 1914 fire that destroyed the Barton-Folsom department store building. In the 1970s the Merchants Bank building was demolished at the time of the expansion of the Amoskeag banks.

On February 19, 1916, Judge wrote: "Our first baby, John Roy Jr. born at 7 a.m. weighed 8 lbs, everything went finely." In accordance with the custom of the times, the birth occurred at home.[10] Later in February, Judge met in Boston with several Dartmouth alumni to discuss his nomination as an alumni trustee, a position to which he was subsequently elected. He notes attending a meeting of the Alumni Council with the trustees in New York City in April to consider the election of Ernest Martin Hopkins as president of Dartmouth College. In June, the National Guard was called up for duty on the Mexican border; the Milford troop, in which Judge's brother Clinton, an officer, was assigned, went first to Concord and in October to San Antonio. Clinton was followed in December by his wife, Dorothy, and their three children.

Judge spoke at public meetings from time to time on a variety of subjects, often social welfare or politics. In the November 1916 presidential

*Elisabeth and Judge*, wedding, June 12, 1915 at Pasquaney.

election, Judge notes on Election Day, "Hughes seems to have won," followed by the entry two days later, "Wilson won California and the Election."[11] During the summer there were mountains to climb around the lake and baseball in Manchester with the Doctors vs. the Lawyers. Judge caught and hit a single and a homer, but who won?

In January 1917, William Starr (father of the William Starr presently in the Wadleigh firm) joined the firm, which became Taggart, Tuttle, Burroughs, Wyman, McLane & Starr. It was probably the largest firm in the state at that time.[12]

At the end of March, Sherman Burroughs decided to run for Congress to fill a vacancy caused by the death of long-term congressman Cyrus Sulloway of Manchester, who was known as "The Tall Pine of the Merrimack." Burroughs' resignation from the firm precipitated discussion about creating a new partnership. Burroughs defeated P. H. Sullivan in late May and went to Washington.

Other concerns occupied Judge. The McLane Manufacturing Company continued to have its problems. Judge noted in March that "business is discouraging" and in April, "Crisis on hand. Looks like the

*Pasquaney about 1917–1918.* From left: Dr. Bancroft, John McLane, Jr., Judge McLane, Jane Shiverick, and Dick Harris, a friend.

end." But the company hung on into the mid-1930s. Judge worked on a number of litigated cases, on the excess profits tax, a wartime measure, and a war agency contract for shoes for G. P. Crafts Company. In December, he took the train to Sanbornville, where he stopped for the night with Judge Sawyer. The next day he rode the caboose to Ossipee, Conway, Intervale, and Bartlett on the case of Roberts vs. Conway Lumber Company. He gave a series of law lectures at the YMCA. In May, Judge started training me, at fifteen months old, for the legal profession: "Baby came down to the office for the first time." Judge was elected a trustee of St. Paul's School in Concord and clerk of the board, a position he held for thirty-five years, until 1952.[13]

In early February 1917, Judge reports a crisis with Germany; diplomatic relations were severed the next day. On April 2, President Wilson asked Congress for a declaration of war, which was voted the following day. About a week later, Judge and about twenty-five others started drilling on the recreation grounds and kept it up at least once a week, frequently more often. Judge enlisted in the State Guard in May, was made corporal in June, and received uniforms in September. Judge gave a number of four-minute speeches at the Palace Theater urging the purchase of War Bonds. In mid-December, he spoke at the Lebanon Town Hall on support for the Red

Cross; it was twenty degrees below zero and there was only a small gathering. Later that night his hotel room pipes burst. On December 29, he wrote: "Too cold to stay in house, so went to Concord" [to the Bancrofts'].

In January 1918, Judge fell down the stairs with me (I was not quite two), with no serious damage to either. He continued to give four-minute War Bond talks at the Palace Theater. January 28 was a "heatless Monday in court," an apparent effort to extend the weekend heat conservation measures. On January 31, the temperature hit twelve degrees below zero, the coldest temperature for that date on record. On February 5 Judge notes, "So cold that we closed the house & went to Concord." Judge had two cases against the street railway, one of which produced an $1,800 verdict; the other was lost. He also worked on the Crafts Company's tax returns.

In February, Judge received a telegram from Ernest Martin Hopkins (on leave from Dartmouth College, where he had recently been installed as president), assistant to the quartermaster general (War Department) in charge of labor relations, asking Judge to join him in Washington. Judge talked it over at lunch with "Hoppie" in Boston a few days later and decided to go. On March 20 he left for the capital.

In his new position Judge dealt with a number of labor problems in a variety of industries: a hat company in Reading, Pennsylvania; garment factories in East New York City and Brooklyn; textile mills in Lowell, Massachusetts; a spongers' union strike in New York City; motor transport during a street railway strike in Buffalo, New York; textile mills in Providence, Rhode Island; shoe shops in Brockton, Massachusetts; garment shops in Cleveland, Ohio; longshoremen in Buffalo and New York City; towboat men and longshoremen in New Orleans; and longshoremen in Savannah. There were jurisdictional disputes between the Garment Workers Union and the Amalgamated Clothing Workers Union. Judge visited raincoat shops, dress and suit houses, and garment shops to try to straighten things out. In addition he met with the War Labor Policies Board, military intelligence officers, and the National Adjustment Commission.

On November 11, 1918, the armistice was signed and the kaiser abdicated. On the eighteenth, Judge wrote: "Seems likely I can wind up by 12/1." A trip to San Juan, Puerto Rico, in December changed the timetable for getting out to December 31. Judge sailed for Puerto Rico on December 7, arriving on the twelfth. He had talks on longshoremen matters and also with the Cigar Makers Union. After business the group had a beautiful ride across the island to Central Aguirre, a sugar plantation. They visited some longshoremen's houses, returned to San Juan, and sailed back to New York. They arrived on December 23 in time for Judge to head to Concord for Christmas with the family. Then he returned to Washington on the twenty-sixth to wind up matters by the thirtieth and came home on the thirty-first, having completed his war service.

While Judge was in Washington, he found classmates and acquaintances to socialize with and went to the theater many times. Elisabeth and I came down for part of the time. Life didn't sound all that bad.

# Notes

1. See page 1 for origin of the nickname "Judge."

2. This was the year of William Jennings Bryan's famous "Cross of Gold" speech at the Democratic National Convention.

3. Judge, with the most education on the Milford team, was elected treasurer, collected the income, and made the disbursements. At the end of the season, Judge divided the surplus among the players. It was only after he had paid everyone off that he realized that he had forgotten to count himself, so he received nothing for all his work.

4. From the guest book of Pasquaney Lodge.

5. Appendix B.1, The Bancroft Family.

6. Appendix A.2, The H. Towner Deane Family.

7. I must admit to playing in "new houses" that were under construction around our neighborhood when I was about five. We ran around and probably threw lumber down stair openings to hear the loud noises, but I don't remember any defacing. We were lucky nobody fell down and got hurt.

8. The Palace served through the 1920s as a legitimate stage and vaudeville theater for shows traveling the circuit and showed movies as they became popular. After World War II, outdoor theaters and home TV caused the closing of many inner-city movie houses. In the 1960s, the Palace was purchased by a group interested in New Hampshire College, then housed in the same building, which used the theater until the college moved to a fine new campus on North River Road. The seats in the theater were removed and the property was used for light manufacturing and storage for grocery products until the building was put on the market in about 1971. A nonprofit group, the Palace Theater Trust (in which I was very active), purchased the theater and restored it to its former glory. It reopened with a full season of activity in November 1974 and has been very active since then.

9. Chapter Six, Governor John McLane and the McLane Manufacturing Company.

10. All subsequent children and grandchildren were born in maternity wards of hospitals. Later, both great-grandchildren, Derek and Rebecca McLane, were born in a midwifery and at home, respectively, in England.

11. Election returns were not instantaneous as they are today.

12. James P. Tuttle had been a member of the firm before Judge joined it in August 1912 but resigned to become attorney general from 1912 to 1917. He then rejoined the firm, retaining his seniority position.

13. Judge was succeeded by his son John (this author) who served as trustee and clerk for thirty-one years. In 1983, he was succeeded by his brother Malcolm, who served until 1993. Then Malcolm's daughter Annie McLane Kuster, who had attended the summer Advanced Studies Program, was elected assistant secretary to the board.

# TWO

# Background
### 1870–1920

This history deals with the fifty-year period from 1920 to 1970, which includes the final years and the demise of the Amoskeag Manufacturing Company, the principal industry of Manchester. It also covers the transition from a predominantly textile and shoe town to a city with a broader business base, including electronics manufacturing and financial and professional services. The city became a center for the distribution of goods in northern New England. This brief review of the preceding history, highlighting some of the major developments, will assist in understanding the period from 1920 to 1970.

## POPULATION

In the 1830s the Amoskeag Manufacturing Company bought some 3,000 acres of land on both sides of the Merrimack River to build canals, mill buildings, and housing for its employees. The city of Manchester was not incorporated until 1846, at which time the population had grown from 3,000 in 1840 to about 10,000 people, almost entirely Anglo-Saxon and Protestant. Manchester, since the 1830s, has been the largest city in the state. During the period from 1850 to 1930, the population grew as follows.

|  | MANCHESTER | | NEW HAMPSHIRE | |
|  | Population | Growth Rate, % | Population | Growth Rate, % |
| --- | --- | --- | --- | --- |
| 1850 | 14,000 | | | |
| 1870 | 23,500 | 60 | | |
| 1880 | 32,000 | 36 | | |
| 1890 | 44,000 | 37 | 376,530 | |
| 1900 | 57,000 | 29 | 411,588 | 9 |
| 1910 | 70,000 | 22 | 430,572 | 4 |
| 1920 | 78,000 | 11 | 443,000 | 2 |
| 1930 | 77,000 | -1 | | |

Whereas the cities and towns having waterpower grew with new industries, agriculture declined as the farm folk abandoned New England for the more fertile lands in the Midwest and Far West; thus the state population barely increased.

The Scottish, Irish, and French started to immigrate to Manchester in the 1850s. The Germans and other northern Europeans began arriving in the 1860s after political upheavals in Europe. Beginning in the 1870s, there were immigrants from these areas as well as from Greece, Poland, and the Ukraine. According to the 1920 census, about 99 percent of the population of Manchester was white (80 percent were native white and 20 percent were foreign white); 50 percent were of native parentage, 19 percent were of foreign parentage, and 10 percent were of mixed parentage. Also in 1920, of the foreign born, 44 percent were French Canadian, 11 percent Greek, 10 percent Irish, 7 percent Polish, 6 percent other Canadians, 4 percent German, 3 percent English, 3 percent Swedish, 2.5 percent Russian, and 2 percent Scottish. In a more recent census (1950), the larger foreign-born groups in Manchester were from French-speaking Canada, 7,500; Greece, 1,300; Poland, 1,200; other than French-speaking Canada, 1,000; Ireland, 750; Great Britain, 700; and Germany, 500.[1]

During the period from 1870 to 1920, the ethnic diversity of the city was much more evident than now. The French Canadians were by far the largest ethnic group. Most of them lived on the West Side, where their children could attend parochial schools taught in French. Sales personnel in stores were frequently required to be bilingual. Many clubs, a few of which survive today, located on downtown side streets served liquor and were strongly ethnic in their clientele. Certain center-city areas, once predominantly Anglo-Saxon, changed as the original inhabitants followed the new electric streetcar (trolley) routes to the recently developed tracts where they built larger homes. As the original Anglo-Saxon population moved out, the newly arrived Irish moved in and dominated the area from the 1850s to the 1890s, only to be replaced by the recently immigrated Poles and Greeks.

These ethnic centers were important when the society was pedestrian and relied on public transportation. Today, the automobile makes it easier for people to visit with one another regardless of residence, so the distinct ethnic neighborhoods are less noticeable. However, there are still a number of Greek coffeehouses in the Spruce–Chestnut Street area. Hispanics and Asians who arrived in the 1970s introduced yet more ethnic diversity.

## ENERGY

The primary source of energy for the mills in the 1830s and 1840s was the waterpower generated by the fifty-two-foot drop at the Amoskeag Falls of the Merrimack River. Two canals channeled the water from the river to penstocks, or large tubes, under the mills on the lower side of the canals. The water fell twenty-five feet, hitting turbine blades that turned large shafts linked by leather belts to other shafts on each floor. The shafts transferred the power all over the mill, ultimately to each individual machine. The spent water from the upper canal exited into the lower canal and was used once again as it dropped another twenty-five feet back into the river through more penstocks under the buildings lining the lower canal.

Prior to the 1840s, wood had been the major fuel used in home stoves and fireplaces for residential cooking and heating. In the late 1840s, steam power became available when coal from Pennsylvania and West Virginia arrived by rail. Steam was used in the mills to supplement the hydropower as well as for heat and process steam (used in manufacturing processes such as washing and scouring, and in the dye house). Steam power also led to the generation of electricity by the first electric company in 1883, which provided energy for mills, stores, homes, and streetlights. By 1891, Manchester was acclaimed as "one of the best lighted cities in the United States which is perhaps one reason why it is also one of the most orderly."[2]

About 1900, several competing electric companies were consolidated into the Manchester Traction Light and Power Company. In the 1920s, this company merged with others in the state to create Public Service Company of New Hampshire (PSNH). The Amoskeag Manufacturing Company, following a policy of self-sufficiency, built the Amoskeag dam and hydroelectric station in 1922. The Amoskeag Manufacturing Company owned most of the water and flowage rights up and down the Merrimack River and its tributaries within ten miles of Manchester to prevent other mills from being built that would compete for Amoskeag's labor market. Amoskeag Industries, Inc., acquired all of the waterpower, electrical generating plants, and distribution system of the Amoskeag Manufacturing Company as part of the Amoskeag bankruptcy sale in 1936 and immediately resold them to PSNH, as previously agreed to.

The Manchester Gas Light Company manufactured coal gas in 1850 and distributed it in pipes, primarily for the gas mantel lamps installed in the mills to increase production by extending the working hours during the short days of winter. Coal gas was used secondarily for home lighting. The original ten miles of gas transmission main in 1852 were extended to 125 miles with 15,000 customers in later years. Natural gas became available after World War II.

## WATER AND SEWERAGE

When the Amoskeag Manufacturing Company commenced operations in the late 1830s, there was no town or city to build streets and provide other infrastructure services. The company built and maintained the streets between Elm and Canal from Granite to Dow Streets. This continued into the 1920s, when the squeeze on corporate profits became severe as the result of the six-month strike and increased competition from the southern mills. The company requested the city to assume responsibility for these streets, but the city refused. The company petitioned the superior court to lay out the streets as public ways and force the city to maintain them; the company won the case.

Amoskeag retained title to this area and built tenements for the "operatives" and other employees of the mills. Until a municipal sewer service was installed, each tenement had its own holding tank located near the back alley. The "honey wagon" came at night to empty the tanks. Children were admonished to be good, otherwise "the honey wagon man will get you."

Water for fire-fighting purposes came from a group of natural ponds that were given to the city by Amoskeag and are now city parks, namely, Merrimack Common and parks on Hanover and Bridge Streets. The Amoskeag Manufacturing Company, prior to the incorporation of the city in 1846, developed its own water system, pumping from Lake Massabesic to its own reservoir (two city blocks bounded by Oak, Harrison, Russell, and Blodgett Streets). The water flowed by gravity in pipes laid in easements in city streets to the mills and tenements for fire protection, process water, and sanitary use. The Manchester Water Works was organized in 1871 as a municipal corporation and acquired about 4,000 acres of land around 2,500-acre Lake Massabesic, with its excellent water. The water works built a pumping station, reservoirs, and a distribution system throughout the city. The Manchester Water Works provided city water to Amoskeag after the Amoskeag system was discontinued following the 1936 bankruptcy.

## TELEPHONE

There were a few telephones and private telephone lines prior to 1879. It was not until 1882 that the first directory, with 375 regular patrons, was published by the Bell Telephone Company.

## TRANSPORTATION

Prior to 1875, people moved around in Manchester on foot or by horse-drawn vehicle. Good intercity train service was available. The only paved streets were in the downtown and mill areas, where paving blocks of granite were used. Streets in residential areas were dirt until the expanded use of macadam (tar) in 1908.[3] Cement was used for major highways beginning in 1918.

Horse-drawn trolleys on tracks made their appearance on Elm Street in 1877 and expanded from the downtown area in all directions as the city grew. This mode of transportation rapidly became obsolete as the electric trolley came into favor starting in 1895, when the Manchester Horse Company was acquired by the Manchester Traction Light and Power Company.

Home construction followed the trolley lines, and real estate prices dropped off as the distance from the trolley line increased. Trolleys were the dominant method of public transportation in the city until the auto and buses replaced them; the last trolley ran in 1940. (I remember taking the trolley to go downtown to the YMCA, to my violin lesson, or to visit my father's office. In the summer, I took the open trolleys to go swimming at Pine Island Park. We, the children, sang lustily as we rode down Elm Street through the middle of town and loved to see all the people turn and stare at us.) There were what were known as "interurban" lines to Concord, Nashua, and Goffstown, with further connections. For $1.26, one could go from Concord to Portsmouth, 102 miles via Manchester, Nashua, Pelham, Haverhill, Amesbury, Salisbury, Seabrook, and Hampton. It was also possible to go by trolley from Wilmington, Delaware, to Waterville, Maine, with only three breaks: the Delaware River, the Hudson River, and the Piscataqua River at Portsmouth! Ferries took passengers across the rivers.

Automobiles were just making their appearance in 1900. In 1892, J. Frank Duryea of Springfield, Massachusetts, demonstrated a single-cylinder gasoline-engine-propelled "horseless carriage." In 1895, there were only four operable automobiles in the nation. The Stanley Steamers were produced in Newton, Massachusetts, in 1897. The steering wheel was introduced in 1900. The first mass-produced car, the Oldsmobile, appeared in 1901, along with the first license plate.

Judge's father, Governor John McLane, owned an auto in 1905. Judge wrote in his diary on July 6, 1905: "To Boston in the Machine." The photos of the Treaty of Portsmouth celebrations in the summer of 1905 show many new (antique looking to us) cars. At that time, there were 704 car and truck state registrations, which grew to 13,449 by 1925. By 1908, the Model T had been introduced by Henry Ford, and the General Motors Company was incorporated.[4]

Judge and Elisabeth acquired their first car, a Maxwell, about 1925. Prior to that they used trolley cars within the city and trains for trips to Boston and elsewhere. Most people employed in Manchester lived within walking distance of their jobs and stores. The towns of Bedford, Goffstown, Candia, Auburn, and Londonderry were farm communities then rather than residential locations for workers from Manchester. They didn't become suburban communities until the 1930s.

Until the 1920s, all delivery wagons for milk, ice, wood, coal, and such

*Cygnet Boat Club about 1912*, Manchester. Credit: Manchester (N.H.) Historic Association Photo Archives.

*Cygnet Boat Club*, tennis courts during match play, about 1920. Jack Nelson in right back court, Ed. B. Stearns and sons Bill and Dick on bench. Credit: Manchester (N.H.) Historic Association Photo Archives.

were horse drawn. During the 1920s and 1930s, there was a shift to trucks, but it was not until the late 1930s that horses were a rarity on Manchester streets.

The Nashua and Lowell Railroad opened a rail line to Nashua in 1838, and the Concord Railroad Company continued it to Manchester in 1841, and thence to Concord. The Northern Railroad extended the tracks to Franklin in 1846 and to Lebanon in 1847. The Boston, Concord and Montreal Railroad erected tracks up the Pemigewasset and Baker River valleys to Wells River in 1844. In the meantime, the Concord Railroad Company controlled the Manchester and Lawrence Railroad, which in 1849 completed the line between those two cities. So by 1870, New Hampshire was nearly crisscrossed with railroads radiating from Boston. In 1840 in New Hampshire there had been only 22 1/2 miles of railroad track, but this expanded to 893 miles by 1874, 1,000 miles by 1880, and a peak of 1,200 miles in 1920.

The early railroads were built by small companies with substantial capital raised from local communities. Many of these smaller lines went by the numerous lakes and ponds of southern New Hampshire, where, in the winter, blocks of ice, cut and packed in sawdust, were loaded onto freight cars and hauled to the port of Boston for shipment in schooners and other vessels to southern ports in the United States, the Caribbean islands, and Central and South America for use in refrigeration.

In the 1870s, 1880s, and 1890s, there were many railroad consolidations, with the Boston & Maine Railroad (B&MRR) involved in bitter legislative battles over corporate charters, legislative control, regulation, and taxation.[5]

By 1920, the railroad companies had started to abandon their less profitable lines that had lost riders because of the increased use of autos, buses, and trucks. The first interstate bus service commenced in 1923. In order to protect the railroads, the Public Utilities Commission (PUC) granted a bus franchise only if the area was no longer served by the railroad.

It was not until 1934 that the first scheduled commercial passenger airline service was started among Boston, Manchester, Concord, and Burlington by the airline formed by the B&MRR and the Central Vermont Railroad.

During this period, the railroads reached their zenith and then started a long decline, and electric street railways came and went. The automobile, bus, truck, and airplane rose to dominate transportation for the rest of the century.

## ENTERTAINMENT

As Manchester grew, theaters were built downtown. One of the first was the 1,200-seat Strand on Hanover Street, built about 1885 as an opera house although it was used for vaudeville and lectures rather than opera. The stage was shallow and there were only minimal facilities for flying scenery and drapes. In later years it was used as a movie house; it survived until the late 1980s, when it was vacant and burned down. The blue-and-white-tile entrance survived and still bears the impressive name STRAND clearly visible from the sidewalk.

The Park was a vaudeville house at the corner of Spring and Elm Streets. Unused for many years, it stood where the Hampshire Plaza is now located. The Palace was built in 1915 as an excellent legitimate stage theater with all the contemporary facilities of an urban theater. It was a part of the Keith circuit and received prepackaged shows, vaudeville, touring stage shows, and, later, movies.

Movies were first shown about 1910, and soon thereafter movie houses were built without stage facilities. By 1920, theaters were advertising in the *Manchester Leader* (evening paper): the Eagle, in the block at the northwest corner of Elm and Bridge (torn down in 1989); the Crown, on Hanover Street (converted in the 1970s to house Child & Family Services); and the Star (location unknown). There were other outlying theaters such as the Empire in East Manchester and one on Granite Street near Granite Square. The Art Deco State, on Elm Street where Wall Street is now located, was the last theater built just before the depression. Its gaudy stone face of the theatrical muse was moved to the Dana Center at St. Anselm College after the theater was torn down in the 1960s to make room for the Manchester Bank.

There are numerous references in Judge's diary to the times he and Elisabeth attended performances at the Palace. The Palace was abandoned in the late 1960s; in 1974 it was acquired by a nonprofit group that restored it to contemporary standards. The theater now (1996) operates a busy twelve-month season.

There were a number of amusement parks accessible by trolley car, such as Pine Island Park in Goff's Falls, near the present airport. The park had a roller-coaster and other rides and amusements as well as swimming and boating on a small man-made pond. Trolley cars ran out to Lake Massabesic, where there was a dance pavilion and boats, including an excursion steamer. In addition, there was the Uncanoonuc Incline Railway, accessible by street railway from Manchester. Developers aspired to have a large colony of summer cottages at the summit. In spite of the promotional enthusiasm of Henry Laxon, president of the railway, few cottages were ever built. With a pavilion for dancing and a dining hall, Uncanoonuc Mountain was a popular place to visit on weekends, but the buildings burned in a spectacular fire visible all over Manchester on a dark evening about 1920. (I remember seeing the flames from our house on Carpenter

Street.) The incline railway was used for skiing before the war; it was accidentally burned about 1945 and was never repaired.

The Cygnet Boat Club was located on the west bank of the Merrimack River just above the Amoskeag Bridge; from the 1880s until World War I, it provided rowing shells, rowboats, and canoes for rent. Six tennis courts were added in the early 1900s and two squash courts and a badminton court about 1930. It was a very active place, hosting many regional and state tennis tournaments, until the 1936 flood washed away the courts, leaving a fifteen-foot-deep trench. The club never recovered.[6]

The city had several parks for both active and passive recreation. Textile Field, now Gill Stadium, at the corner of Valley and Maple Streets was a stadium with covered seats. It was built by the Amoskeag Manufacturing Company for its employees and was a popular athletic field, the scene of many games between the Doctors and the Lawyers. Judge played regularly for the Lawyers. Across the street were the circus grounds, where traveling circuses came about once a year. There were several parks with ponds, good for skating and some large enough for swimming, such as Dorrs Pond, in the northern part of the city, and Nutts Pond, off South Willow Street.

There were many male-oriented social clubs, catering to national groups such as German, Greek, Polish, Ukrainian, and French. These clubs frequently functioned as hiring halls for work in the textile mills or the shoe shops. The German club, Turn Verein, was a gymnasium and a school for German language. Although the United States is called the "melting pot," many religious and national groups clung fiercely to their own cultures, even to the point of preventing children from playing with other groups or marrying outside their own.

# Notes

1. "Manchester, 'The Queen City,'" The Manchester Chamber of Commerce, 1955.

2. James Duane Squires, *The Granite State of the United States*, Vol. II, p. 461.

3. Appendix A.1, Memories.

4. Hobart Pillsbury, *New Hampshire, A History* (New York: Lewis Historical Publishing Co, Inc., 1927) Vol. II, p. 578.

5. The novel *Coniston* by Winston Churchill was written about this turbulent era.

6. See Chapter Eleven, Interlude 1930–1939.

# THREE

# Lawyers and Office Space

In this section, the comings and goings of lawyers in the McLane law firm are noted as well as various changes in office location.

Judge returned to Manchester on December 31, 1918, having finished his work for the War Department in Washington. During January 1919, he was approached by attorney P. A. Sullivan to enter practice with him in Manchester. Later that month Judge went to Hanover at the behest of Dartmouth president Ernest M. Hopkins, for whom he had worked in the War Department, to talk with him and Professor Dixon about taking a professorship in economics. Judge turned down the position because of his growing family and the greater potential of income from a law practice. He anticipated returning to his old firm, but after a disturbing number of sessions with respect to partnership percentages of participation, he learned from General Tuttle on February 17 that "it was no go with the firm." On the eighteenth, Judge traveled from Concord, where his family had been staying with his in-laws, the Bancrofts, while he was on duty in Washington. That day Judge rented offices (rooms 418 and 419) on the fourth floor of the Amoskeag bank building at 875 Elm Street. He ordered stationery, moved in furniture, hired a secretary, mailed out announcement cards, and recorded: "Feel as if I were really in practice."

Judge noted in his diary on April 1, 1919, "Ralph Davis coming in to work for me," and on April 7, "Ralph W. Davis came in office to work for me." Davis studied for the bar, passed the exams in 1920, and became an associate with Judge. Ralph was twenty-nine, a 1913 graduate of Dartmouth College and later of the Yale Law School, and had served in the U.S. Navy in World War I.

The year 1922 started off with the formation of the firm McLane & Davis. They took additional adjoining space in the bank building. During 1921 and 1922 the firm picked up a substantial amount of litigation representing plaintiffs and was reasonably successful. It was a general observation in the profession that law firms that did a substantial amount of defense work for insurance companies were not attractive to plaintiffs, who tended toward more flamboyant, colorful, and hard-hitting attorneys. Whereas Judge was the theoretician—the "law man"—Ralph Davis was rapidly acquiring a reputation as a forceful trial lawyer for plaintiffs. Now well established with the firm, Ralph married Marion Sullivan on November 18, 1922.

In 1923 Judge had a call from Mr. Tuttle, senior partner of his old firm, asking him back. Judge refused, undoubtedly because in the three years he had been practicing, he had built up a good business and was expanding. He was also probably concerned about Ralph Davis, who was developing into an able plaintiff's trial lawyer, and wondered how he would get along with Louis Wyman, who was also becoming known as a top defense lawyer. My recollection from talking to my father is that Ralph was not invited into the Tuttle firm. Judge's diary doesn't speculate, just recites the offer and his refusal. Ralph Davis and Louis Wyman had some grand battles before juries in later years.

In the summer of 1925, Winthrop Wadleigh worked as a summer intern while at Harvard Law School. His family and Judge's were old friends in Milford. Winthrop had graduated from Dartmouth. He practiced with the Wyman firm (Wyman, Starr, Booth, Wadleigh & Langdell, later known as the Wadleigh firm) for many years. John P. Carleton, a native of Hanover and a Dartmouth graduate, arrived as an associate in October 1925 from England, where he had been a Rhodes scholar studying law. The firm was getting very busy and needed a competent office manager. Harriet Mansfield started her lifetime legal career in 1925 as secretary-bookkeeper and soon became office manager. Later she studied law by correspondence course, passed the bar in 1931, and continued as an associate until 1944, when she became a partner. She continued in active practice until the early 1980s.

In 1928 John Carleton was appointed assistant attorney general by Governor Huntley Spaulding, a full-time job under the part-time attorney general. The firm moved from the fourth to the ninth floor of the Amoskeag bank building as more space became available.

On May 1, 1929, Ralph Davis became attorney general, a part-time job, having been appointed by Governor Charles Tobey. John Carleton returned from his assistant attorney general's post on September 1, when the new firm of McLane, Davis & Carleton was formed. Peter Woodbury joined the firm as an associate and in 1932 was appointed as a judge on the superior court, one of the youngest ever at age twenty-nine. Peter subsequently became a supreme court judge and then was appointed to the First Circuit Court by President Roosevelt.

So as the decade of the '20s ended, the firm of McLane, Davis & Carleton had three partners, one associate, and Miss Mansfield studying for the bar.

In the 1930s, others joined the firm. The office moved to larger space on the tenth floor. Kenneth F. Graf arrived as an associate, having worked

*40 Stark Street.* Home of the McLane law firm from 1936 to 1992. Originally a four-apartment tenement row house for the families of foremen of the Stark Mills.

in the office summers while at law school; he became a partner in 1936. Dudley Orr graduated from Harvard Law School in 1933. Although half the class could not find jobs because of the depression, Orr came into the office at twenty-five dollars per week and in 1936 left to become an assistant attorney general. Bill Phinney, one of the founders of the firm of Sheehan, Phinney, Bass & Green, came in 1936 for a year.

In the spring of 1936, when the Amoskeag Manufacturing Company filed for bankruptcy, many parcels of the Amoskeag real estate became available to purchase at reasonable prices. The firm was growing out of its ninth-floor space in the Amoskeag bank building and no long-term leases were available. Judge records in late March that the firm was considering buying a site for a new office and, about ten days later, that 40 Stark Street had been bought from the trustees in bankruptcy. The building was a handsome brick four-apartment row house, originally for foremen of the Stark Mills, built in 1838. At first Mrs. Elizabeth Manning of Boston was considered as the architect, but Judge writes in late April that the firm was "shifting to Fred Larson on remodeling." (Larson was the architect for Dartmouth College.) Judge comments in his diary on October 20, "Busy days getting new building ready"; on November 1 and 2, "Moving"; on the sixth, "Getting settled in office"; and on the twelfth, "The firm had a dinner in Boston to celebrate." George Nelson, William Harrington, and Perkins Bass arrived as associates in 1938 and 1939.

In 1941 this author passed the bar exams, was sworn in, and started practice in August, having spent summers at the firm while in Harvard Law School. In July, Ralph Davis had a sudden heart attack and was taken to the hospital. His activities were greatly reduced after that.

World War II took its toll. In 1942, associates Perkins Bass and I left for the various services, to be followed by John Carleton in 1943 and George Nelson and Ken Graf in 1944. Robert Bingham and Arthur A. Greene arrived the same year to fill some of the gaps, and John Carleton returned.

On April 7, 1944, Judge notes that he and Ralph Davis had completed twenty-five years of practice together. Shortly thereafter, Bill Phinney, friend and former associate in 1936, a little homesick toward the end of the war, called Judge from Africa. Many of Bill's friends were quite accustomed to receiving his calls at any time of the day or night from any part of the world to talk about old and better times. Ken Graf left for the judge advocate general (JAG) school just ahead of the draft on April 25. On the next day Harriet Mansfield was asked to become a partner on May 1. Later in the month, I dropped in the office while on twenty-four-hour leave from the Navy before sailing for the Mediterranean. John Carleton visited in September en route to a new assignment in Ann Arbor before being released from active duty at the end of the year. Ken Graf received his JAG commission in September.

In early 1945, Ralph had a "shock," a continuing problem of his high blood pressure, and was taken to the Elliot Hospital. Ken Graf returned in the summer and Bob Bingham, who had filled in for a year, left. I returned in October; Stanley M. Brown, fresh out of the Navy, joined the associate ranks in November. Both Perkins Bass and George Nelson, who had been associates before the war, decided to practice elsewhere.

On November 1, 1948, Arthur Greene, Stanley Brown, and I became partners.

The following joined the firm as associate (A), summer associate (SA), or partner (P), or left (X) or died (D) as indicated.

Prior to 1930: John R. McLane (Judge), 1919 (solo practitioner), 1922 (P), 1961 (retired), 1969 (D); Ralph W. Davis, 1921 (A), 1922 (P), 1945 (retired), 1951 (D); John P. Carleton, 1925 (A), late 1960s (retired), 1977 (D).

In the 1930s: Harriet E. Mansfield (secretary 1925–1931), 1931 (A), 1944 (P), 1986 (D); Peter Woodbury, 1929 (A), 1932 (X); Kenneth F. Graf, 1932 (A), 1936 (P), 1991 (D); Dudley Orr, 1934 (A), 1936 (X); William Phinney, 1936 (A), 1937 (X); George Nelson, 1938 (A), 1944 (X); William Harrington, 1938 (A), 1940 (X); Perkins Bass, 1939 (A), 1942 (X).

In the 1940s: John R. McLane Jr. (this author) 1941 (A), 1948 (P); Arthur A. Greene, Jr. 1944 (A), 1948 (P), 1980 (X);[1] Robert Bingham, 1944 (A), 1946 (X); Stanley M. Brown, 1945 (A), 1948 (P), 1974 (X).[2]

In the 1950s: Malcolm McLane, 1951 (SA); Robert A. Raulerson, 1952 (A), 1956 (P), 1994 (D); Wesley Whitney, 1952 (A), 1955 (X); Arthur Mudge, 1955, (SA); Larry Spellman, 1956 (A), 1958 (X); Jack B. Middleton, 1956 (A), 1962 (P); G. Marshall Abbey, 1958 (A), 1965 (X); David Nixon, 1959 (A), 1961 (X).

In the 1960s: G. Peter Guenther, 1960 (A), 1966 (P), 1986 (D); John A. Graf, 1961 (A), 1968 (P), 1994 (D); Charles A. DeGrandpre, 1961 (A), 1968 (P); Clifford Moody, 1963 (A), 1964 (X); John T. Franklin, 1964 (A), 1965 (X); Robert O. Kelley, 1964 (A), 1966 (X); James R. Muirhead, 1966 (A), 1972 (P), 1995 (X); Peter B. Rotch, 1966 (A), 1974 (P); Jon Groetzinger, 1967 (A), circa 1969 (X); Arthur G. Greene, 1967 (A), 1974 (P); John P. Griffith, 1966 (A), 1972 (X); Robert Upton II, 1968 (A), 1972 (X); Charles Douglas III, 1969 (A), 1971 (X).

In the 1970s: John J. Ryan, 1970 (A), 1972 (X); Edward Mulligan, 1970 (A), 1971 (D); Grenville Clark III, 1971 (A), 1979 (X); Judith Mulligan, 1971 (A), 1976 (X); Robert A. Wells, 1971 (A), 1977 (P); R. David DePuy, 1971 (A), 1977 (P); Michael P. Hall, 1972 (A), 1975 (X); Bruce W. Felmly, 1972 (A), 1979 (P); Steven J. Selden, 1972 (A), 1979 (P), 1981 (X); James C. Hood, 1972 (A), 1979 (P), 1995 (X); David B. Sullivan, 1973 (A), 1977 (X).

As of the beginning of 1970, when this history of the firm ends, the partners were Kenneth F. Graf, Harriet E. Mansfield, John R. McLane, Jr. (this author), Arthur A. Greene, Jr., Stanley M. Brown, Robert A. Raulerson, Jack B. Middleton, G. Peter Guenther, John A. Graf, and Charles A. DeGrandpre.

The McLane law firm started out on the fourth floor of the Amoskeag bank building in 1919 and moved to larger quarters on the ninth floor in 1928. In 1936, the law firm moved into the recently purchased and thoroughly renovated 40 Stark Street in the center of the city, its home for the next fifty years plus. After World War II, the law practice expanded and more lawyers joined the firm, necessitating further expansion of office space. A wing was added to the south end of the building toward the back alley, which added four lawyer's offices with space for secretaries. A few years later a slightly larger wing with a usable basement for lounge, et cetera, was added to the north end of the building.

By 1970, the firm was running out of space again. After considerable negotiation, the adjoining former bank building to the south on Market Street was purchased; in 1971 a connector was built to join the two structures, which were on different levels, and to furnish access to the large central secretarial space, affectionately called the "gold room." In 1979 and 1980, a reception area, a basement climate-controlled space for the new computer, three lawyer's offices with secretarial spacc on the second floor, and a new entrance off the brick passageway between Stark and Market Streets

*The Office I, 1981.* Seated in front row: John Graf, Harriet Mansfield, Ken Graf, Bill Zorn. Seated in second row: Dick Samuels, Carol Conboy, Charlie DeGrandpre. Standing in back row: Rich Snierson, Wayne Breyer, Bob Raulerson, Tom Donovan, Bruce Felmly, Jim Muirhead, Peter Guenther.

were added. Through the inspiration of Charles DeGrandpre and his influence with the city, the walkway adjacent to the former Hillsborough County Courthouse, now (1996) converted to the Manchester District Courthouse, and our office was attractively landscaped. In 1985 the firm made its final addition by joining the two wings, utilizing the former parking space to create an interior three-story atrium, a basement library, and three floors of lawyer's and secretaries' offices. The firm continued to add staff, to include sixty-plus lawyers and a similar number of support personnel. Several architects made many studies trying to find space to add to our complex and rabbit warren, but to no avail. In the 1980s, the firm looked at new sites, in existing buildings and open space, from the mill yard to brand-new office space. We were a very desirable tenant, and interesting deals were offered.

In 1990, the firm decided on four floors in the NYNEX twenty-two-floor tower with appropriate long-term options on additional space. In 1991 we watched the progress of construction, and in June 1992 the office moved into its fine new quarters on the ninth, tenth, eleventh, and twelfth floors, leaving with nostalgia the space it had occupied for fifty-six years. The Stark Street office space was subsequently sold.

*The Office II, 1981.* Front row: Bob Wells, Debby Ritter, Jack Middleton, John McLane, Jr., Linda Connell, Dave DePuy. Standing in back row: Peter Rotch, Arthur Greene, Jim Hood, Chris Marshall, Rob Jauron, Dan Lyman, Chuck Grau.

Following are biographies of partners during the 1920–1970 period who died prior to 1996.

## JOHN R. McLANE
### 1886–1969

Judge was born in Milford, New Hampshire, in 1886 and grew up there with his parents, an older brother and sister, and a younger brother. Judge's father, although educated in schools only until age twelve, was a very intelligent and well-read man. He was a Baconian theorist on the subject of the authorship of William Shakespeare's writings.[3] It is safe to assume that he educated his children well at home, preparing them for the prep schools and colleges they attended. Judge became an ardent baseball player in the Milford schools, where he usually was catcher. Playing that position he broke his nose on three different occasions. (See Estate of Patrick J. O'Conner in Chapter Twenty-three for the story of this period.)

At St. Paul's School, a boarding school in Concord, New Hampshire, Judge studied the classics, Latin and Greek, math, history, and literature; he took top honors. An Episcopal school, although not affiliated with any diocese, St. Paul's had daily chapel services and one or more services on Sundays with Holy Communion, choirs, and congregational singing of hymns.

Judge picked up his lifelong dedication to the church at St. Paul's School. His parents were not particularly religious. While at Harvard Law School, Judge frequently took the train to Milford on weekends in order to "take" the service at the little Episcopal church, which had no regular minister because the congregation was too small. When he moved to Manchester, he became active in the Grace Episcopal Church, serving over the years as vestryman and warden and also on diocesan boards and committees. Judge and Elisabeth brought up their children with regular attendance at church and Sunday school. In the summertime, Judge and Elisabeth loved to paddle on Sunday mornings over to the north end of Newfound Lake and up the Cockermouth River, pull the canoe up on the bank, and walk through the fields to the little, classically austere white colonial nondenominational community church in Hebron. On occasion, Judge led the family in a simple ceremony at Pasquaney Lodge of hymn singing, Bible readings, and prayers, which his invalid mother-in-law, "Gaga" Bancroft, always enjoyed.

When Judge attended St. Paul's School, it was isolated from other boarding schools, making an interscholastic sports program almost impossible. For this reason the school developed an intramural system of athletic clubs (Delphians, Isthmians, and Old Hundreds) and rowing clubs (Halcyons and Shattucks). Every boy participated on an organized and coached team. Judge played football, hockey, and baseball and somehow managed to squeeze in tennis. On weekends, masters and boys frequently went for four-to-six-mile walks around the countryside on back roads. Judge never lost his love for outdoor exercise, which is described in the chapters entitled "Interlude."

At Dartmouth, Judge was a top student, a Phi Beta Kappa, and a member of Delta Kappa Epsilon fraternity. He was manager of the football team and played on the tennis team. He received his A.B. degree in 1907.

Judge at some point developed an interest in music—whether at home in Milford or at St. Paul's School is not clear. He took violin lessons for several years and played reasonably well as an amateur. Elisabeth played the piano, so they frequently played together. Elisabeth's father enjoyed music, particularly opera, and had quite a collection of old 78 RPM records (including recordings of Enrico Caruso), which were played on a hand-cranked Victrola. Judge and Elisabeth exposed all of their children to piano, violin, or cello. They took them to Boston to hear the Boston Symphony and the Metropolitan Opera when it came to Boston on tour. In later years, Elisabeth regularly attended the Friday-afternoon Boston Symphony concerts. The family went to the Tanglewood concerts in the

Berkshires with a group of Manchester friends who combined tennis and music in their jaunts. The family made up lyrics for many songs on special occasions (births, weddings, trips, mountain climbs), adapting the music of popular songs, frequently in medley form.

Judge had a keen intellect and read vociferously. He was a history major at college and continued his interest as a Rhodes scholar at Magdalen College, Oxford, from which he graduated in 1909. In particular he studied the French Revolution. Whenever he was alone, he read books, frequently one a day, especially while traveling on his many business trips in the 1920s to and from Texas. At home, he always kept a book by his bedside. His favorite author, popular in the 1920s, was Thomas Hardy, whose first editions Judge collected and gave to Dartmouth College. He read the Greek classics in translation after having studied classical Greek at St. Paul's School and in college. He enjoyed British authors, including Galsworthy, but eschewed mystery stories and contemporary writers such as Hemingway, Lardner, and Dos Passos. He read the *Atlantic Monthly* and the *New Republic*, a liberal periodical, and there always seemed to be a copy of *Foreign Affairs* around the house. Before its demise the *Boston Transcript* was a favorite newspaper, and the *Manchester Union* had to be read if one was to be informed, although Judge rarely agreed with any editorial of William Loeb. Judge read the *New York Times* at the office daily and at home on Sundays.

Judge had wonderful concentration, directing his energies to the task at hand, whether it was dictating a letter, reading a document, or talking on the telephone. His secretary of many years, Alice Linehan, later Martel, stated that Judge rarely had to revise anything he dictated, whether a letter, a contract, or an agreement; usually it was correct on the first go-around. He was a fast reader. He regularly read each volume of the New Hampshire Reports of the state supreme court decisions and made his own headnotes in ink. When engaged on the telephone, he shut out everything else and concentrated on the conversation, even though there may have been distracting extraneous noises. Occasionally he would go to the office on a weekend for a couple of hours if he had a brief to write and needed uninterrupted time, but that was rare, at least as he grew older. He practically never took work home from the office or went back to the office in the evenings; instead, he enjoyed his family, outdoor exercise, and avocational reading. He didn't fret about his work and rarely spoke of problems, only the interesting aspects of his work.

Judge did not despair over problems in general. From time to time, various of his children had problems of their own. Judge was understanding, supportive, and rarely critical and usually came up with a creative solution to get over the hump. He applied the same techniques when dealing with clients and the large number of organizations with which he was from time to time connected. He was quick to analyze what needed to be done and then acted with firmness to conclude the matter, no matter how distasteful. It is not surprising that Judge was not only a director of many organizations but was also on the executive committee of the board, of National Life Insurance Company, Boston & Maine Railroad, Dartmouth College, and St. Paul's School. He was chairman of the board or president of New Hampshire Children's Aid Society (later Child & Family Services of New Hampshire) and the Manchester Savings Bank.

Judge corresponded with many of his classmates, and, if he was traveling in their area, he called or met with them. He frequently acted as class secretary or in some other position. When fund-raising had to be done, Judge enjoyed the opportunity to communicate with his friends. He seemed to convey an opportunity rather than an obligation to contribute to the cause. His approach was warm and personal; it is no wonder that he was a very successful fund-raiser.

Judge was very active up to age sixty-five, when high blood pressure and frequent nosebleeds mandated that he take life a little more leisurely— longer lunch periods at home, more days off, and more frequent trips. He had a difficult hospitalization and recovery following prostate surgery in the 1950s. He had a severe stroke in November 1961 that left him speechless and immobilized his right arm and leg. Although this put an end to his professional career, he and Elisabeth (affectionately called "Ibus") led an active and full life for nearly another nine years.[4] Ibus read aloud from Judge's diary and they relived many trips and happy times of years gone by. Judge understood everything and was able to grunt his approval or disagreement when some statement was incorrect. He had a problem with his vision so he was unable to read. However, Ibus read aloud to him, continuing a lifelong pattern when he had read to her. Fortunately they had Eva Hill, who faithfully came in daily to cook and help with canning and the housework, so Elisabeth and Judge were able to continue their entertainment at lunches and dinners for family (children and grandchildren) and friends. This contact with other people was a blessing for Elisabeth, who would not leave Judge alone. Judge loved to listen to the conversation, particularly if the visitors were from the office, such as Miss Mansfield or Ken Graf, and talking shop. They also entertained the younger associates such as the Raulersons and the Middletons.

Judge and Elisabeth traveled extensively. At home, the sporting convertible, usually with top down, took them exploring on back country roads on spring and fall afternoons, sometimes with a picnic lunch. In the summer they spent much time at the lake in a small waterfront house Ibus had built to accommodate Judge's infirmities. In the fall, they continued to make their annual trip to Canada and Quebec, enjoying the late fall foliage. Elisabeth made plans for several trips abroad to favorite places in Scotland

(October '62 and April '66), Greece (April '63), England (October '63), and the Italian hill towns (April '64). In Greece they hired a car and driver through the American Express agency and traveled extensively in northern Greece, staying at small government-run hotels. Elisabeth was afraid that something might happen to her—accident or stroke—and feared for Judge, who couldn't talk, so she sewed into his coat pocket a list of complete instructions—Judge's name, address, health problems, itinerary, and persons to contact in case of emergency. Judge and Elisabeth certainly had a good time together and never let his stroke slow down their life. There was little change in their lives those last eight years until Judge had a second stroke, from which he never recovered. He died on April 21, 1969.

# RALPH W. DAVIS
## 1890–1951

Ralph W. Davis was born in Derry, New Hampshire, on June 28, 1890, and attended local schools before matriculating at Dartmouth receiving an A.B. degree in 1913. He received a B.S. degree the following year. He went on to Yale Law School, graduating in 1916. His professional career was interrupted by World War I, when he served as an ensign in the Navy as a submariner. After the war, he joined Judge McLane on April 7, 1919, and studied for the bar, being admitted in 1920. He became an associate until January 1, 1922, when he became a partner and the law firm of McLane & Davis was formed. In the fall of that year, Ralph married Marion Sullivan.

Ralph was a trial lawyer and a practical courtroom fighter. He was not a theoretical legal scholar, and he had little interest in business law or an office practice. He was happiest when in trial in the courtroom. In the early years, Judge and Ralph made a very successful trial team, with Judge as the "law man" and Ralph the "trial man." They soon established themselves as one of the foremost plaintiff trial lawyer teams in the state. Arthur A. Greene, Jr., who came into the office during World War II, described Ralph as a "lawyer's lawyer"; he received many referrals from other attorneys who would rather have Ralph try the case than attempt it themselves. Arthur also commented that Ralph had a lot of energy and worked with equal forcefulness for the little cases as well as the big ones. In court, when cross-examining, Ralph was aggressive in interrogating the witness, trying to detect a flaw in the witness' statements. If he found one, Ralph was relentless in discrediting that witness. Arthur Greene says, "In court, Ralph was as tough as they come, but outside court he was friendly, likable, and easy to get along with."

Ralph participated in the Progressive Republican group with Judge and the others and served as chairman of the Republican Party Convention in

*Ralph W. Davis, 1890–1951.*

September 1928. Charles W. Tobey, the liberal Republican candidate, won the governorship in 1929 and appointed Ralph attorney general (then considered only a part-time position, with the younger assistant attorney general being the top full-time officer), a position Ralph held until February 1932. An important case, which was overseen by the attorney general's office, was the boundary dispute litigation between the states of Vermont and New Hampshire, initiated in the U.S. Supreme Court (the court of original jurisdiction, because the case involved a dispute between two states) in 1905 by Vermont. The firm of Warren, Howe & Wilson, later Wiggin & Nourie, had earlier been appointed special counsel for the state. The U.S. Supreme Court in October 1933 decided the case in favor of New Hampshire, establishing the boundary line as the Vermont shore of the Connecticut River.[5]

    The most important event during Ralph's term was the closing of the Merrimack River Savings Bank in Manchester on June 9, 1930, on petition of the attorney general. John P. Carleton was immediately appointed attorney for the bank commissioner.[6] On July 3, Judge Sawyer ordered immediate liquidation of the bank and appointed Judge the liquidating agent. While

Judge was suing the bank's treasurer and CEO, Arthur Hale, for $3 million for his defalcations, Ralph Davis, as attorney general, was obtaining indictments and preparing for trial, which commenced on January 27, 1931; it ended on April 8 with a guilty verdict.

Ken Graf recalled a humorous incident that took place while the criminal trial was going on. Hale was represented by the Warren firm,[7] which had its law offices on the tenth floor of the Amoskeag bank building. (Ralph and the prosecuting team were using the McLane office, on the ninth floor.) On one occasion, Ralph and Ken got on the down elevator at the ninth floor en route to the courthouse to resume the trial after a break, only to find Hale and his defense counsel already in the elevator. Hale was an affable and well-respected man, and to make conversation he asked Ralph, "Keeping you busy these days, Mr. Davis?" Ralph and Ken got a great kick out of that and couldn't help retelling the story many times.

Hale's conviction was appealed. On February 3, 1932, Ralph argued before the New Hampshire Supreme Court, which on March 1 upheld the verdict in its decision, a great victory for Ralph. Hale served several years in the state prison. Ralph had resigned as attorney general the day before the decision to resume the private practice of law. Judge and Elisabeth gave a dinner party for Ralph and Marion Davis and John and Alicia Carleton to celebrate Ralph's return.

Ralph Davis' first contact with the Rockingham Racetrack came in 1931. As Ken Graf told the story, a New York group led by Lou Smith had acquired the interests of the old Rockingham Racetrack in Salem and spent a substantial amount of money in refurbishing the track. Since direct horse betting was illegal, their New York attorneys had advised them of an alternate plan: They could sell a ticket to the racetrack that gave the holder the right to exercise an option to purchase the horse named on the ticket, or, in the alternative, to share in the proceeds of the sale of tickets on that horse. This, their New York attorneys advised, did not constitute a wager under New Hampshire Statutes. "Not so," said the attorney general, Ralph Davis, "and if you try, we'll close you down." They did try and the attorney general got an order from the Rockingham Superior Court to close the track. Ralph didn't trust the Rockingham County "machine," who were very unenthusiastic about shutting down the track. Ralph feared they would botch things up in serving the papers (such as maybe losing them), so Ralph got "Mac" O'Dowd, high sheriff of Hillsborough County,[8] to serve the papers (in Rockingham County). The track closed down and the New York group paid all its bills and debts and left. It returned two years later to obtain legislation to authorize horse racing and legalize parimutuel betting. By that time, Ralph was in private practice. Because Lou Smith had been impressed with Ralph Davis' ability as an adversary, he sought him out to be the corporation's counsel, and thereby began a fifty-year successful relationship with a client. Lou Smith had substantial backing from legitimate financial interests and always maintained an operation that was above reproach. The Rockingham Racetrack reopened on June 21, 1933, in the middle of the depression. It found the going tough, but with persistence and imagination in getting special trains to the track from Boston and Lawrence, the track became profitable and over the years made substantial amounts of money.[9]

During the early 1940s, Ralph started to have problems with his blood pressure and heart and had to be careful about his activities. Although he reduced his working hours and got plenty of rest, he had a heart attack in July 1941 and a "shock" in 1945. In those days, medical understanding of the causes and treatment of high blood pressure was in its infancy. Arthur Greene recalls that Ralph was on a rice diet but no medication. There were long periods during the war years when Ralph was not able to get to the office. From about the end of the war in 1945 until his death on September 14, 1951, he remained at home. Ralph's effectiveness as a lawyer really ended at the age of fifty-one, ten years before his death, a tremendous tragedy to lose such talent at such an early age.

Ralph and Marion owned a summer house in a colony of uninsulated summer cottages known as Pine Crest set in a pine grove on the westerly side of Union Street at the top of the hill. In the 1930s, the North End of Manchester ended at Trenton Street just beyond the end of the trolley car line on Elm Street. North of that on both Union Street and River Road were working farms and dirt roads. Ralph and Marion's house was called "Ginbar," which not only suggested a vacation spot but also combined the names of their daughters, Virginia and Barbara. Jim Shanahan remembers being invited by the girls to parties there. In the winter after a snowstorm that left an unbreakable crust, there was marvelous sliding on the north slope through open hay fields all the way to River Road. This area was built up after the war. Judge and Elisabeth also bought land a little farther out Union Street on which they built a tennis court, playhouse, and garden for summertime use, and later, after the war, a permanent home.

Ralph and Judge were a study in contrasts. Judge was the philosopher type, well read and a generalist with long-range views. Ralph was the pragmatist and wanted action with results. I don't think I ever saw my father with a screwdriver, hammer, or any other tool in his hand. Ralph was never so happy as when he was tinkering with his automobile, taking this apart or changing that. Ralph and Marion bought the house across the street from Judge and Elisabeth on Chestnut Street,[10] which was the identical plan but reversed. As a young boy, I well remember, on weekends, seeing the hood of Ralph's car raised and Ralph leaning over the engine working away, seemingly for hours at a time. Judge and Elisabeth were always walking, climbing mountains, or taking European trips, none of which interested Ralph and Marion. They each had their own social friends and activities.

After Ralph's death, Marion continued to live in Manchester until her death in the mid-1980s. They had two daughters, Virginia Atwater, who lives in Pompano Beach, Florida, and Barbara Sawyer, who lives in Wellesley, Massachusetts.

## JOHN P. CARLETON
### 1899–1977

John Porter Carleton, the only child of Dr. Elmer H. Carleton and Louise Carleton, was born in Hanover, New Hampshire, on September 13, 1899. His father, a native of Maine, graduated from Bowdoin College in 1893 and the Dartmouth Medical School, class of 1897. While he was at medical school, he was a director of gymnastics and an instructor in physical culture. Judge notes in his diary that he played tennis with "Doc" Carleton on June 20, 1905, the end of his sophomore year at age nineteen, when Doc would have been thirty-five. Doc returned to Dartmouth Medical School from 1910 to 1914 as a clinical instructor in eye and throat and then entered private practice. In the late 1920s, he received an infection resulting from his operating that ultimately necessitated the amputation of his arm. From that time, he became affiliated with Dartmouth Medical School as a teacher. His wife, Louise Carleton, was a collector and dealer in English antiques, which she collected on her many trips to Great Britain.

John Carleton attended Hanover High School and took after his father in athletic ability. His close friends were sons of Dartmouth faculty, many of whom excelled in athletics, particularly skiing. This sport was enjoying a burst of popularity under the leadership of Fred Harris, who in about 1910 founded the Dartmouth Outing Club and the popular Dartmouth Winter Carnival. Two of John's closest friends were Jack and Dick Bowler, sons of Dr. Bowler, a leading Hanover physician and trustee of Dartmouth. When Jack Bowler was a junior or senior, on the Dartmouth ski team in 1914 or 1915, he went to Montreal to compete against McGill University and took along his younger brother, Dick, and his friend John Carleton, both in Hanover High. The boys brought their skis, hoping for a little exercise. When it turned out that the Dartmouth team was short a couple of members, the two Hanover High kids were plugged in to help out. It would have been fine if they hadn't done well, but they were much better than many of the college skiers, which caused some problems. Should they be counted on the Dartmouth team? If so, the results might have been drastically changed. About this time the Bowler boys and John Carleton learned how to somer-

*John P. Carleton, 1899–1977.*

sault off a ski jump, sometimes side by side. This spectacular event brought out huge crowds to winter carnivals all over northern New England and elicited cheers for these intrepid high school kids.[11]

John did a postgraduate year at Phillips Andover before entering Dartmouth in the class of 1922. While at Dartmouth, he excelled at college sports, particularly skiing and tennis. He was a Phi Beta Kappa recipient and was elected a Rhodes scholar; as a result he "read" law at Magdalen College, Oxford University, receiving his degree in 1925. He was on the lawn tennis team all three years and captain the last. In 1924, he was captain and coach of the U.S. Ski Team at the first Winter Olympic Games, held in Chamonix, France, the only non-Norwegian on the team.

John returned to the United States, took the New Hampshire Bar examinations, was admitted to practice in the fall of 1925, and joined the McLane law firm as an associate. He worked extensively with Judge on business matters and wrote appellate briefs. In April 1928, Governor Huntley Spaulding appointed him assistant attorney general, a position he held until September 1929, when he returned to the firm and was made a partner. The firm name then became McLane, Davis & Carleton.

John was an ardent skier and introduced Judge and Elisabeth to the sport, persuading them to hang up their snowshoes. He also taught their children how to ski. There were no tows, lifts, or even trails. Downhill skiing took place on open slopes used for pasture and hay fields. Cross-country skiing was carried out on abandoned woods roads. Picnic lunches of hot dogs or hamburgers were cooked over an open fire. Hanover High graduates John Carleton and Charlie Proctor, Dartmouth, class of 1929, pioneered skiing in Tuckerman's Ravine, the glacial cirque on the southeast slope of Mt. Washington. They may well have been the first ones over the headwall, in about 1929 or 1930. Judge and Elisabeth watched them come over the headwall on April 30, 1933. John continued his vigorous tennis, playing in tournaments and as a frequent partner of Judge, Ken Graf, Perkins Bass, and me. In later years, John was prone to accidents; on many Monday mornings, when John arrived late to work with his leg in a cast or an arm in a sling, no one asked what happened or offered any sympathy.

In 1931, John married Alicia Skinner in Paris, where she had been studying during her junior year at Smith College. She was the daughter of Prescott Orde Skinner, professor of romance languages at Dartmouth, and Mrs. Skinner. They had four children, Janet, Anthony (Tony), Alice, and Margaret; Margaret died during childhood.

In 1930, the Merrimack River Savings Bank was closed on order of the court. John was appointed counsel for the bank commissioner, who took over possession of the bank until Judge was appointed liquidating agent by the superior court. John worked extensively for two to three years on bank matters; he also had a number of business clients and did some litigation. A lawyer in those days was expected to do a little bit of everything.

During the war, John was commissioned in the Air Force and served for several years on active duty in an administrative position. After the war, he was active in politics behind the scenes and ran Sherman Adams' campaign for governor. He was a trustee of both Camp Carpenter and New England College and served on the Manchester Finance Commission and the Maine–New Hampshire Bridge Authority.

Toward the end of his career, John had health problems and retired in the late 1960s to live with Alicia in their attractive colonial brick house in Bedford. John died on January 21, 1977. He was posthumously admitted as one of the first members of the National Ski Hall of Fame in Ishpeming, Michigan.

## HARRIET E. MANSFIELD
### 1899–1986

In 1925, Harriet Mansfield gave up a good secretarial job with the Merchants Bank to accept a lower-paying job with the neophyte law firm

*Harriet E. Mansfield, 1899–1986.*

of McLane & Davis. Judge had given a commercial law course for bank personnel at the request of the Manchester banks and Harriet Mansfield had been the brightest student in the class. At the same time, McLane & Davis needed a senior secretary and office manager to organize the growing business. Judge knew what Miss Mansfield was earning at the bank and knew he could not match that pay, so he never approached her. But he put an advertisement in the paper and, guess what? Harriet Mansfield answered it. When advised of what the salary would be, she responded, "That's not important. I'll take my chances with Mr. McLane." So Miss Mansfield became Judge's secretary, supervised the other secretaries, did the hiring and firing, kept the books, and attended to the myriad of other duties necessary to run a successful and growing office.

In the fall of 1925, Judge and Elisabeth planned an eight-week trip to Scotland and England to visit friends that Judge had made during his years at Oxford as a Rhodes scholar, to see the ancestral Maclean home at Duart Castle on the Isle of Mull, and to bicycle amid the mountains and lochs of Scotland. Miss Mansfield, not being accustomed to sit and twiddle her thumbs, asked Judge what she was to do during his absence. "Well, why don't you study law?" he suggested, so she subscribed to a correspondence law course from La Salle University and, with the assistance of Ralph Davis and John Carleton, she plunged in. She never actually finished the course, because in 1931, while she was still plugging along, Judge and the others encouraged her to try the bar exams just to learn what they were all about. To her own surprise and the delight of the partners, she passed, was admitted to the New Hampshire Bar, and became an associate of the firm. This called for a celebration in Boston consisting of a gourmet dinner and a baseball game. She became an expert practitioner in probate and tax and won the respect and admiration of her colleagues in those fields. In fact, Judge William Treat, probate judge for Rockingham County, wrote a three-volume treatise on probate law in New Hampshire and asked Miss Mansfield to read the manuscript for accuracy and to check his references. Miss Mansfield's office at 40 Stark Street faced the probate courtroom (now the City Hall Annex), so the register of probate would pull down the window shade, then signal Miss Mansfield by raising the shade when the judge was free, so she did not have to stand around in court and wait a long time like the rest of the lawyers. Miss Mansfield, as she was known to all but a few personal friends, had many clients, mostly women, many widows, some wealthy and others poor, to whom she gave of her time freely and without discrimination. Those who could afford to pay received a bill; those who couldn't received no bill or at most a token one. Miss Mansfield was frequently the first person in the office in the morning and the last to leave at night and was invariably at her desk on Saturdays and Sundays. The word *vacation* was not part of her vocabulary; except for one trip to Europe with a friend, she traveled very little.

Miss Mansfield was born in the Province of Quebec, Canada, in 1899, the youngest of seven children. The family moved to Bedford, New Hampshire, and later to Mammoth Road in Manchester, where she graduated from Central High in 1918. For many years, she lived with her sister and brother-in-law; after their deaths, she moved to an apartment in the Women's Aid Home until her death in 1986.

## KENNETH F. GRAF
### 1906–1991

Kenneth Folsom Graf was born in Manchester on April 22, 1906, the son of Mary Folsom Graf and Harry Graf, a postal supervisor. Ken's grandfather, Johann Adam Graf, a fifteen-year-old weaver, left his parents and ten brothers and sisters in Bavaria (later a part of Germany) and came alone to the Amoskeag Mills, Manchester, in 1863 to work as a mill hand. He worked his way up the ladder in the next twenty-five years, became an overseer (foreman), and was responsible for setting up the new #11 mill on the West Side on McGregor Street opposite the present CMC Medical Center. In the 1890s he is said to have lived at 40 Stark Street, then the Stark Mills housing for foremen (later the McLane law firm office for 50 years). He served as an alderman, and his name appears on several school plaques—in the Classical Building at Central High and in the Parker-Varney School on South Main Street, now used by the Visiting Nurses. Johann Adam Graf was also a leader in state politics, serving in the state house of representatives in 1897 and the senate in 1905, when he was appointed by Governor John McLane (Judge McLane's father) to be a member of the governor's delegation to the Portsmouth Russian-Japanese peace treaty deliberations.

Ken graduated in 1924 from Central High, where he distinguished himself as an athlete—a quarterback in football and an earnest player in basketball and baseball. He made up in spunk and spirit for what he lacked in size; he was always scrappy and fighting to win. He played on Hubie McDonough's football team, which didn't lose a game for two years. At Dartmouth, Ken played on the famous 1925 undefeated varsity football team in all games but not enough to win his letter. He also played basketball and baseball during his college years and was a champion tennis player.

After college, Ken went to Harvard Law School and then to the law firm of McLane, Davis & Carleton. Judge McLane knew of Ken's prowess in sports and commented in his diary in 1924, Ken's senior year in high school, that Ken had been awarded the Manchester Dartmouth Club Scholarship, and that he played tennis with Ken at about the same time. Ken worked in the McLane law firm office during his summers while at law school and started full-time employment after taking his bar exams in the summer of 1932. He became a partner in 1936. For years Ken played tennis and squash with people in the office and others. Ken went fly-fishing, spring and fall, for fifty years in Forest City, New Brunswick, frequently taking associates from the office with him.

Mutual friends introduced Ken to Mary Eaton of Wakefield, Massachusetts. The daughter of a Boston attorney, she was a graduate of Smith College and an athlete. They married in 1934. John Adam Graf was born the following year and Sally (Sarah Danforth) in 1938. There are numerous entries in Judge's diary in those early years of inviting Ken and Mary to dinner or playing tennis with Ken.

In 1935 and 1937, Ken won a seat in the New Hampshire legislature and was appointed clerk of the Judiciary Committee. He also tackled the entire life insurance industry by espousing savings bank life insurance. This low-cost plan, offered in Massachusetts by banks, eliminated expensive selling commissions and was particularly attractive to young couples with children. However, it was anathema to the life insurance agents, who called on

*Kenneth F. Graf, 1906–1991.*

all their customers to kill the bill. It mattered not to Kenneth Graf that he had stirred up a hornet's nest of bigwigs; he stuck to his guns, put up a brave struggle, and went down fighting with only a few votes in addition to his own. In 1938, Ken attended the constitutional convention and was a member of the legislative committee. He also was appointed a commissioner for the Promotion of Uniformity of Legislation in the United States. Much of Ken's early trial experience was learned through his work with Ralph Davis, a very effective plaintiff's attorney and former attorney general.

In 1943, Ken served in the U.S. infantry and became a captain in the Judge Advocate General Corps, stationed with the New York Port of Embarkation in New York City. Tom Clark, later a U.S. Supreme Court justice, was his commanding officer. The most exciting case arose out of the capture of two spies who landed on the coast of Maine, who were tried, convicted, and sentenced to death. (See Appendix C.4, Ken Graf and the German Spies.)

After the war, Ken returned to his practice of law. One of his big cases was the prosecution as special counsel for the state of Stephen Story, former state controller and respected civil servant, and Donat Cote, a

Manchester contractor who connived with Mr. Story in overcharging for
work costing $700,000 at six different state institutions. The criminal trial
lasted some thirteen weeks and ended with convictions on all counts, which
were upheld by the supreme court. Prison terms were imposed on and
served by both men. Ken tried the case with his partners Stanley M. Brown
and Arthur A. Greene. Stan later recalled: "At that point, Ken Graf without any question was the most effective trial lawyer."

Ken Graf took over from Ralph Davis—who was in poor health—representation of the Rockingham Racetrack and its head, Lou Smith, in the
late 1940s. He subsequently became a principal stockholder and director;
after Lou Smith's death in 1969, Ken became the CEO. He attended all
sessions when the track was open and spent nearly all of his available time
on track business. The track suffered from a disastrous fire in 1980 that
resulted in the liquidation of the company, with a good return to the stockholders. For many years, Ken was a director of the Thoroughbred Racing
Association of America.

Prior to his intense involvement with the track, Ken had as clients a
number of shoe companies, particularly Shaer Shoe and its affiliate, Myrna
Shoe. Ken represented the industry employers in negotiations with the
union and was also involved with the pension fund. He successfully represented Dartmouth College in colorful litigation over a large bequest to the
college by Leon Williams involving thousands of acres of ranch land in
New Mexico.

Ken always put his clients' cases above any other consideration,
whether his friends, family, or self.

Nat Bigelow, who had a long association with Ken at the track, said,
"Ken Graf was a tough advocate, but one of great integrity and unques-
tioned loyalty to his clients and business associates." Judge Marty Loughlin
commented that Ken "was fair, just, and compassionate." One of the
younger associates in the office spoke of Ken as "gruff, but fair." Ken was
modest and unassuming, frequently belittling his own accomplishments
and contributions. He rarely served on boards of nonprofit organizations
but was a quiet benefactor to his college, community, and many charitable
organizations, preferring an anonymous role. He once anonymously supplied the Straw School team with baseball uniforms. Harry Lichman
recounted a landlord and tenant case he was trying with Ken in which their
clients, the tenants, were impoverished. At lunchtime, Ken invited them to
eat with the lawyers, which they did for the duration of the trial. Harry
found out that they would not have eaten had it not been for Ken's gen-
erosity. His charity was frequently private and personal.

Ken lived a full life; he came to the office regularly during his retirement years, giving advice when asked, keeping up on what was going on,

*Peter Guenther, 1931–1986.*

and staying in touch with his friends. He suffered a stroke, which necessitated going to a nursing home, where he died after an additional stroke at the age of eighty-five.

# PETER GUENTHER
## 1931–1986

Peter Guenther was born in Hamburg, in upstate New York. He graduated from Dartmouth College in 1952 and from Cornell Law School in 1955. He served in the U.S. Marine Corps as a legal officer from 1956 to 1960. In 1960, he joined the McLane law firm, becoming a partner in 1966 and specializing in corporate law, particularly public utilities matters and securities law.

Peter was a philosopher and enjoyed the writings of Sophocles. He rarely accepted things on faith but sought out in his own mind the rationale for what was being done. He could not be hurried in the deliberations he felt necessary for a decision. He systematically explored all of the options available to him. He exasperated his partners at times, but his ultimate conclusion was usually the right one.

Peter enjoyed restoring old houses, not renovating them but redoing them to the manner in which they originally existed. Peter and his first wife, Betsy, and their two children, Peter and Elizabeth (Lizzie), lived in Hopkinton in such a restored farmhouse with horses, goats, and other farm animals. He read architectural history to learn authenticity and meticulously re-created what had been. For him there was only one way to do a thing—and that was the right way.

Peter loved solitude and the wide open spaces. In the mid-1970s, he purchased four hundred-plus acres of old farmland high on the hills of Corinth, Vermont, overlooking the Connecticut River valley. Although the land was mostly wooded, there were three or four sizable fields, once farmed but growing in, over which he skied, snowshoed, or walked depending on the season, exploring the old cellar holes and stone walls and absorbing the beauty and remoteness of the land.

Peter also loved the wide open spaces of the West. In the early 1970s, with his young son, Peter, he went on a boat trip on the Snake River in Wyoming and saw for the first time the majestic towering Tetons in which they later hiked. Peter returned to climb there several years later and then hiked solo for about a week in the Wind River range, also in Wyoming. Later in 1984, when he had "extended leave," Peter and his friend Dani returned to the Tetons and the Wind River range to camp and climb. For a week or more, they trekked above tree line in the Beartooth range just outside Yellowstone National Park, without seeing a soul, hiking from one little glacial lake to the next, fishing for trout, photographing the ubiquitous wildflowers, and absorbing the majesty and wildness of this remote mountain range.

Peter died after a long bout with cancer on September 20, 1986.

## JOHN ADAM GRAF
### 1935–1994

John Adam Graf was born in 1935 in Manchester, New Hampshire, to Kenneth and Mary Graf. He attended local schools, then graduated in 1954 from Phillips Andover Academy in Massachusetts and from Dartmouth College in 1958, in both of which schools he excelled as a swimmer and tennis player. In 1961, he graduated from Boston University School of Law and was admitted to the New Hampshire and federal bars, including the right to practice before the U. S. Supreme Court. He joined the McLane law firm in 1961 and specialized in commercial and business law and more recently international law. John was very proud of his German ancestry and on his own studied German so that he could communicate with some of his German clients. Although his German may not

*John A. Graf, 1935–1994.*

have been the best, his clients were impressed by his tenacity to learn. In fact, John threw himself into everything he did: law practice, community activity, athletics. He was a tiger and persistently strove for perfection.

In his business connections, John served on the board of directors of the following organizations: Small Business Association of New England; New Hampshire Legal Assistance; Kluber Lubrication of North America, Inc.; Blue Cross and Blue Shield of New Hampshire; Disogrin Industries Corporation; and Twin State Cable Television, Inc.

He held many positions of leadership in the New Hampshire Bar Association and state government—a term in the state legislature, chair of the Ballot Law Commission, the commission to study the laws of eminent domain, and the commission to codify criminal law. He chaired the New Hampshire Advisory Committee on International Trade and served on the advisory committee of the New Hampshire College advanced degree program in international law. He was active in the Business & Industry Association. In 1986, he received the New Hampshire Bar President's Award for Distinguished Service, and in 1991 he was honored for his continuing work on behalf of the IOLTA[12] program.

In community affairs, John served nearly thirty years on the YMCA board of directors or trustees. He worked on the board of trustees of Derryfield School from 1976 to 1989 and was chairman for two years. He was on the board of the Manchester Institute of Arts and Sciences and president of the board of the New Hampshire Symphony. John enjoyed fundraising and giving people the opportunity to contribute to a good cause. He assisted with the Soup Kitchen; St. Anselm College; the Derryfield School campaign, which he chaired in 1982; and annual campaigns for United Way, Federated Arts, YMCA, Channel 11, and New Hampshire Legal Assistance. Jim Muirhead said of John, "Being an attorney was a privilege and meant you had to return something to the community. He met those obligations with enthusiasm."

John greatly enjoyed his Dartmouth connections—his classmates and fellow alumni. He was chairman of the Dartmouth Club of Manchester.

In addition to his love of tennis, John was an avid fly fisherman and often went to New Brunswick with his father to fish for salmon. Charles DeGrandpre, who frequently fished with John, called him a consummate fly fisherman who took pride in his accomplishments: "He had the patience of Job and would never give up."

John and his wife, Ann, a lifetime member of the board of trustees of the Currier Gallery of Art, lived in Bedford and raised their three children, Ted, Peter, and Julie. John died of lung cancer at the age of fifty-nine on January 31, 1994.

## ROBERT ALVIN RAULERSON
### 1926–1994

Bob Raulerson was born in Athens, Pennsylvania, in 1926, graduated from Antioch College in 1950, and received his law degree from Cornell Law School in 1952. Before joining the firm in 1952, Bob served with the National Labor Relations Board in Washington.

At the firm, Bob had a labor practice and was also involved with corporate and business law and probate, trusts, and estate planning. He was always meticulous and competent and believed in maintaining the highest standards of professionalism. During the 1970s, he was the first chairman of the New Hampshire Supreme Court Committee on Professional Conduct and served on the New Hampshire Bar Association's Ethics Committee. After his passing, several of his legal colleagues described him as a "gentleman" and "gentleman's gentleman," very high praise indeed. Although a very private individual, he had a wide interest in and concern for others.

Bob was an avid tennis player and also liked to hike[13] and ski. He was also an ardent Democrat and he hung permanently in his office a photograph of his hero, Franklin Roosevelt.

Bob reached retirement age in 1991, when he became a nonequity partner and was looking forward to a more relaxed practice of the law.

*Robert A. Raulerson, 1926–1994.*

Bob died suddenly in his sleep of a heart attack on March 6, 1994. He is survived by his wife, Jane, and his two children of his first marriage, John P. Raulerson of Bedford and Rebecca R. Hillis of Auburn.

## Notes

1. Arthur A. Greene was brought up in North Conway, went to Dartmouth, class of 1936, and then to the University of Michigan, where he graduated with distinction in 1939 after serving as editor of the *Michigan Law Review*. He practiced several years with his father in the north country before a brief stint with the Sheehan office, then joined the McLane law firm in 1944. Ken Graf was leaving for the judge advocate general's office in the U.S. Army and recommended Arthur to Ralph Davis. Arthur became a partner in 1948 along with Stan Brown and me. He retired in 1978. Arthur was an excellent trial lawyer. He successfully got acquittals for two murder defendants in separate cases. He participated with Ken Graf, as special prosecutor for the state, and Stan Brown in the famous thirteen-week Story-Cote case, which resulted in the convictions

of the state controller and a Manchester contractor. Arthur also practiced business law and was involved in Securities and Exchange Commission filings, public offerings, and regulatory matters. His calm and tempered advice was frequently sought. Arthur summered on Lake Winnipesaukee and, after retirement, wintered in Stuart, Florida. He was an avid fresh- and saltwater fisherman. He and his wife, Jerry, now (1996) reside in Manchester.

2. Stan Brown was a remarkably effective trial lawyer who decided he could do better with his own firm, so in 1974 he resigned from the McLane law firm. Stan grew up in the small town of Bradford, New Hampshire, where he worked after school to assist his widowed mother. After graduating from high school, he worked as a carpenter building houses. I remember my father, as a trustee of Dartmouth College in 1936, telling us about an interesting application from a hardworking and outstanding student from Bradford who also had been a good football player. Judge followed Stan's career through Dartmouth College and Cornell Law School with great interest and was able to assist him by making scholarship loans in later years. Judge was always impressed by the prompt payment of amounts due by Stan's wife, Thalia. Judge offered Stan a job in 1945 when he returned from a distinguished career as a Navy pilot. In addition to being a top-notch trial lawyer, Stan was very active in both the state and American bar associations. He was always a colorful and forceful individual.

3. The Baconians believed that Francis Bacon was the real author of the works of William Shakespeare.

4. See Chapter Twenty-six, Interlude 1960–1969.

5. Appendix C.1, State of VERMONT v. State of NEW HAMPSHIRE, 289 U.S. 593 (1933).

6. The stock market crash of October 29, 1929 ("Black Tuesday"), and the collapse of speculative real estate values were beginning to affect the banks.

7. Forerunner of the Wiggin & Nourie firm of 1993.

8. Later and for many years O'Dowd was the chief security officer for the track.

9. Ken Graf succeeded Ralph as general counsel and, after Lou Smith's death on April 19, 1969, became president and CEO of the track through the period of the disastrous fire on July 29, 1980, and the ultimate liquidation of the track.

10. Ralph hired me to shovel his walks and driveway when I was about twelve. I heartily agree with the current conjecture that the frequency and depth of snowstorms today are nothing compared to those of the 1920s and 1930s!

11. The obituary of John Carleton in the *Manchester Union* of January 24, 1977, states that he double somersaulted with Charlie Proctor, who was the son of a Dartmouth physics professor and a great skier. Since Charlie was in the class of 1929 and John and Dick Bowler were in the class of 1922, I suspect that it was Dick Bowler rather than Charlie Proctor who was involved. I know that Dick Bowler somersaulted, but I do not know about Charlie. For a picture and story

of John Carleton somersaulting on skis, see the *Manchester Union*, February 11, 1921. There also was a series of four sequential pictures of him somersaulting on skis in an issue of the *National Geographic* magazine in the 1920s.

John Carleton was a great inspiration to the next generation of McLanes as he taught diving, skiing, and ski jumping, but we never achieved his excellence in somersaulting—although we tried, inadvertently. I remember going out to the Dartmouth ski jump (which I had been off several times as a member of the freshman ski team) the Sunday of carnival weekend, a glorious warm day with a number of students jumping for fun and lots of guys with their dates looking on, which helped overcome the fear of the hill. I climbed to the top and started down. Unbeknownst to me, the sun had melted the snow on the lip of the takeoff, so when I hit it, my skis practically stopped and I kept going in sort of a swan-dive position. I still can hear in my mind the astonished gasp of the folks watching, wondering what was going to happen. Having been trained by John Carleton to dive and tumble, gymnastically speaking, I doubled into a "tuck" to roll over and landed on the hill kind of on my back with my skis over my head. My skis came off as they hit the landing hill and I rolled to the bottom with a shaken ego but little else injured. When I stood up I realized that I had bent over so quickly and hard that my suspenders had pulled out the buttons on my pants, which then had nothing to hold them up—more embarrassment! Several years later, I was told that my brother Malcolm, when jumping at Hanover as a member of the ski team, had jumped late, causing him to rotate backward about half a turn and land on his back, again with no injury. Thus the McLane brothers could say that they had somersaulted—John doing half a front one and Malcolm half a back one!

12. IOLTA stands for "Interest on Legal Trust Accounts." Lawyers hold clients' funds for a variety of reasons, such as fee deposits or judgments on monetary settlements awaiting some required act prior to disbursement. These funds are required to be held separately and may not be commingled with the lawyers' funds. Usually the amounts are not large and the time of holding is short. It would be uneconomic to deposit these funds in separate interest-drawing accounts or to compute and pay interest on a pooled account. The Bar Association, with the courts' approval, established the IOLTA program, which authorizes such funds to be deposited in a pooled account and the interest transferred to the Bar Association to be used for a charitable purpose, such as Legal Aid to Indigent Clients.

13. He went trekking in Nepal in the Himalayas.

## FOUR

# Politics,
# the Progressive Movement,
# and John G. Winant

J udge McLane was greatly influenced in his political thinking by the activities of the Progressive movement. Judge's father, the governor, was dedicated to Teddy Roosevelt's political viewpoint as a Republican and as founder of the Progressive Party; Judge was aligned with the Progressive wing of the Republican Party, to which he made many contributions during the 1920s.

The Progressive Party in New Hampshire was short lived, as are most third parties. It lasted from the "Bull Moose" Convention of 1912 until 1916, when it polled only .05 percent of the votes cast. Receiving less than the required 3 percent, the Progressive Party was removed from the New Hampshire list. However, the reform movement, which the Progressive Party represented, lived on in the Republican Party for twenty years.

Although there were many different reform efforts being made during the latter part of the nineteenth century throughout the nation, it was the increasing power of the railroads and the abuse of that power that triggered the growth of the Progressive movement. Early in railroad development, New Hampshire Democrats feared that "business and monopoly had contrived legislation to divide transport services into small sections . . . By 1870, a thousand miles of track were cut up among thirty-two separate companies."[1] Consolidations took place, some the result of bankruptcies of the smaller railroads. By 1883, two companies emerged as the dominant carriers, the Boston & Maine Railroad (B&MRR) in the eastern part of the state and the Concord Railroad, which controlled the Merrimack Valley south of Concord. The Concord Railroad planned to acquire the Northern Railroad, which owned the track from Concord to White River Junction, and the Boston, Concord and Montreal Railroad, which operated the line from Concord through Laconia, Plymouth, Woodsville, and on to Montreal.

Monopoly was anathema to the "first" New Hampshire Progressive, charismatic William E. Chandler. Many years earlier, in 1865, he left New

Hampshire for Washington to seek his fortune as a young lawyer. Chandler represented some distinguished clients, among them the Union Pacific Railroad, the Western Union Telegraph Company, National Life Insurance Company, and the interests of Jay Cooke. Chandler was active in the Republican Party and served as secretary of the Navy (1882–1885) before returning to New Hampshire, where he became embroiled in state politics. He was a U.S. senator from New Hampshire from 1887 to 1901. From his home in Bradford and his office in Washington, Chandler kept up his attack on the railroads, particularly the B&MRR, the "Great Corporation." In 1901, Chandler was defeated in his reelection bid for the senate by Henry Burnham, "a polished and colorless personality who faithfully represented railroad attitudes."[2] Chandler made countless speeches and wrote a pamphlet entitled "New Hampshire, a Slave State" in which he sought to describe how a rich and powerful corporation could capture both political parties. He suggested a solution, namely: "abolition of passes, election of Railroad Commissions, accurate evaluation of railroad property, a corrupt practices act and publishing campaign contributions, registration of lobbyists and publication of their retainers."[3]

In November 1904, Theodore Roosevelt was elected president (having become president in 1901 upon the assassination of President McKinley). Roosevelt introduced many reform ideas in the Congress. John McLane of Milford was elected governor in November 1904, defeating Henry Hollis, Democrat, of Concord.[4] McLane had served two terms in each of the house and senate. He was elected president of the senate for an unprecedented two terms. It was here he became friendly with William E. Chandler and was influenced by his reform ideas. McLane also was a delegate to the 1900 Republican National Convention and had helped to nominate McKinley for president and Theodore Roosevelt for vice president. Governor McLane was impressed with Roosevelt. Squires comments that Governor McLane presented "a liberal and enlightened viewpoint in public affairs."[5] Programs to improve the state road system and to introduce forest conservation were commenced.

A curious incident occurred when a group interested in establishing horse racing at Salem introduced legislation, ostensibly for the purpose of improving the breeding of horses, authorizing the construction of a track for horse racing at Salem. The measure passed the legislature and was signed into law by Governor McLane. Only when $1 million of fancy horse racing and gambling machinery arrived in the summer of 1905 was the true nature and the New York backing of the project revealed. The legislature and the governor had been duped! Public reaction was immediate, vocal, and effective: Only one horse race "meet" was held and legalized gambling collapsed, not to be renewed until 1936.[6] (Ralph W. Davis and the McLane law firm became heavily involved, representing the racetrack from 1936 until its termination some fifty years later.)

As governor, McLane played a leading role in inviting and hosting the Russian-Japanese peace treaty conference in Portsmouth in 1905.[7]

Another influential voice in the Progressive movement was that of Winston Churchill, a native of St. Louis, a graduate of the U.S. Naval Academy,[8] and the author of historical novels whose best-known book was *Coniston*, published in 1906. The power of the railroads in New Hampshire is illustrated through the book's central character, Jethrow Bass, modeled after a real character, Ruell Durkee of Croyden. Material for the book was developed while Churchill served two terms in the New Hampshire House from his hometown of Cornish.[9] Thrust into the public limelight by his popular book, Winston Churchill was invited to run for governor in 1906 by a group of liberal Republican political neophytes who called themselves The Lincoln Republican Club. With William Chandler's assistance, they wrote a platform that would eliminate railroad passes, elect railroad commissioners, provide for accurate evaluation of railroad taxable property, endorse a corrupt practices act and publicity for campaign contributions, and provide for registration of lobbyists and publication of their retainers. Senator Robert LaFollette of Wisconsin, a friend of Chandler's, was fighting for the same reforms in his state.

Churchill, however, was defeated in his bid to get his party's nomination for governor. The party convention system was still in control: After eight ballots at the Republican Party convention on September 19, 1906, Churchill was leading, so the party faithful rallied to the "machine" and on the ninth ballot elected the least competent candidate (Charles M. Floyd of Manchester) by a narrow margin and pushed him into office in November.[10]

In 1908, the liberal Republicans, following Roosevelt's lead, supported Taft at the national convention and locally pushed Henry Quimby of Laconia for governor because Winston Churchill could not be persuaded to run again. The 1908 platform included the "reform" elements of 1906, and the legislature adopted the direct primary law and abolished free railway passes. A legislative committee under the chairmanship of Robert P. Bass of Peterborough studied state expenditures, some of which had standing authorizations (thereby evading biennial review). The committee's recommendations later became the foundation for a modern state budget system.[11]

By 1910, the Progressive Republicans were active again. A small group of influential liberals tried to prevail on Sherman E. Burroughs, an attorney in Manchester, to run for governor, but he was unavailable, so the group turned to Robert P. Bass of Peterborough, who accepted the offer. Bass was originally from the Midwest but was educated at Harvard College and Law

School; he then moved to New Hampshire where he ran a dairy farm and managed timberlands. He was influenced by the liberal conservation ideas of Gifford Pinchot and the leadership of Theodore Roosevelt. In the early 1900s he served two terms in the house and one term in the senate. During his governorship in 1910 the primary system was enacted; it was passed in 1908 to break up the monopoly power of the railroads and their control of the political party conventions. Bass was a notoriously poor speaker (as was liberal John Winant, a few years later) but was honest and sincere and won the election aided by campaign visits to the state by President Roosevelt.

Under Bass' leadership, the legislature passed a number of important acts: It established the Public Utilities Commission, one of the first in the nation, to regulate utilities, including the railroads; it required campaign contributions and expenses to be made public; it passed a pure food law; it provided for safety inspections of factories; it enacted a child labor law; it created a state tax commission with power over corporations; it enacted a workmen's compensation law; and it strengthened the administration of forestlands. In 1911, Governor Bass became president of the American Forestry Association and worked for the expansion of forest fire lookout towers throughout the state to halt the devastating forest fires that resulted from sloppy timber practices. While governor, Bass married Edith Bird, whose father, Charles Sumner Bird, was the leader of the Progressive Party movement in Massachusetts. In 1912, Governor Bass was prevented from running for reelection on the Republican ticket because of an ancient convention that a governor could run for only one term.

Although Sherman Burroughs was unable to accept the candidacy for governor in 1910, he ran for Congress against Manchester's ten-term incumbent Cyrus Sulloway, "The Tall Pine of the Merrimack," who won the election. Burroughs, a law partner of Judge McLane in 1912 when the latter started practice in Manchester, became a congressman in 1917 when he won a special election to fill the vacancy caused by the death of Cyrus Sulloway.

In the national political arena, it will be recalled that Roosevelt had supported William Howard Taft as his successor in 1908, but upon Roosevelt's return from an African hunting trip in 1909–1910, the Progressive members of the Republican Party complained to him of Taft's conservatism and urged him to get back into the political fray. By 1912 the latent hostility between Roosevelt and Taft had burst into the open.[12] Roosevelt sent out feelers and got the endorsement of seven Republican governors, including Robert P. Bass of New Hampshire. Political attacks between Roosevelt and Taft became legion. Both Taft and Roosevelt campaigned in New Hampshire in the spring of 1912 for the Republican National Convention candidates. (Former Progressive William E. Chandler stuck with Taft!) The Republican National Convention was held on June 18 in Chicago, where Taft was easily renominated. Roosevelt bolted the party and on August 5 was nominated for president by the new Progressive Party at its convention, with the bull moose as its emblem; – hence its historic name "Bull Moose Convention."

In New Hampshire, Governor Bass and Winston Churchill, both staunch Roosevelt supporters, convened the New Hampshire Progressive Party. Judge notes in his diary on August 26, 1912, "Proposition from Churchill and Bass to become State Chairman of Progressive Party and to manage campaign quarters here. Shan't go into it." I suspect that the reason was that, as of August 1, he had accepted his first employment as an attorney with the prestigious law firm of Taggart, Burroughs & Wyman in Manchester, and accepting the chairmanship of the Progressive Party would not be compatible with his new job.[13]

In September, the New Hampshire Progressive Party Convention was held; it nominated Winston Churchill for governor and adopted a platform that, among other things, said: "In the campaign of 1906, the Lincoln Republicans under the leadership of Winston Churchill were beaten in the state convention only by the use of methods similar to those which have made the Republican National Convention of 1912 notorious. Four years later they were victorious under the leadership of Robert P. Bass . . ."

At the national elections on November 5, 1912, Democrat Woodrow Wilson defeated Progressive Roosevelt and Republican Taft. In the New Hampshire race for governor, Democrat Felker defeated Progressive Churchill and Republican Worcester, but, since there was no majority, the election was thrown into the legislature, where a combination of Progressives and Democrats elected Samuel D. Felker governor. In the last election of U.S. senators by the legislature, Attorney Henry F. Hollis, Democrat, of Concord was elected on the forty-third ballot and served until 1919.[14] The Progressive Party had been urging direct election of U.S. senators, which finally passed and became effective with the 1914 election. Some of the planks in the Progressive Party platform were 1) support initiative, referendum, and recall; 2) abolish discrimination on the grounds of sex in the exercise of suffrage; 3) direct election of U.S. senators; 4) presidential preferential primary; 5) permanent legislative drafting bureau; and 6) public record of all votes.

In 1914, Judge was elected secretary of the Progressive Party, which had been weakened by the losses of 1912. Rolland Spaulding, a conservative Republican businessman, was elected governor. Judge ran for representative to the state legislature on the Progressive Party ticket in Milford and was defeated, his first and last taste of elective politics.

In 1916, with a war in Europe, President Wilson was reelected easily. The Progressive Party in New Hampshire polled only .05 percent of the vote cast, substantially below the 3 percent required to remain a recognized party. Many Progressives continued their activities as the liberal wing of the Republican Party for many more years. The Progressive Party at the national level disbanded in the summer of 1916.

From age five to age twenty-one, Judge grew up in a political environment. His father served in the house for two terms in 1885 and 1887 and in the senate as president in 1891 and 1893; he was a delegate to the 1896 McKinley-Roosevelt Republican National Convention; and he was elected governor for the 1905 to 1907 term.

Politics was dear to Judge's heart. Like his father, he was an activist in the Progressive wing of the Republican Party, although he never aspired to elective office after he was defeated in the race for state representative from Milford in 1914 on the Progressive ticket. In February 1919, after returning from a stint in the War Department in Washington, Judge, who had just hung out his shingle as a solo practitioner, was asked by his Progressive friends to draft a women's presidential suffrage bill; it passed the legislature in September. Judge loved to talk about the Progressive branch of the Republican Party and its political candidates and platform with his clients former Governor Robert P. Bass, future governor John G. Winant, and future governor and congressman Charles Tobey.

In early 1920, Huntley Spaulding,[15] a wealthy fiberboard manufacturer, of Rochester, New Hampshire, asked Judge to survey his chances against incumbent U.S. Senator George Moses in the Republican primary. Huntley had worked with Judge on the New Hampshire Children's Aid board, where Huntley was president and Judge was treasurer. I suspect Huntley admired Judge's ability even though they espoused different political philosophies— Huntley being a conservative and Judge a Progressive Republican. Judge accepted and had some twenty-three daily entries, including interviews with the following: 1) Huntley's brother, Rolland, who had been governor from 1915 to 1917; 2) John Gilbert Winant, a young aspiring politician who served in the legislature in 1917, returned to New Hampshire after World War I, and served in the state senate in 1923; 3) Irving Drew, a prominent attorney in Lancaster, New Hampshire, which at the time was an important center for the lumber and railroad industries; 4) Ernest Martin Hopkins, president of Dartmouth College, who kept his political ear close to his many friends; 5) Frank Knox, editor of the *Manchester Union*, a statewide morning newspaper, and the *Leader*, a Manchester afternoon newspaper; 6) a Mr. Lessard; 7) John Barry, a labor person; 8) former Governor Robert Bass of Peterborough; 9) Arthur Rotch, publisher of the *Milford Cabinet*;[16] and 10) a Mr. Hinman from Milford.

Judge finished the report, which I conclude was not more than mildly encouraging, and then had a series of meetings: one with Huntley, another with Huntley and his "agents," dinner with Mr. and Mrs. Spaulding, another couple of days in Manchester with Huntley, and an all-day conference in Manchester with Huntley "et als." In August, Judge spoke for Huntley at a rally in Milford and later at rallies in Dublin, Harrisville, Troy, Marlboro, and Exeter. Judge confided to his diary on August 5: "Spaulding campaign doesn't stir up great excitement." His prediction was correct; the primary results showed Moses with 28,000 votes to Spaulding's 15,000. George Moses was a popular politician from Concord and was well known around the state, having attended Phillips Exeter and graduated from Dartmouth College in the class of 1890 and received a graduate degree in 1893. He was secretary to Governor McLane in 1904–1905 and was elected to the U.S. Senate in 1918, 1920, 1926, and 1932. He was defeated by Charles Tobey in 1938.

Judge became involved in local politics affecting construction of the Queen City Bridge. In early 1921, the bridge, designed to span both the railroad tracks and the Merrimack River, was ready for construction. It was a substantial piece of work for Manchester, one of the city's largest contracts. The mayor was Democrat Moise Verette, who had been elected in 1917 when the Democrats acquired undisputed control of the city government. Rumors began to circulate that the bridge contract was heavily padded with excessive expenses, money for which was going to end up in the pockets of some local politicians. Local Republicans swung into action. Even before the bridge affair hit the papers, efforts were begun to rewrite the city charter to limit the authority of the mayor and heads of departments. Louis Wyman (Judge's former law partner) asked Judge to work on a revision to the city charter. By the end of that month, there was a "stir about the Mayor's action on the bridge contracts," and a Saturday-evening meeting was held with a Chamber of Commerce committee to decide on a course of action. The next day, Judge, after teaching Sunday school in the morning, worked the rest of the day preparing an injunction petition. A temporary injunction was issued on Monday to restrain any action by city officials with respect to the bridge contracts or construction. Judge and Louis Wyman drafted a bill to create a finance commission, to be appointed by the governor, to approve all city expenditures. Judge worked several days on the city charter legislation providing for a new highway commission to be appointed by the governor. He also prepared a permanent injunction, which was granted, restraining the city from engaging in any bridge construction. The finance and the highway commission bills sailed through the Republican legislature; for thirty years thereafter, the state government (mostly Republicans) had veto power over the expenditures approved by the Manchester Mayor and Board of Alderman (mostly Democrats). The city engineer was fired. The new highway commission rewrote the Queen City Bridge contracts, and the bridge was built at a savings of tens of thousands of dollars over the original contract. John Carleton served on the finance commission in the late 1930s; the commission was abolished after the enabling legislation was repealed in the late 1940s.

Because John Gilbert Winant at this point in time becomes an important New Hampshire political figure as well as a client of Judge's, it is appropriate to relate something of his background. Winant was perhaps the most charismatic individual of twentieth-century New Hampshire. He was Republican governor of New Hampshire for an unprecedented three terms, a confidant of President Franklin D. Roosevelt, first chairman of the Social Security System, organizer of the International Labor Office in Geneva, and U.S. ambassador to the Court of St. James in London during World War II from 1941 to 1946.

Born in 1889, John Winant was the oldest of four sons of Frederick Winant, a successful real estate broker in New York City. The Winants spent summer vacations on Long Island, in Connecticut, or in Europe. Frederick sent two of his younger sons to a highly recommended school in upstate New York and was shocked, as a good Presbyterian, to discover (after the boys were all enrolled) that it was a Catholic school. John went to St. Paul's School in Concord, New Hampshire, an Episcopal school, more to his father's liking. "Gil," as he was known to all his friends, was never a great student. But he developed "an extreme sensitivity toward, and an intense interest in, his fellow human beings in and outside the classroom."[17] At St. Paul's School, he was captain of one of the two boat club crews (Halcyon); he received one of the school's highest awards, the School Medal, and graduated in 1908. He was tutored at home that fall and in 1909 entered Princeton, where he soon became involved in campus politics concerning Princeton President Woodrow Wilson. Wilson was becoming more visible as a Democrat to oppose the feuding Republicans, Taft and Roosevelt, for the U.S. presidency in 1912. At the end of Winant's sophomore year (1911), he dropped out of Princeton and went back to St. Paul's School to teach. He returned to Princeton in February 1912, immediately became embroiled in politics, and dropped out again to work for Roosevelt in the "Bull Moose" campaign of 1912.

Winant taught history at St. Paul's School from 1912 to 1917 and became a Vice Rector, with additional administrative duties. But the lure of politics was too much. He was elected to the state legislature in 1917.

In World War I, Winant entered the Army Air Forces and became a pilot, rising from the rank of private to captain. He served in France and was cited for gallantry under fire. While he was in the Army he met Arthur Coyle, his commanding officer, with whom, in 1921, he became involved in the oil business in Texas. Together they formed the Coyle Concord Oil Company.

*John G. Winant*, pilot, World War I, in France.
Credit: St. Paul's School Archives.

After demobilization, Gil married Constance Rivington of Princeton and returned to the St. Paul's School faculty from 1919 to 1921. He was again elected to the legislature in 1921 and to the state senate in 1923.

Judge became a trustee of St. Paul's School in 1918 and most certainly became intimately acquainted with Gil and Constance. In June 1921 Judge became involved with Winant and the Coyle Concord Oil Company. He saw Gil on a regular basis. They and their wives met socially as well. In 1923, Gil became godfather to Elisabeth (Lilla), Judge and Elisabeth's daughter.

In November 1922, Judge notes that he talked to John Winant and (Jim) Langley about the purchase of the *Concord Monitor* newspaper. I suspect that Winant knew he was going to be involved in politics, and control of the local newspaper could be a very valuable asset. In fact the week before, Judge had lunch with former Governor Robert Bass and future Governor Charles Tobey; I assume that politics was the topic of conversation. It is not surprising to find Judge meeting in 1923 in Concord with Gil, Jim Langley, and a Mr. Gallagher to continue the earlier conversations concerning the purchase of the Concord *Patriot* and *Monitor*. Later, he met with Gil, Robert, and John Bass to interest the Basses in investing in the papers.[18] Judge worked with Gil and Langley on the purchase of the papers, which was consummated. Judge then incorporated the business.

Especially in New Hampshire, 1924 was a big election year. Fred H. Brown, a Democrat, had been elected in 1922, and the Republicans wanted to get him out.

A little background information is necessary. During the nineteenth and early twentieth centuries, politics was controlled by the parties, which held conventions to select candidates for office. The party in turn was controlled by the party "machine," active members who were frequently officeholders from the counties, such as the register of deeds, the register of probate, the sheriffs, and the county attorneys. Toward the end of the nineteenth century, things had gotten so bad that the B&MRR was able to control both parties and get its agenda approved. This domination led to the rise of the Progressive movement and reform in the election process. In 1908, the legislature passed the direct primary law, which abolished party conventions as determinants of party candidates and replaced them with the direct primary election. Congress passed legislation requiring the direct election of U.S. senators starting in 1914, rather than have the state legislatures elect them. This was another blow to "machine" politics.

John Gilbert Winant, a Progressive Republican, had the funds, ambition, and ideas to be governor. He began building an organization. As Gil organized his campaign, Judge became a member of his "executive committee." Judge notes in July that he along with Charlie Tobey and Gil spent one day campaigning in Wilton, Milford, Greenville, and New Ipswich. He went to Exeter to see John Scammon and "General" Greene, who controlled the Rockingham County "machine." In early August, Judge met in Peterborough with, among others, young Styles Bridges,[19] a protégé of Robert Bass, who was helping on the campaign. In mid-August Judge confided in his diary that the Winant campaign was keeping him busy. At the end of the month he spoke at Milford and presided at a "great" rally at Manchester City Hall at which Gil and former Governor Robert Bass spoke.

The primaries on September 2 gave Winant a victory (tantamount to election) over Frank Knox, editor and owner of the *Manchester Union* and *Leader* newspapers. Judge and Elisabeth went to Concord in the evening for the election returns, which were telephoned in from each voting precinct. Later in the month, Judge and Ralph worked on Gil's expenditure return and had conferences with the attorney general. I surmise they had some concern that Gil might have exceeded his spending limits established by the state and wanted to be up front with any problems. Because the law was relatively new, definitions of what were permissible or impermissible contributions and expenditures were not clear. In October, there were more rallies, talks, and fund-raising. In early November, Gil won the general election, along with Coolidge on the national ticket.

Winant had been elected with the strong support of the Progressive Republican group. It included former Governor Robert Bass, who was a key leader of reform coalitions;[20] Charles Tobey, who was elected president of the senate; and Judge McLane. Winant was inaugurated governor in January 1925, an exciting event because this was the first Progressive Republican to hold a high state office.

Progressives had an opportunity to pass the legislation they had been fighting for, for a decade. Judge worked on drafting the liberal Republican platform, which included: 1) a new accounting system for the state and an audit of the old state accounts; 2) an inventory of all state property; 3) a tax commission to provide for uniform state evaluation of taxable property; 4) a state publicity board to advertise the state for recreational and industrial purposes, which introduced the promotional magazine the *Troubadour*; 5) support for the establishment of the New England Council to promote regional development; and 6) a state road survey to develop a comprehensive state highway system. The reform group lost on its effort to pass a forty-eight-hour work week and ratification of a U.S. child labor constitutional amendment, but it did fight back an attempt to repeal the primary election law passed several years earlier. Winant's administration was successful in purchasing the Old Man of the Mountain for the state from a lumber company.

Judge was Winant's personal adviser and spent much time with the governor in Concord at meetings, with or without meals, at any time of the day or night, discussing and drafting legislation, advising on appointments, and generally listening to the governor's ideas. They were in touch by phone on a daily basis. As an adviser, whether to Governor Winant or others, Judge was attentive, tolerant, and understanding. He rarely expressed his personal position but rather analyzed the proposal, seeking its pluses and minuses, and developed options to counter problem areas. In those days, there were minimal paid staffs, probably only a secretary or two, supplemented by volunteer friends and advisers.

Judge had a number of political meetings in 1925: a long talk with Charles Tobey in February; in June, a meeting at Judge's house in Manchester with Winant, Bass, Arthur Rotch, Winthrop Wadleigh, Fuller, and Ralph Davis; another meeting in Manchester in August attended by Bass, Tobey, James Richardson, Ben Worcester, Ben Orr, Coolidge, Parmenter, Davis, Briggs Felton, Cowan, Wadleigh, and Bridges; and several individual meetings, including one with "Rob" Bass in Peterborough to talk about his senatorship announcement. Presumably at these meetings, the legislative agenda, gaining control of the Republican Party (which had been in the hands of the conservatives), party finances, and future candidates were

*John Winant*, governor of New Hampshire, 1925.
Credit: St. Paul's School Archive.

the topics of discussion. In March, Ralph Davis and Judge were engaged in drafting a new primary election law, and Judge spent a number of days on a change in the way the state treasurer accounted for state trust funds, including arguing before the supreme court on a request from the legislature for an Opinion of the Justices on the matter (Opinion of the Justices, April 16, 1925, 81 NH 573). Judge met with Gil, Jim Richardson, a political science professor at Dartmouth, and former Governor A. O. Brown on the state budget. During the fall, there were many meetings with Rob Bass and the announcement in November of his candidacy for the U.S. Senate. In late November, Judge Plummer of the supreme court died, and Gil asked Judge "about taking a seat on the supreme court," but he declined.[21]

With Gil as governor and George Moses as senator,[22] 1926 was a hot year for politics. Rob Bass decided to run for conservative George Moses' senate seat as a liberal Republican. Huntley Spaulding felt that Winant was too liberal as governor, so decided to run against him. The slate then was Conservatives Spaulding and Moses versus Liberals Winant and Bass.[23] There were many political organization and fund-raising meetings. As summer came, there were town rallies. At the September primaries, unfortunately, Spaulding defeated Winant and Moses swamped Bass. Spaulding and Moses were easily elected in November. The Progressive platform had gone down to defeat. The Progressive wing had fought for the primary system of party nominations, replacing the party convention. They believed in professional administration of public welfare by the state rather than by the county government's politically appointed welfare administrators. They wanted a state police force of professionally trained officers rather than the politically appointed sheriffs and deputy sheriffs.

The day after the election, Judge confides in his diary, "Glad to be off politics and at law again."

The defeat of the Progressives presaged a quieter political year for 1927. One of Judge's first January jobs was to help Gil write his swan song speech.

In 1927, with the conservatives in control, efforts were made by the Republican machine to abolish the primary elections and revert back to the "machine" convention system, anathema to the Progressives. There were several meetings, and legal research was conducted to stop the conservatives in January and February. In March the legislature killed the bill: "a fine victory," notes Judge. During the remainder of 1927, there were a number of political meetings spearheaded by Charles Tobey, who was gearing up to run for governor.

In 1928, Tobey was busy. In August Judge wrote: "Political pot boiling and looking good for Tobey." Tobey was a far more effective speaker than prior Progressive standard-bearers Bass and Winant. There were many rallies. Judge spoke at Laconia and presided at a rally at Manchester City Hall the night before the primary election, which Tobey won handily. Then in late September, Ralph Davis presided at the Republican convention, which adopted the platform that Judge had drafted. Judge states in his diary, "Everything our way." In the November election, Tobey won the governorship, but Bass again lost the senate race to Moses. Nationally, Hoover defeated New York Governor Al Smith.

In January 1929, Judge helped Charlie Tobey on his inaugural address as governor and had a couple of talks with him during the year. Otherwise, the year was fairly quiet politically. In December, Judge attended a luncheon in Nashua at which the future of the Republican Party was discussed, with Tobey, Francis Murphy, Winant, Worcester, and Bridges present.

In January 1930, Judge met with Gil Winant, Governor Tobey, and Attorney General Ralph Davis (appointed on May 1, 1929, by Governor Tobey) to decide on candidates. Apparently Tobey did not want to run for reelection but had his eyes on Congress. Gil was anxious to avenge his defeat for reelection as governor and announced his candidacy in early February. Judge had several political sessions during the spring and summer and notes in early September, "Political situation warming up." Albert W. Noone ran for both governor and the U.S. Senate and lost both. (What would have happened had he won both?) Winant won both the primary and the general election for governor when the country made a huge Democratic sweep for Roosevelt. Tobey waited until 1932, when he ran successfully for Congress.

In 1931, shortly after taking office, Winant created a State Unemployment Committee to alleviate the problems of the unemployed. He utilized available federal funds from the Reconstruction Finance Corporation (RFC) to stimulate a highway building program. He sponsored legislation to create and fund the New Hampshire League of Arts and Crafts to stimulate home industry with quality control. He brought in the Brookings Institute to conduct a survey on the efficiency of state government. He promoted the state Parent-Teacher Association (PTA) as an aid to education and the Daniel Webster Council of the Boy Scouts to develop character building in the young boys of the state. He pushed an agricultural program to eradicate bovine brucellosis.

In June 1932, Judge, returning from one of his numerous business trips west, was a New Hampshire delegate to the Republican National Convention at the Edgewater Beach Hotel in Chicago and was elected chairman of the delegation. The only item of note was the rejection by the convention of the minority committee report to immediately repeal Prohibition. Fortunately, the Democrats voted for 3.2 beer by Christmas. Shortly thereafter, the country repealed Prohibition. Hoover and Curtis were nominated by the convention and were swamped by the election of Franklin D. Roosevelt. Shortly after returning to New Hampshire, Judge hosted a group of the Progressives—Winant, Bass, Tobey, Attorney General Ralph Davis, Styles Bridges, Gerry Waldron, Jim Langley, Arthur Rotch, Bob Burroughs, and John Carleton—at Three Acres on North Union Street in Manchester. This group decided on the liberal Republican candidates. In the November election, Winant was reelected to an unprecedented third term. Longtimer Senator George Moses was unseated by Brown, and Charlie Tobey was elected to Congress.

After the 1932 election, Winant utilized many "New Deal" programs to benefit the State.[24] There were a number of Civilian Conservation Corps (CCC) camps that built walking and ski trails in the mountains. Federal matching grants were used to inaugurate aid to the blind, child health services, aid to dependent children, and old age assistance. The FDIC (Federal Deposit Insurance Corporation) was started to protect bank deposits. With the repeal of Prohibition, a state liquor store system was established.

In 1934, the political arena was active. Roosevelt had been elected in 1932 and the Democrats were pretty popular, making it necessary for the liberal wing of the Republican Party to work hard. Winant had been elected in 1932 but did not stand for reelection, and Styles Bridges, a pro-tégé of Bass and Winant, was tapped by the group to run for governor. On July 12 Bridges gave a speech in Durham that got Gil Winant upset. Judge met with a number of the group at his Three Acres and got the matter straightened out. There were additional sessions at Three Acres on July 19 and July 30. Bridges won the primary in September; then there was the platform to be determined and drafted. In October there was a mix-up on the platform, and Judge had a session with Bridges to get that straightened out. Judge spoke at rallies in Winchester, Marlboro, and Troy on October 19 and later at Ward 8 in Concord. It was an exciting election, with Bridges beating out popular Democrat John Sullivan.

This was the effective end of the Progressive movement in the Republican Party. From this point on, candidates announced their own plans. There was no group action with respect to candidates or platforms. The New Deal and World War II completely dominated national politics from 1932 until Roosevelt's death in 1944.

Shortly after Gil ended his term of office in early 1935, Harold Butler of Great Britain, director of the newly established International Labor Organization (ILO) in Geneva, Switzerland, of which the United States became a member in 1934, wished to secure a prominent American as an officer. He asked Winant to be the assistant director. Winant moved to Geneva in May 1935, but in August he was called back by President Roosevelt to become the first chairman of the recently created Social Security Board. He then toured Europe to study the systems over there, which were already in place. He remained in Washington until 1937, when, after consultations with Roosevelt, he resigned to return to the ILO.

Winant had sensed the heating up of an imminent war in Europe. Because the United States lacked a listening post in Europe—this country was not a member of the League of Nations—Winant suggested to Roosevelt that he would be more valuable at his old post at the ILO. The president agreed. The following year, 1938, Harold Butler retired and Winant was appointed the director. In 1940, Roosevelt asked Winant to be secretary of war, but Winant responded that he could not leave the rela-tively new ILO, which was in the process of being moved to Montreal.[25]

Winant continued as director for three years, when once again he was called home by the president, this time to be appointed ambassador to the Court of St. James in London to succeed Joseph Kennedy[26] in February 1941. President Roosevelt had previously gone out of his way to meet the new British ambassador on a warship off the East Coast and welcome him to the United States. The king of England reciprocated and met Ambassador Winant at the railway station in London to welcome him to Great Britain. During air raids, Winant walked the streets, giving comfort where he could. On one occasion in 1941, he and Mrs. Winant went onto the roof of the embassy to watch an air raid in progress and had a narrow escape when a "blockbuster" exploded not far away. Winant, having been a combat pilot in World War I, did not flinch at danger. In April 1941, while at the Embassy, he was reviewing a speech brought to him by John Colville, assistant to the prime minister, Winston Churchill, which was to be delivered the next day in the House of Commons. The speech was about the United States becoming involved in the war on a more active basis than it had been, a touchy subject. Colville writes: "He [Winant] made four pertinent observations in respect of the effect on U.S. opinion and I was deeply impressed by his unassertive shrewdness and wisdom. I afterwards explained these points to the P.M. [prime minister] who accepted them. While I was with the Ambassador a blitz started. He did not even raise his head."[27]

When Mrs. Winant was back in the United States with the children, Winant spent many a night with the Churchills and the Edens in London or "Chequers," where they discussed the reconstruction of Europe after the war. The war struck home to the Winants when their oldest son, John, was shot down on a combat mission in the fall of 1943. He was held as a POW until the end of the war. The ambassador stayed on in London until 1946.[28]

As the end of the war became nearer and the establishment of the United Nations (UN) was being considered, Winant talked with President Roosevelt about becoming the first Secretary General of the UN. The president promised to support Gil's ambition. However, everything changed with Roosevelt's sudden death in the spring of 1945. President Truman would have other plans. Moreover, New York was selected as the UN site, which precluded consideration of a U.S. citizen as the Secretary General. Winant did serve as the U.S. Representative to the UN Economic and Social Council in 1946. He resigned in December to return to life as a private citizen in Concord.[29]

A number of people have commented on Gil Winant's character. When governor, his door was always open to talk to anyone. "He always gave the impression then, and afterwards when he was Ambassador, that he was more interested in his visitor and what he was saying than anything else. He never allowed himself to seem important."[30]

I remember meeting him a number of times in the 1930s. He was tall and had tousled black hair and thick dark, bushy eyebrows, a distinctive soft voice, large hands, and a hefty handshake. People often referred to him as "Lincolnesque." He would look me square in the eye and say, with great sincerity, "Now tell me, John, what are you up to these days?" and he would listen attentively to my answer. He was a very impressive person, although a terrible public speaker. In his halting way, he would stop in the middle of a word or sentence, as though stuttering, struggling to find the right word. You wanted to shout out the word to him, so he could get on with his speech.

There never was any question about his sincerity. His biographer, Bernard Bellush, says:

> Winant had little sense of timing for eating, sleeping or family responsibilities, rarely stopping for a hot meal or a leisurely break during long exhausting workdays. He became totally immersed in administrative decisions and, at times, with the personal problems of troubled visitors … Exhilarated by increasing responsibilities, the Governor frequently overlooked commitments to his wife to host a houseful of dinner guests. This grueling schedule likewise kept him away much of the time from his young children, even though he regretted missing a full family life.
>
> Winant would frequently sit up much of the night reading Ruskin, or conversing with Robert Bass or lawyer friend, John McLane, about intra-party developments, world affairs, the unique personality of Calvin Coolidge or oil investments in Texas. Well along into the morning, an exhausted, droopy visitor would finally take his leave of a vibrant talkative host. Burning this tremendous store of energy would eventually take its toll. With too few relaxing avocations, he seldom shared the joys and change of pace of sports, camping or other outdoor activities.[31]

Gil was unconcerned about many details of his life. When going off on an intercontinental trip, he needed to be reminded about money, foreign exchange rates, and clothes (he frequently was expected to be in formal dress). He was quite oblivious to the necessity of taking a raincoat if he was traveling to the tropics, or a heavy coat if he was going to London or Geneva in winter. He was not a good money manager. His various business ventures were only marginally successful, and he sometimes had to borrow money. His close friends who loaned him money may have been disappointed in not receiving prompt and full payment, but they rationalized that it was a small contribution to ensure having a person of Winant's quality and stature in national and international policymaking positions.

In Concord, Gil Winant worked on his memoirs. He completed them in the fall of 1947. He was not in good health, suffering from stomach ulcers, nervous tension, and extreme fatigue. Furthermore, he seemed frustrated with life. On November 3, 1947, he shot himself while in his house at Concord—a tragic end to the life of a great American.

John Winant was one of New Hampshire's and the nation's greats—

idealist, egalitarian, interested in major policy decisions, confidant of many leaders, effective administrator, and an inspiration to all who knew him.

Appraising and disposing of John Winant's estate took considerable time. There was a very interesting and valuable library, which Judge had appraised by Mr. Goodspeed from Boston. Judge discussed purchase of the library with Gil Verney, who had just bought the Pierce Farm in Bennington as part of the purchase of the Monadnock Paper Mills. Gil Verney acquired the library. The personal property likewise included many interesting and valuable pieces. Constance Winant loved her family's property in Princeton, New Jersey, which she had inherited; she had stayed there frequently with the children while Gil was on many of his overseas assignments, particularly during the war years. Thus, she had little interest in the Concord property, which the state acquired for a children's psychiatric treatment center. It was never used for that purpose but was subsequently acquired by the Unitarian Church, which removed the buildings to make way for a new church.

# Notes

1. Elizabeth Forbes Morison and Elting E. Morison, *New Hampshire* (New York: W. W. Norton & Company, Inc., 1976), p. 170.

2. Morison, *New Hampshire*, p. 175.

3. Morison, *New Hampshire*, p. 177.

4. Appendix B.2, Henry French Hollis.

5. Squires, *Granite State*, Vol. II, p. 597.

6. Squires, *Granite State*, Vol. II, p. 600.

7. Appendix B.3, Treaty of Portsmouth.

8. Pillsbury refers to him as "Colonel" Churchill. Pillsbury, *New Hampshire*, p. 701.

9. Winston Churchill's beautiful estate in Cornish served as the summer White House for President Woodrow Wilson. Pillsbury, *New Hampshire*, p. 701.

10. Morison, *New Hampshire*, p. 178. "Pandemonium reigned [at the convention] . . . and the battle ebbed and flowed all day and all night. On some ballots, more votes were cast than the total number of delegates eligible to sit at the convention." Pillsbury, *New Hampshire*, Vol. III, p. 732.

11. Squires, *Granite State*, Vol. II, p. 602.

12. Squires, *Granite State*, Vol. II, p. 607.

13. Judge did, however, work for the Progressives, attending a rally on September 26 at which both Churchill and Bass spoke. On October 11, 12, and 14, he worked evenings at headquarters, and on the sixteenth, "he spent a.m.

in Concord on Progressive ballot tangle–hdq in evening." He attended a hearing before the Ballot Law Commission the next day. On October 18, he was at headquarters. October 22, "Governor Bass with us (in Milford) for supper and a fine rally." October 31, "Busy preparing speech for rally in Milford." November 1, "Home (Milford) at 5:30. Made my first political speech at rally with Winston Churchill and Rev. Daniel Gross speaking." He spoke at Henniker on the fourth and went home on the fifth to vote for Roosevelt. "Wilson carried the country by a big margin."

14. Appendix B.2, Henry French Hollis.

15. Appendix B.4, Huntley N. Spaulding.

16. Grandfather of Peter B. Rotch, a partner in the McLane law firm.

17. Bernard Bellush, *He Walked Alone* (The Hague: Mouton, 1968), p. 13.

18. Former Governor Robert Bass and his brother, John Bass, both of Peterborough, were well-to-do liberal "Bull Moose" Republicans, as was Gil Winant.

19. Later governor, elected in 1935, and U.S. senator elected in 1936, 1942, 1948, 1954, and 1960.

20. James Wright, *The Progressive Yankees* (Hanover, N.H., and London: University Press, 1987), p. 183.

21. Judge reasoned that he had a better chance to educate his four children (three boys, one girl) the way he and Elisabeth thought they should be educated if he stuck to his law practice rather than accept the security of a court appointment.

22. In January 1926 Judge met for breakfast with President Hopkins of Dartmouth and Rob Bass, later talked with Governor Winant about the campaign, and at the end of the month talked with Bass about the progress in Manchester. During the summer, there were more political talks, and Judge spoke at several rallies for Bass and Winant in Canaan, Milford, and other towns.

23. Then ten years old, I remember being at Newfound Lake for the summer and stuffing envelopes for Winant and Bass by the hour, my first exposure to practical politics. Winant was running against a fifty-year tradition that a governor should hold office for only one term.

24. Squires, *Granite State*, Vol II, p. 695.

25. Obituary notice, *Manchester Union*, November 4, 1947.

26. Mr. Kennedy was an Irishman, hardly an Anglophile, and lacked the qualities of John Winant as a confidant of Roosevelt, Churchill, and Eden.

27. John Colville, *The Fringes of Power* (New York, London: W. W. Norton & Company, Inc. 1985), p. 372.

28. I remember that at the end of the war, in 1945, I was relieved of my command of a naval vessel in the Mediterranean for rotation back to the States and further assignment to the Pacific. I went to Paris en route home and stayed with my brother Charles, who was stationed there in the Army. My brother Malcolm, an Air Force pilot, who had been shot down the preceding December during the Battle of the Bulge, had been in a POW camp in Germany and had been released. However, we did not know his whereabouts, but we suspected he might have been sent to Camp Lucky Strike, near Paris, where most POWs went before being returned to the States. We took a chance and called the U. S. embassy in London. We talked to Gil, who characteristically treated this as of great personal importance and put us in touch with the office that might be able to help. Unfortunately, things were too confusing and rushed, and the information had not been processed, so we didn't locate Malcolm then.

29. Obituary notice, *Manchester Union*, November 4, 1947.

30. Obituary notice, *Manchester Union*, November 4, 1947.

31. Bellush, *He Walked Alone*, p. 73.

# FIVE

# Coyle Concord Oil Company

Judge's long client relationship with John Winant began in June 1921. Oil had been discovered in east Texas before World War I. During and after the war the oil business expanded rapidly with the drilling of wells and the construction of refineries and petroleum plants. Houston developed its ship canal and became the major center of the oil industry. After World War I, oil exploration moved west to central Texas, where new wildcat wells encouraged the further development of oil fields. The anticipated wealth of the west Texas fields never materialized, at least for Winant and his partner, Arthur Coyle, founders of the Coyle Concord Oil Company.

Arthur Coyle was the prime mover and CEO of the Coyle Concord Oil Company. He managed it from San Antonio. Coyle's colorful life began in Berlin, New Hampshire, where he was born about 1900. When quite young his family moved to Concord. In 1914, tensions between Mexicans and U.S. citizens along the Mexican border in Texas began to heat up[1] to such an extent that several National Guard outfits were called up to maintain peace and order, including units of the New Hampshire National Guard. Arthur Coyle wanted to see the world and experience some excitement, so he faked his age and enlisted shortly before the outfit departed for Texas in 1916.[2]

At that time, flying was in its infancy, but the use of airplanes as an intelligence-gathering device about enemy troop movements and deployment was not lost on the Army. The Army was also impressed with the ideal flying conditions (clear skies, few clouds, and no fog) in the southern part of Texas and therefore located a number of training fields around San Antonio. The Army Air Forces expanded their numbers, encouraged flight training, and offered transfers from state National Guard outfits on favorable terms. Learning to fly appealed to Arthur, so he volunteered for flight training. First he was assigned by the adjutant general of the New Hampshire National Guard to take a course in flight training offered by the Aero Club of America. (Flying was so new, the Army had no teachers and relied on a private company to do the training.) Coyle was one of the very first Army pilots. The early mission of the Air Force was largely observation and reconnaissance; combat missions were introduced later. Early in

1916, at the time of the Mexican trouble, Arthur's unit was "federalized" along with other National Guard units and sent to Mineola, on Long Island, New York, for further training.[3]

In September 1917, five months after the United States declared war on Germany, Coyle, as a pilot in the First Aero Squadron, arrived in England. Three days later, he was in France. In October, he began aerial spotting over the battlefront. In May 1918, he was made flight commander of the First Aero Squadron. He was the first American Expeditionary Force aviator to be cited for superior performance of his duties. In mid-June the First Aero Squadron was assigned to the First Army Corps and served during the offensives in Château Thierry, St.-Mihiel, Remicourt, and Argonne. Coyle was decorated with the Distinguished Service Cross and left the service in January 1919 as a captain.

One of the pilots in Coyle's command was John G. Winant, a competent, courageous, and able young man but not, according to Coyle, a good pilot; he cracked up three planes in France.[4] On the way back to the States on a troop transport, Winant and Coyle talked of their futures. Winant indicated he would return to New Hampshire as a schoolmaster at St. Paul's School in Concord, where he had taught before the war, and perhaps get involved in politics. Coyle opted for Texas and a life involved with oil and airplanes, which is where he saw the future action to be. Arthur was well aware of the developing oil industry in Texas; he had seen the discovery oil wells in east Texas. He knew of the construction of refineries to make gasoline for the few new airplanes and the much larger number of autos and trucks that were beginning to roll off Detroit factory assembly lines.

As the troop transport approached New York City, Winant asked Coyle where he was going to stay that night. Finding Coyle had no plans, Winant offered him a bed at his family's house in Princeton, New Jersey, a stop on the Pennsylvania Railroad that would be on Coyle's route to Texas. They took the train to Princeton. Coyle, as he told the story, expecting to find a modest house, was overwhelmed to be met by a huge car with a liveried chauffeur who grasped Winant's bag and welcomed "Master Winant" home. The drive up the half-mile-long family driveway to a luxurious house was impressive, and the hospitality and accommodations were regal. Coyle boarded the train to Texas the next day with a comment from Winant to let him know if he ever found a worthwhile oil investment opportunity in Texas.

In the early summer of 1921, Coyle contacted Winant to advise him of a very interesting new wildcat[5] development in central Texas. I recall the story, probably apocryphal, that Arthur called Gil on a Friday reporting some red-hot opportunities to quickly grab some leases, get a drilling contract, and drill a wildcat well in a geologically interesting new area. Gil looked over his busy calendar and suggested to Arthur that they meet in New York City in about two weeks and talk it over. Arthur exploded on the phone, saying, "Hell, Gil, I need the money by Monday morning and plan to line up the leases starting tonight." Gil responded that he'd see what could be done. First, he called Judge to get him started on a corporation; then he called some of his Concord friends who were interested in putting up some cash for stock and told them to get their checks to him by Sunday noon. Judge corralled a secretary over the weekend and had the incorporation papers ready for a Sunday noon corporate organization meeting. He called the attorney general at home to have someone approve the corporate organization record that afternoon, then alerted the secretary of state that they would bring the organization record for recording at 8:30 Monday morning. He advised the bank president at home that he would have checks to deposit in the new corporate account and wanted to have a bank check payable to Western Union by 9 A.M. so he could wire the funds to Arthur by 10 A.M. According to the story, everything went like clockwork. The account of what actually happened follows. Gil consulted with Judge. Presumably, Gil expressed personal interest and put up money so that Arthur could negotiate to pick up some options on oil leases.

Things looked good by the end of the summer, so in early October, Judge went to Winant's home in Princeton to go over the "Texas proposition." The next day, in New York, they arranged a power of attorney (I assume running from Gil to Judge) and made a bank deposit before Judge took the evening train to St. Louis. Later Judge arrived in Dallas and continued on to Mexia (in central Texas, south of Corsicana and east of Waco), where he met Coyle. Coyle had obtained oil leases, and they went out to the oil field— "great sight, all excitement"—as several oil wells were being drilled. Arthur and Judge drove to Corsicana to meet the National Petroleum people and the next day drew a contract with Beaman Company (I assume to drill a well); returned to Mexia; set up a system of accounts with their agent, Rodney; and went out to the field again.[6] On October 12, they drove to Corsicana, took the trolleys to Dallas to the state fair, and saw one-quarter of the SMU (Southern Methodist University) vs. A&M (Texas Agriculture and Mechanics) football game before Judge caught the train back to St. Louis and then Princeton to report to Gil Winant. Judge continued to Boston and on to the Pasquaney Lodge at Newfound Lake for the weekend. On October 20, Judge confided to his diary, "Hard to work in office when my mind is on oil wells at Mexia."

The opportunity to go back to Texas came at the end of the month when Arthur Coyle telegraphed that the well (Coyle #1) was completed. For some tax reason peculiar to Texas, oil wells are rarely registered in the name of a corporation but are in an individual's name, thus this was "Coyle #1."[7] So Judge got the night train to New York, "getting things lined up,"

*Oil Well, Coyle #1* with Arthur Coyle (wearing hat) and Judge McLane, Mexia, Texas, in November 1921.

then went back to Dallas on November 3. He met with bank officers and Mr. McGhee, then went to Mexia at midnight and out to the well. "It's a corker. Good for better than ten thousand barrels."[8] The next day, they "spent day in the field getting familiar with operating problems. Lots of prospective buyers." Judge studied tax problems, went out to check on the well, then returned to Dallas, met with McGhee and the bank, and returned to Mexia at night. November 8 was spent on tax matters and in the field. Ben Lindsley from Ardmore, Oklahoma, arrived to appraise the well, then they drove to Corsicana and took the trolley to Dallas.

The taxes were complicated because this was a "discovery well" entitled to special tax treatment. A calculation was made of a selling price of the well of $750,000, of which $500,000 would be cash and the balance in oil. The estimate for possible recovery from the sixteen-acre lease was 800,000 to 1,200,000 barrels with a price of about sixty-five cents a barrel, or a potential of $780,000. (Compare the 1996 price of oil, about $18 a barrel or a potential of $21,600,000.) Judge caught the train home from Dallas. His diary entry for November 11, 1921—Armistice Day— "All day on train. Stopped two minutes outside St. Louis for ceremony of burial of unknown soldier." On Thanksgiving, Judge took the night train to New York with Coyle and Orr.[9] First, they met the Frankel brothers, who offered $250,000 in cash and the balance in oil. However, their credit reports were not satisfactory, so Judge and Arthur next talked with a Mr. Irwin, a wartime aviator buddy of Gil Winant and Arthur Coyle who had saved Coyle's life. However, Irwin's business honesty was questioned, and Gil would have nothing to do with him. They finally talked to Governor Haskell and others for a couple of days about a sale of the well, "made some progress," and then went home. After bargaining by wire, Ben Orr and Judge returned to New York and on December 1 reached a deal, selling the well to Haskell's Wichita Petroleum Company for $250,000 cash and $400,000 in oil. The next two days were spent drafting contracts and satisfactorily signing them. The form of the agreement was critical, because Judge figured that if it were done correctly, $100,000 could be saved in taxes.[10] Later in the month Judge spent the day in New York City "going over plans for business" and made up incorporation papers for the Coyle Winant Company, which were the subject of an all-day conference with Gil, Ben Orr, and Fred Colburn. The Coyle Winant Company apparently was a construction company connected to oil drilling, different from the to-be-formed Coyle Concord Oil Company. Possibly there was a desire to separate the risky drilling business from the valuable oil leasing company.

A substantial portion of the year 1922 was devoted to a continuation of the affairs of Coyle Concord Oil Company.[11] Judge went to New York in early January to talk business with Gil, and collected $60,000 from Governor Haskell of Texas for the oil production payments. He met Gil in Concord and again in New York before sailing on February 25 (with his wife, Elisabeth) on the SS *Momus* for New Orleans, a pleasant voyage on which they saw whales, the Florida coast, and porpoises and flying fish in the Gulf before entering the Mississippi River and disembarking on March 3 at New Orleans. They had dinner at Antoine's[12] before taking the train to Houston and then continued on to the well at Mexia, where they met Arthur Coyle and Gil Winant to line up the work to be done. After spending about four days on tax returns with Ben Orr, they went to Dallas on March 9 and then to Denison to see some oil people, then returned to New Hampshire via St. Louis and Cleveland (where Elisabeth stopped off to be with her sister, Jane Shiverick). Judge spent three days in New York City with Gil on oil and other business and observed the Ayrshire Association officers inspecting the Winant dairy herd on the family property in Princeton. Ben Orr and Judge discussed the new corporation, Coyle Concord Oil Company, which was signed up on April 3, although it was not recorded with the secretary of state until June 20. Judge met Gil in New York City on April 10 to see Cannon of Wichita Petroleum Company to collect the April oil payments and learned that they disputed the contract. The initial payments had been made on time; however, payments due in April were partial. Haskell said, according to his interpretation, the payments for oil produced would not be made until the cash payments were completed, claiming that this was the custom of the trade. The Winant-Coyle interests denied this interpretation. Six months earlier, in November 1921 when the well "came in," it was judged to be an excellent opportunity, and Wichita Petroleum Company bought it in December for a substantial price in those days. However, the well quickly petered out—it was just a "pimple," lots of pressure but very little oil—so naturally the buyers sought to get out of their substantial contract commitments. Judge obtained the name of an oil attorney in Houston, made an appointment, left for Houston on April 14, and worked until the twentieth with Judge Parker and Palmer Hutchinson on bringing suit, filing a bond, and arranging service and garnishee (attaching the funds of Wichita in the hands of banks), all apparently successfully. After returning to Manchester, Judge was off to New York City on May 5 to see Cannon, who agreed to pay half of the March and April oil runs. Judge saw Cannon again in New York City when he tried to get Cannon to have the contract guaranteed by Middle States (an oil company). Judge worked on the guarantee with Gil and Judge Parker in New York City.

Judge was back in New York City in late September to meet with Gil on an option offered to Wichita. On completely separate business Judge met a Mr. Hummel on a "Persian red oxide" proposition. (I have no idea what that is.) Judge also worked on Constance Winant's will (Gil's wife, who had substantial assets of her own), and was back again in New York City with Gil and an Arthur Gammel. A financial reorganization was effected to raise additional capital, to which Gil subscribed. In November Judge was busy on the reorganization papers before heading back to Texas late in the month. The suit against Haskell was successful in *step one* when Haskell's pleadings to dismiss were thrown out. The group had fun duck hunting on the weekend at Eagle Lake. They shot forty-eight ducks among them. Judge spent Thanksgiving with his sister-in-law Jane B. Shiverick in Cleveland en route to New York City to report to Gil. Later Judge spent several days (December 9 to 12) in New York City with Texas counsel taking depositions of the parties and key witnesses, then on to Houston for depositions of more witnesses. *Step two*, a court hearing, was held on December 22 in which the judge threw out the opponent's pleading, so Judge, Gil, and Ben Orr took the train back to New Orleans, then through the Carolinas, and, on Christmas Day 1922, passed through Washington to Boston. Judge notes, "Stocking on train in upper berth." I'm sure it was a happy reunion when "Elisabeth, Constance and Mrs. Orr met us in Boston."

In March 1923, the Texas court refused to annul the contract between the Winant-Coyle interests and Wichita Petroleum Company. In April, in *step three,* Judge and others tried the case in Texas and won a judgment for the full amount of $162,000. The judgment was appealed. In June, efforts were made to collect seven months of oil payments (separate from the above judgment) from Haskell in New York City. The partners were finally successful when Judge received a check for $56,800. Judge kept pursuing his debtor and was back in New York in August and October for more oil payments.

In early November 1923, Judge started for Texas once again via St. Louis. He arrived at Rockdale, where he met Arthur Coyle to go over the "Three Rivers proposition," a new project. They straightened out the books with Cassidy, then went on to San Antonio and later drove to Three Rivers to see Calligan's Frio riverbed lease. Judge tried to sell some locations before returning to San Antonio and going on to Houston on the night train. Arthur and Judge worked on the Wichita case with Palmer Hutchinson,[13] then took the train to Eagle Lake Club for another weekend of duck hunting. They were up at 5:15 and got thirty ducks by noon on Saturday and twenty at Sugar Mill hole on Sunday before returning to Houston. On Monday, Judge again worked with Palmer Hutchinson and Judge Garwood on the argument, then took the night train to Fort Worth and argued, *step four,* the Wichita Petroleum Company case before the circuit court of appeals on November 14, 1923. Then he headed for home via St. Louis and Cleveland, where he had arranged an all-day arbitration hearing. The arbitrators reached a decision the next day, and Judge continued his trip home. Judge tried unsuccessfully to get an oil rent check out of Haskell in New York City. Word of winning the Wichita case came through *step five,* then Judge met Cannon in late December, collected royalty payments for October and November, and talked settlement of all outstanding issues.

Wichita Petroleum was slow as usual in sending the royalty check, requiring Judge to go to New York City to collect. In February 1924, Judge spent a day in New York City negotiating a settlement with attorneys Cannon and Saklatvala and was close to an agreement. On March 10, he was again in New York City *(step six),* wound up the Wichita Petroleum Company case, and returned with a check for $196,827.95, which he delivered to Gil Winant the next day in Concord. This ended the Wichita Petroleum Company's Mexia oil well problem.

In May, Judge went to Texas, met Arthur Coyle in Austin, and "got in touch with Frio River affairs." The case started on May 5: "Case complicated and difficult to get parties in to start." On May 6, "Another day trying to untangle the situation, seem to be on the right track tonight." On the seventh, "Judge Calhoun ruled with us today and put case in shape for trial on merits tomorrow." The company put Dion, their surveyor, on the stand as witness. Judge recorded in his diary that Dion was "a very poor witness." The case wound up the week on Saturday noon, so Arthur and Judge drove to San Antonio (Arthur's home) and got an early start Sunday morning for Three Rivers to see the oil field, returning in the evening. They were up again early on Monday to drive back to Austin, finished giving their evidence, and started the defendant's case, which took a couple of days. The diary does not disclose what the controversy was about, but my recollection is that it involved the location of a boundary line. The question was whether the course of the river, the boundary line, had changed from the time of the original deed. Since this area of Texas is relatively flat and subject from time to time to tremendous amounts of rainfall and consequent flooding, it is not unusual for streams to alter their courses by as much as a mile or so. Resort had to be taken to ancient Spanish deeds (two hundred to three hundred years old) to resolve the dispute. Judge notes in his diary on June 12, "Won riverbed case."

In July 1924 Judge met at Newfound Lake with the Winants and one Lars Ostnes on his placer mining scheme. There is no further comment. Placer mining, common in the goldfields, uses great quantities of water to wash gold-bearing soils from the riverbanks into streams, where the gold can be recovered.

From 1925 to 1926, Governor Winant was the firm's most important client. There was virtually no activity of Coyle Concord Oil Company cited in Judge's diary for these years. However, Judge not only gave Gil policy and political advice but also paid considerable attention to Gil's personal and other business problems. For instance, in January 1926, Judge met with Gil, Constance, Fred Winant (Gil's brother), and Arthur Coyle on the Texas oil business of Coyle Concord Oil Company and went with Gil to Boston to meet Attorney Channing and Governor Fuller about New England Gypsum Company.[14] This was followed by many more meetings during the summer as they put together and incorporated the Atlantic Corporation, a gypsum company, which I assume was a subsidiary of New England Gypsum. At the end of the year, Judge worked with Gil on a federal tax deficiency assessed against him for the years 1921 and 1922 arising from a dispute over oil well deductions.

In 1927 there was a fair amount of legal work to be done for Winant—meetings in Washington with Arthur Coyle and a hearing before the IRS on the disputed 1921–1922 income taxes involving treatment of oil well drilling and other expenses, which went to the Board of Tax Appeals in May. Constance Winant had problems with the IRS on farm losses. There were several conferences during the year on Texas oil leases dealing with such matters as renewals and extensions and land rent and oil royalties, as well as a new automobile dealership in Concord and the Boston-Atlantic Co. involving gypsum, the details of which are not stated.

The year 1928 was a busy year. Judge made four separate trips to Texas. In January, he went to Washington to meet with Harvard Law School classmate, Jim Ivins, a tax expert, on Winant's tax case involving oil well costs. He also went with Gil and Constance to San Antonio, where they met Arthur and Lydia Coyle. Vaughn Griffin and Jack Nelson of Manchester, stockholders in Coyle Concord Oil Company, accompanied them. They talked for a day about the general situation with respect to oil production, leases, and profitability, then they drove to Corpus Christi to see the Gulf Gypsum Company deposit, since Gil had interests in New England Gypsum. Eight of them in two cars drove 265 miles by Sonora to St. Angelo (northwest of San Antonio) and 85 miles the next day to see a lease in the Chalk Field in Howard County, spending the night in Big Springs. The next day they reviewed the lease before returning to San Antonio.

En route they drove to Garwood to see the Colorado County Development known as the "Dallas Project."[15] In Houston they met with Tom Talliaferro and Palmer Hutchinson, their attorneys, and also the seismograph and Torsion Balance people.

In mid-October 1928, Judge went to Dallas, Fort Worth, and San Antonio, where at first good reports were received on a well being drilled on the Dallas Project. Later reports were discouraging, then, later still, more promising. There were meetings with several people including the Torsion Balance folks. Then Coyle and Judge approached several prospective purchasers of leases. Later they decided to acquire more leases, so they went to Eagle Lake (Colorado County, between San Antonio and Houston) and Beaumont (east of Houston) looking for owners. They apparently kept in touch with the drillers and the testing outfits, because on different days Judge enters in his diary: "Readings unfavorable," "Better readings tonight," "Good news on Dallas," and "Prospects good." They picked up an additional eight hundred acres and finally closed the sale of the well with Sweetwater Oil Company for $250,000 cash and $250,000 in oil. With the success of the Sweetwater trade, the company expanded the Dallas Project in Colorado County by obtaining more leases.

In November 1928, Judge traveled again with Gil and Constance to Houston to see the Torsion Balance people. Judge used the car, bus, and train in Texas to get around, picking up the Lehrer lease (720A) in Abilene, then headed to Sweetwater (near Abilene) and Lubbock and traded for the Curry lease (167A), then went to Amarillo and on to Denver and traded with G. G. Gordon for 430A and picked up 640A at Salida from F. L. Ream. He took the train through the Royal Gorge to Pueblo, then Fort Worth and San Antonio, where he picked up more oil leases before heading home once again, arriving for Thanksgiving.

He was off again for Chicago on December 4 to get oil leases signed, then out to Rochelle, Illinois, for the W. P. Landon lease, then to Streator to see Inez Strite, and to Indianapolis to see Mrs. and Miss South, thence to San Antonio. It was necessary to transfer all contracts, fifty leases, and other documents and rights to the new Coyle Concord Oil Company, a tedious job that took several days. He came home via New Orleans and had dinner at Antoine's before taking the train to Washington and Boston, arriving December 22—"happy to be home."

Fortunately, Judge loved to read. During his four train trips to Texas in 1928, he completed a book a day and enjoyed the seclusion of the train ride. In 1928 he recorded in his diary the following books read, almost entirely during the train trips: Thomas Hardy, *The Return of the Native*;[16] Sheila Kaye Smith, *Iron & Smoke*; Margaret Kennedy, *Red Sky at Morning*; Florence Hardy, *Life of Thomas Hardy*; Morley's *Rousseau*; Ludwig's *Napoleon*; Butler's *The Way of All Flesh*; Turgenev's *Torrents of Spring*; Conrad's *Chance*; Creavey's *Fifteen Decisive Battles*; Belloc's *James II*; Fisher's *Napoleon*; Beveridge's *Lincoln*; Gibbon's *Autobiography*; and Willa Cather's *Death Comes to the Archbishop*. He enjoyed history through biography.

Why did the Coyle Concord Oil Company hire Judge McLane from New Hampshire to make many extensive trips to Texas over the years—four trips in 1928 alone—instead of hiring a Texas law firm or employing in-house personnel? The company did engage Palmer Hutchinson, an oil specialist in the prestigious firm of Baker, Botts in Houston, to deal with technical legal matters relating to oil problems and to draft legal documents such as leases and well drilling contracts. Arthur Coyle was the company's only employee in addition to a secretary—this was not a big operation. Judge subscribed to trade magazines and newsletters and kept in touch with industry developments, new oil field activity, rental prices for leases, drilling costs, and a myriad of other information. Arthur Coyle was a very practical, invaluable, and hardworking man. Self taught, he lacked any formal education beyond high school. He may have felt uncomfortable in negotiating with "big shot" professional lawyers and accountants, oil engineers, et cetera, and preferred to be assisted by someone such as Judge McLane, who had extensive negotiating experience and who also was close to the stockholders from New Hampshire who were putting up the money. I suspect that it was a mutual decision of Winant and Coyle to have Judge so extensively involved; they had great admiration for him, both professionally and personally.

The year 1929 started off with Judge's extended trip across the country to acquire more leases for the Dallas Project in Colorado County. Judge left Boston in early January, meeting Gil in Albany and continuing on via St. Louis to San Antonio, where they met Manning Jacobs and stayed at the Maverick House (a good Texas name). After catching up on business, a group decided to go to Los Angeles on the Waite lease purchase and the

Root oil royalty agreement. They headed out by train at 2 A.M., spent all day crossing Texas, passed through El Paso in the evening, and arrived the next afternoon at Los Angeles, where they made an initial call on Mr. Root.

They drove with a friend, "Zandy" Zanderhoff, through Hollywood, Beverly Hills, and along the beaches, presumably sight-seeing. The next day, Judge attended a Dartmouth luncheon at the University Club and went to Pasadena with Zandy to see open golf and the great Walter Hagen. (Judge wasn't much of a golfer either before or after this experience.) They met Root again, with no success. The next day was spent driving up the coast to Santa Barbara, and calling on old Manchester friends and former clients Dr. and Mrs. Varick. In the first session with Waite, Judge tried to negotiate a lease on some Texas acreage. After another session with Waite, Judge went on to San Francisco and traded with one McMeans in Oakland, but that fell through at the last minute, so he returned to Los Angeles and struck out on another attempt to get a lease from Waite.

His task completed, Judge headed east on the *Argonaut*, arriving in San Antonio two days later. After catching up with Judge, Gil went to Houston to negotiate with the Marland Oil Company while Judge spent the day in the San Antonio office and a day with Vertrees, geologist for the Marland Oil Company. Judge took the train with Vertrees to Fort Worth and Ponca City, where they met Moran and Nichols of Marland, who offered $100,000 cash and $500,000 in oil and a quarter working interest for another well in Colorado County. Judge notes, "We didn't take," so they went on to Chicago to see the Pure Oil people, who expressed an interest in buying the well. But at the meeting the following day, the deal, which had seemed promising, suddenly fell through. On the whole it sounds like a disappointing trip; they failed to sell the well and also were unsuccessful in obtaining the leases they wanted. They left for Boston, having been gone about a month, arriving in time to accompany Elisabeth to the Chicago Opera production of *Carmen*.

In March 1929, Judge went to New York City to see Sloane Colt to arrange a $130,000 loan for Winant. The precise nature of the loan is not known, but in view of the unsuccessful attempt to sell the well and get additional leases, Gil may have needed more money for business as well as for political purposes. Gil was thinking of running for governor again.

Judge spent two days arranging the sale of Gil's stock in the Concord *Monitor-Patriot* newspaper. He spent one day with purchasers Jim Langley, who had been editor, and Stuart Nelson and successfully closed the sale. Jim Langley was in the Progressive Republican group and was a supporter of Winant. He wanted to own his own paper. Winant therefore had the opportunity both to ensure that the paper would be in friendly hands and to retrieve his investment.

In August, Judge met Gil and Constance in New York City and arranged payment of a part of the 1918 trust to Constance. While in England on vacation in September, Judge received a cable that he had won Gil's IRS tax case allowing well drilling and other expenses as business deductions on Gil's 1921–1922 corporate tax returns.

The Coyle Concord Oil business heated up again in 1932 after a couple of quiet years. Judge made three trips to Texas in 1932. The first trip in July started the day following a telephone call from Governor Winant. Judge took the bus to Eagle Lake in Colorado County, met Arthur Coyle, and went to a new well in the Dallas Project where the drill crew was "attaching pipe to transform to a smaller size tubing." The next day they drove to Garwood, a nearby small town, to see Mr. Landon; then they returned to the well, where the drill crew "broke down drill stem and set in [the smaller] tubing." (The drill stem is made up of sections of pipe screwed together and has the cutting tool at the bottom end. It is turned by a rotating turntable at ground level. The tubing is set in the drill hole and the drill stem rotates inside the tubing. In order to "set in" tubing, the drill stem has to be unscrewed as it is pulled out; the tubing then has to be set in the hole and the drill stem reset inside the tubing.)

The sixteenth was a "hectic day"; they built a Christmas tree (an array of pipes, control valves, meters, and gauges attached to the pipe as it comes out of the ground) and started to "bring in" the well. Normally, when "bringing in a well," if there is oil pressure, oil "mud" (a specialized mixture of water weighted with sand, clays, and metal dust) is pumped into the well casing as the stem is withdrawn to counterbalance the oil pressure and keep the oil underground. Then the mud can be pumped out slowly to permit the oil to rise to the surface under control. Here, since the pressure was low, they pumped water instead of mud. The flow was very low and turned to saltwater at midnight (a very discouraging sign, usually indicating no gas or oil). Judge notes, "Pressure back and made gas well about 3:00 a.m." The pressure built up the next day and, with the sand coming up, too, blew out the choke,[17] so they had to shut down (turn off all control valves to keep the gas and oil in the ground) until new parts could be installed.

As is frequently the case, when a new well is being "brought in," a lot of people are present. Wells that are expected to "come in" are listed in the oil and gas news in the daily papers. The curious come to the site, which may be way out in the flat country, miles away from a road. Some scouts representing buyers are prepared to bid right on the spot. On the eighteenth, Judge records, "Lost pressure again from 1325 pounds to zero. [Probably because of] Sand or frozen tubing." Arthur and Judge returned to Houston, saw their attorney, Palmer Hutchinson, and the Humble Oil people before Judge returned east, reporting to Gil Winant on his arrival.

In October 1932, Judge met Gil in New York City and tried to interest Union Sulphur Company in the well, then went on to Pittsburgh to talk to Gulf Oil. Later in the month, he was back in Pittsburgh to see Heald and Bothwell of Gulf Oil, who expressed mild interest in the Dallas Project well. Judge caught up with Arthur Coyle in San Antonio, "where paying current bills was a bothersome problem."

They had made a big play for the Dallas Project, assembling leases on some 18,000 acres in Colorado County and drilling several wells (which had not been too successful). Their capital was being depleted. Arthur and Judge drove to Houston, arriving at 1 A.M., and visited several refineries the next day to find a market for gas. The only gas pipelines at this time were short ones in Texas from the wells to the refineries.

The great expansion of natural gas pipelines to distribution companies in the North and West didn't come until after World War II, in the 1950s. Until the "big inch" pipelines were built, gas prices were very low, and many gas wells were "shut in" (filled with oil mud and all valves closed) until better prices could be obtained. If there wasn't much gas, the well was "flared" or burned. Arthur and Judge submitted a proposal to Consolidated Oil, who, two days later, offered $100,000 cash for a half interest. Coyle Concord countered with $200,000 cash and $100,000 in oil. The next day Arthur and Judge met with Slim Barrows of Humble. (Arthur knew him when they were both in the field scouting new developments. Barrows later became president of Humble.) Humble submitted a figure of $250,000 cash and $1,750,000 in oil plus a 1/24 overriding royalty; they agreed to meet the next day. Arthur and Judge drove to Garwood to pay the lease rentals. Judge writes on November 3, "Heavy trading all day with Garrett of Gulf in morning and Barrows of Humble in the afternoon. Both seem interested. Showdown tomorrow."

On the next day the Gulf people were complimentary about the leases but thought they were priced too high. Slim Barrows' boss was out of town until the following week, so, disappointed, Judge left for home; he arrived late on November 6 and reported to Gil. After a few days at home, he returned to Houston on November 12, caught up on developments with Arthur, and met the Consolidated people on the morning of the thirteenth and Barrows from Humble in the afternoon. Judge wrote, "Looks good for tomorrow," and it was: "Agreed with Barrows of Humble for $150,000 cash, $150,000 when oil is found, $1,750,000 out of one quarter oil, plus after oil payment, 1/24th over-riding royalty. Happy enough." The contract details were worked on over the next couple of days; then on the nineteenth, Judge records, "Contract in form—few remaining points agreed. Signed 1:30 and left at 2:00. Finished." He spent a half day with Gil going over the contract after getting home. About a month later, the Humble contract was approved (by the regulatory agency—the Texas Railroad Commission, I believe) and the money paid. Judge and Gil spent an evening on Coyle Concord Oil Company business just before the annual stockholders' meeting on December 30. Thus, at least for the time being, the company was solvent and the pressure was off.

Gil Winant was inaugurated governor in January 1933 for his third term (not consecutive). Judge had a couple of Coyle Concord Oil Company meetings in February and a trip south in October. He went with his close friend Dan Sortwell, who had a continuing interest in some silver mines in New Mexico near Albuquerque, which they visited, and found things brighter than in 1926. They had some good interviews with lease-holders there, then returned to Eagle Lake, Texas, on the February 8. There Judge met Arthur Coyle and visited the Powell #2 well in Colorado County, which was running low, with casing at 6,160 feet where they lost the core because of shale. The core was retrieved and a drill test was sug-gested. Arthur and Judge went to Houston to try to continue to sell the well, but the prospective purchasers "grew cold." The well was drilled to 6,189 feet, where they got sand and "some odor of a well," so they decided to do a drill stem test with a Halliburton tester, which "failed because the seat broke through." A second test was tried with a Johnson tester, but that failed to hold. On the twelfth, Arthur and Judge returned to Houston and agreed with the prospective purchaser to a third test, which was conducted on the fourteenth. It proved a failure—"very disappointing." Judge went to San Antonio, reported by phone to Gil, and spent time preparing a speech for St. Paul's School. When he returned to the well, they were coring from 6,200 to 6,235 feet. They got an oil-bearing sand at 6,232 (a potentially good sign). On the sixteenth they cored at 6,235 to 6,239 feet and got sand with a salt taste. (That's a bad sign; there is no oil with salt water.) Then it was back to Houston to consult with the prospective purchasers, who wanted a sixty-day extension, which was granted. Judge mentions, "Saw Lou Smith," a client with Rockingham Racetrack; but doesn't indicate whether it was a planned or accidental meeting. Judge stopped in Chicago for business with client Rob Bass en route home.

In March 1934, Judge went to Houston and with Arthur Coyle headed out to El Campo, where another well was being drilled to the 6,000-foot level. They had hard luck—"Cored at 6,086 feet but it jammed, so cored at 6,102 feet but got a no show and again at 6,117 feet." The next day, they cored to 6,132 feet and still got a no-show, so they drove in to Garwood and El Campo while the well was drilled to 6,147 feet where they "hit what seemed the top of hard sand." "Too low," Judge says. The next day the sand gave out on a seven-foot core at 5 A.M. and there was a no-show at 3 P.M. "At 1:00 a.m. found sand 6,171 feet, no odor, must be first sand too low means dry hole." On the eighth, "Cored to 6,174-80 feet, back into shale, ready to quit." He took the bus to Houston and the next day to Dallas and then to San Antonio by train to see business clients, but not necessarily Coyle-Concord clients. He returned to Houston and "Met Barrows and Teas [from Humble, one of the large oil companies] about drilling more wells. They are about decided to give back the lease. Our backs to the wall." The next day, "Two sessions with Humble, they decide to quit drilling. Offer to pay leases another year," and so home. It was obviously a very disappointing trip. Judge records no activity in 1935 or 1936.

Coyle Concord Oil Company continued to be active in Texas in 1937, and Judge made two trips there during the year. In February he sailed from New York City on the Clyde Mallory line for Galveston, stopping in Miami en route and going out to the El Campo field. The well was in good shape, and the crew was coring for sand at the 6,034-foot level. The next day when they returned to the well, they "found to our dismay core of hard sand, which proved to be full of cement." There is no explanation of what happened after that. Judge returned via New Orleans, and a dinner at Antoine's, before taking the train to Washington. There he stopped for lunch with Gil and Constance Winant and met several social security executives. (Gil had been appointed by President Roosevelt to be the first chairman of the Social Security Board.) In August Arthur Coyle called to report a good drill stem test. In December, Judge received a telegram from Arthur stating that the Texas Crusader deal was on. Judge returned by train to Houston. He says he had a pleasant conversation on the train with Professor Austin Scott of the Harvard Law School, an eminent authority on trusts. In Houston, he met with the Crusader attorney and the company lawyer—Shepard from Baker, Botts—and on the twenty-first signed up a sale. Judge then headed for home, having to change trains outside Cleveland because their train had broken down.

Coyle Concord was relatively quiet in 1938, although Judge spent several days in New York City with Arthur Coyle negotiating oil contract adjustments with Southern Cross Oil Company and had a couple of long talks with Gil in May about the oil company. In early 1941, Judge went to Texas in connection with a new well in the Garwood field, which looked favorable. He met Arthur Coyle and made calls on several oil companies with the results of a recent drill stem test that was favorable, but no concrete action resulted. Judge traveled east and reported to Gil Winant, who had returned from his post as ambassador to Great Britain for a brief visit with President Roosevelt.

The oil business was pretty quiet during the war years. In 1947, upon the death of Gil Winant, Gil's son, John, Jr., assumed financial control because the Winant family had always maintained majority interest in the company. In 1948 Arthur Coyle got a big gas well, after which Judge and John McLane, Jr., went to Houston, met Arthur, and made calls on several oil companies with data on the new well. They traded with some with undisclosed results. They inspected the field, visited San Antonio, and took a long weekend trip to Monterey and Saltillo in the mountains of Mexico, a hot, dry, and rugged country. In 1951, Judge made a fast trip to Texas to negotiate a lease between San Jacinto Oil Company and Arthur Coyle. He took the train out; two days later he flew back, his first reference to flying to or from Texas.

In the fall of 1952, Judge met Arthur in Houston. For three days they visited oil companies. Once again they had a favorable drill stem test. I can only assume that if a good deal had resulted, the diary would have disclosed that fact. Because it says nothing, I assume that the marketing results were inconclusive.

At the stockholders' meeting at the McLane office in Manchester in 1952, president Arthur Coyle reported that recently 3,100 acres in Colorado County had been leased to the Ohio Oil Company, which had completed three producing wells. He stated that there were now 600 "proven" acres, which could be extended to 1,000 acres if planned drilling was successful. He concluded that the company anticipated "substantial revenue for several years to come."

At the 1954 stockholders' meeting, the sale of stock to Arthur Coyle at a nominal price was authorized to "in part make up to him for many years devotion to the Company at a nominal salary" and to bring him up to the 2 percent ownership he formerly enjoyed.[18]

In 1957, Ohio provided $40,000 of royalties, but the forecast was for a decreasing amount. Some wells were "shut in" gas wells awaiting pipelines and therefore produced no income.

In 1958, all indebtedness was paid off, clearing the way for dividends. During the year, Ohio drilled six shallow gas wells and three dry holes. A dividend of one dollar a share was paid in 1958; two such dividends were paid in 1959, 1960, and 1961.

At the annual meeting of stockholders in May 1962 in Manchester, president Arthur Coyle reported and the minutes state:

> Over the years some $4,000,000 has been spent on drilling at the Garwood field but with very little success. Many companies have drilled wells which were either dry or produced insufficient quantities of oil and gas to make them feasible and subsequently pulled out. In 1952 the Ohio Oil Company found some production and will just about recover their investment in the wells. Because of the FPC [Federal Power Commission] regulations it is very difficult for

an operator to make connections to a pipe line and because of the low cost of developing wells in the great newly discovered fields in the Middle East and Africa, oil production is not profitable. About two years ago, the company made a favorable trade with Crescent Oil Co. by which the company received $105,000 in cash which has enabled all debts to be paid and a cash surplus which has been invested in short term securities . . . The outlook for the future is bleak. The speculative value of the field is about exhausted. Royalty income is decreasing and expenses remain the same. It is unlikely that there will be sufficient cash income to enable dividends to be paid much longer.

Arthur Coyle continued that the Winant and Coyle interests own 80 percent of the stock and "feel that it is appropriate that the minority be given the opportunity to sell their shares to the Company and the Board of Directors will consider the matter and possibly vote to make an offer to purchase at $52 a share. The book value of the stock is $37.97, however the lease investments carried at cost are on the books at $24,018.67. By increasing the value of the lease investment to approximately $80,000 the book value of the stock then becomes $52 a share."

There was discussion, and questions were asked. Several minority stockholders concluded that the offer was a fair one. The board of directors at its meeting following the stockholders' meeting voted to approve the offer, which subsequently was accepted by all of the minority stockholders. Their stock was repurchased.

The company continued to pay modest dividends. In 1967 it sold off some properties acquired for the oil business at a good profit and invested in marketable securities, from which it received investment income. Some of the remaining stockholders wanted to be in the company, but only if it was going to remain in the somewhat risky oil business, so two more redemptions were effected in 1968 and 1975.

By the late '70s, the company participated in well drilling as a working partner providing up-front funds, with indifferent results. Profits paid the drilling costs and modest dividends. About a third of the wells were dry holes.

By 1980, gas pipelines came close enough so that gas from shut-in wells could be sold. In 1982, gas was in an oversupply because of reduced demand and low prices. In 1984, some seismic tests indicated no productive areas in the Garwood field. There was some talk about drilling down to the Wilcox formation at about 15,279 feet at a cost of $5 million, with the company taking a 5 percent working interest. However, in 1985, before that was done, the stockholders (members of the Coyle and Winant families) voted to adopt a Plan of Complete Liquidation and Dissolution. They ceased to do business as Coyle Concord Oil Company, a corporation, but continued as a partnership. Thus ended the McLane law firm connection with the Coyle Concord Oil Company—a relationship that spanned the years 1921–1985.

To recapitulate, in 1923, when the oil company was formed and the excitement of the first well gripped everyone, there were dreams of great profits, which never materialized. Just enough money kept flowing in to pay the bills and enable Arthur Coyle, the eternal optimist, to look for better deals. Because no one had to advance any cash, it was only natural to keep going, hoping, hoping, and hoping. Dividends weren't paid until 1957 and then only in small amounts. In 1962, the minority stockholders were paid $52 a share, which had cost them $100 a share in 1922, with only a minuscule amount of dividends during the forty-year interim period.

As for the legal business, Judge spent many hours on the company's affairs, making some eighteen trips to Texas between 1921 and 1937. Each trip lasted between ten and twenty-one days. In addition there were numerous trips to New York to negotiate deals or to collect payments due. There were trips to Washington on tax matters. Bills went unpaid for several years. Creditors had to wait for the sale of a well or the receipt of oil royalties. Judge had to advance most out-of-pocket expenses for travel. My general impression is that Judge was adequately paid, but Coyle Concord was never a lucrative client. Both Gil and Constance Winant and Arthur and Lydia Coyle remained lifelong personal friends of Judge and Elisabeth (all now deceased). My second wife, Betsy, and I have carried on the friendship with John Winant, Jr., until his death in the fall of 1993, and his wife, Janine, and with Arthur's daughter, Sister Elizabeth, with correspondence, Christmas remembrances, and an occasional visit.

# Notes

1. Mexico in 1910 had a revolution to throw out its dictator, and an ineffective government was established. In 1912, U.S. Marines stormed ashore at Veracruz to rescue some Navy personnel who had been arrested for disorderly conduct and were not released to their respective commanding officers.

2. Judge's brother Clinton had been an officer in the Guard in Milford and was called up for duty in June 1916. The unit trained in Concord and in October was sent to San Antonio, Texas. Clinton's wife, Dorothy, with three small children (including Martha McLane, mother of Peter Rotch, a partner in the McLane law firm), followed in December.

3. *Air Power*, March 1919, p. 422. My father and I went to Texas on Coyle Concord business in the late 1940s and had a four-day trip with Arthur and his wife, Lydia, into Mexico to Monterey and Saltillo. On the long auto ride,

Arthur regaled us with stories of his early flying experiences. There were no flying maps because there was practically no flying. There were no road maps because the automobile rarely traveled anywhere other than in its own neighborhood. Arthur would tear out a page from an atlas; that was his "guidance system." Later, towns proudly painted their names on a warehouse or barn roof readable from the air. But when Arthur started to fly, he had to fly along the railroad tracks, keeping just above the telephone wires; he read the town's name on the end of the station platform and then turned to his map to get oriented. There weren't many airfields, and sometimes a farmer's field had to function as one. There was no radio communication with the ground, and the weather forecast was what you could see with your own eyes. Formation flying was fun until you got lost in a cloud, but these early flyers were all young, with plenty of courage, energy, and enthusiasm.

4. Dudley Orr reported this conversation with Arthur.

5. A wildcat well is a new well in an unproven area.

6. The "field" was probably several thousands of acres out on the Texas plains—semiarid, undulating, grazing terrain without trees and hardly any buildings in sight, except the "wildcatter's" drilling rigs. A telltale cloud of dust rose behind every moving vehicle. It was hot and dry in the summer and windy and cold in the winter.

7. Some wells were registered in Judge's name as "McLane #10," et cetera. These were transferred to my name on Judge's retirement. I received royalty checks monthly in varying amounts, sometimes in thousands of dollars, which I would endorse and forward to the Coyle Concord Oil Company in San Antonio and think no more of it. Imagine my surprise when I received notice from the IRS assessing a deficiency tax of thousands of dollars with interest and penalty for failing to report income. I had completely forgotten about those royalty checks and quickly responded. I was immensely relieved when I received notice from the IRS confirming my explanation, accepting my original return as filed, and canceling the deficiency assessment and penalty.

8. "Bringing in" a well in the 1920s was exciting. The driller could usually tell from the feel of the drilling cable what kind of rock the bit was in. When he thought he was in an oil-bearing "sand," the drill stem was gradually withdrawn and replaced with weighted drilling "mud" to keep the oil pressure under control. As the "mud" was slowly pumped out, the various gauges indicated the pressure and other vital information. Fluids could be withdrawn for testing by feel or taste—for saltwater (very bad) but hopefully for oil. Scouts from various oil companies would invariably be there, having read about the well "coming in" in the published reports carried in the newspapers.

9. Dudley Orr's father, who served in the senate with Winant. Dudley said that the group felt that his father's knowledge of pipes gained from his plumbing and heating contracting business would make him an invaluable member of the stockholder group that was about to invest in the oil well business, which also

used pipes. Dudley expressed doubts about the logic used in making the connection between the two.

10. This became a thorny issue, which wasn't resolved until 1929 when the U.S. Board of Tax Appeals upheld Coyle Concord's position that they were entitled to depletion allowance, because the transaction with Wichita Petroleum Company was not a contract of sale. The IRS had disallowed the depletion deduction and made a deficiency assessment against the taxpayers of about $148,000 for the 1922 tax year. *Arthur J. Coyle et als v. Commissioner of Internal Revenue, 17 B.T.A. 368 (1929)* and for construction of the contract between the parties *Wichita Petroleum Co. v. Winant, 295 Fed. 67 (1923).*

11. Although Winant was the principal mover and largest stockholder, he wanted to use the name Concord because there were several stockholders, all from Concord, New Hampshire. Using Arthur Coyle's name gave him some stature in Texas in negotiating and transacting the company's business.

12. A famous, old gourmet restaurant in New Orleans, still going strong with fifth-generation owners.

13. The Palmer Hutchison boys went to Camp Mowglis, a summer boys' camp on Newfound Lake. The boys' parents dropped in at Pasquaney Lodge for a visit with Judge and Elisabeth when they were either leaving or picking up the boys at the camp.

14. Gypsum is a mineral that is mined and is extensively used in the building industry in the manufacture of wallboard. The gypsum is covered with a tough building paper. The resulting product is light in weight, easy to install, and fire retardant.

15. The Dallas Project was a plan to assemble a block of about 18,000 acres in Colorado County, bringing together land and leases acquired by Gil Winant in his own name (which were to be conveyed to Coyle Concord Oil Company) plus land and leases either acquired or to be acquired by Coyle Concord Oil Company. An agreement was made on July 13, 1928, between Coyle Concord Oil Company and Torsion Balance Exploration Company to conduct "torsion balance" testing on the lands to attempt to locate a subterranean salt dome where oil might be found.

16. Judge was a great admirer of Hardy. He and Elisabeth walked and biked a number of times in the Hardy country of southern England. He collected first editions when he was in England and from book dealers in the United States. He gave this collection to the Dartmouth College library prior to his death.

17. A conical heavy iron piece inserted in a pipe opening as a safety valve in the event of excessive pressure.

18. Occasionally, Arthur Coyle acted as a consultant to others with respect to oil matters. Dudley Orr reported that Arthur had assisted his client United Life in connection with the foreclosure of oil property in the Los Angeles area in 1955. He also assisted the McLane office in connection with the Williams

estate, which owned sizable real estate holdings, including the Diamond A ranch in New Mexico, which had potential oil property and in which Dartmouth College had a substantial interest. Judge referred Coyle to the Brown Paper Company of Berlin, New Hampshire, which owned forest acreage in Florida on which there was some oil potential. Arthur consulted with Andrew Marshall, Jr. (John McLane's brother-in-law) about the Ames family's Fort Union ranch, adjacent to the Diamond A ranch, mentioned above, which had oil indications on the Turkey Mountain structure.

# SIX

# Governor John McLane and the McLane Manufacturing Company

One of Judge's clients from the start of his law practice in 1912 was the McLane Manufacturing Company in Milford, New Hampshire. Incorporated in 1907, it was a successor to the individual proprietorship started by Judge's father, John McLane, in 1876. The history of John McLane and his manufacturing company is an interesting one. John McLane was born on February 27, 1852, in Lennoxtown, Scotland, a small manufacturing town nestled in a valley surrounded by the 1,000-foot treeless Campsey and Darcey Hills,[1] about thirty miles northeast of Glasgow. Judge's great-grandfather was Malcolm Maclean, of Dumbarton, Scotland, a small town near Glasgow on the Clyde River where Judge's grandfather, Alexander Maclean, was born in about 1820.

Alexander became an "expert" wood engraver and moved to Lennoxtown, Scotland, where he was presumably employed by the print works there to carve or engrave the wood pattern blocks. Originally the engraved woodblocks were hand inked, and hand pressed on the cloth to transfer the pattern. The Industrial Revolution introduced a mechanized large roller to which the engraved woodblocks were attached. As the roller turned, the block passed over the ink pad, then the inked pattern was transferred to the cloth as it passed under the rotating roller. This new process greatly expanded the potential for textile design.

The Amoskeag Manufacturing Company in Manchester, New Hampshire, is believed to have sent an agent to Scotland to recruit key personnel knowledgeable in the print cloth industry to man the recently completed Manchester Print Works. Alexander Maclean is reputed to have been hired to work for the Manchester Print Works as a wood engraver. Alexander and his wife, Mary Hay(e), came to Manchester in the summer of 1854 with their two sons, Malcolm, age four, and John, age two.[2] Alexander unfortunately drowned in Black Brook while swimming after work on September 4, 1854, only a few weeks after he arrived in the United States.[3] In later years Judge reported to the family, with considerable embarrassment, that the city librarian had found a news clipping of the event that read approximately as follows: "Alexander Maclean, a recent immigrant to Manchester, was drowned in the river while swimming after work. He was known to have been a frequenter of the taverns."

John McLane was two years of age at the time. In the absence of any family or any government welfare programs comparable to Aid to Dependent Children, the two boys were packed off to a foster farm family, where they were expected to work for their keep when they grew older. Their mother, who went to work in the mills, paid support as well. There is no hard evidence of what happened to John McLane between the ages of three and twenty-one, nor is there any record of when the name was changed to McLane.[4] I recall my father telling me that his father lived with a family in Dunbarton until the age of twelve and that he walked to Manchester, about twelve miles, to get books out of the public library. He was always known to have been an avid reader and a well-informed person. There is little information about his brother, Malcolm, only that later he was an iron molder or monger (a trader in iron) in Massachusetts.

Historian Hobart Pillsbury[5] says that John McLane attended Manchester schools in the winters and worked summers learning the cabinetmakers' trade, becoming an "expert" journeyman at age twenty-one and a part owner in a furniture factory in Milford. In 1876, at the age of twenty-four, he became sole owner, having completed seven years of apprenticeship.[6] In 1880, he added the business of manufacturing post office fittings and supplies in accordance with U.S. government standards.[7] By 1886, he was very successful in his expanding business. Needing additional space, he purchased the Fuller mill in Milford on Nashua Street, formerly (1849) the Souhegan Manufacturing Company, a textile operation, together with all buildings, machinery, boiler and engine, shafting, belting, and tools and the waterpower rights and the dam. In order to provide additional production in 1885, he started a factory with twenty-five employees in Chicago, where he already maintained a sales office. Upon expiration of his lease there, he moved the machinery to Milford in 1888, continuing only the sales office in the Windy City. Other sales offices were maintained in Boston and Washington.

In 1890, John McLane sold a part of the Fuller mill property to P. Bartlett & Son for a hosiery mill. On his own adjacent property, McLane added a two-story building for the manufacture of boxes for the hosiery mill. In 1899, John McLane purchased the hosiery mill and machinery from Frank Kaley, trustee in bankruptcy of P. Bartlett & Son, and started a basket business, known as the Standard Basket Shop. The mill produced 12,000 baskets a month made of native oak. The business was sold, in 1904, to a Mr. Needham, who moved the machinery to the old piano factory building in Peterborough. It subsequently was named the Peterborough

*McLane post office front*, originally in Springfield, Vermont, post office, now in Milford (N.H.) Historical Society. Credit Manchester (N.H.) Historic Association Photo Archives.

Basket Company, which became a client of the McLane law firm when it was owned by Richard Pierce from 1950 to the 1970s.

An advertising booklet published by John McLane in 1899 stressed the quality of his products: "For 25 years I have been in the business of supplying postmasters with everything required in a first class office." In the larger cities, the U.S. Postal Service owned and operated the post offices, but by far the largest number of post offices were found in country stores operated by an appointed postmaster or postmistress who owned the equipment. The postal service paid rent to the store owner and a salary to the postmaster and sold stamps and other postal supplies at a discount so that the agent could make a profit on sales to the public.

The earliest system for distributing mail in post offices was for the patron to rent a box or space, which usually had a glass front so the patron could see whether he had any mail. But patrons had to ask the postmaster for mail, and it was available only during regular business hours. One of the first patented improvements introduced by John McLane was a box with a wire mesh bottom instead of solid wood, permitting the dirt and dust to drop down to dust collectors, thus saving the postmaster much time in cleaning. McLane, in his 1899 sales brochure, indicates the existence of 5 million wire-bottomed post office boxes. The next improvement was a lock box opened with a key, which permitted the customer to get his mail without assistance from the postmaster. These boxes, known as Harvard boxes, had sturdy bronze doors to minimize tampering with the lock. The disadvantage of this system was that the postmaster had to keep records of cash key deposits, and frequently keys were lost or mislaid and had to be reordered.

The next important improvement was the introduction of the Franklin Keyless Lock Box, a patented device on which John McLane had the exclusive rights. The lock was activated by moving a dial and a pointer to the preset combination for that box. No more lost keys or bookkeeping for key deposits. McLane in the brochure states that "10,000 post-offices are supplied with my Patented Lock and Call boxes"—an increase from the 7,000 built as of 1890. By 1900, the total post office fronts sold is given as 12,000.[8] The flyer quotes letters dated in 1898–1899 from Maine, Vermont, Massachusetts, Pennsylvania, Ohio, Kentucky, North Carolina, Missouri, Minnesota, Indiana, Illinois, South Dakota, North Dakota, Kansas, Nebraska, Oregon, Washington, and "Indian Territory" (Oklahoma) and Ontario, Canada, all praising the equipment.[9]

In the early years, the machinery in the McLane mill was turned by waterpower, wheels, and belts. In 1909 electric motors were installed to run the machines. The waterpower rights were conveyed to Milford Light and Power Company in exchange for a supply of electricity.

In the 1880s, before the introduction of a public telephone system, John McLane installed a private line between the shop and his house. Whether it was a question of "keeping up with the Joneses" or just latching onto a good idea, William B. Rotch, publisher of the *Milford Cabinet*, also installed a line from the shop to the house, but who was first, we'll probably never know.[10]

John McLane's business was conducted as an individual proprietorship and was not incorporated as the McLane Manufacturing Company until 1907. John McLane deeded the property to the new corporation on June 5, 1908.

After John McLane died in 1911, the business declined—whether due to lack of leadership or functional obsolescence, I cannot say. Certainly the use of stamped metal was coming into vogue, cutting manufacturing labor costs and providing lighter-weight units.

Judge continued to be involved in the business as a director. He approved a reorganization, but his comments became progressively gloomy: In 1917, he writes, "The end is at hand." In 1919, the business was sold to Robert and William Bourn of Templeton, Massachusetts, who continued only the furniture part of the business. Judge continued to be on the board and attended five meetings in 1920 and 1921, which makes me think that the family had not been paid all of the purchase price. He also arranged a meeting with Senator George Moses of New Hampshire about a new type of letter carrier desk for the U.S. Post Office. There were additional directors' meetings in 1922. That year Judge went to Boston to get the contract for equipment for the new Manchester Post Office, at the corner of Chestnut and Hanover Streets.[11] Judge worked on a reorganization of the company in the 1920s. The business managed to hang on until the 1935 depression, when it went bankrupt.

John McLane was active in several other business organizations. He organized the Milford Granite Company, about which I know nothing, but it was probably one of many small granite companies that worked the granite quarries around Milford. He was a director of the New Hampshire Fire Insurance Company in Manchester and the Milford Building and Loan Association. He was president of the Souhegan National Bank in Milford from 1892 until his death in 1911.[12]

Once John McLane had his business well established with qualified people in charge, he was able to devote more time to politics. He served as town moderator from 1892 until his death. He served two terms in the New Hampshire House of Representatives in the 1885 and 1887 sessions, and an unprecedented two consecutive terms as president of the senate in 1891 and 1893. On June 26, 1894, at the one hundredth anniversary celebration of the incorporation of Milford, John McLane gave a short, stirring oration as president of the senate. He proclaimed that the people of New Hampshire and New England owed much to Scotland and the Scottish people.

> . . . I cannot claim this town as the place of my birth, but for a quarter of a century it has been my home. One of your daughters honored me by becoming my wife, and here my children have been born . . . And yet I cannot forget that where I first saw the light many of your ancestors were born and the Scotch blood that flows in my veins is still traceable in yours . . . The few moments of your time which have been assigned to me will be spent in some reflections on what the people of New Hampshire and New England owe to Scotland and the Scotch.
>
> First to be considered and of the most vital importance is the character of the early settlers which Scotland sent to people these shores. They were strong and rugged in health, inured to hardships

from their birth, prone to industry, and cultivators of the moral virtues. Their great national characteristic, which is manifested in all conditions of life, is and always has been, love of God and human liberty. These fundamental principles of life are taught by the songs they sing in the Highland hut, and from the lips of the preacher in the Lowland kirk . . . From such a people came John Knox and the great reformation, and the fires of religious liberty and toleration enkindled by John Knox and his faithful followers will continue to burn brighter and brighter as long as man shall exist with a brain to think or a heart to feel. Scotland furnished New England with her common school system, without which an enlightened people and a free government would be impossible. The schoolhouse is the rock on which is founded our security for the present and our hopes for the future ...

The military spirit and love for home and country shown by the Scotch people have been demonstrated on countless occasions . . . From such a race came the pride of New Hampshire, the brave General Stark, who commanded the troops from New Hampshire at the battle of Bunker Hill, and it was his countrymen who thrice that day repulsed the British at Pebbly Beach, on the Mystic. The battle of Bunker Hill was won by New Hampshire soldiers, commanded by generals from the old Granite state; the same John Stark saved the day at Bennington, which was one of the most decisive battles of the war ...

Friends and citizens, we who have the red blood of Scotland in our veins may well be proud of the achievements of our countrymen wherever they may be found, in town, state, or nation. Twelve of the presidents of the United States, five of the chief justices of the Supreme Court, claim to be of Scotch origin, while the grand list of scholars, orators, and statesmen who have the same blood in their veins are without number . . .

Friends and fellow-citizens of Milford, time will not permit further discussion of this, to me, vastly interesting subject, for I am a Scotchman and am proud of the fact, and as a citizen of this one hundred years old town, I am proud of its past history and hopeful for its future prosperity. May our descendants be loyal to the principles of truth, loyal to justice and liberty, and loyal to the blood of their ancestors!

John McLane was a delegate to the Republican National Convention in Philadelphia and endorsed Theodore Roosevelt for vice president on the McKinley ticket.

In 1903, John McLane was elected governor, defeating Democrat Henry Hollis of Concord (Appendix B.2). The state was expanding its tourist industry as the railroads pushed into the mountains, and resort hotels and boardinghouses sprang up. A new road was built on an old logging railway bed from Twin Mountain to Franconia Notch. That road greatly shortened the distance between Crawford and Franconia Notches. Governor McLane negotiated with President Roosevelt to have the Russian and Japanese peace delegates meet in New Hampshire at Portsmouth and was the official host of the peace conference, which resulted in the Treaty of Portsmouth.[13] The state was the beneficiary of a tremendous amount of free publicity.[14]

In 1880, John McLane married Ellen Tuck, both of whose parents had died before she was seven. She and her brother, Edward, were brought up in Milford by Mr. and Mrs. Clinton S. Averill, whose house, which was built in 1838 by Calvin Averill, Ellen inherited on their deaths.[15] It was here that John and Ellen raised four children, Clinton Averill McLane,[16] Hazel McLane,[17] "Judge" John Roy McLane,[18] and Charles Malcolm McLane.[19] Although John McLane never received much education, having stopped school at the age of twelve, he was adamant in providing his children with what he had missed.

John McLane was active in the Scottish Rite Masonry, going through all the steps—a 33rd degree and Grand Master of the Grand Lodge of New Hampshire. He was also an Odd Fellow. Ellen McLane was active in a number of organizations and was state regent of the Daughters of the American Revolution (DAR). John and Ellen attended the Congregational church. John McLane died of cirrhosis of the liver in 1911, at the age of fifty-nine, in South Carolina while on a trip to restore his failing health. Ellen McLane lived until 1927.

# Notes

1. John McLane and his wife, Ellen, owned two Gordon setters, named Campsey and Darcey, in Milford when their children, including Clinton and Judge, were growing up. Many years later when their children were young, Judge and Clinton each bought a Gordon setter. Judge named his Campsey and Clinton named his Darcey.

2. Squires, *Granite State*, Vol. II, p. 210.

3. Judge's diary at the end of years 1945-1949 states, "Alexander McLane (my grandfather) drowned September 4, 1854 in Black Brook per newspaper account September 9, 1854."

4. In Scotland, the diphthong "ea" is pronounced as a broad "a," but in England and America, it is pronounced as a broad "e"; thus, "Maclean" in Scotland is pronounced "McLane." John McLane was apparently so aggravated by the constant mispronunciation of his name that he anglicized the spelling in order that it be pronounced correctly. When we were recently traveling in Scotland, I mistakenly pronounced "Sleat," the southernmost tip of the Isle of Skye, as "sleet," until I was corrected by some of the natives who told me the name was "slate."

5. Pillsbury, *New Hampshire*.

6. "Men of New England," Vol. II, American Historical Company.

7. "Thirty-four Years In Business," *Milford Cabinet*, December 16, 1909.

8. Wright, "Granite Town," p. 228.

9. In our family's travels around the United States, we have kept our eyes open for the McLane post office fronts in museums and have located them in the following locations: the abandoned mining town of Columbine in northern Colorado; the Chisholm Trail museum in Kingfisher, Oklahoma; the Museum of the West in Bozeman, Montana; and museums in Wenatchee and Cle Elum on the Columbia River in Washington. Various members of the family have located some: My brother Malcolm located one from Melvin Village, New Hampshire, which is at Pasquaney Lodge, Newfound Lake, New Hampshire; Patty McLane Rotch donated the one in the Milford Historical Society in Milford, New Hampshire, and we have one that came from East Surrey, New Hampshire.

10. Rotch's grandson, William Boylston Rotch, married McLane's granddaughter, Martha McLane. Their oldest son, Peter, is a partner in the McLane law firm (1996). Their son John and daughter Elizabeth were the seventh generation to publish the *Milford Cabinet*. The paper is now published by William B. Rotch's son-in-law.

11. The "new" post office of Victorian design built in the early 1920s was demolished in the 1940s for a new contemporary-style post office. In the 1980s, this was abandoned in favor of a new post office nearer the interstate highway and the airport. The old post office was sold to the law firm of Devine & Millimet, which made substantial attractive renovations.

12. Pillsbury, *New Hampshire*, Vol. III, p. 706.

13. Appendix B.3, Treaty of Portsmouth.

14. Governor McLane appointed J. Adam Graf of Manchester as a delegate to the treaty. He was Kenneth Graf's grandfather and the great-grandfather of our own John Adam Graf! J. Adam Graf was an Amoskeag Manufacturing Company overseer and a local politician.

15. Clinton Averill's brother, Thomas, on April 13, 1874, married Mary Hay(e), the widow of Alexander Maclean, her first husband, and one Jondro, or Jonsalo, her second husband.

16. Clinton was educated at St. Paul's School and Harvard University.

17. Hazel went to Baldwin School, outside Philadelphia, a private preparatory school, and then to nearby Bryn Mawr College. At age sixteen, while her father was governor, on June 30, 1906, she christened the battleship *New Hampshire* at the launching at Camden, New Jersey, and received a gold bracelet with three diamonds, suitably inscribed, a gift of the New York Shipbuilding Company. This bracelet descended to her granddaughter, Linda Clark McGoldrick, of Littleton, who wore it until her untimely death. Linda advised me that she thought her family still had wrapped up in paper bags glass remnants that remained from the champagne bottle that Hazel broke across the bow as the ship started her slide into the Delaware River. Hazel married Jack Clark, a Dartmouth graduate and friend of Judge's, who was in the brokerage business in New York City. The family lived in New Canaan, Connecticut.

18. John, who was christened Roy John and had his name changed at a very early age, attended St. Paul's School, Dartmouth College, Magdalen College at Oxford University (Rhodes scholar), and Harvard Law School.

19. Charles attended St. Paul's School; while a student there, during a vacation, he visited an amusement park at Revere Beach, Massachusetts, where he was thrown from a revolving platform. He struck his head and fractured his skull, which resulted in his death a few days later.

# SEVEN

# Interlude 1920–1929

Highlights of the personal life of Judge and Elisabeth McLane are included in the chapters entitled "Interlude," each covering a decade, to give a more intimate insight into the life of Judge McLane.

## HIGHLIGHTS OF 1920

The winter of 1920 was slow in coming, but it came with a vengeance in February. Judge had to thaw frozen pipes, and cold and snow prevented him from getting the train to Hanover for a meeting there. Spring came in March: The fire whistles blew, announcing that the ice was going out of the river—a great sight at the old Amoskeag Bridge to watch large sheets of ice break up as they plunged over the dam.[1] Judge and Elisabeth snowshoed in the woods or fields, taking picnic lunches or suppers and enjoying sunlight or moonlight as the case might be.

When their son, John (this author) was four years old, he went to his first Sunday school, attended his first circus, and swam in the ocean (very salty) for the first time. Judge recorded all kinds of firsts for John but never mentioned the other children when they were the same age. Young John fell on the ice and hit his cheek, which developed an abscess. The doctor lanced and stitched it on the kitchen table without anesthesia; Judge fainted.

During 1920, Judge and Elisabeth moved three times: from a triple-decker on Prospect Street to a house for the winter on Beech Street on the trolley line, back to Prospect Street, and then to a rental at the corner of Carpenter and Chestnut Streets.

Over Memorial Day, Judge and Elisabeth climbed Osceola in the Waterville Valley. On the next day they climbed Mt. Tripyramid, wallowing in two to three feet of snow at the top. In the summer they hiked the Lafayette range twice, returning to their house on Newfound Lake by walking the ten miles from Plymouth over an abandoned wood road up over the hills past abandoned farms. Since they did not own a car, they depended on public transportation or a ride with the Bancrofts' chauffeur. In the fall they rode the logging railroad, sitting on an empty flatcar up the Pemigewasset

River valley to operating Camp 2.[2] Then they hiked through the
Pemigewasset wilderness on old logging roads to Ethan Pond and down to
the Willey House railroad station, where they rode the train to the Sawyer
River station. Then they walked up to the logging town of Livermore (long
since abandoned and reclaimed by the forest) and climbed Mt. Carrigain,
where they slept out in the open. The next day they descended to the
Sawyer River and hiked over to Waterville—a rugged trip. In the fall, Judge
and Elisabeth hired a horse and buggy and rode up over Hackett Hill, north
of Manchester, and back. Christmas was traditionally spent with the
Bancrofts in Concord. Judge took the children over to the state hospital
farm, which was across the street, to see the cows and pigs.

## HIGHLIGHTS OF 1921

Judge was elected to the vestry of Grace Episcopal Church in Manchester.
He presided at a conference of the Federated Council of Charities to organize a new Conference of Social Welfare in response to the call for reform
in the administration of public welfare by the Progressive branch of the
Republican Party. Previously public welfare had largely been administered
by the county and municipal governments, whose staffs were appointed
more for political influence than for professional qualifications.

Judge continued his activity for the New Hampshire Children's Aid
Society, the Elliot Hospital, and the Society for the Preservation of New
Hampshire Forests. Judge and Elisabeth snowshoed in winter and walked
around the Manchester outskirts during the spring and fall with picnics,
sometimes with children and sometimes by themselves. One of their
favorite walks was around the "flatiron," that is, Union Street, River Road,
and Carpenter Street. The young married couple led an active social life,
enjoying a few dances and attending the Palace and Strand Theaters. They
traveled around town on the trolley cars. The traveling circus came to the
circus grounds, on the northeast corner of Valley and Maple Streets.[3]

In May, Judge and Elisabeth stopped their wanderings from one rented
home to another and purchased a 1900 vintage house at 940 Chestnut
Street (still a dirt street) between Clark and Carpenter Streets, not far from
the #1 green line, the "Elm and A Street" trolley car. It would be their
home for the next fifty years. Judge records inspecting the house, seeing
the workmen painting, moving in, spending the first night, and having
their first party. They bought the house just in time. Their third child,
Elisabeth (Lilla), was born on July 2, and mother and child came home
from the hospital on the twenty-second! (No complications, just time to
recuperate according to the fashion of the day.) John (this author) at age

five got his usual attention—first fishing, first camping out for the night, swimming lessons at the lake, dangling from a broomstick with a rope around his waist, and diving headfirst into the water. He had pneumonia in the spring, and at a summer picnic at Newfound Lake's Crescent Beach (now Wellington Beach State Park) he stepped with bare feet onto some live picnic coals that had been covered with sand to put out the fire, with no catastrophic effects.

## HIGHLIGHTS OF 1922

Judge and Elisabeth were amateur bird-watchers. They loved to identify the warblers in the spring migration. They kept a feeding station for the birds outside the dining room window. In the winter of 1922 rare visitors from Canada came—two white-winged crossbills—and spent several weeks in a large spruce tree by the dining room. Word got around and soon there were ornithologists from all over New Hampshire and Massachusetts arriving to see the birds.[4] There was lots of snow that winter and the family went sleighing several times. In the spring, Judge took me at age six to Boston to see Ty Cobb play baseball! Judge played second base for the Hillside Inn team against the Hebron team in the summer and caught for the Lawyers in a game against the Doctors, in which he pulled tendons in both legs running to first base. Judge and Elisabeth bought their first car, a Maxwell.

Judge and Elisabeth sailed for England on the *Pittsburg* on June 24 for a six-week vacation. Judge had promised Elisabeth that as soon as he got a substantial fee, he would take her to England and show her some of the wonderful places he had visited during the two years he was a Rhodes scholar at Oxford. The fee arrived from Coyle Concord Oil Company, following the sale of the Mexia well in Texas. They hiked and biked in the Lake District and the Cotswolds and then took the train to Oxford.

In an account of their trip, Judge wrote:

> We arrived about six and found our room ready for us at the Eastgate. It is hard to describe the mingled feelings of eagerness and apprehension I experienced in reaching Oxford. My two years from 1907–1909 had left me with the deepest sentiment for Oxford's charm. I wanted so much to share it with Elisabeth—it was the chief object of our visit but as we neared it, I began to wonder if the charm mightn't be too elusive—should we be able to catch it? Should I not feel a stranger after so many years? Happily all these doubts were brushed away—we made it our headquarters for nearly two weeks—and when we left, not only did I have the satisfaction of knowing that it had the same attraction for Elisabeth

that it had for me—but I believe I know many sides of Oxford now far better than I ever did as a student. We have come away with definite hopes, tho' we say little of them—that our boys may have the same opportunity to come to this beautiful place."

Judge showed Elisabeth his college, Magdalen, "with its beautiful and familiar features, the cloistered quadrangle—my home for two years—the deer park, Addison's walk, the matchless tower." Judge and Elisabeth called on the Wylies. He was secretary to the Rhodes trustees, kept in touch with all of the Rhodes scholars and remembered "McLane." (The British use last names only.) The Wylies, "gracious as of yore," invited them to tea on the lawn where they met some of the current Rhodes scholars. Judge also found out that the current Dean of Magdalen was an old classmate, S. G. Lee, with whom they also had several pleasant visits.

Judge introduced Elisabeth to Lady Rosfrith Murray and her daughter, Rosfrith, in whose home Judge had had many happy times when a student. Judge writes: "They were so glad to see us and Lady Rosfrith quite fell in love with Elisabeth, kissing her each time we went there." A dinner guest a few nights later told Judge and Elisabeth that the Murrays have been called the finest family in the British Empire. Judge wrote: "There is much to say for this claim. Eleven children all of whom have taken part in the nation's life with honor. We could hardly have visited in a more wholesome English home: simple and unaffected people of great worth." Her husband, Sir James Murray, deceased in 1922, had worked on editing the Oxford Dictionary. When Judge was a student the family consisted of one son, Jowett, "the only triple first (high academic honors) since Gladstone, now teaching in China," Judge writes, and three daughters, Elsie, now in South Africa, Gwyneth, now living in Vancouver, and Rosfrith, at home taking care of her mother. Of the other children, "the oldest was Second in the Admiralty (Pepy's old job), the second son was Chief Inspector in the School system (a job which Matthew Arnold had), the eldest daughter was Mistress of Girton Hall, the finest of the Girl's colleges at Cambridge, the next son was Registrar of the University of Capetown." One afternoon, Judge and Elisabeth took Rosfrith out to tea in a punt on the Char—very fashionable. (A punt is a flat-bottomed boat that is propelled by standing and pushing a pole into the river bottom.)

After nearly two weeks in and around Oxford, they rented a canoe and spent several days on the Thames paddling about fifty miles down to Oxford. They spent a few days in London, before continuing on to the Devon coast, where they walked and biked some more. They sailed from Liverpool, July 28, on the *Montrose* and had a cold and rough passage with many icebergs in sight off the Straits of Belle Isle.[5] The boat took them up the St. Lawrence River to Montreal, where they caught the train to Plymouth and found the children gleefully waiting on the station platform.

In the fall, Judge and Elisabeth entertained Ralph Davis and "Miss" Sullivan for dinner and the Palace Theatre about a month before their wedding.

## HIGHLIGHTS OF 1923

This year had a good old-fashioned winter with lots of snowshoeing and picnics in the woods with their young sons John (this author) seven, and Charles, five. In mid-January there were thirty-one inches of snow on the ground. At the end of the month Judge and Elisabeth took the train to Bristol, snowshoed up to "Pikes" at the foot of Newfound Lake for the night, then the next day hiked fourteen miles up and over the Bridgewater Hills on old roads, cooking lunch en route, and down to Plymouth to catch the train home. In February they enjoyed a weekend of sleighing, skiing, and snowshoeing in Wiscasset, Maine, with Judge's friends the Sortwells. Winthrop Wadleigh, son of family friends in Milford and a Dartmouth senior (who later came to Manchester to practice with Louis Wyman), came over to supper with Janet Shaw,[6] then they all went to the Palace Theatre. Judge worked on soliciting funds for the Burroughs Memorial at New Hampshire Children's Aid Society; Sherman Burroughs, the first president of the society and a former law partner of Judge, had recently died while a congressman. I came down with chicken pox in May; in June, Charles and Elisabeth followed. Over the Memorial Day weekend, Judge and Elisabeth stayed at the lake and climbed Skyline one day, Mt. Lafayette the next, and Starr King the following day. In the fall, Elisabeth and Judge went to Waterville, where they spent the night before heading for Mt. Carrigain. They intended to go over Mt. Kancamagus but lost the trail and bushwhacked through heavy woods. They finally struck a trail but lost it. They had to abandon the trip up Carrigain and wound up in the logging village of Livermore. All of this area was being actively logged, and trail markers were frequently destroyed. (The loggers probably didn't know what the signs were.)

I had my tonsils and adenoids out at the Elliot Hospital, a completely obsolete procedure now. Elisabeth and the children went to the lake for the summer on July 3; Judge went on weekends by train to Franklin, where he changed to the Bristol branch and was met at the end of the line. There was hiking and camping on Cliff Island and Belle Isle, now owned by the state as part of Wellington State Park and closed to the public.

Judge and Elisabeth went to Newfoundland, traveling by boat from

Boston to Yarmouth, then by train up the Annapolis valley (Judge notes "Window fell & smashed in night"), through Cape Breton, and by night boat ("Rough and stayed in dining salon") to Newfoundland. They fished Spruce Brook, catching twenty trout in one day, and walked, canoed, complained about the flies, and admired the lady's slippers. When they were to leave for home, they "waited all day for the train but it went off track & 24 hours late." They read Henry James' *The American*. They finally got the overnight boat—"Routed out at 3 a.m. but couldn't get off boat til 6." They took the train to Halifax for a couple of days, then down the coast to Yarmouth and boarded the boat back to Boston.

During the summer, Judge played second base for the "old-timers" in Milford and caught for the Lawyers vs. the Doctors at Textile Field (Gill Stadium) in Manchester. Thanksgiving was celebrated at Manchester in their new house with "Granny" McLane, Gaga and Grampa Bancroft, and the Clinton McLane family, all six of them. Dr. Bancroft, Elisabeth's father, had a stroke in early December in Hanover, where he had been a psychiatric consultant to Dartmouth students.[7] Judge, Elisabeth, and Mrs. Bancroft took the midnight train to Hanover and found the doctor in very serious condition. Judge went to Boston on December 14 and received a message on the train back that Dr. Bancroft had died, so Judge went through to Hanover and returned to Concord with Elisabeth and Mrs. Bancroft on the midnight train. Funeral services were held in Concord (Appendix B.1, The Bancroft Family). A sad and snowless Christmas was spent at Concord. Word was received that the house at the lake had been broken into; fortunately, not too much was stolen or damaged.

## HIGHLIGHTS OF 1924

This year had another good old-fashioned winter—two feet of snow in January and the temperature went down to nine degrees below zero. On Judge's birthday, the family had a celebration. Judge played the violin while Elisabeth accompanied on the piano. The dog apparently ate a lot of candy and barked—"kept us up all night." On the author's eighth birthday (February 19) the family went sliding at Pinecrest and cooked an outdoor supper. Pine Crest was a development of summer cottages in a pine grove west of North Union Street near Whitford Street at the height of land. The modest log cabins have long since been replaced by substantial homes. The Brown farm, with acres of cleared fields, extended northerly down the long and gradual slope where Chestnut, Adams, and Bay Street extensions are now located. The farm provided wonderful sliding and tobogganing, when the conditions were right, for about a half mile to River Road.

Over the Washington birthday holiday, Elisabeth and Judge took the train to Bristol, snowshoed up over Bristol Peak and down to Newfound Lake to Pikes for the night, and then climbed over the Bridgewater Hills and down to Ashland (eight miles). They took the train home. Elisabeth's sister Miriam arrived home from China following the death of her father the preceding December. She stayed through the summer before returning to China with her mother.

A popular eating place downtown was Barton's, a department store where the new Amoskeag bank building, now First New Hampshire, was located. On the top floor, the fifth, there was a restaurant that had lots of Tiffany glass, a waterfall with palm trees, and tanks with goldfish. In early March, Judge and Elisabeth had dinner at Barton's and then went to the Palace, probably to a vaudeville and traveling stage show on the Keith circuit.

## HIGHLIGHTS OF 1925

Another good winter, with sleigh rides, tobogganing, and a snowshoe trip from Canaan over the shoulder of Mt. Cardigan to Hebron for the night with the Walter Braley family and then over Plymouth Mountain to Plymouth for the train home. Judge and Elisabeth were delayed four hours in Ashland because of a train wreck. In the summer they drove to the lake in their new car, a Maxwell. They left the children at the lake and continued on to climb Mount Washington, spending the night at the Lakes-of-the-Clouds huts. Judge and Elisabeth took the train to Quebec in late August, then sailed for Liverpool on the *Regina*, took the train to Edinburgh, and visited the Nicholsons at Arisaig House (See Appendix A.5, Sir Arthur Nicholson and Arisaig House) on the west coast of Scotland. They biked for four days in the Fort William–Oban area; took a boat to the Isle of Mull, the ancestral home of the Macleans; and visited Duart Castle, home of the clan chief—"The Maclean"—a spectacularly situated and beautifully restored castle overlooking the Sound of Mull. Then there was more biking, a couple of days in London, five days in and around Oxford, then on to Wales for walking, including climbing Mt. Snowden, before embarking on the *Montcalm* at Liverpool for the six-day trip across the Atlantic to Quebec. They took a train to Montreal and another train back home through a heavy blizzard.[8]

## HIGHLIGHTS OF 1926

Judge celebrated his fortieth birthday by taking a group of family friends with children in two buses to the Dunbarton Grange Hall for supper and an evening of square dancing, with an old-fashioned fiddler calling the dances. In February, Judge and Elisabeth, along with John Carleton, who had arrived in the office in the fall of 1925, skied from Bristol to Newfound Lake at Pikes, then over the Bridgewater Hills to Ashland. This trip on skis ended their snowshoeing days. Over the Memorial Day weekend, Judge and Elisabeth climbed the Franconia Range, crossed over to Livermore, the logging town, climbed Carrigain, and spent the night in the vacant fire lookout's cabin. During the summer, the circus came to town under the big tent at the corner of Maple and Valley Streets. Pasquaney was as busy as ever with lots of tennis, boating, beach picnics, walks on the high hill roads, and games of kick-the-can.

For many years the McLane family had occupied at the lake a wall-tent on a wooden platform set in the trees, located between the main house and the garage. During the preceding winter, a new and larger garage had been built on a different site, which included an apartment for help and a play-room for children. The old garage (now christened "Twin Oaks") was enlarged and converted into comfortable living quarters for the McLanes, who abandoned the tent.

In the fall, the family took in the Dartmouth-Harvard football game in Cambridge, followed by a trip to New Bedford and General Greene's estate to see the old whaling ship *Charles W. Morgan*. The ship was subsequently moved to the new Mystic Seaport Museum in Connecticut, where it still is the central attraction.

## HIGHLIGHTS OF 1927

Over New Year's weekend, Judge and Elisabeth took the train north and had a "long hard day's walk (on skis) from Canaan over the shoulder of Cardigan and down the Groton valley to Hebron and the Braleys," then the next day another fifteen miles "over the high road" to Plymouth. Then they took the train home. In the spring, Judge and Elisabeth took the boys by steamer from Boston to Norfolk and by another boat up the Potomac River to Washington. The peacefulness and ambience of boat travel have largely disappeared from our lives. The family took in all the customary sights in the capital and Mt. Vernon, rented a car with driver to tour the Gettysburg battlefield, and went by train to Annapolis before taking the sleeper back home. They started to dicker for land on North Union Street and finally bought what became "Three Acres." Judge and Elisabeth climbed Mt. Mansfield in Vermont over Memorial Day and Mts. Osceola and Tecumseh in Waterville Valley during the summer. There was tremendous flooding in the fall, particularly in Vermont on the Winooski and Lamoille Rivers. The family gathered at the McLanes' for Thanksgiving and went to Concord for Christmas with Gaga Bancroft.

## HIGHLIGHTS OF 1928

The family spent New Year's Day and two weekends in March at Hillside Inn, Newfound Lake. The inn, run by the Smith family, had started as a summer boardinghouse adjunct to the operating farm. When skiing became popular, the inn opened on weekends, when reservations were made. It was very comfortable, with open fireplaces in the several public rooms (no bar), and the food was sumptuous and delicious. The group skied in the open fields and pastures (now all grown over with trees) and on the abandoned wood roads, frequently cooking lunches out in the snow. There were no ski tows in those days. During the summer, Judge played tennis with John Carleton, Jack Nelson, Arthur Rotch, and Frank Sulloway, his most frequent partners. He bought a new Packard to replace the old Maxwell. Judge and Elisabeth hiked the Presidential Range over Labor Day weekend, spending nights at the Lakes-of-the-Clouds and Madison Spring huts of the Appalachian Mountain Club. In the fall and winter, Judge played squash at the Bow Brook Club in Concord. Thanksgiving and Christmas were traditional.

## HIGHLIGHTS OF 1929

The family spent a couple of winter weekends at Hillside Inn on Newfound Lake. One weekend there was breakable crust followed by a hard rain the next day. The other weekend Judge and Elisabeth skied with others from Canaan over the shoulder of Cardigan and down to Hillside Inn for the night and then, the next day, over Plymouth Mountain to the railroad in Plymouth. While attending the Dartmouth Winter Carnival after a trustees' meeting, they visited the new Carpenter Art Gallery, the gift of Frank P. Carpenter of Manchester. On the May 30 weekend, with children, they hiked into the Carter Notch hut for one night, returned for a night at Pinkham Notch, and then made the long climb up Madison Gulf to the Madison Spring huts for the third night, arriving in snow and twenty degree weather.[9] The family made trips to Boston to see the operas *Carmen, Cavelleria Rusticana,* and *Pagliacci* and a violin recital by Fritz Kriesler, for the benefit of this author, who was taking violin lessons, emulating his father. In June, the new YWCA was dedicated. On June 12, Judge and Elisabeth's fourteenth wedding anniversary, they hired a carriage and team and took a picnic out on a back country road. While Elisabeth was at the lake with the children during the summer, Judge "batched" it in Manchester with John Carleton, playing much evening tennis at the Cygnet Boat Club at the west end of the Amoskeag Bridge.[10] Bob Booth, Dartmouth class of 1922, a partner in Wyman, Starr, Booth, Wadleigh &

Langdell in Manchester, and a friend of Judge and Elisabeth's, was married to Lois Rundlett, a friend of Elisabeth's, at Pasquaney Lodge in August.

At the end of the month, Judge and Elisabeth embarked at Quebec on the Canadian Pacific liner *Duchess of York* for France, passing through the Straits of Belle Isle, where they sighted two icebergs. After several days in Paris, they traveled south to the Pyrenees, back to the walled city of Carcassonne, and returned to Paris. There they called on Mr. Edward Tuck, statesman, whose gifts to Dartmouth established the Tuck School of Business Administration and whose gift to the New Hampshire Historical Society made possible its impressive headquarters building in Concord. After visiting the theater and opera in Paris, they crossed the Channel to London, where Judge notes he purchased a first edition of Thomas Hardy's *Woodlanders*. In Oxford, they renewed acquaintance with S. G. Lee, secretary of the Rhodes Trustees in the new Rhodes House. They toured south to Stonehenge, which they visited at night, and Devonshire. Then they engaged in the search for the missing Flynn heirs (a case in the office), which took them to Liverpool and Ireland. They sailed from Belfast on the *Duchess of Richmond* back to Quebec.

Interestingly, Judge makes no reference to the stock market crash on Black Tuesday, October 29, 1929.

Judge notes that they attended the "talkies" at the new State Theater.[11] Christmas, as usual, was celebrated at Concord with Mrs. Bancroft. On New Year's Eve, Ralph Davis gave a big dinner party at the Statler Hotel in Boston, followed by the show *Naughty Marietta*.

Judge notes that his three-quarter interest in the McLane & Davis firm had grown from $10,000 on January 1, 1925, to $28,000 on January 1, 1929. He also writes that his forty shares in McLane Manufacturing Company, which were not previously listed, had a value of $4,000 as of January 1, 1929.

## Notes

1. Today, the steam-generating plant of the Public Service Company in Bow discharges warm water into the river, so that ice rarely forms below that point. This has resulted in the occupation of the lower Merrimack River by a number of wintering bald eagles, evidence of the reestablishment of many bird species threatened by the spraying of DDT in the 1950s.

2. The author and his first wife, Blanche, were ending a camping trip in the 1940s and walking out of the "Pemi" wilderness trail on the logging railroad when an old Ford station wagon with flanged wheels substituted for tires came up the valley on the railroad tracks. There were two men in the vehicle. They said that they were going up to a logging camp to deliver materials, have lunch,

and return to Lincoln and could take us. Because it was raining, we were in no rush, and because we had never seen a logging camp in operation, we accepted with pleasure, threw our packs in back, and sat on the tailgate. Logs were then hauled out of the woods to the mill by truck. This was the only vehicle that still used the tracks, which had not been maintained, as we could easily see as the rails spread apart and converged as we went along. Fortunately, we stayed on the track. The logging camp was housed in a couple of old, unpainted, single-story wood buildings, in a field of tall grass with pigs, cats, and dogs running around. Inside the cook shack was a long, wide table made of coarse lumber covered with a much-used oilcloth with utensils and dishes laid out and long benches on either side. The food was put on family style—baked beans, pork chops, mashed potatoes, peas, applesauce, canned peaches and pears, home-baked bread, doughnuts, and tea, coffee, and water in pitchers. When the gong sounded, the men came and went to work on the food, which was plentiful and simple. There wasn't much ventilation, and the air was close and hot from the large wood cookstove. In the dormitories, originally there was a long bench with blankets sewed together so that one crawled into a space between two other men and slept. The result was a very high incidence of TB, until better sanitary practices were introduced. We were lucky to witness the end of an era.

3. I can remember what fun it was to get up at 5 A.M. and bike down Canal Street to the railroad freight yards, where the circus trains had arrived during the night. We would watch, goggle-eyed, as the elephants pulled and hauled the circus wagons, brightly colored in many hues, off the train and got them in line. Some wagons had wild animals occasionally roaring. We would ride along with the wagons to the circus grounds and watch the wagons being placed in their assigned positions. Out would come the huge tent poles, the ropes, the guy wires. The canvas tent cover would be laid out and hoisted into place, and the bleachers would be assembled and the chairs put in place. The black roustabout gangs would go around the big tent pounding in the tent poles with their giant mallets to a rhythmic chant. Tired and dirty, we would bike back home for breakfast, hardly able to wait for the big parade with the steam calliope and the show in the afternoon.

4. The only other time I have ever seen a white-winged crossbill was at the Great Gulf shelter on Mt. Washington, which is located in a wooded area with evergreens at an elevation of about 4,000 feet. The birds were scrounging for food around the fire pit.

5. Icebergs "calve" off the glaciers and ice sheets of Greenland and are caught up in the southerly flowing Labrador current, sweeping down the Labrador coast and past the Straits of Belle Isle. When they hit the warmer waters of the Gulf Stream off the Grand Banks, they melt and disintegrate, although some continue, far out to sea, to the latitude of New York.

When this author sailed up the Labrador coast in 1990 with the Barringers on their thirty-five-foot sloop, we occasionally stopped near an iceberg, always spectacular in shape and color, to find some floating remnants, which we scooped up to replenish our refrigerator and supply our drinks with what were called "berger bits." The water in these pieces of ice was thousands of years old, having dropped on the Greenland ice cap as snow, then taking years and years to move ever so slowly from several hundreds of miles inland down to a fjord and out to sea, where it became an iceberg.

6. Janet Shaw, then a junior at Manchester Central High School, was one of the "Shaw girls"—daughters of Winfield and Lois Shaw, who lived on Salmon and Bay Streets. "Win" was a client of Judge, and the families were social friends. Win had been with W. H. McElwain Shoe Company in Massachusetts, which also had a plant in Manchester. W. H. McElwain was merged into International Shoe Company with headquarters in St. Louis near the stockyards, the source of shoe leather. Win was made manager of the Eastern Division, with headquarters in Manchester. There was a separate and independent company, J. F. McElwain Shoe Company, with plants in Nashua operated by W. H.'s brother, J. F. Win and Lois were supposed to be a model corporate executive couple reflecting the high standards of their employer. But Lois was an active and ardent suffragette, and when she was arrested for parading in Cambridge for the right of women to vote, and thrown into the Charles Street jail, the Manchester newspapers picked up the item and made the most of it. Mary Shaw Shirley tells me that as a result of the incident, some of her close friends from upper-class families in the North End were forbidden to invite any of the Shaw girls to their houses, for fear they might be contaminated by too liberal thinking.

The Shaws had five daughters, who made quite a splash in Manchester for a number of years. The oldest, Janet, vivacious, an outdoor girl, and very popular, attended Vassar College, following in her mother's footsteps, but she was tragically killed in an automobile accident at the end of her freshman year. Kate was artistic, never went to college, and specialized in children's pastel portraits. She married Elmer Greene, a well-known portrait painter whose subjects included, among others, Herbert Hoover, Pope Pius XII, Cardinal Spellman, Dartmouth president John S. Dickey, and John McLane Clark. The third daughter, Rhoda, also went to Vassar, and married John McLane Clark, Judge's nephew, son of his sister, Hazel. John graduated from Dartmouth, worked with Gil Winant in the International Labor Office, and acquired the Claremont, New Hampshire, *Eagle* newspaper. He and Rhoda had five children. John was accidentally drowned while canoeing with his children in the Sugar River in Claremont. The fourth daughter, Mary, also went to Vassar, then returned to Manchester to marry Larry Shirley, who owned the West Side Lumber Company and lived on Shirley Hill. Their son, Jim, is a lawyer with Sheehan, Phinney, Bass and Green. Mary, now a widow, was active as a trustee of the Currier Gallery of Art for many years. Lois, more familiarly known as "Chiggy," lives in the Lake Sunapee area.

7. I believe that this was the first psychiatric consultation service for students established by a college in the United States.

8. This blizzard was the same one in which a later client, Max Englehart, was lost on Mount Washington. He was luckily found in Tuckerman's Ravine by Joe Dodge, Jack Middleton's future father-in-law (Appendix C.2, Max Englehart).

9. The author, then age thirteen, still remembers the slippery snow and rocks and how cold knees can get in short pants.

10. After the disastrous spring floods of 1936 that destroyed the tennis courts, there was little enthusiasm, because of the depression, for rebuilding them anywhere, so some of the tennis fans built their own courts. Judge convinced Mary Fuller and Parker Straw to join him in hiring one company to build courts for each. Judge's court on North Union Street (where Bill Gannon now lives) is the only one left. See Appendix A.1, Memories—Cygnet Boat Club/Calumet Club.

11. The State Theater, an art deco 1,000-seat movie house, was located on Elm Street at Spring Street where Bankeast was located until 1991. As movie patrons declined, the theater was subdivided in the 1960s into, I believe, three theaters, but that could not stem the tide, and the theater was closed and torn down in the 1970s. The art deco Greek theater mask that decorated the entrance of the theater was saved and is now in front of the Dana Center, St. Anselm College, as a piece of historic preservation of Manchester.

# TIME LINE, 1925

A calendar for a particular representative year will give a good idea of the scope of Judge's activities. The years 1925, 1935, 1945, and 1955, at ten-year intervals, have been selected.

| | | |
|---|---|---|
| *January* | 4 | Concord to play squash with Sulloway. |
| | 5 | Night train to White River Junction, Lyme Center, back, sleigh ride for children in Dunbarton. |
| | 7 | Boston on McLane Company. |
| | 8 | Concord for Winant inauguration. |
| | 10 | Concord for squash. |
| | 11 | Concord, walked to St. Paul's School. |
| | 15 | Boston. |
| | 16 | Concord to argue in Supreme Court. |
| | 17 | 12-mile walk with Elisabeth over Mt. Cardigan to the Lake. |
| | 18 | Rested. Over to Plymouth and train down. 4-hour delay on account of wreck. |
| | 19 | Boston to take mother for X-rays. |
| | 21 | Milford for Annual Meeting McLane Manufacturing Company. |
| | 26 | Concord. |
| | 28 | Night train to New York City. |
| | 29 | White Plains on Estate. |
| | 30 | Washington on McLane Manufacturing Company. |
| | 31 | Home, miserable with cold. |
| *February* | 3 | Concord, hearing before Judiciary committee. |
| | 8 | Concord, Church. |
| | 10 | Concord with Rob Bass on incorporation. |
| | 11 | Milford. |
| | 13 | Boston and 2 o'clock for Cleveland. |
| | 14 | Labor hearing on right to control manufacturing methods. |
| | 15 | All-day conferences in Cleveland. Night train home. |
| | 18 | Milford on McLane Manufacturing. |
| | 19 | Concord, Rob Bass business. |
| | 20 | New York City Labor case from Cleveland. |
| | 21 | Holt Estate (Camp Mowglis). Home. |
| | 23 | Concord, Lunch with Governor Winant. |
| | 25 | Gave law class. |
| | 26 | Boston on Shattuck affairs. |

| | | |
|---|---|---|
| *March* | 1 | Goffstown to see mother. |
| | 3 | Concord on Milton Leatherboard tax case. |
| | 4 | Exeter and Portsmouth to search titles. |
| | 6 | Boston on Atlantic Corp. (Winant). |
| | 9 | Concord on Bass incorporation. |
| | 14 | Concord for weekend with Bancrofts. |
| | 18 | Milford on business. |
| | 19 | Boston to see Elwell on Holt Estate. |
| | 20 | Nashua on Anderson-Murphy sale. |
| | 21 | Concord for dinner at Tollands'. |
| | 23 | Concord for budget conference with Gil. |
| | 24 | Goffstown for view in Shuttoe Company case. |
| | 30 | Spoke at Lions Club on Cleveland agreement. |
| | | |
| *April* | 2 | Boston train for Schenectady, evening on Frear case. |
| | 3 | Saw witnesses. Home. |
| | 4 | Portsmouth with family. Busy on Atlantic Corp. case. Over to York beach to play in sand. |
| | 5 | Gil Winant down and up with him to Concord on trust fund argument. |
| | 8 | Tried case all day in Concord. |
| | 9 | Argued trust fund case before Supreme Court. |
| | 17 | Lake with Elwell to appraise Mrs. Holt's estate. |
| | 18 | Stayed at lake, down in p.m. |
| | 21 | Concord for hearing at PUC on Hudson Water. |
| | 22 | Milford on business. |
| | 23 | Boston on business matters. |
| | 25 | Train to Parker Station and walked back to Goffstown. |
| | 29 | Milford to see bank directors on Bourne (McLane Manufacturing). Boston for trustee meeting. |
| | 30 | Concord all day on Franconia Notch sale. |
| | | |
| *May* | 5 | Concord to argue Nelson Dowling before Supreme Court. |
| | 6 | Finished argument. Hanover on evening train. |
| | 7 | Talked to Keir's labor class on Cleveland agreement. |
| | 12 | Portsmouth on Atlantic Corp. |
| | 14 | Milford for Board of Trade dinner with Chas. Tobey. |
| | 15 | Boston to see Mrs. Shattuck. |
| | 17 | Took car to Marblehead for picnic with family and friends. |
| | 22 | East Washington for weekend on farm. |
| | 25 | Boston on Greenville Lighting. |
| | 27 | Wilton. |

| | | |
|---|---|---|
| *June* | 2 | Concord Tax Comm. |
| | 5 | Nashua on Murphy Anderson deal. |
| | 6 | Hanover for tennis match. Too hot for singles. |
| | 8 | Boston on Esterbrook loan. |
| | 9 | Exeter with Ralph to try Butman. |
| | 11 | Boston on various matters. |
| | 12 | Boston various. |
| | 13 | Boston with Taft on Greenville. Back via Greenville, Lyndeborough, and New Boston. |
| | 14 | Milford. |
| | 15 | Concord. Night train to New York. |
| | 16 | Out to Princeton. On sale Edgerton. Drove to New York City with Gil. |
| | 17 | Drafted contract. To Springfield. |
| | 18 | Drove home from Springfield. |
| | 19 | Family to lake for summer. Drove up in Maxwell (car). |
| | 20 | Hanover. |
| | 21 | Hanover. Called on Mrs. Carleton and Ames. Back to lake. |
| | 22 | Crawford House. |
| | 23 | Groveton to see Jordans. Climbed Mount Washington to Lakes-of-the-Clouds huts for night. |
| | 24 | Climbed to top and down Crawford trail. Drove to Swift River Inn. |
| | 29 | Boston with Bill Taft. Peterborough for dinner with Bass. |
| *July* | 3 | Concord, then lake. |
| | 7 | Boston, midnight to New York City. |
| | 8 | Breakfast, Gil and Constance Winant, who are off to Bogotá. |
| | 9 | Farragut House in Rye. |
| | 10 | Lake, Palmer Hutchison from Houston, Coyle Concord, stopped. |
| | 15 | Milford. |
| | 17 | Lake, stopped in Franklin on business. |
| | 18 | Hanover. |
| | 20 | Boston, met Bill Taft. |
| | 22 | Boston to meet Ned French on Souhegan Woolen. |
| | 23 | Kingston and Concord. |
| | 24 | Candia selectmen. Lake. |
| | 27 | Boston with Rob Bass. |

| *August* | 7 | Cummings Pond, Dorchester. |
| | 11 | Wilton, Souhegan Woolen directors. |
| | 12 | Concord to see Insurance Comm. |
| | 14 | Milford on French estate. |
| | 15 | Windsor to see Evarts. |
| | 16 | Night train to New York City. |
| | 17 | Trenton and Newark on Edgerstowne sale. New Haven to see Puffer. |
| | 18 | New York City. Met Gil and Constance on *Majestic*. |
| | 19 | Worcester to look up L.A. Corp. Win Wadleigh met Judge and drove home. |
| | 20 | Candia on appraisal of Moore estate. |
| | 21 | Concord on Edgerstowne. Lake. |
| | 28 | Lake. Judge and Elisabeth, night train from Plymouth. |
| | 29 | Quebec at noon. Sailed at night on *Regina*. |
| | 30 | Down St. Lawrence River. |
| | 31 | Straits of Belle Isle. Enjoy table companion. |
| *September* | 1 | Quiet, smooth. |
| | 2 | Fog, danced in evening. |
| | 3 | Fog again, have read *Glorious Apollo*, the Kenworthys, and Galsworthy's *Caravan*. |
| | 4 | Sea on today but not too heavy. |
| | 5 | Fine day, sail along Irish coast with Scotch islands on other side. |
| | 6 | Docked Liverpool. To cathedral. Train to Edinburgh. |
| | 7 | Shopped all day for children and us. |
| | 8 | Train through lochs to Fort William and Arisaig to visit Sir Arthur Nicholson at Traig. [Appendix A.5, Sir Arthur Nicholson and Arisaig House]. |
| | 9 | Gathered shells for children. Drove to Loch Morar and walked with Sir Arthur and Helena (his daughter). Round of golf. |
| | 10 | Golf. Drove to Arisaig House. Visit Prince Charlie's cave. |
| | 11 | Left early, got bicycles at Ft. William and rode via Spean Bridge, Tulloch to Loch Laggan. Swim in Rough Burn. Heather at its height. |
| | 12 | Rode 38 miles to Dalwhinnie, Glen Garry to Blair Atholl. |
| | 13 | Up Glen Tilt to Forest Lodge. To Pass of Killiecrankie. |
| | 14 | Rode over to Kinloch, Ramnoch and back via Struan. |

| | |
|---|---|
| 15 | Rode to Kenmore, steamer on Loch Tay to Killin, train to Oban. |
| 16 | Steamer to Tobermory on Isle of Mull (ancestral home of the Macleans), biked down to Aros. |
| 17 | Ride across island and steamer back to Oban. Biked to Taynuilt to Inverary. Caught in rain. |
| 18 | Ferry to St. Catherine's and over "Rest and Be Thankful" Pass, train to Edinburgh. Helena Nicholson to dinner. |
| 19 | Shopped. Holyrood and up High Street. Night train to London. |
| 20 | Brown's Hotel. Out to Kew Gardens. Tate Gallery. |
| 21 | Bought service plates. Saw Hardy's *Tess of the d'Urbervilles* at theater. |
| 22 | Oxford at noon. Tea with Lady Murray. Had Weston and Salman, new Rhodes scholars, for dinner. |
| 23 | Called on Sir Hubert Warren, Lee and Mr. Wylie. Miss Aldrich in for lunch. [Note: These were old friends of Judge's from Rhodes scholar days, and he wanted Elisabeth to meet them and vice versa.] Train to Chipping Camden and biked to Stow-on-the-Wold. |
| 24 | Bicycle to Naunton. Bus to Cheltenham, biked to St. Cerney, spent night with Cripps. |
| 25 | Reading, met Ogilvies for lunch. Back to Oxford for tea with Lees. |
| 26 | Wylies for lunch, took Murrays for ride over Cunmore. Trout (Inn) for dinner. Walked down towpath. |
| 27 | Train to Shrewsbury. Evening service at St. Mary's. |
| 28 | Wales by train, up coast to Portmadoc. Walked down Pass of Aberglaslyn for tea. |
| 29 | Walked in mist to Pen-y-Gwryd hotel for lunch and through Pass of Lamberis. Night at Carnarevon. |
| 30 | Visited castle. Train along coast to Bettys-y-coed. |

| | | |
|---|---|---|
| October | 1 | Fine clear day. Climbed Snowdon. Train to Chester. |
| | 2 | Into Liverpool. Sailed on *Montcalm*. |
| | 3 | Called at Greenoch for mail and passengers. |
| | 4 | Sunday Service. At table with typical young Englishman. |
| | 5 | Stiff sea, pitching. Shuffleboard, deck tennis, and dancing. |
| | 6 | Another disagreeable day, cold and windy. |
| | 7 | Southwest gale, heavy seas. Quieted in evening, danced. |

| | | |
|---|---|---|
| | 8 | Through Straits of Belle Isle. Fancy dress ball. Judge won prize for best dressed gentleman as Highlander (in kilts). Elisabeth in plaid skirt. |
| | 9 | Docked Quebec at 8. Midnight to Montreal. |
| | 10 | Train down in heavy blizzard and home to children all happy and well. [Note: See Appendix C.2, Max Englehart, who was lost on Mount Washington in this storm.] |
| | 13 | Boston on Souhegan Woolen, Concord for dinner. |
| | 16 | Concord for annual meeting SPS Trustees. |
| | 18 | Lake. |
| | 23 | Boston, Dartmouth smoker. |
| | 24 | Cambridge for Dartmouth, 32–Harvard 9 game. |
| | 27 | Boston to see Shattucks. Dinner with Gil and up on train. |
| | 29 | Concord for talk with Rob Bass. |
| | 30 | Milford on French estate. Nashua to talk on Cleveland arbitration. |
| | 31 | Bedford, Goffstown, Dunbarton and Concord. |
| *November* | 1 | Drive Hampstead to see Mrs. Butman. |
| | 2 | Nashua to start trial Owen v. Eliot Hospital. |
| | 5 | Peterborough to Bass to talk senatorship announcement. |
| | 6 | Lake for night. |
| | 7 | Hanover, Dartmouth 62, Cornell 13. [Note: This was the great undefeated 1925 Dartmouth football team.]. Back to lake. |
| | 10 | Claremont on trial preparation with Ralph. |
| | 12 | New York City on night train. |
| | 13 | Saw Constance (Winant) re fees on tax refund case. |
| | 15 | Concord for supper, saw Gil. |
| | 16 | Boston, guest of Dr. Drury at Headmaster's dinner at Harvard Club. |
| | 20 | Nashua to argue motions. |
| | 22 | Drove to Concord over Hooksett and Bow hills. |
| | 24 | Londonderry on Annis Grain case; Concord to meet Rob and John Bass, Larmon and Gil. |
| | 25 | Out to New Boston for supper. |
| | 27 | Concord for dinner. Gil and Pearsons. |
| | 28 | Portsmouth to see navy yard. |
| *December* | 3 | Concord with Rob Bass. |
| | 4 | Concord to dinner. Went over business with Mrs. Bancroft. |

| | |
|---|---|
| 7 | Concord for dinner at Fred Winant's. |
| 8 | Farmington with Ralph on railroad abandonment. |
| 11 | Candia with selectmen. |
| 13 | Goffstown for dinner with mother. |
| 14 | Boston. Saw George Arliss in *Old English*. |
| 15 | Boston. Worked on Esterbrook claims. Concord to convention to elect new bishop. |
| 17 | Lawrence with Constance on Aiken loan. |
| 19 | Concord and back. |
| 22 | Lowell to take Christmas presents to Benners. |
| 26 | Boston on NE Gypsum. |

# EIGHT

# Amoskeag Manufacturing Company

The Amoskeag Manufacturing Company was the dominant force in Manchester from the mid-1830s until its bankruptcy on Christmas Eve 1935. The company exemplified the flowering of the Industrial Revolution in the textile industry in New England and was the reason for the growth of Manchester.

Judge did legal work for Amoskeag starting in the 1920s, first with labor problems and later against the city of Manchester with respect to taxes and property. A review of the early development of Amoskeag will provide helpful background and a better understanding of Manchester and a context for Judge's work.

The Merrimack River has been used by man for about 6,000 years. The Amoskeag Falls, with a drop of fifty-two feet, was a fishing ground used by Indians for salmon and other anadromous fish. It was the scene of encampments of different tribes who traveled from what is now New York and the New England states to fish and exchange goods. Several archaeological sites surrounding the falls have produced evidence of this early use. The river was used by Indians and later by whites for transportation by canoe and raft. A cotton textile mill was built on the westerly shore in 1804, but it proved a failure. In 1807 Samuel Blodgett completed his canal and a series of locks around the falls on the east side of the river to enable traffic to connect with the recently completed Middlesex Canal, which connected the Merrimack River at Lowell with Boston. These canals were heavily used and then abandoned after the arrival of the railroad in the mid-1840s.[1]

In 1822, the three-story Bell mill was built on an island below the ancient partial, or wing, dam. The mill was sold in about 1825 to Samuel Slater of Rhode Island, a famous and successful textile entrepreneur.

In 1825, the Amoskeag Manufacturing Company was incorporated by a group of Rhode Islanders, including Slater, to further develop the water-power available at the Amoskeag Falls. They purchased over 1,000 acres of land on each side of the river and started construction of the upper and lower canals on the east side, the former a mile in length and the latter a mile and a third long. Later they purchased about 2,000 additional acres on both sides of the river. The textile mills at Lowell had just started operating in 1825 and served as the model for the proposed new city. Work was started on a wing dam extending out from the east bank of the river. The dam funneled water into the canals. When sluice gates in the upper canal were opened, the water dropped twenty-five feet through the penstocks under the mill buildings, turning turbines that activated belt shafting, which in turn transferred the power throughout the mill to the individual machines. The spent water flowed back into the lower canal, and then dropped through more penstocks under the lower set of mills another twenty-five feet to the river. The right to draw water from the canal was called a "mill privilege" and was controlled by the Amoskeag Manufacturing Company.

In 1835, the Rhode Island group sold their stock in the Amoskeag Manufacturing Company to members of the Boston Associates, a loosely organized group of Boston merchant families who had been very successful over a period of fifty or more years in maritime trade, marine and fire insurance, banking, railroads, and other enterprises. The families involved with the Boston Associates included Amory, Appleton, Cabot, Dwight, Jackson, Lawrence, Lowell, and Lyman. The principal business offices of the Boston Associates were in Boston.

Their first textile venture was in Waltham in 1815, where a ten-foot head, or drop, of water was utilized successfully to power mills. Several operations previously performed in the home were then brought into a factory building for greater efficiency. The associates next moved to Lowell in 1815. Lowell had a thirty-two-foot head of water. There they developed a much larger concept of mass production that necessitated the building of an entire community, including employee housing. The third move was to Manchester, where the fifty-two-foot Amoskeag Falls enabled the Amoskeag Manufacturing Company to become the largest textile complex in the world, and the city of Manchester to grow.

The Amoskeag Manufacturing Company was initially a development company that sold waterpower and land, or leased its real estate. The initial industrial area was developed along the canals and the river. There was no previously existing community. Amoskeag planned and created a new community. Worker housing, owned and operated by the mills, consisted of three-story brick tenement boardinghouses for the "operatives," as the female workers were called, and brick row housing for the families of the foremen and second hands. The housing was located between the mills and Elm Street, a wide street designed for the "downtown" commercial area. There was some residential use of the upper floors over retail establishments in the downtown area. Residential housing spread out in all direc-

tions from the town center. Until the arrival of mass transportation by
horse-drawn trolley cars in the 1870s, Manchester was essentially a pedestrian community. Trains provided good intercity travel after 1841.

Amoskeag was self-sufficient. It had its own construction crews to build
its mills and housing and machine shops and a foundry to provide metal
goods and to make and repair practically everything, including the textile
machinery. It had its own water system to provide water for drinking, sanitary purposes, process application, and fire protection. Before municipal
sewerage systems were built, the company collected the sewerage in horse-
drawn tank vehicles, known as "honey wagons."

The first operating mill of the new Amoskeag Manufacturing Company
was the Stark Mills, which opened in 1838 at the foot of Stark Street.
Handsome three-story brick dormitory buildings for the "operatives" and
row houses for the "foremen"[2] and "second hands" lined both sides of Stark
Street. Because the railroad did not arrive in Manchester until 1841, all of
the brick for the mills and houses was floated down the river from Hooksett
on rafts and transported to its destination by horse and wagon.

The Boston Associates over a period of some fifteen years caused a
number of corporations to be formed, each to manufacture a distinct type
of textile cloth, such as gingham, ticking, duck, and print cloth. There was
considerable interlocking of directors and overlapping of stockholders. All
mill operators purchased their building sites and received their waterpower
from the Amoskeag Land and Development Company. There were eleven
of these textile manufacturing mills, including the Stark, Langdon, Amory,
and Manchester Mills and the Manchester Print Works. (The latter is
where Alexander Maclean, Judge's grandfather, came in 1854.)

The Amoskeag Machine Shops and Locomotive Works was one of five
distinct departments of the Amoskeag Company. The original machine
shop (381 feet by 36 feet, three stories high), built in 1840,[3] was located in
the mill yard where the University of New Hampshire, now (1996) has its
Manchester mill yard campus. In 1848 another shop was added, which was
320 feet by 40 feet and also three stories tall. Because there were no established machine shops in the area, Amoskeag had to have its own facilities
to repair its machinery. It also made many improvements and developed
new machines. In addition to the machine business, metal parts for the
construction trades were fabricated for the building of mills, tenements,
and houses as the city expanded. A foundry was built in 1842 north of the
machine shop and replaced by a new foundry (154 feet by 80 feet) in 1848.
Circular metal stairs with the name AMOSKEAG embedded were made at the
foundry and can still be seen in many of the mill yard buildings.

Amoskeag saw the possibility of making money by manufacturing
steam locomotives for the railroads, which were penetrating practically

every river valley in New England and beyond. In 1849, Locomotive #1, the *Etna*, was built for the Northern Railroad, which ran from Concord to White River Junction. It weighed about twenty tons and remained in service on this road for about thirty years. The business expanded so that in 1856 sixty locomotives were built under the aegis of Aretas Blood, superintendent of the machine shops.[4] In about 1853, Amoskeag made an experimental locomotive, the *Mamaluke*, with a single pair of exceptionally high drive wheels, seven feet in diameter, compared to the standard five-foot wheels. Engineers were scared of it, but in a test run between Manchester and Concord, it covered a mile in forty-five seconds, or eighty miles per hour. Between 1853 and 1859, Amoskeag produced 232 locomotives. In 1859, the locomotive business was sold to the Manchester Locomotive Works (see Chapter Nine) because, as the Locomotive Historical Society says, the depression of 1857 caused the discontinuance of building locomotives.[5] The last six engines were built on speculation, and were finally delivered to the Grand Trunk Railway in 1858.

In the same year (1859) that the locomotive business was sold, Amoskeag became interested in a new product—the steam fire engine pumper, which had been developed by Nehemiah S. Bean, a graduate of the Massachusetts Institute of Technology. Until 1844, he had worked in the Amoskeag Manufacturing Company (AMC) machine shops building carpet looms. He moved to Lowell and later to Lawrence, where between 1857 and 1858 he designed and built a steam fire engine, the *Lawrence*, the first in New England. It weighed four tons. By early 1859, he returned to Amoskeag and worked on a pumper, *Amoskeag #1*, ordered by the city of Manchester. It was to be delivered in two months, in time for the firemen's muster, to be held on July 4, 1859, on the Merrimack Common in Manchester. It was tested on the common at the muster,[6] where there was a pond and a flagpole suitably marked to measure the height of the pumped stream. The *Amoskeag #1* raised water to a height of 203 feet within seven minutes of lighting the boiler. That pumper continued in active service for the city of Manchester until October 1876. The steam pumpers were pulled by one, two, or three horses and were used into the 1930s when the gasoline engine fire trucks became more reliable and less expensive and the horse-drawn vehicles were phased out. (See Appendix A.1, Memories— Fire Engines.) Business boomed between 1859 and 1876, during which period 550 fire engines were built and delivered all over the world, with a peak production in 1867 of fifty-nine.

In 1867, Nehemiah S. Bean[7] was superintendent of the machine shop and in charge of the development of the first "horseless carriage" (fire engines were also known as "self-propellers"). The vehicle utilized the steam generated by the boiler both for pumping and to provide locomotion, thus eliminating the need for horses. In 1872, during the great Boston fire, the Boston fire chief appealed to many communities for aid. Amoskeag put the "self-propeller" on a flat railroad car and rushed it to Boston, where it did yeoman service on Washington Street. It was said that other horses pulling fire engines were frightened, not so much by the steam engine itself but by the fact that it had no horses pulling it![8] In 1876, Amoskeag closed this branch of the machine shops. The Manchester Locomotive Works acquired the rights to manufacture the self-propellers.

During the Civil War, the mills were hard up because they could not get any southern cotton. The price of cotton skyrocketed, thus stimulating other sources. Egyptian cotton production expanded along the fertile banks of the Nile River.[9] Without a large supply of cotton, the AMC machine shops were busy turning out some six hundred McKay sewing machines between 1863 and 1866. The Northern Army ordered 25,000 .45-caliber Springfield rifles and 17,000 breech-loading carbines. Fortunately, Amoskeag had a large number of well-qualified machinists, including many Germans, to manufacture all these goods. The machine shops also had a giant lathe, twenty-one feet in diameter, on which were turned the brass rings for the gun turrets for the Monitor class of Union gunship.

The machine shops had plenty to do after the war with the expansion of the textile business, so Amoskeag discontinued most of its nontextile endeavors.

Amoskeag was a good example of absentee ownership. Its corporate office, with its all-powerful treasurer, was located in Boston, as were all of the purchasing, selling, and financing departments. William Amory was treasurer for thirty-nine years and built a highly successful complex of mills. The operation of the mills themselves was left in the hands of a local person, who held the title of agent. For three generations in the case of Amoskeag, this was a member of the Straw family. The first, Ezekiel Straw, was a young civil engineer who worked for Amoskeag. In 1838 he laid out the city, then rose to become agent of the Land and Water Power Department in 1851 and general agent in 1858, a position he held until 1885, just two years before his death. He kept his finger on the pulse of the state and protected the interests of the mills in the legislature by serving in that body in 1859–1863 and in the senate in 1864. He was elected governor for 1872–1873.[10] He was succeeded as agent by his son, Herman F. Straw, who served as agent from 1885 to 1929. He was followed by his son, William Parker Straw, agent from 1929 to 1935, when the mills closed down. The agent was the only visible corporate person in Manchester. There were few, if any, stockholders residing in the city. Most lived in the Boston area, at least until Amoskeag went public in the 1920s.

As the city grew, Amoskeag provided land at a low cost for schools, churches, civic buildings, bridges, and public parks with ponds (for fire protection, not recreation or aesthetics). In many instances, the Amoskeag deeds contained a right of reverter, providing that, if the land ceased to be used for the stated purpose, the deed was null and void and the title would automatically revert to Amoskeag. Since there were no building codes or zoning laws at that early time, Amoskeag frequently imposed obligations in its deeds for center-city property requiring the landowner to build with brick and install a slate roof for fire protection. Also there were setback restrictions prohibiting construction a set number of feet from the front, back, and side lot boundaries to prevent overcrowding and for fire safety. These restrictions were enforceable through the reverter clauses.

Amoskeag Industries, Inc., as the successor to the Amoskeag Manufacturing Company by virtue of the purchase of all the assets in 1936 from the bankruptcy court, is the current owner of the reverter rights. In recent years, Amoskeag Industries at the request of landowners has released building restrictions because the city now has adequate building codes. In the case of city-owned land, Amoskeag has modified the restriction where the city wanted to substitute one public use for another, such as use of Merrimack Common for parking, or Victory Park for a parking garage, or the Franklin Street School for municipal offices. However, where the city sold property to third parties, Amoskeag released its reverter interest in exchange for a percentage of the sale price. Such was the procedure in the sale of Amoskeag, Maynard, and Straw schools.

Amoskeag Manufacturing Company made purchase of land easy for its employees who had five or more years of employment. The company offered low down payments, and a second mortgage with low interest, frequently waived for the first couple of years. Loans were subject to a bank mortgage, which financed the construction of a home, usually the ubiquitous triple-decker tenement in which the employee occupied one floor and other members of his family or tenants the other two. As part of its paternalistic policy, the company provided athletic fields (particularly Textile Field, now Gill Stadium), playgrounds, and gardens and sponsored a textile club, athletic clubs, a welfare program, and medical and dental clinics. Because of these policies, the company, at least until World War I, was able to attract and hold a superior class of loyal workers. The apparent humanitarian policy of the company had its practical aspects in that it kept labor agitation by outsiders to a minimum. Amoskeag bought up all the available waterpower sites up and down the river to keep out any other manufacturing establishments that might try to increase wages and lure Amoskeag workers away. Humanitarianism was applied more because it was economically feasible rather than because of any ethical considerations; witness the fact that northern mill owners in the 1830s, '40s, and '50s supported slavery in the South since it meant a lower-cost cotton.

The pre-1855 labor supply was drawn from local farm families. The community at this early stage of growth was predominantly white, Anglo-Saxon, and Protestant. In Rhode Island, entire families were hired and the children were expected to work too. Boston Associates mills, on the other hand, employed mostly women who were hardworking and loyal. The early mill managers felt a duty in looking after the welfare of the young female mill workers. High moral standards were maintained, such as curfews at night; the girls, or operatives, as they were known, were expected to be in their dormitory buildings at bed-check time. Girls were expected to attend the church of their choice on Sundays. In the 1840s there was a church for about every three hundred people. There were a number of erudite societies offering lectures, recitals, and other intellectual forms of entertainment. By the mid-1850s the rules were relaxed, and the mill girls no longer were required to live in the dormitories. The moral standards were maintained by the existence of a blacklist on which were reported any girls or men of undesirable character. These lists were circulated to the mills in Nashua, Lowell, and Lawrence. In 1850, of 4,575 employees in New Hampshire mills, 3,900 were female.

Hours in the mills were long by present standards, but most of the workers came from farms, where long hours were standard. Work began at 6:30 A.M. and ended at 7:30 P.M. Monday through Friday, and at 4:30 P.M. on Saturdays.

In 1847, the first four hundred Irish families arrived as the result of the potato crop failures at home. In the mid-1850s, the French arrived from Canada. With the arrival of foreign workers, the local farm girls turned to the more professional and higher-paying jobs of office secretaries, bookkeepers, and schoolteachers.

About the time of the Civil War, there was a great influx of northern Europeans (predominantly Germans) as the result of political turmoil. More countries attempted to overthrow autocratic governments and espouse the cause of democracy, which was prevalent in the United States and struggling in France. Toward the end of the century, the southern Europeans (Greeks and Italians) came to America in large numbers.

There was agitation for a ten-hour workday in the 1840s; some laws were passed, but they were ineffective and largely ignored. It wasn't until 1874 that the length of the working day was reduced—to ten hours for women and children only. In the 1880s the minimum age for children to work in the mills was set at thirteen.

The labor movement grew in the North toward the end of the century. In 1912 there was a violent strike in the American Woolen Mills in Lawrence, where the International Workers of the World (IWW) was active. There, after a sixty-three-day strike, labor won. During World War

*Circa 1883, Amoskeag Mills from West Side.* Note extensive gabled roofs, which were replaced by flat roofs, probably because of sliding snow damage. Credit: Manchester (N.H.) Historic Association Photo Archives.

I in 1918, 35,000 workers belonging to the United Textile Workers in New England struck for as long as five months in Lawrence. In the South, labor was white and homogeneous. Mill owners and employees didn't want northern carpetbaggers or those "communist unions"; the southerners ran the northerners out of town if they appeared.

Between 1900 and 1920 a dramatic shift in textile production and competition took place, which many people in Manchester failed to notice because of the continual growth of the local textile mills. Between 1900 and 1916, Amoskeag employment soared to its maximum of 16,000 (54 percent male). More spindles (620,000 cotton and 50,000 worsted) were turned than in any other mill complex in the world. Daily production was 471 miles of woven cloth. Annually that consumed 27,000 tons of cotton and 131,000 tons of coal. There was 6 million square feet of mill space on 137 acres of industrial land. Then, in 1916, Amoskeag completed the construction of the Coolidge Mill on the West Side; its new machinery increased production from 160 million square yards of cloth a year to 240 million square yards.[11]

Amoskeag was very profitable through the nineteenth century, paying substantial dividends. However, textile production was shifting to the

*Amoskeag Mill Yard, 1880s.* Credit: Manchester (N.H.) Historic
Association Photo Archives.

South. In 1900 the southern mills had 33 percent of the number of spindles in the North, which accelerated to 66 percent by 1910, to 85 percent
by 1920, and to 200 percent by 1932. World War I, with its huge demand
for khaki cloth, kept the northern mills busy, particularly Amoskeag, but
once the war ended, competition between North and South became acute.
Southern mills went to multiple forty-eight-hour shifts, and Amoskeag and
other northern mills increased machine speeds and workloads.

The reasons for the rise of the textile industry in the South and its
decline in the North are many and complex. The South had a competitive
transportation advantage: Raw materials were closer to the South; both
Amoskeag and many southern mills made "coarse goods" of short staple
cotton, which was grown in the South. Both the North and the South used
coal for power generation, and coal was on the South's back doorstep.
(Waterpower was only marginally effective by 1900 in both the North and
South.) The newer, single-story southern mills and their newer machinery
were more efficient compared to the North's multistoried buildings[12] with
old and obsolete machinery. The northern mills overstated profits by failing to make adequate provision for depreciation reserves; thus they had no
cash reserves to modernize machinery, because a large percentage of the

profits had been paid out in cash dividends. As for the labor cost differential, after the Civil War, the South had an abundance of cheap white labor (nonunion), which was paid about half that of the North, but the southern employee produced only half as much as the northern laborer, so, according to some, labor cost per unit of production was a wash. However, Arthur M. Kenison, professor of economics, St. Anselm College in Manchester, feels that the labor cost differential was by far the most important factor in making the South more competitive than the North.[13]

The South wanted industry after the Civil War to diversify from an agricultural economy. The North was tired of the textile industry with its low technology and low wages and wanted to shift to high-tech industries, such as the manufacture of engines, machine tools, instruments, and goods for the growing electrical industry. Some of the early disadvantages of the South were overcome by technology, that is, automatic humidifiers overcame the drier climate, water softeners made the South's hard water usable, and the telephone and telegraph provided instant communication with the selling markets in New York. At the hearings conducted by Congressman Sabbath in the fall of 1936 to determine if mill owners were profiting by declaring bankruptcy at the expense of creditors, it was suggested that one reason for Amoskeag's decline was the change in women's styling and the abandonment of gingham cloth, one of Amoskeag's principal products.[14]

There were many national labor problems in 1921 that spilled over to the Amoskeag Mills. The high wartime production slowed drastically, southern mills continued to expand with greater efficiency, competition was fierce, and there was overcapacity in the industry. Many of these facts were not believed by the northern unions in Fall River and New Bedford, which pushed for even higher wages, already much higher than those in southern mills. Amoskeag tried to keep a contented and loyal labor force, but this finally became impossible.

William Parker Straw (always known as Parker), working in the office of the agent for Amoskeag (his father, Herman F. Straw), hired Judge to be "consulting labor adviser" because he had worked during World War I in the industrial labor section of the Quartermaster Corps of the U.S. Army (see Chapter One).

The younger Straw was well acquainted with the McLanes. Straw was born and brought up in Manchester and attended St. Paul's School before going to Harvard. He was on the military staff of Governor John McLane as an aide-de-camp and was a frequent tennis partner, social friend, and client of Judge's. He was about eight years Judge's senior. Judge investigated labor conditions in Manchester and particularly in Amoskeag, consulting a number of people presumably both within and without the company (their names are not known). Judge made a report to management.

Labor problems in 1921 were a forerunner to the great strike of 1922. The McElwain Shoe Company had some discontented labor groups, and Judge worked on strike and boycott problems for them in Nashua, where he observed picketing at their plant.

Judge also did legal work in 1921 for Amoskeag related to the Amoskeag street layout. Amoskeag originally owned almost all the land on both sides of the Merrimack River. It sold most of it for development and conveyed to the city the land it had laid out for public streets. The streets adjacent to the mills and mill housing remained the company's. Thus, since the 1840s Amoskeag had retained ownership to and assumed responsibility for the maintenance and construction of the streets west of Elm Street, between Dow Street on the north and Granite Street on the south, because the company houses and tenement blocks were built on these then-private streets. In 1921 profits for the mills were falling. The company approached the city to assume responsibility for these streets. Because negotiations were fruitless, the company hired Judge. The firm petitioned the mayor and Board of Aldermen to lay out and accept as public streets those lying west of Elm Street and east of Canal Street (which was already a public street). A road hearing was held and was adjourned to a later date, when the aldermen voted to accept the streets by a seven-to-five vote. Some of the aldermen thought that all the city got was a lot of expense and no benefit, overlooking the substantial real estate taxes paid.

The textile industry had labor problems in New England in 1922. The unions were well entrenched and militant, but either they did not comprehend or they ignored the competition with the nonunion South, where overall costs were less. Judge notes in his diary on February 13, "Amoskeag Co. strike on today." Labor had asked for a wage increase, but the company had established the terms as a 20 percent pay cut and an increase in the work week from forty-eight hours to fifty-four hours, a position from which they never budged. The strike lasted for nine months. When winter arrived, the employees reluctantly accepted the company's terms. In October, Judge started to advise Parker Straw on labor matters and spent several days with him and others, including a citizens' committee.

Judge was asked to represent Amoskeag before the legislature but turned the job down, without citing any reasons. Throughout his law practice, Judge had a strong aversion to lobbying. Amoskeag lost many old customers during the long 1922 strike to southern mills, and they never returned. Many buyers felt that the northern unionized mills were unreliable because of union labor unrest, whereas nonunion southern mills could deliver their contracts on time.

The year 1923 was the high-water mark for the northern textile industry. It achieved the greatest number of spindles ever, but it was only on a fifty-fifty basis with the South. Thereafter there was a precipitous decline in the number of spindles in the North but continued growth in the South. The textile industry by the mid-1920s was overbuilt; the first mills to go were the most inefficient, usually the old, small-town mills with multistory buildings that required considerable material handling labor cost. Between 1922 and 1932, seventy-three mills were liquidated in Fall River, Massachusetts and seventy-five percent of that city's textile capacity was lost. New Bedford, Massachusetts, lost 23,000 textile jobs. There were many bankruptcies in both cities.

Amoskeag Manufacturing Company provided Judge with a substantial amount of legal work in 1923 and 1924 in connection with its tax abatement cases against the city of Manchester. The company was desperately trying to trim operating expenses and sought to lower its tax liability. The case started when Judge had a conference with Parker Straw and his father, H. F. Straw, and was retained to represent Amoskeag. Although none of the records is available, the issue as I understand it was that the company claimed that the ratio of assessed value of Amoskeag property to its fair market value was higher than comparable ratios of other taxpayers in the city. The company claimed that this difference was unfair and illegal. Case preparation required a tremendous amount of investigation with respect to the valuations of both real estate and personal property, including machinery, inventory, work in process, and finished goods, not only for Amoskeag but also for other tax-payers. One of the methods for determining fair market value was to examine the purchase price as revealed by the federal documentary stamps (based on consideration) placed on deeds recorded in the county Registry of Deeds. Frederick Demond, of Demond, Woodworth and Sulloway in Concord, represented the city. There were twenty-three entries in Judge's diary during the year, mostly on preparation of the case.

The case also occupied a substantial amount of time in 1924. The trial started in early January with Judge and Ralph Davis as the trial team. The trial included "views" of Amoskeag properties located both inside and outside the mill yard. In legal parlance, a "view" is a visible inspection of a site or an object by the trier of fact, either a jury or a judge, in the company of the attorneys, who are permitted to point out features that will be the subject of later testimony. In this instance, the tenement houses and the mill buildings and machinery would have been pointed out because their value was going to be the subject of testimony by expert witnesses on both sides. The Amoskeag agent, Herman F. Straw, was on the stand for five days on direct and cross-examination. He was followed by accountants, engineers, et cetera, intermittently during February. The plaintiff, Amoskeag, finished in early March after twenty-five days in court and was followed by the city for nine days. Then followed fourteen days out of court on argument preparation and three days of oral argument. During May and June, Judge worked on the brief, or written argument, for ten days. In October, Amoskeag received a judgment for abatements totaling $132,000. There followed several conferences with Demond and Woodworth (now the Sulloway law firm) before litigation started on the 1924 tax abatement case with a hearing before the city assessors.

There was a small amount of additional work for Amoskeag during the year: a couple of sessions with Parker Straw and two Spaniards on Casablanca patents, some advice on seniority rights, and attending the annual meeting. Judge also conferred extensively with Parker Straw on the proposed "forty-eight-hour week" legislation, which provided for a compulsory maximum forty-eight-hour workweek. In the 1922 Amoskeag strike, the union had sought to retain a forty-eight-hour week but was forced to accept an increase to a fifty-four-hour workweek. The union finally won via the legislature what it lost in the strike.

Judge formed a personal holding company for Herman F. Straw, which bore the name of "H.F.S. Investment Co.," so that Mr. Straw could put his Amoskeag stock into the holding company.

Judge, in connection with his work for Amoskeag in 1925, formed Moore's Falls Corporation, a subsidiary of Amoskeag Manufacturing Company, to acquire the waterpower and flowage rights at Moore's Falls, located on the Merrimack River below Goff's Falls. Amoskeag had no desire to develop anything there but wanted to control the site so that no one else could, in order to be sure that Amoskeag dominated the labor market. Judge was clerk of Moore's Falls Corporation for some thirty years and was succeeded by an official of Amoskeag in Boston. Judge reported that the Amoskeag tax case was near settlement and that he worked on contracts for the purchase of rayon machinery. Rayon was one of the new miracle fibers made from cellulose, a wood derivative.

As treasurer of Amoskeag, Frederick C. Dumaine masterminded the fate of the company since 1905. In 1925, the company was restructured into the Amoskeag Corporation, a holding company whose stock is still traded on exchanges, and its subsidiary, the Amoskeag Manufacturing Company, the operating company.[15] During the ensuing several years, about $30 million of surplus was transferred by way of cash dividends from Amoskeag Manufacturing Company to its parent, Amoskeag Corporation, which enabled the latter to invest in nontextile businesses rather than modernize Amoskeag.

Synthetic yarns began to become important after 1920. Generally speaking, the South leapt at the opportunity to develop new markets, whereas the North was less interested. Amoskeag established a rayon division in 1926, which made money for seven years and then was liquidated rather than go through a necessary expansion. Woven fabrics (made on looms) had been predominant prior to 1920: Now knitted goods blossomed due to new machinery (rotary knitters) and styles. Again, the South was innovative with the addition of knitting whereas the North was slow to react.

Thus by the end of the 1920s, northern textile manufacturing was exhibiting signs of creeping senility, nepotism, and lethargic management. When the 1929 stock market crash upset the economy, bankruptcy claimed many more northern mills than southern mills, which had increased their competitive advantage in terms of geographic location, newer single-story mill buildings, greater adaptation to change, and improved machinery. Amoskeag tried unsuccessfully in 1932 and 1933 to restructure its debt. Orders continued to decrease as the depression spread. Buildings closed. Employment fell drastically. Unemployment and the welfare roles rose. Judge wrote in his diary in April 1932, "Amoskeag seems to be shutting down." Hope waned during 1934 and 1935. The depression showed no signs of ending. In September 1935, former Mayor Arthur Moreau (owner of J. J. Moreau and Son hardware store) assembled a citizens' committee of thirty-four people together with the New Hampshire Textile Commission (two members of the Executive Council, Roman Catholic Bishop Peterson, general manager Ned Jewell of the *Union-Leader*, and Avery Schiller, president of the Public Service Company of New Hampshire). The committee discussed the Amoskeag situation but took no action. The company negotiated with the bondholders for concessions on the terms of the bonds, without success. The company also dealt with the city with respect to tax relief, also without success. Finally, in desperation to protect its waning working capital, the company filed bankruptcy to gain time to work out an acceptable solution, with the reasonable hope of reopening the mills. The Manchester newspaper made the bankruptcy announcement on Christmas Eve 1935. Amoskeag's doors were closed. No one thought that could ever happen. Would they remain closed forever?[16]

## THE STRAW FAMILY

*Ezekiel A. Straw* was born in 1819 in Salisbury, Massachusetts, and went to the schools of Lowell before attending Phillips Exeter Academy. In July 1838 at the age of nineteen, he was hired by the Amoskeag Manufacturing Company as a civil engineer; he worked on the layout of the Amoskeag lands and construction of mill buildings, canals, waterpower development, and housing and tenements for the employees. In 1841, Straw was sent by the company to England to obtain information on the construction and operation of a print works that was about to be built. The city of Manchester was chartered in 1846. In 1851, Straw was made agent for the Land & Water Power Department; in 1856, he was made general agent for the mills, a position he held until he had to resign for reasons of health. From 1856 to 1864 Straw was a part owner of the Namaske Mills in Manchester and then became sole owner. In 1851 the Manchester Gas Light Company was formed to provide manufactured gas for lighting. The Amoskeag Mills were the largest customer: Light was provided to extend the hours of work of the operatives in winter. Ezekiel Straw was one of the original directors and was president from 1856 to 1876. Straw was also one of the founders of New Hampshire Fire Insurance Company when it was chartered by the legislature in 1869 as the first stock-owned insurance company. Other fire insurance companies were mutual companies. Straw received the honorary degree of master of arts in 1860 from Dartmouth and was ex officio a trustee during his term as governor. He lived in the agent's house, a large brick structure on Temple Court, behind the Masonic Temple on Elm Street, which is still standing and used as an apartment house. Ezekiel Straw died in October 1882.

*Herman F. Straw*, son of Ezekiel, was born in 1849 and attended Manchester schools before enrolling in St. Paul's School, from which he graduated in 1868. He attended Harvard University. In 1885, he was appointed general agent of the Amoskeag Manufacturing Company, a position he held until 1929. The Straws lived in the brick-and-timber house on Chestnut Street, now occupied by the Goodwin Funeral Home. Judge worked for "HF" on the city tax bill against Amoskeag and also on compelling the city to assume responsibility for the care and maintenance of the streets formerly belonging to Amoskeag between Elm Street and Canal Street. He also represented Straw in connection with the taxability of gains realized on distributions from the Amoskeag Manufacturing Company.

In 1929, *William Parker Straw* succeeded his father, HF, as general agent until the bankruptcy of Amoskeag in 1936. Parker, as he was known, also attended St. Paul's School in the form of 1895 and Harvard University. During the governorship of John McLane in 1904–1905, Parker Straw served on the military staff of the governor. He was appointed as one of the liquidating agents of Amoskeag in the bankruptcy proceedings in 1936 and was the first president of Amoskeag Industries, which purchased all of the assets of the bankrupt Amoskeag Manufacturing Company. Parker was involved with the Amoskeag banks for many years. Parker married Mary Perkins from Rye, New Hampshire, and built a beautiful home with a tennis court at 282 River Road. Judge was a frequent tennis partner. The house is now the Cullity, Kelley and MacDowell law office. About 1930, Mrs. Straw developed a mental illness characterized by intense paranoia aimed at Parker Straw to the point of becoming violent. I remember my father saying that one of the saddest days in his life was the day he took

Mary Straw to the New Hampshire State Hospital in Concord, where she remained for the rest of her life in attractive private quarters that Parker had built for her. In the 1950s, when I was on the board of trustees of the hospital, I had pleasant visits with Mrs. Straw on several occasions.

Parker and Mary had two children: Mary, who married "Rocky" Flanders, a doctor in town who specialized in corporate medicine, and *Ezekiel Straw*. Judge has a number of entries in his diaries about the year 1913 concerning tutoring "Zeke," as he was known, to prepare him for St. Paul's School in the form of 1920. After his education, he returned to Manchester and ran a brokerage business, E. A. Straw & Company. He married Virginia Slayton in about 1928, one of Manchester's more colorful weddings, with a large tent for the reception on the lawn in front of the large Victorian Slayton house on Elm Street, just above North Street. This made quite an unforgettable impression on me. The Straws purchased the house on River Road that the Carl Fullers had built and installed a squash court. The house was torn down in the 1980s to make way for an apartment complex.

Zeke and Ginny Straw had five children, including *Ezekiel A. Straw Jr.*. who went to St. Paul's School in the form of 1943 before graduating from Dartmouth after the war. Prior to his father's death, Ezekiel, Jr. was known as Pete; then he took the family nickname of Zeke. Zeke was a popular and active community leader and worked his way up to CEO of the Manchester Savings Bank (see Chapter Fifteen). He died prematurely from lung cancer in 1972.

# Notes

1. Gary Sampson, *The Merrimack Valley, New Hampshire* (Norfolk, Va.: The Donning Company, 1989).

2. Including 40 Stark Street, which together with its several additions for over fifty years was the McLane law firm office.

3. Charles E. Fisher, "Locomotive Building at Manchester, New Hampshire," scrapbook collections, Manchester Historic Association, Manchester, New Hampshire.

4. George Waldo Brown, *Amoskeag Manufacturing Company*. Printed and bound in the mills of the Amoskeag Manufacturing Company, Manchester, New Hampshire, 1915.

5. Railway and Locomotive Historical Society, Baker Library, Harvard Business School, Boston, 1935, p. 5.

6. There are a number of prints in existence showing the firemen's muster on Merrimack Common on September 15, 1859, which involved volunteer hand pumpers from all over New England. There were many musters on the

Merrimack Common, which was a popular place because it was in midtown, so everyone could see the event, and it had a large pond from which the pumpers could pump. The official judges occupied a third-floor room of the Manchester House, a hotel on Elm Street, where they could observe with binoculars the height of the pumped stream against markers affixed to the flagpole.

7. Nehemiah S. Bean was the father of Norwin S. Bean, for many years treasurer and chief executive officer of the Manchester Savings Bank, an important client of the McLane law firm. (See Chapter Eleven, Manchester Savings Bank.)

8. L. Ashton Thorpe, *Manchester of Yesterday* (Manchester: Granite State Press, 1939).

9. The greatly expanded export of cotton brought in huge sums of money to the coffers of the Khedive of Egypt. He spent the money in building universities and all manner of public works, inspiring a national fervor and pride in the country's past. A new opera house was built in Cairo to rival that of Paris, and an opera that would extol the virtues of Egypt's past was commissioned to be composed by none other than Italy's virtuoso Giuseppe Verdi. The result was the magnificent *Aida*. Singers, orchestra, costumes, stage sets, choruses, dancers, and even elephants were imported from many countries to create one of the most magnificent opera productions of all time and a favorite the world over, even today—a serendipity of the American Civil War.

10. The agent's house for Ezekiel Straw was the large three- or four-story mansion on Temple Court, behind the Masonic Temple on Elm Street. Herman F. Straw lived in what is now the Goodwin Funeral Home on Chestnut Street across from what used to be the Straw School. William P. Straw built the handsome house on River Road in the 1920s now occupied by the law firm of Cullity, Kelley and McDowell.

11. Arthur M. Kenison, "An Economic and Financial Analysis of the Factors Leading to the Closing of the Amoskeag Manufacturing Corporation." Unpublished paper, St. Anselm College, Manchester, New Hampshire, 1980s, p. 8.

12. Moving goods from floor to floor on clumsy, old, slow freight elevators was labor intensive and inefficient.

13. Kenison, p. 41.

14. Kenison, p. 31.

15. Kenison, p. 17.

16. For subsequent events, see Chapter Ten, Amoskeag Industries, Inc.

# NINE

# Manchester Locomotive Works, the Aretas Blood Family— Carpenters, Frenches, Fullers, and Mannings

## MANCHESTER LOCOMOTIVE WORKS

The Manchester Locomotive Works was started as a partnership in 1853 by O. W. Bailey[1] (who had been head of the machine shops of the Amoskeag), along with Aretas Blood and J. M. Stone under the name Bailey, Blood & Company. The company was known as the Vulcan Works. It was incorporated in June 1854 as the Manchester Locomotive Works, with Mr. Bailey as agent and Mr. Blood as a foreman. In 1857, Mr. Blood succeeded Mr. Bailey as agent and in 1864 was named superintendent; he continued as CEO until his death in 1897. The five-acre plant was built in 1854 at the corner of Canal, Dow, and Dean Streets. For several years prior to 1992 it was the Pandora store. Their first locomotive, the *Pioneer*, with sixty-inch drivers (drive wheels; a sixty-inch diameter was standard) and weighing twenty-four tons, was completed in 1854 but was without a purchaser. In 1855, it was renamed the *Cossack* and sold to what is now the Chicago, Burlington and Quincy railroad.

The capacity of the plant was three locomotives a month. By 1857, forty-six engines had been built; then the depression caused discontinuance. The plant was leased to Mr. Blood, who ran it as a general machine shop in his own name. In October 1864, during the Civil War, limited production of locomotives was started again by the corporation, primarily for the northern military. After the Civil War, locomotive production was resumed in earnest. Between 1865 and 1897, 1,793 locomotives were produced, starting at the rate of 20 engines a year and increasing to 120 after the plant was expanded to employ about 700 people. Aretas Blood was so intimately involved with the company that it was frequently called the Blood Locomotive Works. After Aretas Blood's death in 1897, the business was sold in 1901 to the American Locomotive Company, which continued to build locomotives and perform repair work for the Boston & Maine Railroad.

In 1876, the fire engine business of Amoskeag, known as Amoskeag Engine, was purchased by Manchester Locomotive Works. In that year, the New York Fire Department purchased its first "self-propeller," which had a differential gear on its rear axle, similar to the present gear on automobiles. When the locomotive business was sold in 1901, Manchester Locomotive Works contracted with American Locomotive Company to manufacture fire engines at the Manchester plant. In 1908 the business was transferred to Providence, Rhode Island.[2] Thus ended a little-known but important aspect of the industrial history of Manchester.

Aretas Blood acquired substantial wealth and was a benefactor to Manchester, as were his descendants.

## ARETAS BLOOD (1816–1897)

Aretas Blood was born in 1816 in Weathersfield, Vermont. A few years later he moved to Windsor, where he had his early schooling.[3] At the age of seventeen, he was apprenticed to a blacksmith with whom he worked for about three years. Then he took up the study of mechanics. At age twenty-four, in 1840, he went to Evansville, Indiana, for a year but returned to New England, first at North Chelmsford, then Lowell for seven years in the Lowell Machine Shop. Then he moved to Lawrence, where he was in charge of building a large new machine shop. In 1853, at age thirty-seven, he moved to Manchester, where he remained for the last forty-four years of his life.

Mr. Blood had many business interests in addition to the Manchester Locomotive Works:

a.  Second National Bank—director and president in 1897 at the time of his death
b.  Ames Manufacturing Company in Chicopee, Massachusetts, manufacturer of bicycles, et cetera—president and director
c.  Globe Nail Company, Boston—president
d.  Manchester Print Works, print cloth—president
e.  Nashua Iron & Steel Company—treasurer
f.  Amoskeag Paper Mills—president[4]
g.  Manchester Hardware Company—treasurer
h.  Manchester Sash and Blind Company
i.  Columbia Cotton Mills and Columbia Water Power Company, Columbia, South Carolina—an investment he made after reaching the age of seventy

Mr. Blood died intestate in 1897, leaving his two daughters, Elnora, who married Frank P. Carpenter, and Emma, who married Dr. L. Melville

French. The only probate record is a petition for administration and bond for $1 million indicating a substantial estate in 1897, before there was any estate and income tax at the federal level.

The Bloods attended and were substantial supporters of the Franklin Street Congregational Church, on Market Street, as was their granddaughter, Mary Carpenter Manning. She gave the funds for the parish house, which was purchased and remodeled in the 1980s by the Wiggin & Nourie law firm, which also acquired the adjacent site of the old church for a parking lot. Mrs. Manning gave her house, "Brookside," on North Elm Street, for the new Brookside church when the parish decided that a downtown location was no longer viable. Mary Manning built a new house on the top of Union Street hill. Later her daughter, Priscilla Sullivan, built a house just to the north, which is adjacent to the Zimmerman house (now owned by the Currier Gallery of Art), a Frank Lloyd Wright house. The Bloods also took a great interest in the Women's Aid and Relief Society, later the Women's Aid Home, providing the funds to enable it to purchase land on Pearl Street and build a home there. Harriet Mansfield, a partner in the McLane law firm, spent the last years of her life there. Many of the Bloods' children, grandchildren, and great-grandchildren have been outstanding benefactors to the city of Manchester.

## CARPENTERS, FRENCHES, FULLERS, AND MANNINGS

These four closely connected families related to Aretas Blood were prominent citizens of Manchester during the last quarter of the nineteenth century and the first half of the twentieth century. They invested in the manufacturing life of Manchester and its financial institutions and were among the city's chief benefactors. They invested wisely in the nation's economy and accumulated substantial wealth. From time to time, Judge McLane counseled most of them.

### The Carpenters

Frank P. Carpenter (1845–1938) was born in Manchester but moved to Concord, where he received his education. He started his career in Manchester. Mr. Carpenter's life is covered in Chapter Seventeen.

Mr. Carpenter had two children, the elder being Aretas Blood Carpenter, born in 1875, who lived in Manchester. He was treasurer of Amoskeag Paper Company and president and director of Mechanics Savings Bank and Amoskeag National Bank. He was a director of Amoskeag Industries, Inc. During all the years I attended meetings as secretary, at which "Reet" Carpenter was a regular attender, I do not recall ever hearing him utter a word, which confirmed his reputation of being a taciturn fellow. Aretas Carpenter married Alice Burnham of Manchester, daughter of a prominent Manchester attorney and U.S. senator from New Hampshire from 1910 to 1913. They had two daughters. Elnora married Harry Jackson, for many years deputy secretary of State. The other daughter, Elizabeth, married William Floyd, who ran a hardware store. There is no probate record of the estate of Aretas Carpenter, leading to the conclusion that his estate was held in inter vivos trusts, trusts created during one's lifetime that are not subject to probate court jurisdiction and are not on public record.

## The Mannings

Mr. Carpenter's other child was Mary Elizabeth Carpenter, born in 1882, who married Charles Bartlett Manning. Tragedy struck Mary Manning in 1924 with the accidental deaths of her husband and his two brothers while hiking in a snowstorm along the train tracks in the White Mountains near Glencliff, New Hampshire. They were hit by a special train run for Henry Ford. The hikers had stopped at the train station and received assurance that no trains were scheduled to use the tracks while they would be hiking. Judge refers to this tragedy in his diary for February 11, 1924. A few years later, Mary Manning's only son, Frank Carpenter Manning, who was then between ten and twelve, developed an infection in his ear that resulted in his premature death.[5] Mary Manning's daughter, Priscilla, who died in 1994, married John Sullivan of Manchester, a product of Manchester Central, Dartmouth class of '21, and Harvard Law School. He was a prominent citizen, Democrat, and lawyer, practicing in both Manchester and Washington, who served as Secretary of the Navy under Franklin D. Roosevelt. Although their principal residence was in Washington, they built a home next to Mrs. Manning's on Union Street, both of which are still maintained. The Mannings also had a beautiful summer home in Rye, New Hampshire. Mary Manning was a gracious and generous person supporting many institutions in the community. Her benefactions to Manchester were recognized in 1956 when she was named Citizen of the Year at the annual Chamber of Commerce dinner. She was particularly active with the Currier Gallery of Art and the Manchester Historical Society. She provided flowers from her greenhouse for functions at churches, museums, and other institutions.

## The Frenches

In 1887 Aretas Blood's other daughter, Emma Blood (1853–1932), married Dr. L. Melville French (1849–1914). They lived in a gracious French-style house on a spacious tract running from River Road and Clarke Street westerly to the railroad tracks and the river bordering on Ray Brook on the south. Mrs. French was an energetic lady and took an active interest in the District Nursing (forerunner of the Visiting Nurses Association); NHTB Association; the Institute of Arts and Sciences, for which she gave the building, opened in 1916; the YWCA; the Children's Home; the children's wing of the Elliot Hospital; the American Red Cross;[6] and the Shakespeare Club. The Kiwanis Club bestowed upon her a Distinguished Service Medal for her contributions to the people of the city of Manchester.

Dr. French was born in Ashby, Massachusetts. He received his undergraduate education at New York University and his medical training at Dartmouth. He practiced in Manchester for some thirty years as a member of the Elliot Hospital staff. Mrs. French died in 1932, leaving a will drawn by Judge McLane and a gross estate of just over $2 million, with stocks totaling $1.8 million, of which the largest holdings were National Biscuit Company ($426,000), Hanover Fire Insurance Company ($153,000), Chicago Junction Railroad ($152,000), and Consolidated Gas Company of NY ($111,000).[7]

## The Fullers

The Frenches' only child, Margaret, maintained a lifelong interest in two organizations supported by her parents and grandparents, namely, the Women's Aid Home, of which she was president for twenty years, and the Manchester Institute of Arts and Sciences. In 1910 Margaret married Carl Fuller, a Bowdoin graduate, who was a dye chemist for the Amoskeag Manufacturing Company. Carl took a great interest in the Elliot Hospital, serving on its board for twenty years, of which ten were as president. They had two children, Mary Spencer (born 1911), married Malcolm Russell and lived in Rye, New Hampshire, until her death in 1995. She maintained the family interest in the Manchester Institute. Henry Melville Fuller (born 1914) lives in Manchester and Nelson, New Hampshire, having retired from a career as a New York City broker. He maintains contact with Manchester through the Currier Gallery of Art, of which he is a trustee and to which he has been a generous contributor.

# Notes

1. J. D. Van Slyke, *Manchester Locomotive Works*. (Boston, Mass.: Representatives of New England Manufacturers, 1879), Vol. II, p. 337. Van Slyke spells Bailey, "Bayley."

2. Charles E. Fisher, "Locomotive Building at Manchester, New Hampshire," scrapbook collections, Manchester Historic Association, Manchester, New Hampshire.

3. Col. James A. Ellis, editor; "Aretas Blood," *Memorial Encyclopedia of New Hampshire*. (New York, N.Y.: American Historical Society, 1919).

4. In 1872, Frank P. Carpenter married Elnora "Nora" Blood, one of Aretas Blood's two daughters, and had two children, Aretas Blood Carpenter and Mary Carpenter, later Manning. Frank P. Carpenter acquired substantial ownership of Amoskeag Paper Company; subsequently his son, Aretas B. Carpenter, "Reet," became treasurer.

5. I remember playing football with Frank and a raft of other boys from the North End on a large field along Clarke Street where the Brookside Church parking lot is now located. I vaguely remember that we had a high school or college student who functioned as coach, probably paid for by Mrs. Manning.

6. The American Red Cross for years was a tenant in the former Frank P. Carpenter house, which was owned by his family. In 1995, the American Red Cross purchased the property and renovated it.

7. The similarity in stock portfolios between Mr. Carpenter and his sister-in-law, Emma French, suggests that either Mr. Carpenter was advising her or they utilized the same investment adviser, most likely the Amoskeag Trust Company.

# TEN

# Amoskeag Industries, Inc.

Amoskeag Industries, Inc. (AII), was incorporated in New Hampshire, on September 2, 1936, by Judge McLane for the purpose of acquiring all of the assets of the Amoskeag Manufacturing Company (AMC) from the referee in bankruptcy. AMC filed for bankruptcy on December 24, 1935.

On January 20, 1936, the court ordered AMC to prepare a plan of reorganization. In late February, with the approval of the bondholders, the plan was filed. It provided for the scaling down of debt obligations and the resumption of operations. F. C. Dumaine, CEO of AMC, wrote a letter dated March 9 indicating that the plan had a reasonable chance of success. However, disaster struck a week later when torrential rains combined with a snowmelt in the entire Merrimack watershed brought floodwaters to Manchester. "Worse than the 1927 flood," wrote Judge in his diary on the eighteenth. The next day, he wrote: "Water sixteen feet over the dam, McGregorville Bridge out" (Bridge Street bridge). On the twentieth, he wrote: "High water was at 17.1' over the dam, Elisabeth and I at Red Cross Relief tent by Amoskeag dam."[1] The bottom floors of the mills along the river that were full of machinery were covered by the floodwaters. The second floors were about half filled with water, damaging machinery to the tune of hundreds of thousands of dollars. On April 27, the bankruptcy court referred AMC's reorganization plan to Arthur Black, special master, for a report on the plan's fairness. On June 10, a public meeting was held at the same time that Mr. Dumaine withdrew the plan as no longer feasible because of the flood damage and the lack of working capital. On July 8, Judge recorded, "The Master reports for liquidation." The master stated to the court that there was 25 percent industry overcapacity even after twelve years of industry losses and many terminations in New England and that it would be impossible for the reorganization plan to work. The bankruptcy court accepted the report of the special master and ordered immediate liquidation. A complete inventory of all assets had been in process for some time. On August 8, auctioneers and liquidating trustees were appointed to sell everything. By mid-August, brochures were available describing in detail all that was to be sold. A date was set and the auction was advertised

*1936 Spring Flood,* Bridge Street bridge carried away. Note first-floor windows, barely visible. Credit: Manchester (N.H.) Historic Association Photo Archives.

all over the world. Manchester's only sizable hotel, the Carpenter, was full of prospective purchasers from Europe, South America, Asia, and Africa, speaking many foreign languages, coming to inspect the machinery. It soon became apparent that these buyers had no intention of operating in New Hampshire and planned to remove the machinery. What would Manchester do with 6 million square feet of empty mill space? That became a tormenting question to the city leaders.

In early August, former Mayor Arthur Moreau initiated conversations with a group of citizens to discuss the situation. The group included the CEOs of the Public Service Company, several banks, and the New Hampshire Insurance Company, philanthropist Frank P. Carpenter, and Judge McLane, Arthur Moreau's personal attorney, who was asked to be the attorney for the new corporation. In a sense, this was a continuation of Arthur Moreau's efforts begun in September 1935 to alert the citizenry to the plight of Amoskeag Manufacturing Company. In an extraordinarily bold move, the group decided in a desperate effort to save Manchester by approaching referee Black and offering to purchase all the AMC assets. A committee met referee Black in Boston on August 21 and indicated that they wished to purchase the bankrupt property as is, "lock, stock and barrel," stating that the city had about 85,000 people, that 15,000 used to work for Amoskeag—the principal employer in town— and that if the machinery were removed, the city would probably go bankrupt and it would be almost impossible to restore employment. The referee indicated that he was aware of the city's plight—it was not unlike that of other New England communities—but he had to protect the rights of creditors (mostly bondholders). He also stated that the time was late, that many potential buyers had spent substantial sums to come to look at the machinery, and that he was not sure that the property could be sold other than at a public auction. However, he concluded that the minimum price would be the appraisal price of $5 million and that he would need a cash deposit of 10 percent, or $500,000, of the purchase price (forfeitable if the deal fell through) within ten days (September 3) together with firm letters of commitment for the balance of the purchase payable prior to October 15.

The group returned to Manchester and started to do some hard figuring and pencil pushing. First, the group held conversations with the Public Service Company of New Hampshire (PSNH), which would be devastated if the mills were empty and there was no employment in town, because the company would lose many of its customers. The Amoskeag Industries group attempted to convince PSNH to buy the waterpower rights and electrical distribution system for $2.5 million, the banks having indicated they would make real estate loans if the balance of the purchase price did not exceed $2.5 million. But PSC would only agree to purchase all of the system for $2,250,000, which included the Merrimack River dam, the canals, the coal-burning generating plants, the Piscataqua River Kelley's Falls dam, and the distribution system within the mill yard. This was finally agreed to by all on September 3. A consortium of banks, with the Amoskeag National Bank acting as trustee for all, relented and agreed to a mortgage loan of $2.8 million, which included working capital of $550,000 secured by a mortgage on all of the real estate, which included the mills as well as the tenements, personal property, and machinery. Stock totaling $500,000 was subscribed, about 50 percent by PSNH and New Hampshire Fire Insurance Company and the rest by individuals and companies in Manchester. The entire transaction was put together in about a week—an extraordinary show of community strength and support.

The committee returned to Boston on September 3 with a certified check for $500,000 and firm commitments from PSC to purchase the waterpower rights for $2,250,000, the banks to loan $2.8 million, and confirmed subscriptions of stock for $500,000. Judge wrote in his diary, "Boston—long hard day making offer at $5k with 1/2k deposit." Amoskeag Industries, Inc., was incorporated on September 2, with Arthur Moreau as president, Frank P. Carpenter as vice president (the largest individual stock subscriber at $100,000), Harry L. Davis as treasurer, and Judge McLane as clerk. Approximately 5,500 shares of common stock were issued, of which Public Service Company of New Hampshire, New Hampshire Fire Insurance Company, and Frank P. Carpenter subscribed to 1,000 shares each at $100 per share. The remaining shares were subscribed to by a large number of Manchester's business community and individual citizens. Judge McLane subscribed to 110 shares. Many of these shares have been passed down two and three generations. Referee Arthur Black confirmed the sale on September 15, set October 9 as the closing date, and called off the liquidation auction sale. Thankfully, the foreigners in the Carpenter Hotel lobby went home empty-handed.

On September 10, Judge records a long evening continuing into the eleventh with Nate Robinson and Cook. Nate Robinson of New York City was a professional liquidator of mills that had ceased operations. On the fourteenth, Judge had all-day negotiations with the Atherton group, which consisted of Attorney Percy Atherton of Boston and his clients from New York City including a Mr. Gale, who also were liquidators. My understanding is that these two independent groups wanted to buy the textile assets (not the PSNH assets) and liquidate them. The board turned the offers down, preferring to retain control for the protection of the city. Amoskeag Industries wanted to retain as much of the good machinery as possible to attract manufacturers to Manchester to occupy the mills.

Now began the work of drafting documents with the Boston attorneys for the old Amoskeag and the bankruptcy court and planning for the future. On the twenty-sixth, there was a meeting with the appraisers, Freeman Company. On October 17, Judge and Mr. Carpenter had lunch in Boston with Mr. Dumaine, longtime CEO of Amoskeag. The details of the meeting are not stated in Judge's diary.

U.S. Representative Sabbath of Illinois was chairman of a subcommittee of the Select Committee on Investigation of Real Estate Bondholders' Reorganizations. Sabbath held hearings in New England, including one in Manchester on September 30 to determine if there were any shenanigans going on by the bondholders who would file for bankruptcy and wind up back in control. Judge testified and assured the committee that the new owners had no relationship with the old crowd.

The first two weeks of October were devoted to preparation of closing papers with the attorneys for old Amoskeag and Public Service Company, including title searches, deeds and mortgages, and bills of sale. All papers were passed at the closing on October 13. The McLane law firm participated in the preparation of all of the initial purchase and sale agreements and documents required therein, corporate minutes, and so forth. The real estate deeds were particularly difficult because the property was located on private land, not on public streets (the city of Manchester refused to accept the streets in the mill yard). Thus rights-of-way and easements had to be defined and described in the deeds, both those that were of benefit to and those that were a restriction on the described land. Fortunately, the Amoskeag Manufacturing Company had maintained excellent engineering surveys and maps of its properties, which had been acquired by Amoskeag Industries, Inc., and sold to Amoskeag Machine Company, formed by several former engineers of the old company.

The purchase by AII of all the assets of AMC from the bankruptcy court received a lot of publicity in the metropolitan and trade papers, both in the United States and abroad. Thus there was considerable interest in the AII advertisements offering mills and machinery for sale or lease, and inquiries started arriving soon for substantial transactions.

The principal concerns that moved into the mill yard the first year were: Pacific Mills, Johnson & Johnson's Chicopee Mills, Amoskeag Worsted Mills, Arms Textile Mills, and Waumbec Mills.

In November 1936 talks were initiated with Pacific Mills for the purchase of 1722 Draper "X" looms and the lease of a substantial mill. After seven days of negotiations, the transaction was consummated on November 27. Judge wrote, "Great lift over Pacific Mills deal," the first major disposition of property. A little over a year later, in April 1938, Pacific Mills advised AII that because of soft market conditions, Pacific had an overcapacity with its two owned mills (in Massachusetts) and the one leased mill (in Manchester) and would have to let the leased mill go. AII made inquiries in the trade and concluded that the condition was as stated and was not a bargaining ploy. Unfortunately, in spite of several very favorable offers by AII, Pacific advised that it was reluctantly leaving. Even before the Pacific sale was closed, Judge along with Arthur Moreau, Parker Straw, and Arthur Roberts went to Boston to talk with Pepperell Manufacturing Company about additional space. (They did not take the offer.)

Johnson & Johnson (J&J), headquartered in New Jersey, a large manufacturer and marketer of medical products including gauze, bandages, and adhesive tape, negotiated at the end of November 1936 for the lease of the #4 Mill, Central Division, together with the purchase of the machinery. At the directors' meeting on December 4, Mr. Straw reported that J&J, through a new subsidiary to be formed, Chicopee Mills, was now definitely interested in buying the much larger and most recently built Coolidge Mill (300,000 square feet) on the west side of the Notre Dame Bridge. On January 7, 1937, the contract for the sale of the mill and machinery was signed; papers passed a week later. Substantial employment started soon thereafter for the manufacture of surgical gauze, to the relief of everyone in the city. Once the deal was struck, Chicopee hired Judge to be its local counsel and to form Chicopee Mills, a New Hampshire corporation and subsidiary of J&J. Chicopee was so happy with the Manchester operation that in May 1937 it expressed interest in acquiring the #11 Mill, adjacent to its plant, but that transaction came to naught. In 1940, Chicopee expressed an interest in some of the new blends of rayon and wool and the desire to enter that market, possibly by the purchase of Amoskeag Fabrics and Raylaine Worsteds, but nothing materialized. Chicopee Mills operated the plant for about forty years.

In December 1936, Mr. Straw reported interest on the part of one Mr. Hamburger for the Worsted Division: "Mr. Hamburger's principal is L. Bachman & Company, who owns the Uxbridge Worsted Company and is a large factor in the Worsted trade."[2] In January 1937, AII gave Hamburger an option to purchase for $600,000 the buildings south of Granite Street housing the Worsted Division. The offer was extended several times to Mr. Hamburger, but he was apparently having problems putting a deal together. In early April the transaction fell through.

In August 1937, a new proposal was considered. AII and L. Bachman would each subscribe to $100,000 of stock with a $750,000 mortgage to buy the Worsted Division with 200 looms, employing 800 to 1,000 employees on a three-shift basis, with the possibility of expanding to 500 to 600 looms. This proposal moved along slowly. In late January 1938 and again in early February, Judge, Parker Straw, and Arthur Roberts went to New York City to negotiate with Hamburger, L. Bachman, and the CIT Corporation on the formation of a worsted mill, Amoskeag Worsted Mills, Inc., to be owned jointly with Amoskeag Industries, Inc. In April 1938, talks were instituted with the RFC for a loan. In July the proposed terms were again changed to a Reconstruction Finance Corporation (RFC)[3] loan of $600,000, with Bachman and AII each subscribing to $75,000 of stock. In August 1938 a final agreement was reached to drop the RFC, substitute local banks for a $650,000 loan, and increase the stock purchases by AII and Bachman back to $100,000 each.

Philip Scheerr & Sons of Philadelphia, a manufacturer of interlining fabric—a stiffener, frequently made of mohair (Angora goat), inserted between layers of garment cloth, especially coat lapels—in December 1936 expressed interest in the #2 Mill, Southern Division. The company changed its mind to the #9 Mill, Central Division. In June 1937, consideration was being given to moving all of its Philadelphia operation to Manchester. The company took an option on the #9 Mill and River Dye House. The transaction was closed in November 1937 with the sale to ARMS Textile Manufacturing Company. ARMS stood for the initials of the four Scheerr sons who owned the mill—Alvin, Robert, Maurice, and Stanley. In January 1938, AII loaned money to build a new boiler plant for the mill. During the war years the company imported, probably from central Asia (Iran, Pakistan, et cetera), mohair, some of which was contaminated with the deadly anthrax bacillus, which caused the death of several workers. As a result the building was demolished in the 1950s and the bricks were buried in a distant location. The site is now known as ARMS or Riverfront Park.

Cantor-Greenspan, a factor in New York City, bought greige (pronounced "gray") goods, shipped them to commission dyers, and then sold the cloth to manufacturers of clothing and drapes. One of the family, Saul Greenspan, came to Manchester in 1936 to run the U.S. Silk Mill, which the Greenspan brothers had acquired for debt in about 1931. In June 1937, Cantor-Greenspan leased the second floor of the #4 Mill for three years with two further renewal periods plus an option to purchase the entire building. Cantor-Greenspan's manufacturing subsidiary, Waumbec Mills, occupied the space and manufactured high-grade rayon fabrics. In 1939, Waumbec needed more space and leased an additional 15,000 square feet. In August 1945, Waumbec wanted to exercise its option to purchase the 300,000-square-foot building, so AII helped Hampshire Worsted Mills (Harry Wheeler) to find new space. They had been a tenant in the Waumbec building. Waumbec installed new machinery and manufactured parachute fabrics under war contracts for Cantor-Greenspan. Saul Greenspan, who had acquired sole ownership, sold the mill to Berkshire-Hathaway (Warren Buffet) in 1974 but continued to reside in Manchester.

The fall of 1936 and the spring of 1937 were very busy times for the McLane law firm. The board of directors of Amoskeag Industries was very active, meeting eight times in September and two to six times a month for the rest of the year. Parker Straw, who had been agent for old Amoskeag and who was very familiar with all aspects of the old company, was appointed agent for Amoskeag Industries. Many of the tenement properties were sold, frequently to tenants. AII often took back second mortgages. A number of tenements conveniently located in the downtown core city area were converted from residential to office and other commercial uses. As an example, the McLane law firm purchased, from the trustee in bankruptcy in the spring of 1936, 40 Stark Street (a four-apartment foreman's row housing building), which it completely gutted and restored with contemporary construction standards to a law office. It occupied the site (along with several additions) for fifty-six years before moving into the Market Square Tower (NYNEX building) in 1992.

The textile machinery was divided into categories. The very usable and salable remained in Manchester. (My recollection is that there was a restriction placed in the bills of sale of this machinery that it could not be sold or removed from Manchester within a stipulated time frame without the approval of Amoskeag Industries, Inc.) Marginal machinery, which might be obsolescent or cannibalized, was sold where possible. Scrap (anything broken or damaged by the flood) was sold. Sales were pushed aggressively.

Strong efforts were also made to advertise the space and machinery in trade journals in the United States and abroad. Very favorable terms were offered on leases and options to purchase. Representatives were engaged in England to promote the sale or lease of mills and machinery. At the end of 1936, to attract more interest in the space available in the mill yard, Amoskeag Industries invited a group of manufacturers and industrial real estate people to view the properties and attend a dinner party at which speakers described the property, the prices, and financing that was available.

When making their initial purchase agreement, a number of the new arrivals in Manchester had their own legal counsel from either outside the state or outside Manchester. After completing the transaction, some of them asked Judge McLane to be their New Hampshire counsel. The McLane law firm really hummed at this time with the work for Amoskeag Industries and the other manufacturers who wanted to be incorporated. I remember Judge reporting that the secretary of state told him, perhaps apocryphally, that the McLane office was filing more corporations than all the rest of the lawyers in the state combined. Some of those new clients were the Chicopee Mills, Gilbert Verney, Mack Kahn, and Ben Mates.

By February 1937, after six months of operations, 900,000 square feet of floor space, $750,000 of machinery, and $500,000 of scrap iron had been sold, enabling some debt to be repaid. This was a remarkable result, far exceeding expectations. In the spring, AII transferred its water system to the city, including the water mains from Lake Massabesic to the reservoir on Oak, Russell, and Harrison Streets and thence to the mill yard. The company negotiated with General Foods Corporation to store one hundred railcars of raw chocolate.

The State Board of Health was concerned that the intake of raw water from the river for humidification purposes might be injurious to the health of the employees because of the amount of raw sewerage dumped in the river upstream. Testing was done under the supervision of engineers from the Massachusetts Institute of Technology; the report concluded that the water was not hazardous to employees. Forty new tenements on Canal Street built only a few years prior to the bankruptcy were sold to Arthur Moreau's Acme Warehouse Company, Inc. There were a number of inquiries from persons acting on behalf of undisclosed principals, which produced much competition. One of these was Clark Thread, a subsidiary of J. P. Coates of England; another was Goodyear Tire & Rubber Company. Onyx Knitting Company of Philadelphia bought machinery and leased for three years 70,000 square feet of space in the #10 Mill.

In August 1937 the state of New Hampshire, having appropriated $400,000 for a new armory—provided the state could acquire the site without cost—proposed that AII convey some 23,500 square feet on Canal

Street between Salmon and West Pennacook Streets "to be used exclusively as a site for a State Armory, title to revert to Amoskeag Industries, Inc., its successors and assigns, if it ceases to be used as an Armory." Upon completion of the new armory, the old armory (now part of the Center of New Hampshire) reverted back to AII by virtue of the reverter rights in the original deed. One Mr. Rauch requested that the rent on his property be postponed to January 1, 1938, because there was a serious slump in the knitting goods business due to changes in styles in bathing suits and it would not be possible to commence manufacturing before January 1!

Harrison Abrasives bought the foundry on the west side in August 1937 to be used for a polishing shop process (for ammunition shell casings). This property was subsequently acquired by Hitchiner Manufacturing Company, Inc., and used for the investment casting process. Later, the company moved to Milford.

Now Amoskeag Industries was embarrassed with a plethora of riches. It had sold so much real estate and machinery, substantially above its cost, that it was faced with a "humongous" tax on its net profit of $800,000 for its first year of operation, ending August 31, 1937, unless it could devise a way to reduce its profit. Cash was shy because of the many deferred payments on sales, and the company was already borrowed to the hilt. A scheme was developed by James A. Shanahan, the company's independent auditor, to declare a 125 percent dividend ($650,000, a deductible expense)—payable $25 in cash, and four promissory notes of $25 each, bearing interest, payable one note in each of the four consecutive following years, 1938–1941. Since this was an unusual arrangement, Judge, Jim Shanahan, and Parker Straw went to Washington and were successful in clearing the plan with the IRS. The dividend was declared by the directors on August 27, just before the end of the fiscal year.

So at the end of the first year of operation (August 31, 1937), the stockholders had received promissory notes with interest for their original investment plus a 25 percent cash payment—a remarkable turnaround in one year.

In the fall of 1937, Judge and Elisabeth hosted a dinner at Three Acres, their playhouse on North Union Street, for the board of directors of Amoskeag Industries to celebrate its first year of existence, which was successful beyond the wildest dreams of the board.

During the fall of 1937, Silver Bros. (Morris and Henry) acquired several buildings in the Southern Division and a couple more in January 1938 for its wholesale grocery and expanding beverage business. Federal Shoe moved into town, taking two floors of the #3 Southern Division, and employed about four hundred people. There was an inquiry from a doll manufacturer who wanted space to make Shirley Temple dolls and would employ five hundred to eight hundred people, but it did not materialize. A petition to the city was authorized to lay out streets in the mill yard. Since the Amoskeag Reservoir on Oak Street had been abandoned, it was offered for sale for housing development.

At the end of the second year of operation in September 1938, there were fifty-four industries in the mill yard providing employment to 3,000 employees and greatly reducing the welfare cost of the city. The company had a slight loss of $25,000 as the volume of sales of property decreased.

As the political situation in Europe continued to deteriorate, purchases of textile war goods, such as uniforms and clothing, accelerated. In 1938 Amoskeag Industries started four wholly owned subsidiaries to increase employment, realizing that it would be easier to sell a going concern than empty space. Raylaine Worsteds started in 1938 and wove a fifty-four-inch-wide fabric that was 40 percent wool and 60 percent rayon. The company was quite successful, making $100,000 in 1940. In 1941, 51 percent of the stock was sold as well as the mill and machinery. Amoskeag Mohair Spinning Company started with $35,000 capital and employed 125 in the #7 Central Division. It lost money for the year ending in 1939 and was liquidated in 1940 with a loss of about $69,000. Amoskeag Fabrics, started with $100,000 capital and a $150,000 loan, wove a thirty-four-inch-wide fabric that was 20 percent wool and 80 percent rayon, getting off the ground in late 1938. In 1940 Amoskeag sold 51 percent of the stock at a profit to Wellington, Sears and ran very profitably in 1941, when substantial payments were made on the purchase price of the mill and machinery. Langdon Mills was started with $100,000 capital and manufactured a 40 percent wool and 60 percent rayon fabric.

Two things were happening that redounded to the benefit of Manchester. First was the gradual end of the great depression. For seven years there had been many plant closings, foreclosures, and downsizing, resulting in the elimination of excess manufacturing capacity. The real estate market, both residential and commercial, ground to a virtual halt during those years. When the pent-up demand began to loosen and business started to pick up in 1936, Amoskeag Industries was able to furnish space and machinery at very reasonable prices because their acquisition cost in the bankruptcy court was at rock-bottom prices. The second factor was a transformation of organization in the textile industry, which traditionally had been organized on a "horizontal" basis, that is, a "top" mill performed the scouring, carding, and combing functions; then the product was shipped to a spinning mill, which spun the fiber into yarn; then other mills, such as the dye house, the weave mill, and the finishing mill, each performed its separate operation. Usually each mill was independently owned.

The revolution in the textile industry was the shift to a "vertical" organization, where a single corporation owned and controlled the entire manufacture of the product from start to finish. This was introduced by the merchant houses in New York City that were facing stiff competition and wanted to control cost as well as quality. With unified control, they could eliminate multiple profits at each stage of the manufacturing process, substituting a single profit and thereby reducing the cost. They could also control production quality much more easily.

ARMS Textile and Cantor-Greenspan's affiliate, Waumbec Mills, were examples. Another was Mack Kahn, who was engaged in the design and sale nationally of foundation garments from its New York City sales headquarters. Mr. Kahn bought the Amoskeag-Lawrence Mill and machinery in 1942, established a latex plant for the manufacture of rubber elastic thread, essential in foundation garments, and controlled his own operation. He also acquired plants in a number of other New England states. Mack Kahn, who teamed up in partnership with Ben Mates, leased the north half of the large Coolidge Mill on the West Side and established Manchester Knitted Fashions. It had rotary knitting machines that turned out, in addition to other products, thousands of sweaters and knitted watch caps for the Navy.

In the spring of 1939, Amoskeag-Lawrence Yarns, Inc., was formed to acquire the yarn department of the Lawrence Manufacturing Company in Lawrence, a producer of knitting yarns (some of which were sold to Raylaine), because the company had decided to liquidate. Amoskeag Industries sold the Amory Mill and machinery to Amoskeag-Lawrence Yarns, Inc., and subscribed to some of the stock. The latter company bought some of the Lawrence Manufacturing Company machinery and work in process.

In the fiscal year ending in August 1939, the New Hampshire Timber Salvage Administration leased office space to handle the disposition of millions of board feet of timber that was destroyed by the hurricane of September 1938 and that had been stored in ponds all over the state to protect the wood from beetles and other insects until it could be sold. Habitant Soup acquired space in the mill yard. Myrna Shoe (Shaer family) leased the Langdon Mill. Several shoe companies in Lowell and other Massachusetts cities inquired about space because their CIO labor contracts were expiring and they were thinking about moving to nonunion Manchester. At year end, August 31, 1939, the company had a loss of $80,000 but employment had jumped to 4,600, with an annual payroll in the yard of $4.5 million.

In early 1940, inquiries were received from the federal government about administrative space for the possible location of a National Military Cemetery to be located somewhere in New England. Also, representatives of manufacturers from France, Belgium, and Great Britain sought information about possible manufacturing facilities; they were considering moving some of their operations to the United States because of war

losses in Europe. An Atwood Corporation looked at space for the manufacture of pontoons for Navy seaplanes. Several inquiries came from people with no capital who were willing to run a business provided AII agreed
to furnish the mill, machinery, and working capital. AII declined. Scrap
iron prices soared, and Amoskeag Industries scrounged around all of the
mills for obsolete and broken machinery that could be sold. Tenement
properties and vacant land continued to be sold. In 1940, there was considerable request for storage space: The First National stores needed
50,000 square feet, and the U.S. government inquired about 1 million
square feet for cotton. This became something of a political hot potato,
and nothing materialized. By year end, August 31, 1940, there was practically no good vacant space left in the mill yard; the mills were running two
and even three shifts and were lighted up all night—a wonderful sight
after all those years when the mills were dark. Amoskeag Industries
showed a profit for the year ending August 1940 of $100,000, with 6,000
employed in the mill yard, an increase of 1,400 over the year before.

For the following year, August 31, 1941, the profit was $74,000. Of the
original 7.2 million square feet purchased, 4,885,000 had been sold and
570,000 leased, with 1.7 million left on hand. AII's 51 percent interest in
Raylaine Worsted was sold profitably for $102,000 together with the mill
and machinery. In March 1941, Gilbert Verney negotiated to lease the
southerly half of the #11 Mill to establish a rayon plant with two hundred
Draper looms plus the new Whitin spinning frames. He obtained a loan
from AII for $118,000 for five years to finance the purchase of the machin-
ery. Amoskeag Metal Products, Inc., was formed in the spring of 1941 with
a Mr. Marsh for the manufacture of 20mm shell casings, but dealing with
Mr. Marsh was almost impossible because he frequently exceeded his
authority in purchasing and hiring employees. AII's position in Amoskeag
Metal Products, Inc., was taken over by Johnson Automatics in the fall.
There were now 8,400 employees, up from 6,000, in eighty-four companies.

In the fiscal year ending August 31, 1942, AII sold its stock interest in
Manchester Narrow Fabrics for a profit. Verney paid off its debt and repurchased its stock at a profit. Three buildings were sold for wool storage.
Maurice Shaer bought the Myrna Shoe building (Langdon #2), which it had
been leasing for a number of years. A lease was executed to the Atlantic
Parachute Company. Judge McLane was authorized to appeal to the superior
court to force the city to take over maintenance of the streets in the mill yard.

Although the welfare of the city depended on the health of the
Amoskeag Manufacturing Company and its successor, Amoskeag
Industries, Inc., there was a history of continuing hostility between the city
politicians and its largest taxpayer. The local politicians resented the fact
that Amoskeag Manufacturing Company was owned almost entirely by

affluent Boston families who had no interest in Manchester. This feeling was carried over to Amoskeag Industries, Inc., even though they were local people. In October 1941, the stock of Amoskeag-Lawrence Yarns, Inc., was sold to Mack Kahn, who also purchased worsted spinning machinery. In December, the north half of the #11 Mill was leased to Mack Kahn and Ben Mates for the latter's Manchester Knitted Fashions, Inc. Profits increased $60,000 and employment increased to 9,300.

In 1943, the war was nearing its height as far as production was concerned, and Manchester was booming. Many mills were operating three shifts, which meant a good income for the workers and the mills were still lit up all night long. Along with the rapid buildup of production, shortages started to appear. For instance, 43 percent of Raylaine looms were idle for a time because of a temporary shortage of yarn, and construction materials for new construction were hard to get. So Ferretti bought a Stark mill to raise chickens and Max Myer rented another mill for a chicken slaughterhouse—new businesses for the mill yard. Limerick Yarn Mills ran into a labor shortage at its mills in Limerick, Maine, so it came to Manchester to lease with option to buy. For the year, profits for AII were off $100,000.

In the fall of 1943, Atlantic Rayon Corporation was planning to manufacture tire yarns for the government in the #10 Mill, which it wanted to buy. General Motors was looking for land on which to build a ball-bearing plant and looked at the circus grounds on Valley Street, but it came to naught. The circus grounds were also considered for a helicopter field. The U.S. government had taken over the Manchester airport and built a much larger Air Force base known as Grenier Field. A number of Air Force officers were transferred from Presque Isle, Maine, to Manchester. There was a critical shortage of housing for them, which was discussed by the AII directors, but it is not clear what action was taken, if any. There also was a lack of information about the labor supply, so the AII voted $2,500 to the city for a survey of available labor. The year ending August 31, 1943, wound up with a profit of $153,000, up from $100,000.

In the spring of 1944, the New Hampshire Supreme Court affirmed the lower court finding that the city was obligated to take over the millyard streets because a public necessity had clearly been shown. There was very little space left in the mill yard, and practically all other real estate had been disposed of, leading to a consideration of liquidation of the company. The war in both Europe and the Pacific was going better, and the end was nearing. The board considered the uncertainties that would follow the end of the war and concluded that the company should stay in existence to cope with whatever might happen even though the original mission of the corporation to sell off all of the old Amoskeag assets had been achieved.

The old Amoskeag Manufacturing Company had three large boiler plants—Northern, Central, and Southern Divisions—which burned coal or oil and manufactured electricity and steam for heat and processing. When Amoskeag leased or sold mills, there was also executed a contract to furnish steam. Public Service had acquired all of the electrical-generating capacity of the old Amoskeag, so AII had nothing to do with generating electricity. However, the boiler plants were getting old, and various options were considered. One was to form a new steam company to operate the boilers and sell steam. This was never carried out. The easiest solution was to have each company have its own steam plant. Fortunately, the newer boilers were compact and efficient and quite feasible for the job; most businesses followed this option.

During the depression, the Manchester Country Club had fallen on hard times; memberships were off, loans were defaulted, and the bank foreclosed. But as business in the city picked up there was more demand for a good country club. Under the leadership of J. D. Smart, president of New Hampshire Fire Insurance Company and a director of AII, efforts were started to purchase the country club from the banks, with New Hampshire Insurance Fire Company, Public Service Company of New Hampshire, and AII as the largest stockholders, owning about 50 percent. AII subscribed to $15,000 of stock, which it still owns.

In the spring of 1945, the city was considering a new city hall and talked with Amoskeag Industries about waiving restrictions on some of the city parks under consideration, but the discussions were dropped. Textron wanted 36,000 square feet of space with a concrete floor on which to install new high-speed knitting machines. At the end of the war and the fiscal year—August 31, 1945—the profit was just under $100,000, down $50,000 from the preceding year.

In the fall of 1945, U.S. Rubber exercised its option to buy the Manchester Locomotive Works, at the corner of Dow and Canal Streets. After the war ended in August 1945, there was a huge influx of returning servicemen, many of whom, now married, found an acute shortage of housing; there had been little building from 1929 to 1936 during the depression, and during the war years materials had been in short supply if not nonexistent. Because of the critical housing shortage, AII published a list of available building lots and appropriated $50,000 to purchase second mortgages and $5,000 to improve housing.[4] After ten years of operation, Amoskeag Industries' sales of real estate totaled $6,292,000, with a net profit of $1,619,000 and dividends paid of $166 per share. The company owned or leased practically no real estate. For the year, there was a profit of $121,000, and the book value of the stock was $135.50 per share. Employment in the mill yard was approximately 12,000.

The restrictions on the western part of Victory Park were released to permit municipal parking. Land on South Main Street was sold to the Navy for a reserves training space. Because there was a shortage of manufacturing space, AII considered building a small industrial building on Commercial Street. With the abandonment of the Southern Division Boiler Plant, the space was sold to Amoskeag Steel Company for a foundry. AII participated in a survey of the airport as the U.S. government contemplated the abandonment of Grenier Field. Adjusted profit for the year ending August 31, 1947, was $24,000 and book value of the stock was $160 a share.

AII sold its stock interest in Amoskeag Fabrics at a profit. It had owned the stock since 1939. It also sold the Jefferson Mill. In 1949 it loaned $100,000 to Northeast Engineering, which planned to manufacture a bulk milk vending machine but faced substantial problems in getting operating approval because of health codes in various cities. The loan was defaulted and, in 1952, $50,000 was written off. In 1958, the remaining loan and stock were sold for $45,000, a substantial loss. Brookshire Knitting (Pandora) purchased the #3 Mill, Southern Division, with the help of a $125,000 loan from AII. Hitchiner Manufacturing Company, which made investment castings on the West Side, needed more space and moved to Milford in spite of efforts to satisfy its demands. General Electric leased a floor of the new manufacturing building on Commercial Street. For the year ending in 1950, AII had a modest profit and a net worth of $711,000.

In the 1951 fiscal year, Tam-o-Shanter, a children's textile manufacturer, built a single-floor plant at the corner of Lincoln and Auburn Streets and received a $125,000 loan from AII. At the annual meeting, it was reported that the small industry building had not attracted customers so it had been leased for storage. A net worth of $729,000 was reported.

In the summer of 1952, the directors turned down a request of the city to release restrictions on the easterly portion of Merrimack Common (site of the present Hillsborough County Courthouse) for a parking lot. AII believed that the city should acquire land for parking and not use up city parks. AII had released restrictions on Victory Park for parking the year before. At the end of the fiscal year, the company suffered a loss of $31,000, and the surplus sagged to $54,000.

In 1952, Textron terminated its textile operation—precursor to the general collapse of the northern textile industry in the latter part of the 1950s. It removed its machinery and sold the building to AII for $250,000, having spent $600,000 in rehabilitation costs. In 1953, several shoe concerns expressed an interest in the space but nothing happened until the end of the year, when the Textron building was sold to Mylsher Realty Company for $280,000, with a $150,000 mortgage loan for building improvements. Mylsher was the real estate corporation for Insuline

Corporation of Long Island City, which ...anufactured about 5,000 different products, mostly electronic, for the radio, TV, and auto industries and employed about six hundred people. At the end of 1954, Insuline requested a five-year moratorium on its loan, stating that the restoration had been more expensive than contemplated. It was granted a one-year extension. In June 1955, Insuline sold out while in default on its loan. The city continued its interest in providing more downtown parking, and in 1953 AII approved a plan to use the westerly half of the Merrimack Common for two hundred cars.

In January 1954, William McElroy, who had much experience in manufacturing real estate, was appointed agent. It was apparent that the multistory hundred-year-old buildings in the mill yard were not meeting the needs of contemporary industry and were becoming functionally obsolete. Industrial parks, with ample land for vehicular access and parking and single-story construction, were in great demand. Mr. McElroy, after consultation with the mayor, city planning board, and the Manchester Housing Authority, started to assemble for AII what subsequently became the Brown Avenue Industrial Park, by buying a number of large undeveloped lots financed by AII, starting with a thirty-two-acre lot in 1954 and some thirty acres more in 1962 for use as the municipal sewerage treatment plant. AII, at the request of the city, released a number of city lots from the old Amoskeag restrictions. At the end of 1954, there was a modest profit of $18,000 and a surplus that had grown to $84,000. There was talk about the government abandoning five-hundred-acre Grenier Field and not renewing its lease with the city, which expired June 30, 1957. At the 1955 annual meeting, there was talk again about liquidating the company, but the directors concluded that it was in the best interests of the city to continue the corporation to encourage industry to move to Manchester.

About 1956, winds of change were blowing in Manchester. The northern textile industry, which was on its knees during the depression, survived and won a reprieve during World War II for the manufacture of war materials and for another period of eight years for the manufacture of civilian goods, which had been in short supply during the depression and the war. But time was running out. Southern mills were more modern, closer to raw materials and markets, and were able to deliver the goods at lower prices. Textron moved out in 1952. Shortly thereafter Verney Corporation sold out to Gera Corporation, a conglomerate based in Cleveland, which in turn sold to Peter Fuller from Boston in 1957. Fuller closed the operation in 1958, resulting in litigation with AII over the terms of the AII loan relating to a prepayment loan premium. International Shoe in 1956 sold its plant on Queen City Avenue to a plastics company from Leominster, Massachusetts. The Frederick E. Everett Turnpike was started in 1956 and the Brown

Avenue Industrial Park in 1957. Although some outfits were having difficulty, others were doing well, such as Tam-o-Shanter (Syd Rosenberg) and Brookshire's Pandora line (Saul Sidore). Arrow Needle built a new plant on South Willow, and AII agreed to purchase its old plant on Hollis Street. In 1959 Arrow Needle sold the new plant to AII, which resold it to Sylvania Electric together with land previously owned by Faltin Trucking.

In 1961, Chemical Chains, which manufactured a variation of sponge rubber, negotiated for land on Perimeter Road at the Airport Industrial Park. In early 1962 the company requested from AII a $85,000 loan, which in December was approved for $50,000. In September 1963, Chemical Chains went bankrupt, and AII foreclosed on the mortgage and resold the property to American Felters, which manufactured insulation for the automotive industry.

In the 1960s, the city embarked on a gigantic plan of industrial renewal of the mill yard, which was in deplorable condition, with inadequate access, exposed railway tracks, road surfaces that were mostly dirt and potholed, poorly lit streets, and inadequate provision for parking, pickup, and delivery of goods, to name just a few problems. The six-year plan involved filling in both the upper and lower canals, removing most of the narrow buildings lining the lower side of each canal, relocating the railroad tracks to the west over the filled-in upper canal, widening Canal Street to four lanes, utilizing the discontinued railroad bed, and providing parking in the mill yard. These much needed changes greatly improved the appearance and efficiency of the mill yard. There is something like 5 million square feet of space there now, which is about 1 million less than when the old Amoskeag was running full blast, but there is still about 1 million square feet of empty space available for rent or sale. There continues to be discussion about the best use of the space. Amoskeag Industries owns no property in the mill yard.

In the 1970s, in addition to purchasing the land for the development of the Brown Avenue Industrial Park, Amoskeag Industries acquired the old Pine Island Park property and conveyed it to the city. Originally planned for a technical high school, it became an office park, occupied first by Home Insurance Company and in 1993 sold to Blue Cross–Blue Shield. Since the 1970s, AII has been practically quiescent. There have been other sources of funds, both state and federal, for industrial development; therefore, there has been little demand for AII participation.

The most recent activity of Amoskeag Industries was in connection with the acquisition of land in the mill yard for the University of New Hampshire facility in Manchester. Amoskeag Industries took a third mortgage of $300,000 behind the banks' first and the city's second (purchase price). Although occasionally an individual stockholder seeks liquidation of the company to realize a quick profit, the larger stockholders feel that the maintenance of a modest capital pool of funds is desirable and that the organization can perform a catalytic role for the benefit of Manchester.

# Notes

1. I was on vacation from Dartmouth at the time and remember going down River Road and seeing the water lap up over the railroad tracks under the Amoskeag Bridge and commence to wash away the tracks toward Dow Street. Men were filling burlap bags with sand hauled in by truck and making a dam from the end of the canal gatehouse to the high land by River Road to keep the water in the river and prevent it from washing out the tracks. They were successful! I also remember driving the next several days for the Red Cross, particularly to the streets west of the railroad tracks in South Manchester, below the present Sundial or Hesser building, where the houses had been badly flooded and were full of silt, mud, and sand, warping the floorboards and ruining furniture, pianos, et cetera. It was very heartrending.

2. Minutes of the Amoskeag Industries, Inc., board of directors' meeting, December 26, 1936, p. 71.

3. A government agency created during the depression by the New Deal to loan money to start-up businesses.

4. Prior to the war, there had been an active federal public housing program, developed as part of the New Deal, which financed construction of thousands of housing units across the country by local housing authorities. John McLane, Jr., this author, had been appointed to the Manchester Housing Authority in 1941 after starting the practice of law. The program was in suspension after Pearl Harbor. After the war, the American Legion Housing Committee consisted of many real estate operators and realtors who were dead set against any government housing, which they thought smacked of socialism if not outright communism, and fought in Congress against any appropriation for government housing even if it was for veterans. As the result of this inaction, here in New Hampshire, the AVC (American Veterans Committee, which was accused of being dominated by leftists) included an active group of lawyers from Manchester, including Joseph Millimet, Murray Devine, Stanley Brown, and the author. The group approached both Republican and Democratic candidates for governor and received their pledges that, if elected, they would support the establishment of a New Hampshire State Housing Authority modeled on the federal plan, with appropriations to build housing for needy veterans. Governor Charlie Dale stuck to his promise; he established the State Housing Authority (and appointed the author as one of the members), which financed the construction in Manchester of the Rimmon Heights project of some 120 units. Although Rimmon Heights later in the 1970s had a high proportion of Central and South Americans and was known for drug traffic, in 1946 it was a boon for returning veterans.

# ELEVEN

# Interlude 1930–1939

## HIGHLIGHTS OF 1930

Skiing was a major winter diversion for Judge and Elisabeth. They skied at Schilling Hill in Grasmere; Mt. Kearsarge in Warner on old carriage roads (this was prior to the days of the CCC, the depression Civilian Conservation Corps, created by President Roosevelt, which cut many of the early ski trails); Hillside Inn and Tenney Hill at Newfound Lake; the Uncanoonucs in Goffstown; Pomfret in Vermont; St. Sauveur, north of Montreal; up the Mount Washington Carriage Road above the halfway house; Berthoud Pass, Colorado, at 12,000 feet (Judge only); and finally, on Christmas Day, skijoring behind a two-horse team.

Judge was an avid tennis player in college and took up squash and badminton in winter when courts became available. The new badminton court opened at the Cygnet Boat Club (at the west end of the Amoskeag Bridge), a welcome addition to the two squash courts. (See Appendix A.1, Memories.) There were several squash matches with the Bow Brook Club in Concord and a team of St. Paul's School students.

The family bought a twenty-acre woodlot in Bedford for taxes and had a great time in the winter skating on the small pond. In the spring they swung on birch trees and dammed up brooks; in the fall, they cut wood and burned brush. Charles, with the assistance of a wonderful French Canadian carpenter, built a log cabin, about eight feet by six feet, with a smoky old stove. Jack Middleton bought the property many years later for his family and finally sold it to the state when the highway was widened and relocated, covering the little pond.

Elisabeth and the children with a camp counselor spent the summer at Pasquaney swimming, playing tennis, and climbing mountains close at hand or in the White Mountains. Elisabeth's sister Jane B. Shiverick and her three children usually spent summers there too, to avoid the heat of Cleveland.

Judge read extensively at home and also on his frequent train trips. In 1930 he read *The Virginians, Henry Esmond, Pendennis, Pair of Blue Eyes,* and *June Moon.* Generally speaking, Judge stuck to the classics, eschewing mysteries and science fiction. He enjoyed history, biographies, historical novels, and books with character development.

## HIGHLIGHTS OF 1931

Judge and Elisabeth always loved exercise and the outdoors. In 1915 they had spent their honeymoon climbing and hiking in Waterville Valley, a place they returned to almost every year. In the winter they loved to ski. There were no tows or lifts in 1931, so it was cross-country skiing or a long climb up a road in the woods and a fast run down. Hillside Inn, on the shores of Newfound Lake in Hebron, one mile from the Bancrofts' summer home Pasquaney Lodge, was a favorite spot. The inn was a year-round working farm that took in boarders in the summer, operated a large dining room for the general public, and with a little advance notice welcomed skiers in the winter.

Typically the New Year's holiday was a time for a family ski trip. Judge, Elisabeth, and those children old enough to ski plus other couples, mostly childless, such as the Carletons, Bob and Lois Booth (Bob was an attorney in the Wyman, Booth, Starr, Wadleigh & Langdell office), Bob and Dotty Burroughs, and others, formed a ski party. There was a variety of old abandoned town roads leading from the valleys to the higher hill farms, honeycombed with ancient cellar holes of the 1840–1880 era, which made for excellent cross-country skiing. There were still a few open hill pastures, such as Tenney Hill and Sheep Knob, that provided good open-slope skiing. (Fifty years later they are densely wooded.)

In 1931 Judge and Elisabeth returned to Hillside Inn for two weekends to ski. In February they attended the Dartmouth Carnival. On a winter weekend they skied the Pomfret, Vermont, area. During the week, as a break from the long Hale trial,[1] Judge skied in Goffstown and at Charles' cabin in Bedford after work and another time by moonlight at Pine Crest. Judge records that the winter had many snowstorms with lots of snow. For spring skiing they went to Pinkham Notch. They spent nights at the AMC huts and skied on the Old Jackson Road, the Mount Washington Carriage Road, the snowfields just above the Half Way House, and the Nineteen Mile Brook trail.

Squash and badminton at the renewed Cygnet Boat Club provided more exercise. Judge notes that Elisabeth bought a bicycle. They both biked. They also took time to play the piano (Elisabeth) and violin (Judge) together.

On Memorial Day weekend, they spent the night at the lake, swam (brrrrr), drove to the abandoned lumber town of Livermore, and climbed Carrigain, spending the night at the forest ranger's cabin. In June they walked the Wild River and Evans Notch trails and fished the East Branch.

From the lake, they climbed Mt. Cardigan with Malcolm, then five and a half years old, Mt. Moosilauke, spending the night at the Dartmouth Outing Club (DOC) cabin at the summit, and Mt. Lafayette.

In June, Judge and Elisabeth saw John Carleton and his mother off on the train to New York City for the boat to Paris, where John and Alicia Skinner (a student at Smith College) were to be married. The Carletons returned in August from their honeymoon. Elisabeth gave a tea for Alicia, a newcomer to the community. Her home had been Hanover, as had John's.

Judge comments that Harriet Mansfield "was ill and makes us worry" and again in December that he visited her in Rutland, Massachusetts, at a sanatorium. My recollection is that she either had TB or a somewhat similar bronchial condition, probably the result of being an inveterate smoker.

The family celebrated Thanksgiving at the newly finished Three Acres on North Union Street. It was a rustic, Cotswold-type cottage with a large living room with cathedral ceiling built with barn beams, a spectacular chandelier for about a hundred candles, and an ample fireplace. A tradition was established of serving breakfast to the assembled multitude of twenty plus or minus children home from school and college and family friends who lived too far away to go home. The group tore up accumulated newspapers to lay a trail for a hare and hound chase through the then-undeveloped abandoned farm fields of North Union Street. Fresh cider welcomed the runners, who finished off the morning with field hockey, soccer, or touch football to get up a good appetite. The main Thanksgiving dinner was served back at 940 Chestnut Street, followed by a country square dance at Three Acres in the evening. This tradition continued for nearly fifty years until Elisabeth died in 1983 and the Union Street property was sold. Then the family started a new "Thanksgiving" tradition at Pasquaney, Newfound Lake, celebrating over the Columbus Day weekend at the height of the foliage season, when the houses are still open with beds for about forty. Kilts and turkey dinner are still traditional.

## HIGHLIGHTS OF 1932

The year 1932 was a good winter for skiing, starting off with a snowstorm at Hillside Inn that produced twenty-two inches of snow in six hours. The family skied at the lake for two weekends and on the Mt. Moosilauke Carriage Road for another two. In April, they tried Tuckerman's Ravine on Mount Washington and Judge notes on April 9: "Bumped[2] into a tree and to North Conway Hospital," and on the tenth: "Spent day in hospital and drove home." Dr. Ezra Jones pronounced the injury to be a bruised bone. During July, weekends were spent at the lake. The family, that is, Judge, Elisabeth, and the three oldest children, sailed from Quebec to Glasgow on the *Montcalm;* toured the Highlands of Scotland and then England, then to Oxford for tea in Judge's old room at Magdalen College; and biked in the Cotswolds and climbed in Grindelwald, Switzerland. Judge and Elisabeth wanted to provide son Charles with more of an educational challenge than they thought he was getting at Central High School in Manchester. They had researched foreign schools, talked with parents, and decided on Sillig Institute in Switzerland. The school was located at Vevey on Lake Geneva for spring and fall terms and at Villars in the mountains near Montreux for the winter term. The opportunity to learn at a young age a foreign language in a foreign country was a motivating factor. The experience was so successful that the three younger children all enjoyed comparable schooling in France or Switzerland. The family left Charles at the school in Vevey and returned home on the *Carinthia* to New York, where Ken Graf met them. Traditions continued with Thanksgiving in Manchester and Christmas in Concord, concerning which there is a little story.

It was traditional for Judge to give to each of his children a $2.50 gold piece, which he placed in the bottom of each Christmas stocking. Each child gave the coin back to Judge, who deposited it in that child's bankbook. It was also traditional for Gaga Bancroft to invite the Congregational minister and family for Christmas dinner. Everything went according to plan. The McLane children played with the minister's children, who were about the same age. They had a great time running all over the large Victorian house. However, when Judge was getting ready to return to Manchester the next day, the gold pieces were missing from his dresser! Everyone looked everywhere, without success. The children then were confronted by our father: "Did you touch the money?" to which each answered in the negative. All spent a very uncomfortable night. The mystery fortunately was cleared up early the next day when the minister called Mrs. Bancroft and said that he and his son wanted to come up to the house immediately because the son had something he wanted to say. So up they came, and the son apologized for having taken the "bright pennies" from Judge's dresser top.

## HIGHLIGHTS OF 1933

In the winter the family skated, built many bonfires, and chopped wood at the woodlot in Bedford. Skiing remained an important activity. They skied at the "German's" (Schilling) in Grasmere on winter afternoons, Hanover during Dartmouth functions, Hillside Inn in March, and Pinkham Notch in late winter and spring, where both the carriage road and Tuckerman's Ravine provided excellent slopes. John Carleton and Charlie Proctor, both Dartmouth ski greats, came over the spectacular headwall on April 30.

The drive to Pinkham Notch took about three hours; there were numerous frost heaves in March and April, and the roads then were more narrow and curvy than now. Frequently we stopped by the side of the road to cook a hamburger or eat a picnic supper. Judge did most of the driving. Partly to keep himself awake and partly to entertain us, he talked about the interesting cases in the office. I loved hearing about these cases and find that I still remember many of them. I was a student at St. Paul's School, so Judge would interrogate me about my studies. This led to interesting conversations and an occasional argument. Coming home Sunday afternoons, after a couple of days in the sun and wind, made staying awake very difficult. The conversations were much less animated, and there were frequent driver changes. Judge and Elisabeth's son Charles, spending the year in school in Switzerland, wrote about breaking his leg while skiing.

There were several parties, including dances and plays, at Three Acres. Judge notes that he met Elisabeth in New York City and went to a speakeasy before repeal of Prohibition. Charles returned from his year in Switzerland with a fair command of the French language and enthusiastic stories of life abroad. During the summer, there were traditional activities at Pasquaney—picnics, blueberrying, mountain climbing (Lafayette, the Twins, Zealand and Carrigain Notches), and a trip to Maine with the family to visit around Mt. Desert. John sailed with Judge's St. Paul's School classmate, historian Samuel Eliot Morison, from Halifax to Southwest Harbor, Maine. They anchored in the harbors of little fishing villages at night. The "Admiral" cooked supper and then relaxed after dinner and read aloud about the history of Nova Scotia while the crew washed the dishes and cleaned up. During the summer midweek, Judge was alone in Manchester and played tennis with Frank Sulloway and Ned Toland from Concord, Arthur Rotch from Milford, and John Carleton, Ken Graf, Bob Booth, Bob Burroughs, and Ellis Straw from Manchester. Little Elisabeth, "Lilla," was a freshman at Central with a rather uninspiring group of friends. Charles' experience at a Swiss school had been so positive that Judge and Elisabeth decided to send Lilla there for the balance of the school year. This time their research indicated that Château Brillamont in Lausanne met their requirements. After Christmas in Concord, Judge and Elisabeth took Lilla and me to New York and put us on the German liner *Bremen* for France so Lilla could attend the school in Lausanne, Switzerland. I was her escort.[3] Judge and Elisabeth spent New Year's at the Ravine Camp of Dartmouth College at Mt. Moosilauke.

## HIGHLIGHTS OF 1934

In January 1934, Judge and Elisabeth skied on Tenney Hill at Newfound Lake, then continued on to Russell Mountain in North Woodstock, spending the night at Peckett's on Sugar Hill. The next day they skied on

Kinsman Hill and its trail with Harold Paumgarten as teacher.[4] Judge and Elisabeth gave a party at Three Acres at which Mr. Stewartson, a fiddler, taught everyone and called old-time contradances. They went to Mt. Cardigan in deep snow, which resulted in many stuck cars. The next day, they had a sleigh ride with the Mudges in Northwood, where the car got stuck and froze. (Roads weren't plowed well in those days, and antifreeze was primitive.) I arrived home from putting Lilla in school in Switzerland and told of the North Atlantic storm on the SS *Bremen*.[5] Judge and Elisabeth skied with Peter and Margaret Woodbury on Kearsarge (on a carriage road) and cooked lunch outdoors. There were weekends of skiing on Tenney Hill and climbing Mt. Tecumseh in Waterville Valley. Judge records in early February that there were ten days with the temperature below zero. On February 26, the newspapers told of the tragic death of nine Dartmouth students who were asphyxiated from a defective heater in their dorm during the cold weather. Judge attended a meeting of the Uncanoonuc Ski Club at the Cygnet Boat Club in February and skied on the mountain in mid-March. Judge and Elisabeth spent three weekends in April at Pinkham Notch, skiing Wildcat or the Ravine, including watching the Hocheberger "Inferno" ski race on Mount Washington from top to bottom.

During the summer months, Judge and Elisabeth, usually with children and friends, climbed Whiteface, Osceola, Lafayette and the Franconia Range, Carrigain, the Presidential Range to the Lakes-of-the-Clouds, down to Great Gulf and up to Madison Spring huts, and over Adams to Jefferson and down the Castellated Ridge trail. Judge notes that John drove for Styles Bridges[6] during the latter part of his gubernatorial campaign in August before matriculating at Dartmouth as a freshman; Lilla started in Concord Academy in Massachusetts. Throughout the year there were theater and musical events, including the New York Metropolitan Opera Company on tour in Boston for a double bill of *Pagliacci* and *Emperor Jones*.[7] In the fall, the Ravine Camp at Mt. Moosilauke was a favorite weekend spot, with trips in mid October and early November in six inches of snow with another five inches the next day while walking to Jobildunk Ravine. Judge and Elisabeth wound up the year skiing on Tenney, then "tough going in the dark" skiing in to the Ravine Camp on December 30, with two runs on Hell's Highway the next day.

## HIGHLIGHTS OF 1935

The year 1935 was a good winter for skiing, starting off with New Year's at the Ravine Camp at Moosilauke and a snowstorm and skiing on supersteep Hell's Highway (since abandoned). Uncanoonuc Mountain, including the North Mountain, was popular, with five visits, some on weekday

*1930s, Old Ravine Camp, Mt. Moosilauke,* Dartmouth Outing Club.
Burned in September 1935. Visited by the McLanes for New Year's
parties and other occasions. Credit: Dartmouth College Library.

afternoons. Judge, Elisabeth, John Carleton, and Bob and Lois Booth skied
up over the shoulder of Cardigan from Canaan and down to the AMC
camp at Alexandria. They spent a weekend at Laconia and another at
Hillside Inn and Tenney Hill. The winter season wound up with three
weekends at Pinkham Notch in March and April.

Judge and Elisabeth purchased an abandoned farm pasture, well grown
over, in the town of Webster near Little Hill, which they named "High
Stoy" from a place in England. The Little family had been great friends of
the Bancrofts at the New Hampshire Insane Asylum, as it was then known,
in Concord. Dr. "Squash" Little,[8] a psychiatrist, a favorite of young
Elisabeth Bancroft, became the first superintendent of the Laconia State
School in the early 1900s before going on to New York to start Letchworth
Village, a pioneer institution for the care of the "feebleminded." His
younger brother, Ben, had remained to run the family farm in Webster.
Judge and Elisabeth made plans for Charles, then a student at St. Paul's
School in Concord, to spend the summer working on the farm, an arrange-
ment that was replicated with daughters Lilla and Mary and son Malcolm.
For these "city" kids it was a memorable and rewarding experience to work
on a real dirt farm.

Judge and Elisabeth entertained frequently. They invited St. Paul's
School or Dartmouth trustees to stop en route to or from meetings for the
night in Manchester. There were several Dartmouth functions in the
Manchester area at which Dartmouth administration or faculty people
spoke. Judge frequently arranged for them to spend the night at 940

Chestnut Street. Judge invited many clients with their wives as well as his law partners or younger associates. The delicious dinners were accompanied by some of Henry Hollis' wine, and the conversations flowed. During the depression years, Elisabeth usually had live-in help.

In the latter part of June, Judge and Elisabeth drove to Quebec with my wife, Blanche, and me, as chauffeurs, then embarked on the *Montrose*. They spent a couple of days in Paris before pushing on to Geneva, where they stayed with Gil and Constance Winant.[9] In Austria, they hiked in the Otztal valley and visited Kitzbuhl before taking the train to Berchtesgaden, Konigssee, Munich,[10] Nurnberg, Heidelberg, and down the Rhine River to Brussels. They crossed the North Sea by boat to London, then on to Oxford, the Cotswolds, the Lake District, and Wales for hiking and biking before catching the *Duchess of York* at Greenock in Scotland. The rest of the summer there was tennis with John Carleton, Ken Graf, me (I was working at Felton Brush for the summer), Frank Sulloway, Ted Foster, Bob Booth, and others at the Cygnet Boat Club courts. They spent weekends at the lake climbing Cardigan, Lafayette, Garfield, Stinson, and other mountains. The old DOC Ravine Camp at Mt. Moosilauke burned in September; in December, Judge went with a group to scout a site for a new camp. Twenty-three kilted McLanes feasted at the traditional Thanksgiving in Manchester. Christmas was celebrated as usual at Gaga Bancroft's in Concord. The year ended as it began—at the site of the old Ravine Camp skiing. The group stayed at Fordy and Peggy Sayre's Spyglass Farm, which had been hurriedly fixed up for large groups immediately after the Ravine Camp fire.

## HIGHLIGHTS OF 1936

Over New Year's, Judge, Elisabeth, and available children stayed at Spyglass Farm and skied in the Ravine where it was snowing hard, then went on to Sugar Hill the next day. There was hard rain on January 3, so we took a trip into Littleton to bowl and play pool. We skied on the fourth on the Taft trail. Judge and Elisabeth took Malcolm and Mary to the Robert Burns birthday dinner of the clan MacKenzie in Manchester with bagpipes playing. This must have been a good skiing year because the family skied on the Uncanoonucs or in Hanover practically every weekend through January, February, and up to the floods of mid-March.[11]

Judge and Elisabeth attended the dedication of the remodeled Dartmouth Hall after the big fire of a couple of years before. They trekked north to Pinkham on three weekends in the spring and skied Tuckerman's Ravine, Gulf of Slides, and Bear Mountain. During one week, a "tremendous avalanche covered the brook," making it impossible to get into Tuckerman's. In late April, Judge hiked into Jobildunc Ravine at

Moosilauke with Dartmouth Outing Club officials Dan Hatch and Ford Sayre and found four feet of snow on the ground. In June, after school, Judge and Elisabeth sent Charles, Lilla, and Malcolm off in the family car on a trip to Washington, Virginia, and Cleveland, sight-seeing and staying with relatives and friends. Charles then went to work for the second year on the Ben Little farm in Webster, haying, milking, tending the cows, and performing other farm chores. The Winants visited the lake several times in the summer. Judge and Elisabeth climbed Mt. Tripyramid in Waterville Valley, then went to the Dartmouth College grant[12] in northern New Hampshire in September. They climbed over East Peak of Mt. Moosilauke from Jobildunc Ravine in November. Judge records after Christmas in Concord that there was neither snow nor ice.

## HIGHLIGHTS OF 1937

The family spent New Year's in Jackson skiing on the golf links at the Eagle House until the snow was spoiled by a hard rain. Judge notes on January 15, "Terrible weather, no snow." He celebrated his fifty-first birthday with a dinner and dance at Three Acres. The next day Judge and Elisabeth went to a party at Arthur Moreau's.[13] They put Mrs. Bancroft on the boat in New York City for Cape Town, South Africa,[14] and then they sailed for Galveston, stopping for an afternoon in Miami, where Colonel Henry Teague "did the honors."[15] They had "a perfect day in the Gulf, balmy and smooth," but later it was "dull and turned rather rough again." Judge notes when they landed, "Glad to get off, bus to Houston."

During the school winter vacation, Elisabeth went with Malcolm, Mary, and seventy-five other children to Spyglass Farm at Mt. Moosilauke for a ski school run by Fordy and Peggy Sayre. In the spring they skied at Pinkham on the Sherburne, Gulf of Slides, and Wildcat trails (no lifts). In mid-May, a group went up the cog railway on Mount Washington to the summit and had a grand clear day skiing on the snowfields. (My wife, Blanche, sunburned her eyeballs, which were extremely sore for several days.)

On May 25, Judge, Elisabeth, Ken Graf, and Mary Fuller christened Judge's new tennis court at Three Acres. After the disastrous flood of March 1936, which ruined the Cygnet Boat Club and its six tennis courts, it was impossible to find the money during the depression to restore the courts; therefore, Judge, Parker Straw, and Mary Fuller decided to build their own courts and hired the same outfit to install them.

The summer of 1937 was apparently the hottest on record, but for Judge, trips to the lake on weekends made it bearable. In September, Judge, Elisabeth, and Malcolm sailed from Quebec on the *Duchess of Richmond* for Glasgow and a week of hiking and biking in Scotland before going to London, Oxford, and the Cotswolds for more biking. Then it was on to

Europe via the Dover-Calais boat, then Paris, and a stop in Geneva to see the Winants, where Gil was director of the International Labor Office. The school year abroad had been so successful for both Charles and Lilla that they continued the experience for Malcolm, whom they dropped off at Sillig Institute in Vevey, Switzerland, following in Charles' footsteps. They drove around the Swiss Alps before returning to Paris, called on Mr. Edward Tuck, a benefactor of Dartmouth and the New Hampshire Historical Society, and embarked on the *Queen Mary* for the trip to New York. The year ended as it began, with a weekend of skiing at Intervale and the Gulf of Slides in Pinkham Notch.

## HIGHLIGHTS OF 1938

Judge and Elisabeth opened the year skiing with the children in heavy snow on Black Mountain at Jackson. Later in the month they skied over the shoulder of Mt. Cardigan and down to Hebron. On January 19, the temperature in Manchester was minus thirty-four degrees, a record low. In March they hiked up and skied down the new Mt. Tecumseh trail in Waterville Valley, which is now part of the Waterville ski area.[16] Both in March and April, Tuckerman's Ravine was their skiing destination. Judge notes that Frank P. Carpenter, Manchester's wealthiest citizen, died. He had been a client of Judge's with respect to tax problems, but Judge was not involved in the settlement of his estate. (See Chapter Seventeen, Frank P. Carpenter.) In June, Judge and Elisabeth went to Concord with Charles and niece Jane, and her husband, John Hall, to celebrate some event with Gaga Bancroft at her house at a festive meal. Champagne was served with dessert. Judge proposed a toast for the occasion and quaffed down his drink; before anyone else could drink, he spat his out all over the table with a great exclamation. The "champagne" bottle was immediately examined; the label read "Champagne de Bain"—toilet water!

The great hurricane of 1938 rolled across the state on September 21, leaving $20 million worth of destruction to trees and buildings. Substantial tree damage was sustained at the lake on the Bancroft property, which Judge and Elisabeth inspected on September 23. Much of the fallen timber was purchased by the government, cut as fast as possible (to avoid damage by bugs and worms), and stored in ponds until it could be salvaged. Judge noted that the war scare was serious again in late September.

On November 3, Judge records, "Great to-do about Harrington Gates. Ralph went to see him." The next day, "Gates stops at RWD [Ralph W. Davis] on way back to college." "Heavenly Harry" Gates was a sophomore at Dartmouth who excelled in football as a backfield runner and defenseman. (Players then played both offense and defense.) He was a very evangelical and religious student and a member of a small biblical sect that had a number of centers in New England, including one in New Boston, New Hampshire. He would not stand any swearing on the football field and is reputed to have swung at one or more teammates who did swear. My recollection is that at the Harvard game he excelled, but then God spoke to him and, upon returning to Hanover, Harry turned in his uniform and announced that he was leaving college. Because he was attending college on some form of athletic scholarship, this was practically a traitorous act. Many people talked to him during that week, and the newspapers had a field day speculating whether he would see the light by the next Saturday for the Yale game, when the Dartmouth team desperately needed him.

That Yale game was dramatic; I saw it. (It was in my first year at law school.) Everyone could see Gates' number on the sidelines, but he wasn't playing. Yale took the opening kickoff and ripped through the Dartmouth team like cottage cheese, making first down after first down nearing the Dartmouth goal. Then, with a tremendous roar from the Big Green side, out ran "Heavenly Harry" to substitute in the linebacker position. He was so charged up that he leapt over the Yale line and was in their backfield before the ball was snapped; he was twice penalized for being offside. By now all of the Dartmouth players were charged up. On the next two plays, Yale was thrown back some twenty yards and never could get up momentum again. My recollection is that Dartmouth won, but Harry decided that his original decision was the correct one, and he never played football again.

## HIGHLIGHTS OF 1939

The year 1939 was a good year for skiing, and Judge and his family made the most of it, skiing New Year's and the following weekend at Cannon Mountain and two other weekends in early April. The new Dartmouth Ravine Camp at Moosilauke opened, replacing the burned one, so the family skied Hell's Highway, a precipitous trail laid out several years before by Dartmouth coach Otto Schneibs. The trail has long since been abandoned because of avalanches. Judge records: "Swell fun on Hell's Highway." One weekend was shared with skiers from the Boston area who were members of the ski club Old Carriage Road Runners. They were veterans of skiing on the Moosilauke Carriage Road, over which at the turn of the century passengers in wagons were taken to the summit to spend the night in the Tip Top House.

The old Ravine Camp was a primitive one-story logging camp, built of tarpaper and wood, with a low ceiling. It had bunk rooms with double- and triple-deckers, and outside toilets. It could accommodate about fifty people. Ford[17] and Peggy Sayre ran it for Dartmouth College for several years, starting a very popular children's ski school, before the camp burned down in September 1935. Ford and Peggy bought a farmhouse on a hill just off the Warren-Woodstock road that they named "Spyglass," where they continued the ski school and a ski inn.[18] Dartmouth decided to rebuild the old Ravine Camp on its original site, which commanded a great view of the mountain, but in a contemporary massive log-cabin style with accommodations for a hundred or more. A new road was built in from the Warren-Woodstock highway, making the place accessible by car. Previously one had to ski in about a mile and a half and lug one's clothes. The new Ravine Camp, with its peeled native logs, is massive and handsome. College groups use it frequently throughout the year for meetings, seminars, and parties. For years it was a favorite spot for New Year's Eve celebrations for the McLanes and a host of friends from Manchester.

In 1939 they stayed three weekends at Pinkham Notch AMC huts and on one weekend watched the fabulous Inferno Race from the top to the bottom of Mount Washington, held only a few times because of the difficult weather problems. They watched Swiss skier Toni Matt schuss the headwall (never done before) and win the race with a time of six minutes, twenty-seven seconds. If the weather was not auspicious in the ravine, the family skied the Wildcat trail. There was occasional skiing at Oak Hill in Hanover when Judge was attending Dartmouth trustee meetings or at Cardigan Mountain as well as a few late-afternoon climbs on Uncanoonuc Mountain in Goffstown. In late January, Judge was able to ski in the streets of Manchester! Apparently it was a cold winter because Judge and Elisabeth skated at Dorrs Pond, the Bedford woodlot, and Lake Massabesic. On Elisabeth's birthday in May, Judge presented her with the title to an additional two acres of land abutting the original Three Acres on North Union Street.

In the summer, Judge and Elisabeth went to England on the *Montrose* and bicycled along the Devon coast, including St. Ives,[19] then crossed to the Continent and traveled in Burgundy, Provence, and the valley of the Dordogne, and returned to Paris via Chartres amid gloomy war news. They dined with Henry Hollis and ordered wine. (See Appendix B.2, Henry F. Hollis.) On August 30, they sailed from Cherbourg on the *Queen Mary*; on the thirty-first, the ship was blacked out; on September 1, Germany invaded Poland; on September 3, England declared war. British cruisers off Halifax met and escorted the ship, which had drastically changed its route. The *Athena* was torpedoed; Malcolm and I met Judge and Elisabeth when the ship docked in New York City on the fourth.[20]

Judge comments that he went to a Dartmouth trustees' meeting in Hanover "on Ned French's new railroad car to White River Junction." The presidents of most railroads had their own cars complete with bar, dining

*1930s, Summit House, Mt. Moosilauke,* Dartmouth Outing Club. Burned in winter in the 1930s. Visited by Elisabeth in her youth and by the family in the 1920s and 1930. This author spent a night during Christmas vacation in about 1933. Credit: Dartmouth College Library.

room, parlor, and sleeping accommodations. The private car was added to the rear of a train going to their destination and put on a side track if the train was going farther. Much business could thus be accomplished in relative comfort.

Judge and Elisabeth went to the Dartmouth-Harvard football game in Cambridge as usual and enjoyed dinner afterward at the Hofbrau House, a German beer hall, as they had done in 1938. Several years later it was revealed that the Hofbrau House had been a meeting place for German Nazis during the war, some of whom were in the United States on espionage missions. (See Appendix C.4, Ken Graf and the German Spies.) Thanksgiving was traditional at Three Acres with a hare and hound chase and a square dance with a fiddler who called the dances. There were twenty-eight for a turkey dinner. The year ended with the family and other Manchester friends at the Dartmouth Ravine Camp at Mt. Moosilauke.

## Notes

1. Arthur Hale; see Chapter Sixteen, Merrimack River Savings Bank.

2. Note Judge's use of the delicate "bumped," probably an influence of his British training at Oxford, rather than the more macho American "smashed" or "slammed."

3. This author remembers how cold it was when we got on the boat, well below zero and windy, but the next morning we were in the Gulf Stream and it was pleasant. Nazi swastikas were everywhere, and the crew gave the Nazi salute to the officers. I didn't know what to make of it. Max Schmeling (world heavyweight champion boxer) was a passenger in first class. We were traveling third class, but there were very few people on board and I found a way to get up to first class and look around and see the great boxer. After a couple of days with the Sortwells in Paris, we took the sleeper to Lausanne, where I enrolled Lilla in school and went shopping with her. Then I continued on to the winter school in Villars (where Charles had spent the preceding year) for a week of skiing before making a final check on Lilla, who by now was well settled in, and returning home on the *Bremen*.

4. Harold Paumgarten came from St. Anton, Austria, and was a member of the Austrian ski team in the 1932 and 1936 Olympics. He went into business, moved to Philadelphia, and married a Philadelphian whose family had St. Paul's School connections. Very tragically, Harold was killed while skiing by an avalanche at St. Anton close to his home in an area where he had skied all his life. A number of his children and, I believe, grandchildren attended St. Paul's School.

In the mid-1950s, my wife, Blanche, and I went skiing with our son, Sandy, on leave from the Army in Germany, at St. Anton and stayed at the pension run by Gerta Paumgarten, sister of Harold, and her father. We were guided by Gerta, who had been a member of the Austrian women's ski team in the 1936 Olympics.

5. This author, after skiing at Villars, checked in on his sister and sailed on the return trip of the *Bremen*, one of the largest oceanliners of the day, sailing from Cherbourg, normally a five-day crossing. The ship hit force 10 winds on the Beaufort wind scale (a nautical wind scale originally used in the days of sail and still used that grades winds from 0 to 12, the latter being a hurricane) and was obliged to turn off her two outboard propellers and continue on the two inboard props because the huge waves lifted the stern out of the water. I was able to get out onto the topmost deck above the bridge and watch the bow of the ship plunge down into an oncoming wave, a substantial portion of which was cut off and crashed into the superstructure, making the entire ship shudder and shake. I watched one wave pass off the stern before the next wave hit the bow, meaning that the length between crests of successive waves was over 1,000 feet, the length of the *Bremen*. The tops of the smokestacks were white from the salt spray. The vessel was thirty-six hours late in arriving in New York. The passage was an unforgettable experience.

6. I remember driving Styles to various rallies, meetings, and factory visits and to the National Guard training at an encampment in Webster. When not driving, I worked in the office stuffing envelopes, licking stamps, and doing other odd jobs. I was at the office on election night, collecting returns and posting them to bulletin boards. I remember one embarrassing moment. My recollec-

tion is that Styles' brother called on the phone to congratulate him, and I was dispatched to find him in the *Patriot* building, where we all were located, using offices on several different floors that night. I guess I was somewhat euphoric and maybe a little loudmouthed and returned to the office to report. All of a sudden a nursery rhyme came into my head and I blurted out, "'I've looked upstairs, downstairs, in the ladies chamber' and can't find him." Of course there were great guffaws of laughter and I realized what I had said—and have never forgotten it.

7. Judge and Elisabeth loved the theater and music. They also exposed their children to both. I took violin lessons; Charles, Lilla, and Mary took piano; and Malcolm took cello. Mary was the only one to become an accomplished musician. We also went to the opera in Boston. The Boston Symphony used to have a special concert for its pension fund on the Sunday after Christmas. We sat on the curve of the balcony just above the orchestra so we could plainly see all the instruments being played. We attended Dartmouth night at the Pops from time to time. Elisabeth had studied drama at Smith College and encouraged Charles to write when he showed some innate abilities. Even before he was a teenager, Charles authored several plays, which Elisabeth produced at Three Acres or at Pasquaney. I remember playing minor parts in some of these or working on sets, lighting, costumes, et cetera. Charles was quite a dramatist at college.

8. Charles Sherman Little from Webster, New Hampshire, graduated from Dartmouth in the class of 1891 and the medical school in 1896.

9. Gil was then with the International Labor Office.

10. Judge and Elisabeth picked up an open car in Munich to see the sights—it was sort of like one of the Nazi "staff" cars. They were leaving the city by a wide boulevard on which there were few cars and were somewhat confused by all the German signs, which they couldn't read. (Later they decided the signs said something like "Reserved for official vehicles only.") As they approached a narrow underpass, a noisy column of army cars, trucks with troops flying Nazi swastikas, armored personnel carriers, and tanks suddenly appeared on the other side of the pass with engines roaring. They both couldn't get through at the same time. The lead car, an open staff one, stopped, and a tall, monocled officer quickly jumped out and approached Judge, barking some incomprehensible language. He looked like he wanted to see some papers, so Judge reached in his coat pocket and extracted his Boston & Maine Railroad pass (Judge was a director at the time). The pass, a plastic card, had very fancy scroll writing in red and black on a white background with large letters at the top, then the person's name in distinctive print with a colored serial number and below, the date and the unreadable but impressive signatures of the president and treasurer of the railroad. The German officer was duly impressed, clicked his heels together with a loud crack, returned the card to Judge, executed a snappy salute, roared a "Heil Hitler," and waved them on while the German Wermacht was stopped in its tracks. Both Elisabeth and Judge gave the stony-faced German soldiers and officers broad smiles and waved enthusiastically as

they passed. Their story when related back home improved with each telling.

11. These were the floods that caused the Merrimack River to rise seventeen feet over the Amoskeag dam in Manchester and did such tremendous damage to the mills that the reorganization plan under consideration was withdrawn and the property was liquidated by sale to Amoskeag Industries, Inc.

12 The Dartmouth College grant, consisting of several thousand acres in Coos County, New Hampshire, was a gift of the king of England in the eighteenth century prior to the American Revolution to the trustees of Dartmouth College as an endowment, the income from which would help defray the expenses of the institution. I am not sure there was any substantial lumbering prior to World War I. Timber prices reached high levels at that time. The college sold all timber rights to the Brown Paper Company, which logged it over within a few years. The funds, several millions of dollars, were invested to produce income. The college withdrew income and enough principal to amortise the fund over a forty-year period, at which time it was expected there would be merchantable timber again. In the 1930s, the college reviewed its forest policy, hired expert advisers, and developed a plan to encourage sustained yield. A college forester, Bob Monahan (whom Judge interviewed in California), was hired to manage the woodlands, negotiate timber sales, and monitor logging operations. The grant produces net income to the college. There is a center where guests can be accommodated.

13. Arthur Moreau, a client, merchant, and owner of Moreau's Hardware store, was the motivating force in starting Amoskeag Industries, Inc., to purchase the assets of the Amoskeag Manufacturing Company from the bankruptcy court. Mr. Moreau was a beloved and outstanding citizen of Manchester. It is interesting to note that Arthur Moreau's great-grandson, Scott Moreau, married Judge McLane's granddaughter, Virginia McLane.

14. Mrs. Bancroft was a great traveler, frequently taking a relative as a companion. She patronized the Thom. Cook Travel Agency and signed up for their cruises. She sent numerous postcards home, which in the 1920s I collected and used in the stereoptican shows I put on in our house for the benefit of the neighboring children. The running commentary was by yours truly.

15. Colonel Teague took the Mount Washington Cog Railway off the hands of the Boston & Maine Railroad and ran it in the summers. In the winters, he operated the Venetian Hotel in Miami by the Venetian Causeway. During World War II, the Navy Department took over the Venetian as a barracks building for the Submarine Chaser Training Center (SCTC) and I was billeted there in 1943 for about four months.

16. In the days before lifts, most people used "skins" to climb up trails. Real sealskins were best but expensive, but a plush fabric became an effective, cheaper substitute. The skins had straps to attach them to the skis; the skis slid forward easily and were held from slipping backward when stopped. The skins were tied around one's waist for the trip down.

17. Ford Sayre went to Dartmouth in the class of 1933 and was active in Dartmouth Outing Club affairs. My first contact with him was in the winter of 1934–1935 when my parents gave my brother Charles and me ski lessons with Otto Schneibs, the Dartmouth ski coach, during the Christmas holiday. Otto had organized an overnight trip to the top of Mt. Moosilauke for a group from the Dartmouth Outing Club and the Smith College Outing Club, to which we were invited. Two of the people on the trip were Fordy Sayre and Margaret (Peggy) Lincoln, whose romance blossomed into marriage.

18. After the Sayres established themselves in Spyglass, the college hired Fordy as general manager of the Hanover Inn, which was owned and operated by the college. (I graduated in 1938.) In my last year or so at Dartmouth, Blanche and I had children the same age as the Sayre children and saw them on occasion. Because of Elisabeth's attendance at several ski schools at the Ravine Camp and Spyglass and Judge's position as a New Hampshire trustee of the college and a frequent visitor to the inn, Judge and Elisabeth formed a warm friendship with the Sayres. During the war years, Fordy entered the service and Peggy ran the inn. Very tragically, Ford was killed in an airplane accident; Peggy continued at the inn with the three children. Andrew Marshall, my former wife's brother, moved to Hanover to establish a business after he was discharged as an officer in the Army. His first wife, Lee McKean, had died of cancer, leaving two children. Andy and Peggy soon established a warm relationship that resulted in marriage. The ceremony was attended by Peggy's three and Andy's two children. Soon thereafter, Andy was asked to take a position managing family properties in Colorado and New Mexico, so the two families moved to Colorado Springs in the late 1940s. Andy and Peggy had a child of their own. Andy died in March 1996.

19. St. Ives may be remembered from the ditty:

"As I was going to St. Ives,
I met a man with seven wives,
Each wife had seven sacks.
Each sack had seven cats,
Each cat had seven kits.
Kits, cats, sacks and wives,
How many were going to St. Ives?"

20. John and Malcolm remember going to the New York World's Fair the day before the ship docked and hearing over the loudspeakers that England had declared war. In the evening they sat on the grass at the World's Fair with thousands of other people and listened to President Roosevelt address the nation.

# TIME LINE, 1935

The time lines cover one year in each decade and summarize Judge's activities away from home.

| | | |
|---|---|---|
| *January* | 1 | Ravine Camp, Moosilauke, skied in snow on Hell's Highway. |
| | 4 | Hanover, evening train. |
| | 5 | Rhodes committee. |
| | 6 | Ski North Uncanoonuc. |
| | 8 | Boston—passed papers in Carpenter–Mead Morison case. |
| | 11 | Peterborough—taking statements in Bass case. |
| | 12 | Concord, dinner Mrs. Bancroft. |
| | 16 | New York by train. |
| | 17 | Northport to see Adele Breaux. |
| | 18 | SPS meetings in New York City. |
| | 19 | Hanover—skied on golf links in moonlight. |
| | 20 | Alexandria—skiing. |
| | 25 | Skied Uncanoonuc. |
| | 26 | Skied Uncanoonuc. |
| | 28 | Concord to see Styles Bridges. |
| | | |
| *February* | 2 | Train to Canaan and skied over shoulder of Mt. Cardigan to Alexandria AMC Lodge. |
| | 3 | Skied Alexandria trail, "swell skiing." |
| | 6 | Boston on NH Breeder's case. |
| | 9 | Skied Uncanoonucs. |
| | 10 | Laconia to ski Rowe Mt. |
| | 12 | Laconia to ski. Boston to see Walter Houston in *Dodsworth*. |
| | 13 | Boston at Ritz for Dartmouth XC meeting. |
| | 14 | Concord for NH Foundation meeting. |
| | 16 | Hillside Inn, Hebron. Icy skiing on Tenney. |
| | 17 | New snow, fine skiing on Tenney. |
| | 21 | Boston to see Andrew Marshalls. |
| | 22 | Skied Woodstock. |
| | 23 | Skied Woodstock. |
| | 25 | Brattleboro, for Blanche and John's marriage. |
| | 26 | Skied Dr. Faulkner's hill in Grasmere. |
| | | |
| *March* | 2 | Uncanoonuc. |
| | 3 | Ski in Laconia. |
| | 5 | Dinner with Mrs. Sortwell in Cambridge. |
| | 7 | Boston for Alumni dinner. |

|    |    |
|----|----|
| 8 | Up on train to Hanover with Hoppie. |
| 9 | Hanover, skied golf links. Drove to Concord, Massachusetts, to see Lilla in *Iolanthe* at Concord Academy. |
| 10 | Concord, NH, to ski with Malcolm. |
| 14 | Boston to meet Fred Howland and Vic Cutter on Hoppie's retirement allowance. |
| 16 | Elis. and I out to Ravine trail. |
| 18 | Wilton to see Abbott on Souhegan River case. |
| 19 | Concord for Charles' birthday dinner at SPS. |
| 20 | Hanover with Elisabeth to visit John. |
| 22 | Boston. |
| 23 | Hanover and Ravine Camp with Lilla, Malcolm, picked up John. Skied Hell's Highway. |
| 24 | Moosilauke—skied all day. |
| 25 | Boston, conference EM Chase tax case. |
| 26 | Concord—elected President, NH Conference on Social Welfare. |
| 30 | Pinkham, skied new Tuckerman trail to Hermit Lake shelter. |
| 30 | Clear warm day in Ravine. |

| April | 1 | Charles down to see Dr. Shedd with infected hand. Skied Wildcat Trail. |
|----|----|----|
| | 4 | Boston—Metropolitan Opera. |
| | 5 | With Elisabeth, Bob, and Lois Booth to Pinkham. |
| | 6 | Picked up Charles from hospital in North Conway, skied to Little Headwall. |
| | 7 | Grand day in Ravine, best skiing. |
| | 17 | Concord to PUC on Greenfield Lighting Rate case. |
| | 18 | Hudson to see Water Co. property for bank loan. |
| | 19 | Hanover to dinner with John and Blanche in Parker Apartments. |
| | 20 | Hanover for trustees' meeting. |
| | 23 | Whitefield—night with Dodges at Mountain View. |
| | 24 | Lancaster for hearing on divorce case and conservatorship. |
| | 25 | Train to New York City. |
| | 26 | St. Paul's School trustees. |
| | 27 | Back to Dover, Pinkham Notch, skied at Glenn House. |
| | 28 | Raining, climbed into Ravine and good run down. |

| May | 2 | Laconia on Moosilauke project. |
|----|----|----|
| | 5 | Church. Lake, all-day picnic with Charles and SPS |

friends.

| | |
|---|---|
| 6 | Boston all day FP Carpenter tax case. |
| 8 | Train to Burlington on Englesbury case with Guy Page. |
| 9 | Burlington all day making settlement. Boston. |
| 10 | Conference IRS on FP Carpenter 1932–33 taxes on Brown Co. stock. |
| 11 | Fessenden School for Malcolm's (Mickey Mouse) baseball game. |
| 12 | Concord for SPS Evensong service. |
| 13 | Salem Race Track with Ralph to close tax case. |
| 14 | Concord. |
| 15 | Concord on NH Federation matters. |
| 17 | Hanover to get John, who has measles. |
| 18 | Picnic at High Stoy in Webster—arranged for Charles to farm with Littles. [Judge and Elisabeth picked up at tax sale several acres of old pastureland with a view.] |
| 20 | Spoke at SPS on law. Hanover on Park case. |
| 22 | Concord before PUC on Hudson Water case. |
| 24 | Boston on Straw block lease. |
| 25 | Took three children to Boston for Dartmouth-Harvard baseball game, dinner at T—Wharf overlooking harbor and to Pops. Night in hotel. |
| 26 | Left Elisabeth at Concord Academy, Concord, Mass., to Concord, NH. |
| 28 | Concord before Governor and Council on Mississippi Bond matter. |
| 29 | Lake in p.m. |

| June | | |
|---|---|---|
| | 1 | SPS Trustees. |
| | 2 | SPS Anniversary chapel, Boston, Pops, and New York night train. |
| | 3 | Met Rob Bass, to Washington in p.m. |
| | 4 | Conference in Washington on Bass Estate, dinner with Bass and Tobey—hot politics. |
| | 5 | Session on EM Chase and FP Carpenter tax cases. To New York City. |
| | 6 | Home in a.m. |
| | 9 | Picked up Chas at SPS and took him back. |
| | 11 | Nashua to Proctor Bros. machinery sale. Boston to Summerfields'. |
| | 12 | Celebrate 20th Wedding Anniversary. Buggy ride and picnic supper in Goffstown. |
| | 13 | Hanover tennis doubles, trustees' meeting. |

14    Alumni Council.

15    Lake.

16    Saw tanagers and many birds. Paddle in the moon-
      light.

17    Hanover for commencement.

18    Boston on sale of race track.

19    Boston. Train to New York City.

20    Out to Summit, New Jersey, to see Gen. Kaley on
      Souhegan Bank matters.

22    NH Bar Association at Rye.

23    Drove Charles to Ben Little's to start farming.

25    Took Malc and Mary to Grey Rocks at Lake. Drove
      to East Angus, Quebec, with John and Blanche.

26    Quebec at noon, dinner at Kerhulu, sailed on
      SS *Montrose*.

27    Very tired, foggy day.

28    Cabot Straits.

29    Deck tennis, foggy, smooth.

30    Church, routine of sleep, eat, and deck tennis.


*July*        4    Paris, Petite Palais, Folies Bergéres.

5    Place du Tetre, Carnavalet Museum.

6    Versailles, Jeu de Paume, Sainte Chapel.

7    Geneva by train to see Gil and Constance Winant.

8    Train Berne, Zurich, Tyrol to Innsbruck.

9    Train to Otztal, bus to Solden.

10    Grand all day walk above tree line.

11    2 1\2 hr walk up to Obergurgl. Glorious views.

12    All-day trip to Carlsruhe Hut at foot of Gurgl glac-
      ier.

13    Out of mountains, back to Innsbruck.

14    Sightseeing.

15    Shop for Tyrolese dresses. Train for Salzburg via
      Kitzbuhl.

16    Hired car to Berchtesgarden. Konigssee. Too trippy.

17    Wolfgangsee—walk, tennis, and swim. Boat on Lake
      and bus back.

18    Mozart House. To Munich and Hofbrau Haus for
      dinner and concert.

19    New State Gallery a disappointment.

20    Hired car, drove Nurnberg, night at Rothenberg.

21    Dinkelsbuhel, Augsberg.

22    Lunch at Lowenbrau, Deutsche Museum.

23    Heidelberg via Ulm and Stuttgart. Saw castle.

24    Train to Mainz—down Rhine to Cologne to

|    | Brussels. |
|----|-----------|
| 25 | Saw bit of Brussels and Antwerp. Night boat to Harwich. |
| 26 | London, Brown's Hotel. |
| 27 | Helen Nicholson with us. [See Appendix A.5, Sir Arthur Nicholson.] Davis Cup tennis matches. |
| 28 | Oxford, lunch with Wylies. Walked to Trout Inn. |
| 29 | Bikes, train to Camden, lunch Burton-on-the-Water, night at Stow-on-the-Wold. |
| 30 | Swells and Slaughters. (See Chapter Twenty-six.) Into London. |
| 31 | Train to Windemere, bus to Dungeon Ghyll in Langdale Valley. |

| *August* | 1 | Climbed Scafell, down to Westdale. |
|----------|---|-----------|
|  | 2 | Over Black Sail Pass, Scarf Gap to Buttermere. Bus to Cockermouth. Train to Penrith and Glasgow. |
|  | 3 | Sailed from Greenock on *Duchess of York*. |
|  | 4 | Deck tennis every day. |
|  | 7 | Reached Belle Isle—lots of ice. |
|  | 8 | Up gulf and into river at night. |
|  | 9 | Quebec in the morning and on to Montreal. |
|  | 10 | Landed in a.m., train to Plymouth, everyone met us, to Lake. Picnic at Belle Isle. |
|  | 11 | Church in Hebron. |
|  | 14 | Concord for dinner with Mrs. Bancroft. She and Elisabeth (Lilla) back from North Cape cruise. |
|  | 21 | Boston on EM Chase taxes, Longwood tennis. |
|  | 22 | Boston for tennis, rained out. |
|  | 23 | Longwood—National Doubles, dinner in Concord, to Lake. |
|  | 24 | Picnic at Belle Isle. |
|  | 25 | Mary McLane first climb up Cardigan. |
|  | 27 | Peterborough to meet Doc Bell on Shattuck Estate. PM with Bass. |
|  | 28 | Nashua before Judge Bourque on French and Heald. |
|  | 30 | Lake. Pasquaney Associates meeting on Zoning. |
|  | 31 | Lake tennis and swimming. |

| *September* | 1 | Climbed Lafayette and Garfield to Galehead Hut for night. |
|-------------|---|-----------|
|  | 2 | Walked out. |
|  | 4 | Lake to see Asa Shiverick, who is in from Cleveland. |
|  | 6 | Lake. |
|  | 7 | Lake, tennis, and swimming. Picnic at Belle Isle. |

| | | |
|---|---|---|
| | 13 | Clin died in Concord [Judge's brother]. Went to Concord to see Dot. |
| | 15 | Milford for Clin's funeral. |
| | 17 | Boston. Dinner at Plaza with Charles and Elisabeth and to see *Macbeth*. |
| | 21 | Concord tennis. |
| | 25 | Washington with FC Carpenter on tax case. |
| | 26 | All-day conference on tax case, then to New York City. |
| | 27 | Day train to Boston and home. |
| | 28 | Left children at Lake. To Sugar Hill for opening of St. Mary's School. |
| | 29 | In to see ruins of Ravine Camp at Moosilauke, which burned down. |
| *October* | 1 | Boston on EM Chase tax case. *Porgy and Bess*. |
| | 3 | Boston on Colonial Mining with Sortwells. |
| | 5 | Peterborough for tennis and dinner. |
| | 7 | Laconia. |
| | 11 | Train to Franklin and to lake. |
| | 12 | Moosilauke and Hanover for Bates game. |
| | 13 | Climbed Stinson. |
| | 16 | Nashua and Boston on Sussman case. |
| | 17 | Presided at NH Bar Association meeting. |
| | 18 | Boston on EM Chase tax case. |
| | 19 | SPS trustees' meeting in Concord. |
| | 21 | Nashua on Bean v. Quirin. |
| | 23 | Keene to see Bell on Brahm case. Hanover. |
| | 24 | Hanover for trustees' meeting. |
| | 25 | Ralph Davis and I to Concord to see Page on Bean v. Quirin. |
| | 26 | Picked up Elisabeth at Concord Academy, saw Malcolm play Fessenden, Dartmouth 14, Harvard 6 game, dinner at Plaza. |
| | 29 | Hanover, DOC, met with Cabin and Trail. |
| *November* | 3 | Hanover to take Blanche and new baby. |
| | 4 | Derry to vote Nutfield Savings Bank liquidation. |
| | 7 | Hanover to see Mrs. Natt. Emerson. Keene on Brahm case. |
| | 9 | Milford for Gen. Kaley funeral. Concord for League of Nations Association dinner. |
| | 10 | Climbed Crotchet Mountain. |
| | 11 | Took Mrs. Bancroft to Boston to see *Romeo and Juliet*. |

| | |
|---|---|
| 12 | Fitchburg in a.m. on Paper Co. case. |
| 16 | Hanover. |
| 17 | Dartmouth Outing Club meeting. Drove Elisabeth back to Concord, Mass., in hard snowstorm. |
| 18 | Motored to Exeter, train to Portland on Babcock Wilcox case for Brown Paper Co. Home. |
| 19 | Noon train to Boston, off to Cleveland. |
| 20 | Cleveland. Good day with Jane and Asa. |
| 21 | Saw Paul Holden on FPC tax case. Also Industrial Rayon people. Night train to New York City. |
| 22 | Met Elisabeth in New York City. Dartmouth Alumni Council meeting, FPC tax case. Saw Lunt and Fontanne in *Taming of the Shrew*. |
| 23 | Princeton for Dartmouth game, lost 26-6 in snowstorm. Dinner at Rainbow Room. |
| 24 | Breakfast at Longchamps. VanGogh exhibit. New Canaan to see Mr. Thayer and Jack and Hazel [Clark—his sister]. Home. |
| 26 | Hanover to see Mrs. Natt Emerson. |
| 29 | Nashua on Tilton Co. receivership. |
| 30 | To Spyglass Farm with Fordy and Peggy Sayre. |

| | | |
|---|---|---|
| *December* | 1 | All-day tramp with JPC and DOC boys scouting for campsites in Jobildunk Ravine. |
| | 2 | Woodsville by train to prove Natt Emerson's will. |
| | 6 | Boston to see Mrs. Curry regarding divorce. Dinner at Sortwells', stay at Ritz. |
| | 7 | Elisabeth in from Concord Academy with two friends for lunch. |
| | 12 | To Hanover with Miss Mansfield on Natt Emerson estate. |
| | 13 | Boston. Charlie Proctor and I lunched with Mr. Parkhurst on Moosilauke. Chase tax case. Rhodes committee for dinner. |
| | 17 | Derry on Nutfield Savings Bank liquidation. |
| | 23 | Boston on Hambleton tax case. |
| | 24 | Concord for Christmas. |
| | 26 | Night train to New York City. |
| | 27 | Met Dan. We saw Hart re sale of Mogollon mine. Saw Javitz and Javitz regarding Amoskeag bankruptcy committee. To Boston. |
| | 30 | Nashua on Emerson v. Bank. Conference Brahm case. |
| | 31 | Spyglass Farm with family. Rowdy Mallory party. |

# TWELVE

# Labor Relations

Judge's law practice grew rapidly in 1919 and kept him busy. As the result of his wartime experience in labor relations, Judge soon acquired a number of clients in this field. In 1919, he was asked to serve as a permanent member of a Textile Industry Arbitration Panel for seven textile companies in Cleveland, Ohio, and six more in New York City. He had been involved with these companies on Army contracts during the war. His membership on the panel took him to New York City many times; on one trip here he met with Samuel Gompers, president of the American Federation of Labor. He also went three times to Cleveland—four days visiting textile shops and garment manufacturing establishments (once dropping off this author, at four years old, to visit Judge's sister-in-law, Jane B. Shiverick, while he worked). Later in November, another three days were spent in Cleveland, and in December five long days were consumed mediating between labor and management. A settlement resulted.

In May 1919, he was offered the job of secretary of the (National) Shipping Board. He turned down the job but did write the wartime "History of the Industrial Service Section of the Quartermaster Corps" for his old wartime boss, Stanley King. In July he had talks with two sons-in-law of R. G. Sullivan about a strike at the "7-20-4"[1] cigar factory in Manchester. Peripherally, Judge spoke about being in Boston for a Felton Company directors' meeting during the Boston police strike, and comments that the city was "in great disorder."

Judge spent a substantial amount of time in 1921 as master or referee. He was appointed receiver in the bankruptcy of Emma Daniels and arranged a sale of Marcelle's shop, all of which took four days. He was a master in *Mayo v. Shattuck*, which took eight days. On one of them, he writes, "Mrs. Shattuck fainted and broke up trial."

Judge served on an arbitration committee with Judge Wagner and Bill O'Brien on a plumbers' strike and made an award; he was on another panel to settle a painters' strike.

Work continued in 1921 on labor problems in Cleveland for the Textile Industry Arbitration Panel. There was an appeal from a referee's decision that necessitated a trip to Cleveland for an all-day wage hearing and later a trip to New York to make the award and write the decision, which called for a 15 percent wage cut, a downsizing from wartime wage scales. This was a forerunner of what was to come in 1922 at Amoskeag.

The Textile Industry Arbitration Panel was active again in 1922. There was an all-day hearing in Judge Mack's office (in New York City) with the Cleveland people concerning wage differentials. Later in Cleveland, stopping on his way back from Texas, Judge spent two long days at hearings. Judge notes that it is "almost impossible to decide either way." In New York City, the arbitrators spent more time trying to arrive at a decision. Everything was quiet until late October, when there was another meeting in New York City on renewal of the labor agreement. Then at the end of the year, Judge was in New York City for an afternoon and evening of hearings and a morning making a wage decision.

Judge kept on with his labor arbitration for the textile industry in 1925, spending about three days in Cleveland on issues involving the right of management to control manufacturing methods.

In June 1926, Judge went to Cleveland on wage hearings in the textile industry. This time he took his five-year-old daughter, Elisabeth (Lilla), with him to visit with Jane Shiverick, his sister-in-law. Judge lectured in Professor Malcolm Keir's labor course at Dartmouth on the Cleveland labor arbitration decision, which had acquired notoriety. Judge and Keir had worked together in Washington on labor matters during the war. Judge also spoke to the Manchester Lions Club and the Nashua Manufacturers Association on the same topic. The passage of time has dimmed the importance of the Cleveland decision.

In 1930, Judge went to Cleveland with the panel for an appeal on a case involving the guaranty fund.

Labor matters intensified in the late spring of 1933, when Judge spent an evening with Ann Weinstock on the shoe strike involving shops in Manchester. On May 19, the Amoskeag Manufacturing Company went out on strike; on May 22, Judge records, "Exciting labor situation. Troops called out tonight. Session with John Barry [commander of the troops?] and [police] Chief Healy, et als. Keeping Gil posted." Judge remained busy on the strikes for the next couple of days, noting on May 24 that things were a little more promising. On the next day, he drove to Lowell to see Nolan, president of the Shoeworkers Protective Union. On the twenty-sixth, Emile Lemelin (later Hillsborough County probate judge) arranged for conferences between the shoe manufacturers and the workers, which continued for the next two days with fair progress. On June 1, three of the shoe companies agreed on a settlement.

In 1934, Judge served on the Minimum Wage Board and had seven days of hearings on the laundry industry.

Judge had a number of labor cases in 1939. One involved the Abbott Worsted Company of Wilton. Another was Waumbec Mills of Manchester. This case took Judge to Washington for arguments before the National Labor Relations Board (NLRB), preparation of an appeal, meeting in Boston with his clients, the Greenspans, to discuss settlement, and early in 1940 arguing the case in Boston before the Circuit Court of Appeals— "heavy day," as Judge described it. Many textile mill managers, having been accustomed to acting independently in hiring and firing, disliked the militant unions and government interference. They were not particularly tolerant of the New Deal labor relations policies. They thought they were right in their actions, although fifty years later those actions seem pretty unjustifiable labor relations.

In 1941, Judge had an NLRB discrimination case in Wilton involving Hillsborough Mills, a woolen mill operated by E. J. Abbott. (See Chapter Eighteen, E. J. Abbott and the Abbott Companies.)

In 1942, Amoskeag-Lawrence Mills was involved with a union election. The Abbott Worsted Company settled its NLRB discrimination case.

Although the New Hampshire Jockey Club was primarily Ralph Davis' and Ken Graf's client, in 1942 Judge assisted them in dealing with some labor problems, including a hearing before the War Labor Board in Boston that resulted in a good settlement, as Judge notes in his diary. Judge also negotiated a labor contract with the CIO for the Abbott Worsted Company in Wilton. Judge had a hearing before the War Labor Board for the Abbott Machine Company. In the following year, Judge made trips to Boston for more hearings before the War Labor Board and to negotiate with the CIO for the two Abbott companies.

In 1947, Judge was busy negotiating a labor contract with the CIO on behalf of G. P. Craft's shoe shop. He later arbitrated a dispute between the Claremont Paper Company and Bemis Bag Company.

Ken Graf represented a number of shoe manufacturers in labor negotiations involving elections, annual contracts, or pension matters. My recollection is that Ken represented the employer group in an industry-wide pension fund.

In the early 1950s, I worked with Monadnock Paper Mills on labor contracts. On one occasion, there was a wage reopening clause at the end of each year of a three-year contract, which the union indicated it wished to exercise. A meeting date was set and the parties assembled. The union national representative from Fitchburg was late in arriving. Rather than waiting, the meeting started and the union outlined its demands, which included a 15 percent wage increase, far above the industry standard and the company's expectations, which were for a 5 percent increase. The company made no response then but listened to the rest of the union demands, many of which were operational and not money oriented. The union national representative arrived, apologized for being late, and indicated he hadn't talked to the union; he asked the local union steward to repeat the union demands, which he did. The national representative then requested that the meeting be adjourned for a half hour so he could meet with his people. When the meeting reconvened, the national representative stated that the local steward had misread his notes and that the demand for a wage increase was supposed to have been 5 percent, and not 15 percent. One can imagine that the national representative at the union meeting had said something like: Look, guys, don't you know that Fitchburg Paper settled for a 4 percent increase, Holyoke got 5.5 percent and they are a very efficient mill. There is just no way that you're going to get 15 percent and Monadnock knows all this. You should be happy with a 5 percent increase.

The company responded they would agree to a 3 percent increase. If the union would change some of the operational rules that the company found burdensome, they might consider a 4 percent increase. It didn't take long for an agreement to be reached.

It is not uncommon to see that the local union people have exaggerated hopes and are not as knowledgeable about industry standards and history as the national representative is.

Bob Raulerson, before joining the McLane firm, had worked for the NLRB and was very informed on labor law matters.

# Note

1. "7-20-4" was the brand name of a popular handmade cigar made by the R. G. Sullivan Cigar Company, which employed some five hundred people at its factory on Canal Street (more recently known as the Indian Head Shoe building). The company also had twenty-eight other plants in the East. The name originated from the street number of its retail store on Elm Street. R. G. Sullivan had three daughters, whose husbands all worked for the company and were prominent citizens, namely, Joseph Epply, James Driscoll, and Joseph Flynn.

## THIRTEEN

# Felton Brush Company

Felton Brush Company was founded sometime before 1847 in Marlborough, Massachusetts.[1] Presumably it was an individual proprietorship of Samuel A. Felton, an old Yankee shoemaker who had to deal with a paucity of brushes in his business and therefore decided to do something about it—make them in his house. There are practically no records of the company until the 1920s, although it is known that the company moved to Manchester in the late 1890s, a time when the textile industry was booming and the shoe shops were rapidly growing, both of which industries needed industrial brushes. During the next ten to fifteen years, the company grew rapidly and supplied the United Shoe Machine Corporation (USMC), headquartered in Beverly, Massachusetts, with many of its brush requirements. The USMC corporate purpose was to sell or lease machinery for manufacturing shoes. Leasing required less capital, and new improved machines could be more quickly exchanged for the old leased machines than owned ones. There was a substantial foreign market for leasing the superseded machines. USMC also controlled practically all the supplies used in shoe manufacture—thread, glues, leather, lasts, and the like. In order to fulfill this plan, USMC acquired an interest in many companies that had developed expertise in some aspect of the shoe business. Thus in 1911, USMC acquired a 52 percent controlling interest from the Felton family. USMC improved management and poured in substantial new capital, thus enabling the company to grow from a regional supplier to a national one with greatly increased sales.

Judge McLane became a director of the company representing the Felton family, now the minority stockholders. J. Briggs Felton, the CEO for many years, and Judge had attended St. Paul's School together in Concord, and were business associates, tennis partners, and social and political friends. Judge mentions in his diary attending meetings of the board in Boston in 1920 and 1921. In the 1930s, the company acquired several other brush companies, such as the Atlanta Brush Company in Georgia, which made brushes for the textile trade. One of the principal products was brushes for cleaning lint from the combing machines. Another acquisition was the Royal Brush Company in Hamilton, Ontario, which had manufactured brushes for the shoe and textile industry in Canada. The third purchase was the Quimby Company in Boston, which made wire brushes.

During the years of split ownership, there was a difference of opinion with respect to dividend payout policy. The minority family members wanted more cash dividends, whereas the USMC wanted to plow the profits back into acquisitions and expansion. The minority were vocal but amicable; they really didn't have control.

In 1947, USMC was faced with a massive lawsuit by the federal government under the Sherman Antitrust Act. The government claimed that USMC was exerting monopolistic practices, controlled the sale and lease of machinery and supplies, dominated the marketplace, and established prices. The lawsuit dragged on for seventeen years, and a court order tied the hands of USMC from purchasing minority interests in its subsidiaries or selling its majority interest. It was prohibited from acquiring any greater interest in the shoe industry for ten years. This prohibition expired in 1974, at which time it purchased the Felton family minority interest, which was represented by Kenneth F. Graf of the McLane law firm.

In the late 1970s, USMC was acquired by the Emhart Corporation, which decided to raise cash to pay for the purchase by selling some ten subsidiaries, including the Felton Brush Company. It was at this time that Dick Godfrey and three other management people decided to purchase the company; they closed the deal on December 30, 1980.

The company's only plant is in Manchester on Lake Avenue, where it employs 220 people. Its product line includes a standard line of brushes, which it sells to supply houses for the janitor trade, et cetera, and a made-to-order division, which makes specialty brushes for the computer industry, brush seals for the automotive industry, and a variety of brushes for the agricultural industry. Some brushes are still made for the shoe shops and repair stores, but shoe manufacturers use far fewer brushes because of changes in methods and materials.

I worked one summer vacation while at Dartmouth in the 1930s in the cost accounting department. I became familiar with the manufacturing process and the materials used, some of which were quite exotic. At that time brushes usually were made from either tropical vegetable fibers, known as Tampico (Mexico), where many of them came from, or animal bristle, mostly pig bristle from China. The farther north in China the bristle came from, the colder the climate and the stiffer the bristle. Siberian pig bristle was the coarsest. It was said that Siberian peasants went into the forests in the spring and collected the pig bristle at the foot of the trees where the wild pigs had rubbed to rid themselves of their winter coats. Human Chinese hair was purchased in queues about three feet in length;

apparently, according to Dick Godfrey, it is still being used in the candy industry to put the indicating swirls on the top of chocolates, to spread sugar on cookies in the bakery business, to mark vitamin pills in pharmaceutical factories, and in the shoe industry to put the final smooth coating on patent leather pumps. The company also bought whale whiskers from the Norwegian whaling fleet. They came in bundles like a hearthside broom and were black and very stiff. They were used to make brushes for the hat industry, principally centered in and around Danbury, Connecticut.

The basic ingredient in felt for a man's hat is the skin of rabbits caught in gigantic roundups in the outback of Australia. The animals were gutted and the pelts baled and shipped to the United States, where they were laid out on a cement floor in the factory basement to be cleaned of the remaining dried flesh. A caustic cleaning agent was used with the whale whisker brush to do a good job; apparently all other brushes had very short lives. It was said that black men were preferred for the job since they had thicker skins than other races.

Another exotic bristle was that of the civet cat from Ethiopia, in Africa. When excited, the civet ejects a musky fluid with a skunklike odor. Surprisingly, the fluid is used in the making of perfume. The civet's fur consists of a very soft bristle (I can't remember what it was used for). Badger hair, which has a split end, makes top-quality men's shaving brushes. In addition to these smaller brushes, large rotary brushes, four feet in diameter, were made for street cleaning trucks, and small typewriter brushes were made for IBM, Underwood, et cetera. Dick Godfrey says the company has drawings and other documents for something like 78,000 different brush applications.

The Felton Brush Company still operates in Manchester on Lake Avenue as an independent company and has been a client of the McLane law firm off and on over the years.

# Note

1. I am greatly indebted to Dick Godfrey, the present principal owner since 1980 and for many years the president and chief executive officer, for sharing with me the history of the company, which he has gleaned from many sources during the fifty-plus years he has had a relationship with the company.

# FOURTEEN

# Public Utilities

In 1919, Judge had the Milford Light and Power Company as a client on a rate case before the Public Utilities Commission (PUC). Apparently the company was not doing too well, because Judge discussed being the receiver for the company with Judge Anderson in Boston, but nothing materialized. In January 1920, Judge spent several days preparing a rate case for Milford Electric Company, which was heard before the PUC. This was a separate company from the Milford Light and Power Company and may have been its successor.

The firm represented the Salmon Falls Manufacturing Company of Somersworth in 1920, primarily a textile manufacturing concern, but its water business was conducted as a separate water company offering water to the public, subject to PUC jurisdiction.

In 1921, Judge represented the Derry Electric Company in a rate proceeding that involved time in Derry, a trip to Boston, a conference with the PUC in Concord, and a settlement meeting—six days in all. Philip Lockwood, in the insurance business (Lockwood-Bodwell Agency), became interested in the Contoocook Telephone Company, which resulted in a series of meetings in April and May, including one with the PUC, but the result is not disclosed.

By 1925, the expansion of railroads had run its course and the less profitable ones were being abandoned. Judge was involved in the abandonment of two railroads. One was the New Boston branch of the Boston & Maine Railroad; the other was the Farmington branch in connection with which Ralph and Judge talked with various town committees about discontinuance of service.

## HUDSON WATER COMPANY

Hudson Water Company, a subsidiary of Consumers Water Company of Portland, Maine, for whom Judge had done some title work in 1912 just after starting the practice of law, issued bonds for the construction of wells, standpipes, and a distribution system, which required PUC approval because it was an expansion of the plant. Sometimes, the company borrowed from the Manchester Savings Bank and secured the loan by a mort-gage of its assets. Later, as is common in the utility industry, the company issued a bond indenture with a trustee to whom was mortgaged all of the company's present and future fixed plant. The bond indenture authorized additional series of bonds to be sold from time to time secured by the mort-gage in accordance with formulae stated in the bond indenture. The PUC authorized the issuance of the bonds. This system greatly simplified the raising of capital by public utilities to expand a plant where the population was growing. Hudson Water Company subsequently became Southern New Hampshire Water Company as it expanded its area of operation, but it remained a subsidiary of Consumers Water Company. It has remained a client since 1919.

## GREENVILLE ELECTRIC LIGHTING COMPANY

The Greenville Electric Lighting Company in Greenville, New Hampshire, was owned by the Taft family. It consisted of power dams and hydro stations as well as a supplemental diesel generating facility. James Chamberlain (Bill) Taft was a fellow Dartmouth alumnus of Judge's. The floods of the late 1930s wiped out one of the hydro plants, and a new hydro plant was built. In addition, a diesel plant was added, but these new facilities were not of sufficient capacity to take the load alone. The size of the town together with surrounding communities did not warrant a substantial installation. There were several textile mills in town in the 1930s that operated with water-power, generating their own electricity. They were not substantial cus-tomers of Greenville. The solution was to scrap the hydro and diesel plants and change to a distribution company with power purchased from Public Service Company of New Hampshire at bulk rates at a lower cost than Greenville could generate. Finally the entire plant was sold to PSNH. The office settled the estates of Mr. and Mrs. Taft. Their son, Robert Taft, was an associate in the McLane office for a couple of years in the 1950s, before he went to practice in Peterborough, where he is still located.

## WILTON TELEPHONE COMPANY

Wilton Telephone Company has been a client since the late 1930s. Elmer Draper was a native of Wilton and came from a large family. His father died when he was quite young and he had to work to help his mother bring up the family. Elmer liked figures and wanted to become an accountant. He went to Boston to attend Bentley College while he held down a job as a meat cutter. Upon completion of his training, he returned to Wilton and became a bookkeeper with the Whiting Company, which had several enterprises, such as a box factory that made boxes for the Whiting Milk Company in Boston, a dairy farm, and a fuel business selling wood left over from the box company. Elmer Draper also worked on the side doing bookkeeping for the Wilton Telephone Company, an independent company with about five hundred phones. During the depression of the 1930s, the Whiting Company went bankrupt and Kenneth Graf became the liquidating agent, thus bringing him into contact with Elmer Draper, to whom he sold the fuel business, which included coal and oil in addition to the wood. At about the same time, Elmer became the principal officer and manager for the Wilton Telephone Company as well as a stockholder. He ran his fuel business from his home. The telephone company then had a manual system and required operators to receive and switch calls twenty-four hours a day, seven days a week. By the mid-1940s, the Guernsey Cattle Club in Peterborough was expanding rapidly and hiring all available female clerical help in the area, with the result that Elmer Draper was hard-pressed to fill his operator requirements. Elmer and his wife took turns at times on the hard-to-fill night shift. There was a bed by the telephone switchboard with an electric light that turned on when the phone rang. Getting a good night's sleep was tough. Finally, to solve his problem, Elmer installed the first automatic dial system in the state of New Hampshire on May 1, 1951.[1]

Elmer obtained quotes on the dial equipment from several manufacturers and arranged bank financing. With this author he visited the Connecting Lines Department at NET&T and obtained information on a new tariff schedule, maintenance costs, and operating procedures. This information was germane to petitions to the PUC for approval of capital expenditures for the installation of a dial system, authorization for the loans, and authorization for an increase in capital, which was subscribed by the existing stockholders. Elmer paid attention to detail, he did the bookkeeping and his wife did the cleaning, and he always paid his bills when due. He expected his customers to do the same and reminded them in a day or so if they were late. The result was that he wrote off practically no bad debts in either the telephone or fuel business. In 1958, he bought an apartment complex, which his wife supervised. They had one son, Stuart, who came into the office after school and filed papers or did other chores. Like his father and mother, he had to be doing something useful.

Now that both Elmer and his wife have long since passed away, Stuart continues the family tradition of running the energy company and the Wilton Telephone Company, of which he is the largest stockholder. The family picked up shares as they became available when the older stockholders died. Elmer worked hard and rarely took a vacation. He was an active Mason and participated in town government on the budget committee.

Elmer's one relaxation was finding a good restaurant and having a "good feed." He knew just about every restaurant within fifty miles of Wilton.

## NEW ENGLAND TELEPHONE
## AND TELEGRAPH COMPANY

The New England Telephone Company has been a client since 1959. Franklin Hollis of the Sulloway law firm in Concord was the state's most experienced public utilities attorney. He represented both the Public Service Company of New Hampshire and the New England Telephone and Telegraph Company. The telephone company apparently thought that there were or might be occasions when the interests of the telephone company might be different from that of Public Service Company of New Hampshire. There might be a conflict-of-interest situation if the same attorney represented both utilities. In order to avoid any such occurrence, the telephone company decided to seek independent counsel, without indicating any lack of confidence in Mr. Hollis' abilities. It hired Kenneth Graf.

Most of the work for the telephone company in the 1960s and 1970s involved rate cases before the New Hampshire Public Utilities Commission. The McLane law firm was responsible for the entire case, preparing testimony and exhibits and presenting the witnesses for the company as well as cross-examining opposition witnesses. The firm also assisted in preparing testimony in the AT&T lawsuit, which resulted in the divestiture of the "Baby Bells."[2] By the mid-1980s, the company's in-house legal department had greatly expanded and took over the rate case work. The McLane firm did some securities work and was involved with employment law issues. As is generally the case with large utilities, they are self-insurers with respect to tort claims arising from the operation of their own motor vehicles. They also self-insure claims against the company by drivers or passengers of other motor vehicles alleging, for instance, that the company was negligent in placing its poles in the public highway, thereby resulting in an accident. For many years, the firm represented the company throughout the state in connection with its tort litigation. In 1990, when the firm was looking for new office space, it was only natural to consider the new NYNEX building (parent of NET&T) and negotiated a lease for the ninth, tenth, eleventh, and twelfth floors.

## MANCHESTER GAS COMPANY
## (LATER ENERGYNORTH, INC.)

In 1970, the firm became involved in a proxy fight for control of the Manchester Gas Company representing holders of the company's common stock who were disaffected because of a loss of confidence in the president and the CEO. The firm's clients prevailed in the proxy fight, resulting in the office becoming general counsel to the Manchester Gas Company. The legal work involved rate cases before the PUC and securities matters. As the result of several years of discussions, in the 1980s Manchester Gas Company and Gas Service, Inc., supplying the Nashua and Laconia areas, became subsidiaries of a new publicly traded holding company, EnergyNorth, Inc., through a statutory share exchange. A few years later a similar transaction was negotiated with Concord Natural Gas Corporation. In 1987 the three separate subsidiaries were merged into a single, more efficient natural gas distribution utility, and a separate retail propane subsidiary was created by combining the retail propane operations of each of the three utilities.

# Notes

1. Fortunately, the NET&T Company maintained a Connecting Lines Department to provide technical assistance to the independent companies to ensure that they operated efficiently and remained independent. The NET&T Company realized that the Public Utilities Commission would exert tremendous pressure on NET&T to take over an independent if it wasn't providing satisfactory service. NET&T had more urgent uses for its available capital.

2. The American Telephone & Telegraph Company (AT&T) grew into a giant holding company by becoming the owner of all or part of the stock of many operating companies and controlled a majority of the telephone business in thecUnited States. The Company was highly successful, but its regulated monopoly power was seen as a detriment to free competition and lower consumer costs. The federal government, under its antitrust powers, instituted suit to break up the AT&T monopoly. Eventually, a consent decree was agreed to by the parties and approved by the court, which broke up AT&T into a number of separate companies with stipulated territories and powers. These separate companies became known as the "Baby Bells." New Hampshire is served by the New England Telephone Company, which covers all of New England and is a subsidiary of NYNEX, one of the Baby Bells. NYNEX also includes New York Telephone Company, which serves the metropolitan New York area. The Baby Bells are highly competitive and offer a wide range of communication services, such as local and toll telephone, mobil phone (wireless), cable TV, et cetera.

# FIFTEEN

# Manchester Savings Bank, Bankeast, Walter Parker, and Norwin S. Bean

Judge became a trustee of the Manchester Savings Bank in 1923 when he was in his late thirties, had been in law practice for over ten years, and had established a reputation for being an able lawyer. It may have been that the bank wanted a new legal affiliation. In addition to his legal abilities, Judge had many political connections either through his father, who had been governor, or through his affiliation with the Progressive Republicans, such as former Governor Robert P. Bass and John Winant, who was active in the house of representatives and the state senate. These factors may not have been lost on Walter Parker, the CEO and treasurer of the bank, who was a fellow alumnus of Dartmouth. In any event Mr. Parker invited Judge to become a director of the bank; thereafter, he did much legal work for the bank and Mr. Parker personally.

The Manchester Savings Bank was a mutual state-chartered savings bank founded in the 1840s. Mutual savings banks were intended to encourage thrift and the accumulation of capital by the ordinary man in a rapidly expanding but capital-poor economy. Because it was a mutual bank, it had no stockholders; the surplus, in theory, belonged to the depositors. Its investments were regulated by statute. The bank commissioner had regulatory oversight. Most of its investments were in local residential mortgages or in marketable securities included in the bank commissioner's "Legal List," which was generally made up of high-rated corporate first mortgage bonds, preferred stock with little or no senior debt, and common stock with a proven dividend record and no debt. Most of its depositors were local individuals, not corporations. There were other mutual savings banks in Manchester: Amoskeag (the largest) and Merchants. Until about 1950, neither mutual savings banks nor mutual insurance companies were subject to federal income tax. Each of the mutual savings banks organized a national bank and owned no more than 25 percent of the national bank stock as limited by statute. The savings bank, with its larger asset base, usually owned the bank building and leased a portion of the banking floor to the national bank, so that the national bank was located on one side of the banking floor and the savings bank on the other side. The national banks were regulated by various agencies of the federal government. They maintained demand deposits (checking accounts) for individuals and corporations and made commercial loans, both of which were forbidden to the savings banks.

The trustees met once or twice a month to vote on loan applications, appraise the value of the homes being mortgaged,[1] approve the purchase and sale of securities, and review the list of delinquent accounts. Prior to 1950, the Manchester Savings Bank had no independent auditor, so the trustees periodically counted the securities in the bank vault. The McLane law firm did the legal work for the bank such as real estate title opinions after searching records at the Registries of Deeds, preparing the loan documents, attending closings, and making the loan disbursements. This work fell on Miss Mansfield or an associate, such as George Nelson before the war.

In 1894 Walter Parker (see the section on Walter M. Parker later in this chapter) succeeded his father, Nathan Parker, as treasurer and CEO of both the Manchester Savings Bank and the Manchester National Bank. After Judge joined the board in 1923, the bank and Walter Parker became increasingly important clients. After Mr. Parker's unexpected death in 1927, Judge spent a substantial amount of time finding executives to fill Walter Parker's shoes in the two banks. Ed Stearns at the Manchester National Bank succeeded Parker. Norwin S. Bean became treasurer and CEO of the Manchester Savings Bank. Judge recommended both men after he had consulted with Mrs. Parker, who owned a substantial amount of the national bank stock.

Norwin S. Bean was born and raised in Manchester, graduated from MIT, and became a federal bank examiner in the New England area (see the section on Norwin S. Bean later in this chapter). In 1928, Judge worked on the Walter Parker estate, preparing the probate inventory and valuation of the estate assets, preparing the federal estate tax and income tax returns, and discussing matters relating to the Walter Parker estate with Mrs. Parker and her daughter, Charlotte Milne. Judge had a conference with his friend Jim Ivins,[2] a tax practitioner in Washington, on some issues dealing with the Parker federal estate tax return.

In 1929, Judge was involved with distributions, taxes, and investments for the estate. Mrs. Christine Parker was very ill in a Boston hospital for about a week in October. Judge visited her on October 23, when she was recovering, but she died suddenly the next day, October 24, just five days before the stock market crash on October 29, 1929. Ten days of entries include trips to Washington and another conference with Judge's law friend

Jim Ivins. Judge also went to Scituate, Massachusetts, where I assume the Parkers had a summer home.

Norwin S. Bean, treasurer and CEO of the Manchester Savings Bank, came to see Judge on May 17, 1932, to report the defalcation of one of the bank officers. Both went immediately to Concord to report to Governor Winant and bank commissioner Rand. Judge and others in the office spent a considerable amount of time investigating what had happened and recuperating losses. Mr. Bean, although in no way implicated, pledged his personal assets to keep the bank free from any loss. It was also discovered that the culprit had an active brokerage account with a prominent local broker who had connections with Manchester Savings Bank. The broker should have been suspicious of the account activity and size, knowing the salary and the bank position of his customer. When confronted with the facts, the broker executed a guaranty to hold the bank harmless. The entire affair was presented to the board, which approved the action taken.

In 1947 Judge was elected president, tantamount to chairman, of the Manchester Savings Bank. The CEO of savings banks was traditionally the treasurer. The bank board met, if I remember correctly, biweekly or monthly Monday mornings at nine o'clock. George Nelson, an associate, had done much of the bank legal work before the war, consisting largely of completing residential home mortgages by searching the title, preparing a title opinion, preparing the mortgage deed and promissory note, attending the closing, and disbursing funds. Miss Mansfield replaced Nelson and his duties. After the war I took over from her. Earl Dearborn was hired to do this work in the McLane office. He became in-house counsel to the bank and handled the routine residential mortgage business, leaving the McLane firm to deal with the more complicated commercial, industrial, and participation loans, a new area for bank investments.

In 1949, Judge negotiated the purchase of the vacant Summerfield store on the west side of Elm Street practically next to the bank's old, narrow, and overcrowded banking quarters at the corner of Market and Elm Streets (the site in 1992 of the NYNEX building and the McLane law firm offices).

Congress passed legislation in 1950 imposing an income tax on mutual institutions, which, since the passage of the income tax in 1913, had escaped taxation. The new tax law applied to both mutual insurance companies (National Life of Vermont) and mutual savings banks (Manchester Savings Bank). Up to this time the Manchester Savings Bank had never had an outside independent auditor. It filed no tax returns, and it was audited by federal and state banking agencies. Now, however, because of the complexities of the income tax law, the bank engaged James A. Shanahan & Company to help. The bank had a substantial portfolio of investments of marketable securities, both equities and fixed-income securities, which had been acquired over the years. Because the bank had never been subject to income tax, it had never kept or computed figures for determining the "tax cost basis." This now became very important, because any gains realized after the effective date of the act would be subject to tax. Any losses could be offset against income or future capital gains. Therefore, it was important to identify the gains and sell those securities before the effective date of the act to realize the gains free of tax. The bank also wanted to retain the securities with losses for future use.

Some mutual banks, overwhelmed by the analysis process, either sold their entire portfolio or retained it, in either event to their disadvantage. I well remember spending many a day, evening, and weekend with CPA Jim Shanahan, Jr., in the dusty basement of the bank in the old Summerfield building poring over the musty ledger records of the bank to arrive at the tax cost basis for all of the bank's current holdings, including the entire history of that security. I and some bank personnel attended a three-day seminar in New York City on the implications of the act.

A typical transaction ran as follows. Many years ago, say 1920, the bank purchased a first mortgage, 10 percent, twenty-year bond of, say, the Louisville and Nashville Railroad at a time when the railroads were at the height of their financial success. A first mortgage bond was the most conservative and prudent investment possible. If the purchase was made prior to March 1, 1913, the date when the income tax became effective, the value as of that date had to be determined, since prior gains or losses were disregarded. If the purchase was subsequent to that date, the purchase price determined the tax cost basis.

In the depression years of the 1930s, many railroads defaulted on their obligations. Special legislation was passed, enabling them to reorganize their debts, under plans approved by the bankruptcy courts. In our case, let us assume that for each defaulted $1,000 first mortgage, 10 percent bond, the holder was issued in its place a $500, 5 percent income bond (interest payable only if earned), $250 of 6 percent preferred stock, and $250 of common stock. The IRS issued rulings stating the percent value of the tax cost basis to be assigned to each new security issued in the tax-free exchange. Thus, 60 percent might be the value attributed to the income bond—30 percent to the preferred stock and 10 percent to the common stock. These figures were obtained from IRS publications or the Commerce Clearing House (CCH) Capital Gains Tax Service and were applied to the original tax cost basis to determine the tax cost basis of the securities still retained. It was possible once all these tax cost basis figures were obtained to recommend to the bank the securities with gains that they should sell before the effective date of the act. Some securities with gains that were sold were repurchased with a new stepped-up tax cost basis. Securities having losses were retained to offset gains in future tax years.

The Manchester Savings Bank had been a member of the Savings Bank Association, which for several years maintained an insurance fund to protect depositors from loss, but the fund was very small and would provide no help in the event of major losses. The Federal Deposit Insurance Corporation (FDIC) had been recently established and in 1953 was soliciting memberships from the savings banks. After considerable discussion the Manchester Savings Bank joined, as did most banks.

The Manchester Savings Bank took a hard look at where it was going and in 1954 hired the McKinley Company to do a professional survey of the bank and its operations. Mr. Bean, the treasurer and CEO, was getting along in years but had made no plans for retirement. A small group of the board met privately for dinner to discuss plans for Mr. Bean's retirement, followed by a lengthy discussion by the entire board. The result was to encourage Mr. Bean to make a definitive plan for his retirement and to start the search process for a successor. In the meantime, the directors hired Ezekiel Straw from the Amoskeag Bank as a junior executive. Ezekiel had a strong Manchester background (his forebears had been agents or key employees for the Amoskeag Manufacturing Company for one hundred years). He was a Dartmouth graduate and a popular community leader. In the summer, the bank made contact with Charles Nims, another Dartmouth grad and banker, then head of a bank in southern Massachusetts. In December, Charlie Nims was elected executive vice president of the bank and understudy to Mr. Bean, who had made his retirement plans.

The Manchester Savings Bank actively pursued a new bank site in 1955 and negotiated with Maurice Brams for his building on the corner of Spring and Elm Streets. The bank also wanted to acquire from the city the adjacent old Spring Street school, which was no longer in use. Under the city charter, surplus property had to be sold at public auction. Some speculators, knowing of the bank's interest in the property, bought it. The bank was compelled to buy it at a far greater price than the appraised value. The bank, in anticipation of playing a more aggressive role in banking, greatly expanded the number and role of incorporators by including many community leaders and keeping them informed of the bank's plans and general economic conditions.

As the plans for the new building went forward, there were increasing differences between the two banks. The national bank did not want to put up any of its own money and be an owner, only a lessee; it did not want to run the safe deposit business, which it had run in the old building, so the savings bank took on that task; and it was not interested in consumer loans, normally the province of national banks and forbidden to the savings bank. The savings bank wanted a full-service facility. The national bank didn't care. The two banks were competing with each other, as were savings and national banks in general; normally the savings bank had time deposits and specialized in mortgage lending whereas the national bank took demand deposits (checking accounts) and made short-term loans. Savings banks introduced what were known as NOW (negotiable order of withdrawal) accounts so they could have demand deposits and checking accounts; the national banks sought time deposits (CDs).

In 1956, Judge led the effort to bring the Manchester Savings and National Banks together operationally in anticipation of a new bank building. The existing CEOs, Norwin S. Bean and Edward Stearns, were approaching retirement. In July a plan seemed to have been approved looking to merge the CEO positions of each bank, but Mr. Stearns of the national bank failed to resign as contemplated. However, by the end of July, Messrs. Bean and Stearns became chairmen of their respective boards, and Charles Nims became president and CEO of both banks. The Manchester Savings Bank owned about 25 percent of the stock of the national bank, so it was in a position of considerable influence. Charlotte Parker Milne owned or controlled a large block of the national bank stock, which she had inherited from her father, Walter Parker, who had been CEO of both banks, and which she voted with the Manchester Savings Bank interests.

The national bank owned the Manchester Trust Company, which was state chartered in 1891 with broad banking powers and which operated a small trust division with relatively few accounts. The national bank was not at all aggressive about promoting the trust business; however, the savings bank felt that a strong trust operation was essential for a full-service bank.

In December 1967, the banks negotiated for the exchange of the stock of the Manchester National Bank owned by the savings bank for the stock of the Manchester Trust Company owned by the national bank with a cash payment to make the transaction equal. The national bank was glad to get rid of the savings bank as a stockholder because it wielded considerable influence. The savings bank now owned a state-chartered bank with much broader banking powers than the mutual savings bank had. In February 1968, the savings bank decided to explore the feasibility of converting the savings bank, with deposits of $121 million, into the trust company because of the vastly greater powers of the trust company.

The savings bank had accumulated a substantial surplus, 10 percent of its deposits. The question arose as to who was entitled to it. A mutual savings bank has no stockholders; generally the depositors are entitled to receive the surplus on liquidation. Then the question arises, What depositors—the depositors on the liquidation date? Was there to be a time-waited computation to allow for depositors who held for a long time frame? It was decided, based on practicality and on what precedence there was, to use a specific cutoff date—July 31, 1968. It became very important to keep that date a secret so people would not deposit moneys just prior to the cutoff date in order to share in the windfall distribution of the surplus. Only certain officers and employees of the bank were informed; likewise only a limited number of consulting attorneys and accountants were informed, and neither they nor their families were permitted to participate in the distribution of surplus. As it turned out, there were no leaks.

There was one problem: The New Hampshire statutes provided that a savings bank could own no more than 25 percent of another bank, and the bank commissioner moved to order the savings bank to divest itself of 75 percent of the trust company stock, which had a fair market value of about $375,000. The bank obviously did not want to lose control, so it looked for a "white horse" and found one in the Norwin S. and Elizabeth N. Bean Foundation, with assets of around $5 million, which had been created by Norwin Bean, former head of the savings bank, who died in 1958. The trustees of the Bean Foundation were also trustees of the savings bank and had been personal friends of Mr. Bean for many years. In December 1968, the savings bank and the Bean trustees agreed that the foundation would purchase 350 shares (75 percent) of the trust company for cash at its fair market value with an option to the bank to repurchase the stock for cash prior to December 31, 1972, at its then fair market value, by which time the Plan of Merger should be completed.

The Plan of Merger involved the following steps:

1. Savings bank (MSB) transfers all of its assets (except the trust company (MTC) stock and cash to purchase Foundation's trust company (MTC) stock) to Trust.

2. MSB then owns 125 shares of MTC and has option to acquire foundation 375 shares, which it exercises, or total of 500 shares (all).

3. MSB transfers to Holding Corporation (HC), recently formed, its only asset, namely 500 shares of MTC stock, in exchange for 236,146 shares of HC stock, being all of the HC stock.

4. MSB transfers to a Voting Trust (VT) the 236,146 shares of HC stock in exchange for 236,146 Certificates of Beneficial Interest (VTC) in the VT. (Note: the Voting Trust, which had a life of ten years, prevented anyone from raiding or buying up substantial amounts of the stock to gain control of the trust company to the possible detriment of the holders of the VTCs, because the only securities traded were the VTC. The stock in the MTC was owned by the HC, which was controlled by the VT.)

5. MSB distributed the 236,146 VTC to its depositors at the rate of one VTC for each $500 of deposit plus scrip for fractional shares

for amounts not divisible by 500. The scrip, which had a short life, was pooled through an agent to make whole shares or sold to realize cash for stockholders wanting to sell their fractional shares for cash.

6. At the expiration of the ten-year life of the Voting Trust, stock in the Trust company was issued, one for one, to the holders of the Voting Trust Certificates, which then became worthless.

The result was that the depositors owned the VTC in the VT, which owned 100 percent of the stock of the trust company, which in turn owned the assets of the old Manchester Savings Bank. The value of the VTC was equivalent to a 10 percent dividend on the individual's savings bank deposit. The VTC were listed on a stock exchange and were transferable. Initially there were a huge number of holders of VTCs, but many of the small accounts were bought out by the trust company on favorable terms, thus reducing the cost of servicing them.

The petition to the New Hampshire Superior Court requesting approval of the proposed merger between the Manchester Savings Bank and the Manchester Trust Company was filed August 16, 1968, and was referred to a master, Arthur Nighswander. He submitted his report on August 7, 1969, after several days of hearings in March 1969 at which the New Hampshire Association of Savings Banks and the National Association of Savings Banks both appeared in opposition. The master's report found that the proposed union of the two banks "will promote the public convenience and advantage of the institutions, their members, stockholders, and depositors; that the plan of reorganization and distribution was legally adopted and is fair and equitable" except for a minor amendment to provide for cash distribution to school savings depositors. The report of the master was accepted and approved by the superior court and a decree issued on November 26, 1969. The plan was consummated on October 31, 1970, after other regulatory approvals were obtained. The Manchester Trust Company changed its name to the Manchester Corporation. The McLane law firm was heavily involved with these proceedings. There were usually two to four lawyers working on the bank's problems.

During the 1970s, the bank prospered and the VTCs increased in value and paid dividends. Prior to the consummation of the merger, Charlie Nims died suddenly of a heart attack at a relatively young age. He was succeeded by Ezekiel Straw, who in turn died in 1972 from lung cancer, also at an unusually young age. Walter N. DeWitt, who had been with the bank for about ten years, became the new CEO.

In 1974, the Manchester Corporation changed its name to First

Financial Group. In 1976, it started on a plan of expansion by acquiring the Colonial Trust Company in Nashua after considering several alternative banks. As of the end of 1976, the value of a VTC was $11.875. In 1981, First Financial Group changed its name to Bankeast, and in 1982 it merged with the Heritage Banks.

The early 1980s saw considerable expansion within the state. Ski areas were developed with associated second-home developments and condominiums, and residential developments expanded around major cities. Although there was a decline in manufacturing, there was growth in the service sector. Real estate prices escalated and there was considerable speculation in land, bank, and other stocks. Loans were made based on appraisals of fair market value, which in turn was based on comparable sales. Recent comparable sales were at prices that were highly inflated compared to those of five to ten years before and compared to prices five to ten years in the future; however this did not deter anyone from buying and borrowing at the inflated prices. Everybody was euphoric. Bankeast split its stock 3-2 in 1983, 2-1 in 1984, and again in 1985.

According to the New Hampshire bank commissioner reports, gross loans of New Hampshire banks grew rapidly in 1986 and 1987, slowed in 1988, peaked in 1989, and declined in 1990. Equity capital as a percentage of year-end assets declined from 7.50 percent in 1986 to 4.90 percent in 1990, and loan loss reserves increased from less than 1 percent of gross loans in 1986 to 3 percent in 1990.

By 1990, real estate prices were dropping sharply and unsold real estate increased drastically. The value of the security for loans dropped below permitted limits (i.e., appraisals that reported inflated prices) although payments were punctual, creating a technical default in many loans, a condition known as a "performing, nonperforming asset." Bankeast's deposits increased from $429 million in 1986 to $518 million in 1987 and peaked in 1989 at $822 million before dropping to $659 million in 1990. Its net income dropped from positive figures in 1986 and 1987 to losses of $19 million in 1989 and $23 million in 1990, as loan loss reserves were set up to cover nonperforming assets. In October 1990, Bankeast sought protection from some of its pushing creditors by declaring bankruptcy under Chapter 11 of the Bankruptcy Act and filed a Plan of Reorganization in September 1991. On October 10, 1991, Bankeast, along with other insolvent banks, was taken over by the FDIC, which paid the depositors in full. Later the FDIC transferred some of Bankeast's assets to, and some of its liabilities were assumed by, First NH Bank. In effect, FDIC kept the bad assets and tried to salvage what it could. The FDIC reserves built up from the premiums paid by the banks were completely inadequate to pay the depositors. The Federal Government had to appropriate billions of dollars to protect the depositors. First NH Bank also acquired Amoskeag Bank, Bank Meridien of North Hampton, and Nashua Trust Company. The stock of Bankeast and the other banks became worthless.

The McLane law firm acted as general counsel for the bank during its growth and decline. After the takeover by First NH Bank, the firm represented the FDIC and some of its liquidating companies in disposing of former bank assets.

## WALTER M. PARKER

Walter M. Parker was one of Manchester's wealthiest individuals in the early 1900s, a leading banker and businessman.

Walter Parker, born in 1850, was the son of Charlotte and Nathan Parker, chief executive officer of the Manchester National Bank and the Manchester Savings Bank, a mutual bank. He was educated in the Manchester public schools before attending Dartmouth College, from which he graduated in 1871. He immediately went to work at the Manchester National Bank, where his father was president. At that time it was common for a stock-owned national or state-chartered bank and a mutual savings bank to share the same office space and officers. Frequently the mutual savings bank owned a substantial amount of the other bank's stock (the statutory limit was 25 percent).

In 1894, Walter Parker succeeded his father as president of the national bank and soon after as treasurer (chief executive officer) of the Manchester Savings Bank, positions he held for thirty-three years, until his death from pneumonia in 1927, at the age of seventy-six. This period was at the height of Manchester's growth. As might be expected, Mr. Parker was active in the business life of the community and served on many corporate boards of directors, including the following: New Boston Railroad, Suncook Valley Railroad, Concord & Portsmouth Railroad, Concord & Montreal Railroad, Boston & Maine Railroad, Manchester Street Railway, Nashua Manufacturing Company, Methuen Manufacturing Company, Meade-Morrison Corporation, Public Service Company of New Hampshire, New Hampshire Fire Insurance Company, Manchester Safety Deposit & Trust Company, and the Manchester Gas Company, of which he was also treasurer. With respect to nonprofit organizations, he was treasurer of the University of New Hampshire and the Manchester City Library and on the boards of the Currier Gallery of Art and the Manchester Opera House Association. He served on the Manchester School Board, in the state legislature as a Republican in 1883, and as a member of the City Parks and Playground Commission. Mr. Parker was a Congregationalist, a Mason, and a member of the Derryfield Club and the Manchester Country Club.

Mr. Parker came to know Judge McLane perhaps because of their common interest as Dartmouth alumni. Judge became a trustee of the Manchester Savings Bank in 1923 at the behest of Mr. Parker. This was the start of Judge's representing the bank and Mr. Parker personally. Judge made wills for Walter and Christine Parker and prepared their tax returns in the mid-1920s. Walter Parker died, suddenly, in March 1927, and Mrs. Parker immediately sought Judge's help. Judge spent two to three days each month, frequently with Miss Mansfield, on matters relating to the settlement of the estate, with trips to Boston to work with Norman Milne, Mr. Parker's son-in-law, who had married his only child, Charlotte. Judge argued an income tax case, which "succeeded in getting a good settlement." The Parkers owned a substantial Victorian brick house on the southeast corner of Elm and Webster Streets in Manchester, since torn down. They also had a beautiful "showcase" mansion in Auburn located on 1000 acres of extensive farmland with greenhouses and forest property overlooking Lake Massabesic and Manchester with panoramic vistas westerly to the Uncanoonucs. The house was started in the 1890s and finished in 1903.[3]

When Mr. Parker died in 1927, the newspaper reported that he was the largest individual taxpayer in Manchester; of course this did not include the house in Auburn.

Walter and Christine Parker had one daughter, Charlotte, who graduated from Smith College and married Norman Milne, who had an insurance agency and brokerage business in Manchester. After the death of Christine Parker in October 1929, Charlotte and Norman moved into the Auburn house and continued the farm operation. They had three children, Norman Milne, Jr., who with his wife, Ann, lives in Auburn; Madeline Girolomon, now deceased; and Marjorie Winston, who with her husband, Manny, also lives part time in Auburn.

## NORWIN S. BEAN

Norwin S. Bean was born in Manchester in 1873 to Nehemiah and Ruhmah Bean. Nehemiah was the inventor of the first steam fire engine and later became involved in the manufacture of fire engines by the Amoskeag Manufacturing Company and the Manchester Locomotive Works. Norwin Bean graduated from the Massachusetts Institute of Technology in 1894 as an electrical engineer but spent most of his professional life in the field of banking. He was a national bank examiner for New Hampshire from 1906 to 1926. In August 1927 he was elected treasurer (CEO) of the Manchester Savings Bank following the death of Walter Parker. Bean held the position for twenty-five years. In those days, a substantial part of the investment portfolio of a mutual savings bank was in local residential mortgages. Mr. Bean was active in the business community, serving as president of Amoskeag Industries, Inc., and the Manchester Gas Company and as a director of the Public Service Company of New Hampshire and the New Hampshire Fire Insurance Company.

Mr. Bean, particularly in his younger days, was active athletically. He played tennis and golf. He rode horseback with his friend Frank Knox, owner of the *Manchester Union Leader* and at one time Secretary of the Navy. He hiked extensively in the White Mountains and was a supporter of the Boys' Club, the Boy Scouts, and the YMCA. For sixteen years, he served as president of the Family Welfare Society, which later, through merger, became a part of Child & Family Services of New Hampshire. He served as treasurer of the Manchester Community Chest, the Manchester Institute of Arts and Sciences, and the Currier Gallery of Art.

In October 1901, Norwin S. Bean married Elizabeth N. Nichols in the Congregational church in Amherst. For the next half century, they spent the fall and winter at their Manchester home and the spring and summer in Mrs. Bean's colonial brick 1825 ancestral home in Amherst at the corner of the Boston Post Road and Horace Greeley Highway. This house had been purchased by Mrs. Bean's maternal grandfather, Barnabas B. David, a manufacturer of buggy whips in Boston and Amherst. Mr. Bean was able to commute from Amherst by train if he didn't want to drive.

Mrs. Bean was a gracious and quiet lady, participating with Mr. Bean in the cultural events of the two communities. She was interested in her Congregational church, local organizations, the Colonial Dames, and the Daughters of the American Revolution. Mr. and Mrs. Bean had no children.

Mr. Bean died in 1957, leaving a substantial estate, a result of his astute and careful investments. He left his estate in trust for the benefit of Mrs. Bean for her life. Upon her death in 1967, the trustees paid certain charitable bequests. The remainder formed the principal of the Norwin S. and Elizabeth N. Bean Foundation, a permanent charitable trust fund the income from which was to be distributed to institutions operating in Manchester and Amherst for broad charitable purposes. The original trustees were fellow trustees with Mr. Bean at the Manchester Savings Bank. Judge McLane drafted the document and was an original trustee; however, he had suffered a stroke prior to Mrs. Bean's death and was unable to serve as a trustee of the charitable trust. His place was filled by this author on petition of the trustees and appointment by the judge of probate. Subsequently, guidelines approved by the director of charitable trusts and the judge of probate were adopted, which provided for two senior trustees and three term trustees; the latter serve a three-year term plus a year of "training" and a year as "trustee emeritus." There must always be an Amherst trustee, two Manchester trustees, and at least one female trustee.

The foundation started out in 1968 with approximately $4 million, of which $3 million originated with Mr. Bean and $1 million as the residue of Mrs. Bean's estate. During the first thirteen years ending December 1979, the foundation distributed over $2.5 million of income to charitable organizations. This is described in the report "The Norwin S. and Elizabeth N. Bean Foundation: The First Thirteen Years," published in 1980, which was distributed to libraries and public officials as well as many charitable organizations. A similar report, "The Norwin S. and Elizabeth N. Bean Foundation: A Ten-Year Report 1980–1989," shows the foundation assets increased to $8.3 million by the end of 1989 and a distribution during the decade of over $4 million in income. As of the end of 1994, the assets further increased to over $10 million. The books and records of the foundation are maintained by the McLane law firm; the foundation is an Affiliated Trust of the New Hampshire Charitable Fund, which functions as the foundation's secretary with respect to grant-making activities, investigating applications, making recommendations, attending all meetings of the trustees, and carrying out the decisions made. The trustees retain investment control and over the years have utilized several different investment advisers.

## Notes

1. Frequently on Saturdays or Sundays, one or more of the trustees would walk around the city to inspect the properties that were to be voted upon and make a "sidewalk" appraisal.

2. Ivins had successfully represented the Coyle Concord Oil Company interests in the IRS 1922 tax case decided in 1929.

3. About a third of the house was taken down in the 1950s to save on taxes. The house was sold to Edward Socha, a local builder, about 1983, after Charlotte Milne's death, and burned down in 1984. It was subsequently determined to have been arson to collect about $1 million of insurance. Edward Socha went to prison. In 1991 additional persons were scheduled to be tried as accomplices. Norman Milne, Jr., and his sister, Marjorie Winston, built houses on remaining land, taking advantage of the spectacular location with views over Lake Massabesic to the west to the Uncanoonuc mountains and beyond.

# SIXTEEN

# Merrimack River Savings Bank

The big news in Manchester in 1930 following the stock market crash of October 1929 was the closure of the Merrimack River Savings Bank on Monday, June 9, by order of the superior court. The crisis started on Saturday, June 7, when Judge met with Attorney General Ralph Davis and bank commissioner Arthur Dole, who believed the bank to be insolvent. They continued their review on Sunday. The first thing on Monday morning, the ninth, the bank was closed so that no funds could be withdrawn. Judge records, "Spent hectic day on closing Merrimack River Savings Bank." Presumably, on Saturday, a petition had been prepared and filed by special arrangement in superior court accompanied by affidavits alleging the insolvency of the bank. The petition requested that the bank be closed, that no withdrawals be permitted, and that present management cease all activity with respect to the bank. The court probably issued an ex party order after a hearing either Saturday or Sunday with the petitioner, the bank commissioner. John Carleton was appointed by Governor Charles Tobey to be counsel to the bank commissioner. (Although not mentioned in Judge's diary, Winthrop Wadleigh, an assistant attorney general, went to Colorado with someone from the bank commissioner's office to locate and appraise the land involved in some of the bank's mortgage loans.)

Later, Judge had a session with Ralph Davis and John Carleton about bank affairs. On June 26, Judge notes, "Arranged to be appointed liquidating agent of Merrimack River Savings Bank." This probably meant conferences with the bank commissioner and his attorney (Carleton), the attorney general (Davis), the governor (Tobey), and the court. After full days on the thirtieth and on July 3, the diary notes that Judge Sawyer "ordered immediate liquidation and I am appointed liquidating agent." On July 10, Judge records, "Preparing to sue Hale for three million dollars." The next day he writes, "Brought suit against Hale and made attachments." On July 17, Hale's diaries were found. On the eighteenth, Judge went to Keene on an entirely different matter. Summer intern Ken Graf drove him. In 1990 when this author interviewed Ken about his recollections of his first experiences in the office, Ken recalled driving Judge to Keene so that Judge could read the just-found Hale diaries, which contained some very damaging evidence against Hale.

It was customary in the New Hampshire banking world at that time for a mutual savings bank, which was subject to state regulation, to form a national bank, subject to federal regulation, and to own 25 percent (statutory maximum) of its stock and share office space. The mutual savings bank was limited in its investments, which were primarily real estate mortgages. Its customers had passbook savings accounts. The national bank could accept time deposits and provide checking accounts and invest in a much more liberalized way, that is commercial loans, et cetera. As of June 30, 1929, the Merrimack River Savings Bank owned 907 shares of the stock of the First National Bank (of Manchester), which had a book value of $90,000.[1]

Judge notes on August 12, "Working on sale of National Bank stock"; August 13, "Session with Judge Sawyer and bankers on First National Bank stock"; August 14, "More rowing on First National Bank stock, evening at bank"; August 15, "To Judge Sawyer on Bank"; August 17, "Night train to New York with Arthur Dole (Bank Commissioner)"; August 18, "Met Gibson[2] at New York Trust Company about bank stock." More time was spent on bank matters during the rest of August.

In early September, Judge saw Judge Sawyer and Dole. He notes on the thirteenth, "Long session with Judges of Superior Court on bank matters"; on the eighteenth, "Governor Tobey and Council demand Dole's resignation as Bank Commissioner" for failure to properly supervise the Merrimack River Savings Bank; on the nineteenth, "John and I up to see Arthur Dole"; on the twenty-second, "Saw Tobey on Dole matter"; and on the twenty-fourth, "Dole resigns as Bank Commissioner." On September 26, John Sullivan (Democrat) was named the new bank commissioner by Governor Tobey (Republican). Presumably this would take the heat off the Republicans. Judge went to Concord on October 3 to see Sullivan and on the sixth notes, "Hot session with Judge Hunt[3] about his withdrawal of deposits at Merrimack River Bank." On the ninth, Judge had a "hectic day selling bonds of Merrimack River"—part of the liquidation of the bank's assets. The next day John Sullivan and Judge called on Roman Catholic Bishop Guertin to let him know what was going to happen to the Church's substantial deposits. By this time, a reasonable estimate had been made of the expected recovery from the liquidation of the assets and the extent of liabilities. Thus a preliminary figure of the liquidating dividends could be made to large depositors. Ultimately, the bank paid out approximately seventy-five cents on the dollar. John Carleton went to Tennessee for two weeks in early October, but the purpose is not stated; it could very well have been to check on bank assets. Judge spent most of the fifteenth and sixteenth on bank affairs and the seventeenth in Boston with Gibson and

Howard on the sale of the national bank stock. He notes that the twentieth was the last day for proving claims; he held a long conference in preparation for Hale's trial. Judge sold the bank's municipal bonds to raise cash, anticipating that a liquidating dividend would soon be paid. There was a lot of bank work on the twenty-eighth and twenty-ninth, and on the thirtieth the court issued an order to pay a 16 1/3 percent cash dividend to depositors. This was just before the gubernatorial election. Judge comments that Noone, the Democratic candidate, was making the connection of the McLane law firm to the bank his main issue; however, it availed him naught; Winant won by a whopping 20,000 votes. (The country generally, however, was strongly Democratic in 1930, notes Judge.)

The First National Bank stock issue got hot again. Judge notes that on November 12 and following, "All day with Sullivan and Wyman [Louis Wyman, probably representing Gibson] on proposed sale"; "Still at bank stock sale"; "On bank sale. Concord with Wyman to see Judge Sawyer"; "Sawyer, Young and Matthews[4] here on bank sale"; "Bank stock matter very interesting"; "F. P. Carpenter getting interested in bank stock"[5]; "Mr. Carpenter coming into picture as buyer of bank stock"; "Mr. Carpenter offers $140 for the stock. Working to get it accepted"; November 24, "Sold First National Bank stock to F. P. Carpenter for $140 per share. Glad to get it off my mind."

Judge notes that he spent all day on Hale's motion to get at a safety deposit box (which seems not to have happened). This occurred just before Judge left for a three-week trip west to locate bank property. He left in late November for Denver, where he met the bank's attorney and four people who knew about the bank's real estate holdings. He went to Alamosa, toured the Gibson lands (pretty arid and speculative), then to Saguache and on to Monte Vista. A Homer Holland met them, and arrangements were made for him to be a witness at the Hale trial. They looked at several properties on which the bank had made loans south of Alamosa, took the night train back to Denver to meet a couple of men from Wichita, and spent a day on the Kansas and East Colorado lands on which the bank held mortgages. Judge took an afternoon train via Cheyenne and all the next day through Utah, arriving at Los Angeles, where he looked at property there with their agents, concluding there was a "fair chance of salvage." The next day he "visited the Del Rey Development and the oil field. Session with D-G people. Night train to San Francisco." There he spent the day on land owned by the Winchester Estate Land Company with a group, then took the night train to Seattle. John Carleton had been doing some independent investigation of bank property and joined Judge on the train at Oakland. Judge saw some people in Seattle and Bainbridge Island while John was tracking down some other leads.

On the trip home, they began with the night boat to Vancouver. In the morning, they took the train east up the spectacular Fraser River canyon in British Columbia, through the mountains, stopping at Banff for the day, where they climbed a little mountain near town. They drove up to Lake Louise before catching the train east, spending all night and the next day crossing the wheat fields and flatlands of Alberta and Saskatchewan provinces. John got off at Minot, North Dakota, while Judge continued to Minneapolis, where he spent the day investigating bank property. He was joined again by John for the trip to Chicago, where they caught the *Century* for Boston, arriving on the twenty-first. After Christmas, Judge went to Concord to report to John Sullivan, the new bank commissioner, on the results of the western trip, that is, the current values of the properties compared to their cost, the likelihood of sale or other disposition, and expected cash realization.

The Merrimack River Savings Bank continued to be the major attraction for 1931, particularly the criminal trial of Arthur Hale. Judge and Ralph went to Concord in early January to see Judge Parsons to discuss the trial. Judge recorded spending four days on preparation. There was a long final session with Judge Young the day before the case started on January 27. On the first day, all the defendant's motions were denied and a jury was selected. On the next day Ralph opened and put on his first witness. The case continued four days a week through February with the state resting on March 3 when the defendant started putting on witnesses. Hale took the stand on direct examination for four days and then Ralph went to work on cross-examination, which caused Judge to note that Hale was very evasive. On the thirtieth, "Hale broke badly on cross on Alabama steel trade." The evidence was closed on April 7. Arguments were made the next day. The case went to the jury and a guilty verdict was returned at 10:30 that evening. Quite a victory for Ralph.

Later, Judge worked on bringing suit against the bank directors. He filed the suit in early July. Judge reached settlement agreements with most and collected a substantial amount of additional money for the depositors. Hale was released under bond pending appeal. In September, the court approved another liquidating dividend of 16 2/3 percent.

In the fall, Judge sailed for Los Angeles to search out bank properties; he stopped in Havana for a day; transited the Panama Canal, "Wonderfully interesting"; sailed up the Mexican coast; saw whales; and arrived in San Diego, where he took a day trip to Tijuana and Agua Caliente before continuing to Los Angeles. Several members of the Leighton family, whose family trust Judge managed with a Boston bank, entertained him. He took a deposition in the Peterborough Basket Company[6] case (a separate client unconnected to the bank) and met people in connection with the Merrimack River Savings Bank's real estate.

The Merrimack River Savings Bank business continued to be important in 1932. Arthur Hale appealed his criminal conviction. Judge prepared the brief and Ralph's oral argument, which Ralph gave before the New Hampshire Supreme Court. The court upheld the verdict the day after Ralph resigned as attorney general. In May, Judge prepared for taking depositions in the West for the suit against the directors. In early June, he took the train to Denver, then drove south to Alamosa and through the Gibson lands, taking depositions before a commissioner for a couple of days. Judge returned to Denver, where he held conferences with Dickenson and Gillespie on their promissory notes. Next he traveled to Chicago and the National Republican Convention at the Edgewater Beach Hotel, where Judge was a delegate.

The Merrimack River Savings Bank liquidation continued to take much time in 1933. In March, final settlement on the Hale civil case was reached. In July, Judge started working to get a federal Reconstruction Finance Corporation (RFC) loan to pay liquidating dividends before the assets were liquidated. He had conferences with the bank commissioner, the superior court, and the RFC people in Boston on this matter. Judge also was trying to collect on assets, sell mortgages, and collect from the directors. He notes that he went up to the state prison to take Hale's deposition in connection with the Higgins case.[7] Entries appear in the diary on twenty-six dates during the year.

The banking business was extraordinarily busy in 1934. The liquidation of the Merrimack River Savings Bank continued. Judge went on with his efforts to obtain a loan from the federal RFC. The loan closed in January, the dividend was distributed, and the loan was repaid in May. In June, Judge went to see Judge Sawyer about the firm's fees; he notes "a very discouraging reception." About a month later, Ralph Davis saw Sawyer; Judge says it "was more promising." In August, Judge and John Carleton "had a successful session with Sawyer, CJ." The firm's fees were approved, maybe not as much as submitted but satisfactory enough. Office procedures for recording time and computing bills were extremely unsophisticated compared to the computer-generated billing procedures of today.

An additional liquidating dividend was paid in 1935 and the liquidation proceeded slowly, winding up in 1938 with payment of the final liquidating dividend. All dividends totaled about seventy-five cents on the dollar for depositors. Final assets representing uncashed dividend checks were turned over to the state treasurer, and Judge filed his final account and was discharged on his bond as liquidating agent.

# Notes

1. New Hampshire Bank Commissioner's Report 1929. National banks were subject to federal, not state, regulation.

2. Harvey Gibson was head of Manufacturer's Trust Company in New York and somehow had connections with New Hampshire and the North Conway area, where later he purchased the Eastern Slopes Inn and developed the Mt. Cranmore Ski Area, with its one-of-a-kind skimobile.

3. He probably was a bank director.

4. All superior court judges.

5. Frank P. Carpenter was one of Manchester's wealthiest individuals. He was a client of Judge's on limited matters but obviously not in connection with this transaction.

6. In 1886, John McLane purchased the "Fuller Mill" in Milford for his expanding cabinet business. The Fuller Mill had previously (1849) been the Souhegan Manufacturing Company, a textile operation. In 1890, McLane sold a portion of the Fuller Mill that he didn't need to P. O. Bartlett for a hosiery mill and then built a two-story building on his own land to make boxes for the hosiery mill. The hosiery mill eventually went bankrupt. McLane bought back the property from the trustee in bankruptcy in 1899 and started a basket factory known as Standard Basket Shop, which produced 12,000 baskets a month. In 1904, McLane sold the business to a Mr. Needham, who moved the machinery to the old piano factory in Peterborough and changed the name to Peterborough Basket Company. Later, in the 1950s, when Richard Pierce became the principal owner, the company once again became a client of the office.

7. This was probably a suit against one of the directors.

# SEVENTEEN

# Frank P. Carpenter

Frank P. Carpenter (1845–1938) was born in Manchester but moved to Concord, where he received his secondary school education. He never did attend college. He started his career in Manchester as a flour and grain merchant with J. S. Kidder & Company but soon branched out and acquired a major interest in Amoskeag Paper Company; for a number of years he was its chief executive officer. At some point, he also acquired most of the preferred stock of the Brown Paper Company in Berlin, New Hampshire. Over the years, Mr. Carpenter was a director (and stockholder in most) of the Amoskeag National Bank, the Mechanics Savings Bank, the New Hampshire Fire Insurance Company, the Amoskeag Manufacturing Company, the Burgess Sulphite Fibre Company of Berlin, New Hampshire, and the Boston & Maine Railroad. He was one of the federal trustees for a number of years of the Boston & Maine Railroad stock owned by the New York, New Haven & Hartford Railroad.

In 1915, Dartmouth College conferred on Mr. Carpenter an honorary degree. He gave to the city of Manchester the beautiful public library in memory of his wife, Elnora Blood, whom he married in 1872 and who died in 1911. Elnora was one of the two daughters of Aretas Blood. The library, designed by Edward Tilton of New York, was completed in 1914 at a cost of about $1 million. It followed the popular style of the time, Italian Renaissance, made famous by the well-known firm of McKim, Meade & White, who designed the Boston Public Library.

Frank Carpenter was involved in creating the Currier Gallery of Art. Upon the death of Hannah Currier in 1915, the desires of both Moody Currier, who predeceased his wife in 1898, and Hannah that their home become an art gallery became a reality. The trustees first met in 1917 at the Amoskeag National Bank; Frank P. Carpenter became a trustee. The gallery was incorporated in 1919. The trustees determined to build a new building on the site of the Currier homestead. Prestigious Ralph Adams Cram of the Boston firm of Cram and Ferguson was commissioned to design a suitable structure; however, after twenty-five drawings and two years of deliberations with the trustees, he was discharged in 1922.[2] Within a month, another Boston architect, R. Clipston Sturgis, was invited to develop alternative concepts. The trustees approved them in April 1924 and moved toward a construction contract, but in June Sturgis was advised to stop all work and await further instructions. He was fired in early 1925, for reasons unknown. Later in that year, Frank P. Carpenter became chairman of the building committee. It is not surprising that his architect for the Manchester City Memorial Library, Edward Tilton and his partner Alfred Githens, were asked to prepare drawings, which were accepted. A contractor was chosen in 1927. The building was completed in 1929.

Judge's first client contact with Mr. Carpenter (who was then eighty-two) came in 1927, although they undoubtedly knew each other before that. Frank P. Carpenter and Herman F. Straw sought Judge's opinion about the tax consequences of the receipt of stock of the Amoskeag Corporation contained in an option offered in connection with the 1927 reorganization of the Amoskeag Manufacturing Company (AMC). Judge had numerous dealings before with H. F. Straw, both personally and with the Amoskeag Manufacturing Company, for whom Mr. Straw had been agent for many years. In 1925 AMC had reorganized by creating the Amoskeag Corporation, which acquired most of the stock of AMC in exchange for its stock. In 1927 the Amoskeag Corporation offered to its stockholders the option of receiving, in exchange for each share of its stock, $52 in cash, $40 in 6 percent bonds, and one share of AMC stock. In 1928, Judge wrote opinions on the transactions, presumably for the company's tax returns, and in 1929 did some more work for them, including attending a hearing before the IRS in Boston.

In 1928, Mr. Carpenter gave Dartmouth College $300,000 to build the Carpenter Art Gallery and Library attached to the Baker Library. Although Judge was a trustee of the college at the time, he did not play any known role with Mr. Carpenter in connection with the gift. Judge and Elisabeth visited the newly completed structure while in Hanover for the Winter Carnival and a trustees' meeting in February 1929. In the same year, Judge worked on a lease for the Barton building (a department store located on Elm Street where First NH Bank, formerly Amoskeag National Bank and Amoskeag Savings Bank, is located). The ownership of the building was divided among the Quirin family, Norwin S. Bean, Mr. Carpenter, and possibly others. It is not clear just who Judge's clients were.

In 1931, Mr. Carpenter gave the funds for the construction of the new Manchester Historic Association building on Amherst Street facing Victory Park. The building was also designed by Edward Tilton. Mr. Carpenter was a director of the New Hampshire Fire Insurance Company, then on Hanover Street. That company selected Mr. Tilton as the architect for its building.

In 1932, Mr. Carpenter acquired, at $140 a share, all of the stock in the First National Bank of Manchester, which was owned by the bankrupt

Merrimack River Savings Bank, of which Judge was liquidating agent. In 1929 the bank owned 907 shares; however, it is not clear how many shares Mr. Carpenter bought or whether there were capital changes subsequent to 1929, which would have caused a change in the per-share value in 1933. Assuming Mr. Carpenter bought 907 shares at $140 per share, the purchase price would have been $126,950. In 1938, 251 shares were inventoried in his estate at $60 per-share, or $15,060.

In February 1932, Frank P. Carpenter asked Judge to represent him in connection with his interest in the Meade-Morrison corporate matters. It is assumed that Mr. Carpenter was a substantial investor and that the corporation was in financial difficulty. The diary notes conferences with stockholders, a blocked loan attempt and the inevitability of receivership, and numerous trips to and meetings in Boston. The ultimate outcome is not disclosed.

In 1933, Meade-Morrison matters involved a number of meetings in Boston and in Montreal for the Canadian subsidiary, of which Judge was made a director. The Meade-Morrison Corporation continued to have financial problems in 1934. Mr. Carpenter had a suit against them on which Judge spent a week or more, much of it in Boston, negotiating with attorney Goodhue, counsel for the company. He finally settled in December for $25,000, the amount suggested by the trial judge, McLellan. The Meade-Morrison Corporation and the Canadian Corporation were both listed in 1938 in Mr. Carpenter's estate as worthless. A personal holding company for Mr. Carpenter was formed.

Mr. Carpenter first brought his tax figures to Judge for help in 1933. In the following year, Mr. Carpenter had a problem on the audit of his tax returns for 1932 and 1933 with respect to the allowance of losses he claimed on the sale of his Brown Paper Company stock. (See below, Frank P. Carpenter Tax Case.)

In 1935, Judge did a fair amount of work for Mr. Carpenter, probably Manchester's wealthiest individual and most generous philanthropist. In January, he worked on a mortgage for the Hotel Carpenter, which Mr. Carpenter had built in 1924. Judge also had meetings in Boston on the Meade-Morrison Corporation. In April, Mr. Carpenter came to the office to talk about the Pepperell Company. In May, Judge went to Boston twice on the tax cases for the years 1932–1933, spent more time in June, wrote a brief in August, and in September went to Washington with Mr. Carpenter. They had an all-day conference with the IRS and two more conferences in New York City in November—all on the Brown Paper Company preferred stock sale. Judge also represented Mr. Carpenter's paper mill, Amoskeag Paper Company, in a claim against Fitchburg Paper. The claim continued into 1936. The Brown Paper Company was having financial problems in

*Frank P. Carpenter, 1930*, philanthropist, one of Manchester's prime citizens. Judge's limited client. Credit: Manchester (N.H.) Historic Association Photo Archives.

the middle of the depression. It petitioned the federal court in Portland, Maine, for reorganization under the Bankruptcy Act. Mr. Carpenter, as the largest holder of preferred stock, asked Judge to represent the Preferred Stockholders Committee. Judge attended a number of committee meetings and court sessions in Portland over a period of several years. Judge also represented the Brown Paper Company in a case, which took a couple of days, against Babcock & Wilcox, manufacturer of large industrial equipment and machinery, particularly boilers.

In 1936, Mr. Carpenter was a key director, vice president, and one of the largest stockholders (1,000 shares at $100 per share, next to Public Service Company of New Hampshire and New Hampshire Fire Insurance Company) in Amoskeag Industries, Inc., during its successful effort to purchase all of the Amoskeag Manufacturing Company assets from the referee in bankruptcy and keep those that were useful in Manchester. In September, just prior to the "closing," Judge and Mr. Carpenter had lunch in Boston with Frederick Dumaine, the CEO of the Amoskeag Corporation, the holding company of Amoskeag Manufacturing Company, but the topic discussed is not stated in Judge's diary.

The Brown Paper Company of Berlin, New Hampshire, continued its reorganization efforts in 1937. Judge made a number of trips to Boston, New York, and Montreal for committee and board meetings to discuss various plans, trying to reach a satisfactory agreement among the stockholders, bondholders, and other interested parties. These efforts finally culminated in a meeting in Boston in late November at which all sides were represented and came closer to agreement. Frank P. Carpenter frequently accompanied Judge on trips to meetings. In 1937 Mr. Carpenter's 1934 tax case (not involving the Brown Paper Company preferred stock) was finally settled following a favorable and controlling tax court decision in another case.

The Brown Paper Company continued its reorganization efforts in 1938, the year in which Mr. Carpenter died. Judge made a number of trips to Boston, spending thirteen days at committee and board meetings to discuss various plans, trying to reach a satisfactory agreement among the stockholders, bondholders, and other creditors and draft a reorganization agreement. Judge took depositions in the F. P. Carpenter tax case.

In 1939 Judge, as counsel for the Preferred Stockholders Committee, made numerous trips to Boston and the federal court in Portland for committee hearings, negotiations, and arranging for an RFC financing and SEC securities registration pursuant to the reorganization agreement. Ralph Davis and Judge tried a tax case in the Federal District Court in Concord before Judge Morris involving claimed losses on the sale in 1932 and 1933 of Brown Paper Company preferred stock to F. P. Carpenter's son, Aretas. The court disallowed the loss. The case was appealed and argued in November in Boston before the Circuit Court of Appeals, which upheld the lower court's decision. (See Frank P. Carpenter Tax Case, below.)

In 1940 the Brown Paper Company reorganization plan made headway during the year. In October there was a hearing in Portland on the final decree. Some eighteen days were devoted to this project during the year.

The Brown Paper Company reorganization moved slowly toward completion in 1941, requiring monthly meetings. Judge found to his chagrin that he failed to get adequate fees for all his time because of poor office recordkeeping. He did not have detailed daily time sheets to substantiate his charges. Thus ended Judge's representation of the Preferred Stockholders Committee.

Although Judge's primary contact with the Brown Paper Company was through Mr. Carpenter in connection with the preferred stock, he got to know the management and some of their problems. Because of his extensive knowledge of the oil business through Coyle Concord Oil Company, he was able to provide some advice to the Brown Paper Company about its woodland acreage in Florida acquired for wood pulp production. When oil was discovered in Florida, the company wanted to explore that business. Judge went down with W. R. Brown in 1943 and met Arthur Coyle of the Coyle Concord Oil Company, traveled through the Everglades, visited a Humble Oil Company well, and talked with the Humble Oil people, whom Arthur Coyle introduced to W. R. Brown. Subsequently, Judge was invited to the Brown Paper Company directors' meeting to report on the oil potential of their landholdings. In 1944 Judge worked with the company as it negotiated for oil leases on its Florida land.

Mr. Carpenter was an original trustee of the Currier Gallery of Art in 1918 and was president of the board for a couple of years before his death in 1938. The inventory of his estate shows a Monet *Coast of France* valued at $2,500, which is still held by the family.

Mr. Carpenter died on April 13, 1938, leaving an estate consisting of $100,000 in real estate and $3 million in personal property, of which over $2 million was in stocks. The largest holdings were New Hampshire Fire Insurance Company ($400,000), National Biscuit Company ($346,000),[3] Amoskeag Paper Company ($169,000), and United Fruit ($124,000); the rest was in a diversified group of well-recognized companies.

Mr. Carpenter had two children, Aretas Blood Carpenter and Mary Elizabeth Carpenter Manning, whose lives are covered in Chapter Nine.

## FRANK P. CARPENTER TAX CASE

The case of Manning et al. v. Gagne, 308 Fed. Rep. 2d, 718, was decided on December 29, 1939, by the CCA, First Circuit. Judge represented the appellant, F. P. Carpenter.

The case involved the tax returns of Frank P. Carpenter, deceased, for the years 1932 and 1933, in which losses on the sale of stock of $194,221 and $186,221, respectively, were disallowed by the district court. The judgment was affirmed on appeal.

Frank P. Carpenter had owned 4,000 shares of the 6 percent preferred stock of the Brown Paper Company, paper manufacturer in Berlin, New

Hampshire. The Brown family owned nearly all the common stock and the Carpenter family nearly all the preferred stock; the two families had maintained very close relations for many years.[4] The stock had deteriorated in value from a cost of about $95 a share to $3 a share, and Mr. Carpenter wished to take a loss on his income tax return. Mr. Carpenter wanted his son, Aretas, to have the stock to maintain it in the family.[5] Mr. Carpenter, in early December, "consulted a lawyer"[6] as to a possible method of procedure. He was advised that R. L. Day Company, a reliable brokerage firm in Boston, held weekly auction sales of stock and that a sale might be made through this company. In accordance with the suggestion of counsel, arrangements were made to place 2,000 shares of the Brown Paper Company on sale. Mr. Carpenter and his son went to Boston; Mr. Carpenter made arrangements for the sale and the son left an order to purchase at market the 2,000 shares. The auction was held on December 21 as planned, and Aretas purchased the stock. He received a bill for $6,000, the cost of the stock, and sent his check in payment. He told his father that he had mailed the check, and Mr. Carpenter made out his check for $6,000 payable to Aretas. He left it on Aretas' desk, although Aretas had plenty of funds of his own to cover the purchase.

The same procedure was followed in the sale of an additional 2,000 shares in October 1933, establishing a loss that was claimed on F. P. Carpenter's 1933 return.

The trial court stated: "I find that it was the purpose and intention of Frank P. Carpenter to make a transfer of the stock in question in such a manner as to make it appear that he was entitled to a loss on its sale without transferring it outside the members of his own family and that while in form a sale, in fact, it was a gift from Frank P. Carpenter to his son Aretas B. Carpenter."

The appellate court stated that the trial court's findings were not clearly erroneous and must stand.

## Notes

1. Possibly, Mr. Carpenter acquired the Brown Paper Company preferred stock in exchange for his common stock in the Burgess Sulphite Fibre Company.

2. Aurore Dionne Eaton, *The Currier Gallery of Art, A History*, 1929–1989 (Whitman Press, 1990).

3. I am not sure whether this investment had anything to do with the fact that Mr. Carpenter started business in the 1870s as a flour and grain merchant. His sister-in-law, Emma French, died in 1932, owning $426,000 of NaBisCo stock. This would seem to indicate that this was a popular investment of the times.

4. It is not clear how Mr. Carpenter acquired the Brown preferred stock. One possibility is that Mr. Carpenter owned common stock in another paper mill that the Brown Paper Company wanted to acquire and did so in exchange for the preferred stock. Mr. Carpenter did own the Amoskeag Paper Company in Manchester.

5. The preferred stock may have contained provisions for voting equally with the common stock or exclusively in the event of default in the payment of preferred stock dividends, which would have made retention of the preferred stock valuable.

6. Who the attorney was is not stated.

# EIGHTEEN

# E. J. Abbott and
# the Abbott Companies

Edward J. Abbott was born on June 15, 1884, in Philadelphia, the son of William G. Abbott, a veteran of the Civil War. William was rumored to have been a drummer boy; he was only eleven years old. He may have simply marched in a parade as a drummer boy after the war, which mushroomed into a bigger story.[1] William attended school in Germany and served as a German in the Franco-Prussian War of 1870 and as an American in the Spanish-American War in 1898.

E. J. Abbott attended local schools preparing for college, but family finances dictated a practical training instead.[2] He indentured as an apprentice in the Baldwin Locomotive Works in Philadelphia, where he was paid five cents an hour for a sixty-hour week. He attended Drexel Institute, taking night courses in math and mechanical drawing.[3]

William G. Abbott is believed to have been a principal in a textile "factoring" concern in Philadelphia. A factor solicited orders for a manufacturing concern at prices determined by the mill, then loaned working capital funds to the mill secured by an assignment of the accounts receivable and a general mortgage on all the mill assets. In the business recession of 1907, the Hillsborough Mills of Wilton, New Hampshire, which had a factoring arrangement with the Philadelphia concern of Mr. Abbott, defaulted on its obligations and was taken over by the factor.[4] Wishing to recoup his losses and believing that with proper management there was good money to be made in the textile business, William Abbott acquired a half interest in the mill and moved to Wilton in 1910 with his family. The same recession caused drastic cutbacks at Baldwin Locomotive, resulting in Edward J. Abbott being laid off. He moved to Wilton to help his father run the mill and soon purchased his father's original half interest in the stock. Jacob (Jake) Frederick Brown, a wealthy man, sold his half interest to William Abbott on condition that E. J. would be the principal manager. E. J. familiarized himself with the manufacturing processes and mill operation. Although business at Baldwin subsequently picked up, resulting in a request to E. J. to return, he was then so involved at Hillsborough Mills

that he refused. When William G. Sr. died in 1926, he willed the half interest he had acquired from Brown, one-third to each of his children, William
G. Jr., E. J., and Caroline, a maiden lady who lived in Wilton. Thus,
Edward Abbott, known as "Ned" in the community but as "E. J." in the
shop, wound up with a two-thirds interest; his sister and brother each
owned a one-sixth interest. E. J. became intrigued with textile machinery
technology, which he felt to be quite outdated.

In October 1910, E. J. married Dorothy Delano from Northampton,
Massachusetts (daughter of prominent lawyer Charles Delano), whom he
had met in Wilton while she visited a cousin, Jessica Stuart Swift. E. J. was
so enamored of her that he proposed on their first date. The cousin, Jessica,
whose father was governor of Vermont, put on the wedding at her place in
Middlebury, Vermont. Dorothy bore three sons, James in October 1911,
William in July 1914, and Samuel in August 1915. The marriage soured,
however. Around 1920 they were divorced, E. J. retaining custody of the
three boys. Dorothy moved to Florence, Italy, where she lived with her
twin sister, Marie Donati, for the next fifteen years. Dorothy studied
singing to the point of auditioning at La Scala opera house in Milan. She
returned to the United States in 1933 with the Donati family. Her boys saw
her from time to time at her home in Mount Vernon, New York;
Middlebury, Vermont; or Wilton, New Hampshire. She died in 1972.

E. J., just under forty at the time of his divorce, hired several different
ladies to keep house for the first five years following his divorce. In about
1925 he hired two Irish sisters, Eileen (who started as a sixteen-year-old
high school girl) and Julia Shea, to run the house and take care of the boys.
They remained in his household until E. J.'s marriage in 1940. With good
help at home, E. J. spent his days and many evenings at the mill, which was
within walking distance of the house. Often, after the boys were in bed, he
worked at his drafting table. E. J. participated in the life of the community.
He served on the school board for many years and also on the town finance
committee. He was generous in assisting many town organizations.

The original Hillsborough Mills bought noils and waste from worsted
mills and manufactured yarns to make a line of low-cost products, including horse blankets, which were widely marketed. The mill was not
profitable. E. J. over time successfully changed the production to high-
grade worsted weaving yarns.

The Hillsborough Mills was known in the trade as a "top" mill. It
received raw wool, usually from Australia. In the first stage it was washed
and scoured to remove impurities. In the second stage the wool was carded
and combed to straighten the fibers so they were all parallel. Next, the wool
was gathered into a strand about the thickness of a thumb and was slightly
twisted to hold it together. The wool was now "top" and ready for the next

process, a spinning or yarn mill. There the top would be spun into yarn by a series of processes that would stretch or attenuate the strand and impart more and more twist.

In about 1920, Hillsborough Mills had added spinning frames, so it qualified both as a top mill and a yarn or spinning mill. Two strands could be combined to make a two-ply yarn. Wool yarns were relatively loose, good for sweaters, heavy socks, and sport coats. Worsted yarns were more tightly twisted and wore longer; they were used for men's business suits and trousers. Yarns could be top dyed or yarn dyed.

Originally most of the textile industry was organized along horizontal lines where each mill performed a completely separate function. Ownership was usually separate too, that is, top mill, yarn mill, dye house, and weave mill. In the 1920s, however, there was a move to organize along vertical lines so that the product could be controlled as to quality at all stages of manufacture and also to reduce the cost by eliminating the profit margins at every stage. E. J. was interested in making his production vertical. To do this, Hillsborough had added both a dye house and a spinning division.

One of the first inventions that E. J. patented in the 1920s was a pressure dye kettle. "Top" or yarn was wound onto large metal spools with a perforated central shaft. Each spool was lowered into a large enclosed metal chamber, which was then sealed shut. The dye solution was forced by impeller blades up through the central shaft, out the perforations, and through the yarn. This provided a faster and more even distribution of the dye material through the yarn. The mill had a machine shop that manufactured the dye kettles that E. J. used in his manufacturing. The kettles were also sold to other textile companies.

During the depression of the early 1930s, a local worsted weave mill ceased operations. It was acquired by the town for taxes and then bought by E. J. This now gave him a vertical operation from raw wool to finished product. Because there were relatively few looms, the mill could run small quantities of a particular pattern and guarantee exclusivity to the buyer within a five-hundred-mile radius of his retail store. Abbott Worsted specialized in fine yarns and sold fabrics to the most exclusive stores: Hickey Freeman; Hart, Schaeffer & Marx; Brooks Bros.; et cetera.[5]

E. J.'s brother, William G. Abbott, Jr.—"Uncle Bill," as has been noted—graduated from MIT, then worked for General Electric at Lynn, Massachusetts, until World War I, when he served in the Army as a major in the Chemical Warfare Service. After the war, he joined the family in Wilton and worked at the Hillsborough Mills, of which he was treasurer for many years. Uncle Bill had an inventive streak and perfected a "grease" recovery system for Hillsborough Mills. Raw wool in the first stage, scouring, is washed in a series of baths consisting of warm water and soap to remove from the fleeces the dirt, excrement, and natural body oils of the sheep. The effluent was dumped into the river, where it gummed up the rocks and riverbanks and undoubtedly deprived the fish of oxygen. "Uncle" developed a centrifuge machine that caused the lighter oil or lanolin to rise to the top of the liquor, where it could be easily removed and sold at a profit. Incidentally, the device cleaned up the river.

E. J.'s most famous invention was the traveling spindle winder. In the spinning operation, the yarn is wound onto a bobbin made of a hard wood, usually maple. Because the metal parts are fitted into the wood to guide and control the spinning process, the bobbin is expensive and does not hold much yarn. After the yarn completes the spinning process, it is shipped to the weave mill and may wait a considerable period of time before being used. Therefore, at the end of the spinning process, the bobbins are put on "winders," machines that transfer the yarn from the bobbins to cardboard "cones," which are light in weight and inexpensive. Before the Abbott winder was built, the operator, usually a woman, walked about fifty feet up and down the aisle between rows of winders, pushing a large basket cart on wheels. When she noticed an empty bobbin on the machine, she "doffed" (removed) it, threw it into a bin in her basket, removed a full bobbin from a separate bin, and placed it on the machine. She then found the loose ends of yarn from the full bobbin and the cone and tied them together with a weaver's knot, so the winding process could continue. A cone, sometimes called a "cheese" or "package," contained the contents of some ten or more bobbins.

E. J. observed that the operator walking up and down the aisle pushing the cart consumed time and energy and was unproductive. He reasoned that if Henry Ford could introduce a moving assembly line to the automotive industry, why couldn't he do the same to the textile industry? In the quiet of his own house in the evenings, he worked at his drafting table trying to solve the problems of designing a traveling spindle winder. First, he located the chair for the operator. Then he placed a rail on which a traveling unit holding the full bobbins and empty cones could travel in an ellipse, long enough for the bobbin to be emptied, so that when it came back by the operator, she could doff it and reload with a full bobbin. He next developed an automatic doffer. When the bobbin was empty, the arm on which it had been placed was tripped and popped up, and as it passed a bin, a wiper blade knocked it off into the bin. There was a problem when the operator tried to find the loose ends of the full bobbin and the partly filled cone as they were moving by her on the rail. Sometimes she had to stop the machine. E. J. solved that problem by introducing a vacuum suction tube that wiped over the cone and picked up the loose end. The operator then only had to find the loose end on the new bobbin and feed it into another vacuum tube that merged with the first tube, bringing both ends to an automatic knot tier that tied a weaver's knot and set the unit on another trip around the circle. There were about a hundred independent duplicate units traveling around the track.

E. J. had an experimental shop with a couple of ingenious mechanics who could make anything. As his machine developed to operational status, it was erected in the mill and tested. Careful comparative cost figures were developed with the old-fashioned machines, which assisted in marketing.

The companion machine was the Abbott Traveling Spindle Quiller. In the weaving operation, the warp threads run lengthwise; as some are raised and others lowered, the shuttle bobbin is thrown back and forth at right angles to and between the warp threads. The shuttle bobbin contains the weft threads on a spool. The quiller machine fills the shuttle bobbin spools from the cheeses or packages, which were made on the winder. The process is the same but in reverse. The traveling unit has a full cone or cheese and unwinds the thread onto the empty shuttle bobbin spool, which is doffed when full. The operator installs the new empty spool and the process is repeated.

E. J. perfected the machines in about 1930 and formed the Abbott Machine Company to manufacture them. His brother, Uncle Bill, set up the design for the shop. However, the depression arrived; many mills closed and hardly anyone wanted to buy new machinery. Because these were revolutionary machines, when customers started buying again in the late 1930s, they bought only one, to see if the machines were really as good as the company claimed. They were. By the time repeat orders were coming in, World War II was nearing. Raw materials were rationed and operations were curtailed. The machine shop partially shifted to manufacture critical defense products. As soon as rationing eased at the end of the war, large orders poured in. The company was hard-pressed to keep up production. Uncle Bill set up the southern sales and service organization in Greenville, South Carolina, the textile center of the South, to accommodate the expanding mills there as the northern mills wound down. As the market in the South became saturated, the sales effort was shifted to foreign markets. Orders doubled every year for about four years. Every year additions were made to the plant by the company's own work crews, machine tools were ordered, and many new employees were added. The business was highly successful.

The Abbotts' family life was as interesting and complicated as their business life. In the mid-1930s, E. J.'s sons were away at school and college. Jim went to MIT, where he received his master's degree in chemical engineering, then returned to work at Hillsborough Mills and the Abbott Worsted Company. Bill attended the University of New Hampshire and MIT for a short time and returned to work at Abbott Machine Company. Sam went to MIT for two years, and after a bout with pneumonia transferred to the University of Florida for his degree. Sam worked in California for three years before returning to the Hillsborough Mills.

The Abbotts became linked with the Wilder family in Lyndeboro. That family was struck by tragedy in 1920 when the father, William, died of pneumonia. In 1921 his wife died as the result of an infection. Three of their seven children were independent and could manage alone. The younger ones were split up.

Lena, in her early teens, lived with her mother's sister, Ruth Stephenson, in Lyndeboro and stayed through college. She married William M. Abbott and moved to Wilton, where they raised three boys. The two youngest children, Charlotte and Francis Wilder, were adopted by the Chauncey Ryders. He was a successful landscape painter who summered in Wilton. After William and Lena were married, his father, E. J., became interested in Charlotte, Lena's younger sister. In 1940 E. J. and Charlotte married. Marriage worked wonders on E. J.'s personality. He had been cantankerous and difficult to get along with. After marriage, he became much more relaxed, friendly, and interesting. The marriage was a very happy one, despite the substantial age difference. But all of this ended abruptly when Charlotte gave birth at Phillips House at the Massachusetts General Hospital in 1944 to a baby girl, Charlotte Mary, and developed severe hemorrhaging, which sadly resulted in her death. E. J. continued to live in the big house with baby Charlotte, assisted by the faithful Eileen and Julia Shea, who returned in 1946 from positions at St. Paul's School in Concord. Eileen and Julia remained with the family for the rest of their lives, about thirty years.

In the late 1930s, E. J. Abbott, when he was contemplating marriage to Charlotte, sought Judge's advice with respect to estate planning. In 1941, he worked with Judge concerning a discriminatory labor practices charge made by the NLRB against Hillsborough Mills (which was settled the next year), a tax case involving Abbott Worsted Company (which continued into 1942 when Judge worked on a tax brief), and a patent infringement case for the Abbott Machine Company against Universal Winding Company.

In 1944, Judge negotiated a labor contract with the CIO for the Abbott Worsted Company and attended a War Labor Board hearing for the Abbott Machine Company, which may have involved obtaining a higher priority for metal for the traveling spindle winders and quillers. Judge also prepared estate planning documents following the birth of Charlotte Mary Abbott and the death of Charlotte Ryder Abbott in 1944.

Jim had a falling out with his father in 1945 and left Wilton with his wife and family for an excellent textile company, the Kendall Company, in Massachusetts. He later moved over to the Gillette Company.

E. J. had been a heavy smoker all of his life and in 1949 died after a long illness. Sam had recently married Mary, whom he had met in school in Florida; with no children of their own, they stepped in to take care of five-year-old Charlotte Mary. Sam and Mary soon started a substantial family of seven of their own.

Sam had been assuming more and more managerial responsibility for Hillsborough Mills, Abbott Worsted Mills, and the Abbott Machine Company. In 1948, Judge worked with Sam and his father to enable Sam to purchase a substantial block of Hillsborough Mills stock. There were talks between Universal Winding and the Abbott Machine Company about a possible merger; the talks were terminated on E. J.'s death in 1949. Fortunately, Sam was well prepared to become CEO. Judge had done legal work for E. J. for a number of years, including labor problems and estate and tax planning. Both Judge and I worked on the many problems that existed or arose as the result of E. J.'s early death.

One problem was the assertion by the IRS of an undistributed profits tax on the substantial earnings of Abbott Machine Company for the years 1946, 1947, and 1948. E. J. was the majority stockholder (the minority interest was held by E. J. as trustee of a 1944 irrevocable trust for the benefit of little Charlotte), so a dividend would have been taxed to him at very high rates. Therefore, it was better to retain the earnings and hope to work out a favorable settlement with the IRS, because the undistributed profits tax rates were lower than the individual rates.

The second problem was the formation of a charitable foundation into which could be paid the maximum amount of corporate profits allowed as a charitable deduction under the Internal Revenue Code, thereby reducing taxable income. The foundation over the years paid for an addition to the Wilton School, paved the main street, provided movies in the town hall, created a park, and supported a number of nonprofit organizations providing services to the townspeople.

The third problem was the settlement of E. J.'s estate, which encompassed a number of interesting legal and tax questions, such as the valuation of the Abbott Machine Company stock, which depended on the settlement of the undistributed profits tax issue. The problem included the exclusion from E. J.'s estate of the 1944 Charlotte Mary Abbott Inter Vivos Irrevocable Trust, the issue being the retention of extensive managerial powers by the grantor-trustee.

The fourth problem involved a gift in 1944 to the C. M. Abbott Trust from E. J. in the form of a minority interest in the Abbott Machine Company at the formation of the trust, as mentioned above. In 1949, upon the death of E. J., the trust received the remainder of the stock as the residuary beneficiary of his estate. A new Abbott Machine Co. Inc. was formed in 1950 by Sam, Bill, and key employees to purchase for cash from the old company its assets subject to liabilities, so that the C. M. Abbott Trust, upon liquidation of the old company, would have cash to invest in marketable

securities rather than ownership of all of the stock of a manufacturing corporation in the dying New England textile industry. John McLane, Jr. subscribed to some of this stock.

The Abbott Machine Company tax case on undistributed profits was
holding up the settlement of the E. J. Abbott estate because no valuation
could be put on the company. A series of meetings with the IRS in Boston
in 1953 resulted in a settlement that saved the company several hundreds
of thousands of dollars and broke the logjam with respect to settlement of
the estate.

However, after World War II the steam had just about run out of the
northern textile industry. The 1950s and 1960s witnessed the almost complete liquidation of what was left. Manchester's old Amoskeag mill yard and
the Wilton-based Abbott companies were no exceptions.

In 1952, Abbott Machine Co. Inc. negotiated with SACM, a large
French manufacturer of textile machinery, for a license to manufacture the
Abbott traveling spindle winder and quiller. Because Judge was going to
Paris on a pleasure trip, arrangements were made for him to see the SACM
people there. Sam Abbott briefed Judge for the visit in Paris and also a visit
in London with other licensees.

The Hillsborough Mills, instead of manufacturing for its own account,
shifted to the less risky commission spinning business. Abbott Worsted
hung on as long as it could but finally wound down production and sold its
plant in 1971. Hillsborough Mills was sold in 1979. Abbott Machine Co.
Inc. did not have available the money necessary to engage in gigantic
research into new ways to manufacture textiles using sophisticated electronics, as the Germans and Swiss were doing. As the new machine business fell
off, a larger percentage of production was geared to the spare parts business.
The Abbott machines were ingenious, practical, and affordable and served a
very useful niche in the industry throughout the world for twenty years.

Sam Abbott died of cancer in May 1976. The leadership of the company had served well for some thirty years and made decent profits, but the
old products had run their course and there was nothing to replace them.
The Abbott Machine Co. Inc. plant was sold in 1979 and the textile business of the Abbott family ended.

# Notes

1. William M. Abbott, "Memories of E. J. Abbott," typescript, January 10,
1992.

2. There was enough money to educate only one son, so the elder, William G.
Abbott, Jr., graduated from MIT.

3. Obituary, Edward J. Abbott, *The Milford Cabinet*, April 7, 1949.

4. The mill manager was one Nash Simonds. One story is that payroll checks were made out to names from the cemetery.

5. In the 1970s, when this author was doing work for Sam Abbott, he would occasionally give me a piece of cloth, maybe a "yard end," (too small to sell), of wonderful worsted material. I took it to excellent tailors in Lawrence, the Salvo Bros. The two brothers and their wives, all Lebanese, custom-made suits. They would take measurements, make patterns, finalize them at the second fitting, and keep making adjustments as you grew older and usually bigger. The advantage was that you needed only one fitting for subsequent suits. I bought top-quality suits for one hundred dollars that would have cost three hundred to five hundred dollars in a store. I remember the first time I went to the shop, all four Salvos were sitting cross-legged on their benches sewing and cutting. I had a piece of excellent worsted flannel and without saying anything placed it on the counter. One of the brothers came over (he didn't know me), felt the cloth, and said, "So, I see you have some of Sam Abbott's private stock." They made wonderful suits and would tell me that Judge Kenison just picked up a suit yesterday, that attorney so-and-so was coming in for a fitting tomorrow, and so forth. They made a set number of suits a week, so that when you came in they entered your name in the next spot and could tell you when the suit would be ready, frequently not for three to six months. It was sad when they announced they were retiring.

# NINETEEN

# Gilbert Verney

Gilbert Verney was born in England in 1905. After spending four years as a midshipman in the British Merchant Marine, Verney emigrated to the United States. His sailing experience gave him a love for the sea for the rest of his life. He was probably exposed to the textile business through his export-import experience with the merchant marine. Thus he entered the textile industry working for the Waypoysett Manufacturing Company in Central Falls, Rhode Island. In 1928, Mr. Verney moved to the Warwick Mills, a Wellington Sears company, in West Warwick, Rhode Island, where he advanced to the position of vice president and general manager. He started mills for Warwick in Manchester, Greenville, and New Ipswich, New Hampshire, and Natick, Rhode Island. It is probable that Judge McLane's first contact with Gilbert Verney was the acquisition of the mill in Manchester.

In 1940, with the war on in Europe, there was an increasing demand for all kinds of textile products, and there were new synthetic, or "miracle," fibers coming on the market. Gilbert Verney decided to form his own company. He resigned from Warwick and formed Verney Corporation, with headquarters in Boston. The Verney company acquired from Amoskeag Industries, Inc., in Manchester, the southern half of the so-called #11 Mill, on the West Side, opposite the Catholic Medical Center. The stone door lintel of that mill still bears the carved name VERNEY. In July 1940, Judge incorporated Verney Mills, Inc., as a subsidiary. The Manchester mill was the most important mill in the entire operation. In those early years, Verney resided in Manchester and Bedford but later moved to a Boston suburb. For many years Judge was connected with Gil Verney's affairs. During 1942, Judge assisted Gil Verney in arranging more loans to finance his expansion plans. Judge had meetings with the RFC, the First National Bank of Boston, and banks in New York City and finally closed a loan agreement in December.[1] Additional mills were bought in West Peterborough, New Hampshire; Brunswick, Maine; and Warwick, Rhode Island.

In 1943 and 1944, in Manchester, the war effort was going full blast. Judge was very busy with Gil Verney. Verney bought additional mills in Newmarket, New Hampshire; Taunton, Massachusetts; and Granby,

Quebec. The directors, including Judge, held their meetings at these sites and inspected them. There were meetings also in Boston, New York City, Montreal, and Manchester.

In 1945, as the war wound down, Judge spent a lot of time on Verney Mills matters, including shifting production from rayon to cotton, purchasing a mill in Greenwich, Connecticut, and refinancing through White, Weld investment brokers. This work involved many trips to Boston and New York City. Judge recorded some forty diary entries, many of which were working with Abe Berkowitz of Ropes & Gray in Boston, Verney's lead counsel.

In 1946 and 1947, Judge continued to attend monthly meetings of Verney Corporation, usually in Boston, with the annual meeting at one of the mills; he also worked on some refinancing. In 1948, Judge was very active on Gil Verney's affairs. Gil had been quite successful in his textile business using the new synthetic fibers, particularly rayon, a cellulose product made from wood fiber. He thus became familiar with the wood pulp business, which also supplied the paper industry.

The Verney mills were busy. Judge attended meetings in New York City and one meeting in Montreal to visit the Granby textile plant. It was a good time for Gil to sell some of his stock publicly—the business was successful and the market was right—so he registered and sold 100,000 shares in September 1948.[2] This was the top of the market for textile stocks, which shortly thereafter started a long downward trend, as the war demand was over and the pent-up civilian demand was satisfied. Southern and foreign mills were able to manufacture at lower cost.

At this time Colonel Arthur Pierce, owner of the Monadnock Paper Mill in Bennington, New Hampshire (which had been in business since 1819), died, with no family members interested in operating the mill. His estate was anxious to sell it. The plant had two paper machines, but one of them was not operative; during the war years, when it was impossible to get parts, the #2 machine was cannibalized to keep the #1 machine running. Colonel Pierce had hired Arthur Bell (who had his own paper mill a few miles away) to run the mill for him as he got older and more infirm. The result was that the mill was considerably run down and could be bought for a very reasonable price. The challenge intrigued Gil Verney, who had just acquired substantial funds from the sale of his Verney Corporation stock. He had some of his friends in the paper business look over the mill. Judge negotiated for Gil with Dudley Orr of Orr and Reno in Concord, who represented the estate. Mortgage financing was arranged through the Manchester Savings Bank, and the closing was held in late April 1949. Along with the mill buildings was included a magnificent active farm with a beautiful spacious house and extensive grounds, fields, and timberland.

In 1949, Judge was settling the estate of John Gilbert Winant, who had a very fine and valuable library in his home in Concord. It contained many volumes with comments and notes by the many friends of the Winants—prominent people who had presented books to him. Judge had the library appraised by Mr. Goodspeed of the famous Boston bookstore of the same name. Judge finally convinced Gil Verney that the library would make a handsome addition to his new home on the Pierce farm.

In 1949, Judge attended bimonthly directors' meetings of Verney Corporation, mostly in New York City. He also spent a day in Bennington seeing the new paper mill and the plans for improvements. Monadnock was a small mill and could not compete with the paper giants. It had to produce small runs of quality and specialty papers to be successful. This meant considerable research and experimentation, which Gilbert Verney financed. The mills had extensive laboratories to test its products, and Verney relied on consultants in paper manufacturing. As a result, the mill became one of the country's finest producers of text, cover printing papers, and industrial specialty papers.

By 1950 the decade of boom years in the northern textile industry began to come to an end. Verney Corporation was an example of the decline. After a period of falling profit margins, the decision was made to sell the Taunton, Granby, and Greenwich plants to reduce debt. This still left plants in Manchester, West Peterborough, and Brunswick.

In 1951 Judge spent a lot of time with Gil Verney, more on his new Monadnock Paper Mills than on the Verney Corporation textile operation. Elizabethtown, Tennessee, made attractive overtures to locate a new paper mill in the Tennessee Valley Authority (TVA) area, where there was cheap power, a nearby pulp supply, and plenty of employees. In April, Judge went south with Gil and his wife, Virginia, and Abe Berkowitz of Ropes & Gray in Boston, a longtime friend and adviser to Gil. They visited the Tennessee site, then went on to Atlanta to look at a paper mill for sale.[3] The Monadnock directors met in New York to further consider the Tennessee offer. In May, representatives from the South visited in New England, but the offer was eventually rejected.

In 1952, Judge worked on a dispute with the tax assessors in West Peterborough on the appraised value of the property. He attended several meetings of the board of directors.

Gil Verney, as an entrepreneur in both the textile and paper industries, was frequently approached with properties or businesses for sale. If they looked at all interesting, he would visit them. One such offer was in Savannah. The directors scheduled a meeting there and visited properties including a former plantation called "Richmond Hill," a beautiful estate along a river with rich bottomland probably once used for cotton and rice production, and acres of surrounding land that were undoubtedly used to grow tobacco. A magnificent colonial mansion stood at the end of a broad driveway lined with ancient huge southern live oak trees festooned with Spanish moss. Slave quarters, a laundry building, tobacco sheds, and other agricultural buildings surrounded the main house, all reminiscent of the movie *Gone With the Wind*.

Unfortunately, all buildings were vacant and abandoned. The house had no furniture or furnishings and obviously had seen better days. Probably it had belonged to a well-known southern family that owned it for many generations and kept it as long as possible, but labor costs and changing agricultural practices made it financially unprofitable. The only salvation was a wealthy northern gentleman who would be overcome by the romance and beauty of the place and see it as an entertainment center for friends. Gil Verney did not bite, and I do not know what became of it. I was fortunate to have been along on the trip.

The problems of the northern textile mills continued to increase in 1954. Judge noted that the Verney southern division was having hard going and a few days later that "Verney financially full of problems." Meetings were held in Yarmough; Brunswick, Maine; and Peterborough, New Hampshire. Meetings were also held with the banks in New York City, where the company was told it had to get into the black in the last two quarters of the year or the loans would be called.

Judge recorded more than twenty days working on Verney matters in 1955. That year, the Verney Corporation was faced with liquidity problems. The Brunswick Mills in Maine, a subsidiary, were targeted for sale, although the Celanese interests objected. However, arrangements were made to liquidate through the Crescent Corporation of Fall River, a major liquidator of northern textile companies. The rest of the Verney Corporation was sold to Gera Corporation, a conglomerate based in Cleveland, through a stock swap. This precipitated a minority stockholders' suit, in which the court upheld the position of the company. Many stockholders had paid a much higher price for the stock when the company went public in 1948 than they received from Gera and consequently were unhappy. What was happening in Manchester was also occurring in nearly all the northern textile cities, such as Fall River, New Bedford, Lowell, and Lawrence. The end of the textile industry in the North was practically complete.

In 1956 Judge met with representatives of the dissenting stockholders in New York City and a settlement agreement was eventually reached, thus concluding Verney's textile activities. Verney poured substantial amounts of money into the Monadnock Paper Mills to increase its productivity and profitability. Verney's two sons, Richard and Geoffrey, went into the paper business, holding a number of positions over the years. Richard, the older, became president and CEO on his father's death in 1978, and Geoffrey assumed the responsibilities of marketing manager. Monadnock continues to be a successful family-owned mill and a client of the McLane law firm.

Gil Verney maintained his principal residence at the farm in Bennington after its acquisition. He also had a summer residence on Nantucket Island, Massachusetts. Gil loved to sail and over the years owned several ocean-racing boats, which he entered in the Bermuda, Halifax, and other ocean races. Gil was a member of the New York Yacht Club and frequently participated in its cruises along the New England coast. He attended most of the America's Cup races in Newport and was a participant in one or more syndicates sponsoring an America's Cup defender. He frequently chartered a yacht and invited as his guests personal friends or business associates to watch the races off Newport.

Gil Verney died suddenly of a heart attack at age seventy-three while on a trip to Miami.

## Notes

1. Judge was a trustee of Dartmouth College and adviser to the Dartmouth Outing Club (DOC). In 1942, Judge records after a DOC meeting: "Dumping Hans Pascher overboard." For what reasons (German background?), this author does not know. Judge may not have approved of the dismissal or, in any event, sympathized with Hans, because a couple of weeks later Hans spent an "interesting evening" with Judge and Elisabeth telling them about his involvement in the rescue of one Picard from a bomber that crashed near the top of Mt. Jim, a spur of Mt. Moosilauke. Judge also put Hans in touch with his client Gil Verney, for whom Hans started to work in June.

2. Judge owned three hundred shares of Verney stock which I assume he acquired when the company went public.

3. While in Atlanta, Judge went to All Saints Episcopal Church to hear the Rev. Matthew Warren preach. Warren was under consideration for headmastership for St. Paul's School and eventually was selected to that position.

# TWENTY

# Boston & Maine Railroad and Mount Washington Cog Railway

Judge McLane became a trustee of Dartmouth College in 1926. Ernest Martin Hopkins, president of the college, was a director of the Boston & Maine Railroad (B&MRR) and the National Life Insurance Company of Vermont. Ned French, president of the B&MRR, was also a trustee of Dartmouth. Fred Howland, president of National Life, was a director of the B&MRR. The result was that Judge intimately knew many of the B&MRR directors, who wanted him on the board. When his name was first proposed in 1932, Frederick C. Dumaine, president of the Amoskeag Company, blocked it for several years, for unknown reasons. In 1933 Judge had a talk with Mr. Dumaine, presumably covering the B&MRR election. Judge was finally elected a director of the B&MRR in 1939 and of National Life in 1943.

Ned French, president of the B&MRR, in the early 1930s asked Judge and his law firm to represent the railroad in southern New Hampshire. The B&MRR, like most railroads, was self-insured because liability insurance is frightfully expensive, if it can be obtained at all. In the 1920s and 1930s there was a substantial amount of tort litigation involving the B&MRR. A large percentage of these cases dealt with automobile accidents at railroad crossings, many of which were not protected. These were tough cases to win. There was no great love on the part of the juries for the railroads, which were seen as large and wealthy and could afford to pay for the injuries they caused. The juries tended to overlook evidence of contributory negligence on the part of the automobile driver. Furthermore, the B&MRR employees usually were terrible witnesses. Working for a big corporation somehow made them feel superior to other people, which manifested itself in a certain arrogance on the witness stand, creating a negative impression on juries. Many railroad employees thought their employer and their fellow employees could do no wrong. They usually considered the automobile driver to be at fault, claiming he didn't stop, look, and listen. There were three or four such cases a year coming into the office, which Ralph Davis, John Carleton, and Ken Graf tried. Many cases lost in the trial court were appealed to the New Hampshire Supreme Court, which ruled on trial errors. Some cases were reversed, some were sent back for new trials, and some were affirmed. Awards in second trials were usually larger.

Judge attended monthly meetings of the board of directors and in September was elected to the executive committee, which had additional meetings. The war years were busy ones for the railroad.

In 1941, Bob Burroughs, a client of Judge's from Manchester and an insurance agent for National Life of Vermont, son of Judge's former law partner, pioneered the development of retirement programs for large corporations. These programs were funded by insurance policies, a new field. Judge helped Bob Burroughs by accompanying him to Washington to obtain tax approval from the IRS for several of Bob's clients. Judge also went with Bob to Cincinnati to sell the pension program to Cincinnati Milling Corporation. The B&MRR and its subsidiary, Maine Central Railroad, were also customers. Judge spent a considerable amount of time developing a retirement plan for the railroad.

For several years, the Boston & Maine Railroad had been working on a stock reorganization plan, which was finally approved by the court. Over the years, the company had bought out many of the small regional railroads and had issued a separate class of preferred stock for each acquisition. This conglomeration of issues created extra expense, confusion, and a weakened market for its securities. The reorganization plan, among other things, consolidated all of the different classes of preferred stock into a single class of stock, which was issued in exchange for the older stock at rates that reflected the differences in market value of the various issues of preferred stock.

The Boston & Maine Railroad kept Judge busy with an average of two meetings a month in Boston. He attended directors' or executive committee meetings. He was part of special meetings on the new reorganization plan and the Wilton, New Hampshire, branch railroad. Judge noted the completion of a new automatic signal system in the freight yard in Boston and a modification to the pension plan.

In 1946, with the end of the war, there were massive changes in the railroad industry in the East. Judge was appointed to a special committee on capital reorganization, which dealt with the New York, New Haven & Hartford Railroad (NY, NH & Hartford) and the new Pennroad. There were many meetings in New York and Boston, frequently with John Hall of Choate, Hall and Stewart, counsel for the NY, NH & Hartford. The railroads had enjoyed a great deal of business during the war but were faced with high debt and increasing competition from the growing trucking industry. They also had to cope with many unions and regulatory authorities, which greatly limited management's ability to operate efficiently. In 1947, the B&MRR adopted a stock reorganization plan. In 1949 the plan was heard before the Interstate Commerce Commission (ICC). Judge attended. He also worked on equipment trust financing.

During the 1950s, Judge continued attending about two meetings a month. In 1953, the B&MRR was still before the ICC straightening out its finances. In 1954, the board voted to eliminate all steam engines in favor of diesel power.

In early 1955, the B&MRR directors met over the NY, NH & Hartford control with the McGinnis group. A proxy fight appeared imminent. There were several negotiating meetings but without result. While Judge was away in Europe on vacation skiing and sight-seeing, there was a stockholders' meeting at which the McGinnis faction won control and elected a new board of directors. Judge's connection with the B&MRR ended with a final dinner of the old board of directors on June 29, 1955.

## MOUNT WASHINGTON COG RAILWAY

The Mount Washington Cog Railway, a tourist attraction, was built in the mid 1800s.[1] It was the first cog railroad to overcome steep grades. The 1880s was the era of growth of the large hotels in the White Mountains— the Bretton Woods, Fabyan, Crawford House, Twin Mountain, and Profile House—all serviced by the ubiquitous railroad that whisked customers overnight from New York City and Boston to the mountains. At some point in time the B&MRR developed service to the mountain hotels and acquired the cog railway. Much of the construction and maintenance work on the engines and cars, all of which were unique, was done thereafter at the B&MRR machine shops at Tewksbury, Massachusetts.

During the depression years, the railroad passenger business fell off as more people used automobiles to get to the mountains. Many of the big hotels fell on hard times. Some closed; others burned down. The cog railway suffered too and became an embarrassment to the B&MRR, which decided to get rid of it so that the Public Utilities Commission regulators would not reduce the railroad's allowable earnings by the amount of the cog railway losses.

For many years there had been a close association between Dartmouth College and the B&MRR. Ernest Martin Hopkins, president of Dartmouth, Ned French, president of the B&MRR, and Judge McLane were directors of both corporations (maybe there were others). All knew Henry Teague, a charismatic individual and Maine woodsman who owned and operated hotels in Florida and New England. Dartmouth, by virtue of its outing club and mountain trails and cabins, had a distinct interest in the welfare of the White Mountains. It negotiated with Henry Teague to help him buy the cog railway from the B&MRR by loaning him money on favorable terms. The loan was secured by a mortgage on the property and a pledge of the stock, 100 percent of which Henry owned, plus Henry's promise to bequeath the stock to the college on his death. (Henry was unmarried and had no family.) The deal went through in the 1930s.

The cog railway had a long-term lease to substantial acreage at the summit, which was valuable as a tourist attraction, for radio and TV transmission towers, and for research on the unusual atmospheric conditions year-round at the summit. Many research projects were carried out there over the years for government agencies and private enterprise.

The 1938 hurricane did a tremendous amount of damage to the trestles and tracks of the cog railway. About the same time, Yankee Network was anxious to obtain exclusive broadcast rights for radio and other forms of communication at the summit. Yankee Network negotiated with Henry Teague a long-term lease that extends into the twenty-first century. It provided that a substantial portion of the rent was to be paid up front, which enabled Teague to repair the hurricane damage and get his trains moving again.

Judge and I went to Mount Washington in the summer of 1946 to investigate an accident on the cog railway in which several people were severely injured. A flatcar used for hauling supplies to the Tip Top House had been left at the top for unloading supplies and loading trash to be brought back down. A cold front with high winds hit the mountain and somehow started the flatcar moving down the tracks, accelerating as it went. About a quarter of a mile from the summit, it crashed into the passenger car of an ascending train (the passenger car is pushed up the mountain by the engine, which is in the rear), making a jumble of car seats, windows, wood, and passengers, who were sprayed with the contents of the trash barrels as they were catapulted into the wrecked car. Fortunately, there were no fatalities.

Judge and I arrived at the base station late at night and ascended the mountain on the train in the early morning with representatives of the Public Utilities Commission. The commission had supervisory jurisdiction over the railroad, including matters of safety. My recollection is that the injured had been evacuated from the mountain by ambulances down the carriage road and that the flatcar and passenger cars had been cleared from the track. We were able to observe what was left and conjecture what had happened. I don't remember whether the cause was ever determined, but we suspected that summer camp juvenile visitors may have climbed on the flatcar and somehow undid the brakes (supposedly securely locked), not realizing what might happen. There was no evidence of malicious or intentional conduct. Settlements were eventually made with all injured passengers.[2]

The railway was a colorful and seasonal enterprise that gobbled up huge quantities of money in track maintenance and custom machining to make parts for the engine and cars, which took a lot of abuse going up and down the mountain. Henry Teague, in order to keep expenses down, hired college students to run the railway. During the depression years, these young folks were mighty glad to get a job and were as loyal to Henry as he was good to them. Although they worked hard, they also had a memorable time. After the war Henry befriended a North Carolinian, Arthur Teague (no relation), who had a brilliant and much-decorated war career in the Army. Henry hired him and over the years gave him increasing authority in managing the operation. As Henry got older, he wanted to make it possible for Arthur to buy the company. In October 1950, Judge met with Henry and Dartmouth College to see what might be worked out. The transaction was not consummated before Henry's death in October 1951. The college received the stock from Henry's estate, and Arthur ran the railway for the college. John Carleton was counsel for the cog railway. In 1953 the firm won important litigation for the college against Yankee Network. The suit involved a long-term lease on the top of Mount Washington for broadcast purposes. Because of the exposure to liability from the railroad operations, the college very much wanted to dispose of its ownership. It negotiated with Arthur Teague to buy the railway. Nevertheless, the college retained ownership of the summit, which had value because of the long-term Yankee Network lease for a TV tower and the potential rent on space for experimental testing in the extreme weather. About 1960, Ken Graf represented the college in the sale to Arthur Teague. In spite of conflict questions that were raised and waived, Arthur Teague asked Jack Middleton to represent him, which he did. Jack represented the cog railway for the next twenty-five years until Ellen, Arthur's widow, sold it.

Arthur ran the railway with modest success. It came as a tremendous shock when, in August 1967, he committed suicide. Jack counseled Ellen, who picked up the reins and discussed liability insurance, which Arthur had never carried although Jack Middleton and the accountant had urged him to. Ellen, convinced by their arguments, authorized Jack to obtain coverage, which he did, buying two policies providing over $1 million coverage. Just over a month later, there was a serious train crash on the mountain in which eight passengers were killed and about eighty injured. All claims were settled within the policy limits. The cog railway was sold in the 1980s to some local businessmen, and the McLane law firm connection with the railroad came to an end.

Governor John King engineered the purchase of the summit for the state from Dartmouth College, which was represented by Ken Graf. The college sold about half of its property, retaining ownership of the Yankee Network lease property and some other parcels. Because of his connections with the mountain, Jack Middleton was appointed in 1969 to the Mount

Washington Commission and is still a member. Jack also continues his longtime interest in the Mount Washington Observatory, of which he has been secretary since 1957.

# Notes

1. Subsequently, in Switzerland, several different cog systems were developed for difficult grades, and many are still in use.

2. The *Boston Globe* newspaper printed a story of a man who was on top of the mountain the day of the accident. He had observed the flatcar and expressed definite ideas how the accident happened. Winslow Melvin, transportation director for the Public Utilities Commission, and I had both read the *Globe* article, so we made arrangements to take his statement in Boston with a public stenographer. He was a man in his sixties, very sincere, apparently honest with no interest in the matter, cooperative in answering questions, and had no bias against the railway. He was very definite about what he had seen and was able to make diagrams as to where the flatcar was located on the top of the mountain and the location of other buildings and objects around. I interrogated him about the brake mechanism, which I understood pretty well from shop drawings, photographs of the flatcar after the accident, and personal observation at the top of the mountain the morning after the accident. I asked him about the linkage between the brake control wheel on top of the flatcar and the chains and cables under the car that led to the brake shoes, which acted on the wheels. He answered all of my questions clearly and positively just as though he had a photograph in front of him. I even gave him options asking whether something was A or B. He never waffled and was always perfectly sincere. I did not try to confront him when I thought him to be wrong, but asked him for more detail or whether he was positive that what he said was correct.After we had finished with the questions, we left and marveled at how absolutely inaccurate his entire story had been. He even had the brake wheel and the mechanism at the wrong end of the flatcar. His description of the brake mechanism was very logical and clear but it bore no resemblance to what was actually on the car. We concluded that he had been on the mountain that day and probably did see the flatcar and had a very vivid imagination. We decided that this would be a good case for a psychiatrist or psychologist to analyze.

# TWENTY-ONE

# Interlude 1940–1949

## HIGHLIGHTS OF 1940

The war news in 1940 dominated everyone's thoughts. The news was grim. Judge records in his diary the following events: April 4, "Germans invade Norway and Denmark"; May 10, "Germans invade Holland, Belgium and Luxembourg, Chamberlain out, Churchill premier"; May 14, "Holland gives up"; May 16, "Most distressing war news"; May 21, "Darkest day of war, Nazis near Channel ports"; June 10, "Italy enters war, Nazis 35 miles from Paris"; June 13, "Paris falls"; June 17, "France surrenders." Judge was particularly sensitive to the war news because he had spent two years at Oxford as a Rhodes scholar. He knew and liked many English people. He had traveled extensively in France and studied French history in detail.

Despite the depressing war news, Judge and Elisabeth carried on their normal life. They loved their skiing and made the most of the excellent winters of the late '30s and '40s. In January they enjoyed two weekends at Moosilauke and two weekends at Franconia. They frequently stayed at Sel and Paulie Hannah's Ski Hearth Farm. In March, they watched the Hochebirge Club ski race on the Taft trail. Charles raced for Dartmouth. They took Lilla and friends from Smith College to ski on the "Thunderbolt" trail on Mt. Greylock, towering above Williamstown, Massachusetts, and enjoyed a weekend in undeveloped Waterville Valley. In March, they went to Grey Rocks in the Laurentians and skied Mt. Tremblant. Tuckerman's Ravine and Wildcat beckoned for four weekends in the spring. The weather forced the cancellation of the Inferno Race, which Judge and Elisabeth had witnessed the year before. In mid-May they experienced a rare treat when they ascended Mount Washington on the cog railway as guests of owner Henry Teague and skied the cone in perfect spring weather.

In July Lilla and a Smith College friend welcomed four Austrian Jewish refugee girls for two weeks at the lake and ran a camp for them. The family dog, Campsey, returned to Pasquaney after a three-year absence, having been "found" and taken by tourists staying at the Whippoorwill Motel.

250

*Circa 1940, Elisabeth "Lilla" McLane* on
pack trip in the High Sierras of California
with the Bradley family, including future
husband, Dave Bradley.

Because Campsey didn't have on an identification collar, they thought he
had been abandoned. Three years later the tourists returned to the same
motel with the dog for a week's vacation. The McLane family recognized
the dog walking along the road with his new masters. When the children
called him by name, Campsey came running and climbed all over them,
licking their faces and whining with joy. There was no question to whom
he belonged. In early August, there was a long tennis and music weekend
at South Egremont and the Tanglewood Music Festival. The family made
an expedition to the Dartmouth College grant in northern New
Hampshire to hike the ten miles in to "Hellgate," an old logging camp. A
small forest fire, started in the duff by a lightning strike several days before,
was put out with shovels and water from "handy billies." A visit to future
son-in-law Dave Bradley and family at Woods Hole produced a sail in
Dave's Herreshoff "S" boat, the *Mischief* (built in 1926 and still sailing in
1996), through the Hole to Quisset Harbor. In mid-October, Judge

*1950s, New Ravine Camp, Mt. Moosilauke,* Dartmouth Outing Club. Built in 1939 to replace old burned Ravine Camp. Site of numerous New Year's parties. Credit: Dartmouth College Library.

finished the Community Chest campaign as chairman and just made it over the top of $87,250. As usual, the family attended the Dartmouth-Harvard football game and had dinner at the Hofbrau House. Later in the fall, Judge and Elisabeth took the train and their bikes to Montpelier Junction and biked to the Pavilion Hotel for the night. Next day, they covered forty-four miles, going through Barre, Williamstown, and South Royalton to Terrace Lodge. The next day they biked fifteen miles down the White River back to their car.

In late October, they climbed Mt. Moosilauke. They saw the famous Dartmouth-Cornell fifth-down game in Hanover. Thanksgiving sported a hare and hound chase in six inches of new snow and a turkey dinner for twenty-three. Skiing was good at Cannon in December. The traditional Christmas was held at Concord with Gaga Bancroft. The family headed for the Ravine Camp for New Year's just as the year had begun.

*War Years. Charles McLane*, U.S. Army Reserve, in 86th Mountain Infantry Regiment (Ski Troops) before Pearl Harbor, later commissioned and assigned to SHAEF in France.

## HIGHLIGHTS OF 1941

The new year started at the Ravine Camp, then a couple of days at Stowe, Vermont, with rides up on the new chairlift and down the toll road and the "Nose Dive." Later there were trips to Cannon, the Ravine Camp, the Uncanoonucs, Cardigan, and, at the end of the season, Pinkham Notch and Tuckerman's Ravine. They enjoyed a week in February at Mt. Tremblant—always relaxing with a feel of a foreign country in French-speaking Canada.

Charles, a senior at Dartmouth and captain of the Dartmouth ski team, competed in the nationals at Sun Valley, Idaho. In June, Charles gave the Class Day address to the college, which precipitated Judge's diary entry: "Proud of him." After graduation Charles entered the Marine Corps Officer Training School at Quantico, Virginia, but, unfortunately, the summer pollens incapacitated him with hay fever, resulting in his being "drummed" out

*Judge and Elisabeth, 1941*, picnicking on trip to Wisconsin to visit Lilla and Dave Bradley.

of the corps. In the fall, he joined the newly formed Mountain Troops and was temporarily assigned to the Arkansas National Guard stationed at Fort Lewis, Washington. On December 7 he took the bus to Mt. Ranier to go skiing, oblivious of the attack on Pearl Harbor until he came off the mountain. Several months later, he was transferred to SHAEF (Supreme Headquarters Allied Expeditionary Force) because of his linguistic ability, particularly in French. After the invasion of France, he was assigned to southern France, dealing with the French civilian population to stimulate the war effort.

Lilla was married in Manchester in the spring to David Bradley, from Madison, Wisconsin, a Dartmouth graduate in the class of 1938 with this author. Dave, a skier, had taken a graduate year of study at Cambridge, skiing and jumping with the Finns. He volunteered as an ambulance driver at the end of the Russian-Finnish war, helping where he could in the backcountry of Finland in the winter. Unable to return to the United States via Europe because of the war, Dave went to Moscow. He took the Trans-Siberian Railway to the Pacific at Vladivostok, then a boat to Japan. From there, he took a Japanese steamer across the Pacific to the West Coast, arriving in the summer of 1940.

During the summer, Judge and Elisabeth took the mail boat from Port Clyde to Monhegan Island off the coast of Maine, where they spent the night. They climbed Mount Washington and descended over the Southern

Peaks. They spent a weekend playing tennis and listening to the music at Tanglewood. That summer, they enjoyed several climbs on Mt. Moosilauke. In the fall, they traveled by train to Washington, D.C., drove down the Blue Ridge Parkway, visited Monticello, and returned to Alexandria. Later they took another trip through the Poconos and the Alleghenies to Cleveland to visit Elisabeth's sister Jane Shiverick. From there they went to Madison, Wisconsin, to see the Bradley family and newlyweds Dave and Lilla, who were enrolled at the University of Wisconsin. (Lilla transferred from Smith College.)

The year ended with the attack on Pearl Harbor, the mobilization and expansion of American forces, the increasing movement of troops and supplies to Great Britain, and the immersion of the United States in a two-ocean war. In Manchester, the mills were operating two and three shifts as orders for textiles and shoes, mostly military, increased tremendously.

## HIGHLIGHTS OF 1942

The United States was now engaged in war, and that dominated everything. The state's judicial system slowed to a crawl as lawyers, litigants, and witnesses left for the military service. Most law firms were shorthanded, as Judge notes in his diary, when John Carleton left in September. To make matters worse, Ralph Davis, who had been hospitalized in 1941 for high blood pressure, was advised in April by his doctor not to try any more cases. The war news during the first part of the year was grim. The Allies suffered defeats in Africa and Russia. Bataan and the Philippines fell. In the fall of 1942, good news started to come: The Germans were bogged down at Stalingrad after forty-five days of bitter hand-to-hand fighting; the British pushed Rommel back at El Alamein in Africa; the Americans landed in Africa; and the U.S. Navy won a big battle in the Solomon Islands in the South Pacific.

The year 1942 started out with the family again at the Dartmouth Ravine Camp on Mt. Moosilauke for New Year's Eve festivities but shifted to Cannon for skiing, where the tramway was operating. Later in the month, Malcolm and two friends took the family car to ski at Cannon, starting off at six on a bright, cold morning. Just outside of Plymouth, the windshield fogged over and Malcolm attempted to clear it. He took his eyes off the road, with the result that the car hit a tree, smashed the radiator, and banged up the boys' knees. I was drafted from my associate position in the office to go on an errand of mercy. The roads north of Concord were deserted, so I went breezing along until a trooper stopped me and ticketed me for speeding. Well, that wasn't too bad. I picked up the boys with sore knees, checked out the car, got an estimate on repair cost, and started home. When we were going through Hooksett, talking away,

*War Years. John McLane, Jr.*, U.S. Navy
Reserve, Naval Intelligence, 1942–1943.
Patrol Craft, USS PC1246 1943–1945 in
Caribbean and Mediterranean Seas.

another trooper gave me a warning for speeding! I pleaded to the judge in
the Concord municipal court that I had been on an errand of mercy and
not on a frolic of my own and sought leniency, which fortunately was
agreeable with the judge. Then I went to see the commissioner of motor
vehicles and argued with him that my license should not be revoked for two
offenses in one day; fortunately, the commissioner agreed.

Skiing played a major weekend role in Judge and Elisabeth's lives:
Cardigan two times, Cannon five times, Mount Washington Valley four
times, and a week at Mt. Tremblant in Canada—just before national gas
rationing went into effect.

The new Air Force Base, Grenier Field (a greatly expanded Manchester
airport), was dedicated in February. It was a training facility and jumping-
off place for bombers headed for England. Judge and Elisabeth entertained
soldiers and pilots on a fairly regular basis, inviting groups of three to ten
for skating on the river, to play tennis at Three Acres, or parlor games and

*War Years. Malcolm McLane,* Fighter Pilot
in P-47, participated in Normandy land-
ings and other missions, shot down
December 23, 1944, listed "missing in
action" for five months, taken to prisoner-
of-war camp, which was freed by Russian
troops in 1945.

lunch or dinner. They also chaperoned a dance at the colored USO. (Still
segregated at that time!)

Departures for the service became common events. Associate Perk Bass
left in April for the Army, this author for the Navy in May, and John
Carleton joined the Air Force in August.

In May, gas rationing began and changed everybody's lives. People
brought out long-unused bicycles from garages and walking shoes from
closets. They depended on the trolley cars, buses, and trains. This did not
hold up the McLanes. In late June, Judge and Elisabeth took the train to
Bath, Maine, biked to Wiscasset to visit the Sortwells, took the train to
Rockland, biked to Lincolnville, rode the ferry to Isleboro and then
Castine. Then they biked to Ellsworth and Winter Harbor, where they

stayed at the Grindstone Inn, then biked around Schoodic Point, took the train to Machias, biked to Cutler and Lubec, took the ferry to Eastport and Perry Island to visit, then biked back to Calais and took the train home— an energetic week! In late August, the McLanes bused to Franconia Notch, climbed Lafayette, and hiked over to Garfield and the Galehead Hut, where they spent the night. The next day, they hiked over Twin Mountain to the Zealand Hut for another night. They ended their hike at Crawford Notch, where they picked up the bus to Meredith and caught the train home.

This author, in Naval Intelligence, came home after completing indoctrination school at Cornell and headed off for "spy school" in Washington for a few weeks before returning to Boston. Judge was asked to go to Washington on the Board of Economic Warfare, but declined because of the shortage of lawyers in the office.

Judge mentions the holocaust at Coconut Grove in Boston in November, in which 440 lives were lost. A traditional Thanksgiving at Three Acres for twenty-three and Christmas in Concord closed out the year.

## HIGHLIGHTS OF 1943

The family had icy skiing at Hanover over New Year's. On January 2, Gil Winant and his family came to Manchester for "a delightful dinner." Gil was home from his post as ambassador to Great Britain in London to visit his family. It did not seem advisable for his family to accompany him to London, although Constance was there on many occasions. One can assume that Gil had many fascinating stories to tell about the Battle of Britain and dinners with the Churchills and Edens, with whom he frequently stayed when alone. On January 4, Charles headed west to Camp Hale in Colorado to rejoin the 10th Mountain Division. On January 7, Malcolm headed south for Air Force training. And in May I left my Naval Intelligence post to start training for sea duty. The fuel at 40 Stark Street was so low that the office was closed for a day. Judge and Elisabeth made the most of a wonderful winter by skiing across the fields many times to Three Acres, taking a picnic lunch or cooking out. They took the train to Plymouth, where they spent the night, caught an early bus to Woodstock, arranged for a car to take them to the Ravine Camp at Mt. Moosilauke, and on the return trip stayed at the Pemigewasset Hotel (now demolished) and skied on the Frontenac slopes (now a veritable forest). On a February weekend, they stayed at Sel and Paulie Hannah's Ski Hearth Farm in Franconia and enjoyed deep powder snow skiing on Cannon and returned home to minus-thirty-degree cold—a record for that date.

Judge and Elisabeth took the night train to Montreal and arrived in the Laurentians in the evening, where they enjoyed a week of skiing at

Mt. Tremblant. A last skiing weekend started with the train to Laconia, then the bus to Pinkham Notch AMC huts, with excellent skiing on the Tuckerman's Ravine headwall.

Judge served on the Navy V-12 Selection Committee, an officer training program in colleges. He had dinner with Hoppie and Ned French, who asked him to be a director of National Life Insurance Company of Vermont, which Judge accepted. Hoppie was interested in running for the U.S. Senate seat held by Styles Bridges and was sounding out opinions around the state. Judge held meetings at Three Acres in June and again in July at which the group considered the candidacies of Hoppie and Foster Stearns. The latter turned out to be the favorite, a great disappointment to Judge, I am sure.

In June, Judge and Elisabeth had a "commission" to deliver a car in Mississippi, so went west via Cleveland to visit Elisabeth's sister Jane Shiverick, then to Richmond, Indiana, to visit a Smith College classmate, then to Louisville, Memphis, and Vicksburg. They enjoyed seeing Malcolm at his airfield in the South, delivered the car, and returned home by train. During the summer, they spent weekends at the lake, taking the train to Plymouth and biking from there. They picked plenty of blueberries in the hill pastures. They put bikes in the canoe and paddled and biked to church in Hebron. During the week, there was tennis with Grenier soldiers or pilots and picnic suppers at Three Acres, where the new shower house had just been completed from lumber salvaged from the 1938 hurricane.

In October, Judge went south on oil business. He met Malcolm at his airfield in Florida, and met me in New Orleans where I awaited my new ship, which was under construction at Nashville, Tennessee.[1]

A new McLane tradition was started at Thanksgiving: namely, the family had a skewered lamb supper at Nick's Macedonia restaurant on Wednesday evening. The new tradition helped Ibus by getting everyone out of the house, and expressed gratitude for Nick's support of the Community Chest drive. Nick donated the receipts of a special day. Judge had been chairman of the fund drive. Several years later, Nick's Macedonia was demolished in connection with an urban-renewal project. In the intervening years the family has visited several different Greek restaurants. In 1993 the family held its fiftieth Wednesday- night dinner at a Greek restaurant, now the Athens.

Three Acres was the site of the traditional hare and hound chase. During the war years, Judge and Elisabeth had various kinds of livestock there—usually two pigs and hens. Judge notes collecting seven eggs from eight hens, also in the fall after the pigs were slaughtered changing the salt brine for the salt pork. On another occasion, he talks about getting a flitch of bacon from the cold cellar at Three Acres. (I remember doing this.

Usually the flitch, hanging from a hook in the ceiling of the dark, moist, and dank cellar, was covered with a green mold, which quickly disappeared when dragged across the snow to the car.)

December was cold: Judge records on December 23, "Cold, but pleasant wood fire in office." He skated on Lake Massabesic on December 26 and on the river on the thirty-first.

# HIGHLIGHTS OF 1944

The year started off with excellent skating on the river. Judge and Elisabeth with groups of friends took the Concord bus to the bridge in Hooksett-Suncook and skated back to Manchester on January 1, 2, and 3.[2] When the snows came, because of gas rationing, skiing frequently was limited to cross-country across the fields to Pine Crest and Three Acres. Judge and Elisabeth did, however, take the train to Plymouth and taxi to Cannon for "swell skiing." In February they made their customary sojourn for a week to Mt. Tremblant in the Laurentians. There was another weekend at Cannon, and on three April weekends they traveled by train to Laconia and bus to Pinkham Notch for excellent skiing in Tuckerman's Ravine. Judge writes in his diary, "Funny time chasing new pigs, Gaston and Josephine, over in Leach's pasture."[3] In September, they hiked the Presidential Range, climbing up Tuckerman's Ravine to the Lakes-of-the-Clouds hut for the night. They hiked over the range the next day to Madison Spring huts for the second night, then back to Pinkham Notch via Madison Gulf.

Governor Herbert Lehman of New York called from Washington to ask Judge to be deputy director general of the United Nations Relief and Rehabilitation Administration (UNRRA) in London. Judge went to Washington to meet with the governor and Sir Arthur Salter but notes in his diary the next day that he had "pretty well decided against" the position.

Judge notes on November 23: "Strange Thanksgiving. Elisabeth and I to Grenier Field for day on Red Cross canteen." However, on Saturday, the twenty-fifth, there were twenty-two for dinner in a postponed Thanksgiving celebration. On Christmas, Judge writes, "Quiet but pleasant day (in Concord) observing all the time-honored traditions. Back to Manchester and Elisabeth and I to Grenier as of 10 p.m." At the time they did not know that Malcolm had been shot down over enemy lines during the Battle of the Bulge on December 23; they did not receive the telegram from the War Department advising that he was missing in action until January 5, 1945.

# HIGHLIGHTS OF 1945

Judge and Elisabeth kept on with their lives after receiving the news about Malcolm. They received a letter from a fellow pilot who said that it had been reported that Malcolm's parachute had opened after his plane was hit, so there was hope. Their daughter, Lilla Bradley, and granddaughter, Kim, age one, came from San Francisco for a number of weeks to comfort Judge and Elisabeth. Lilla found them to be "strong and brave." They all went skiing at Cannon in twenty-degree weather. Apparently there was much snow that winter, because they frequently skied across the fields to Pine Crest or to Three Acres. Mt. Tremblant beckoned again for two weeks in early March. Judge fell and cracked a bone in his wrist, but that did not prevent him from skiing.

In April, Judge and Elisabeth had planned a trip to San Francisco to the United Nations convention to interview John Dickey, a candidate for the presidency of Dartmouth College, to succeed Ernest Martin Hopkins, who had announced his desire to retire. Elisabeth McLane Bradley was living in San Francisco, where Dave was doing his medical residency, so this was also an opportunity to see the grandchildren. Judge and Elisabeth started their trip by taking the night sleeper to Montreal. They were scheduled to take the transcontinental Canadian Pacific train late in the afternoon, so they were killing time window-shopping on St. Catherine's Street when they bumped into Bob Kiely, an attorney with whom Judge had done business on Verney matters, en route to lunch. He said that Judge's office had called and had an important message for him, so they all returned to Bob's office. Judge was overjoyed to learn that a postcard in Malcolm's handwriting had been received, indicating he was safe and sound in a POW camp.[4] Bob Kiely corraled some of his partners and they all went out for lunch and drank champagne toasts to Malcolm's safe return.

Judge and Elisabeth boarded the train and had a beautiful trip west with a great load lifted from their hearts. They enjoyed a couple of days skiing near Banff, met friends in Vancouver, and stopped in Seattle for a visit on Bainbridge Island. In San Francisco, on May 1, there were rumors of peace and the news that Hitler had been killed. On the next day Berlin fell as Judge attended a plenary session of the United Nations. Judge met with John Dickey and discussed the presidency of Dartmouth College. Germany unconditionally surrendered and there were V-E Day celebrations across the land. Judge and Elisabeth visited with Dave and Lilla Bradley and the grandchildren. Lilla recalls that she went window-shopping with them in downtown San Francisco. Elisabeth admired a contemporary glass statue of a Madonna and Child in a window. Next day Judge sneaked back, bought it, and had it shipped to Elisabeth as a surprise. Lilla writes, "It meant so much to them for somehow it represented knowing that Malcolm was alive." Judge and Elisabeth arrived back home in April and had a little niche built in the living room, lighted from top and bottom, for the beautiful little "Madonna and Child," which resided there for the rest of their lives. It now (1996) graces Lilla's mantelpiece in Hanover. I returned on leave in May, and Malcolm, all discharged, returned in July. On August 6, the atom bomb was dropped over Hiroshima, and on the fourteenth Japan surrendered.

In Hanover, Hoppie's planned resignation after some thirty years as president was accepted. On November 1, John S. Dickey was inducted as Dartmouth College's twelfth president. Malcolm returned to Dartmouth to finish his war-interrupted academic career. The traditional Thanksgiving events were renewed at Three Acres. The traditional Christmas was held in Concord after the midnight candlelight service at the Episcopal church in Hopkinton.

## HIGHLIGHTS OF 1946

Charles arrived home from France discharged from the Army. Judge records a family day with piano (Elisabeth), violin (Judge), and voices (the children). On January 7, Judge celebrated his sixtieth birthday with the office in for punch in the afternoon. The Dartmouth trustees approved plans for proceeding with the Hopkins Center. Judge and Elisabeth went on weekend ski trips to Cannon and Tuckerman's Ravine as well as the usual week at Mt. Tremblant. The family livestock at Three Acres was enlarged by the arrival of Modestine, a taciturn and docile donkey, which Judge describes as a "feature" at Three Acres, particularly for the neighborhood children, who loved to ride her. In July, Elisabeth and Judge climbed Lafayette and spent the night at the Greenleaf Hut, where Malcolm had been a "hutman."[5] They spent the night and continued over the range in beautiful weather.

Judge and Elisabeth bought more land adjoining Three Acres in Manchester. Judge notes the explosion of an atom bomb at Bikini Atoll in the Pacific, where their son-in-law, Dr. David J. Bradley, was a radiological monitor flying in an observation plane. In the fall there was much activity cutting ski trails on Uncanoonuc and building a ski jump in Bedford as the returning soldiers and sailors caught up on the fun things in life they had missed during the war years. In November, Judge and Elisabeth went on a trip up the Maine coast, visiting the Sortwells in Wiscasset, then up through the Maine woods to Jackman and into Canada, returning via the Connecticut Lakes to Hanover. At Thanksgiving the family ate at the Macedonia restaurant for the traditional Wednesday-evening skewered lamb supper, then twenty-eight sat down the next day for a turkey dinner at Three Acres after the hunger-generating hare and hound paper chase.

There was a white Christmas in Concord for the candlelight midnight service at the Hopkinton church. Christmas afternoon, Judge and Elisabeth walked out toward St. Paul's School to call on Constance and Gil Winant and their family, who had returned to their home in Concord after the war. Fourteen inches of snow fell during the week before a large group from Manchester celebrated New Year's at the Lincoln Inn.

## HIGHLIGHTS OF 1947

There were bountiful winters with plenty of snow and cold in the postwar years. On New Year's Day the family drove from Lincoln to Waterville for skiing. Later they went to Cannon Mountain and the Ski Hearth Farm of Sel and Paulie Hannah in Franconia, where the temperature hit twenty-one degrees below zero. Judge and Elisabeth made their annual ten-day skiing pilgrimage in January to Mt. Tremblant. They went west for ten days skiing at Sun Valley, watching the Olympic trials on Mt. Baldy, and dined with Lowell Thomas, whose son, Sonny, roomed with Malcolm at Dartmouth. In California, they joined up with Dave and Lilla Bradley to ski at the Sugar Bowl and Donner Pass before enjoying San Francisco and the grandchildren. They boarded the eastbound train, which passed through Ogden, Utah, crossed Wyoming the next day, arrived in Chicago in a storm, and pulled into Boston—"glad to be home."

Ralph Davis, plagued with high blood pressure, had another hemorrhage and had to take it easy. He rarely came to the office anymore. Charles' engagement to Carol Evarts was announced in the spring, and they were married in September at Carol's family house in Garrison, New York, up the Hudson River. Carol's father, William Evarts, attended St. Paul's School and Harvard Law School with Judge, practiced law with Winthrop, Stimson in New York City, and was this author's godfather.

The Manchester community was mystified by the disappearance on July 23 of college student Ann Straw, adopted daughter of Eunice and Ellis Straw, prominent citizens of Manchester, all close friends of Judge and Elisabeth and their daughter Mary. Ann was spending the summer with her family at their place on Lake Winnipesaukee and was thought to have gone swimming alone about 10 P.M. from the dock; some of her clothes and belongings were found there. No trace or sign of her ever materialized, leading to theories of kidnapping, running away, drowning, murder, or suicide. Because of the prominence of the family and Ann's attractiveness, the press let its imagination run rampant, much to the distress of her family. As late as October, Judge went to Boston at the behest of the family to talk to the press.

Judge records in his diary that he and Elisabeth had a delightful dinner at Three Acres with Gil Winant and the Sam Brooks. A few days later Gil came to dinner with John Dickey, president of Dartmouth College, and Tom Braden. Just six weeks later the world was saddened to learn on November 3 that John Gilbert Winant had shot himself at his home in Concord. He had a distinguished career as a public servant—three times governor of New Hampshire, first chairman of the Social Security Board, head of the International Labor Office in Geneva, and ambassador to the Court of St. James in London during the war years. He was highly respected for his vision, integrity, and idealism. He had been a good client and close personal friend of Judge's for thirty years. (See Chapter Four, Politics, the Progressive Movement, and John G. Winant.) Judge had a number of meetings with coexecutor Geoffrey Smith of Philadelphia; Constance Winant, Gil's widow; and Arthur Coyle on business matters and in later years with others searching for a biographer of Winant.

Judge and Elisabeth over the years took several late fall trips to Canada, usually in their convertible with the top down, all bundled up in ski pants and parkas to keep warm. In November 1947, they took a trip to the Connecticut Lakes, then to Quebec and St. Anne de Beaupre, and back to Manchester by way of Sherbrooke and Colebrook. Winter came early, with skiing in Amherst on December 6. Malcolm was elected a Rhodes scholar to spend two years of study at Oxford, at Magdalen College, where Judge had studied when he was a Rhodes scholar. With all of the children away and Mrs. Bancroft infirm, Judge and Elisabeth celebrated a white Christmas alone in Manchester with a foot of new snow on the ground. The year ended with a group of forty people from Manchester at the Dartmouth Ravine Camp at Mt. Moosilauke.

## HIGHLIGHTS OF 1948

In early 1948, Judge started having rather heavy nosebleeds along with high blood pressure. He was examined at the Hitchcock Clinic and received a good report. So far as I know, he did not take medications. I do remember that he always put a lot of salt on his food. All of this was a precursor to the stroke he suffered in the early 1960s. Judge and Elisabeth went off on their annual two-week trip to Mt. Tremblant in late January in one of the coldest winters with record snow. Temperatures hit twenty and thirty degrees below zero, which did not stop the skiing. Lowell Thomas broadcast twice while they were there, and they enjoyed skiing with him.[6] Malcolm and Susan Neidlinger of Hanover were married in April and left in the fall for England to start Malcolm's Rhodes scholarship. In July, Judge and Elisabeth drove to Quebec and boarded the *Empress of Canada* for a trip to Scotland, including the Isle of Skye, then England and France. In England, they bicycled in the Cotswold Hills and enjoyed London before taking the boat to France, where they visited Chartres, the Valley of the Dordogne, Vezelay, Auxerre, and Fontainebleau in Burgundy. Then they returned to Paris and home. Thanksgiving was traditional with Wednesday night at the Macedonia Greek restaurant, hare and hound paper chase at Three Acres, twenty-one for turkey dinner, and a square dance in the evening. After Mrs. Bancroft's death, the Christmas celebration shifted to Manchester, but Judge and Elisabeth continued to attend the midnight candlelight service at the stone church in Hopkinton on Christmas Eve.

# HIGHLIGHTS OF 1949

There was not much snow in January, even at the Ravine Camp, where New Year's Day exercise consisted of walking on old logging roads. In Manchester, Judge and Elisabeth cooked lunch on the ice at Charles' cabin in Bedford and took a walk around the back side of the Uncanoonucs. In Boston, Judge picked up French wines that he had ordered from Henry Hollis in Paris the preceding summer. (See Appendix B.2, Henry French Hollis.) Finally some snow came in late January, so Judge and Elisabeth were off to Cannon, staying at the Hannahs' Ski Hearth Farm and visiting Paulie in her new house.

Tremblant beckoned in February, even with marginal snow. Judge, always the optimist, writes in his diary, "Two inches wet snow. Good heavy skiing." The day before they left after two weeks, there were "3 inches at last." In late March, they tried Cannon but it was "rain. All trails closed."

Judge attended an MIT convocation at the Boston Garden at which Winston Churchill spoke. A few weeks later he had lunch with Constance Winant in New York City, at which she produced "a fascinating letter to Gil from [Anthony] Eden."[7]

In April, Judge and Elisabeth took the *City of San Francisco* from Chicago, west through Wyoming, to Ogden and San Francisco, where daughter Lilla met them. They hiked and biked in Yosemite. Judge spent a day in Stockton on the Arthur J. Conner case talking to witnesses. (See Chapter Twenty-Three, Probate and Tax Practice.) The family explored the Pacific Coast down to Monterey, walking on the beaches with the grandchildren. They were home in mid-May in time to get the customary little piglets for Three Acres.

In midsummer, Judge had meetings of National Life in Montpelier, after which he and Elisabeth visited with the Towner Deanes at Squabetty in Underhill, Vermont, then on to Wiscasset, Maine, to see the Sortwells before taking the boat out to Matinicus Island for five days. One day they saw a flock of white-winged crossbills, a Canadian bird usually seen in the States only at higher elevations.[8] The crossbill looks as though someone had cruelly taken a pair of pliers and twisted its bill—it appears almost deformed. One wonders how the bird feeds, although actually it is an ingenious natural adaptation for eating seeds. Judge went out with Howard Bunker early one morning to haul lobster traps, an interesting experience for neophyte Judge.

For several years a group of Manchester families went to Tanglewood in the Berkshires for a delightful long weekend of music, tennis, and swimming. Judge and Elisabeth, with whatever children were around, spent weekends at the lake. They climbed Mt. Moosilauke. It rained at the top. They walked into the Franconia Brook shelter, in the Pemigewasset Wilderness, and swam in the glorious pool just above the falls. Then they rode up the Cannon Tramway with the grandchildren and hiked down to Lonesome Lake. They climbed again with grandchildren up Cardigan over the steep, rocky ledges loaded with blueberries. Nice as the grandchildren are, Judge notes in his diary: "Children wore us out."

Judge presided at the 46th Annual Meeting of the Forestry Society. Then Judge and Elisabeth took off for the customary fall trip to Quebec in November. They returned in time for the Thanksgiving festivities, including the Wednesday-evening dinner at the Macedonia and the next day hare and hound chase followed by the dinner and dance at Three Acres. The plans for the new house proved too expensive, so the architect, Elizabeth Manning, and the contractor, Ernest Swanburgh, pared down the plans. A chimney fire at 940 Chestnut Street caused by burning Christmas wrappings created a lot of noise and excitement—many firemen but only a little smoke. As the firemen, clad in their bright yellow raincoats and hard hats, came up the porch steps to enter the house, Elisabeth's visiting sister, Jane Shiverick, commanded each fireman to open his mouth and she popped in a delicious Christmas chocolate. There was no snow, so Elisabeth and Judge went looking for large stone front-door steps from abandoned farmhouses in Candia, Ashland, and Tilton. On December 30, the papers told the story of the euthanasia killing of a comatose patient by Judge's doctor, Hermann Sander. Judge testified as a character witness. The doctor was ultimately acquitted. Once again the family headed for the Ravine Camp for New Year's.

# Notes

1. At Thanksgiving that year, I called the family at Ibus' house, talked for a , and then asked to talk to Blanche, my wife. Ibus kept on talking, ignoring my request. I finally figured that Ibus thought that she was talking to Malcolm and so advised her, which turned out to be the case. Ibus roared with laughter at her mistake and dutifully turned over the phone to Blanche, stating she couldn't

understand why Malcolm (then unmarried) was so interested in talking to Blanche.

2. This was prior to the construction of the Bow steam-generating plant, whose discharge cooling water now warms the river and keeps it from freezing over, to the joy of the wintering bald eagles.

3. During the war years, Judge and Elisabeth bought a pair of pigs (to stimulate competition for food) each spring, fattened them up in the summer, and had them slaughtered in the fall to provide them with meat, which they froze or had smoked (bacon and hams). The pigs were named Gaston and Josephine for the twins in *Babar*, the delightful French children's book series. Another pair were Castor and Pollux, from mythology and the stars.

4. The postman who delivered the mail to Judge's house saw the foreign postcard and read it, then brought it to my wife, Blanche, only two doors away, and said he brought good news. Blanche took the postcard, recognized Malcolm's writing, and got in touch with Alice Linehan, Judge's secretary, to try to get in touch with Judge and Elisabeth. Alice then called Bob Kiely, and by the greatest of coincidences the message got through.

5. One of Malcolm's escapades while a hutman is still legend in the mountains. At Lonesome Lake on the other side of Franconia Notch, where there is also a hut, the AMC had been loaned a canoe on the condition that it be given good care. At Greenleaf Hut there is a small mountain tarn. The Greenleaf crew thought it would be nice if they had the canoe at Lonesome, so in the dark of night, some of the boys descended the mountain, climbed up the 1,000 feet to Lonesome Lake, purloined the canoe, lugged it on their backs back down to the notch, and climbed up the 3,000 feet to Greenleaf, depositing the canoe in the tarn. Of course, news of such an event travels fast, and it wasn't long before the crew at Lakes-of-the-Clouds hut on Mount Washington arrived in the dead of night and removed the canoe once again. When the owner heard about the treatment accorded his beloved canoe, he was irate, demanded its immediate return, and vowed never to assist the AMC again.

6. Lowell Thomas' son, Sonny, was Malcolm's roommate at Dartmouth.

7. So far, I have been unable to identify the letter.

8. Judge and Elisabeth had a pair that wintered in 1922 at 940 Chestnut Street. (See Chapter Seven, Interlude 1920–1929, Highlights of 1922.) I saw several at the Great Gulf shelter on Mount Washington several years later.

# TIME LINE, 1945

The time lines cover one year in each decade and summarize Judge's activity away from home.

| | | |
|---|---|---|
| *January* | 6 | To Plymouth, Cannon Mt. and stayed at Sel Hannah's 20 deg. below. |
| | 7 | Good day skiing. |
| | 8 | Skied all day. |
| | 9 | Boston to talk new financing with Gil Verney. |
| | 11 | Boston to meet Lilla and Kim, train six hours late, stayed over at Copley Plaza. |
| | 16 | Boston for B&MRR meetings. |
| | 18 | New York City at night. |
| | 19 | Breakfast with Gil Verney on refinancing. St. Paul's School (SPS) trustees' meeting. |
| | 20 | Day with Steve Stackpole. Home. |
| | 22 | Montpelier. Evening with Fred Howland [president of National Life]. |
| | 23 | National Life directors' meeting. Home. |
| | | |
| *February* | 7 | Boston with Verney on order to change from rayon to cotton. |
| | 8 | Hanover, concert. |
| | 9 | Lovely ski by Reservoir and over Balch Hill. |
| | 10 | Ski on Oak Hill. |
| | 11 | Ski on Oak Hill. |
| | 13 | Boston for B&MRR meetings. |
| | 18 | Skied Uncanoonuc Mt. |
| | 21 | Boston to take over securities in Ida Folsom estate. |
| | 25 | Skied Uncanoonuc Mt. |
| | 27 | Boston for B&MRR meetings. |
| | 28 | Concord to speak on adoption bill. |
| | | |
| *March* | 2 | Evening train to Plymouth and Lincoln. |
| | 3 | Rain and cold, tram not running. Home. |
| | 4 | Night train to New York City. |
| | 5 | All day with Verney and Berkowitz on White Weld financing. Dinner with Ben Tomlinson [Rhodes classmate]. |
| | 6 | Concord for Supreme Court argument on Amoskeag highway case. |
| | 8 | Newport for hearing on Deery case. Off to Tremblant in sleeper. |
| | 9 | A.M. train from Montreal to Tremblant. Skied. |

| | | |
|---|---|---|
| | 10 | Skied, icy, fell in rut and cracked bone in wrist. |
| | 11 | Watched Standard Course race. Skied in p.m. |
| | 12 | Snowed all day. |
| | 13 | Beautiful snow on all trails. |
| | 14 | Turning warm. |
| | 15 | Very warm and soft on some trails. |
| | 16 | Set slalom. |
| | 17 | Montreal. Shop. Night train home. |
| | 20 | Boston with JPC and Berkowitz on Verney financing. |
| | 23 | Drive to Laconia and found Berlin bus not running. Home. |
| | 26 | Spoke in Amherst on Dumbarton Oaks conference. |
| | 27 | Boston on B&MRR and Verney. |
| | 28 | Boston with EJ Abbott for War Labor Board hearing. |
| *April* | 1 | Concord for Easter dinner with Mrs. Bancroft. |
| | 9 | Boston to see Verney. Dartmouth Alumni fund dinner. |
| | 11 | Boston Annual meeting of B&MRR. Dinner at Algonquin Club to honor Ned French [president of B&MRR]. |
| | 13 | Hanover for XC. |
| | 15 | Night train for Montreal for start of western trip., |
| | 16 | Bumped into Bob Kiley who advised my office trying to reach me. Called office and learned postcard received signed by Malcolm, who is alive and well. Happy Day. Lunch celebration and caught train west. |
| | 17 | Through northern Ontario, along Lake Superior. Happy about Malcolm. |
| | 18 | Quiet day crossing the plains of Manitoba and Saskatchewan. |
| | 19 | Glorious ride from Calgary into mountains. Off at Banff, 24 mile bus to Sunshine Lodge, ski run. |
| | 20 | Ski toured up Cairns in a.m. |
| | 21 | Glorious snowfield and run down. |
| | 22 | To top of Brewster in a.m., top of Standish in p.m. Five ptarmigan up there. |
| | 23 | To top of Brewster, last runs, down to Banff, saw 5 deer on road. |
| | 24 | Noon train west. Very interesting day through mountains. |
| | 25 | Blacks met us in Vancouver and drove us to Seattle, over to Bainbridge. San Francisco Conference opens. |
| | 26 | Most enjoyable visit. Saw city. |
| | 27 | Spent day on Island. Met many friends. |

| | 28 | Noon train to Portland to visit the Rockeys. |
| | 29 | Quiet day. |
| | 30 | Lunch at Albermarle Club. Night train. |
| *May* | 1 | San Francisco. Lilla met us. Dartmouth dinner. |
| | 2 | United Nations Plenary Session. Molotov presiding. |
| | 3 | Took babies to Golden Gate Park and Zoo. |
| | 4 | Quiet pleasant day of visiting. |
| | 5 | Golden Gate Park, Fisherman's Wharf. |
| | 6 | Biked down coast. Delightful dinner with John Dickey. |
| | 7 | Unconditional surrender by Germany. |
| | 8 | V-E day celebration. Dinner at Officer's Mess, Treasure Island. |
| | 9 | Drove across Golden Gate Bridge into Marin County. |
| | 10 | Quiet day with babies. |
| | 11 | Lunch at Cliff House. Streamliner *City of San Francisco* up through Donner Pass. |
| | 12 | Lovely sunrise approaching Salt Lake City. |
| | 13 | Chicago at noon. |
| | 14 | Boston at 3:00. Home. |
| | 15 | Boston on Verney, B&MRR. |
| | 23 | New York City. |
| | 24 | All day with Verney on White Weld, then Brown Co. |
| | 25 | Breakfast John and Blanche in Boston. John back from Navy in Sicily. Ross tax case. |
| *June* | 2 | Concord. SPS trustees. |
| | 5 | Boston all day. |
| | 6 | To Franconia for Mary's graduation from St. Mary's. Mary did the Admiral in *Pinafore*. |
| | 7 | Mary graduated. Hanover for Fincom meeting. "Hop" [president Ernest M. Hopkins] to resign. |
| | 8 | Hanover. Trustee meeting. |
| | 9 | Lake. |
| | 13 | Boston for CIO–Abbott Worsted hearing.d |
| | 19 | Boston for B&MRR Directors' meeting. |
| | 21 | Swim and supper in Hampton. |
| | 23 | Canterbury for picnic and swim at Burroughs. Lake. |
| | 24 | NY train. |
| | 25 | Very hot. White Weld on completion of Verney financing. |
| | 26 | SPS committee meeting. Berkowitz from Boston on Verney. |

| | 27 | Another day on Verney. Dinner with Bill Evarts and Pick Bennet [Harvard Law School classmates]. |
| | 29 | Federal Court on Shapiro OPA case. Lake. |
| | 30 | Lake. |
| *July* | 1 | Lake. Gaga [Mrs. Bancroft] over for church service in house. |
| | 2 | Peterboro to confer with Rob and Joanne Bass. Our dear Malcolm came tonight, to Lake. |
| | 3 | Happy, happy day. Swims and picnic. Malc's stories keep us enthralled. |
| | 4 | Clement's Hill for kick-the-can. We hang on Malc's every word. |
| | 5 | Lake. |
| | 6 | Typical Pasquaney days—with delightful evenings with Malc. |
| | 7 | Cardigan–lovely day. |
| | 8 | Church in Lodge. Crescent Beach picnic, home. |
| | 9 | Boston. |
| | 10 | Boston. |
| | 12 | All day and evening in Boston on Verney—Bank. |
| | 13 | Verney in a.m. Home, Rob and Joanne Bass in p.m. Lake. |
| | 14 | Lake with Woodburys. |
| | 15 | John's leave over, off to New York City. Home. |
| | 16 | Montpelier with Ned. Evening at Howlands'. |
| | 17 | Directors' meeting. Home. |
| | 20 | Boston, then Lake. |
| | 21 | Lake, blueberrying, picnic at Crescent Beach. |
| | 22 | Church. Down in p.m. |
| | 23 | New York City. Met John and Blanche for dinner. |
| | 24 | All day on financing. |
| | 25 | All day with Gil. Flew to Boston. |
| | 26 | Worked with Abe Berkowitz. |
| | 27 | Lake in evening. Very tiring work. |
| | 28 | Belle Isle picnic. |
| | 29 | Church. |
| | 30 | Boston and New York City. Met John and Blanche. |
| | 31 | Philadelphia to clear up with SEC. |
| *August* | 3 | Boston to execute bonds and mortgage. |
| | 4 | Lake. John and Blanche up. Picnic at Grey Rocks. |
| | 5 | Boston and New York City. |
| | 6 | All day to get ready for closing. Atom bomb dropped on Hiroshima. |

| 7 | Closed Verney deal. Plane to Boston and home. |
| 10 | Boston for Dartmouth trustees' meeting to meet John Dickey. |
| 11 | Lake. |
| 12 | Walked. Down to Manchester. |
| 14 | Boston. Japs surrender. War over. Lake. |
| 15 | Walk over Skylands. |
| 16 | Picnic lunch above Lincoln. Walked into Zealand Hut. |
| 17 | Good day climbing Mt. Hale. |
| 18 | A-Z trail, over Willey to Willey Station, home. |
| 21 | Concord at St. Paul's School with Fred Larson, architect. |
| 22 | Concord, long meetings on State Council of Social Agencies. |
| 23 | Peterborough for dinner with the Basses. |
| 24 | Boston for Dartmouth trustees' meeting, accepted Hoppie's resignation and elected John Dickey, President. |
| 25 | Lake. |
| 26 | Lake. Cold, rainy day, burn brush. |
| 28 | Boston, B&MRR meeting. |
| 29 | Portsmouth to start settlement of Elizabeth Elwyn Langdon estate. |
| 30 | Portsmouth and Exeter on Langdon. |
| 31 | Lake in evening. |

| *September* | 1 | Rainy day. John here [from Navy in New York City]. |
| | 3 | Boston, to meet Dave, Lilla, and family from San Francisco. |
| | 7 | Lake. Hot, picnic Grey Rocks. |
| | 9 | Onaway beach with children. |
| | 11 | Boston, B&MRR meeting. |
| | 12 | Spaulding's for lunch, visit Langdon House. |
| | 18 | Drove Malc to Fitchburg for train to Deerfield as junior master. |
| | 20 | Boston, various matters. |
| | 24 | Concord for meeting State Social Planning Council. |
| | 25 | Boston, B&MRR meetings. |
| | 26 | Dublin with JPC to meet Greenville Clark on Monadnock case. |
| | 28 | Concord on various matters. High Stoy [pastureland with view that Elisabeth and Judge bought] in Webster and Lake. |
| | 29 | Quiet day. Walked old Orange road. |

|       |    |                                                                                                  |
|-------|----|--------------------------------------------------------------------------------------------------|
|       | 30 | Clear day. Climbed Plymouth mountain, home.                                                      |
| *October* | 4  | Interesting day on appraisal of Langdon House in Portsmouth.                                 |
|       | 6  | Deerfield to see Malcolm, and Northampton to see Mary.                                           |
|       | 7  | Lunch at Deerfield, lovely ride via Goshen, walk on hills, home.                                |
|       | 9  | Boston on B&MRR meetings.                                                                        |
|       | 12 | Lake.                                                                                            |
|       | 13 | Walk over "Kriegie" path. John Jr. home and out of the Navy.                                     |
|       | 15 | Hanover.                                                                                         |
|       | 16 | Early drive to Montpelier for National Life meeting.                                            |
|       | 17 | Concord for Forestry meeting and NH Historical Society meeting on Langdon House.                 |
|       | 19 | Concord to PUC with Bill Taft on Greenville Electric.                                            |
|       | 20 | Concord SPS trustees' meeting.                                                                   |
|       | 24 | Boston and New York City.                                                                        |
|       | 25 | Delightful meeting with Bishop Manning on Langdon Estate. p.m. with executors. Went to *Carousel*. |
|       | 26 | Boston with Gil Verney.                                                                          |
|       | 27 | Deerfield and Northampton to see Malcolm and Mary.                                               |
|       | 28 | Malc and Mary home. Big family dinner.                                                           |
|       | 29 | John Jr. back in office after 3 1/2 years in Navy.                                               |
|       | 30 | Boston, B&MRR meeting and Whiting tax suit.                                                      |
|       | 31 | Hanover. Dartmouth trustees' meeting.                                                            |
| *November* | 1  | John Dickey inducted 12th President of Dartmouth College.                                    |
|       | 3  | Concord on CB Little tax refund.                                                                 |
|       | 9  | Hanover, presided at Dartmouth night.                                                            |
|       | 10 | Drove Ravine Camp, walked on Snapper trail, on to Colebrook.                                     |
|       | 11 | Clear day, up to Dartmouth College Grant, new road toward Hellgate. Lunch there and drove to Intervale. |
|       | 12 | Fine ride home on dull day.                                                                      |
|       | 13 | Boston on B&MRR. Stan Brown in office to begin work.                                             |
|       | 16 | Hanover. Paul Robeson concert.                                                                   |
|       | 17 | Football, Cornell 20, Dartmouth 13 in snow.                                                      |

|    |    |                                                                          |
|----|----|--------------------------------------------------------------------------|
|    | 25 | Concord for dinner with Mrs. Bancroft.                                   |
|    | 26 | Portsmouth and Exeter on Langdon and Folsom cases.                       |
|    | 27 | Boston B&MRR meetings, Langdon estate.                                   |
|    | 30 | Boston with Abe Berkowitz on Verney. Dartmouth lunch at Union Club on War Memorial. |

*December*  

|    |    |                                                                          |
|----|----|--------------------------------------------------------------------------|
|    | 1  | Boston, all day, on Verney purchase of Greenwich Worsted Co.             |
|    | 8  | Walk with Elisabeth 10 miles over Grasmere Dunbarton Road.               |
|    | 9  | Terribly lame today.                                                     |
|    | 11 | Boston on Whiting tax case, New York City in p.m. saw *The Bloomer Girls*. |
|    | 12 | Conference on distribution to Cathedral-Langdon. Fly home.               |
|    | 14 | Met NH Historical Soc. committee on Langdon House.                       |
|    | 15 | Cannon Mt. good skiing, stayed at Hannahs'.                              |
|    | 16 | 5 runs on good trails.                                                   |
|    | 18 | Boston B&MRR.                                                            |
|    | 19 | Stormy. Drove to Fitchburg to get Mary on vacation.                     |
|    | 20 | Boston to see Crocker on Langdon.                                        |
|    | 24 | Concord to trim tree. Hopkinton for midnight service.                    |
|    | 25 | Concord. Lovely Christmas.e                                              |
|    | 27 | Boston on Folsom Estate. Saw *The Late George Apley*.                    |
|    | 28 | All day on Verney buying Greenwich Mill.                                 |

# TWENTY-TWO

# Miscellaneous Business Clients

## A. ABRAHAM MACHINIST
### 1882–1976

Abraham Machinist was a dry goods merchant in Manchester who started out as a wholesaler of hosiery and remnant Amoskeag Manufacturing Company textiles to small dry goods stores all over New England. He later expanded into the retail business. For some fifty years he was Judge's client.

Mr. Machinist was born in Romania in 1882 to Moses Steifleman, a tailor, and his wife. Moses, wanting to know what machinery and tools were available in his business, traveled to Hamburg, Germany, to attend a trade show, where he saw and bought his first Singer sewing machine. After that he was called "Moses, the Machinist." A few years later, Moses and his sizable family emigrated to America, landed in New York, and passed through immigration at Ellis Island. When asked to give his name, he responded "Moses," and, somewhat confused by the foreign language (English), when asked the rest of his name, Moses said, "I am Moses, the machinist. So the family's official papers named him "Moses Machinist," and his children were also "Machinist."

Moses got a job in a sweatshop garment factory on the Lower East Side. He lived in one of the multistory tenements with his wife and six children (three others having previously died in infancy). Moses' health failed under those conditions and his neighbors urged him to get out of New York City. A friend in Worcester, Massachusetts, invited him to come there. The older children were moving out, to Cleveland, Tennessee, and other places. Moses, with his wife and two children, Abraham and Sarah, traveled to Worcester and established a home in a basement apartment on Green Street. Moses continued his tailoring. Abraham went to the Worcester schools and helped in the tailor shop by taking samples of cloth to show to Holy Cross students and soliciting orders for suits. Moses was a tough old bird, a strict orthodox Jew (according to his grandson, Milton Machinist), who insisted that he and his family attend the synagogue daily. He took the Scriptures literally; when he reached the age of three score years and ten, the biblical end of a man's life, he announced he wanted to go to Palestine, the motherland, before he died. He traveled alone. Palestine was then under the control of the Turkish empire. Moses was killed by a runaway horse about two years later while still in Palestine.

Abraham hated being cooped up in a tailor shop. He wanted to be a salesman. He learned of a hosiery mill in Goff's Falls, New Hampshire, just south of Manchester, which sold men's hosiery. He visited the mill, liked the people, jumped at the opportunity to sell, and in 1909 settled in Manchester. He found a Mrs. Siegel (the grandmother of Bill Green of Sheehan, Phinney, Bass & Green), who served kosher meals. He lived next door in Mrs. McCarthy's rooming house. He soon found out that the Amoskeag Mills had lots of remnant cloth for sale. Some may have been seconds with minor defects and some simply yard end goods.

Abe rented the back of a store on Hanover Street, where he could keep his goods. He shared space with Mr. Cronin, who sold shoes; Mr. Bodwell, who ran a coal business; and a house painter. Abe traveled around to dry goods stores in the small towns of New Hampshire showing his fabric samples, taking orders, and collecting accounts, which were payable once a year.

Business was good, and in a few years he took over the whole store on Hanover Street. His first employee, Mrs. Lord, stayed for more than thirty years. He kept expanding—adding sales personnel and collectors for his wholesale business. After Amoskeag failed in 1936, he bought remnants from other textile suppliers.

In 1947, he rented the Mirror Block on Hanover Street. He kept his inventory of fabrics on the upper floors, which could not be used for a store because of the ancient lightweight construction, and started a retail remnant store on the ground floor, specializing in fabrics and accessories. Wholesale customers could come in to see fabric samples and leave their orders. The owner of the Mirror Block, Mr. Cashin, died, and the Manchester Savings Bank controlled the property. Mr. Machinist bought the property in about 1947 with financial assistance from the Manchester bank. A few years later he purchased the adjoining Harrington, Opera, and Smith blocks and expanded his retail store, adding new departments, such as draperies, linens, women's clothes, and gifts. Downtown Manchester was still the retail shopping area for the city.

Abe Machinist transferred his real estate business into a corporation, EBM Realty, Inc. (the initials were those of his wife, Esther B. Machinist). In 1952 the city taxed EBM Realty, Inc., at a much higher ratio of assessed value to fair market value than other taxpayers, an inequitable situation. In 1953 Judge McLane brought suit against the city to abate the tax. The suit necessitated substantial preparation, including examining all deeds of sales of Manchester downtown commercial property at the Registry of Deeds in

Nashua. The fair market value of Machinist's property was established by testimony of appraisers, and the ratio of fair market value to assessed value was compared to that of other downtown property to determine if Mr. Machinist's property was being assessed at a higher ratio than other comparable property. The suit resulted in a substantial abatement.

Almost all of Machinist's financing of his real estate purchases over the years was done through the Manchester Savings Bank. Judge McLane or his office was involved in those transactions. Furthermore, Judge did the estate planning work for Abe Machinist and prepared wills and other documents. The office subsequently settled the estates of both Abraham and Esther.

About 1960 a shopping center was built at the corner of Maple and Valley Streets, which was opposed by the Downtown Merchants Association. In the 1960s, Jordan Marsh came to town in the Bedford Mall. That mall marked the beginning of the large shopping malls on the outskirts of the city and the decline of the downtown retail trade. Abe was getting along in years and retired from active management in 1956. His son Milton became the manager, and Abe sold him the store in 1970.[1] The wholesale business had been declining over the years as many of the small-town dry goods stores closed when shopping moved to the large communities and malls.

Abe always thought that good real estate was an excellent long-term investment. He and his sister, Sarah, bought the block on Elm Street where McQuade's is located. They also bought a block on Central Street where the E&R Laundry is located. Abe added a second floor on that building to get more rent. He also bought more property on Elm Street—the site of the State Theater (now demolished), which he sold to Shea Enterprises, and the site of Lemay's Jewelry Store. Abe rarely bought real estate without consulting Walter Parker, whom Abe called "Daddy." Parker was a very wealthy man and head of the Manchester National and Savings banks.

Occasionally Abe ran into anti-Semitic feeling. Once when he tried to buy insurance on his inventory, he was advised it wasn't available, so Abe went to another agent, Ferdinand Edgerly, and obtained it in no time. Abe assumed that the refusal was an anti-Semitic act, since the insurance was in fact readily available.

Abe and Esther built a fine home on Union Street where they raised their two sons, Burt and Milton, both of whom went to Harvard University. Burt moved to Boston and became a stockbroker, while Milton remained in Manchester and helped his father run the businesses. Milton became a reserve officer in the Army while at Harvard and served on active duty from 1941 to 1946; he became a director of the Amoskeag Savings Bank in 1954, subsequently sold the stores, and continues an active role in the community. Abe was an active Mason and an incorporator of the Manchester Savings Bank. He died in 1976.

## B. SILVER BROTHERS

### Morris Silver, 1897–1986
### Henry Silver, 1900–1988

In 1897 Morris Silver was born in Russian Poland. His brother Henry was born there three years later. They came with their parents and two other children to the United States in 1907[2] and settled in West Roxbury, Massachusetts, where the father, Samuel, worked in the used wool business.

Morris went to Boston public schools and then to work to help his younger brother Henry go to Boston Latin School. Although an honor student, Henry did not complete school because of family financial pressures. The two boys learned the tricks of the marketplace by buying and selling produce wholesale. Then in 1918 they decided to find a quieter market in the New England area that they could expand. They settled on Manchester, New Hampshire, a large textile manufacturing city, and opened a wholesale fruit and vegetable store on Elm Street between Traction and Granite Streets. They bought a truck, which Morris drove to Boston to haul produce from the markets there back to Manchester while Henry did the selling. Soon they added dry groceries such as peas and beans and moved around the corner on Traction Street next to the trolley car barn where there was more room. They moved again to get on the railroad side tracks on Granite Street. In 1933 they entered the wholesale grocery business under the name of Silver Brothers.[3]

When Prohibition was repealed by President Franklin Roosevelt in 1933, Morris and Henry negotiated to get sole distribution franchises for Kruger and Ebling beer for the whole state. Later they added the Ruppert franchise, which became Knickerbocker; later still they acquired distribution franchises for Miller, Heineken, Molson, and some smaller breweries. They were energetic merchants, always expanding their market territory, trying new ways to make a penny here and a penny there, and paying attention to detail. Prior to World War II, the Silver brothers relied on Judge McLane and John Carleton for legal advice, but after the war Ken Graf was their principal adviser and general counsel.

Myer (Mike) Friedman joined Silver Brothers, Inc., as chief financial officer in 1943, having graduated from Boston University and become a CPA in 1936. Mike had several years of experience in the shoe industry and stayed forty-three years with the Silvers. About 1940 they acquired an old mill building from Amoskeag Industries, Inc., called One Seventy Seven Granite Street, which became the name of their real estate company. They hired a new grocery buyer, Eli Rudnick. In the 1940s they merged with the Philip Porter Company, wholesale grocers in Nashua; they changed the name to

Consolidated Foods, Inc., and transferred the Manchester grocery business to Nashua to make room for the soft drink plant inventory. Rudnick was sent to Nashua to do the purchasing temporarily but decided to stay.

Silver Brothers eyed the soft drink market because it would complement the beer business, but sugar was in short supply during World War II so they waited. Henry heard that Cott Bottling in White Plains, New York, was looking to expand its soft drink products. Henry met with John Cott and signed up a distribution agreement in 1947. The Silvers acquired the Cott franchise for distributing carbonated drinks and organized the Cott Bottling Company of Manchester, which expanded from 25,000 square feet and seven employees in 1947 to 400,000 square feet and three hundred employees in 1951 with a capacity of 5 million cases annually, the largest independent bottler in the United States. Henry Silver was able to develop "prestige" accounts and place the Cott products in Jordan Marsh stores in Massachusetts, Gimbel's in New York, and Bamberger's in Newark, New Jersey. The dining cars of the New York, New Haven & Hartford Railroad and the B&MRR served Cott beverages. Morris Silver coined the slogan "It's Cott to be good," which was effectively used in the company's promotions. In 1949, a root beer plant in Natick was purchased as well as an Orange Crush plant in 1952 in Somerville, both in Massachusetts. Bottling plants in Portland, Maine; Perth Amboy, New Jersey; Pittsburgh, Pennsylvania; and Montreal, Canada; were bought in the 1950s, and plants in Miami, Florida; Troy, New York; and Chicago were franchised. The company maintained a fleet of well over a hundred trucks. The Montreal plant introduced Cott beverages to Canada.

In the late 1940s, Cott couldn't keep up with the demand, so the Silvers decided to become a bottling franchisee and formed Cott Bottling Company of New Hampshire. In 1950, the bottling machines were installed at 177 Granite Street and were ready to roll when a bad fire swept the building, causing three floors to collapse on the new machines. Back to square one! The plant was rebuilt and expanded. In a few years, the franchisee, Silver, was bigger than the franchisor, Cott, an unusual occurrence.

Henry's mind never relaxed—he was always thinking of new ideas. He made innovative approaches to stores to encourage them to buy in volume. He made entrepreneurs of his salesmen; he sold them their trucks, assigned a territory, and made them distributors, with the result that they made good money and sold plenty of beverages. When sugar-free food became popular, Henry Silver conceived the idea of producing sugar-free beverages. At first sorbitol was used, but that was declared illegal by the FDA, so the company chemist developed a beverage using saccharin. Henry worked with the canning industry to make a suitable can for soft drinks. (The carbonates in soft drinks are much more corrosive on cans than is beer and

were under greater pressure.) Henry also introduced nonreturnable bottles. He made lots of money on the five-cent deposit paid on the returnable
bottles. This led to a fight with the IRS as to how to treat the deposit. It
was decided to depreciate it over a three-year period. The formula finally
worked out with the IRS became the industry standard. The Silver
Brothers had close relations with the New Hampshire Liquor Commission
because of their beer business. Why not bottle cocktails? thought the
Silvers. Thus was born Jenkins Spirits, named for the traditional English
butler who served fine drinks. At first only cocktails were bottled, but this
was expanded to include straight liquor sold through the New Hampshire
Liquor Commission. Henry cut a deal with Sardi's restaurant in the theater
district of Manhattan, paying them a royalty on the sale of coffee that
Henry attractively packaged and sold.

The beer and soft drink businesses were doing well, so the idea of going
public with the soft drink business naturally came up. Ken Graf and the
McLane law firm performed much of the legal work involved in the registration with the Securities and Exchange Commission (SEC) by Cott
Bottling of New England, the franchisee, preparation of the prospectus and
subsequent securities matters. On the Initial Public Offering (IPO), the stock
was sold at six dollars a share and in time went up to fifteen dollars. Three
years later, the franchisor went public as Cott Corporation. Subsequently,
John Cott suggested that the two companies merge, which they did and were
listed on the American Stock Exchange as Cott Corporation.

Henry Silver used to call John Cott, the principal one of the Cott
brothers, about ten times a day for a couple of years to find out what the
Cotts were doing to increase sales—much to the annoyance of John Cott,
who finally concluded he wanted out. He found National Industries of
Louisville, Kentucky, a conglomerate that had no experience in the beverage industry, to buy out the Cott controlling interest in Cott Corporation
at six dollars a share. The Silver brothers put their heads together and
decided that they would offer to buy out the Cotts' interest for $4 million
and not have to deal with National Industries. The financing was lined up
and the deal looked as though it would move forward, when Henry decided
he couldn't go through with it because of his health. Shortly thereafter,
Henry revealed that he had just seen his doctor, who told him he was suffering from complete exhaustion and if he wanted to live, he'd better quit
the business for the time being. The sale of the soft drink business to
National Industries went through, but the buyer handled the business
poorly, lost money, sold out to two men from Canada Dry, and eventually
went into bankruptcy, thus taking Cott beverages off the market.

Morris and Henry were very different personalities and frequently were
at odds with each other. Mike Friedman was the go-between and sometimes

would consult with Ken Graf. In 1982, Mike Friedman wanted to retire, and gave his notice, but things weren't going well. Cott Canada, which had been formed after the sale to National Industries, Inc., was sold. Morris' son, Bert, and Henry's son, Eddie, were trying to step in to fill their fathers' shoes but without much success. Bert now lives in Bedford and owns Jenkins Spirits; Eddie lives in Montreal, where he has a couple of businesses. Henry convinced Mike Friedman to return to help out, which he did for three and a half more years. By the late 1970s, Morris was suffering from Alzheimer's disease, of which he died in 1986. Henry was slowing up as Alzheimer's took its toll on him, leading to his death in 1988. It became necessary to sell some of the businesses to raise cash to pay federal estate taxes in both estates.

Morris Silver was active politically and in charitable organizations. He was a member and chairman of the city planning board for twenty-eight years, a member and chairman of the New Hampshire State Parole Board for twenty-eight years, as well as chairman of the New Hampshire Prison Board of Trustees. He was a trustee of Bentley College. He was active in a number of local charities, such as the Red Cross, United Cerebral Palsy Foundation, Sacred Heart Hospital, and the Conference of Christians and Jews. Henry and Morris were codonors of the Silver Wing of the Brandeis University physics building, and both were made Fellows of the university.

Henry Silver worked actively on the boards of several educational institutions, including Suffolk University and Nathaniel Hawthorne College in Antrim, New Hampshire. The college's new library was named for Henry and his wife, Hilda, for which they gave generously and where Henry was awarded an honorary degree of doctor of business administration in 1971. Henry was a national board member of the Jewish National Hospital in Denver. He received an award for his good works from the Conference of Christians and Jews. He had a close friendship with Richard Cardinal Cushing, working on behalf of the special children at the Kennedy Memorial Hospital in Massachusetts. When Ted Williams was an active baseball player, Henry worked with him as New Hampshire chairman of the Jimmy Fund. Henry was appointed to the New Hampshire Athletic Commission. He also assisted a number of local Manchester organizations and was active politically.

## C. SHAER SHOE

Sam Shaer has been a client of the office for over fifty years and from the 1940s was a great friend of Kenneth Graf. Sam's father emigrated from Poland in 1910 to Boston and then moved to Worcester, where he had a wholesale and retail shoe business. Sam's father wanted him to be a doctor, so Sam went first to Clark University, then the University of Michigan; but after three years, Sam knew that medicine was not for him and so advised his father. About the same time, Sam's cousin, David Shaer, was working in Nashua as general manager and salesman for a shoe shop, but he wanted to branch out on his own; he asked Sam's father to back him, which he did. David and Sam formed Shaer Shoe Company. Dave was the outside man in charge of sales; Sam was the inside man in charge of production and operations. Mr. Shaer provided the capital. In about 1936 they purchased a mill on Kelley Street in West Manchester and did so well making women's heel shoes they needed additional space. They acquired from Amoskeag Industries, Inc., the Langdon building adjacent to the upper canal at the north end of the mill yard, which is known as the Myrna Shoe plant. Judge, representing Amoskeag Industries, undoubtedly dealt with them on the sale of the building.

Dave was a very colorful person, a wonderful salesman, and a successful businessman, always bringing in orders in the volatile shoe industry. He owned twenty-eight horses, which he raced at Rockingham and other parks, and so knew Lou Smith, president of the track. Dave had a labor attorney in Boston who was available only when he could get to Manchester by train. Dave wanted someone more immediately available in New Hampshire, someone who was a scrapper and could provide better service than the Boston attorney in connection with the effort of the union to organize the plant in Manchester. Knowing that Lou Smith had New Hampshire counsel, Dave talked to him, and he strongly recommended his own attorney, Kenneth Graf. Thus, Shaer Shoe become a client. Dave and Ken got along well. Ken gained further kudos from Dave as the result of reinstating Dave's horse. In a "claiming" race, Dave had won a horse, which was declared a "ringer" (imposter) by the Pinkerton Detective Agency, working for the New York Jockey Club; the agency determined that the horse's name had been changed. Under the New York Jockey Club rules, the horse was thus barred from ever racing again under the auspices of the New York Jockey Club. Ken Graf took on the case and won, getting the horse reinstated—a most unusual event.

Dave died in 1976.

Ken also worked closely with Sam, who ran the business in Manchester, and they became personal friends. For over fifty years, Ken and Sam were familiar faces having coffee or lunch together at the Hotel Carpenter and later at one of Manchester's downtown restaurants. Sam married Eunice Silver, Henry Silver's daughter. Ken did a substantial amount of labor negotiating over the years. In 1960, when the company went public, the firm became deeply involved in securities work. Ken became a director in 1960.

Shaer Shoe, which never lost money, has had plants in several towns. There had been one in Lowell, but Wang Labs pushed the wage rates too high, so the company went to Farmington, Maine. It also had a mill in

Milford, Massachusetts. Manchester became too expensive when the electronics businesses started moving in. Also, in recent years cheaper shoes were made in Thailand and Korea, which forced the closing of many New England shoe shops. The company still owns the Langdon Mill, which along with many other mill buildings in the mill yard, is vacant.

## D. THE HUBBARD FAMILY

In what appears to be the first business with the Hubbard family in Walpole, New Hampshire, Judge met with them in 1952. He subsequently wrote a long brief on their sophisticated farm business, which was then in its second generation and involved the genetic breeding of chicken stock as laying hens and broilers. The firm began representing the business, Hubbard Farms, Inc., initially as a result of a litigation case in which Kenneth Graf was on the other side and bested the Hubbard Farms' attorney. The Hubbards decided that they wanted to hire Ken Graf for the future and thus began a long and productive association.

Eventually the business was sold to Merck Drug Company by means of an exchange of stock, which resulted in a substantial profit. Ken Graf was very much involved in the transaction. As a result, the Hubbard family became owners of a large amount of Merck stock. They gave away much of their newfound wealth and became a very large factor in charitable giving in the state of New Hampshire, particularly assisting the New Hampshire Charitable Fund with its charitable efforts and new building program in 1993. The firm continues to assist the family members with their charitable giving and tax planning.

## E. THE GLEN HOUSE

The Glen House, built in the mid-1800s, is located in Pinkham Notch on the easterly side of Mount Washington at the base of the carriage road. The Libby family has owned the Glen House and the Mount Washington Summit Road Company since its inception. In the 1950s, after the war years, there was a tremendous interest in expanding ski areas in the West and also in the East. One of the areas that was discussed was the Glen House properties. Wentworth Brown, of the Brown Paper Company family in Berlin, was an enthusiastic skier and knew the Glen House terrain, which seemed admirably suited for development as a ski area. He corraled a group of potential investors and developers to discuss the project. The group included Judge McLane. Also part of the group were Sel Hannah of Franconia, whose company, Snow Engineering, planned a number of ski areas; Charles Lovett, innkeeper of Franconia; and Bob Burroughs of

Manchester, in the insurance business and a potential investor. Malcolm McLane, lawyer and later a developer of the Wildcat Ski area with George Macomber and Brooks Dodge, met with the group a few times. There were meetings for about a year, but no great enthusiasm could be generated and the project died aborning.

## F. ELBA CHASE NELSON

Senator Joseph McCarthy, a Republican from Wisconsin, was chairman of several Senate committees investigating communism in the United States after World War II. In 1950, he attracted attention by accusing the Department of State of harboring Communists. He also attacked publicly people and organizations that he claimed were "soft on communism." The enthusiasm for ferreting out communism spread across the country. In New Hampshire the legislature passed a bill directing the attorney general to conduct an investigation determining the extent of communism in New Hampshire. In November, the attorney general subpoenaed Elba Chase Nelson, titular head of the Communist Party in New Hampshire and a perennial candidate for president on the New Hampshire presidential ballot. The attorney general wanted all lists of members of the Communist Party and wanted to interrogate Mrs. Nelson on her personal knowledge of Communists in the state. Judge was at the time president of the New Hampshire Bar Association. Seeking advice, Mrs. Nelson came to see him, explaining she did not understand all this. She thought she needed the advice of a lawyer but she could not afford to pay one. Judge assured her that she would be represented, and he volunteered to help. Judge met with her on December 6. On the seventh, when she was subpoenaed to appear before the attorney general, she refused to produce records of Communists. The attorney general obtained a contempt citation from Judge Wheeler of the superior court. Mrs. Nelson was taken to the county jail.[4] Judge says in his diary, "Tough day for Mrs. Nelson." The contempt order was purged the next day, however.

The criminal trial of Elba Chase Nelson continued. A brief was filed in early January, and Stan Brown argued the case later in the month. An adverse decision was rendered, coincidentally, on May 1 (May Day). At the midwinter bar association meeting, a successful resolution was passed defending the right of lawyers to represent avowed Communists. At the annual meeting, Judge delivered his president's speech and emphasized litigants' rights in connection with subversive investigations.

# G. NATIONAL LIFE INSURANCE COMPANY

In 1947 Judge was elected a director of National Life Insurance Company of Vermont, a mutual company. Fred Howland was the president; some of the other directors were president Ernest Martin Hopkins of Dartmouth, president Ned French of the B&MRR, and at a later date Geoffrey Smith of Philadelphia, president of Girard Trust and a fellow trustee of Judge's at St. Paul's School. Judge admired these men and greatly enjoyed his association with them. For the next thirteen years, meetings of the board and the executive and the salary committees on which Judge sat averaged about one a month. Frequently, there were committee meetings in Hanover or Boston in conjunction with a Dartmouth or B&MRR meeting. Usually one meeting a year was held in the spring or summer at a resort with recreational amenities, such as Murray Bay in Canada, Miami Beach in Florida, or the Swampscott House in Massachusetts, and the spouses were invited. Unfortunately, the diaries rarely explain what happened at the meetings.

In the 1950s, the IRS, along with much support from Congress, sought to tax all mutual enterprises, such as mutual savings banks and insurance companies. The mutual organizations claimed that they had no profits to be taxed because the profits were distributed to the depositors or policyholders. Stock companies, which paid taxes, claimed this was a subterfuge that gave the mutuals an unfair advantage and enabled the mutuals to avoid paying their fair share of taxes and to sell their product at a lower price. While the tax legislation was being considered, Judge went to Washington, to a dinner arranged by the mutual insurance industry at which many senators and congressmen were present, to hear the industry position.

In 1954, National Life was busy on tax legislation pending in Congress. On one occasion, while attending hearings in Washington, Judge met with Congressman Tom Curtis of Missouri, a fellow trustee at Dartmouth, about the proposed tax on mutual insurance companies. On another occasion, I recall Judge talking about the company embarking on a program of investing in mortgages on mobile homes. This was not exactly a high-class investment and was shunned by banks. A marketing study revealed that the owners of mobile homes were a stable lot who paid off their loans in five to ten years. There was relatively little depreciation in value, and the interest rates were 15 to 18 percent, far above comparable investment vehicles.

Over the years Judge spent a considerable amount of time at meetings of the board and the executive and salary committees, for which he was compensated, but so far as I know the McLane law firm did practically no legal work for National Life.

## H. MACK KAHN AND THE AMOSKEAG
## LAWRENCE MILLS, INC.

In New York City in the 1930s, Mack Kahn was marketing "foundation garments" nationally. In about 1940, as New England textile mills became available at very low prices, he became intrigued with the idea of acquiring his own manufacturing facilities and controlling manufacturing from start to finish, a process called vertical integration. This was opposed to the more traditional organization of the textile industry along horizontal lines. Not only could quality be controlled at every step of the manufacturing process, but also expenses could be cut at each level.

In October 1941, Mack Kahn bought the stock of Amoskeag-Lawrence Yarns, Inc., which had been incorporated in 1939 to acquire the yarn department of Lawrence Manufacturing Company in Lawrence, Massachusetts. He also purchased the Amory Mill from Amoskeag Industries, Inc., which also subscribed to some of the stock. The Amory Mill was located along the upper canal just south of Dow Street. After Mack Kahn purchased the property, he hired the McLane law firm to represent him. He established a latex yarn plant for the manufacture of elastic thread, an essential ingredient of foundation garments. Subsequently, as the business expanded, he acquired additional manufacturing properties in Epsom and Suncook, New Hampshire, and in a few other states. In December 1941, Mack Kahn teamed up with Ben Mates to form Manchester Knitted Fashions, Inc., for the manufacture of knitted goods on rotary knitting machines. The company acquired substantial contracts with the Navy for sweaters, watch caps, et cetera. The north half of the #11 Mill on the West Side was leased from Amoskeag Industries and purchased in 1944. (Verney occupied the south half of the mill.) Amoskeag Lawrence Mills, Inc., had some labor problems relating to a union election in 1942 on which Judge worked.

Mack Kahn's enterprises continued profitably throughout the war and during the conversion from wartime to peacetime production. In 1947 Mack Kahn created the Mack Kahn Foundation to receive the maximum charitable deductions from his enterprises and to distribute his fortune to a broad array of charitable enterprises, mostly in the New York City area, where Mack Kahn's main interests were located. Judge was a trustee and attended the one meeting a year held in the fall at Mack Kahn's house on Long Island. I believe that members of the family constituted the majority of the board.

In 1951 Judge presided at a dinner for Mack Kahn at the Manchester Country Club. It was attended by three hundred business leaders and friends of Mack to recognize his accomplishments in textile manufacturing in Manchester and his other mill locations. About this time, Mack Kahn improved his financial condition by consolidating his financing with a number of banks; he created a new single loan from a consortium of banks from New York and Boston, secured by mortgages on his fixed assets and a security agreement with respect to his other assets and paying off his old indebtedness.[5] The New England textile industry was peaking. Conditions were definitely changing. Growth in the industry was occurring in the South and abroad. In September 1954 he gave a party at the Manchester Country Club for his New York City bankers.

As the New England mills struggled to remain competitive with the South and new foreign mills, the banks put pressure on Mack to liquidate some of his interests and reduce bank debt. As a result, Manchester Knitted Fashions was sold in 1955 to a Mr. Prince, with whom Leonard Finder was associated. Mr. Finder had previously been a co-owner with William Loeb of the *Union Leader*, until he was bought out by Loeb.

The collapse of the textile industry in New England continued in 1955. In April, Mack Kahn concluded, after receiving pressure from his banks, that he should wind up operations in Manchester and liquidate his holdings to reduce bank debt. In the fall, Judge met with Mack on his problems, later went to see Felix Pereira at the First National Bank of Boston about Mack's loans, talked for a morning with Mack, and in December spent a long day in New York City on liquidation plans. The business was closed and the properties were sold. Employment had been decreasing, and most remaining employees found jobs in other industries, particularly electronics, which relied on the same type of skill—finger dexterity—used in the textile industry.

Mack Kahn was a born salesman; he was outgoing, friendly, and knowledgeable. He kept himself in good shape. When he visited the office around Christmastime he would get the measurements of the secretaries and on his next trip bring in the wrapped presents of foundation garments (girdles and bras) for the girls and personally hand them out. There weren't all that many secretaries at that time. One time when Judge went to New York City on Mack's business, Mack announced that there was a showing of new styles at the office for buyers from around the country and Judge should see the "show," which was held in a little theater with a runway from the stage through and over the audience. The scantily clad models displayed the latest fashions in bras, girdles, and the rest. Judge made few comments about this show. We never knew whether he was embarrassed or loved it.

## I. CONFIDENCE MAN (CM)

The practice of law is frequently exciting because one never knows what kind of a case is going to arrive with the next telephone call. I recall one morning about 6:30 A.M. getting a telephone call from a distraught client who said that her ex-husband was out in the yard stealing her horses and what should she do. I suggested that she eat a good breakfast and meet me at the office.

On another occasion, the telephone caller was a lawyer from a small town in central New Jersey, Salem, I believe, which I had never heard of, whose client was a local chiropractor who was convinced he'd been had, to the tune of $10,000, by a con artist whose address was the YMCA in Manchester.

Because this event occurred many years ago—in the early 1950s—and I don't recall the names of the individuals involved, and because the files have long since been destroyed, I have only a very skimpy recollection of what happened. I think my only involvement was to locate the culprit if possible and verify that he lived in Manchester. I seem to remember that the confidence man had lived at the YMCA in Manchester for some time but had left several months before with no unpaid bills or complaints. He had left no forwarding address. No one at the YMCA or the police department knew anything about him. What happened after that remains a mystery to me. My New Jersey lawyer, after the initial telephone call and instructions, sent me considerable material in the form of correspondence and statements, from which the following story emerged. I must admit to embellishing it just a little here and there but in no significant detail.

The confidence man, whom I shall call "CM," somehow contacted a chiropractor in Buffalo, New York, and said he had a delicate mission and needed the help of several chiropractors. He represented, he said, a large insurance company, and did not wish to disclose its name at this juncture for fairly obvious reasons. The company was, however, interested in gaining reliable statistical information on the treatment of patients by the chiropractic profession such as patient recovery and mortality rates. Because the American Medical Association (AMA), which treated the chiropractic profession as a bunch of quacks, controlled the state establishments that collected such statistics, the results from the chiropractic profession were not even collected and hence not available to insurance companies, which had an interest in the results of treatment by chiropractors. The AMA wanted the insurance companies to exclude treatment by chiropractors as a covered event and include only licensed M.D.s. Obviously, coverage by insurance health policies was desired by the chiropractic profession.

The insurance company proposed that a nonprofit statistical-gathering entity be incorporated to collect the data nationally from chiropractors, which it would then process and make available, for a fee, to the insurance company and other interested parties. Once the organization got into an operating mode, it would be self-sustaining, and make enough money to pay operating expenses and pay the directors' modest stipends to recompense them for their time, interest, and travel expenses. The organization did require some funding to get off the ground. The insurance company was willing to put up $50,000 as a loan at market interest rates repayable in three to five years to be matched by $50,000 in similar loans from what CM called the "investor group." CM indicated he'd decided to invest $10,000 and was looking for a group of four to eight chiropractors to put up the remaining $40,000. This outline was typed out on stationery that purported to be from an insurance company, but the name and address were blanked out. There was an accompanying "position paper" that told about the statistics as presently collected and how the new information would be compiled and utilized, all of which was presented in a very professional style.

This proposal sounded very plausible and reasonable to the Buffalo chiropractor, who then contacted chiropractor friends of his in several other cities, including the four who finally participated—from Roanoke, Virginia, a town in Ohio, and my client in Salem, New Jersey. Once the participants were identified, CM arranged a meeting in New York City at a hotel, where he procured bedrooms and a meeting room, picking up the tab for the rooms and meals temporarily, as he said, until the organization was completed and in business. At the meeting, which was attended by CM, his "friend from the insurance company," and the four chiropractors, CM was elected chairman pro tempore, and one of the chiropractors was elected secretary pro tem to keep the minutes. The "friend" from the insurance company reviewed the proposal from the company and had more handouts with additional information, which made a lot of sense, including criticism of the American Medical Association's hostile attitude toward the chiropractic profession.

After the "friend's" presentation, including a pledge of support of $50,000 from the company, he excused himself, and the others discussed the proposal, asked questions, and finally voted to organize a nonprofit corporation. They decided on the officers: CM would be the president and treasurer, one of the chiropractors would be the secretary, and another the assistant treasurer. They discussed and decided on a large and prestigious bank in New York City where they would do business. As for a business address, CM suggested that he was in New York City frequently and could pick up the mail, so why didn't they use a post office box at the Grand Central Station branch post office until they established an office in a couple of months? CM indicated he would engage a lawyer to represent them and prepare the incorporation papers for New York state. CM would apply for an ID number from the IRS and order some stationery. They decided on a name—it was something like Health Statistics, Inc., descriptive of their planned endeavor.

Once the business at hand was completed, the group relaxed over highballs and a delicious dinner, which CM had arranged to be served in their private meeting room. They talked of professional sports, their families, and vacations and soon acted like close friends. Before they broke up that evening, the group decided that at the next meeting, when the legal papers were to be signed and the enterprise officially launched, their wives should be invited and they should have another comparable dinner to cement their friendship and celebrate the inauguration of the corporation. CM agreed that this was a splendid idea and the treasury would be able to stand the expense. Each went to bed that night with a warm glow of accomplishment for a noble cause that would be both enjoyable and rewarding to them at the same time.

The next meeting was held about six to eight weeks later in New York City with the wives present. The incorporation papers—including the articles of association and bylaws, the bank authorizations, the application for ID number, drafts of the promissory notes, and various other minutiae—were described by the "lawyer" who attended part of the meeting. The papers were discussed, signed, and attended to, after which CM had more information and reading material from the "insurance company" and more detailed plans of operation. Before the meeting adjourned, the group decided to wait until CM had officially heard from the state of New York that the incorporation was complete and the banking arrangements finalized before holding a "closing" in New York City. They planned to wait for a call from CM. They agreed the meeting would be held in the morning of a day early in the week so checks could be deposited in the bank in the afternoon. Each of the participants, including the "insurance company," would bring his own checks payable to the new organization for deposit in the bank account. The evening and dinner were as enjoyable as ever, and everyone left with a sense of substantial accomplishment.

About six weeks later, after incorporation was official and the banking arrangements were finalized, CM set up the next meeting in New York City. The group, including the representative from the "insurance company," met. Each lay down on the table his check for his promissory note, and votes were taken authorizing the promissory notes from the corporation to each investor, which were then signed and placed on the table too. CM distributed a draft of a lease for a one-room office in a not-too-expensive Manhattan office building. Everyone approved. Copies of all pertinent documents had been assembled in folders and were distributed to each of the participants. CM indicated he would hire a secretary in a couple of days after interviewing a few more applicants. Everyone agreed that the business was about concluded—several participants had trains to catch, and CM indicated he wanted to deposit the checks that afternoon before the bank closed—so they all shook hands and went their various ways.

When my client got home that evening, his wife at supper innocently asked her husband more about his $10,000 investment—a substantial sum for them given their mortgage payments, retirement savings goals, children's education, and other expenses. She expressed interest in knowing more about the project and CM and his background, education, business experience, et cetera, which my client had to admit he couldn't answer. CM had brought an attractive and bright "wife" to the meeting when wives attended, but he had no idea where they actually lived or what he did for a living. CM had said he traveled a lot and gave a mailing address at the Manchester, New Hampshire, YMCA where he could be reached. My client began to have doubts. The next morning he called the bank and asked if it had an account in the name of Health Statistics, Inc. He was advised that was confidential information that could not be disclosed, so my client called the Manchester YMCA and was told that no one was registered there by the name he requested and that they could not give information with respect to the U.S. mail. My client was now thoroughly suspicious. He consulted his attorney, who asked a lot of pointed questions that my client could not answer. He asked the name of the attorney in New York City who had prepared the incorporation papers, but his client said that CM had only introduced him by name when the incorporation papers were signed. He had no business card or document with the New York City attorney's name and address. The attorney telephoned for a search of the New York state records in Albany for incorporations and found no recent filing for Health Statistics, Inc. He also was able to solicit the assistance of his bank in Salem in ascertaining whether there was an account in the New York City bank for Health Statistics, Inc.; he found none. My client's attorney became more and more gloomy about the prospects for recovery. He called the hotel where the meetings had been held and learned that CM always paid his bills promptly in cash, usually maintained a small credit balance, and left no addresses.

At this point, the Salem, New Jersey, attorney called our office, probably taking our name from Martindale and Hubbell, and sought our assistance. I wish that I could report that by skillful sleuthing and dogged persistence we had identified the thief, located his residence, had him apprehended, and recovered the money put up by the chiropractors. Of course by now everyone realized that the insurance company was a figment of the imagination, as was its deposit of $50,000 and also CM's $10,000 investment. The "lawyer" and the "wife" were phonies too. The end of the story is actually an unsatisfactory one—I never heard again from my client or his attorney after reporting that CM was not to be found in Manchester. We submitted a bill, which was promptly paid, and the file was closed.

## J. CONFIDENCE MAN (FALVEY)

In June 1936 Judge had an exciting time recovering 1,100 shares of New Hampshire Fire Insurance Company stock that Janet Brown of Raymond had turned over to a Mr. Falvey, a confidence man. The story goes like this, according to my recollection of what my father told me. Mr. Falvey, perhaps operating under another name, made contact with Mrs. Brown, who was a middle-aged widow and lived alone. Mr. Falvey represented himself as a stockbroker from New York with a number of clients in New Hampshire and had been given Mrs. Brown's name by a client whose name he could not now recall. He was very courteous and a gentleman and gave Mrs. Brown some literature on investments but did not try to push for a sale, nor did he inquire about her holdings. They talked about their respective families and interests for a while and, when Falvey left he said he'd drop in the next time he was in the area. This pattern continued for several more visits three to four months apart, and he may even have invited Mrs. Brown to lunch or dinner in Manchester. I don't recollect whether she ever did any business with him or not. On one occasion he did talk with her about her investments and she advised him of her New Hampshire Fire Insurance Company holdings, which she had inherited from her family or husband and constituted most of what she had. He allowed as how New Hampshire Fire Insurance Company was an excellent company, but perhaps she should consider diversifying some and not have all her eggs in one basket. He said he'd write to her with suggestions for buying new stocks with the proceeds of the sale of a portion of the New Hampshire Fire Insurance Company stock.

Falvey's suggestions in well-recognized companies were good, and she thought that his plan made sense, so it was arranged that on his next trip to Manchester, he would pick up the insurance stock certificates, get the stock powers signed, put in the sell and buy orders, and have the new certificates sent directly to her. All of these things were done on his next visit. Well, as soon as his car was out of sight, she realized she really didn't know anything about him—where he worked or lived or how to get in touch with him. He seemed nice enough, but now he had just about everything she owned. She called the New Hampshire Fire Insurance Company and told them what had happened. They advised her to get an attorney in a hurry and they would try to put a stop order on the sale of this particular stock. She came to Judge, who consulted with Ralph Davis, a former attorney general, and developed their plans. Ralph and Judge took the night train to New York City on June 8, the same day she came in. Judge records on June 9: "Exciting day recovering 1,100 shares New Hampshire Fire Insurance Company stock with the help of (New York) AG [Attorney General] McCall and Koerner." I assume that Falvey had hightailed it to New York City and delivered the securities and stock power to a broker to sell. I don't know how he handled the signature guarantee or order to the broker to pay him. Because of the quick action of Mrs. Brown notifying the New Hampshire Fire Insurance Company and their placing an immediate "stop order," the sale of the stock was not consummated and the police retrieved the certificates. On June 10, Mrs. Brown went to New York City to recover her stock. The New York City Police Department maintains a very thorough Fraudulent Securities Division with files and photographs on just about anyone, anywhere involved in fraudulent security transactions. It is indexed in many different ways: victim, geographical location, modus operandi, et cetera. Judge and Ralph took Mrs. Brown to the rogues' gallery in the police department and, sure enough, she identified her "friend." The police knew of some of his hangouts in upstate New York and put a police officer in the post office where he used to pick up his mail. He was nabbed on June 19. Judge worked on extradition papers in Manchester and on the twenty-fourth he had a long train ride with Mrs. Brown cross-country to Potsdam, New York, where Mrs. Brown was able to identify Falvey in a police lineup. He was arrested on the extradition warrant on June 25. Judge and Mrs. Brown drove along the St. Lawrence River and took the train to New York City and thence home. There is a little mystery because Judge writes on June 26, "Met Allen Fox, Attorney for Williams in court," and on November 16, "Portsmouth with Mrs. Brown on State v. Williams." I conclude that Falvey was an assumed name and that his real name was Williams. There is no further reference to Mrs. Brown, Falvey, or Williams.

## K. NEW HAMPSHIRE CHILDREN'S AID SOCIETY— CHILD & FAMILY SERVICES OF NEW HAMPSHIRE

Judge McLane was active in the New Hampshire Children's Aid Society from its founding in 1914 to his retirement in 1958, forty-four years later. He was its first treasurer, from 1914 to 1953, and then served as president from 1953 to 1958.[6]

In the summer of 1913, Hannah Kimball from New York City, vacationing in Canaan, New Hampshire, became very concerned about the treatment that a seven-year-old neighbor girl received from her family. She sought help from town officials, who indicated they had no authority to act. Nor could she find anyone who did. Wondering how many other children were being abused, Miss Kimball personally engaged the Russell Sage Foundation of New York to conduct a survey of New Hampshire to see if there were any facilities for the protection of children and to determine the desirability of establishing a protective agency. The investigator, Mr. Hubbard, found three humane societies, all for the care of animals. In Portsmouth, there was an impoverished Society for the Prevention of Cruelty to Children, which was affiliated with a well-endowed animal cruelty prevention organization. The SPCC had only three hundred dollars annually for children. The county commissioners had no funds with which to care for children, who were institutionalized when referred to them.

There obviously was a great need for an organization dedicated to helping needy children. The state children's agency was concerned only with child labor and school truancy. Mr. Hubbard, in the course of his investigation, had met Sherman Burroughs and Judge McLane, law partners in Manchester, and urged them to contact Miss Kimball and offer their assistance. This resulted in the founding on January 29, 1914, of the New Hampshire Children's Aid and Protective Society. Mr. Burroughs was president and Judge was treasurer. Directors came from Manchester, Concord, Franklin, and Boston. Miss Kimball had guaranteed the payment of salaries for the first year and a half. The Home for Little Wanderers in Boston helped greatly the first few years. In its first annual report, Mr. Burroughs pointed out that thousands of dollars were spent on foot-and-mouth disease in cattle and for the eradication of the gypsy and brown-tail moths, which were ravaging the trees, but children had to be protected too. In 1916, 537 contributions totaling over $4,000 were received along with assistance from a number of women's clubs and the New Hampshire Federation of Women's Clubs, which has been a consistent supporter over the years.

From the beginning, the society considered itself a statewide agency and offered services anywhere. In 1917, over seven hundred children were assisted, many being placed in a new program of foster homes rather than in institutions or returned to abusive parents. Miss Sarah T. Knox joined the society as a caseworker in 1919 and became general secretary in 1921 following the resignation of Mr. Pittenger for health reasons. Miss Knox filled the position for twenty-seven years. Huntley Spaulding (See Appendix B.4, Huntley N. Spaulding) became a director and succeeded to the presidency on the untimely death of Sherman Burroughs in 1923. Mr. Burroughs' friends raised a Memorial Endowment Fund of $50,000, which, with an endowment gift of another $50,000 from the Greenleafs, hoteliers in New Hampshire and Boston, created a permanent secure financial position for the agency. In 1921, the Coos County branch was opened in Berlin with the cooperation of the Red Cross. In 1922, the society, in a new initiative with Coit House in Concord, used the Coit House facilities for temporary housing for children to permit a thorough case study. Previously, children were kept at Coit House for long periods of time without an adequate plan.

In the 1920s, the agency pioneered legislation requiring the licensing of homes where children under three years of age were to be boarded. In later years licensing expanded to include foster homes for children sixteen and under. The society was asked by the courts to become involved in the determination of custody in divorce cases. The society became one of the charter members of the Child Welfare League of America.

The depression years of the 1930s were difficult. Funds were hard to come by, yet the number of children seeking assistance increased. In 1936, Dr. Douglas Thom, a Boston psychiatrist, completed a study of the agency made at the request of Huntley Spaulding, president. Thom recommended a shift to more professional work on prevention and therapy. The innovative plan was adopted. The agency added psychiatric social workers and a part-time psychiatrist and psychologist, making Children's Aid the first such child guidance clinic in the state. By 1938, the New Hampshire Department of Public Welfare had been given the responsibility for investigating physical abuse and neglect. In 1942 the society dropped its protective program and name, becoming simply the New Hampshire Children's Aid Society.

During the early 1940s, the agency was particularly busy studying the effects of war-created conditions, investigating homes for European refugee children, and maintaining a clearinghouse for refugees. In 1942 Mrs. Jeannette Melton succeeded Sarah Knox as general secretary. In the same year a medical advisory board was established to ensure a competent program of medical care for all children involved with the agency.

In 1945, an affiliate program was established with schools of social work to provide hands-on training for their students. The agency had outgrown its quarters and in 1948 moved into a renovated private home at the corner of Lowell and Walnut Streets.

In 1953, Huntley Spaulding resigned as president and was succeeded by Judge McLane. The society was very professionally run and its leadership built firm financial support from throughout the state, not only in its annual giving campaign but also in the development of a strong permanent endowment fund. Committees were formed in most towns that did the local solicitation for the annual fund-raising and kept the name, mission, and accomplishments of the society before the people. Judge McLane led the Development Committee for many years; with the assistance of Robert Burroughs, Ralph Langdell, Robert Upton, William Scranton, and many others, personal contacts were made with a large number of people who enjoyed comfortable circumstances. One of the results of this organized development program was the receipt of a large number of bequests from persons of all walks of life and financial circumstances.

In the 1950s and 1960s the agency expanded services to children and their families by encouraging the formation of affiliate organizations in Laconia (Lakes Region Family Service) and Keene (Monadnock Area Family Service). Seacoast Family Service was opened in Exeter, as a branch office. Judge McLane resigned as president in 1958 and was succeeded by Ralph Langdell of Manchester. Shortly thereafter, Jeannette Melton died suddenly; and a Memorial Committee raised funds and produced a motion picture that Jeannette Melton had always wanted to do, depicting the life of the agency through its case histories. The movie *Debbie* was widely shown in New Hampshire and in many U.S. locations as well as overseas; it received an award in the 1962 Film Festival. Vallance Wickens became executive director. In 1962, the society entered into an affiliation with the Child Guidance Clinic of the Massachusetts General Hospital for psychiatric services. In 1963, Ralph Langdell resigned for reasons of health and was succeeded by this author. Albert Chicoine became the executive director in 1965 and held the post until his retirement in 1986.

In 1968 the society merged with Family Service of Manchester, headed by Reed Carver, and changed its name to Child & Family Services of New Hampshire. It merged with Concord Family Service in 1971 and inherited Camp Spaulding, a summer camp for 180 students from low-income families, which it still operates. In the same year, it moved into its present quarters, the renovated Crown Theater on Hanover Street. The advocacy program got under way with a grant from the Spaulding-Potter Trusts, which enabled the society to pay more attention to causes rather than cases. Mike Chamberlain arrived as the staff advocate attorney and worked with the legislature to monitor and improve legislation affecting children, such as adoption reform and poverty issues. Jack Lightfoot succeeded Mike in 1975 and still heads up this important activity. A "Children's Lobby" keeps track of legislation affecting children. In the 1970s, runaway and group homes were established to assist children who could not stay in their own home's. Also in the 1970s both the Seacoast and Lakes Region offices became independent organizations, but it is interesting to note that in 1994 the Seacoast once again became a regional office. The North Country had an office in Berlin in the 1920s that was discontinued, but in 1990, the agency opened a branch office in Littleton.

In recent years, the society has established collaborative relationships with other agencies, such as an office in Nashua with a child abuse center, space in Derry with an Adolescent Program, and an outpost in Wilton. Many clients are seen in their home settings rather than in the central office. The staff of two hundred-plus consists of senior-level persons with master of social work degrees, but 50 percent of the direct service staff are paraprofessionals. Trained family volunteer aides also assist in direct service. The adoption program reached a peak in 1971 and has dropped drastically as more babies are retained by their natural parents. However, the agency does provide foster care homes for infants prior to adoption. There are licensed homes for temporary care of adolescents and "mentor" homes for youth between the ages of eighteen and twenty-one. There are many independently arranged adoptions today, and the agency frequently will conduct the home study for the court.

A third generation McLane, Annie McLane Kuster, daughter of Malcolm McLane, former president of the Concord Family Service, has become an adoption expert as well as serving on the board. There is much interest in "roots" today, and many adopted children, now adults, seek information from the agency of their birth parents, and parents look for their babies long ago given up for adoption. As part of its commitment to professionalism, the agency continues its program of field training for students from schools of social work.

The annual budget has grown from $1,300,000 in 1986 to $4,000,000 in 1994, of which $2,260,000 came from state and federal sources. The permanent endowment fund has grown from $2,275,000 in 1969 to $7,400,000 in 1993.

Child & Family Services (CFS) touches many people in the state—staff, volunteers, contributors, clients, and their families. It is their continued support that makes CFS one of the best professional service organizations in the state.

## L. GEORGE ABBOT MORISON FAMILY

The Morisons of Peterborough are descendants of Scottish Presbyterians from the Outer Hebrides who fled in about 1680 from the Catholic populace to Protestant Londonderry in Northern Ireland.[7] About thirty years later they emigrated to America, landing in Boston and settling in southern New Hampshire. In 1739, a group went to explore the Monadnock area, but Indians ate their salt pork and absconded with their provisions, so they returned home. In 1749, Thomas Morison led a group to the present Peterborough and settled on land now a part of Upland Farm, owned by the G. A. Morison family. By 1758, it was apparent that farming was marginal at best, so Thomas built a dam in South Peterborough at Noone's Falls. He used as the core piece a three-foot-diameter pine log that bore the blaze of the king's broad arrow. He risked serious punishment if caught by the British navy, who had marked the tree as belonging to the king for masts and spars for the Royal navy. Interestingly, in 1926 when the dam was being overhauled, the old pine was found to be in excellent condition and was left where it was for another couple of hundred years!

Waterpower ran a grist- and sawmill in the eighteenth century and a textile mill in the nineteenth century. It generates electricity in the twentieth century. Thomas died in 1797, and his grandson, Nathaniel, expanded the mill operation. In 1802, he took "an invoice of chairs" to the Caribbean but found no market, so returned to North Carolina, where he sold them at a profit and started a carriage manufacturing business. In 1804, he returned to Peterborough and married a Scot, Mary Ann Hopkins, who went to North Carolina with him for two years, returning when the elder Morison was ailing.

The War of 1812 was devastating and created a five-year depression that practically bankrupted Nathaniel, who took off for Mississippi to try to collect some large debts owed to him and also to sell goods that he took with him. He was partially successful and returned with new contracts, which unfortunately were repudiated. Nathaniel had contracted yellow fever on one of his southern trips and died at age forty, leaving his widow, Mary Ann, with seven children. She knew she had to educate the children, so she sent the five boys off to Exeter Academy[8] and a daughter to school in Groton. Mary Ann worked in the mill by day and at her own loom at night to earn enough for her children's expenses.

Four of the boys went on to Harvard and entered the professions—ministry, medicine, teaching, and school administration. The oldest son, John Hopkins Morison, was a Unitarian minister and inherited Upland Farm. John's oldest son, George Shattuck Morison (1842–1903), also attended Exeter Academy[9] and Harvard College (1863) and Law School but eschewed the law for engineering. He worked in Kansas City and Detroit and built many railway bridges over the Mississippi and Missouri Rivers as the railroads expanded westerly in the latter part of the nineteenth century. He later established offices in New York City and was instrumental in persuading the McKinley administration to locate the Panama Canal in Panama rather than the originally proposed site in Nicaragua.[10] He inherited Upland Farm, reacquired much of the original farmland that had been sold, and built the handsome three-story Brick House in 1894, which he used as home and office as he commuted by train to New York and Chicago.

Only John and Horace, the descendants of the two oldest brothers, still live on their original land, but for major occasions, the clans gather to become reacquainted "to the mournful tune of the bagpipes."

Upon the death of George Shattuck Morison in 1903, his sister, Mary Morison, lived in the Brick House and raised Jersey cows in a vain hope to make the farm pay. Her younger brother, Robert S. Morison, also a Unitarian minister, introduced apples in 1912 in another attempt to make money. Apples have been a continuing crop since that time. Upon the death of Robert in 1925, his son, George Abbot Morison, born in Peterborough in 1879, inherited the farm and sought to make it profitable, but over the years 1925–1942, the farm produced black ink in only one year. George Abbot Morison lived in Milwaukee, Wisconsin, where he was affiliated with the Bucyrus-Erie Company, a manufacturer of heavy industrial equipment. He spent summer vacations at the Brick House, to which he retired in 1947. Modern methods of apple marketing have been tried with the construction in 1958 of controlled-atmosphere (CA) storage,[11] which enables apples to be marketed year-round, thus benefiting from higher prices. He knew that a New Hampshire farm probably could not be profitable and was impressed with the history of the businesses that sprang up around the waterpower sites of the dams on the Contoocook and Nubanusit Rivers, so he started to look for a small company to purchase. With the help of the state industrial agent, the Hitchiner Manufacturing Company, Inc., in Manchester, a foundry manufacturing investment castings, was purchased by George Abbot Morison and his son John H. Morison, who returned to the States from his job in Brazil. (See below for the history of Hitchiner.)

Upland Farm continues to produce apples; sometimes the trees are leased to an operator who pays rent based on production, and sometimes, as is currently the case, Upland Farm runs the orchard itself. Some of the unused land of Upland Farm was dedicated for the retirement community River Mead.

George Abbot Morison's son Robert and his wife lived in the Brick House for the rest of their lives after Robert retired from a medical career that included being director of the medical and biological sciences program of the Rockefeller Foundation and professor of science and technology at Cornell and MIT. The second son of George Abbot Morison, Elting Morison, retired from MIT, where he taught industrial history, and lived with his wife, Elizabeth, in one of the older houses on the farm until his death in 1995. George Abbot Morison's third son, John H. Morison, who lives in Lyndeborough, has been president, CEO, and chairman of the board of Hitchiner. He has been an active citizen in New Hampshire, playing a prominent role in many civic and cultural organizations, among which are the New Hampshire Charitable Fund and the Currier Gallery of Art.

For over one hundred years the family has gathered from time to time to enjoy the spacious rooms of the three-story Brick House and the spreading lawns and farm fields that overlook the Contoocook River Valley under the shadow of Mt. Monadnock.

Judge McLane and the McLane law firm worked with George Abbot Morison on his estate planning and also for various members of his family. They were involved with tax considerations and other matters having to do with the farm property and, as will be seen below, advised the Morisons with respect to the Hitchiner Manufacturing Company.

## M. HITCHINER MANUFACTURING COMPANY, INC.

Hitchiner Manufacturing Company, Inc., was incorporated by Fred Hitchiner and others in 1946 to operate a small foundry with ten people engaged in the investment casting business in the Amoskeag Mill Yard in Manchester, New Hampshire.[12] The business was purchased by George Abbot Morison and his son John H. Morison from Fred Hitchiner in 1949.

The new owners were dissatisfied with the then-current technology of investment casting and enthusiastically inaugurated improvements that ensured that all processes, systems, and equipment were subject to constant scrutiny. The company moved into larger quarters in Milford in 1951 and ten years later started construction on the first mechanized investment casting facility for high-volume applications, utilizing automated shell-building equipment and both power and free conveyor systems. The company established consulting relationships with MIT, particularly in metallurgy and ceramics. In the mid-1970s, Hitchiner patented the first of its exclusive countergravity casting processes (CLV, CLA), one of the most significant advances in investment casting technology. Previously, casting had always been done by gravity. The new process vacuumed the metal into the molds, thereby reducing the turbulence that had seriously affected the metallurgical quality of the castings.

In 1986, Hitchiner formed a joint venture research and development center with the General Motors Corporation called Metal Casting Technology, Inc., located at the company's headquarters in Milford. The company has four plants in New Hampshire, one in Missouri, and one near Mexico City, with a total employment of over 2,200 people. In addition, it licenses investment casting technology throughout the world.

The company has divided its workforce into four major divisions. *The Ferrous USA Division* has plants in Milford, Amherst, and Littleton, employs 1,400 workers in 250,000 square feet of space, and provides castings to the automotive industry, as well as defense, firearm, pumps and valves, tool, business equipment, golf, and others. *The Gas Turbine Division* was established in 1983 in New Hampshire and primarily services the jet engine component market and specializes in producing parts requiring difficult-to-cast vacuum alloys, with emphasis on thin-walled, high-tech applications. Its customers include Pratt & Whitney, General Electric, the Allison Turbine Division of General Motors, and Textron Lycoming. *The Nonferrous Division*, founded in 1969 in O'Fallon, Missouri, casts a wide variety of aluminum and copper-based alloys where thin walls, light weight, intricate coring, and complex design are involved. The castings are found in aircraft, helicopters, missiles, satellites, and spacecraft as well as in housings for PC boards and radio receivers. *Hitchiner S.A. de C.V.*, the company's first offshore production facility, is located near Mexico City in a very modern 95,000-square-foot plant that primarily makes investment cast automotive parts and golf club heads for such outfits as Taylor Made, Head, Hogan, and other leaders.

Metal Casting Technology, Inc., the joint venture research and development company with General Motors, employs some twenty specially selected mechanical and metallurgical engineers and technicians to generate useful new near-net-shape casting technology. Ongoing research delves into all phases of production and new materials and alloys and has produced dramatic improvements in casting technology. The company is also committed to total quality and was one of the first in the industry to win the prestigious "ISO 9001" award of the International Standards Organization.

Hitchiner is privately owned and has been quite successful. Its board of directors has been small but with several extremely well-informed outside members from the business and professional world. The McLane law firm, initially through Judge McLane, helped the company from the time of the acquisition by the Morison family to the move to Milford and the financing of the new construction. Over the years, legal services have involved environmental problems, personnel management matters, litigation, and general corporate advice.

## N. JOHN IAFOLLA AND THE IAFOLLA COMPANIES

John Iafolla lived in the Beverly section of Massachusetts and was engaged in the highway construction industry in eastern Massachusetts for seventeen years before selling out in 1944. He did most of his financing business with the Norfolk County Trust Company in Massachusetts. Because of the highly competitive nature of the business, John Iafolla looked north to the comparative calm of the New Hampshire business atmosphere. He obtained several construction contracts in New Hampshire. One of the largest involved the New Hampshire approaches to the interstate highway bridge over the Piscataqua River. At that time, 1940–1941, Iafolla acquired a 120-acre quarry of traprock just outside Portsmouth off Peverly Hill Road with 3,000 feet of frontage on Lafayette Highway. This gave him a good base for his construction business in the growing Portsmouth area. He decided to move his business to Portsmouth in 1949. When Pease Air Force Base was under construction, Iafolla leased the quarry and plant to the prime contractor, Morrison-Knudson Company of Boise, Idaho.

In 1932, some years before moving to New Hampshire, John Iafolla married Sarah Bavicchi, a widow, who had been his bookkeeper for several years. The Bavicchi and Iafolla families had been old friends in Massachusetts for many years. Mrs. Bavicchi had three children, John, ten; Pamela, eight; and Ferris, seven. After the move John Bavicchi became a musician and lived in the Boston area. Pamela married an attorney and lived for many years in western New Hampshire. Ferris after the war went to the University of New Hampshire and then to work for his stepfather, John Iafolla. John and Sarah had two sons—Michael, born in 1933, and Robert, born in 1935—both of whom went to the University of New Hampshire and then into the family business.

The McLane law firm first became involved with John Iafolla in about

1950 in connection with his financing needs in New Hampshire when he
wanted to refinance his quarry and rock-crushing plant. His Massachusetts
bank could not make mortgage loans in New Hampshire and recommended that he apply to a New Hampshire bank, which he did. He wound
up with a successful application to the Manchester Savings Bank, which was
represented by this author. After the closing, John Iafolla hired the
McLane firm, which became increasingly involved with his affairs. The
business was expanding and would need financing, which was being
planned. It therefore made sense to engage the services of a recognized
New Hampshire accounting firm rather than rely on the company's prior
accountant in Massachusetts. The James A. Shanahan Company of
Manchester was hired. John Iafolla was an able and likable, swarthy Italian,
short in stature, colorful in speech, with boundless energy.

John Iafolla had conducted his business as an individual proprietor, but
after losses on a New Hampshire road construction project, it made sense
to incorporate the construction business and isolate it from the real estate
and the rock-crushing business. Thus two corporations were formed:
Iafolla Construction Co., Inc., and Iafolla Crushed Stone Co. Inc. The
John Iafolla Company remained an individual proprietorship, which
owned the real estate and was subsequently incorporated. The construction
company got out of the highly competitive and risky road construction
business and concentrated on paving contracts for the new large shopping
malls, the interstate highway system and other public roads, private housing projects, and excavations for drainage and laying utility pipes. One of
the largest jobs was the resurfacing of the Pease Air Force Base runway,
some 12,000 feet long, used by the Strategic Air Command for its bombers
and refueling jet tankers. The crushed-stone company purchased quarry
rock from the John Iafolla Company, paying a royalty, and crushed it into
varying sizes of stone, some of which was used in its asphalt plants. The
product was sold to the construction company for its jobs or to outsiders.

Just when the business was improving, John Iafolla died suddenly in
May 1953. There were substantial federal estate tax issues involving complex valuations of the real estate and the stock of the two operating corporations, which were family owned, and cash-flow problems to raise money
to pay the taxes and run the businesses. There were also corporate management problems. Mrs. Iafolla had not worked full time for many years
and because of her health was unable to do so. Mrs. Iafolla was a very well-
informed person in business and financial matters and kept up-to-date on
corporate taxes. She was chair of the boards of the companies and kept the
family together. Ferris had learned a lot under his stepfather and, although
young, assumed the responsibilities of chief executive officer and dealt with
the public and the community in a public relations and selling role. Mike

was chief operations officer in charge of operations and equipment maintenance. Bob, who had a business management degree, was the chief financial officer and planner for the future. They worked well together.

John Iafolla's will created a trust, with the income being paid to Mrs. Iafolla for life and then to whomever she might appoint. Because she had a general power of appointment, the assets would be taxable at her death. If she could make gifts to her children during her lifetime in the amount of the annual exclusion, she could reduce her estate taxes, but her husband's trust owned all of the assets and there was no way that she could acquire them. So it was decided to petition the court to allow Mrs. Iafolla to encroach on principal for the purpose of making gifts to her children on the basis of hardship and an unintended result (increased taxes) that her husband never contemplated. Because she possessed a general power of appointment, she could give all or nothing to any person; therefore, no one had a vested interest that might be defeated by approving the petition. The petition was approved by the court after a hearing and the filing of legal briefs.

Mrs. Iafolla died in 1975. The executors of her estate had to go through the same questions on valuations as occurred at John Iafolla's death. The federal taxes were eventually worked out and distribution was made to the family. This required some innovative solutions, because the two older Bavicchi children had no interest in being involved in the family businesses. The three boys worked out a solution to acquire their inheritance.

Bob foresaw problems with the three boys continuing together, so he withdrew and successfully developed his own construction supply business, which he subsequently sold. He now has a consulting business.

Ferris and Mike continue to run the business and have weathered the slow economic conditions of the late 1980s and the early 1990s and are optimistic about the future.

Ferris has played an important role in the community of Portsmouth, having served since 1958 as a director of Fleet Bank New Hampshire or its predecessors, Indian Head National Bank and New Hampshire National Bank. Among his civic activities, he has served as president of the Greater Portsmouth Chamber of Commerce and the Associated General Contractors of New Hampshire. He has held key leadership roles in the New Hampshire Charitable Fund, the Greater Piscataqua Community Foundation, the Portsmouth Hospital, the Rye school board, and the Rye Conservation Commission.

Bob has also been a responsible citizen of Portsmouth. He has served on the Portsmouth Housing Authority, the Board of Education and the Economic Commission. He was a founder and treasurer of the Portsmouth Mental Health Clinic and president of the New Hampshire Association of Mental Health Clinics. He has been president of the Portsmouth Chamber of Commerce, the Portsmouth Hospital, and the Portsmouth Police Athletic League, and chair of the Portsmouth YWCA, as well as being a member of a number of other boards of nonprofit organizations.

# Notes

1. I am indebted to Milton Machinist, a loyal client of the office, for the history of the Machinist family.

2. I recall Morris Silver telling me years ago of the trip to the United States. On the sleigh ride from their small town in Russian Poland to the railroad station, they could hear the wolves howling in the forests on the other side of the snow-covered fields. On the train, they sat on hard wooden seats and traveled toward the German border. By prearrangement, they had paid to bribe the train conductor to hide them as the train crossed the border. So when they approached the border, they were herded into the toilet and told to be absolutely quiet; the door was locked behind them. The train stopped at the border and the officials came on to examine the passengers. The Silvers could hear them making their way down the corridor asking questions of the passengers. Then a key was inserted into their door, the conductor pushed it open against the Silvers crowded together on the floor, and in a loud voice announced, "No one there." Then he pulled the door closed and locked it again. As the officials moved on to the next car, it was all quiet again. They all breathed a great sigh of relief. Soon the train started up and headed for Hamburg and the boat that would bring them to a new life in America.

3. I am indebted to Myer (Mike) Friedman, CPA. and chief financial officer to the Silvers' enterprises for over forty years, for the history of their business activities.

4. Judge and Elisabeth took pajamas, toothbrush, and toothpaste to Mrs. Nelson in jail.

5. Two funny incidents occurred in connection with the preclosing of the loan at a bank in New York City. This author was present with the borrower. There were representatives from the participating banks and their attorneys. About twenty-five people surrounded the large table loaded with closing documents and copies for all participants. The documents were all duly signed, and sealed, and acknowledgments were taken before a notary public, a bank employee. The documents were then delivered to a bank "runner" to take to the nearest clerk of court to attach a court certificate, authenticating that the notary public was in fact a notary public. To everyone's dismay, the runner returned, stating that the notary was not in fact a notary since his commission had expired. Apparently, someone in the bank had neglected to have the individual's commission renewed. The signature pages had to be removed, retyped (no computers then), reassembled, and reexecuted by a proper notary public, all of which took about three hours of extra time.

While we were all waiting for the papers to be redone, Mr. Kahn, an imposing gentleman, irked by the delay, stated to all of the attorneys present that he hoped and trusted that the legal bills submitted to him after the closing would be reasonable. The room full of people guffawed when a lawyer for one of the banks, who obviously was very familiar with the provisions of the loan agreement, with tongue in cheek responded, "But, Mr. Kahn, I think you may not be familiar with the provisions of the loan agreement, which simply states, 'The borrower shall be responsible for all reasonable attorney's bills,' and I'm sure you agree that we are all reasonable people. The reasonableness of our bills is clearly irrelevant."

6. Most of the material is taken from *The New Hampshire Children's Aid Society: The First Fifty Years*, by W. Everett Doe, Jr., director of public relations, published in 1964, and a personal interview with the current development director, Ruth Zax.

7. From a talk by John H. Morison to the Peterborough Historical Society, June 26, 1994.

8. The boys were all over six feet tall, so when they walked together, people commented, "There goes thirty feet of Morisons."

9. George S. Morison became a trustee of the school in 1888 at a time when consideration was being given to construction of dormitories rather than housing students with private families in town. In 1891, a committee was formed to prepare plans for a dormitory, and George S. Morison was added to the committee. In 1892, his plans for Soule Hall were accepted and, later, his plans for Peabody Hall in 1896 and Hoyt Hall in 1903.

10. James W. Griswold, "100 Years of Soule-itude: Morison's Vision at the Century Mark," Phillips Exeter Bulletin, Winter 1993, p. 10.

11. Controlled-atmosphere storage is a leakproof space in which the oxygen has been replaced by carbon dioxide gas, which inhibits the growth of bacteria, thus keeping apples stored therein fresh longer.

12. Much of the material for this article is taken from a company sales brochure and a conversation with John H. Morison, until recently chairman of the board.

# TWENTY-THREE

# Probate and Tax Practice

## A. ROSE LEIGHTON

In 1923, Judge drew a will for Mrs. Rose Leighton, a new client. She apparently had lived in Manchester until the death of her husband, George, and then moved to Boston. In 1926, Judge drafted an inter vivos trust for Mrs. Leighton that provided that investments may be made only in bonds[1] and that the income be paid to Mrs. Leighton during her life. Then, because she had no children, the income would be paid to named nieces and nephews for their lives, with the residue going to a church in Maine and a hospital in New Hampshire. The Boston Safe Deposit and Trust Company was the corporate trustee and Judge the individual trustee, to which this author succeeded in the 1960s.

Judge had numerous dealings with the family over the years, visiting family members in Los Angeles when there on other business and receiving some family members at Newfound Lake. Mrs. Leighton became seriously ill in the spring of 1930 and died in August. I suspect that the omitted heirs, nieces and nephews, were objecting to the bequests to named nieces and nephews and the charitable remainder on the basis of lack of mental capacity. Unfortunately, no records exist of these early events. Anticipating a contest over the will, the will was proved in solemn form (all witnesses are interrogated, not just one), which shortens the time for appeals. Judge made trips to Peabody, Beverly, Lynn, and Salem preparing the case. In the fall of 1932 he settled the matter on the courthouse steps in Salem and proceeded to dispose of Mrs. Leighton's possessions at her house in Boston. In 1933 Judge closed out the estate by transferring the securities to the residuary trust at the Boston Safe Deposit and Trust Company, Judge's cotrustee, and payments have been made to the beneficiaries ever since.

In the 1970s, one of the nieces disappeared for several years; her income distribution was retained by the bank pursuant to a court order. The niece was known to have been an alcoholic. A Los Angeles attorney was retained to find her, which he finally did after checking obituaries, vital statistic records, police entries, the morgue, and other sources. She had been a "street person" with no residence and had been taken to a county institution when unable to fend for herself. Arrangements were made to have the county institution manage a small fund for her personal needs during the rest of her life. Her burial expenses were paid out of her accumulated income, the residue of which was distributed to her heirs. The last surviving heir, Mrs. Gertrude Anderson, died in the spring of 1996.

## B. ESTATE OF GEORGE SHATTUCK

Following the death of Dr. George Shattuck in 1922, Judge had extensive contacts in Boston with Mrs. Shattuck and her daughter (believed to be adopted) Althea. These contacts involved the substantial estate of George Shattuck, conferences with Hale and Dorr, meeting Dr. Shattuck of England—a brother of Dr. George —on matters relating to the estate of L. H. Shattuck (possibly the father or brother of Dr. George) and the sale of Mrs. Shattuck's house. There were diary entries on fourteen days. Judge continued on the George Shattuck estate in Boston, making almost monthly visits to Mrs. Shattuck in 1924 to assist her with probate accounts and to advise her on investments. Judge continued these visits in 1925. In 1929 Judge visited the Shattuck family in Boston three times and once in Manchester, after which there were no further entries mentioning the family.

## C. ESTATE OF FLYNN

In 1929, Judge had a case involving missing heirs in the estate of one Flynn; there is no indication of where the decedent lived or how large the estate was. In the fall of 1929, Judge and Elisabeth went to Europe, and in late September Judge made the following entries in his diary:

September 26, "To Wakefield [England], dreary town, spent day on Flynn case. With Stewart and Walker, Solicitors";

September 27, "Train to Liverpool [boat to Ireland]. Looked up Brown in Flynn case";

September 28, "Train via Enniskillen to Manor Hamilton. Saw Solicitor Patrick O'Flynn. Drove to Drumohair-Abbey Hotel";

September 29, "Out to Altrava to see Flynns. Townylea Post Office. Most interesting sight of peasant life. Walked in [illegible] miles to town church";

September 30, "Drove to Manor Hamilton to see O'Flynn and on to Bally Shannon then to Donegal. Walk. Race day, rough crowd."

In 1930, back home in the United States, Judge saw his Rhodes scholar friend Attorney Sam Rinaker in Chicago on two occasions about the Flynn heirs when passing through on other business. Had he forwarded the case to Judge?

Unfortunately, it is impossible to state what this case was all about. There were missing heirs who presumably would inherit something, but whether they did or not, we don't know.

# D. ESTATE OF ARTHUR J. CONNER

The family and guardians of little Arthur Conner, age ten, came to Judge in January 1948 to represent little Arthur in a will contest case against the estate of his grandfather, Arthur J. Conner. Arthur J. Conner (familiarly known as "AJ"), a graduate of the Massachusetts Institute of Technology (MIT) owned the Improved Paper Machine Company of Nashua, which manufactured machinery for the paper industry. It was a very successful company. Arthur Conner had three children, two girls and a boy, from his first marriage, which ended in divorce. His son, Frank, went to Yale, was a star track man, and competed on the U.S. Olympic team in 1936 as a hammer thrower. He placed second, for which his father never forgave him; his father thought he should have placed first. Frank subsequently moved to the West Coast, married into a prominent San Francisco family by the name of Haas, and had a son, Arthur, the only male Conner heir. Frank became an alcoholic; his wife, from whom he became divorced, ended in a mental institution. Frank remarried and lived in Stockton but never put his own life in order. He committed suicide, leaving little Arthur, about eight years of age, who was cared for by his maternal grandparents and attended a private boarding school in Los Gatos, California.

Arthur J. (AJ) Conner sold his Canadian plant in Sherbrooke, Quebec, in the early 1940s and later sold the U.S. plant to Walter Barker of Nashua. He retired to live in the ancestral Conner farm outside of Exeter, which had been in the family for some six or seven generations, a fact of which AJ was very proud. He was crowding eighty and evidenced some signs of senility. Prior to Frank's death, AJ had provided in his will for his two daughters but had left the bulk of his estate to Frank. Then, after Frank's suicide, AJ changed his will, cutting out Frank completely, and left Frank's share to his alma mater, MIT. True, AJ set up a trust of about $200,000 for little Arthur with a bank in Stockton as trustee and also guardian, so little Arthur was not destitute.

Judge contested the will on the basis of lack of mental capacity at the time the codicil cutting out little Arthur was executed. The McLane firm started collecting evidence of mental incapacity. In 1948, there were many conferences with family members compiling the facts of AJ's behavior, depositions were taken of people with knowledge both in New Hampshire and California, medical records were obtained and possibilities of settlement were explored with MIT.

Several examples of mental incapacity turned up. After AJ sold his Canadian plant, under Canadian regulations  he could not take the proceeds out of Canada, so had invested in provincial and dominion bonds, which he kept in a bank safe deposit box in Montreal. About once a quarter, he traveled to Montreal, clipped the coupons, and deposited them in the Montreal bank. He became well known to the train conductor (this was prior to airplane travel), whose deposition was taken and whose testimony was that AJ sat in the coach car (this was wartime and all Pullmans were used for troop transport) shuffling his papers back and forth with no apparent purpose. On one occasion when a new conductor was on duty, AJ refused to give his ticket, which he had with him, saying he had no money, although he always carried several hundreds of dollars. The conductor called the railroad police, who removed him from the train in White River Junction and locked him up in the Wilder, Vermont, jail. The regular conductor found out and called AJ's family,who talked AJ into turning over his ticket. The railroad officials put him on the train to Manchester, where someone met him and took him home to Exeter and placed him in the hospital for observation. He became quite playful in his hospital bed, trying to do somersaults and being a little fresh to the nurses.

On another trip back from Canada, he was supposed to go to Nashua to stay with his daughter, who lived there, but got off the train in Manchester, started walking toward his daughter's house as though he were in Nashua, and became hopelessly confused. When his daughter didn't find him on the train, she called the railroad, which radioed the conductor, who verified that AJ had been on the train past Concord and must have gotten off in Manchester. The Manchester police were alerted and found him wandering about. All of these incidents of confusion were close in time to his executing the codicil to his will that cut off Frank's family and left the bulk of his estate to MIT.

In 1949, the Conner case continued with considerable activity trying to negotiate a settlement. Judge went to Portsmouth and Boston to talk with attorneys and to Nashua to interrogate AJ's doctor. When on a trip west in the spring on other business, Judge spent four days in Stockton and San Francisco interviewing witnesses and discussing settlement options with members of the family. Later I went to Stockton specifically to take depositions with attorney Bill Starr from the Wadleigh law firm on the other side. In September, a case statement was prepared and both sides presented their evidence to Leonard Pierce of the Pierce, Atwood law firm in Portland. His decision, rendered in October, was disappointing to Judge. Several more settlement negotiating sessions were held. On December 8 Judge records, "Finally got a good settlement."

# E. ESTATE OF PATRICK J. O'CONNER

One of Judge's more interesting wills and estates was that of Patrick J. O'Conner, with whom Judge played baseball on the Milford High School baseball team.

Patrick O'Conner was born in Ireland in May 1883 and came to the United States with his family in 1887. He settled in Milford, where he attended the local schools and played baseball. His niece, Helen Bradford of Manchester, recalled Patrick talking about how he loved baseball and had a chance to play professionally, perhaps with the Boston Braves (those were the days when Boston had two professional teams), but never took it up. She did remember that Patrick lived with her family from about 1918 to 1921 in Lawrence, where her father (Patrick's brother) was head of the tannery. The family caught the flu in the 1918 epidemic. After graduating from Milford High in about 1900, Patrick went to work for the B&MRR in Boston as a baggage man, a fairly humble job, and lived alone in Melrose. Patrick was thrifty, well read, particularly the financial news, and talked with friends and B&MRR patrons he came to know about the stock market and investments. He became a shrewd and astute investor.

Judge used to see "Uncle Sam,"[2] as Patrick was known to many, on his frequent trips by train to Boston, and they had a few friendly words together. In 1947, O'Conner came to Judge's office and said he needed a will. He had no immediate family and no one to whom he was beholden. In thinking about his past, he recollected that some of his happiest moments in life had been when he played second base on the Milford High team nearly fifty years before. He recalled the bags of stones they used for bases, which were hard on the feet, and he remembered the catcher's masks they used, which broke pretty easily. (Judge broke his nose three times as catcher.) He wanted the kids to have better equipment and facilities to enjoy sports. He stated he had about $30,000 in investments and wanted to create a trust fund in the Milford High School Athletic Association, not the school board, the income from which was to be used for athletic purposes.

Patrick O'Conner died in June 1949. Judge was named executor and proved the will in Massachusetts. O'Conner's housekeeper and some of his family contested the will, feeling they should have received something. Judge ultimately worked out a settlement, and the estate was closed in 1955 when $50,000 was turned over to the Milford High School Athletic Association as principal with expected earnings of $2,000 annually. The school was able to introduce new sports activities, according to the *Milford Cabinet* (January 20, 1955), including soccer and indoor track. Principal expenses were for transportation and uniforms. The basketball program was expanded so that all students in high school or junior high could play. The school budget was unaffected by the gift.

By 1991, the fund had grown to over $300,000 and the income exceeded $10,000.


# F. ESTATES OF MR. AND MRS. BEN CHANDLER

Judge and Elisabeth on several occasions, while in England, called on Mrs. Ben Chandler and her daughter, Mrs. Whitfield, both of whom lived in Chipping Camden in the Cotswold country near Oxford. He also did a small amount of business for them. They had roots in Manchester through the Chandler family.

George Byron Chandler was president of the Amoskeag National Bank in 1893, when the annual report indicated he had been connected with the bank for thirty-eight years. The Amoskeag Bank commenced business as a state-chartered bank in 1848 when the city of Manchester was just two years old. In 1864, Congress so heavily taxed state-chartered banks that they were forced out of business. Amoskeag immediately rechartered under the Federal Banking Act as the Amoskeag National Bank (which continued until its insolvency and FDIC takeover in October 1991). Banks generally did well, and George Byron Chandler became wealthy. He built the large brick mansion and carriage house on Elm Street just above Carpenter Street, which is part of Notre Dame College.

Ben Chandler, the son of George Byron Chandler, moved to England in about 1900 and married an Englishwoman whose family resided in Chipping Camden. The Chandlers resided there too. They had a daughter who married a Whitfield who also resided in Chipping Camden. Judge from time to time had small amounts of business with the family relating to family trusts in the United States Judge records on the 1948 trip, "Delightful time with the Chandlers and Whitfields."

During one summer in the 1950s when Judge and Elisabeth were in England visiting Malcolm and Susan in Oxford, where Malcolm was studying as a Rhodes scholar, they drove out to Moreton-on-Marsh in the Cotswolds to visit Mrs. Chandler and the Whitfields. Over the years there had been a number of legal problems dealing with the dual citizenship of Mrs. Chandler, who was British by birth but American by marriage to Ben Chandler. The problems related to some trusts created in New York banks by George Byron Chandler for the benefit of his English descendants. I believe transferring the money to England would have subjected the transfer to a substantial tax, hence the creation of trusts in the United States.

In the 1980s, upon the death of Ben Chandler's widow, an interesting international tax question arose. Mrs. Chandler was a British citizen and therefore her worldwide assets were subject to tax by Great Britain, including the New York trusts over which she retained appointive powers. Great Britain moves rather leisurely in assessing death taxes, so the Great Britain tax was not paid until four to five years after her death. Mrs. Chandler was also a U.S. citizen by virtue of her marriage to Ben Chandler, an American citizen. That was the case then under U.S. laws, which are no longer in effect.

Under the IRS rules, Mrs. Chandler's (an American citizen) worldwide assets, including her real estate in the Cotswolds and her British investments, were also taxed by the U.S. federal estate tax, which was due (then) fifteen months from death. Both taxes were paid, seriously depleting the assets of the estate. There was a tax treaty between Great Britain and the United States that was designed to prevent double taxation of its subjects. The treaty delineated in which country property would be taxed; for instance, real estate and tangible personal property would be taxed where situated as of the date of death; other rules pertained to intangibles such as stocks and bonds, et cetera. Thus, the British estate of Mrs. Chandler was entitled to a credit and refund of the U.S. tax paid to the extent of the Great Britain tax paid on the English real estate and the tangible property located in England. Because it took four to five years to determine the British tax, an application for refund could not be made until the tax was determined. Typically, the United States charges interest for unpaid taxes but pays no interest for overpaid taxes, such as the refund. Bruce Felmly, as a young associate in the McLane firm, nursed the procedure for four years or so through a very reluctant International Operations Office of the IRS, finally getting a determination of the amount of the refund—in excess of $100,000. His troubles didn't end there. The U.S. Treasury, which had to issue the refund check, was equally reluctant to part with cash, even to the point of misplacing the issued and signed check on the desk of a departed but unreplaced clerk. It was only Bruce's dogged persistence that resulted in a fee for this firm and a substantial and long-awaited refund for our client.

The most recent contact the McLane law firm has had with the Chandler family was a visit by Mrs. Chandler's grandson, Mr. Whitfield, to Manchester about 1980 to seek out his roots. This author and his wife entertained Mr. Whitfield for a very pleasant lunch with Bruce and Sue Felmly.

## G. GALE ESTATE

An interesting case came in 1950 concerning the Gale will (not drawn by the McLane firm). The will created a trust that provided, in effect, for the income to be divided equally between the testator's children, Arthur and Deborah, during their lives; upon the death of the first to die, the trust would terminate and the trust principal would be distributed to the survivor. At the time the will was drafted, the children were young and unmarried, but after the testator-father's death, both children married and had families. The trust was not insubstantial in size.

It soon became apparent that the will created a horror situation—the children of the first to die would get nothing whereas the other family would take all and purely by chance. The situation was probably not intended by the testator, but it was a good example of sloppy draftsmanship on the part of the attorney. The two children (then married adults with families) came to see what could be done. This was not a question of "cy pres," a court-approved change in a will to more closely attain the intention of the testator. For example, a will gives Dartmouth College a fund for scholarship aid to students from the town of Bath, New Hampshire, but there are no such applicants, so the court applies the doctrine of cy pres and permits the fund to be used for students of Grafton County (which encompasses Bath) with preference to residents of Bath.

In the Gale will, there is no ambiguity or impossibility; the will is clear but produces an unjust result. The will could be reformed by saying that the trust should be divided in half for each child—a more difficult issue because usually the testator's stated intention will be carried out. Another possibility was to terminate the trust and distribute half to each. There seemed to be a conflict-of-laws[3] question or at least a jurisdictional one. The parties both were residents of New Hampshire but the will was admitted to probate in Illinois and the trustee was a Chicago bank. What state had jurisdiction? This required some legal research. A legal brief was prepared that justified New Hampshire jurisdiction and terminating the trust by dividing it equally between the children. A trial was held to establish the factual situation. The Rockingham County Probate Court entered a decree terminating the trust. The Chicago bank filed a final account, and upon allowance of the account, the assets were distributed equally to Deborah and Arthur—a very satisfactory result.

## H. ESTATE OF LEON WILLIAMS

Leon Williams, a Dartmouth alumnus of the class of 1915, was an accountant and partner of Rittenhouse, a national accounting firm. Williams died leaving a will with a very substantial bequest to Dartmouth College. John Meck, treasurer of the college, asked Judge to represent the college; Judge in turn called on Ken Graf, Stan Brown, and Marshall Abbey to work with him.

Williams owned the Diamond A cattle ranch[4] of about 90,000 acres, near Wagon Mound, New Mexico, his legal residence. Mr. Williams left his widow, his divorced wife to whom he had obligations, and sisters, nephews and nieces, none of whom wanted the college to have the ranch. (Williams left no children.) The local populace, including court personnel and other government officials, were mostly of Mexican descent and likewise were not happy about Dartmouth College inheriting the ranch. The scrivener of the Leon Williams will had him execute the original (ribbon copy) and a number of carbon copies of the will. This was most unusual—normally there is only one original of a will; as with a promissory note, there may be conformed copies (signatures typed in) but only one executed (signed) original. The local judge ruled, in accordance with common law, that each executed copy was an original and must be produced in court, that a revocation or destruction by the testator of any copy was a revocation of all copies, unless it could be shown that the testator had no access to the missing copy. Copies of the will had been distributed to the two named executors and interested legatees, including Dartmouth College, at the time the will was executed in April 1958, about a month before Williams died. Wouldn't you know that the ribbon copy that couldn't be located was the one given to Dartmouth College? A long, desperate weekend was spent searching for the will in Hanover and several banks in Boston and New York where the college maintained safekeeping facilities. Fortunately, the will turned up in a safe in Hanover, much to the relief of everyone concerned.

The will was duly probated; a number of problems arose. Under New Mexico law, the executor had to be a New Mexico resident, and neither executor appointed by the court resided in New Mexico. Lawyers advised that the appointments were void, so qualified executors were named by the court.

The widow had executed a prenuptial agreement[5] that she had destroyed, claiming it was not legal, and Leon Williams' executed copy of the prenuptial agreement could not be found. The question was also raised whether a prenuptial agreement could affect community property under New Mexico law.

The widow furthermore contested the will claiming that her husband (Leon Williams) had destroyed the prenuptial agreement, "animo revocandi" (intending to revoke it). If the will were considered revoked, she would lose a $400,000 bequest contained in the will.

There also was a dispute over ademption of bequests to the decedent's sisters and nieces and nephews; that is, did gifts made by the testator after the will was executed reduce the bequest, or was the legatee entitled to keep both the gifts and also the bequest?

There were lengthy negotiations with all interested parties. Ultimately a satisfactory settlement of all outstanding disputes resulted. John Love of Denver, a governor of Colorado, acted as local counsel for the college. The

Diamond A ranch was sold—the college did not want to get into the ranching business—and the proceeds were added to the college endowment. It was one of the largest bequests, if not the largest, ever received.

## I. ESTATE OF GILBERT HOOD

The Gilbert Hood estate in Derry came in 1936 through Norman Bingham, senior partner of Bingham, Dana & Gould of Boston. Gilbert Hood was one of the "sons" of Harvey P. Hood (H. P. Hood & Sons, Inc., the large New England dairy company), who lived in Derry and had a large experimental dairy farm. I suspect that the McLane firm filed papers in the probate court and attended any hearings and worked with the Bingham, Dana & Gould office, which presumably did most of the work.

Several years later, Mrs. Gilbert Hood, who loved the farm in Derry although she also had a residence in Winchester, Massachusetts, decided to give the town of Derry a new high school. She did not trust the town politicians and didn't want to give them the funds, so she created a private foundation, which qualified under the provisions of Section 501(c)3 for tax deductions. She gave to the foundation the funds necessary to build the school, then hired the architect to plan the school, with the advice of the local school board, and put the construction out to bid. When the project was completed, she delivered a deed to the land and buildings and turned over the keys. This was about a $1 million project, a lot of money for the 1940s.

The character of Mrs. Gilbert Hood is further revealed by the following story. In the 1920s, when the gift and estate tax laws were first passed, the law provided that if a person transferred property under a so-called general power of appointment (where the donee of the power may direct that it go to anyone), the property was not subject to tax. In the 1930s the IRS closed this loophole by taxing transfers that were subject to a general power of appointment but providing that if the transfers were subject to a special power of appointment (where the donee could transfer only to a limited class, such as children, lineal descendants, people with red hair—that is, finite and determinable), they would not be subject to tax. The IRS provided a time limit within which a donee of the power could renounce the general power and agree to a special power and thus avoid the tax. Mrs. Hood had a general power of appointment under her husband's will. Mr. Norman Bingham called Mrs. Hood for an appointment in his office so he could explain the necessity of renouncing her general power and converting it into a special power, which would save her estate several tens of thousands of dollars, if not more. Mrs. Hood, a regal woman, listened to what Mr. Bingham had to say and responded: "Mr. Bingham, I appreciate your concern for my welfare, but I want you to know that my country has been very good to me, and I have no intention of doing anything that would deprive my government from receiving any monies from my estate to which they are so justly deserving. Is there anything else you wish to discuss?"

The McLane office helped to settle Mrs. Hood's estate, the residue of which passed to the charitable trust created to build the high school but which had remained dormant after its completion. Gilbert Hood, Jr., his wife, and two daughters were trustees, as were an attorney from Bingham, Dana & Gould and this author. Annual meetings were held at Mr. Hood's house in Winchester at about Christmastime, and the list of distributions prepared by Gilbert Hood was approved. He was always happy to consider any suggestions of contributions from the other trustees. The business of keeping up with requirements for the trust became too great for Mr. Hood, and the trust was terminated by transfer to the Boston Permanent Charity Fund.

## J. MATTER OF EDITH

One of the more amusing entries in Judge's diary is the following: (1920s) "Hunted around Concord for Edith on a binge." I have no idea who Edith was.

## K. ESTATE OF EDWIN NEVILLE

Edwin Neville, a U.S. diplomat, had a place in Conway, New Hampshire ,as well as New York. Judge had been involved in estate planning for him for several years and settled his estate after his death in February 1942. Mr. Neville had been stationed in Japan for several years and had acquired property there, which he had to abandon when he returned to the United States just before the war. After the end of the war, the family received a detailed accounting of the Japan property—all rents received and expenses paid and a check for the difference from the office of the Custodian of Alien Property. The property was found to have been well cared for.

## L. ESTATE OF EDWARD M. CHASE

Edward M. Chase was born in 1874 in Lithuania and migrated with his parents to Lewiston, Maine, in 1889. In the following year, when just sixteen, Edward started work in his father's department store. Two years later, he started his own business as a tea merchant and developed a chain of twenty-one stores in New York and New England. In 1898, he moved to Manchester and for forty-seven years conducted a house furnishings and furniture business under the name of the E. M. Chase Company, located at the southwest corner of Elm and Bridge Streets. (The building was demolished for the widening of Notre Dame Bridge in 1990.) Mr. Chase was very successful and generous with his money. In 1924, he founded and financed the Chase Family Home for destitute families. In 1928, he founded the Edward M. Chase Student Aid Foundation, primarily to assist students with Lithuanian antecedents. Mr. Chase was active in the Scottish Rite Masonic Order and in Jewish organizations. He died late in 1939; his estate was settled between 1940 and 1942. The family continued the business after his death for a couple of decades.

Mr. Chase was a very independent man and, among other things, made out his own income tax returns. It was inevitable that about two years after the return was filed, Mr. Chase would regularly appear in the office with a deficiency notice from the IRS. Judge would then dig into the factual evidence, arrange conferences with IRS agents in Boston, and finally reach a settlement. For instance, in 1935 Judge had conferences in Boston with the IRS in March, August, October, and December and in Washington the following June. In 1938, Judge went to New York City and Washington on Mr. Chase's 1936 tax return, with no resolution. I don't know what the issues were or whether the government or Mr. Chase came out ahead on balance. In 1943, the federal estate tax was finally settled.

Sometime in the early 1900s, Mr. Chase's store was the scene of a spectacular accident in which fortunately there were no personal injuries. The Bridge Street trolley line ran north on Elm Street to Bridge Street where it turned east on Bridge Street and continued to the top of the hill by Derryfield Park and the Catholic Retirement Home. The Concord trolley line turned north on Beech Street. On this particular trip, the last one of the day at about 11 P.M., there were no passengers. Upon arrival at the end of the Bridge Street line, the conductor set his brakes and got out of the car, as he always did, to swing the overhead trolley around from the rear (going easterly) to the rear (going westerly). This he did by pulling on the rope attached to the trolley, disengaging the overhead electric cable, and pulling the trolley around to the other end of the car and reengaging the cable. As the conductor was walking the trolley around, the car started to move downhill, accumulating speed very quickly. Try as he might, the conductor could not stop the car, and he soon was forced to drop the rope and simply watch the trolley disappear down the hill. He probably shook at the thought of what might happen to others and himself. The car picked up speed as it hurtled down the long hill. Fortunately, no one was around at that time of night. The car started to lose speed as it passed Beech, Union, and Chestnut Streets, but it was still going at a fair clip when it came to the abrupt corner of Bridge and Elm. No way could it make the turn. It jumped the tracks and headed for Mr. Chase's big plateglass show windows in his store. What a noise did it make as it hit the building: the breaking glass, the smashing of wood and metal as the store floor sagged under its heavy burden and broke, sending the trolley into the basement, where it was invisible from the street. The noise and vibrations sent consternation into the tenants asleep on the second, third, and fourth floors, who were shaken from their beds and thrown to the floor as the building trembled and shook. They thought an earthquake had struck Manchester, but on looking out their windows they could see that no other buildings were affected nor could they see any damage to their building. As they went out on the street and saw what happened they laughed, and in the chill of the night offered theories as to how to extricate the trolley from the basement!

## M. ESTATE OF SALLY DREW HALL

Sally Hall, longtime friend and client of Judge, died in October 1949. She was the daughter of Irving Drew, a successful and distinguished lawyer in Lancaster, New Hampshire, in the latter part of the nineteenth century when railroading and lumbering made Lancaster a prestigious town. Sally married E. K. Hall, a loyal Dartmouth alumnus and successful businessman in financial circles in New York in the 1920s and 1930s. E. K. and Sally gave Dartmouth "Dick's House" as the college infirmary in memory of their son, Dick, who died while a student at Dartmouth. The firm settled her estate and administered a testamentary trust.

## N. ESTATE OF ARTHUR MOREAU

In March 1951, Judge prepared a will for Arthur Moreau, who ran a successful hardware business under the name of J. J. Moreau & Son. J. J. was Arthur's father.[6] Arthur Moreau was mayor of the city from 1925 to 1931 and was the instigator in 1936 of Amoskeag Industries, Inc., which acquired the assets of the old Amoskeag Manufacturing Company in bankruptcy. Moreau was the first president of Amoskeag Industries. Arthur Moreau, a longtime client of Judge, asked him to be secretary of and counsel for Amoskeag Industries and the firm continues in that relationship in 1996.

Arthur Moreau died on July 4, 1951. His funeral was one of the largest ever held in Manchester; people from all walks of life came to pay final respects to Manchester's number one citizen—a successful businessman, a civic leader, a popular municipal government official, and a leader in the French community and the Catholic Church. Judge and Ken Graf, a college classmate and close friend of Arthur Moreau, Jr., settled the estate and administered trusts under his will.[7] The firm also settled the estate of his widow, Emilienne Moreau, a few years later.

## O. ESTATES OF CHARLES AND ALMA MILHAM

Charles Milham of Hanover, who held an administrative position with Dartmouth College, died in 1952. Judge and Miss Mansfield settled his estate. His widow, Alma Haas Milham, lived on in Hanover and was a client of the office until her death in 1989. This author was the attorney for the estate and a trustee of the Charitable Remainder Trust, which distributed about $4 million to five named charities, namely, Dartmouth College medical and engineering schools, Meharry Medical School in Nashville, Tennessee (primarily a black institution), and Sloane-Kettering Institute for Cancer Research, Lighthouse for the Blind, and the Multiple Sclerosis Foundation, all of New York City.

## P. ESTATE OF JOEL COFFIN

The trust under the will of Joel Coffin of Sugar Hill (now a separate town) in Franconia presented some problems in 1952 in addition to filing annual accounts for the trustee in New Jersey. Mr. Coffin's widow, who remarried, was given a life estate in the farm, which the trustee was required to maintain as it had always been maintained. As the farm lost more money because of economic conditions (not poor management), the trustee was obligated to use more principal, to the distress of the remaindermen—children of Mr. Coffin by a prior marriage. This adversarial position caused numerous conferences and hearings and was litigated in 1954 when the parties and Judge Wescott took a view, but the case was settled before trial, limiting the amount of principal the trustee could spend on farm maintenance.

## Q. ESTATE OF ELIZABETH ELWYN LANGDON

Elizabeth Elwyn Langdon (Mrs. Woodbury Langdon), a resident of Portsmouth, died on August 22, 1945, leaving a will naming John F. Crocker of Milton, Massachusetts, and Arthur Burgess of Philadelphia, Pennsylvania, as executors and trustees. They were both engaged in trust administration in banks. Judge McLane had reviewed Mrs. Woodbury Langdon's will in New York City with her attorney in about 1939. Messrs. Crocker and Burgess engaged the McLane law firm to represent them in the probate of the estate. Judge McLane and Miss Mansfield worked on the case. The principal assets were the historic and well-preserved Governor John Langdon Mansion in Portsmouth along with some other real estate and about $2.8 million in personalty, mostly investments in stocks and bonds. Mrs. Langdon left bequests of $25,000 to several charities in and around Portsmouth, and created trusts for the benefit of family members for life with the residue passing to the residuary legatee, The Cathedral Church of St. John the Divine in the Episcopal Diocese of New York. Mrs. Langdon bequeathed the Governor John Langdon Mansion, which had been her homestead, to the New Hampshire Historical Society, forever, together with furniture therein and an endowment fund of $75,000; however, the society declined to accept the gift, since it was not in the business of managing real estate and it felt the endowment was too small. This raised the question of whether a public trust had been established to which the doctrine of cy pres might apply or whether, upon the failure of the bequest, the property passed to the residuary legatee, the Church of St. John the Divine. The executors had conversations with the director of charitable trusts within the attorney general's office, who indicated strongly that a public trust had been established. A search was made for a charitable organization that was capable and willing to carry out the terms of the will. The Society for the Preservation of New England Antiquities (SPNEA) in Boston filled the bill. The organizations negotiated an agreement by which the Governor John Langdon Mansion would be conveyed to the SPNEA together with the furniture and the endowment fund. Because the endowment fund seemed small for the maintenance and upkeep of the property, the Church of St. John the Divine agreed to pay a supplemental amount provided it was found to be necessary by an impartial committee. A petition was filed in the superior court for Rockingham County by the executors of the estate of Elizabeth Elwyn Langdon naming as petitionees the director of charitable trusts, the Church of St. John the Divine, the New Hampshire Historical Society, and beneficiaries of the estate. This raised the question of cy pres and whether additional funds might be ordered from the estate if the endowment was found to be inadequate. SPNEA moved to be allowed to intervene, which it did successfully. The court decreed as the parties had agreed and thus SPNEA acquired the property and maintains it, keeping it open to the public in the summer months.

    John Langdon was a charismatic and distinguished individual of the Revolutionary period. He was born in 1741, the second son of a hardworking but poor farmer who could not afford a Harvard education for his sons. John went into commerce and became an able businessman, exporting building materials and lumber to eastern seaboard cities to be used in shipbuilding and cargo packaging. While still in his teens, he skippered ships of other owners and took along some of his own goods to sell. In 1763, at the age of twenty-two, he commanded the *Keppel* on a trading voyage to Antigua. He built and sailed his first ship to London and sold it when he was twenty-six; he continued to build and sell more vessels until 1770, when he settled in Portsmouth.

    In 1772, one of his ships was seized by the British in Portsmouth harbor and was charged with false registration to avoid tax. From then on he was a confirmed revolutionary, and in the next year, at age thirty-two, he was the youngest member of the Committee of Correspondence. Langdon learned that General Gage planned to remove the munitions from Fort William and Mary in Newcastle, so Langdon organized a raiding party of four hundred men, overran the fort, took away the munitions, and parceled them out to the surrounding towns. Langdon made a significant contribution in convincing Congress to build a Navy. He built two ships for the Navy, one of which was commanded by John Paul Jones.

Langdon was a shrewd businessman. As administrator of naval affairs for the Constitutional Congress, he received a percentage of the value of prize ships taken and did some privateering himself. No wonder he ended the war a rich man.

In 1777, Langdon married Betsy Sherburne of Portsmouth; they had a daughter, Elizabeth, who subsequently married Thomas Elwyn, thus becoming Elizabeth Langdon Elwyn. John Langdon went to the New Hampshire legislature and was its speaker, and also a justice of the Court of Common Pleas. He financially backed General John Stark's campaign against Burgoyne and was present when the latter surrendered in Cambridge in October 1777.

In 1783, the John Langdon Mansion was started, with John paying attention to all the details of construction. He and his wife moved in in 1784. John Langdon apparently was a charming man and wanted his house to be spacious enough for large receptions as well as intimate gatherings. The south parlor still has the original hand-painted scenic wallpaper.

In 1785, Langdon became president of the New Hampshire Senate; in 1787, he was a delegate to the Constitutional Convention; and in 1788, he was elected to the U.S. Senate and became a supporter of Alexander Hamilton and the pro-French republicans. He was elected the first president pro tem of the senate[8] and officially advised General Washington of his election as president. Both Washington and General Lafayette stayed with John Langdon in his mansion in Portsmouth.[9] In 1800, he ended two terms in the senate and sought the governorship; he lost in 1802, 1803, and 1804, won in 1805, and was defeated in 1809. But then he was reelected and served until he retired in 1812 at the age of seventy-one. John Langdon died in 1819 and left the mansion to his daughter, Elizabeth Langdon Elwyn, who lived there until 1833, when she sold the house to the Reverend Charles Burroughs. In 1877, the house came back to the family when it was purchased by Woodbury Langdon.

Woodbury Langdon was the sixth generation descended from Woodbury Langdon, John Langdon's brother. Woodbury Langdon was born in Portsmouth, New Hampshire, in 1838 but entered business in

Boston, where he was engaged in the dry goods business as a commission house dealing in woolen and cotton goods. He subsequently moved to New York and was successfully engaged in business, being on the boards of directors of a number of corporations. In 1896, he married Elizabeth Elwyn of Philadelphia, who thus became Elizabeth Elwyn Langdon. She was descended from Elizabeth Langdon Elwyn, Governor John Langdon's daughter. Woodbury and Elizabeth Langdon moved back to Portsmouth in 1911 and became an important part of the community. He made many gifts of $5,000 to nonprofits and just before his death he gave $100,000 to the Cottage Hospital Annex building fund.[10] He also put up the money to save the John Paul Jones house. Woodbury Langdon died in 1921. His widow, Elizabeth Elwyn Langdon, kept the house until her death in 1945. It is fortunate that over the years, although there have been additions (servants' quarters), the mansion has remained substantially as built originally and has been maintained in good condition.

## Notes

1. An unusually conservative provision that  I suspect originated with the client. There were times when a balanced portfolio of equities and fixed income obligations would have produced more income. Consideration was given to petition the court for greater investment latitude, but that was never undertaken.

2. Patrick's niece, Helen Bradford, says Patrick was called Sam in school, but she knows of no reason why. Her family always called him "Uncle Sam."

3. Conflict-of-laws questions arise when the laws of two or more jurisdictions could apply to a situation. The question then is— Which law applies?

4. The Diamond A ranch is adjacent to the Fort Union ranch, also of about 100,000 acres, which is owned by the Ames family, of which this author's first wife, Blanche, is a member.

5. A prenuptial agreement, executed before marriage, is an agreement between the parties to the marriage, after full and fair disclosure by both parties of their complete financial assets and liabilities, that purports to divide the couple's properties in the event of divorce. It is usually important that each party be represented by a qualified marital counselor, attorney, or CPA.

6. The Moreau store continued for several years with some downsizing following a disastrous fire in its wholesale lumberyard on Canal and Spring Streets. Then in a reorganization, the family interests were purchased by Gerry Leblanc, Arthur Moreau's grandson, who moved the store from Elm Street, just south of the Numerica building, to lower Elm Street, where there was more parking. Unfortunately, Gerry Leblanc died prematurely and the business was sold outside the family, although many of the store clerks stayed

on. The business continued until the fall of 1991, when it was liquidated. Moreau's hardware store had been a fixture in Manchester for about ninety years, in the same way that Varick's hardware store had served Manchester from the late nineteenth century into the depression years.

7. It is interesting to note that Arthur Moreau's great-grandson, Scott Moreau, married Judge's granddaughter, Virginia (Gigi) McLane, in 1988.

8. The vice president of the United States is the president of the senate.

9. Ray Brighton, *They Came To Fish* (Portsmouth, N.H.: Portsmouth 300, Inc., 1973), Vol. II, p. 426.

10. Brighton, *They Came to Fish*, p. 427.

# TWENTY-FOUR

# Criminal Litigation

## STATE V. STEPHEN STORY
## STATE V. DONAT COTE

The *New Hampshire Sunday News*[1] in its March 7, 1948, issue had banner headlines proclaiming "Story admits 'Bad Business' in State Funds." A headline story by Elias McQuaid, an investigative reporter, asserted that Donat Cote, a Manchester contractor, had obtained $700,000 of state contracts for work at state institutions without competitive bidding as required by statute. There were sixteen separate jobs and only four were competitively bid. Stephen Story, the controller for the state of New Hampshire and the responsible official, stated it was important to get the work done and hence the contracts were awarded to Cote, there not being other contractors who could do the work. Story approved the manifests for payment to Cote, but the newspaper reported that frequently there was no supporting data accompanying the manifest. Donat Cote was described as a former forty-dollar-a-week laborer who had worked under Story as a building inspector in the office of the comptroller, which then, but no longer, oversaw state construction contracts. Story admitted to the newspaper that he and Cote were warm personal friends. Fifty-eight-year-old Steve Story had been city manager for the city of Rochester, New York, before coming to New Hampshire. Donat Cote had three construction corporations and eight businesses using registered trade names through which he conducted his business, which frequently caused substantial confusion in tracing invoices to particular contracts and jobs and resulted in some duplicate payments. Cote employed about two hundred people in his businesses. The newspaper story indicated that after an examination of records at the comptroller's office, it was evident there was a careless handling of accounts, transfers of accounts without proper authorization, confusion as to where records were kept, a lack of entries on the contract ledger, and slipshod bookkeeping. The newspaper also found that Cote owned a car that had belonged to Story. Cote stated that Story had given it to him; Story claimed that Cote had purchased it for $1,100.

The next week's edition, of March 14, indicated that Governor Charlie

Dale of Portsmouth had suspended all work being performed by Donat Cote or any of his companies and was pushing for a vigorous probe of the state work. Contractors had been contacted and assured the newspaper that there were plenty of firms capable of performing the state work, contrary to the assertions of Mr. Story. The newspaper asserted that many of the manifests for payments to Cote simply read, "Labor and materials—$3 M—." with no supporting documents. Cote was paid $715,000 in 1947.

In the edition of April 21, the paper made the revelation that Standard Construction Company, one of Cote's business entities, had received a payment of $10,000 for work that was not sanctioned by the original authorization of work at Keene State Teachers College. Somehow a duplicate manifest was improperly used to authorize the payment. In fact, none of Cote's companies ever did any work at Keene. Story explained it away as simply a bookkeeping error! The governor, with the approval of the executive council on the recommendation of the attorney general, Ernest D'Amours, hired the nationally recognized top-rated accounting firm of Lybrand, Ross Bros. and Montgomery of Boston to make a detailed audit of the Cote-related work.[2] The paper also disclosed that the comptroller was keeping some of the records and papers at his home in Newbury, New Hampshire. Apparently, Donat Cote got pretty hot under the collar as a result of some of the questions asked over the phone, according to the paper. Some parties were beginning to criticize the administration for moving too slowly in the investigation, particularly the Taxpayers' Association and the Democratic Party leaders.

The next week's article revealed that there were no records to show that labor and material were actually expended to support manifests. The article reported that the architect on the Laconia State School project had notified Cote that the specifications were not being followed. It stated that the attorney general was taking steps to seize Cote's records. The article revealed that there was a crew of four auditors at work from Boston and that Steve Story, with a state salary of $6,000, was having trouble in maintaining his schooner, which he purchased on Long Island for under $10,000 and which was wintered in Boothbay Harbor, Maine.

The April 4 edition headlines urged a grand jury probe of the Story case. Two dissident executive councilors, who claimed the investigation was proceeding too slowly, had demanded the probe. A grand jury should be impaneled and a special prosecutor appointed, they urged. The paper also revealed that Cote had loaned an executive councilor money for a new suit and had also given each of the executive councilors a gift certificate for a new hat. The editorial called the investigation slow, unsatisfactory, and evasive.

The next weekend edition revealed that Steve Story had resigned as comptroller at the request of the governor and council. He threatened countersuit if prosecuted.

Subsequent editions stated that Cote was permitted to cash sizable checks out of the treasurer's petty cash account without depositing them in a bank account (thus avoiding a bank record of deposits), a privilege normally reserved as an accommodation to state employees to cash small paychecks. The audit by Lybrand, Ross Bros. revealed that a full audit was necessary. Faulty work by Cote in the installation of a boiler at the state prison was pointed out. The state supreme court approved an order by the superior court making all of Cote's records available to the attorney general.

There were several issues. First, the cost-plus contracts were awarded without competitive bidding, contrary to the statute. Steve Story authorized Donat Cote and his companies to perform cost-plus work in a letter dated December 13, 1946. It outlined the basis of compensation as follows: item A, labor and materials, trucking and transportation at actual cost; item B, supervision, planning, insurance, and taxes computed at 10 percent of item A; item C, profit computed at 15 percent of item A and item B. Work was started on these in 1946 at six different institutions.

What was meant by cost-plus? The state contended that the actual cost of an item meant what Cote paid for it. Cote practically never used the amount invoiced by the vendor as the base cost, but claimed that actual cost called for "the application of various formulas," all of which increased the amount billed to the state. The New Hampshire Supreme Court (97 NH 141) agreed with the trial court that there was no legal definition of actual cost and left it to the jury to decide what the parties meant. The jury agreed with the state's contention—that is, what Cote paid for the item.

In many instances, Cote was also awarded a fixed-price contract for work at the same institution and frequently charged to the cost-plus contract items that were supplied and paid for under the fixed-price contract, thus in effect collecting twice for the same item. Story acknowledged this had happened and claimed he intended to speak to Cote to adjust the matter but never did because, as Story said, "The bell was rung and I was sent home." In some instances Cote represented that he had furnished labor and materials, but examination showed that the state was charged for more items than were delivered. In order to prove these in court, each count of the indictment represented a separate invoice, to which the engineers from Charles T. Main Company testified, identifying and indicating where the item was used in the particular institution and whether it was included in a fixed-price contract or a cost-plus contract. The accountants from Lybrand, Ross Bros. testified as to whether the item was included in the fixed-price contract and also the cost-plus contract or just in the cost-plus contract and whether the computation of cost was in accordance with the contract or not. The paper reported that the accountants found "overbids" of $318,888 on the cost-plus contracts.

In July 1948, Kenneth F. Graf of the firm of McLANE, Davis, Carleton & Graf, as it was then known, was appointed special prosecutor by the governor and executive council upon the recommendation of the attorney general, Ernest D'Amours. The case was presented to the grand jury for Merrimack County during the fall of 1948. Indictments were returned against both Donat Cote and Steve Story. Arthur A. Greene, Jr., and Stanley M. Brown, partners of Kenneth Graf, assisted in the preparation of the evidence and in the trial. One of the longest in New Hampshire court history, the trial ran for something like sixteen weeks, in the summer of 1949, one of the hottest summers on record, without the aid of air-conditioning in the old Merrimack County Courthouse in Concord. The verdict against both defendants was guilty on all counts of the indictments. The defendants appealed, but the New Hampshire Supreme Court overruled all exceptions and upheld the verdicts.

This was a very complicated case involving many separate claims of fraud and misrepresentation, which had to be proved to the jury. Much of the initial investigation was performed by accountants and bookkeepers employed by Lybrand, Ross Bros. and Montgomery and engineers employed by Charles T. Main & Company. Additional investigation was done by the New Hampshire State Police and personnel from the New Hampshire attorney general's office. All of this information was prepared for trial by special prosecutor Kenneth F. Graf and his associates, Arthur Greene and Stanley Brown. The fact that the defendants were found guilty on all counts attests to the meticulous preparation of the case by Mr. Graf and his team and their superb trial techniques.

Both Story and Cote served a number of years in the state prison in Concord.

## STATE V. EDWARD H. COOLIDGE, JR.
### 109 NH 403, June 30, 1969

Pamela Mason of Manchester, age fourteen, was murdered on January 13, 1964. On February 26, 1964, indictments were handed down against Edward H. Coolidge, Jr. Sandra Valade, also of Manchester, was murdered February 1, 1960. Edward H. Coolidge, Jr., was indicted for the Valade crime on March 26, 1964, but was never tried. The court appointed J. Murray Devine of the firm of Devine and Millimet as chief counsel for Coolidge. He was assisted by Matthias J. Reynolds of the same firm and John A. Graf of the McLane law firm.[3] Murray Devine died suddenly from a heart attack on January 2, 1965, just before the scheduled start of the trial. Matthias J. Reynolds became chief counsel and asked that additional attorneys from other law firms be appointed to assist him. The court appointed Robert Chiesa from the Wadleigh firm. The defendant was found guilty.

Pamela Mason, on the night of her death, was picked up at her home at 6 P.M. by a man, believed to be Coolidge, to baby-sit his children, although no one saw him. He had called the Mason home earlier in the afternoon about a baby-sitter and spoke with Pamela's mother, who advised him to call when Pamela would be there. She told her daughter not to accept the job unless a woman was involved. It snowed about ten inches that afternoon, forcing schools to close the next day. Because of the storm, no one was particularly disturbed that Pamela did not return home that evening, thinking she had stayed at the child's home. Pamela's body was recovered from a snowbank alongside Interstate 93 about a week later with twenty to thirty stab wounds, a cut throat, and a bullet in her head. Medical evidence placed death at between 7 and 9 P.M. on the night she disappeared. Her body had been moved from the site of her death and was warm when abandoned by the highway.

Coolidge was a route salesman for a bakery that had suffered losses. The company suspected that some of its route men weren't reporting all their sales and were pocketing cash. The route men were given lie detector tests. It is standard procedure to ask test questions to establish normal reactions of the person being examined. Because the Pamela Mason case was prominent in the news, the test question asked was "Did you kill Pamela Mason?" a negative response and no reaction on the lie detector was expected because the question was considered obviously inapplicable. However, in Coolidge's case there was a strong reaction on the machine, which led the police to immediately treat him as a prime suspect. There was evidence that a bullet recovered from Pamela Mason's body was fired from a gun that was found in Coolidge's house, that knife wounds could have come from knives in Coolidge's possession, that particles of material found in his car matched particles found on Pamela, and that Coolidge's car was seen near the spot where the body was found. Probably the most devastating evidence, which influenced the jury to return a guilty verdict, was the elaborate attempt by Coolidge to establish an alibi as to his whereabouts the night of the murder. There was evidence that Coolidge had called several friends urging them to give false testimony as to his whereabouts. The case went to the state supreme court, which upheld the guilty verdicts.

One of the most interesting incidents in the trial was the testimony of the state's witness, a ballistics expert with the Massachusetts State Police, and that of the defendant's witness from the Mossberg Company, which manufactured the rifle. The testimony of these two witnesses (assumed names) is paraphrased as follows:

S   (state): Lieutenant Smith, will you state your name and employment?

W (witness): My name is Lieutenant John Smith of the Massachusetts State Police. I am a ballistics expert.

S: Will you describe to the jury what a ballistics expert does and how?

W: I examine bullets that are recovered from the perpetration of a crime and try to ascertain what gun they came from. Every gun makes unique and distinctive marks on a bullet fired from that gun that cannot possibly come from any other gun. We test-fire a bullet from the gun in question and compare it with the bullet retrieved from the crime scene by examining the two under the microscope. If the unique and distinctive marks are the same on both bullets, you then can testify that the bullet recovered from the crime scene was fired by the gun in question.

S: How long have you been involved with this bullet comparison and how many trials have you testified in?

W: I've been doing this for about twenty years and have testified in about two hundred cases.

S: Have you written articles about bullet comparison techniques?

W: Oh yes, I have published a number of articles for professional journals and have written several books about the subject.

S: Now, turning to the Pamela Mason case, please describe to the jury just what you did.

W: I was given a bullet that was tagged by the state police as having been recovered at the autopsy from the body of Pamela Mason. I was also given a Mossberg rifle that was likewise identified by the New Hampshire State Police as having been recovered from the residence of Edward Coolidge pursuant to a search warrant. I then test-fired the Coolidge rifle in our laboratory, recovered the bullet, and compared the two bullets under a powerful microscope and concluded that the markings were identical. My opinion is that the Pamela Mason bullet was fired from the Coolidge gun.

S: I have no further questions. You may inquire (addressing the defendant's counsel).

D: (defendant's counsel): Lieutenant Smith, you were one of the first to specialize in this field, were you not?

W: Yes, that is correct.

D: I suppose that you probably know more than any other person about bullet comparison techniques?

W: Well, if there is someone who knows more than I, I would very much like to meet him.

D: As I understand your testimony, every bullet fired from a particular gun will have the same markings on it?

W: That is correct.

D: And it would be impossible for a particular bullet to come from more than one gun?

W: That is true.

D: Now, did you compare a test bullet fired from the Coolidge gun with a bullet from a source other than the body of Pamela Mason?

W: Yes.

There was considerable whispering in the courtroom as this question was asked. It seemed obvious that the defense was going to ask if the bullet from the body of Sandra Valade came from the same gun. Why, people were asking themselves, did the defense want to bring up a different murder that was not involved in this case? The evidence would be pretty devastating to the defense if the expert's answer were that both bullets did come from the same gun. Coolidge had been indicted for the Sandra Valade crime, but no plans had been made for trial.

D: Please tell the jury what the bullet was and what your findings were.

W: I was furnished a bullet that was identified by the New Hampshire State Police as having come from the body of Sandra Valade in 1960, and I performed comparison studies with the test bullet from the Coolidge rifle and concluded that the Sandra Valade bullet came from the same gun.

D: Now, let me see if I understand you correctly. You are testifying that the bullet recovered from the body of Sandra Valade in 1960 and the bullet recovered from the body of Pamela Mason in 1964 were fired from the same gun of Mr. Coolidge. Is that correct?

W: Yes, that's correct.

D: Are you absolutely sure of that?

W: Yes, I am.

D: Is there any way that the bullet that was recovered from the body of Sandra Valade could possibly have come from another rifle?

W: None whatsoever.

D: Do you want to change your testimony about this? Or are you willing to stake your reputation on your testimony?

W: I am correct.

D: I have no further questions.

The prosecution finished presenting their evidence in the case, then the defense presented their evidence. They soon called Mr. Richard Doe from the Mossberg Gun Company.

D: Will you state your name and address and indicate by whom you are employed?

W: My name is Richard Doe and I live at 300 Main Street, Indianapolis, Indiana, and am employed by the Mossberg Gun Company.

D: Please describe your duties at the company.

W: My title is registrar of firearms. My duty is to examine every gun upon completion and record in a special book the make and model of the gun and its serial number. When the gun is shipped from the factory, I record, as a part of the original entry, the date and the name and address of the purchaser.

D: Do you have the registration book with you?

W: Yes, I do.

D: I show you a gun marked Prosecution Exhibit #10 and ask if you can identify that gun.

W: Yes, that is a Mossberg rifle made at our factory.

D: Is that gun registered in your registration book?

W: Yes, it is. I see that the serial number engraved in the metal of the gun is 133458. By looking in the registry book under that number, I find that the rifle was completed in our factory on November 15, 1961, and shipped to Edward Coolidge, Jr., in Manchester, New Hampshire, on December 18, 1961. [Over a year *after* the shooting of Sandra Valade!]

D: Thank you, Mr. Doe, I have no further questions. You may inquire (addressing the chief prosecution attorney).

S: I have no questions.

The Court: That will be all, Mr. Doe, you are excused.

The impact of this testimony was to negate the testimony of Lieutenant Smith that the Coolidge rifle had fired the bullet found in the body of Sandra Valade. Although that testimony was not germane to the Pamela Mason case, it cast into doubt the whole theory of bullet identification by comparison and raised the question of the veracity of the police lieutenant's opinion that the bullet from Pamela Mason's body was fired by the Coolidge rifle. The jury was instructed to consider this testimony along with all of the other testimony. The jury concluded that even if they did not believe the police ballistics expert, there was sufficient other evidence to find Edward Coolidge guilty of the murder of Pamela Mason beyond a reasonable doubt.

As indicated above, the case was appealed to the New Hampshire Supreme Court, which upheld the verdict. The defendant then appealed to the U.S. Supreme Court, which granted Certiorari (the court agreed to hear the appeal), and appointed Archibald Cox as special counsel with the New Hampshire lawyers. The supreme court (Edward H. Coolidge, Jr., v. N.H., 403 US 443, 1971) reversed, on a five-to-four decision, and remanded the case to the New Hampshire courts on the ground that there had been an illegal search and seizure under the Fourth Amendment to the U.S. Constitution and that the "fruits of unconstitutional seizure were inadmissable." The court stated that the warrant authorizing the search of the automobile was invalid because it was not issued by a neutral and detached magistrate. The warrants were issued by the attorney general acting as a justice of the peace. Prior to issuing the warrant, the attorney general personally took charge of all police activities and later became chief prosecutor. The car was searched and vacuumed; sweepings, which were the same as dirt found on Pamela Mason (implying she had been in the defendant's car), were improperly admitted. The court also found that the police knew of the presence of the car and planned to seize it, thus there were no "exigent circumstances" justifying a warrantless search.

The New Hampshire court scheduled a new trial. William Maynard, the original attorney general, was replaced by Warren Rudman and his assistant attorney general, David Souter,[4] but before trial, the defendant pleaded guilty to second-degree murder and served out his sentence.

Edward Coolidge was indicted on March 26, 1964, by the grand jury for the murder of Sandra Valade. On July 13, 1965, Coolidge, through his attorneys (Reynolds, Graf, and Chiesa), sought dismissal of the Valade indictment upon the ground that he had been denied a speedy trial, in violation of his constitutional rights. The motion was denied, but the state was ordered to indicate to the court by August 15, 1965, whether they proposed to try the case. On August 16, 1965, the state filed a *nolle prosequi* (I do not intend to prosecute). The defendant's motion to dismiss the indictment was denied again on the ground that, because of the *nolle prosequi* the case was no longer pending. The case was transferred to the New Hampshire Supreme Court, which heard arguments on December 20, 1968, and decided on June 30, 1969,[5] affirming the lower court ruling, stating that under New Hampshire practice, a *nolle prosequi* operated to discharge the indictment, so that the case is no longer pending.

## Notes

1. Blair Clark and Ben Bradlee came to New Hampshire in 1947 and started the *New Hampshire Sunday News*, working out of a rented second-floor office

in downtown Manchester with a couple of beat-up old tables, some equally used typewriters, and a few ashtrays. They and their staff exercised a lot of imagination, asked a lot of questions, looked into many corners, and learned about the state and its people in a short time. Their paper's statewide circulation grew rapidly as people rushed to buy it for its fresh approach to the news. The Story-Cote case was its most prominent bit of investigative reporting. The *New Hampshire Sunday News* was a client of Kenneth Graf in the McLane law firm. Soon after the Story-Cote case broke, the *Union Leader* made overtures to the *Sunday News* about purchase, but the June 14 edition indicated that the paper would maintain its independence. However, the August 29, 1948, edition contained statements by both Blair Clark as seller and William Loeb as purchaser that the *Union Leader* had purchased the paper as of September 1. The assets plus the subscription list were sold at a handsome profit.

Blair Clark went on with his journalism to the *Boston-Herald* for a couple of years, then fourteen years with CBS News, first in Paris, then New York City, and finally as general manager before moving over to the *New York Post* in 1965 until his retirement.

Ben Bradlee went to the *Washington Post* for three years, then the U.S. embassy in Paris as press attaché for two years, then as European correspondent for *Newsweek* from 1953 to 1957, and in the Washington bureau until 1961. He rejoined the *Washington Post* working his way up the ladder, and took the helm as managing editor from 1965 to 1968 and executive editor from 1968 to 1991.

2. Governor Charlie Dale of Portsmouth did not trust either the "Concord Gang," including Steve Story, who had been a popular state employee for several years, or the state police and hence did not want to talk to any of them about an investigation. Therefore, on his own he determined that, in addition to Lybrand, Ross Bros. and Montgomery as accountants, he needed an equally qualified engineering firm. He ascertained that the Charles T. Main Company of Boston was a thoroughly reputable firm and so personally called them. He apparently informed the telephone operator that he was Governor Dale of New Hampshire, and that he had a serious confidential problem and wanted to speak to one of the senior partners. The telephone operator transferred him as requested, but ever after in the office the governor and the state of New Hampshire were referred to as her clients.

3. Matthias J. Reynolds, in reviewing this material on the Coolidge case in 1995, wrote: "John [Graf] did an incredibly good job with not only his specific assignments in and out of trial, but also a great job of keeping the whole ship afloat with his incredible organization and neverending sense of humor."

4. It is interesting to note that Mr. Justice Brennan's vote played a key role in the majority decision to overturn the verdict and remand for a new trial. He had long been admired by David Souter, who later was appointed to the U.S. Supreme Court to replace Mr. Justice Brennan.

5. State v. Edward H. Coolidge, Jr., 109 NH 426 (1969).

# TWENTY-FIVE

# Interlude 1950–1959

## HIGHLIGHTS OF 1950

Judge and Elisabeth spent New Year's 1950 at the Dartmouth Outing Club's Ravine Camp on Mt. Moosilauke. There was no snow. Many of the group got their exercise by walking the couple of miles to the romantically located Jobildunc[1] Ravine cabin, a little log cabin big enough for four, with stove and bunk beds, nestled among a grove of tall evergreens and surrounded by the steep slopes of the ravine. The next day songs with guitar playing overcame the sound of the rain.

Judge and Elisabeth returned the next weekend to help celebrate the fortieth anniversary of the founding of the Dartmouth Outing Club. It was founded by Fred Harris of Brattleboro, Vermont. Judge was the college trustee adviser to the outing club and so participated in many of its affairs. On the way home, Judge and Elisabeth stopped at the Mary Hitchcock Hospital in Hanover to call on Pauline Hannah from Franconia, who had contracted polio and was badly crippled. Judge and Elisabeth had stayed many times with Sel and Paulie at their Ski Hearth Farm in Franconia.[2] At the end of the month, the trip to Mt. Tremblant was postponed for lack of snow, but two days later a telephone call from Canada indicated it was snowing hard. Judge and Elisabeth caught the night sleeper for Montreal and the day train to Mt. Tremblant. Judge records there was little snow and they had a very bad time walking down from the summit. Apparently, they had taken the chairlift to the top expecting to ski down, but found insufficient snow and were forced to walk. That year there was more eating, sleeping, and reading than skiing. The rest of the winter turned out to have ample snow. They tried Oak Hill in Hanover, a new ski tow in Hooksett (which long ago bit the dust), Cannon, Newfound Lake, Jackson, and Sunapee. Just five days before sailing on the *Queen Mary* in late March from New York City, they skied in twelve inches of new snow on Cannon.

In Paris they met Malcolm and Susan, on vacation from Oxford, where Malc was a Rhodes scholar. Judge and Elisabeth drove through Burgundy to Auxerre, the beautiful hill town of Vezelay where the abbey was started in the middle of the ninth century and where the Second Crusade was staged

334

in 1146. They traveled to Dijon, Lake Geneva, and then to Zermatt, Switzerland, for a week of skiing before heading into Italy, visiting Florence, Pisa, and Genoa. They drove along the Riviera to Marseilles, flew to Ajaccio on Corsica, where they walked and bused around the rugged island for a week, and then returned to Paris. They crossed the English Channel by boat; met Malc, Sue, and Robin in Oxford; and biked in the Cotswolds, stopping to see clients, the Whitfields and Chandlers, before taking the train to Southampton for the boat *(de Grasse)* home. Their crossing was very smooth; Judge notes that a migrating white-throated sparrow rested on deck the day before the ship landed in New York City.

Spring had arrived, and the building season began with clearing at the lake for Lilla and Dave's new cottage. At Three Acres Judge and Elisabeth began their new house, built with Elisabeth's inheritance from her mother. They made trips around the countryside picking up door stones (three-by-six foot slabs of granite, usually found at front and rear doors of eighteenth and nineteenth-century houses) from abandoned cellar holes and other valuables for the new house. In July Malc and Sue returned from two years at Oxford just as Mary sailed for a trip to Europe. In September, Charles, Carol, and Kristin left for two years in Moscow with the U.S. State Department. Judge and Elisabeth sailed with Gil Verney from Woods Hole to Nantucket on his sloop *Sea Lion*.[3] A week later, they sailed one of the Pasquaney sailboats to church. In late October, with top down and ski parkas on, Judge and Elisabeth drove to Pinkham Notch for the night and a visit with the Joe Dodges, then to Bangor and Presque Isle and the Madawaska Valley. At Quebec and Ile d'Orléans, they ran into early snow and wind howling across the wide open fields. They returned home via Sherbrooke and Colebrook. Thanksgiving was traditional with supper at the Macedonia restaurant and twenty for dinner the next day. The weekend was marred by the sad news of the death of Judge's nephew, John McLane Clark, by drowning in Claremont.[4] John had been the publisher of the *Claremont Eagle*.

Judge and Elisabeth attended the Christmas Eve candlelight service in Hopkinton and celebrated a quiet holiday by themselves as their children visited their in-laws. The year ended auspiciously with eight inches of new snow at the Ravine Camp and a good cross-country tour up to the Carriage Road, down to Breezy Point, and back to the Ravine Camp, where ninety were on hand for the New Year's Eve festivities of dinner and singing.

## HIGHLIGHTS OF 1951

On New Year's Day, fourteen of the group had another good cross-country ski tour, which prompted Judge to write, "One of the best New Year's parties." On January 7, Judge's sixty-fifth birthday, Harriet Mansfield entertained the lawyers from the firm for cocktails. There was good skating on the pond at the Intervale Country Club and Lake Massabesic. Judge had meetings with Dartmouth trustees in Hanover, trustees of St. Paul's School at the Somerset and Tavern Clubs in Boston, and trustees of the National Life board in Montpelier. Judge and Elisabeth read aloud Boswell's journal of *A Trip to the Hebrides*. They watched progress of construction on their new house, and moved books into the new library and arranged them. Finally, in late February they moved in from 940 Chestnut Street, their home for thirty years. They made their annual pilgrimage in February to Mt. Tremblant, enjoying the skiing in mild weather. There were lots of things to do to settle into the new house. Friends, including members of the firm, and family came to see and enjoy. Judge notes the first chickadees and juncos arrived at the feeding station, and the first cookout on the terrace, et cetera. Cannon provided good skiing on three weekends, and they visited Tuckerman's Ravine hoping to see the famous Inferno Race,[5] which was postponed because of bad weather.

In mid-April, Judge went to Tennessee with Gil Verney to look at paper mill sites. The local promotional group was most interested to have Verney build and operate a new paper mill. Judge, a member of the selection committee for a new rector at St. Paul's School, detoured to Atlanta to hear the Reverend Matthew Warren, a candidate for the position, preach and to discuss the school. Mr. Warren was subsequently elected rector. Judge took in both *Kiss Me Kate* and *South Pacific* while in New York City en route home.

In May, Judge and Elisabeth attended a shower party for Ralph Davis' daughter, Barbara, just before her wedding. Miss Pattee, a landscape architect, planted new shrubs at 1590 Union Street. The family threw a big surprise party and housewarming at Elisabeth's birthday with the apple blossoms in bloom. The office came up for cocktails. All of the people who built the house and their families came to inspect and enjoy. The neighbors came in for ice cream and coffee. The newly seeded lawns needed constant watering, and they bought two piglets for the new pen to be fattened during the summer and slaughtered in the late fall for hams and bacon. Judge and Elisabeth stopped in Wiscasset, Maine, with the Sortwells, Judge's St. Paul's School classmate, en route to a Verney meeting in Brunswick. After that meeting, they explored on foot the delightful channel called Oven's Mouth on the Sheepscot River, a favorite of Maine coast yachtsmen. Granddaughter Lyn McLane and a group of friends came to the lake for a May weekend, followed by grandson Jock McLane with a contingent of boys from St. Paul's School.

In June, Judge and Elisabeth paddled to church but found it too rough to paddle back, so they left the canoe and walked the four miles home. They picked strawberries and later made them into jam. Judge attended a New Hampshire Bar Association meeting at the Hotel Farragut in Rye. In July, they climbed Cardigan Mountain from the lake, attended a National Life meeting in Montpelier, then climbed Mount Washington en route to Rockland, Maine, to catch the boat to Matinicus. They spent a relaxing week there, swimming in the invigorating water, catching flounder in the harbor, and making a trip with a lobsterman to isolated Matinicus Rock to see the puffins and arctic terns.

In August, Judge and Elisabeth made the annual trip to South Egremont for a weekend of tennis and music at Tanglewood. Malcolm and Susan arrived home from their trip west where Malcolm explored legal possibilities. Malcolm went to work in the office as a summer intern. Weekends were spent at the lake doing the usual things—picnic and swim at Franconia Falls, burning brush, supper picnic at Belle Isle. Dr. Jack Kennard came to talk to Judge about law partner John Carleton's alcohol problems. Later, Judge records, "Difficult to persuade JPC [John Carleton] to go to hospital," and a week later, "Tough day with Alicia [John's wife] at the hospital." Judge and Elisabeth ascended Mount Washington on the cog railway as far as Gulfside, then walked over to the Lakes-of-the-Clouds hut. They planned to walk down through Oakes Gulf, but the weather was too threatening so they descended by an easier route. Charismatic Henry Teague died; he was the owner of the Mount Washington Cog Railway for many years, a hotelier—owner of the Venetian Hotel[6] in Miami—and a friend of Dartmouth. Judge and Elisabeth drove to Mt. Desert, Maine, for the funeral.

In October, Judge and Miss Mansfield went to Whitefield on the Dodge estate and the Mountain View Hotel business, then to Berlin to prove Henry Teague's will. Judge and Elisabeth attended Mr. and Mrs. Norwin Bean's fiftieth wedding anniversary lunch at their home in Amherst. They entertained Mary Manning and her daughter, Priscilla, for tea. Judge presided at Mack Kahn's party for about three hundred of his friends and associates at the Manchester Country Club.

On November 1 in a drizzle they set off for Quebec via the Aziscohos dam and Errol. They had a picnic on Ile d'Orleans and the next day experienced strong winds, snow, and rain. They started home on icy roads, which soon melted as the temperature warmed. Judge and Bill Evarts, a New York attorney and St. Paul's School classmate, made a trip to Texas on oil business for Coyle Concord Oil Company and met Arthur Coyle. The St. Paul's School trustees elected Matthew Warren the new rector. The Thanksgiving holiday started on a clear and cold day with the traditional Wednesday supper at the Macedonia restaurant and nineteen for Thanksgiving dinner and the square dance at Three Acres. The family was glad to receive from Moscow (where Charles was working in the U.S.

Embassy) Charles' special edition of the "Pasquaneyaga"[7] with news of his family.

In December Judge went to New York City on Verney business and the Mack Kahn Foundation and returned direct to Manchester by plane, a first for him. Judge went to Hanover with Elisabeth for meetings and came home via the lake to cut a Christmas tree. They trudged through one and a half feet of snow in the woods to get the tree. They attended the midnight candlelight service in Hopkinton and celebrated their first Christmas in the new house, skating that afternoon on Lake Massabesic. They went to the Ravine Camp on the December 30, in the rain, but the skiing was not bad. On New Year's Eve there were thirty-eight for the festivities.

## HIGHLIGHTS OF 1952

Once again New Year's was celebrated at the Ravine Camp on Mt. Moosilauke. About the January 5, there was a fourteen-inch snowfall, so Desty, the faithful and placid mule, was harnessed to a sleigh to give rides to the neighborhood children. Judge and Elisabeth went to Hanover for meetings and skied on Oak Hill, operated by the Dartmouth Outing Club, with fellow trustee Harvey Hood and his wife, Barbara.[8] The January thaw hit about midmonth, melting the snow, so Judge burned brush by the new house. Ken and Mary Graf came for dinner. Judge, always an Anglophile after his Rhodes experience, notes the death of King George VI and the succession of Elizabeth II.

In early February, they were off for Mt. Tremblant, where there was good snow. Cold and windy weather forced them to tour in the Deer Yard and on other cross-country trails on some days when the lifts were closed. Back home they skied on Temple Mountain, and Judge records, "Most snow in many years." Judge had a National Life meeting in Montpelier and B&MRR, Dartmouth, and Verney meetings in Boston. Grenville Clark, living his retirement years in Dublin, gave a dinner at Boston's Somerset Club for Paul Hoffman. It was a good season for skiing at the lake, on back roads or small hills in Dunbarton and New Boston and over the shoulder of Cardigan to the AMC camp and an outdoor cookout by the new house there. Dwight Eisenhower won the New Hampshire primaries, beating Taft. The Arthur Coyles came north for a Coyle Concord annual meeting. In late March Judge and Elisabeth sailed for Europe from New York City on the *Ile de France*. About two days out, Judge notes, "Rough day. Got done in for the first time on a big ship." In London they stayed at the Brown's Hotel, went to the theater several times, and had lunch at the Ritz with Lord and Lady Dartmouth— "most enjoyable." They crossed the Channel from Dover to Calais, stayed at the familiar Hotel Quai Voltaire, and met Charles in the American Hospital. He had a bad back from a disk injury. They took in *African Queen* with Katherine Hepburn, had lunch with Win and Lois Shaw from Manchester, had a business session with SACM (Société Alsatian Construction Méchanique) on Abbott Machine Company matters, and had several visits with Charles. They drove over secondary roads to Dijon, met daughter Mary, who was studying nearby, then went up over the Jura mountains to Lausanne and on to Zermatt, where they skied for three days. Then they put the car on the train and went through the tunnel to Venice, Italy. They enjoyed on Easter a starry evening ride on the lagoons with songs, then went to Padua and Ravenna with its great mosaics, and on to the hill towns of Assisi and Perugia and a night at Siena before arriving in Florence. They continued north to Lucca and along the Tyrrhenian Sea to St. Margharita, Genoa, and Nice, thence inland to Vence and Digne and the high country of eastern France to Le Chambon and Mary again. Next they went east through the Auvergne to the valley of the Dordogne, where they stopped for lunch at the spectacular Château Romegouse,[9] then continued on to the caves at Lascaux[10] and Limoges for the night. Turning north again, they stopped at the Loire Valley château at Azay-le-Rideau and Blois before heading to Paris, where they had supper with improving Charles and welcomed Mary for a visit. They experienced a Communist May Day celebration, ate at the Place-du-Têtre, drove to Fontainebleau, put Mary on the train back to Chambon, and caught the boat train to Le Havre to meet the *Nieu Amsterdam* for the voyage to New York. The ride home by car was beautiful, with the forsythia and apple blossoms out.

In May, Judge worked on the St. Paul's School Long Pond case, in which the city of Concord closed Long Pond to all use after contamination in the form of *E. coli* was found. It originated with an unsupervised picnic area at the north end of the pond near the public water supply intake. St Paul's School had been using Long Pond for rowing for fifty years or more. Closing the pond was a great blow. The school offered to pay for year-round police patrols and supervision to ensure the pond would be contamination free. There never was any evidence that the school's use of the pond in any way contaminated it. The issue became a political one in the forthcoming municipal election. Candidates pledged that they would not permit rich children from the big cities to contaminate Concord's water supply. It was a no-win situation for the school, which finally worked out a satisfactory rowing course by raising the level of Little Turkey Pond and dredging a channel between Big and Little Turkey Ponds in conjunction with the building of Interstate 89. At the annual meeting in May, Judge resigned after thirty-five years on the board of trustees. His position as clerk was filled by this author. Judge and Elisabeth entertained the board for dinner at Three Acres.

*About 1952, Mary Craig McLane*, guitar on back, with her mother, probably in France.

In late June, Judge and Elisabeth with John Carleton met John Meck and Arthur Teague at the Mount Washington Cog Railway base station, then rode to the top for dinner and the night. In the morning the men attended to business (Arthur Teague was interested in buying the cog railway) while Elisabeth hiked alone over the range to Mt. Madison Spring huts and down to Randolph.

In mid-July, Judge records that Jock and friends arrived home from Memphis, disappointed in finding that jobs that had been promised were nonexistent. They were students at Harvard looking for summer jobs. A couple of weeks later they had a job cleaning out the coal pocket in the Southern Division Boiler House in the Amoskeag mill yard. They arrived home each night covered with coal dust from head to foot and looking like chimney sweeps. Early in the year, the father of one of the boys was flying on business and struck up a conversation with his seat mate, a stranger, who volunteered that his company could use the boys in manning a new tugboat that was practically complete and would be working on the Mississippi River during the summer. The father contacted the boys, who were interested. He wrote his friend and gave him an out, in case this was just airplane conversation. The response was positive; the boys were definitely needed and were given the contact point, date of hire, and their boss' name. On the appointed day they reported for duty and were given the runaround. The boat would not be ready for a week and they could report back then. They conserved their meager cash, stuck around, and showed up a week later with substantially the same story, only the boat would not be in service until late fall. They headed home, disappointed and poorer than when they set out. They did attend several debutante parties in Nashville and Memphis, so the trip was not without its happy moments.

In August, Judge and Elisabeth joined the Manchester group for the annual trek to Tanglewood for tennis and music with Leonard Bernstein conducting. There were a number of large weekend gatherings at the lake. Judge records that thirty-six slept there one night. A large group ascended Mount Washington, with the elders going up by train and hiking over the range to Mt. Madison Spring huts for the night, then descending on the Valley Way. The family celebrated Labor Day with a picnic on Belle Isle, now owned by the state and closed to public use. The "Integrated Naturalists" (Booths, Burroughses, Zopfis, and Woodburys) spent a weekend at the lake walking and hiking. Judge's friends from Oxford, England, the Lees, spent a weekend in October at the lake with gorgeous foliage. In late October, they paddled to church and then headed for Franconia for dinner at the Lovetts' with the Browns, Hannahs, and Lovetts to talk about the possible purchase of the Glen House properties for a ski resort. Later they drove to Marshfield, Massachusetts, to celebrate the one hundredth anniversary of the death of Daniel Webster.

In early November, Judge and Elisabeth were off once again to Quebec, up the Arnold Trail after a night with the Sortwells in Wiscassett. Thanksgiving produced twenty-five for dinner, including Judge's and Elisabeth's sisters (Hazel Clark and Jane Shiverick) and Bishop Dallas, retired and living in Lee, New Hampshire.

Judge made a trip on Coyle Concord business to Texas, visiting oil companies and enjoying lunch at the Petroleum Club in Houston. Judge and Elisabeth drove to the lake to cut a Christmas tree and attended the Hopkinton Christmas Eve service. On December 31, they joined one hundred others at the Ravine Camp to celebrate the new year.

## HIGHLIGHTS OF 1953

Judge's diary indicates that the New Year's party at the Ravine Camp was one of the best, with plenty of snow and good skiing. They skied Waterville Valley on the way home. In mid-January, Judge went to New York City for a meeting with Mack Kahn and Arthur and Lydia Coyle, up from San Antonio. They took in *Guys and Dolls* in New York City and *Dial M for Murder* in Boston the next night. Judge went to Hanover to speak at a faculty coffee hour.

In mid-February, Judge and Elisabeth took the train to Montreal and rode a new Budd liner to Mt. Tremblant. There was good snow, but it turned warm and rained, then cleared and turned cold, making the going "hard and fast. Too hard for fun." It turned better before they returned home.

Huntley Spaulding resigned as president of the Children's Aid Society after thirty years of effective service. Judge took over as president. Judge talked to the Savings Bank Association on the new FDIC program. Sue McLane broke her leg skiing at Mad River in Vermont and was confined to the Mary Hitchcock Hospital for five weeks. Heavy rains and melting snow at the end of March created the highest river waters since the 1938 hurricane. In May, Judge spoke for the college at the class officers' dinner. Judge and I went to Savannah with Gil Verney and some of the Verney directors to see the Richmond Hill properties, an old plantation owned by the Ford family for many years. There were live oaks dripping with Spanish moss lining the drive to the impressive two-story colonnaded house with the slave quarters nearby. The plantation would be a wonderful place for entertaining when fixed up, but the Verney directors did not bite. The group had lunch at the Oglethorpe Club in Savannah. Judge celebrated the fiftieth anniversary of his St. Paul's School form of 1903, which he entertained at Three Acres.

On June 2, Judge records the coronation of Queen Elizabeth II, the first successful climb to the top of Mt. Everest by Sir Edmund Hillary and his Sherpa, and the election of Nathan Pusey as president of Harvard University. On June 9, Worcester was struck by a tornado. A few days later, Judge attended the Dartmouth commencement, at which President Eisenhower received an honorary degree and gave the commencement address. On June 16, Judge and Elisabeth left for New York City to sail on the *Queen Elizabeth* for Cherbourg and Southampton. They traveled around the south of England for several days, stopping to call on Lord and Lady Dartmouth, and then headed for the Cotswolds. They had lunch at Minster Lovell, inventoried in 1086 by William the Conqueror in the Domesday Book. Elisabeth's finger became infected and she had to be operated on in an Oxford hospital, where she stayed for three days. After a rest they flew to Oslo and went sight-seeing, then traveled by bus and steamer on the fjords to Bergen, and by boat up the Sogne Fjord, the largest in Norway. From the head of the fjord, they bused to the Jotunheimer (Land of the Giants) mountains and spent four days walking above tree line by lakes and glacier-covered slopes, stopping at alpine hostels for the night. They traveled by boat, bus, and train to Lillehammer, where they visited the museum of beautiful ancient houses and farm buildings, before returning to Oslo and a flight to Paris, where they met Mary en route to London. They enjoyed a romantic supper at the Place du Têtre under a full moon. Later they took in the Raoul Dufy exhibit before sailing home on the *Queen Elizabeth*.

The lake was busy during August with trips to the Berkshires for music and tennis and to North Conway for Ann Dodge's wedding to Jack Middleton, later to become a partner in the McLane law firm. Judge recorded that his granddaughter Lyn left for her first year at the new Colorado Rocky Mountain School in Carbondale. He noted that Jock returned from a summer in the slums of London with the Winant Volunteers and matriculated at Harvard. He made an entry about Sandy's ruptured spleen from playing soccer at Woodstock Country School.

In October Arthur Coyle visited at the lake, where he and Judge spilled out of the canoe—only damaged egos. Judge and Elisabeth sailed to church over the Columbus Day weekend when they closed the house. Later in the month, they drove to Quebec via the Arnold Trail, had two good days on Ile d'Orléans, took in a hockey game, and went home via the Connecticut Lakes. Judge had Verney meetings in Brunswick, Maine, and National Life meetings in Montpelier. Then Judge and Elisabeth visited the Deanes at Squabetty, building bonfires and swimming in the pool fed by brook water, which must have been freezing. Judge speaks of "salting almonds" in preparation for Thanksgiving. Sixteen showed up for Wednesday-evening supper at the Macedonia restaurant and twenty-seven for dinner at Three Acres the next day. The paper chase and square dance were traditional.

Judge became busy defending Elba Chase Nelson in the attorney general's investigation of communism. Judge was unsuccessful in keeping her out of jail on contempt charges for failing to turn over lists of names to the attorney general. While she was in jail, Judge and Elisabeth brought her a toothbrush, towels, and sleeping gear. Judge got her purged of contempt the next day. Judge spoke at a dinner honoring Robert Upton, a well-respected and prominent attorney of Concord. On Christmas Eve, Judge and Elisabeth attended the midnight candlelight service in Hopkinton and had a quiet Christmas again with no snow. They put on two parties at Three Acres on December 26, stoking fires to make it warm. One party was for Robin McLane and her young friends, the other for Mary McLane and an older group. On New Year's Eve, Judge and Elisabeth joined 125 at the Ravine Camp for a good evening of dancing and singing.

## HIGHLIGHTS OF 1954

The new year began with a paucity of snow, so the group walked the Hubbard Brook trail, but they did ski toward Jobildunc Ravine on what little snow there was. Judge celebrated his sixty-eighth birthday on January 7 with Towner, Speck, and Betsy Deane and some of the family. They went to Cannon, but there was so little snow that they walked on the Hubbard Brook trail again. Later, in Hanover, there was good skiing on the golf course, where they watched grandson Jock on the Harvard ski team in the cross-country race. Judge and Elisabeth attended the Robert Burns Night dinner by the clan MacKenzie of Manchester. Judge went to the bar association midwinter meeting as president. The bar adopted a good resolution about members of the bar representing alleged Communists in the attorney general's investigation. It reaffirmed the obligation of attorneys to render legal services to all defendants, regardless of political popularity.

In mid-February, Elisabeth and Judge went to Mt. Tremblant, where, first, it turned warm with sticky, slow going, then it became cold and very hard, but then it snowed the next day with good skiing. Then Judge says, "Miserable rainy day," then "Pretty good skiing," "Snow," and "Perfect skiing." They bused to Montreal and took the night train home. Then, "Cannon—best skiing in many years."

In late March, they traveled to Florida by train to Hollywood for the National Life meetings, which included a "grand" Audubon tour by boat. Elisabeth went on a trip to Key West while Judge had meetings. They never liked the glitz of Florida and went only on Judge's business. The same attitude held for the Caribbean or cruises. Judge saw a great deal of the United States by train, but it was always in connection with business. Occasionally there was a short side trip of a day or two, but they never spent long vacation time in the United States; they much preferred Europe.

En route home, they stopped to visit Charles and Carol in Swarthmore, where Charles was teaching. Shortly after returning, they learned of the death of Bill Evarts (William M.), a St. Paul's School alumnus, Judge's classmate at Harvard Law School, my godfather, and father of Carol Evarts McLane, Charles' wife. Judge and Elisabeth drove to Garrison, New York, for the funeral at the Evartses' country home.

On a nice warm spring day in April before everything had turned green, Judge burned some grass, but the wind caught it and spread the fire fast, so they called the fire engines—no damage, just scary. The Metropolitan Opera spent a week in Boston on tour. Judge and Elisabeth took in *Don Giovanni* and *La Bohème*.

In early May, Judge went to New York City to attend a farewell dinner for Henry Kittredge, retiring rector of St. Paul's School. He was a vice rector for many years, housemaster of the Lower School, and a master of English, who with his wife, Patsy, was beloved by hundreds of students who knew them during their thirty-seven years at the school. The office came for cocktails under the apple trees in full bloom and humming with bees busy at fertilizing the blossoms. Judge and Elisabeth took a picnic breakfast to cook out in Dunbarton while looking for warblers. Judge arranged to see attorney Burt Cooper in Rochester in time to walk on Ogunquit Beach in Maine before going to a dinner at the Wentworth Hotel in New Castle for the Child Welfare League. Elisabeth attended her fortieth reunion of the class of 1914 at Smith College.[11] Judge always enjoyed the Dartmouth commencements and the fun of escorting the honorary degree candidates in the academic procession. In 1954 it was actress Lynn Fontanne. At a meeting of the B&MRR directors, it was decided to give up all steam power—a decision with many nostalgic overtones. Judge gave his president's address at the annual meeting of the New Hampshire Bar Association. He spoke about representation of persons being investigated by the attorney general.

On July 1, Judge, Elisabeth, and others took the cog railway up Mount Washington. It was a long ride because the cylinder head on the engine was punctured and had to be repaired. After supper at the top, they descended to the AMC Lakes-of-the-Clouds hut for the night, then descended the Ammonoosuc trail in the morning and drove home, stopping for a picnic by Lake Chocorua. They saw a bear crossing the road—an unusual sight. On July 3, Judge records: "Put up peas all day," and on July 11, at the lake, "Typical summer day, three swims, tennis twice, twenty for turkey dinner on the lawn."

Judge and Elisabeth stopped in Wiscasset to see Frances and Marion Sortwell en route to Rockland for the night, and then took the morning boat to Matinicus, where they enjoyed the birds, sighting a Savannah sparrow, walking and swimming at the beach, fishing for flounder in the harbor, and enjoying "a grand picnic at Howard and Rena's new house." Later, at Pasquaney, they paddled to church dressed in old-fashioned gear for Old Home Week. The summer National Life meeting was at the Marshall House in York Harbor, Maine, after which Judge and Elisabeth drove to the Portland Yacht Club with Geoff and Kay Smith and sailed for three days with them on their *Cherry Blossom*, a forty-six-foot yawl. They all spent one night at Harpswell harbor and the next at Oven's Mouth on the Sheepscot River, and then to Boothbay Harbor. The following weekend, they played tennis and listened to the Boston Symphony at Tanglewood. The Integrated Naturalists came to the lake to celebrate Bob and Lois Booth's twenty-fifth wedding anniversary, resulting in a turkey dinner for thirty on the lawn. Bob and Lois had been married at the lake. There were two New England hurricanes. One broke a cherry tree and "knocked the garden around" and the other raked the coast but spared inland areas.

In September, they went to St. Paul's School to hear the new rector, Matthew Warren, conduct his first chapel service. The next weekend they visited the Deanes at Squabetty— "lovely fall day, bonfire, place is very picked up this year, always enjoyable visit." They came home over Lincoln Gap and took back roads, cross-country, to Hanover. About two days later, Judge states, "Lame back from bonfire at Squabetty." Howard and Rena Bunker, from Matinicus, visited, so all the Matinicus group came for breakfast.

In late October, Judge and Elisabeth were off once again for Quebec via the Derby Line and Sherbrooke. Their room in the Château Frontenac was on the fourteenth floor this year. They enjoyed dinner at their old favorite Kerhulu's restaurant, Ile d'Orleans, and a hockey game before returning to the States via Jackman, Maine, and Wiscasset, where Judge had wills to draw for the Sortwells. Judge and Elisabeth took Darby Bradley's twin boys to Boston to see *Old Ironsides* at the navy yard, visit the Natural History Museum, and eat at the Blue Ship Tearoom overlooking the harbor. Back home, they had a rare visitor—a white-winged crossbill from the North. One had wintered in the 1920s at 940 Chestnut Street.

A big crowd turned out in the wet for the Thanksgiving-morning paper chase to generate an appetite, and twenty-three enjoyed the turkey dinner. The firm met at Thanksgiving time to prepare year-end bills. The partners met again at my house to discuss John Carleton's alcohol problems. Judge spent three days in Washington on hearings on the taxation of mutual institutions, life insurance companies, and savings banks. Judge and Elisabeth went to Hebron to church and to cut a Christmas tree. On Christmas Eve there was the traditional candlelight service before a cold and clear Christmas Day. December 30 was a stormy day, which Judge and Elisabeth spent by the fire reading and enjoying a pâté sandwich lunch with a bottle of Beaune wine. The next day, they headed for the Ravine Camp, where 110 participated in welcoming in the new year.

## HIGHLIGHTS OF 1955

Judge and Elisabeth joined twenty-four other skiers at the Ravine Camp for New Year's; they skied cross-country one day and on wood roads in a light snowfall the next. During January, they skied Cannon Mountain and Newfound Lake, skated on Lake Massabesic, and left for Europe on the *Queen Mary*. After a couple of days in Paris, they took the train to Switzerland and skied for several days at Klosters, where Judge pulled a leg muscle in a fall. Then they took the train over the Arlberg Pass to St. Anton and down the valley to Innsbruck, then to Kitzbuhl, where they witnessed a gloomy end of the season. They boarded another train to Vienna and Schonbrun and on to Zagreb, Yugoslavia, where they drove with a female guide to Dubrovnik and the beautiful coastal villages. They went by boat to Venice, then flew to Rome, picked up a car, and drove to Naples, Pompeii, the Amalfi Drive, and Sorrento (where they saw the opera *Boris Godunov*). They visited fabulous Greek temple ruins at Paestum[12] and

*Judge and Elisabeth* about 1955.

returned to Rome via Ravello and Caserte. They had a couple of days in Rome, including the Easter service at St. Paul's, before taking the plane to Athens. There they picked up another car, then drove to Delphi, Olympia, Sparta, Mycenae, Nauplia, and back to Athens via the theater at Epidaurus. They took a five-day cruise through the Greek Isles, returning to Athens for the plane to Paris, then sailed home on the *Queen Elizabeth*.

Judge's leg continued to bother him after the ski spill in Switzerland. He talked to an orthopedic surgeon at the Hitchcock Clinic about operating on the Achilles tendon but later decided against it. Thus ended Judge's active tennis life, a game he adored. He still could enjoy walks on country roads during the bird migration season in the spring and observe the colorful foliage in the fall. In July, Judge and Elisabeth stopped in Wiscasset to spend the night with the Sortwells before continuing to Rockland to board the Matinicus Island boat. After a rough trip out, they walked and explored the beaches, fished for flounder in the harbor, and enjoyed the solitude of this "outer" island.

In August the group went as usual to the Berkshires for the music at Tanglewood. Judge noted that he missed tennis, but he enjoyed paddling to the Hebron church and walking the Kancamagus highway under construction. In late October Judge and Elisabeth went on their traditional Quebec trip, this time via Greenville, Maine. They picnicked on Ile d'Orléans and drove home via the Connecticut Lakes. They went as usual to the Christmas Eve candlelight service in Hopkinton and had a quiet Christmas in Manchester with Mary Craig. The year ended as it began—back to the Ravine Camp for New Year's, where Judge reported that his leg worked fine on cross-country skis on easy terrain.

## HIGHLIGHTS OF 1956

New Year's Day dawned bright and cold—minus ten degrees—at the Dartmouth Ravine Camp at Mt. Moosilauke. This turned out to be Judge and Elisabeth's last year of seventeen at the Ravine Camp extending back to 1932. (The old lumber camp, the first Ravine Camp, burned down and was replaced in 1939 by the current massive log structure.) The Manchester group consisted of five or six Dartmouth families with children of all ages, principally the Bob Burroughses, Peter Woodburys, Bob Booths, Bill Zopfis, Roger Mosscrops, and Randy Childs. There also were families from the Boston and Hanover areas. The crew consisted mostly of Dartmouth students, who invariably had dates for the holiday. They had guitars and music, which provided a festive ambience to the occasion.

On January 7, Judge celebrated his seventieth birthday by skiing the Kimball Pond road in Dunbarton with Elisabeth and then welcoming seventeen from the office, who provided a surprise party and a gift of a TV set, Judge and Elisabeth's first. Judge and Elisabeth swung around by Newfound Lake en route to Hanover to inspect the progress Mr. Glover was making on the little suite for Judge and Elisabeth off their second-floor porch bedroom. Judge reported that grandson Jock and family had returned from two years of study on his thesis in India toward his Ph.D. degree from the University of London's School of Oriental and African Studies (SOAS). In late January Judge and Elisabeth attended the traditional Scottish Robbie Burns dinner complete with kilts and Scottish dancing. Judge tried out his ski leg at Hanover's Oak Hill and found, to his great delight, he could make controlled turns. After a two-week trip to Texas for Coyle Concord Oil Company, Judge presided at a Dartmouth function as acting president, being the ranking trustee, in the absence of John S. Dickey, who was on sabbatical leave. Skiing beckoned at Mt. Tremblant, Hill 70 at St. Sauveur, St. Adele, and Mt. Gabriel in the Canadian Laurentian Mountains. Granddaughters Kim Bradley and Bonnie McLane joined them.

It isn't known what inspired Judge's splurge into classical literature in translation—possibly his performing as acting president of Dartmouth—but in the next couple of months, he had to read himself or aloud to Elisabeth the following books: Aeschylus' *Agamemnon* and *Prometheus Bound*; Sophocles' *Antigone* and *Oedipus Rex, Ajax, Maidens of Trachis,*

*Philoctetes*, and *Oedipus at Colonus*; Euripides' *The Bacchae*; Hippolytus' *Canons*; and Aristophanes' *The Clouds*.

Judge and Elisabeth skied back roads at the lake and around Candia and Dunbarton. There was a giant snowstorm in mid-March that kept them snowbound all day. Judge skied cross-country to the store and back. After an Easter church service at home, the next weekend Judge went to the Glen House, then on to the Dartmouth College grant with Bob Monahan and Sam Brungot, going up the Swift Diamond on skis. They had dinner at Edmund Rouleau's lumber camp on the Dead Diamond and then headed for home.

In April, Judge visited with Charles and his family at Swarthmore, Pennsylvania, where Charles was teaching. They viewed a Toulouse-Lautrec exhibition at the Museum of Modern Art in New York City before taking the train to Buffalo for a Spaulding Fibre Company directors' meeting. This was followed by meetings of the National Life Insurance Company in Montpelier, Vermont, and Dartmouth College in Hanover. Judge records snow on the ground at the end of April, a very late season, but the warblers were arriving at Plum Island, Massachusetts, in early May. Judge presided as acting president at an honors convocation at Dartmouth.

In May, Judge and Elisabeth walked many back roads welcoming the birds back north again. They checked the Bedford woodlot for cutting and bought a new Ford convertible.[13] In June, St. Paul's School celebrated its one hundredth anniversary with several special events. John's family started west on a two-month safari to attend Lyn's graduation from Colorado Rocky Mountain School and a tour of the West. Judge retired as a Dartmouth trustee after thirty years on the board and received many accolades for his years of devoted service to the college. In late June, Judge and Elisabeth motored to Augusta and Houlton, Maine, down the Madawaska Valley in Canada to Murray Bay for National Life Company meetings, and thence home via Quebec and the Connecticut Lakes.

In July, they made their annual pilgrimage to Matinicus Island. Jack Middleton started work in the office in August, and the firm had its annual outing at the Kenneth Grafs at Wolfeboro, complete with horseshoes, waterskiing, and swimming.

In August, Judge and Elisabeth drove to Quebec to embark on the *Empress of France*, sailed down the St. Lawrence River, observed icebergs off Belle Isle, enjoyed the British and Canadian passengers (only one American), landed in London, and proceeded to Oxford. They motored up through the border country and the Scottish Highlands, stopping at the quaint town of Tomintoul before flying to the Shetland Islands for a few days. They drove through rugged Ross Shire on the northwest coast to Inverness and Edinburgh and on to London and Paris, where they attended a Matisse exhibit. By car they visited Fontainebleau, Nemours, and Vezelay again. Keeping on back roads they toured the vineyards of the Côte d'Or in Burgundy, stopped in Beaune for a night, then headed north through the Vosges mountains to Nancy and Strasbourg, around Paris to the north to beautiful Chartres, and back to Paris and home on the *Queen Elizabeth* (they found the boat trip quite dull).

Thanksgiving produced fifteen for the traditional supper at the Macedonia restaurant, twenty-four for breakfast at Three Acres and dinner in the new house, and fifty at the square dance. Blanche and I held the office Christmas party. Judge, Elisabeth, and Mary attended the candlelight Christmas Eve service in Hopkinton and observed Christmas Day at home. It snowed hard on December 30, making for good skiing around the house. For the first time in many years, Judge and Elisabeth observed a quiet evening on New Year's at home.

## HIGHLIGHTS OF 1957

Judge and Elisabeth were at home in Manchester on New Year's Day, which was cold—minus eight degrees. They entertained Pete and Dee Rice, who were considerably younger, for cocktails; they were not social friends—Pete was a client of the bank's. They skied in South Weare in sub-zero temperatures and on Sunapee with the Bob Booths and Peter Woodburys. On January 10, it snowed all day, bringing the season total to sixty inches. In the middle of the month, they went to Hanover for a Dartmouth Outing Club luncheon, then out to the dedication of the new Holt's Ledge ski area and skied it the next day. Throughout the middle of the month, there was unprecedented cold, minus twenty-six on January 14 and minus twenty-eight on January 18, which didn't end until rain arrived on January 22. Judge had three days of meetings in Montpelier on National Life business. Judge and Elisabeth attended the annual Robert Burns Scottish dinner in Manchester. They cross-country skied at the lake twice before taking the train to Canada on February 8; they had a good week skiing part of the time with Lilla and her son, Darby Bradley. In March they walked on two occasions exploring the unfinished new toll road toward Hooksett. Jack and Ann Middleton came to dinner, and Judge and Elisabeth had tea with the Raulersons at their new house in Bedford.

Judge over the years had tough times with his teeth and states in his diary that he had a tooth extraction; the tooth broke in three pieces, which made "tough going." Lyn McLane and four Smith freshmen outing clubbers stopped for dinner en route north to ski. On March 22, Judge and Elisabeth, with grandchildren Bonnie and Angus McLane, skied up the Swift Diamond River in the Dartmouth College grant and then motored down to Wildcat the next day. Blanche and I arrived home from a month of skiing and traveling with Sandy, who was stationed in the Army in Germany. Judge went to New York City to meet Arthur Coyle, saw *My Fair Lady*, and brought Arthur back to Manchester.

This was a favorite year for exploring the Kimball Pond road in Dunbarton, a dirt road that passes Kimball Pond, a low, marshy area with beaver and other wildlife. Judge and Elisabeth were there on April 3, 7, 13, 17, and 28 and May 5, 11, and 13 and recorded seeing a myrtle warbler and a green heron. On one of the trips they picked up along the road a girl in distress who said she was avoiding her drunken husband. The diary does not explain where he was or what Judge and Elisabeth did with the girl. At this beautiful time of the year, if Judge didn't have too much to do, he'd take the afternoon off or leave at three or four to enjoy the out-of-doors. He and Elisabeth spent a half day at Plum Island near Newburyport birding on April 14, pretty early for warblers. The Spaulding matters took a good deal of time—meetings in April and May in New Hampshire and two days in late April in Buffalo.

Grandson Jock McLane and a group of his Harvard senior friends came to Three Acres for a delightful luncheon in early May as the apple blossoms were about to burst. I went to the Mary Hitchcock Hospital for an operation to repair a ruptured Achilles tendon brought about by skipping church and skipping rope on Easter Sunday. Judge and Elisabeth stopped for dinner with the Sortwells in Wiscasset, Maine, on May 20, en route to Rockland for the night and then took the early boat, the *Mary A*, to Matinicus Island, where they caught the main bird migration. They sighted some fifty different varieties of birds, including many warblers and a red-headed woodpecker. On Memorial Day weekend, they spent the night at the lake, took off early for Waterville Valley, cooked breakfast over a driftwood fire among the boulders of Mad River, and then walked to Greeley Ponds. In early June they called on Grenville Clark at his home in Dublin, and the next day collected laurel and evergreens at the woodlot for decorations for Three Acres for the Zopfi-Saltonstall party the next day, prior to the wedding. After the wedding they hustled off for Judge's fiftieth reunion at Hanover before winding up at the lake. In June, Jock McLane and his fiancée, Joan Brooks, came for wine. The next day, Joan's parents, Polly and Ernie Brooks, from New Canaan, Connecticut, visited. Judge and Elisabeth threw a party for Jock and Joan at Three Acres.[14] In late June, Judge and Elisabeth tried out their new apartment at the lake. A small bedroom off their dressing room adjacent to the sleeping porch was converted into a sitting room with a sink, refrigerator, and two electric plates so they could get their own breakfasts or other meals without bothering others in the house, which contained eighteen beds. They paddled to church one day, only to find that there was no service that day. In July, they made two expeditions to scout the Tunnel Brook trail on the west side of Mt. Moosilauke for suitability for cross-country skiing, exploring from the south on one weekend and from the north the next. The firm had a party at the Kenneth Grafs' house on Lake Winnipesaukee in Wolfeboro.[15] Judge drove to Rochester for a Spaulding Fibre meeting, arriving twenty-four hours early.

In early August, Blanche and I drove Judge and Elisabeth and two of their granddaughters, Kim Bradley and Bonnie McLane, to Quebec after a picnic at the Third Connecticut Lake. The next day they picnicked on the Ile d'Orléans and met the *Empress of Scotland* in the evening and boarded her from a lighter. Three days later, they were crossing the Atlantic "in a little roll," which gave the girls some discomfort. They picked up a car on landing at Greenoch, explored Sterling Castle, observed highland games at Strathdon, and visited the Isle of Mull and Duart Castle, ancestral home of the chief of the clan Maclean.[16] (Judge's father anglicized the name to McLane so that it would be pronounced properly; the diphthong "ea" in Scottish is pronounced as a broad "a.") They went to the town of Tobermory and the Isle of Iona, just off the Isle of Mull, seat of Christianity in the fifth century and burial place of many medieval Christian Scandinavian kings, whose bodies were transported by boat from the Scandinavian peninsula.

After Edinburgh and its castles, they drove south to York and the Cotswolds, stopping at Stratford-on-Avon to see *As You Like It*, then on to Stonehenge and back to London for evensong at Westminster Chapel and the play *Peter Pan*. Judge forgot to reconfirm the girls' return flight and found that their reservations had been canceled. After much hustle and bustle, they were able to fly home the next day. Judge and Elisabeth continued to Paris, drove to the Massif Central and the valley of the Dordogne, and back to Paris to meet Sandy McLane, on leave from the Army in Germany, where he was stationed with an atomic cannon outfit. They thoroughly entertained him with visits to the Eiffel Tower, Versailles, the Louvre, the film *Around the World in 80 Days*, and good meals, then put him on the train back to Neckarsulm. Judge and Elisabeth went to London and met Jock and Joan McLane, recently married and getting settled for Jock's four years of study at the University of London's School of Oriental and African Studies, where he would concentrate on Indian nationalism for his doctoral thesis. The *Empress of Britain* brought Judge and Elisabeth home to Quebec, where Towner and Speck Deane met them.

The family celebrated their return at the lake with twenty-three for a big family picnic in late September. Judge went on a tour of the state with the Spaulding-Potter trustees, then made a trip to the Dartmouth College grant and a trip to Maine for a sail with the Sortwells from Boothbay to Outer Heron Island for a picnic lunch. Judge notes in his diary that the

Russians launched a rocket with a dog into outer space and recovered him. Mrs. Norwin Bean, in her eighties, fell and broke her hip and was confined to her bed, but that did not prevent her from enjoying a martini, which Judge and Elisabeth took down to her on occasion.

Thanksgiving included supper at the Macedonia with skewered lamb, breakfast at Three Acres, dinner at Judge and Elisabeth's new house (1590 Union Street) with thirty present, and an evening of square dancing and song—very traditional. The next day, Judge picked up the smoked bacon and hams from the slaughtered pigs. The Spaulding trustees had a meeting in Boston with lunch at the St. Botolph Club and dinner with wives at the Union Club. Blanche and I hosted the office party at 18 Clarke Street. Judge and Elisabeth attended the Hopkinton church service on Christmas Eve and had a mild and snowless Christmas before going to Blanche's family's West Hartford farm with Blanche, me, and the children for New Year's. They watched eight deer browsing on the hill.

## HIGHLIGHTS OF 1958

Bob Raulerson became a partner on the first of the year. Just after Judge's seventy-second birthday, eighteen inches of snow fell. Judge and Elisabeth went to the opening of the Wildcat Mountain ski development in Pinkham Notch in which Malcolm McLane was one of the principals. They also visited with the elderly: They took cocktails to Mrs. Bean and supper to Bishop Dallas in Lee. At the forty-fourth annual meeting of the New Hampshire Children's Aid Society, Judge resigned, having been treasurer or president since its founding in 1914; he was succeeded by Ralph Langdell. In late February Judge and Elisabeth made the annual trek to Mt. Tremblant, where they enjoyed the best week of skiing ever. This was their last trip to Tremblant. When the trains ran, it was very easy to take the sleeper from Manchester to Montreal and then the day train through colorful rural Canada to Mt. Tremblant. Judge and Elisabeth first skied in Canada in 1930 at St. Sauveur, a small town with many open slopes and roads for cross-country skiing. Starting in 1940, they went to Tremblant for eighteen years and stayed most of the time at the hotel run by the Ryans at the foot of the chairlift. They frequently took some of the family, and the same Manchester families that frequented the Ravine Camp also skied Tremblant. The lodge had rooms but there were also little cabins close by with two double rooms and a connecting bath with its own heater and hot-water tank. The rooms were very private and cozy. The food was always good, and there were interesting people. On many evenings there was entertainment, either outdoors on the skating rink or indoors with games, movies, et cetera. It was always a relaxing trip, and because the area was entirely French, it was like being in a foreign country. Elisabeth's sister, Jane Shiverick of Cleveland, a widow for twenty years, married Chester Tripp, a widower, of Chicago. They lived an active and interesting life of travel and enjoyment of cultural affairs.

There were heavy snows in March, enabling Judge and Elisabeth to cross-country ski across the fields from their house to the store for the Sunday papers. Judge banded many birds with his granddaughters Kristin and Robin. Judge and Elisabeth skied the Tunnel Brook trail, which they had scouted the year before on foot, and enjoyed good spring skiing on Cannon in April. They had a "glorious day on Wildcat" the day before they went to Boston for the Metropolitan Opera production of *Don Giovanni*, which Judge confesses he was "too sleepy to enjoy." They attended the new Cinerama theater in Boston. In mid-May they traveled to Matinicus Island for the bird migration, which was smaller than usual; however, they had "a great experience watching woodcock perform."

In May Judge attended meetings of National Life in Montpelier, where he participated in laying the cornerstone for the new building. He was busy on the Dartmouth capital campaign and also the Williams bequest case (see Estate of Leon Williams, Chapter Twenty-three).

In August, they rode the Mount Washington Cog Railway to Gulfside, then walked over the range above tree line, to Mt. Jefferson and back. Later they visited daughter Lilla and her husband, Dave Bradley, in Stonington, Maine, and sailed with them in Dave's *Mischief*, a 1928 Herreshoff "S" boat, in the fog. The new wing to the office at 40 Stark Street was completed.

Judge and Elisabeth scouted the Beebee River in Sandwich Notch for a cross-country ski trail. Then the next week they walked the Guinea Pond trail in the same area. Later they explored the Guinea Pond trail again but never found the pond. In September, Judge went west on Dartmouth's Williams case to Raton and Santa Fe, New Mexico, to meet their attorney, John Love, from Denver, one-time governor of Colorado. They had all-day conferences, then Judge spent the night with Andy and Peggy Marshall[17] at the Fort Union ranch, adjacent to Leon Williams' Diamond A ranch.

Judge notes in October that Sandy McLane returned from three years in the Army in Europe. He served the last winter on the ski patrol and teaching staff at the Army Rest Center in Garmisch, Germany, where he had to be on the slopes from eight to five! In late October, Judge and Elisabeth attended a Capital Gifts Steering Committee meeting in Hanover, then drove up through Vermont to Rouse's Point, New York, down the St. Lawrence River to Kingston, Ontario, then to Toronto and on to Buffalo for three days of Spaulding Fibre meetings. They returned home via Boston for meetings and a dinner of the National Life Insurance Company. Judge noted the last meeting of the Manchester Savings Bank in the old building and recorded the move to the modern new quarters.

At Thanksgiving, the early arrivals had supper at my apartment, breaking their Macedonia tradition. Twenty-seven had Thanksgiving dinner, and fifty attended the evening square dance.

The firm celebrated its Christmas party at the Raulersons' in Bedford with an impromptu orchestra and chorus to play Christmas carols. Judge and Elisabeth attended the Hopkinton midnight candlelight service on Christmas Eve, and celebrated Christmas with John and Mary at home. They skied by Kimball Pond the next week and spent New Year's Eve at home.

# HIGHLIGHTS OF 1959

Four inches of snow fell on January 2, making for good skiing around the house. Judge loved banding birds; he trapped and banded fourteen evening grosbeaks and other birds. He and Elisabeth skied in Dunbarton and Candia. He saw Dr. Hermann Sander, who found Judge's blood pressure very high. Judge says he felt punk. In Hanover he had a checkup, which concluded he needed a prostate operation; it was performed in late February. He was not discharged from Dick's House, the Dartmouth infirmary, until late March. It was a much more difficult procedure than anticipated and permanently slowed Judge from his previous pace. He recuperated in April and went back to the office in May. In June they picked up their new piglets for the summer. Matinicus beckoned in June for a week; they watched birds—followed a mockingbird—and enjoyed a full moon and a lobster and strawberry shortcake supper with Harold and Rena Bunker. On the way home they stopped in Boothbay Harbor to sail with the Sortwells to Outer Heron Island for a picnic.

Traditional salmon and peas on the lawn at the lake was the order of the day for the Fourth of July. They picked raspberries in July and blueberries in August. The Peter Guenthers and the David Nixons, both from the office, came to dinner. Judge and Elisabeth went to a National Life meeting at the New Ocean House in Swampscott, Massachusetts, followed by dinner at the Eastern Yacht Club and a clambake at Marblehead the next day. Elisabeth's great friend Speck Deane died suddenly in August at Squabetty. Judge and Elisabeth flew to Burlington for the funeral. (See Appendix A.2, The H. Towner Deane Family.)

In late October, Judge and Elisabeth drove to Bangor, Maine, for the night, then continued onto Campbelltown, encountering snow above Caribou. The next day was cold, but they dressed warmly and continued on to Gaspé for another night, then returned by Cape Rosier and Quebec, where they had a room on the twelfth floor of the Château Frontenac commanding great views of the river. They returned to their favorite spot, the Ile d'Orleans, for a picnic, took in a hockey game, shopped for coats and sweaters to protect against the cold and wintry weather, and returned to Montpelier in time for a National Life meeting.

In early November, Judge made a trip to Texas on Coyle Concord business with Arthur Coyle and traded acreage in Corpus Christi before flying to Colorado Springs on the Williams case for Dartmouth College. While there Judge called on Louis Benezet, president of Colorado College. Louis was a native of Manchester, where his father was superintendent of schools for a number of years. Both were graduates of Dartmouth College. On the way home, Judge stopped in Cleveland, met Elisabeth, and spent the night with Elisabeth's sister, Jane Tripp, and her husband, Chester. Judge broke a tooth and learned from his dentist that all his teeth had to come out, which was done after Christmas— "a miserable time." At Thanksgiving, twelve showed up for supper at the Macedonia and twenty-three for breakfast at Three Acres and dinner at 1590. Judge banded chickadees and evening grosbeaks. They drove to the lake to get a crib for their great-grandson Derek McLane, who arrived from London with his father and mother, Jock and Joan. There was the traditional Christmas Eve service at Hopkinton, Christmas breakfast with John and Mary, then off to Hanover to celebrate with Charles and Carol and Lilla and Dave and their families. They ushered in the new year at home.

# Notes

1. Jobildunc was the name affixed to the ravine by the first Dartmouth students to explore the area in the 1920s and 1930s, whose names were Joseph, William, and Duncan. In the winter of about 1932, this author accompanied John Carleton, then a partner in the McLane law firm, and two Dartmouth Outing Club officials on skis to Jobildunc Ravine to scout the area for possible ski development. After bushwhacking, we spent the night in the snug little cabin and continued our search the next day. No suitable areas were found. The ravine remains as wild and beautiful today as it always has been.

2. Sel and Paulie Hannah were legendary figures of the Franconia area. Sel hailed from Berlin, New Hampshire, and went to Dartmouth College, where he was captain of the ski team in 1936, a four-event skier. He decided to be a dirt farmer and acquired a good-sized farm in Franconia with bottomland fields bordering the river. He married Pauline Lee of Boston, a Wellesley graduate, who learned how to become a farmer. Sel and Paulie had a sizable dairy herd and milk route but usually lost money on it because of the difficulty of collecting their accounts, mostly hardworking but poor folks. Paulie was in charge of the truck garden, which provided summer vegetables for hotels and restaurants. Sel ran the potato business with over one hundred acres in production, leasing land when he didn't have enough himself. He built a large underground storage facility into a hill to store potatoes in the winter when

prices became better. In addition to the farm operation, they ran Ski Hearth Farm in the winter, taking around thirty people, some of whom slept in bunk rooms. Sel also participated in a consulting company, Snow Engineering, which laid out ski areas and trails all over the United States. Just after the war, Paulie contracted polio in the epidemic. Polio severely paralyzed her legs and arms. She continued with her life uncomplaining, performing many farm business functions from her wheelchair and telephone, and brought up her children and grandchildren. Sel and Paulie had four children: Frank and Selden, who went to Dartmouth; Joan, a ski instructor for many years in the West; and Lucy, who married Paul Pfosi, a Swiss skier, head of the ski patrol and ski school at Waterville Valley. Lucy and Paul had four children, one of whom, Eva, also went to Dartmouth and was a competitive skier. Paul and Lucy separated and Lucy returned with the children to Franconia, where she was killed by a drunken driver while walking on the highway at night. The children went back to Paul, who had remarried and lived at Waterville Valley. Tragedy struck again when Paul, about to take a fine new position with a new California development, was flying with three other employees over the Sierra mountains to a ski operators' convention and was hit by another plane, resulting in the deaths of all four aboard. Sel died in 1993. Paulie then moved from their house to Littleton, where she could receive assistance with her living.

3. Gil Verney had served in the British Merchant Marine and acquired a love of the sea. He frequently made his boat, moored in Portsmouth, available to nonprofit organizations for weekday sails, and it was not surprising to see a boatload of enthusiastic children sailing in the harbor.

4. John McLane Clark was the son of Judge's sister, Hazel Clark, and college mate Jack Clark. Raised in New Canaan, Connecticut, John achieved high honors at St. Paul's School and Dartmouth College, where he was a Senior Fellow. He worked with John Winant at the International Labor Office in Geneva, Switzerland, and developed the Great Issues course with President John S. Dickey at Dartmouth. He published a weekly newspaper in New Canaan and aspired to buy the *Manchester Union-Leader* from Mrs. Annie Knox, without success. He finally purchased the *Claremont Eagle* and moved to Claremont with his family, which consisted of his wife, Rhoda Shaw Clark, and their five children. Several years later, just after Thanksgiving, John went canoeing on the Sugar River with several of his children. The canoe capsized, resulting in his death. It was thought that he might have suffered a heart attack.

5. A race from the summit of Mount Washington to Pinkham Notch via the headwall of Tuckerman's Ravine, a distance of about four miles with a vertical drop of 4,200 feet—one of the world's longest and toughest races. It was scheduled about five times but run only twice because of the weather; it has not been run since the 1950s.

6. The Navy took over the hotel during World War II as an officers' barracks. This author was billeted there for several weeks while attending the Submarine Chaser Training Center.

7. In the summer of 1929 at Newfound Lake, there were five cousins: John, Charles, and Elisabeth McLane and Jane and Asa Shiverick, all between the ages of six and sixteen. The families hired a counselor, a Dartmouth student, to work and play with the children, teaching them tennis, swimming, boating, et cetera. One of the children came down with the German measles and it quickly spread to the rest. Beds were moved into the living room of Twin Oaks and it became a dormitory sick bay. In order to keep the children amused, the counselor published a daily newspaper, *The Pasquaneya*, written in longhand but in column form like a newspaper, with the news around the place ("JOHN FINALLY SUCCUMBS TO MEASLES," "JANIE DECLARED WELL, LEAVES SICK BAY"), make-believe advertisements ("MARY LOOKING FOR SOMEONE TO FILL WOODBOXES," "WANTED: ABLE BODIED LAWN-MOWER"). The paper was peddled for two cents a read. For many years after the initial edition, Charles McLane wrote *The Sunday Pasquaneya*, telling of mountain trips, visitors, and birthday parties. Even after the children grew up, special editions were published on memorable occasions, such as weddings and Judge and Elisabeth's fiftieth wedding anniversary. They have been a priceless joy to the family and a record of events long forgotten.

8. Barbara Hood tells a wonderful ski story. Some years ago she was skiing at a slope that had a rope tow. In the afternoon the temperature was very warm, making the tow rope wet and heavy, but as the day wound down the temperature dropped below freezing, making the rope slippery and difficult to hold. Barbara struggled up the slope on the tow, and as she neared the top she wanted to know whether there was anyone close to her because she didn't want to get in their way, so she quickly glanced around behind her down the slope. She did a double take: A short distance behind her were two gloves frozen to the rope with a ski pole attached to each glove; that was all—no person was in sight. The owner had obviously fallen off down the hill. Barbara managed to get off okay and roared with laughter as the gloves and poles headed for the big bull wheel. I don't know whether they hit the automatic safety stop or not.

9. This author and his wife, Betsy, have spent the night there twice in the 1980s and 1990s.

10. The original caves have been closed because the fresh air and humidity brought in by visitors was affecting the paint of the prehistoric pictures on the walls and ceiling. The French government has built Lascaux II nearby, which is an exact duplicate of the original and is most impressive.

11. Judge and Elisabeth's two daughters, Elisabeth (Lilla) and Mary, attended Smith, although Lilla transferred to the University of Wisconsin to be with her future husband, Dave Bradley. Both of this author's wives, Blanche and Betsy, went to Smith, as did two of his daughters, Lyn and Katie, and both of his mothers-in-law!

12. I had an interesting time with photographs of Paestum. In 1957, Blanche and I went to Europe to meet Sandy on leave from the Army. We met in

Zurich, skied at Klosters and St. Anton for a week, picked up a car in Innsbruck, drove into Italy, and went down the Amalfi Drive to Paestum. I took a couple of rolls of film of the spectacular Greek temples, which I thought were the best photographs I had ever taken; however, when we returned home and had the film developed, the Paestum shots were missing and presumed lost. It wasn't until after Sandy's death in 1984, when I looked over some of Sandy's European photographs from his Army experience, that I discovered that Sandy had mixed up all of my photographs of Paestum with his.

13. Judge and Elisabeth loved their convertibles and toured around the countryside at all times of the year with the top down. They bundled in ski parkas and warm hats when the weather was cold.

14. Jock and Joan were married at the end of the summer at Biddeford Pool, Maine, while Judge and Elisabeth were abroad.

15. The photograph in the McLane Room of the office shows Judge surrounded by many of the lawyers and their wives.

16. The castle, originally built in the twelfth or thirteenth century, was badly damaged when the British tried to stamp out the clans in the Highlands in the seventeenth century but was beautifully restored about 1900 by Sir Fitzroy Maclean, then chief of the clan. The castle welcomes visitors, who ascend to a large second-floor room with magnificent views over the Sound of Mull and are greeted by an attendant, who invites them to register in one of two books. If they are a Maclean or related to one, they may sign in one special book; otherwise, they register in the common book. Visitors may roam around the castle and tour the ramparts. One room in the dungeon has two mannequins dressed as Spanish sailors; history says they were taken from one of the ships of the Spanish Armada in 1588, which encountered terrific storms in the English Channel and were blown up to the Shetland Islands off the north coast of Scotland. Several of the ships made their way back south along the west coast of Scotland and stopped in Tobermory Harbor on the Isle of Mull. One of them, said to be the ship of the treasurer of the armada, with all of the money in gold to pay their crews, while anchored in the harbor was attacked by the Scots to get the gold; the crews were captured and the ship was blown up and sunk. In the 1950s, divers recovered some of the cannons from the ship, which are on display in Tobermory.

17. Andy Marshall was my brother-in-law. Peggy Marshall was married to Fordy Sayre, who ran the Hanover Inn for Dartmouth College prior to his death in the service. Peggy continued to manage the inn until the end of the war, when she married Andy, whose first wife had died of cancer. Andy was named manager of family-owned ranches in Colorado and New Mexico, so they moved to Colorado Springs.

## TIME LINE, 1955

| | | |
|---|---|---|
| *January* | 1 | Ravine Camp, skiing, dancing, and singing. |
| | 2 | Snowing hard. Ski wood road on way home. |
| | 5 | Cannon Mt. lovely day of skiing—new Zoomer trail. |
| | 7 | 69th birthday. Boston to Symphony. Hazel [Judge's sister] visiting. |
| | 8 | Peterborough on Morison estate. |
| | 9 | Hazel's 70th birthday. St. Paul's School [SPS] chapel. |
| | 11 | Boston on B&MRR on New Haven control. Proxy fight looms. |
| | 14 | Hanover for National Life Executive Com. meeting. Dartmouth trustees' meeting. |
| | 15 | Trustees' meeting. |
| | 16 | Ski tour with Dave and Lilla. Home. |
| | 20 | New York City for Verney meeting. |
| | 23 | Lake, toured McClure and Wilson Farm roads. |
| | 25 | Boston, B&MRR meeting. |
| | 27 | Montpelier, Nat. Life meeting. |
| | 28 | Night train to Montreal. |
| | 29 | Train to Tremblent. Chas and Carol there. |
| | 30 | -18 deg. Good skiing. |
| | 31 | -26 deg. |
| *February* | 1 | Best skiing conditions ever. |
| | 4 | Perfect skiing in zero weather. |
| | 5 | Last runs. Bus to Montreal. Train home. |
| | 6 | Boston negotiation with McGinnis interests on RR. |
| | 13 | Rochester to see Huntley Spaulding. |
| | 15 | Boston, B&MRR. |
| | 16 | Boston for Dartmouth dinner. |
| | 17 | Boston, Dartmouth Exec. Com. meeting. |
| | 21 | New Boston, then Hanover. |
| | 22 | Talk John Dickey about Hanover trustee. Nat. Life Exec. Com. meeting. |
| | 24 | Boston, Verney meeting. Train to New York City. |
| | 25 | "Life of Man" photo exhibit at Museum of Modern Art. UN building, *Teahouse of the August Moon*. |
| | 26 | Sailed on the *Queen Mary*. Hazel, Alec, and John saw us off [Judge's sister and her two sons]. |
| | 27 | Church. Smooth sea. Easy to fall into routine. Reading *Iliad* aloud. |

| | | |
|---|---|---|
| *March* | 3 | Landed—comfortable trip. Paris. |
| | 4 | Shopped for Swiss francs. Mireille [friend of Mary] for tea. |
| | 5 | Snow last night. Louvre. |
| | 6 | Van Gogh at Orangerie, flea market. |
| | 7 | Snow and rain, night train to Switzerland. |
| | 8 | Klosters. One run in p.m. |
| | 9 | Met friends, skied together. |
| | 10 | Skied with Hoods. |
| | 11 | With guide to Parsenn Furka, then to Kublis, fondue dinner. |
| | 12 | Parsenn Hut for lunch, Weissflujoch, Parsenn Furka, down to Serneus. |
| | 13 | Fell off tow and strained leg muscle and tendon. Left for Landquart, drove to Maienfeld. |
| | 14 | Good day on train via St. Anton to Kitzbuel and Grand Hotel, gloomy and end of season. Tyrolean singing. |
| | 15 | Ankle and tendon kept me from skiing. Lunch on mountain. |
| | 16 | Lunch at Tennerhof, delightful. Train to Vienna. Reading *Anna Karenina*. |
| | 17 | Belvidere, Schonnbrun. To Strauss *One Night in Venice*. |
| | 18 | Drove into Vienna Woods and old villages. |
| | 19 | Lunch in Vienna Woods. |
| | 20 | Train to Zagreb, long ride enlivened by bright Englishman and Finnish girl, an artist. |
| | 21 | Drove around Zagreb with girl guide, train at night to Sarajevo. |
| | 22 | Drive with guide, picturesque town with many mosques, muezzin calling to prayer from towers. *Traviata* at night. |
| | 23 | 11-hour ride in narrow-gauge RR to Dubrovnik, spectacular scenery. |
| | 24 | Drove along most beautiful coastline. |
| | 25 | All-day tour to Kotor-Budva. Women in costume. |
| | 26 | Market day at Trebinje, good p.m. in old town, great to be here in off season. |
| | 27 | Boat to Split. |
| | 28 | Drove to Soleno. Walked in Diocletian's Palace. |
| | 29 | Again in Palace. Night boat to Rejeka. |
| | 30 | To Venice via Trieste. |
| | 31 | Flew to Rome and Naples, got car. |

| | | |
|---|---|---|
| *April* | 1 | Long day—Pompeii, Sorrento, and Amalfi. Met a priest and drove him to high orphanage—El Deserto—views of Capri. |
| | 2 | Pozzuoli for lunch, fine amphitheater. To Cumae. |
| | 3 | Sorrento. *Boris Godunov* at opera. |
| | 4 | Pompeii, Salerno, and Paestum, back to Amalfi. |
| | 5 | Up to Ravello for lunch at Palumba Hotel—best yet. Over hilly road to Caserta. |
| | 6 | Drove to Rome via Gaeta. Coliseum by moonlight. |
| | 7 | Shopped for garden pottery. Tivoli and Hadrian's Villa. |
| | 8 | Garibaldi monument at Janiculum. St. Peter's. |
| | 9 | Vatican Museum. |
| | 10 | Easter service at St.Paul's. Drive in Borghese Gardens. |
| | 11 | Plane to Athens, Hotel Grande Bretagne. |
| | 12 | Good guide, looked around city. |
| | 13 | Byzantine Church at Daphine, to Delphi for interesting afternoon. |
| | 14 | Ferry to Patras and on to Olympia in rain. |
| | 15 | A.M. at Olympia. Spectacular ride to Tripolis. |
| | 16 | Over the mountains to Sparta and Mystra with frescoed churches. Mycenae. |
| | 17 | Mycenae, Napolia, delightful spot. |
| | 18 | Epidaurus, theater. Old Corinth and back to Athens. |
| | 19 | Sight-see, Cap Sounion and Marathon. |
| | 20 | Sailed on *Semiramis* for Aegean Isles. |
| | 21 | Melos in A.M.—Roman theater and catacombs. Santorini, up to town by donkey. |
| | 22 | Crete. To Knossus, drive to Festus. |
| | 23 | Rhodes—delightful town. |
| | 24 | Delos to Mykenos. |
| | 25 | Piraeus early. |
| | 26 | Most enjoyable morning at Stoa of Attilus. Flew to Paris via Rome and Geneva. |
| | 27 | Lovely spring day. |
| | 28 | Napoleon Exhibit at Invalides. Lunch at Medici grille, boat train and sailed on *Queen Elizabeth*. |
| *May* | 1 | Church. |
| | 2 | Deck tennis. |
| | 3 | Docked, John and Blanche met us. Home. |
| | 5 | Boston on B&MRR and Nat. Life. B&MRR change in management. |
| | 6 | Boston—Nat. Life meeting. Hanover. |

| | |
|---|---|
| 7 | Concord to see Dud Orr on Spaulding Trust. |
| 11 | Lake to open house. To Hanover to consult Dr. Staples about leg operation. |
| 14 | Drove to Dunbarton to get wildflowers and ferns to plant. |
| 19 | Boston for Verney meeting. Celenese objects to sale of Brunswick mill. |
| 26 | Lake. |
| 28 | Boston. Washington 5, Red Sox 3 game. |

*June*

| | |
|---|---|
| 3 | SPS trustees' dinner at Warren's. To lake. |
| 4 | Lake. |
| 5 | Paddled to church. |
| 6 | Candia to get plants. |
| 8 | Hanover. |
| 10 | Checkup with Dr. Gunderson. Picnic on White River. President's reception. Exec. Com. meeting. |
| 11 | Trustees' meeting. |
| 12 | Commencement exercises in gym, rain, marched with Robert Frost. |
| 16 | Bradford with Miss Mansfield on Felton estate. Picking and putting up cherries. |
| 17 | Lake. |
| 18 | Hanover to see Sven Gunderson and decide against Achilles tendon operation. Home. |
| 19 | Francistown to see Winifred Rand [cousin of Elisabeth], who is very frail. |
| 23 | Boston for Verney meeting. Concord to see and hear Pres. Eisenhower give talk in State House Yard. Lake. |
| 24 | Hanover for National Life meeting. |
| 25 | Hotel Wentworth for NH Bar Meeting. Made report on Probate fees. |
| 29 | Boston for old B&MRR board dinner to Ned French. [Old board had been ousted in proxy fight.] |
| 30 | Hanover for Dartmouth Fincom and Execom meetings. |

*July*

| | |
|---|---|
| 1 | Lake. |
| 2 | Hot summer day at Lake. |
| 3 | Church, to Hanover to see Fannie Ames, whose husband, Del, died. |
| 4 | Walk up McClure's road. |
| 5 | Hanover for memorial service for Del Ames. |
| 6 | Boston to see Wolcott and Bigelow on Ames estate. |

| | |
|---|---|
| 7 | Hanover to see Ames family and on to Woodsville on estate matters. |
| 8 | Lake, almost a record hot spell. |
| 9 | Blueberrying in North Groton. |
| 10 | Church. Peterborough to meet Robbie Bass' fiancée, Patricia May. |
| 12 | Beans had party in Amherst for Bank of New York person and trustees. |
| 13 | Bay View for swim and picnic on the Island. [Bay View is on Cape Ann, owned by Blanche McLane's family.] |
| 15 | Wiscasset for supper with Sortwells, on to Rockland. |
| 16 | Rough boat trip to Matinicus. Stay Calhoun cottage, foggy, swim. |
| 17 | Another coldish day but good to be here. Bunkers for cocktails. |
| 18 | Bob Booth and I fished flounder in harbor. |
| 19 | Woodburys came. |
| 20 | Restful day. |
| 21 | Noon boat. 95 degrees on mainland. |
| 23 | Lake. North Groton for berries. |
| 24 | Church, Hanover to see Carol and new baby, Rebecca. Home. |
| 25 | Drive in Dunbarton. |
| 27 | Boston for good baseball game from roof box. |
| 28 | Boston for Verney meeting, Swampscott House for National Life meetings, Eastern Point for supper. |
| 29 | Nat. Life directors. Clambake at Marblehead. Lake. |
| 30 | Canoe in moonlight. |
| 31 | Church. Home. |

| August | | |
|---|---|---|
| | 1 | 100 degrees, no rain for month. |
| | 2 | Manchester, Mass., to Hoods for swim and evening. |
| | 3 | Boston for Finance and Executive committee meetings. |
| | 4 | Berkshires via Francestown and Williamstown. |
| | 5 | Typical day. Miss not playing tennis. Boston Symphony—Beethoven Mass. |
| | 6 | Swim. Wagner music. |
| | 7 | Heat wave broke. Beethoven 5th and 8th Symphonies plus piano concerto. Home. |
| | 12 | Lake. |
| | 13 | To Yarmouth to get Darby and Wendy. |
| | 14 | Good blueberrying at North Groton. |
| | 16 | Newton to Louise Rand's funeral [wife of cousin of Elisabeth]. |

| | | |
|---|---|---|
| | 17 | Boston at Ritz, good ballgame, in the bleachers. |
| | 18 | Verney meeting in Boston. |
| | 19 | Lake, Cornelia Evarts with Carol. |
| | 20 | Lake. New terrace at garage for Malc completed. |
| | 21 | Paddled to church. |
| | 22 | Littleton to prove Ames will. Mountain View for dinner. |
| | 24 | With Norwin Bean to party by NH Fire at Little Bear Island in Winnipesaukee. |
| | 26 | Lake with Sandy McLane. |
| | 27 | Picnic at Belle Isle. |
| | 28 | Walk on Clements Hill. Turkey dinner on lawn. Janie Hall's birthday. Children gave *Hansel and Gretel*. |
| *September* | 1 | Lake. |
| | 2 | Zealand Hut for night. |
| | 3 | Walked out. Left Mary's car in Livermore. (She is hiking with friends and will end up here.) |
| | 4 | Paddled to church. |
| | 5 | Labor Day to New Boston with Hazel for Shaw's 50th wedding anniversary. |
| | 8 | Lake to see Chas. and family off for Swarthmore College to teach. |
| | 9 | Lake for family weekend. |
| | 10 | Tennis, swims, sailing. |
| | 11 | Paddled to church. Singing on the porch. |
| | 12 | Littleton to settle Coffin account. Dinner at Pecketts'. |
| | 15 | Lake alone. |
| | 16 | Hanover for Nat. Life. Drove to Cumming's Pond to see Park girls. Bequest committee dinner. |
| | 17 | Lake for Mary's house party. |
| | 18 | Talk to Wink Tappley on Bristol Community Center. |
| | 19 | Peterborough on Verney tax. |
| | 22 | Lake. |
| | 23 | Lovely paddle across lake and down shore. To Squabetty [Betsy Deane McLane's family place on Mt. Mansfield in Vermont]. |
| | 24 | Quiet, enjoyable day. |
| | 25 | Home via Barry. |
| | 28 | Drove to College Grant. |
| | 29 | Gorgeous fall colors, to Hell Gate, lunch in Brown camp. Drive to Conway. |

|          | 30 | Dover for Spaulding trustees' meeting. To lake. |
|----------|----|----|
| *October* | 1  | Hanover for Exec. Com. meeting. Met party at Tarleton, to Armington Cabin. |
|          | 2  | Up Kancamaugus Highway (under construction), walk toward Hancock Pass. |
|          | 8  | Hanover 50th Reunion planning, to Lake. Deanes there. |
|          | 9  | Mild day, walked Rattlesnake Mt. trail in Rumney. |
|          | 11 | Lake. Alone for pleasant evening. |
|          | 14 | Lake. Carpenters, plumber, and electricians at work on our apartment. |
|          | 15 | Squabetty for dinner. |
|          | 16 | Basin Harbor Club on Champlain for Nat. Life meetings. |
|          | 17 | Nat. Life meetings. Home. |
|          | 19 | Boston on Verney sale. |
|          | 20 | Hanover. |
|          | 21 | Long day of committee and trustees meetings. Hopkins Center a little bogged. |
|          | 22 | Trustee meetings. Dartmouth 14, Harvard 9 in exciting game. Home. |
|          | 25 | Boston all day on Verney-Gera. |
|          | 26 | Saw Huntley [Spaulding] in Rochester. To Wiscasset. |
|          | 27 | Good start via Greenville, Great Northern Paper road by Moosehead to border. Quebec at dark. Crown room in Chateau, best yet. Kerhulu for dinner. |
|          | 28 | Shopped, picnic on Ile d'Orleans. Dinner Savoy, movie *The Virgin Queen*. |
|          | 29 | Drove by Beaupre, back through hills. Kerhulu for dinner. |
|          | 30 | Off at 10:00, home via Conn. Lakes. |
| *November* | 1  | Boston, Verney directors' meeting. |
|          | 5  | Springfield with Whit for Hop's 78th birthday dinner. |
|          | 7  | New York City on Verney minority stockholder matter. |
|          | 12 | Hanover for Dart 7, Cornell 0. |
|          | 14 | Nashua for hearing on Verney-Mintz. |
|          | 16 | Milford to call on Serena Rotch (Arthur died today). |
|          | 17 | To Francestown to see Stuart and Leslie Rand (Winifred Rand died today). To Rochester to Huntley Spaulding's funeral. To Boston. |

| | |
|---|---|
| 18 | Arrived Phila., out to Locksly to see Charles and Carol's new house. |
| 19 | Charles and Judge to Princeton 6, Dart. 3 game in snowstorm. In to Barclay—good party. |
| 20 | Relaxing breakfast, Boston for tea with Mary, then home. |
| 22 | Milford to settle Arthur Rotch estate. |
| 26 | Hanover for Exec. Com. meeting. |
| 27 | Church. Walk in Dunbarton. |
| 29 | Boston for Dartmouth Fin. Com. meeting. |

| | | |
|---|---|---|
| *December* | 1 | Virginia Verney died suddenly yesterday. To Bennington to see Gil and the children. |
| | 3 | Bearer at Virginia Verney's funeral. |
| | 5 | Hanover for Nat. Life Exec. Comm. meeting. |
| | 9 | Boston on Virginia Verney Estate. New York City. Dinner at Harvard Club with trustees: Harvey Hood, Beardsley Ruml, and Congressman Tom Curtis. |
| | 11 | Lake for brush burning party. |
| | 15 | Boston to Ritz. Symphony with David Oistrakh, violinist. |
| | 16 | Shopped. Up with Howie and Cushman for Spaulding trustees' meeting. |
| | 18 | Hanover for Christmas goose dinner and give presents. |
| | 21 | Portsmouth to see Perkins family. |
| | 24 | Francestown to see Rands. To Hopkinton service. |
| | 29 | Boston to see the Lunts in *The Great Sebastian*. Took Diane Verney and Jim Greenway to dinner at Union Club. |
| | 31 | Ravine Camp, record crowd of 172, first skiing—leg worked okay. |

# TWENTY-SIX

# Interlude 1960–69

## HIGHLIGHTS OF 1960

Judge and Elisabeth celebrated New Year's 1960 at home with snow on the ground, which made for good skiing around the house and on various abandoned roads in Dunbarton. When the snow wasn't good, they walked in Candia. They picked up hams and bacon in Dunbarton from their slaughtered pigs and hung them in the cold cellar at Three Acres. They called on Lawrence Whittemore several times in Pembroke; he was bravely facing a long terminal illness from cancer. The Appleton Thayers of St. Paul's School invited them for dinner and told of their trips to Greece; Judge and Elisabeth were beginning to plan for their own trip there in the spring. Since they also planned to spend time in Italy, they started to take Italian lessons. Miss Mansfield had the office for cocktails to celebrate Judge's seventy-fourth birthday. The Raulersons and Abbeys came to dinner. Grandson Jock McLane with wife, Joan, and their first great-grandson, Derek, came to dinner before returning to London, where Jock was working on his Ph.D. from the School of Oriental and African Studies at the University of London. Judge and Elisabeth had Ben Bradlee for a couple of days and took him skiing in Dunbarton and had a cookout in the snow before the annual Robert Burns banquet in late January. Judge made one trip to Montpelier and a couple of trips to Hanover for medical checkups and a National Life meeting. He and Elisabeth went to Boston to the Pops. Judge accompanied Elisabeth, a volunteer driver, on an errand for the New Hampshire Children's Aid Society. In February, they skied and walked around Manchester. They went to Lee to have tea with Bishop Dallas and made calls on Mrs. Norwin Bean and Mrs. Mary Manning. The Thayers came to dinner from Concord to talk further about the trip to Greece. In Boston, Judge and Elisabeth had lunch at the Union Club before attending the symphony, then spent the night; they enjoyed reading *Look Homeward, Angel*.

In late February they sailed from New York on the SS *Queen Fredweica* and had a fairly rough passage to the Mediterranean. They landed in Palermo, Sicily, where they picked up a car and saw the sights around

Palermo, including the mosaics at Monreale Cathedral, before driving to the south side of the island to Segestae and Agrigento, with their impressive Greek temples and theaters. They continued on to Syracuse around Mt. Etna, crossing lava fields, where they had a couple of beautiful days, which caused Judge to write in his diary: "Hated to leave." They drove to Messina and back to Palermo along the north coast.

The boat took them to Naples, where they went sight-seeing and attended the opera. Every city of any size in Italy has its own opera company, where younger singers train for the larger and more prestigious companies. Judge and Elisabeth spent a day around Pompeii at Cumae and Herculaneum before heading down the spectacular Amalfi Drive along the coast, spending a night at Positano[1] and continuing to Paestum and its beautiful Greek temples, built several centuries before the birth of Christ.

They cut across Italy to Bari, where they caught the boat down the Italian east coast, crossed over to Albania and the Gulf of Corinth, then went through the canal to Piraeus and Athens. They spent a couple of days enjoying Athens, then drove to Delphi in the mountains, crossed to the Peloponnese, stopped at Olympia, and went over the mountains where there had been bitter fighting and slaughter by both Greeks and Turks during the many years of Turkish occupation. They returned to Athens to explore the Parthenon and to see *Rigoletto* in the ancient Greek theater outdoors. Next, they went to Istanbul and saw the great mosques. Richard Pattee, nephew of Elisabeth's landscape architect, who worked in the U.S. embassy, invited them for tea in his quarters, an "interesting experience." They flew to Rome for a few days of sightseeing, particularly the Sistine Chapel, then drove north into the hill country around Orvieto and saw Etruscan tombs and walled hill towns. They took back roads to Hadrian's Villa, returned to Rome, and flew to Paris for a couple of days before flying to London. There, they had tea one day and dinner another with Jock, Joan, and great-grandson Derek. They shopped for kilts for grandchildren, did a little sight-seeing, and took the boat train to Southampton to catch the *Queen Mary* for New York.

Spring was just arriving in New England and everything was beautiful. They had their first asparagus, bought strawberry plants to put out, and went to Dunbarton to see about buying their usual two piglets. They entertained the Grafs for cocktails, then Miss Mansfield. They made calls on their old friends Mrs. Bean, Mary Manning, and Margaret and Mary Fuller. The house at the lake was opened. Judge got a physical checkup at Hanover. They picked up Malcolm's children in Concord, went out to Dunbarton to get the little pigs, put them in their pen in Manchester, where the children played with them, then drove the grandchildren back to Concord. Judge attended a couple of New Hampshire Bar Association complaint committee meetings. Judge and Elisabeth attended Lyn

McLane's graduation from Smith College in Northampton. They celebrated their forty-fifth wedding anniversary by going back to Waterville Valley and having a picnic on the rocks by the Mad River.

Judge and Elisabeth were leading such an active life that their knees started to give out. They saw Dr. Staples in Hanover, who prescribed rest and heat treatments for both of them. They succeeded in slowing up a little bit, but then they were off to the customs office in Portsmouth to pick up the rug shipped from Greece. Then they went to the lake for spring cleanup. Judge records in his diary on a Sunday that they went to church in Hebron: "Both have damaged knees—pretty confined—no walking." The next day they drove grandchildren to Stonington, Maine, to sail on Dave Bradley's *Mischief*, while they continued to Rockland to catch the boat for Matinicus for an enjoyable and restful week.

The Fourth of July was celebrated at the lake. A new flag with fifty stars was unfurled and hoisted up the tall flagpole accompanied by the singing of the national anthem and other patriotic songs. One of the grandchildren played the bugle and Malcolm made a speech. Judge records, "Pretty tired with all the celebrating."

Judge called again on Lawrence Whittemore in Pembroke, "who is failing fast." Judge and Elisabeth stopped at the lake en route to Montreal for a National Life dinner at the new Queen Elizabeth Hotel. The next day a special train took them to Montpelier, where they had directors' meetings. They visited the Deanes at Squabetty before returning home. Judge made a last visit with "Whit" in Pembroke before his death in August. There was good blueberrying under the power line in Groton over a period of several weeks, rain or shine. There were weekends at the lake with paddles to church on Sunday mornings, turkey dinners on the lawn at noon, and lots of swimming. Judge listened to the Republican National Convention in Chicago and commented that Eisenhower spoke well. The law firm enjoyed a day picnic at the Grafs' in Wolfeboro. Judge and Elisabeth had more checkups for knees at the Mary Hitchcock Hospital. They drove to Boston with the Bradley family, who flew to Helsinki, Finland, for a couple of years where Dave taught English in the university. In late August, Judge flew to Indianapolis to have an informal reunion with three other Rhodes scholars, class of 1907. Judge records in his diary: "Talked old times; all day in a mellow mood; a unique reunion; a pretty damaged four, but spirits are good." Judge and Elisabeth went to Cambridge to see Marcel Marceau, the perfect mime.

In September, Lyn McLane visited before taking off for two years in Kampala, Uganda, to teach school. This was before the Peace Corps and Uganda's independence. Judge and Elisabeth attended a three-day symposium on "Great Issues of Conscience in Modern Medicine" at the

Dartmouth Medical School, at which there were distinguished scientists and medical people such as C. P. Snow, Aldous Huxley, and Sir George Pickering. Judge recorded that the meetings were most stimulating.

Judge's sister, Hazel Clark, died suddenly in Hanover. Judge and Elisabeth went to the Dartmouth College grant in late September to see the new cabin and walk to Hell Gate on the Dead Diamond River. On the way home, they walked a couple of miles in on the Zealand Notch road for exercise and to enjoy the fall foliage. Later, they went to Montpelier for the dedication of the new National Life office building and stayed at the Lodge at Stowe with Elisabeth's sister Jane Tripp and her husband, Chester. There was a dinner, the formal dedication, and a directors' meeting spread over three days. They returned on back country roads amid the colorful foliage. In late October, they embarked on their annual Quebec trip, going via the Aziscohos dam and the Arnold Trail. They stayed at the impressive Château Frontenac and ate at their favorite Kerhulu restaurant. They saw some 80,000 geese on the river near St. Anne on one day and explored the Ile d'Orleans the next. They returned via the Connecticut Lakes. They attended a meeting of the recreation association in Hanover and went to a World Council debate in Durham. Judge flew to New York to see the American Express about their next trip abroad and also to meet Camp Onaway people about converting the camp on Newfound Lake from a proprietorship to a nonprofit corporation. Judge flew back to Keene to attend Hoppie's (retired president Ernest Martin Hopkins of Dartmouth College) annual dinner of about twelve men. One of the best, records Judge in his diary. Judge and Elisabeth collected the sausage from their pigs in time for Thanksgiving breakfast. Dinner as usual was at the Macedonia restaurant on Wednesday evening. Twenty-one came for dinner on Thanksgiving Day and forty for the evening square dance—all family.

On December 3, Judge records in his diary "John [this author] tells us of his engagement to Betsy Deane[2] and we are all very happy." A few days later, Judge spoke at the dedication of the new Spaulding Library at the New England Conservatory of Music in Boston. The library was made possible by a grant from the Spaulding-Potter Charitable Trusts, of which Judge was chairman. Judge had a bad nosebleed again. The lawyers in the firm had their annual Christmas party. Judge and Elisabeth went to the candlelight service in Hopkinton on Christmas Eve and enjoyed a quiet Christmas. Daughter Lilla Bradley surprised them by flying home from Finland for my wedding. (Betsy Deane's mother was Lilla's godmother.) The firm gave a dinner for me. Then Judge and Elisabeth gave a dinner for the two families at Loch Ober's in Boston. On December 30, Betsy and I were married at a candlelight service in the church in Lincoln with a reception at the Wayside Inn. The year ended with us off for a honeymoon in

*1960s, Thanksgiving with Eva Hill* finishing the turkeys at 1590 Union Street, Manchester.

Bermuda and the other children going to ski at Moosilauke, leaving Judge and Elisabeth to ring in the new year alone.

Judge was definitely winding down. His nosebleeds were becoming more frequent. He turned more clients over to the growing number of partners and associates in the firm; and he spent considerably less time in the office. He enjoyed the meetings of the National Life board and those of the Spaulding-Potter Charitable Trusts.

## HIGHLIGHTS OF 1961

New Year's Day was stormy. After church and a call on Mrs. Bean, Judge wrote in his diary: "Enjoyed being indoors." On January 4, Judge and Elisabeth reread and threw away their Christmas cards. They went to Dover to pick up Eva and sang old-time songs with Mary. On Judge's seventy-fifth birthday, nineteen family members came for a grand dinner party and fifteen cousins arrived for dessert and coffee. Charles' *Twelfth Night* play, which he had written many years before, was reproduced by the family. The next day a group of friends came for lunch, and the law firm came for cocktails. All the excitement produced a nosebleed the following day; Dr. Sander treated it. Judge drove to Plymouth with Lilla to see her son, Darby, at Holderness School. The next day he flew to Montpelier for a salary committee meeting and then to Boston to put Lilla on the plane back to Helsinki. His car gave out in the tunnel to the airport, requiring a tow. The problem was he ran out of gas! He had a nosebleed a couple of days later; he stayed in bed in the morning and banded birds in the afternoon. A day later he skied in Dunbarton and felt good. The annual church parish meeting and a Manchester Bank dinner and meeting kept him busy. On January 20, there was a big snowstorm that kept Judge and Elisabeth marooned for the day, but they went to Boston the following day to see *My Fair Lady*. The weather was very cold, reaching a record low for the date of minus twenty-six degrees, but this did not prevent them from skiing around Black Brook. Judge flew to Montpelier and back for an executive committee meeting. On January 28, Judge and Elisabeth skied with the Burroughses in Dunbarton and the next day went to church, skied, and called on Mrs. Bean. On the thirtieth, they skied on an abandoned railroad track in Candia and entertained the Grafs for dinner. The next day, they returned to Candia to ski and had the Gilmores for dinner.

In February, they drove to Plymouth to see Darby at Holderness—all of his family was in Finland. On the fifth, they went to church, skied, then planned their next trip to Spain. One evening, the Middletons invited them to dinner. After skiing in Dunbarton, they had an automobile collision. No one was hurt, but the car was badly damaged. About a week later, they were involved in another collision in Manchester—again no one was hurt. Judge spoke at the Milford Historical Society. Prudence Gilmore finished a sculpture of Judge. He and Elisabeth visited the Sortwells in Wiscasset and walked on Wells Beach on the way home. They took a picnic lunch to the lake, skied around the place, and stopped in Holderness to see Darby Bradley. Judge took the train to Montpelier for an executive committee meeting, then flew to New York City to catch a plane to San Antonio, Texas, where he met Arthur Coyle on Coyle Concord Oil Company business. He returned home from Dallas by jet airplane. Judge and Elisabeth skied the Black Brook area a number of times and occasionally walked on Candia Road.

On March 13, someone drove them in a snowstorm to the railroad station at Route 128 south of Boston; there they caught the train to New York City. The next day they toured the Guggenheim Museum and boarded the *Queen Elizabeth* in the late afternoon. They shared their dinner table with Jean and John Meck—John was treasurer of Dartmouth College—and played a lot of Scrabble together. They met Merrill Knapp of Princeton College; he had been in the Navy with me in 1942. Judge and Elisabeth had a couple of days sight-seeing in Paris before taking the train to Bordeaux, where they picked up a car and passed through Bayonne and into Spain via the grand Roncevalles Pass over the Pyrenees. They stayed in Pamplona on

Palm Sunday and walked the walled ramparts; then it was on to Burgos, and a dreary ride to Santanda. They rode out to Altimar to see the prehistoric animal pictures; then traveled around, going to Easter service in a cathedral and visiting Santiago, Salamanca, Madrid, and Toledo. They enjoyed the Prado museum in Madrid and the El Greco house in Toledo. Judge had another nosebleed, which was controlled. They drove north and crossed the mountains over the Samport Pass and were glad to be back in France after about three weeks in Spain. After a couple of days exploring back roads in the south of France, they wound up in Bordeaux, where they left the car. They took the train back to Paris and on to Geneva, where they visited Charles, Carol, and their children for a couple of days. They flew to Copenhagen and Helsinki to visit the Bradleys and were charmed by their quaint wood house on an island. Lilla drove them to Leningrad, about one hundred miles, where they enjoyed *La Bohème* in a small opera house. They visited the Hermitage with a good guide and loved the ballet at the opera house. They drove back to Helsinki on April 30 in a snowstorm and were glad to be out from under the Iron Curtain. They observed May Day celebrations in Helsinki on May 1. They went sight-seeing with the Bradleys, shopped, had a boat ride with a picnic lunch, and saw a church designed by Alvar Aalto. They crossed to Stockholm by plane and heard a weird modern Swedish opera. Visiting the quaint Old Town, seeing a ballet, and going on a boat excursion were interesting activities. Judge notes in his diary that New Hampshire astronaut Alan Shepard reached suborbital flight. After saying good-bye to the Bradleys, they flew to London, where they went to the theater with Jock and Joan and later went to Jock and Joan's home to see their great-grandson, Derek, and their first great-granddaughter, Rebecca. Judge met with the Whitfields at Brown's Hotel on business. (See Chapter Twenty-three, Estates of Mr. and Mrs. Ben Chandler.) They had a fast trip home on the *Queen Elizabeth* and were met by Betsy and me.

The next day they celebrated Elisabeth's seventieth birthday with the apple blossoms in bloom at Three Acres. Mary, Malcolm, and Susan came to dinner and tasted the first asparagus from the garden. They opened the house at the lake. Judge flew to Montpelier for National Life meetings. The Manchester Bank directors came to a party at Three Acres. On Memorial Day they took flowers to the Bancroft cemetery lot in Concord. In June, Darby Bradley finished Holderness for the year, so Judge and Elisabeth took him to Boston to catch the plane for Finland. They celebrated their forty-sixth wedding anniversary by going back to Waterville Valley again for a walk. Judge records that Elisabeth gave him new bird binoculars, and they had "a notable dinner and fine wine." Mary had a party at the lake for her faculty friends from the Beaver Country Day School in Boston. Judge states that he and Elisabeth enjoy the privacy of being alone. After meetings with the bank, YWCA, and Children's Aid, they went to Maine and stopped for the night with the Sortwells in Wiscasset, looked at Lilla and Charles' new property in Brooklin, then took the boat from Rockland to Matinicus in the fog. They were glad to see all of their island friends at the store, meeting the boat for mail and provisions. They walked, birded, swam, read, attended a church supper, went blueberrying, and enjoyed the restful life for a week. On the way home, they spent a night with Peter and Margaret Woodbury at Arrowsic.[3] On the Fourth of July at the lake, there were fourteen for lunch, prepared by Eva, whose family occupied the garage apartment. Judge and Elisabeth stopped at the hospital to call on Bishop Dallas that day and again two days later. On July 15, there were seventeen for a turkey dinner on the lawn. Judge indicates they had a swim with me at Sudden Pitch in Manchester, the recently formed family club, which built four tennis courts and a swimming pool. Judge drove to Manchester, Vermont, for a National Life meeting, then returned to the lake. The Raulerson family came up for a day of swimming and boating. On the way home Judge and Elisabeth stopped again to see the Bishop in the hospital and found him failing fast.

On August 14 they celebrated Eva Hill's sixty-fifth birthday[4] at the lake. Two English girls, part of a larger group visiting Manchester, stayed with the McLanes. Elisabeth took her guests on a ride around the lake in a boat. All of the English visitors had a party at Three Acres. Judge's Rhodes scholar friend, "Heff," whom Judge had visited with two other Rhodes men in Indianapolis the year before, stopped with his daughter, Pat, for a couple of days and had a good time visiting the lake, Ogunquit, Maine, and St. Paul's School. On August 30, Judge writes, "Alone for the first time in a long time." But not for long. There was a gathering of the clan starting on August 31, when Kristin, Jerry, and Tii, Charles' children, arrived from Geneva, followed the next day by Jock, Joan, Derek, and Rebecca back from London; Betsy, me, Sandy, and Angus; and Malcolm, Susan, and their family and an Indian boy, Jessie, staying for part of the year. The next week, Charles, Carol, and the rest of their family came, glad to be back home after a year abroad. Judge and Elisabeth visited the lake almost every weekend, but the floats and boats were brought in to protect them against the fall winds. In Manchester, Judge and Elisabeth entertained Stan and Thalia Brown and Bob and Ruthanne Raulerson for dinner and a little later the Jack Middletons and the Marsh Abbeys and later in the fall the Dave Nixons and the John Grafs. In mid-September, Judge had a dizzy spell in the night and called Dr. Sander, who came and gave him a prescription, saying that he had hardening of the arteries in the brain. This author and Betsy's new house in the field was started.

In early October, Judge visited with Miss Stiles, owner of Camp Onaway at the lake, about incorporating the camp as a nonprofit organization that would buy the camp from her. This was subsequently done. The firm had its annual dinner and decided to take in Jack Middleton as a partner.[5] Judge and Elisabeth attended a dinner meeting of the Forest Society at the Crawford House at which Sherm Adams presided. Then they went up the cog railway to the westside station, walked over to the Lakes-of-the-Clouds huts and came down the Ammonoosuc Ravine trail. Elisabeth and Eva closed the house at the lake for the winter on October 9. Judge and Elisabeth went to the Mountain View House in Whitefield for a business conference with the owners, the Dodges. After attending the symphony in Boston, they visited Charles and Carol in Hanover to see their Europe photographs, then continued on to Montpelier for a National Life committee meeting, before returning to Manchester. The next day they drove to Wiscasset for a night with the Sortwells and then had "a grand ride" to Quebec via Jackman, Maine, arriving in time to have a delicious dinner at their favorite restaurant, the Kerhulu. They drove along the St. Lawrence River and saw about 50,000 Canada geese in large bays in the river. The next day they drove around familiar Ile d'Orleans, taking a picnic lunch, and drove home via the Connecticut Lakes the following day.

Their life continued as usual. They went to the lake to see how the painters were coming along on the house and continued on to Hanover and Montpelier, where Judge had executive and finance committee meetings. In Manchester, there was a Manchester Savings Bank meeting and the Dartmouth alumni dinner, at which John Dickey spoke well. Three whistling swans made an unusual appearance at a pond near Manchester, to which Judge and Elisabeth, along with many other people, went on four separate days. Judge went with Elisabeth to a Smith College alumnae dinner in Concord at which President Mendenhall spoke. Judge had a New Hampshire Children's Aid Finance Committee meeting on November 1 in the morning. Betsy and I came for lunch before departing for Nantucket Island for the weekend.

This was Judge's last entry in the diary. He suffered a stroke in the left side of his brain that affected his speech and partially paralyzed the right side of his body. Judge was reading Thomas Hardy out loud to Elisabeth in bed and suddenly stopped. He never spoke again. Elisabeth at first thought he had a cold and wasn't feeling quite right, which she told her daughter, Mary, who had called. Mary sensed something more serious and came to Manchester late to find the next morning that her father was unable to talk and was partially paralyzed. Elisabeth later wrote: "Judge sat on the edge of the bed and made this last entry in his Diary. By morning he could not speak, nor could he use his right side. Weeks went by and gradually the pattern we had lived by for almost 47 years re-established itself. Speech did not come back and there is limited mobility."[6]

Betsy and I called from Woods Hole in the morning and Elisabeth said Judge was all right except he couldn't speak and that she was calling the doctor. She had not called the other children. She was bound and determined that she would take care of him and did not want him to go to any hospital. She also had made up her mind that, to the extent possible, they would continue to live their lives as they always had. Thus, with Eva's help, they entertained family, friends, and the office for tea, cocktails, lunch, or dinner as well as having people for the night. Judge listened to the conversations and could register acknowledgment—his comprehension was good. He occasionally uttered words, but they were invariably wrong. If you asked him what two and two were, the word "five" came out. He would shake his head and indicate no, but the right word wouldn't come. He could nod or shake his head to indicate approval or disapproval.

Elisabeth enjoyed conversations with other people since Judge was mute. She helped Judge to learn to walk with a cane or walker, and he maneuvered around the house very well. Getting in and out of chairs required some help. Elisabeth used the services of physical therapists to help Judge's fingers and hand and occupational therapists to help with living at home for about a year, although there was practically no improvement in his condition. Judge got exercise on a stationary bike when Elisabeth would read aloud, sometimes from the diaries. Elisabeth could help him get into and out of the car, so they could go on errands or ride in the country. They drove with the top down in just about any kind of weather except when it was raining or snowing. The TV, which the office had given him, was a great godsend to them. They enjoyed listening to the news together as well as classical music. They had many classical records and a record player. Elisabeth read aloud extensively from the diaries and they relived their many happy times together. Judge's eyesight was blurred so he could not read easily.

> ... but by October of 1962, we were flying to Scotland, exploring the wild north coast in a Humber Hawk (auto, not plane!) The following Spring to Greece from Salonika across the mountains to Corfu. Again in October to the Thomas Hardy country and Scotland. In the Spring of 1964 to the hill towns of Italy and last fall to Quebec, picnics on Ile d'Orleans and finding the white geese downriver. Reading the diaries together has been fun. We think that the BBC has the slogan for our 50 years, "Not so much a programme, more a way of life.[7]

They went to Scotland in the fall of 1962, Greece in the spring of 1963, England in the fall of 1963, and Italy in the spring of 1964. Elisabeth kept

Judge's diary during the trips to Great Britain and Italy. They arranged the trips through the American Express Company and had a car with a driver; they had wonderful times. On the trips to Scotland and England, they visited familiar areas, but they were more venturesome on the Continent.

The following is paraphrased from Elisabeth's entries in Judge's diary. On October 8, 1962, Judge and Elisabeth flew from Boston to Prestwick, Scotland, where they were met by a car and driver. They drove north to Aberfeldy for the night and continued to Braemar, the site of the royal Balmoral Castle, made popular by Queen Victoria, whose visits started a romantic renaissance of things Scottish. They drove up the Linn of Dee, a quiet valley with a delightful trout stream, for lunch, then continued on over the Highlands to Strathpeffer, in the heart of the district, where are found the many small distilleries that make single malt Scotch Whisky. Here they stayed the night. At Campbell's they bought kilts and wool sweaters for the increasing number of grandchildren and had lunch at an inn, where there was a local wedding reception. They toured along the north coast, passing small towns with little harbors for the fishermen. In rain and fog they drove to Kinlochbervie and Scourie at the northwest tip of Scotland, then around Point Stoer to Inchnadamph for two nights. The next day they explored Lochinver and Loch Assynt and then came back to their inn.

The weather cleared as they traveled to Ullapool with "magnificent mountains" and spent the night on Loch Maree. This corner of Scotland is very rugged, wild, and beautiful with practically no people, only a few crofters' cottages. The treeless mountains rise to around 4,000 feet. In between are deep glaciated valleys filled with lochs, either fresh or salt water from the ocean. The roads are mostly single lane with "lay-bys" located at strategic places where there is a view ahead. They spent nights in typical small Highland inns in the rain and fog. They went to Strome Ferry, lunched at Loch Alsh, where the ferry crosses a narrow strait to the Isle of Skye,[8] and watched the mists swirl around the Cuillins (high hills) of Skye. They continued on to Spean Bridge for the night. There was more rain and fog the next day as they continued to Oban for lunch and Tarbert and its small inn on the harbor. They enjoyed a game of Russian Bank, a card game with two decks, a family favorite that is perfect for two people on a long train ride or an evening alone. Judge was able to master this, as it involves visual acuity, not talking. The weather cleared as they drove down the Mull of Kintyre and saw Ailsa Craig, a volcanic plug that juts high up out of the Firth of Clyde. They spent the night at Inverrary, the seat of the lowland Campbell clan, the enemies of the Highland Macleans. On a perfect day, they sat on a bench overlooking Loch Fyne, enjoying the sunshine and the surrounding hills and mountains. These they crossed, over Rest and Be Thankful pass, stopping at Rob Roy's grave and continuing to Balquidder for lunch and the Buchanan Arms at Dryman for two nights. They cruised around Loch Lomond and Loch Long for a day, then drove to Prestwick to catch the plane home.

In the spring of 1963, they flew to Greece and traveled with a driver and car from Salonica to Corfu over approximately a two-week period. There is no diary of this trip.

On October 7, 1963, Malcolm drove Judge and Elisabeth to Logan Airport, where they caught a PanAm flight to London. They were met by their driver, Harry Abernathy, with a comfortable car. They drove to Winchester, where they visited the cathedral and an old Norman church. The next day, they drove through Hardy country, stopping at Marnhill, home of *Tess of the d'Urbervilles*. They continued to Milton Abbas, a village of thatched-roof houses, then Bere Regis (which they had visited in 1929), and over Egdon Heath to Weymouth for the night. Then they traveled to Abbotsbury, Bridport, and to Portesham seeing Sir Thomas Hardy's monument,[9] and back to Weymouth. On October 11, they visited Dorchester via Maiden Castle and Theatre and on to Wells for the night, where they attended an evensong service and visited the Cloisters and the Bishop's Garden. The next day they went through Cheddar Gorge, lunched in a fourteenth-century hotel, and continued to Fairford and Bibury.

On Sunday they drove through the Cotswold hills, old favorites from hiking and bicycling trips thirty years before. The Cotswolds was a great sheep and wool-producing area in the eleventh and twelfth centuries. The wool and garments made therefrom were shipped all over northern Europe and brought back much wealth to Great Britain. Judge and Elisabeth visited such familiar[10] quaintly named places as Upper and Lower Slaughter, Upper and Lower Swell, Burford-on-the-Water, and Stow-on-the-Wold. They drove to Oxford, lunched at the Mitre, and walked through the grounds of Magdalen College, where Judge spent two very happy years as a Rhodes scholar in 1908 and 1909. After a lazy morning in Oxford sitting in the sun, they motored to Burford, where they picked up a longtime friend, Pamela Redmaine, for lunch at the Lygon Arms in Broadway. They returned to Stow via Stanton. They had another lazy start the next morning, then in heavy mist they passed through Chipping Camden, Stratford, Coventry, and Nottingham. On October 16, they had a lovely day, although they passed through the grim midlands industrial area on the way to high moors and Kirby Lonsdale. Then they headed to Broughton on a very steep and narrow road over Hard Knott Pass to Ullswater in the Lakes District. They lunched on a couple of days in small pubs. They crossed Honiston Pass to Cockermouth for lunch, then went through Carlisle in the rain to Castle Douglas in Scotland. On Sunday they motored to Newton Stewart and Loch Troll over moors and mountains, had lunch at the Black Bull Inn at Straith, then drove along the coast to Ayr (Robert Burns country) and Troon for the night. The next day they caught the plane home from Prestwick.

The next year, on April 9, 1964, Malc and Sue drove Judge and Elisabeth to Boston and put them on an Alitalia flight for Milan, where they were met by their driver Mario and a Fiat limousine. They drove up to Lake Garda and stayed in a hotel with a big comfortable room with a terrace overlooking the lake. The next day they drove along the west shore with its many tropical vegetables, lemon trees, and tall dark cypress trees. Next, it was Trento at the beginning of the Alps with snowy mountains. They took the ferry to Modena and watched women with huge baskets hand scrub the laundry in the lake. Schoolchildren wore blue smocks with white ties. They spent a night in Padua, crossed the Po Valley, and saw many bicycles, canals, vineyards, and fertile farms. They arrived in Ravenna for the night, then they crossed the Apennines over a mountain pass, observed groves of low olive trees with twisted and gnarled trunks, and arrived in Siena, where they watched a soccer game from their room. They drove around the hill towns of Tuscany and on to Florence, where they had lunch at a lovely restaurant on the Arno River and drove around the beautiful city. The next day they went to Volteria, passing fields of red poppies, yellow mustard, olive groves, and vineyards, and on to Pisa, where they visited the Baptistry. They marveled at the Campanile, or bell tower, the famous Leaning Tower of Pisa. They drove north, lunched in the charming walled town of Lucca, and spent the night in Via Reggio. The next day they climbed high into the mountains on winding roads past the marble quarries of Carrara and snow-capped peaks. They lunched on trout and lasagna at Castle Nuova before descending back to Via Reggio. The next day, they continued along the coast, past Shelley's house, where he lived before he was drowned. They spent nights in La Spezia,[11] Portofino, and San Marguerite en route to Genoa, where they took the plane back to the States.

This ended the diary entries and any record of their daily life. They continued their lives pretty much as before with some limitations. There were two trips to Greece, one in the spring of 1963 and the other in 1965 or later, but no diary was kept. Because of Judge's difficulty in walking, they drove in the car with their driver, Ulysses (the same one on both Greek trips),[12] most of the time and went to small towns on back country roads enjoying the scenery and observing the people. They stayed in the excellent government-run small hotels. They had to give up going out to Matinicus, because the boat trip and getting around on the island would be too difficult. They made one more late fall trip to Quebec, observed the geese in the river, and enjoyed a picnic on Ile d'Orleans. They didn't go to Boston to the theater nor did they visit anyone. It was easier for friends to

*1965, Elisabeth and Judge McLane* pose for their fiftieth wedding anniversary.

come to Manchester. Fortunately, both enjoyed good health, and there were very few changes to their lifestyle.

On January 8, 1966, the family celebrated Judge's eightieth birthday with a large gathering at the Dartmouth Outing Club house on Occom Pond in Hanover.

During the years after Judge's stroke, Elisabeth took care of him most of the time, but she took a day off each week for her own R & R. Sometimes she went to Boston for the Friday symphony, had dinner with Mary, spent the night, and came home the next morning. Occasionally she went skiing. Her daughter-in-law Susan McLane, an excellent skier, remembers that in February 1967, she and Ibus went to Waterville Valley the day the Waterville Inn burned down. Judge and Elisabeth had spent their honeymoon there, but that didn't faze Elisabeth; she just wanted to get out on the slopes to ski. Susan said she cut quite a figure in her French snood, kilts, old-fashioned Peter Limmer boots, and fifteen-year-old skis, skiing nonstop up and down that hill. Everybody on the slope stopped to stare at this seventy-six-year-old dynamo!

Elisabeth, with the professional help of Elizabeth Pattee,[13] built a cozy one-room cottage at the lake in 1967. It was close to the water with a deck where Judge could sit and watch the children swimming, waterskiing, or boating in canoes, rowboats, or sailboats. There was an entry ramp so Elisabeth could push Judge in the wheelchair if he didn't want to walk, and there were no thresholds inside. There was a small kitchen alcove, a living room with a fireplace, a dining room table, and a double bed and small toilet, all on one level and separated only by curtains on travelers. The building was insulated and had continuous windows on two sides opening at the bottom to provide good ventilation. A sliding glass door opened to the deck. Judge and Elisabeth used this cottage a great deal. In the spring and fall, they made day trips or overnights on the weekends, particularly if other family members were going to be present. They were there in the summer continuously when family or friends were occupying the several other houses in the "compound."

Judge slowed imperceptibly in the later years. He slept longer in the mornings, had a good nap after lunch, dozed easily in his upholstered chair, and didn't follow conversations as much as he used to—his mind just seemed to be somewhere else unless he was specifically spoken to. He walked around the house, and when the weather was good Elisabeth would walk with him on the driveway. He greeted family and friends warmly but did not react much to their conversations.

In February 1968, Judge spent a number of days at Dick's House, the Dartmouth College infirmary, with a lingering flu. At commencement in

June, Judge sat in the car parked at the edge of the campus behind the stands. A number of the trustees and friends stopped by to say hello, much to Judge's delight. In July, Judge, Elisabeth, and Eva went to visit Charles and Carol in Maine, practically an annual visit. Although Judge couldn't go, Charles and Carol took Elisabeth for a moonlight sail on Eggemoggin Reach—a rare occasion.

The end came on April 21, 1969. Judge had had a second stroke.[14] Elisabeth put him to bed, but Judge wanted no help. For the first time in his life he pushed Elisabeth away when she brought him his food. He had decided that his time had come and that he should go. He died peacefully shortly thereafter in his sleep. Judge lived an active, interesting, and full life. He was an excellent lawyer, a responsible citizen, a devoted husband, a fine father, and a close friend and confidant to many.

# Notes

1. Blanche and I spent a night in Positano in the early 1950s while vacationing with our son Sandy, who was in the Army in Germany. Our six-story hotel hugged the almost perpendicular slope. Each room had a terrace, which was the roof of the room below, overlooking the Mediterranean Sea. The bathroom had a floor-to-ceiling glass wall also overlooking the sea. The foot of the bathtub was cut off and cemented to the glass wall, the exterior side of which was a glass fish tank enclosure holding goldfish. Thus you could sit in the tub, see the fish swimming by your toes, and look beyond to the blue, blue Mediterranean.

2. See Appendix A.2, The H. Towner Deane Family.

3. Peter Woodbury came from an old distinguished New Hampshire family of Democrats. Peter, wounded in the shoulder in World War I, after graduating from Harvard College and Law School practiced with Judge until he was appointed to the New Hampshire Superior Court, one of the youngest judges. He later sat on the Supreme Court of New Hampshire and then the First Circuit Court of Appeals in the federal court system. Peter and his wife, Margaret, were longtime walking, skiing, and social friends of Judge and Elisabeth'ss.

4. Eva Hill first came into the McLanes' life in about 1925 at the lake to baby-sit and help. She was a vivacious and hardworking young lady. On one occasion, she went on a blueberry expedition up a rough abandoned road in high heels. One of her heels broke off. One of the men decided the best thing to do was to break off the other, so she could at least walk decently. Later Eva married and had three girls, but tragedy struck when her husband died at a very early age. There was little money. Eva went to work as a weaver in the mills on the third shift. She went home in time to send the girls off to school, then slept

until they came home, when she had their lunch ready. She slept more in the afternoon, then made their supper. After putting them to bed, Eva went to Mass and then back to work in the mills. Eva was always a part of the McLane family for special events such as Thanksgiving and many weekends as well as summers at the lake, when her children were frequently with her. She was an excellent cook and cheerfully helped with the mending and other household chores. She loved working with Elisabeth making jams, marmalade, and jellies and putting up beans, corn, and other vegetables, which she had done as a girl on the family farm in Canada. Usually she lived with her brother once her girls were grown and married, but occasionally she stayed in the room in the house that was always known as Eva's room. In Elisabeth's last years, after Judge died, Eva was a constant companion at home and in the nursing home. Eva and Mary McLane were with Elisabeth when she died in 1983. Eva said to Lilla, "Le fin de ma vie." Eva died peacefully a year later surrounded by her children and grandchildren.

5. Although this sounds like a democratic action, actually, until Judge had his stroke, all decisions on partnership, salaries, or points were made by Judge alone—after consultation with Ken Graf but without much discussion. Everyone was very happy with Judge's decisions and no one wanted to change the system.

6. Postscript to "Not So Much a Programme . . . More a Way of Life." Excerpts from the diary of John R. McLane from 1915 to 1961. Prepared by David Bradley in connection with the fiftieth wedding anniversary of Judge and Elisabeth McLane on June 12, 1965.

7. Ibid.

8. A bridge now crosses to Skye that is praised by some and cursed by others.

9. Mary McLane recalls her mother telling her that she had thought the statue to be that of Judge's favorite author, Sir Thomas Hardy. When Judge saw the statue, he started laughing with great gusto. Finally Elisabeth figured out that Judge realized the statue was of an *Admiral* Thomas Hardy, a completely different individual who meant nothing to them!

10. They visited the Cotswolds in 1922, 1925, 1932, 1935, and 1948.

11. I had been on a patrol craft in the Navy in the spring of 1945 patrolling a "swept channel" at night off Via Reggio and La Spezia to prevent it from being remined by German or Italian boats emanating from La Spezia. During the day Allied destroyers came up the channel from Leghorn to provide gunfire support to the Allied troops ashore. At night, I could see tracer bullets being fired by both sides up in the mountains. Occasionally a building would be hit and catch on fire. All of this was several miles away and looked like beautiful fireworks. In daylight, it was hard to distinguish between the white marble quarries and snow-capped peaks.

12. Ulysses spoke a little English, was very solicitous of their welfare, and understood their love for the back roads, the small towns and the non-touristy things. When they first met Ulysses, he said to Elisabeth: "You no worry. He my man. I take care." He helped Judge into and out of the car; into the inn to their room or into the restaurant to their table. He also made sure that Judge was comfortable about his toilet situation.

13. Elizabeth Pattee taught landscape architecture at the Rhode Island School of Design in Providence.

14. For Elisabeth's life after Judge passed away, see Appendix B.1, The Bancroft Family.

# APPENDIX A
## *John R. McLane, Jr.*

# APPENDIX A.1

# Memories

*Here are some miscellaneous recollections of the author's boyhood in Manchester and several interesting incidents in my practice of law.*

## THOSE WONDERFUL DIRT STREETS

From about 1920 to 1946, Judge and Elisabeth lived at 940 Chestnut Street. For most of the 1920s Chestnut Street had curbstones and unused hitching posts for horses but was unpaved, which was a delight to us young people. I don't remember any dust during the hot summer days, but I'm sure there was plenty. What I do remember is the winters and springs when we used to make dams of snow or mud across the street and race our matchstick boats down the channels by the curbstones on either side of the street or in the ruts in the middle. There wasn't much traffic—families had only one car and Daddy had taken it to work. Most of the delivery vehicles were either horse-drawn or light auto trucks. Milk, coal, ice, and wood were usually delivered by horse-drawn wagons; groceries were delivered in light trucks. People did their own laundry—there were no central laundries making pickups and deliveries. All of these vehicles wreaked havoc with our dams, so when we saw one coming we filled our shovels with snow or mud, depending on the season, and as soon as the vehicle had passed we plugged the holes in the dam. Most of the kids on our street worked together. We made "crossovers," channeling the water from several ruts into just one to make the boats go faster. We didn't know kids from other streets; I don't remember ever going over to another street to play, and I guess we never expected them over on our street. On warm days when the snow would melt, we made great dams; at night they would freeze solid and in the morning they resembled speed bumps, to the annoyance of the drivers.

The farm kids who lived out on Union Street and River Road were brought to school in the spring and fall in horse-drawn wagons that had steps on the rear and bench seats on either side of the wagon. In the winter, they were brought in a pung, a sleigh holding a large, boxlike structure with benches on either side, a door at the rear, and a couple of tiny windows up high. The driver, wrapped in a fur robe (probably made from horse or cow hide), sat up front outside and drove the two horses. As the pung came down Chestnut Street, we would try to jump on the runners and get a ride. This was forbidden and dangerous; the driver would flick his whip at us and try to dislodge us, usually successfully.

The dirt street was our playground for baseball, skip rope, and kick-the-can. It was neutral territory and belonged to everyone; it was our social gathering place, where we sat on the curbstones and gabbed on the warm evenings. It was the scene of many childhood love affairs. On Halloween, it was a mob scene with little children robed in sheets with their jack-o'-lanterns, accompanied by parents. Older gangs on bicycles were bolder in committing acts of vandalism; we had fun taking rocking chairs off porches and hoisting them up flagpoles, hoping we wouldn't be interrupted by the police, who loved to snap our peashooters not so carefully hidden inside our sweaters. Oh, those were the days!

## CYGNET BOAT CLUB/CALUMET CLUB

The Cygnet Boat Club dates back to the 1880s, when it started as a boating club with canoes and some "single" and "double" shells. Later, six clay tennis courts were added. The Cygnet club became the tennis center of Manchester as boating lost its popularity. Many city, regional, and state tournaments were held there. In 1929, the club added two squash courts and a locker room and showers; at about the same time it converted an upstairs boat storage loft into a badminton court and added a small kitchen. The Cygnet thus thrived until the March 1936 flood,[1] which left a hole in the ground about twelve feet deep where the tennis courts had been and tilted the building and squash courts off their bases. This was at the height of the depression when the Amoskeag Manufacturing Company had ceased its operations and filed for bankruptcy. No one had the money or heart to restore the damage.

Another 1880s club, the Calumet, was a men's club on Lowell Street between Pine and Union. Beside its overstuffed leather chairs reeking with decades of cigar smoke, it had a do-it-yourself bowling alley in the basement and green-cloth-covered billiard and pool tables on the first floor. It also had a bar and a caretaker who served light meals. A deal was struck by which the Cygnet members paid for the cost of moving the squash courts to the Calumet and were admitted to membership—a good deal for everyone. During World War II, when there were few squash players around, the older members converted one of the courts to a cocktail lounge.

As for the tennis courts, there was little enthusiasm for rebuilding them anywhere, so some of the tennis fans built their own. Judge convinced Mary Fuller and Parker Straw to join him in hiring one company to build courts for each. Al DuPont built his court on the West Side. Judge's court on North Union Street, where Bill Gannon now (1996) lives, is the only one left.

## U.S. BOBBIN & SHUTTLE COMPANY

I recall in the late 1940s doing some work for U.S. Bobbin & Shuttle Company of Goffstown. All of the company's maple logs outside their factory in Barton, Vermont, were attached by the Barton Savings Bank, which claimed that it held a mortgage on the real estate from which the trees had been cut and that the logs had been removed without the approval of the mortgagee, as required in the instrument. The bank demanded payment for the value of the logs. The mortgagor, having been paid by my client, had conveniently disappeared with his family and, it was rumored, was headed for Florida. The company manufactured bobbins and shuttles for the textile industry. Spinning frames and looms operate at high speeds, causing a lot of impact and abuse to the bobbins and shuttles used in the machines, so the latter have to be made of hardwood. Northern maple, found extensively in Vermont, is the best material.

I received the attachment on December 24, I believe, and set off on the twenty-sixth in very mild weather for Barton, located near the Canadian border, armed with the documentation prepared to determine the validity of the bank's claim. The farther north I went, the colder it got. I was heading into an advancing arctic cold front.

In Vermont, all deeds and records affecting land are recorded in the town clerk's office, which in a small town means the town clerk's house rather than a substantial heated county courthouse. It also happened that this large piece of timber property, located high on a mountain, was spread over three towns with about thirty miles between the town clerks' offices. In one I had to wait for the clerk to come home from work. In another the records were all kept in a separate unheated building, formerly the milk house; the clerk was very accommodating in getting a fire going in the potbellied stove, which took a little of the chill out of the air. The temperature was about ten above and going down, with a brisk wind out of the northwest. I tried to turn the pages of the big folio volumes with my gloves on while stamping my overshoes to keep my feet warm. I finally accomplished my objective, determining that the mortgages were all properly recorded and that the bank's position unassailable, which would not please my client. I started home, only to discover that my engine was frozen; so I thawed it out in a garage and was about to start again when we discovered that the engine block was cracked and spouting a thin stream of water. The air was thick with unmentionable words for my stupidity, all caused by my penuriousness in not buying enough antifreeze. Not wishing to leave my car to be repaired at this forlorn town in the northern Vermont winter wilderness, I drove it home, stopping every twenty miles or so to fill it with water and alcohol and tighten up the robe over the hood. It was one of my most expensive trips ever—unfortunately, not chargeable to my client.

# FIRE ENGINES

In the 1950s, the McLane law firm had a case for its client Sears, Roebuck & Co. involving a fire that was alleged to have started in a Sears oil furnace in the Sears store on Elm Street in Manchester. Sears leased the property from Mrs. Mooney, the owner. The fire spread to the adjacent Mooney store, doing damage to a truck and some merchandise before being brought under control by the Manchester Fire Department. The suit was a subrogation action by

Mooney's insurer, who paid the claim to Mrs. Mooney, the landlord, and then sued the tenant, Sears, for negligently causing the fire. There was no customary antisubrogation clause in the lease. Mrs. Mooney was irate that her insurer would sue her longtime prize tenant and immediately canceled all insurance with the company.

Bill Green, from Sheehan, Phinney, Bass & Green, represented the plaintiff and the McLane firm represented the defendant. At the trial there was evidence about the fire, where it started, how it spread, how fast it burned, what fueled it, and so forth. Testimony was given by the state fire marshal, the Manchester fire chief, and some others. The case was settled during the afternoon break the first day; it was too late to go back to work, so the lawyers took the witnesses over to the Jolliet Club for a couple of beers. The fire marshal and the chief had started out as rookies together in Manchester at the Webster Street fire station[2] some forty years before and soon were reminiscing about the good old days when they had horses. The more the beer, the better the stories.

The fire horses slept in stalls at the rear of the station. When the alarm went off, they were on their feet in an instant and ready for action. The alarm triggered one of many Rube Goldberg devices that released the stall doors held shut by a spring; the horses rushed out to their proper places under the suspended harnesses and backed up to the whiffletree. The driver arrived from the second floor by sliding down the pole and jumped up into the seat. He pulled an overhead cord that lowered the harnesses onto the horses' backs. Another fireman, usually the newest, reached under each horse's belly, grabbed the cinch, hooked the ends together, and pulled tight. Still another fireman slipped the bit from the reins into the horses' mouths. The firemen jumped onto the wagon. The driver pulled another overhead rope that released the doors, which swung open,[3] and the horses were off. Our storytellers, in stitches of laughter, told of one new recruit who was supposed to do the cinching, but he was overawed under a horse's belly by those pawing feet and couldn't get the cinches together. The driver, thinking that the neophyte had had enough time, pulled the door cord. The doors opened and the horses tore off, side by side, with nothing behind, and, smelling the smoke, headed straight for the fire.

When the fire station had the old steam pumpers, it was an art to get the fire going fast while the horses were pulling the rig to the fire. The pumper was always left in the station with excelsior, paper, and kindling, carefully whittled by the firemen (in their spare time) into scrolls up and down the sides of each stick, in place on the grate. There were dry pine shavings on top and a few larger pieces of kindling on top of that. A bottle with a chemical was suspended inverted inside the fire chamber over the excelsior; the stopper was in place but it was attached by a string to a hook in the adjacent wall of the firehouse. When the fire engine moved, the string pulled out the stopper, releasing the chemical. It burst into flame on contact with the air, igniting the prepared ingredients. The firemen standing on the rear platform from time to time opened the door and plunked in pieces of special coal, redolent with oil, which burned very rapidly. As soon as there was steam pressure, valves were opened to provide a forced draft under the fire to make it burn faster. By the time the engine got to the fire—in, say, five minutes—there was enough pressure to pump water from the hydrants. Smoke and embers were pouring out of the stack; a fireman sprayed water on surrounding awnings. Wet blankets were thrown over the horses so they wouldn't get burned; sometimes the horses were led away a safe distance and tied up. Trigs were placed before and aft all wheels to stabilize the fire engine, which jumped all over the place. To see one of those steam fire pumpers in action was a sight never to be forgotten, we were told.

When the new motor-driven fire engines came on the market, there were no self-starters. The engines had to be hand cranked; to engage the crankshaft, a crank was inserted into a hole in the front of the engine below the radiator. After a couple of hard turns (the crankshaft was usually stiff and ornery), the engine was supposed to fire by itself, although that was not always what happened. Sometimes the engine backfired and the crank sailed out of the hole—very dangerous. The firemen were quite ingenious in developing self-starters. At the Webster Street fire station, they obtained an old engine block and fastened it to a cable that ran through a pulley in the ceiling and down to the engine, where the end was wound around the fire engine flywheel. The engine block was hoisted to the ceiling and locked in place. When the alarm sounded, the driver mounted his seat and pulled a rope that unlocked the block so it could fall and turn the flywheel to start the engine without the necessity of cranking. The throttle and spark levers on the steering wheel had been placed in their proper positions to facilitate starting. When the engine block fell, it landed on a pad made of old mattresses, so no damage was done to the block itself or the firehouse.

The firemen had much time on their hands, so they were always thinking of better ways to do things and were very competitive with the other station crews.

We thoroughly enjoyed those couple of hours of nostalgia from a couple of old pros producing fond memories of a bygone era.

# THE TRIAL OF PROFESSOR FORD

Our client was Professor Ford, retired chairman of the Department of Romance Languages at Harvard University, an erudite, scholarly, and distinguished-looking gentleman in his late seventies. He and his family had spent many summers at their place in Peterborough and were well known in the community. This story took place in the 1950s when Professor Ford was on trial in the Peterborough District Court for breach of the peace. He was accused of attacking his neighbor in what became a sensational and humorous case. The trial was held one summer evening in the colonial town hall meeting room on the second floor, which was crowded with onlookers and the press from the metropolitan-Boston area. Those tabloids were always eager to hear of the transgressions of the Harvard aristocracy.

According to the testimony given at the trial, Professor Ford's house was located on a hill overlooking a field sloping down to a small brook. The brook crossed the professor's land before continuing through a culvert under the town road and thence onto the land of Maurice Belanger,[4] the complaining witness. He was a sturdy laborer of French Canadian extraction well over six feet tall and weighing about 250 pounds. Mr. Belanger observed that the culvert had become clogged, backing up the water onto the professor's land and preventing it from flowing onto his land, so he took his shovel to clear the obstructing debris. Professor Ford, watching from his veranda, observed Mr. Belanger at work on what appeared to the professor to be his land. Ford immediately walked down the road to the culvert and ordered Mr. Belanger off his land. Mr. Belanger calmly advised the professor that from time to time he worked for the town on its roads and was trying to clear the obstruction so that it wouldn't flood the professor's land; instead it would safely flow onto Belanger's land and continue on its course. He also explained that the town road right-of-way was three rods wide and extended about one rod on either side of the traveled portion of the road, so that he was working within the town right-of-way and was not on the professor's land and had no intention of leaving. The professor sputtered something, turned, and briskly set off for his house. Mr. Belanger continued with his work, assuming that the incident was closed. However, in a few minutes, Professor Ford returned carrying what Mr. Belanger described as a "blunderbuss," some kind of a firearm resembling a shotgun. Once again the professor, in a loud and agitated voice, ordered Mr. Belanger off his land, holding the firearm in a threatening position. The burly Mr. Belanger walked slowly over to the professor, who was of slight build, reached out, and grasped the gun, attempting to take it away from him. The professor hung onto the gun tightly and they scuffled. The professor was pushed backward; he lost his balance and fell to the ground with Mr. Belanger landing on top of him, still clinging to the rifle. There was a crack as the professor's collarbone broke; he relinquished the gun. Mr. Belanger helped him to his feet and both returned to their respective homes. I don't recall exactly what happened next; I think that Mr. Belanger gave the police the gun and told them what happened but did not want to prosecute the professor because they still had to be neighbors. So the matter was forgotten—for a while.

Sometime later, whether weeks or months, I don't recollect, Mr. Belanger went into town with his wife to shop in the supermarket. As they emerged from the store with bundles of food, Professor Ford—about to enter the market—spied Mr. Belanger. Ford made a beeline for him and then executed a perfect flying tackle, which he must have learned in prep school sixty years before. He knocked Belanger and his bags to the ground. Mr. Belanger, upon regaining his composure, decided that this was enough. He went to the police station and swore out a complaint against the professor for breach of the peace.

At the trial, the prosecution was represented by eighty-year-old Jerry Doyle, a fiery Irishman, an able trial attorney from Nashua. The defense was represented by the McLane law firm team of John Carleton and this author.

The spectators and press sat on the edge of their seats as Mr. Belanger outlined the above-described events under Jerry Doyle's interrogation. Mr. Belanger was not upset by Mr. Carleton's cross-examination. On direct examination by Mr. Carleton, the professor justified his actions rather than denying them. Then came the battle of the octogenarians. Jerry Doyle cross-examined the professor. He went over much of the testimony about what happened at the culvert, then asked, "Didn't you use some nasty words in talking to Mr. Belanger?" The professor thought for a moment, pulled himself up with his head held high, and said in a clear voice "Yes, I called him several contumelious epithets." The courtroom broke into guffaws of laughter even though no one, including the judge, knew what "contumelious epithets" were. It took a few minutes to restore order. The court found the professor guilty, fined him several hundred dollars (the fine was suspended), and made him post a cash bond of several thousand dollars to keep the peace. The press got the story they wanted and the citizens of Peterborough will never forget those "contumelious epithets."

## JUSTICE UNDER THE SKIES

I tried an "issue to court"[5] case with John Carleton. The case involved a property line dispute on the shores of a pond in Wakefield, near the Maine border. Our client, a lumberman who bought and sold timber lots all over the state, lived in Goffstown. The other side, represented by Burt and Dick Cooper of Rochester, was also a lumberman. I don't remember whether our client was the plaintiff or the defendant. One of the parties was the grantor in a deed and the other was the grantee. Each said he'd been in land dealings for over fifty years and nobody had ever questioned a deed of his. He knew he was right and wasn't going to give an inch. The economic impact was that if one interpretation of the deed prevailed, the grantee had about 2,000 feet of beautiful shorefront on the pond; if the other interpretation held, the line would be moved away from the shore by about 300 feet so that the grantee would have no frontage at all. It was going to be necessary to rely on the testimony of some old-timers who could describe the ancient use of the land and identify old stone walls, barbed-wire fences embedded in trees, and different growths of timber to determine the ownership of several lots and the location of the boundary line. Since these witnesses couldn't get to court easily, it was decided that the attorneys with their clients, the judge (Wescott), and the stenographer would take a view and then go to two old-timers' houses for their testimony.

The appointed day was one of those glorious days in the fall—the morning was crisp and cool, mist rose lazily from the ponds we passed on the drive from Manchester, and the foliage presented a myriad of riotous colors. As planned, the court, the plaintiffs, and the defendants met on Route 16 at a road junction and pulled over to the side of the road. The judge and stenographer stayed in their car to keep warm while the rest of us gathered by the judge's open window. Then John Carleton and Burt Cooper made their opening statements, exuding mist in the cold air as they spoke. Then we drove over to the pond and a picnic area in a grove of pines, swept off the pine needles from one of the tables that was bathed in the early-morning sunlight, laid out our maps, and explained our positions. We took a view pointing out the ancient barbed-wire fences, stone walls, and differences in tree types and age. We offered the maps and deeds in evidence and then proceeded to the first witness' house. His wife was expecting us and had the kitchen table all laid out with a red-checkered tablecloth with plenty of chairs around. She was very gracious, with a plate of freshly cooked doughnuts and a pot of coffee (tasted mighty good) on the back of the big kitchen woodstove, which took up almost half the room and kept the kitchen plenty warm. We got down to business and took the witness' testimony, direct and cross. He was able to relate what the fields and land were like when he was a boy some seventy years before. He recalled whose cows used which field, who owned what, and where the boundary lines were.

Then we moved to the next house, an old cape with paint peeling and window shutters askew. We found our witness sitting in an old rocker on the sagging front porch. It was later in the morning with a rising temperature. He was expecting us. He was older than the first witness and seemed to move with difficulty, so we decided to proceed right there. The stenographer sat on the edge of the porch while the rest of us stood on the porch or the adjacent dirt driveway. As the testimony started, someone leaned on one of the porch columns that held up the roof. The pillar fell down onto the driveway with a creaking of wood as the roof, deprived of its support, sagged. I thought the whole roof was going to fall on our witness and the stenographer. We four lawyers, with the help of the judge, pushed the roof back up with the aid of a long pole, which we found in the attached shed, and slid the column back into place, thus stabilizing the roof again. We enjoyed a good laugh, brushed off our hands, and finished our case.

It reminded me of the medieval "king's courts", where the king rode "circuit" and held court where there were disputes among the king's vassals that needed to be heard by their peers.

I don't remember whether we won or lost the property line dispute, but I shall never forget the beauty of that New Hampshire fall day and the effective administration of justice in the raw at a time when life was more leisurely than it is at the present.

## A SEXUAL INCIDENT

The telephone rang at my home at about seven o'clock one morning.

"John, this is Bill Katz. My brother Sam is in trouble and you've got to help."

"What's the problem, Bill?"

"The police arrived at his house last night after eleven and took him to the station without telling him what it was all about, said they just wanted to ask him some questions. Scared him to death. Apparently two young girls complained that a man picked them up on the way to school and exposed himself to them in the car. They took down the license number and gave it to their teacher, who called the police. Sam told them he'd not been on the West Side and was at work at Varick's at the time, but is supposed to appear in court at eight-thirty this morning."

"Okay, meet me at the office at eight with Sam, and we'll see what we can do."

Sam, about fifty years old was short, heavyset, and weighed about two hundred pounds. He was single and had worked for years for Varick's hardware store on Elm Street. He was upset and surly at the police treatment of him.

"Sam, you've got to understand that the police have nothing against you," I told him at the office. "They are just doing their job investigating a complaint that has been filed." (Being a Jew, he may have believed that he would not get a fair shake from the police.) "Now, you've got to be straight with me if I am going to help you. I understand that this incident took place over on the West Side yesterday morning. Were you ever on the West Side yesterday?"

"No. I practically never go over there. I live and work on the East Side."

"Have you ever picked up any small girls?"

"No."

"Have you ever exposed yourself to anyone?"

"No."

"Sam, I believe you. I think this is a case of mistaken identity. Well, we better get on over to the court."

At the courthouse, we entered the sheriff's office; I directed Sam and Bill to sit down and wait while I went to talk with Tom O'Brien, the high sheriff for Hillsborough County, who was sitting in his inner office. Tom was a good Irishman, sheriff for twenty-odd years, in his sixties, short and rotund.

"Tom, can I have a word with you?" I asked. "I represent Sam Katz and need a copy of the complaint."

"Sure, John, come on in." He shouted to his secretary, "Margaret, give Mr. McLane a copy of the Katz complaint." Then he turned back to me. "What else can I do for you?"

"Tom, I've talked to my client. I'm convinced he's innocent and I think we've got a case of mistaken identity. Do you know what color the car was that the girls got into?"

"Nope, the school principal didn't give me that, just the license number."

"Well, how about the type of car? Was it a sedan, two-door, four-door, or was it a pickup, van, truck, or what?"

"I don't know."

"You mean all you know is the license number that the girls gave to their teacher and the teacher gave to the principal or his secretary who gave it to your office? Pretty easy for someone to make a mistake, and you're going to arrest a guy, maybe ruin his reputation, on that flimsy evidence?"

"Look, John, you're young and new at this stuff." (That was perfectly true, since I had only very recently been admitted to the bar.) "But I've been around and learned a thing or two in my twenty years at this business and I tell you I can spot a guilty guy when I see one, and this is one."

"I don't think that is going to settle this case, but I've a proposition to make to you. I'll have my client bring his car with the license number you have for him to the parking lot out in front of the courthouse and you bring in the girls and have them identify the car. How about that?"

"Fair enough. I'll have them here in half an hour.".

"See you then."

A half hour later, we congregated on the courthouse steps overlooking the parking lot—the sheriff, my clients and me, and the two girls with the deputy sheriff, Tom Pichette, who went to pick them up. There were about twelve cars parked of different types—passenger cars and pickups—different colors. My client's car was among them.

"Now, girls, the car with the license number you told your teacher is out there. I want you to look at the cars, not the license plate, and see if you see the one that picked you up. Look at the type of car and its color." Tom let the girls look carefully; they said it wasn't there. Tom pointed to several cars, one at a time, asking if that was it, including Sam's car, but none was the right car. Tom pointed to the license number on Sam's car and asked if that was the one they remembered, but they couldn't recall.

Tom then asked the girls what the man looked like who picked them up. "Did he look like me?" He pointed to himself—sixties, weight 220 pounds, rotund and short. "Or did he look like Mr. McLane here?" (He pointed to me, not yet thirty, weight 180, taller than the others, and young looking.) "Or Mr. Sam Katz, there?" (Fifties, stocky, weight about 200.) The girls looked at each of us and then pointed to me and said, "He was young and looked most like that man there."

"Okay, Tom, you've got me, I give up." I held my hands together toward Tom as if to be handcuffed. "I'm ready to go, but will you first let my client, Sam, go?"

"To hell with you, John, you win this time. See you later."

Scary, isn't it?

# Notes

1. This was the same flood that "did in" the Amoskeag Manufacturing Company.

2. The Webster Street fire station, built around the turn of the century, was torn down in 1992 to make way for a new and larger station.

3. Somehow, the door opener was rigged to a timer, so that after an appropriate interval, the doors automatically closed, keeping the station house warm.

4. Assumed name.

5. Trial before a judge but without a jury.

# The H. Towner Deane Family

## H. TOWNER DEANE (1890–1976)
## VIRGINIA FLAD DEANE (1892–1959)

*The friendship between the Deane and McLane families started in 1910 when Elisabeth Bancroft and Virginia Flad were freshmen at Smith College. It was renewed in 1960 when Elisabeth's son John McLane, Jr. (this author), married Virginia's daughter, Betsy Deane.*

Elisabeth Bancroft attended Smith College as a member of the class of 1914. One of her closest friends was Virginia Speck Flad from St. Louis. "Speck" (as she was known to all) stayed only one year at Smith, but for the rest of her life she was one of the most loyal members of the class. Speck attended college house parties at Pasquaney with "Bid," as Elisabeth was known at college. Speck was a bridesmaid at Elisabeth's wedding at Pasquaney in June 1915 and was a frequent visitor. She served in France as a nurse's aide in World War I. Her father, Edward Flad, was a civil engineer in St. Louis and a member of the Mississippi River Commission, which oversaw the dams, locks, flood control program, and navigation for the river basin. In 1921, Speck married Henry Towner Deane of Chicago, a graduate of Harvard in the class of 1912. Henry used only his middle name, Towner, which was his mother's maiden name. Towner served in the Navy in New York on board a patrol vessel during World War I. The family lived variously in Chicago, New York, and St. Louis, depending on Towner's jobs, which were mostly in the banking field. They had two children, Virginia and Elisabeth. Elisabeth was named for her godmother, Elisabeth McLane, although Elisabeth Deane has always been better known as "Betsy." In the 1930s, the Deanes purchased an old tumbledown farm and about five hundred acres of land on the northwest slope of Mt. Mansfield in the towns of Underhill and Cambridge, Vermont, for a summer place, known as "Squabetty." It is at the end of an unplowed dirt road almost two miles from the main road. They spent substantial parts of each year there and made many improvements, including the addition of a guest house, tennis court, and swimming pool (fed directly by the mountain brook, guaranteed to be cold); they also rebuilt the barn. Squabetty is still used frequently in the warmer seasons and occasionally in the winter for brief periods.

Virginia and Betsy attended St. Mary's-in-the-Mountains in Littleton, New Hampshire, and then Smith College in Northampton, Massachusetts.

They were frequent vacation visitors of the McLanes, with or without their parents. Virginia taught English and history and assisted in administration for twenty-five years at North Shore Country Day School in Winnetka, Illinois, and another fifteen years at St. Paul's School in Concord, New Hampshire, before retiring in 1986. She was a client of the McLane law firm. Virginia died on January 1, 1993, from emphysema. Betsy was a professional photographer specializing in children's casual photographs until she married me in 1960. Since then, she has been the mother to our four children. Our daughter Virginia (Gigi) attended the University of New Hampshire and was married to Scott Moreau, also of Manchester and a graduate of the University of New Hampshire, at Squabetty in a wild rainstorm in June 1988. Gigi teaches elementary school and Scott is a forester. In 1993 Gigi and Scott had a baby girl, Emilie. Towner, Gigi's twin brother, a self-taught craftsman, is a cabinetmaker living on Lummi Island in the San Juan Islands of Washington near Bellingham, with his wife, Lynn, and daughter, Kelsey. Kathryn, a graduate of Smith College and Washington & Lee University Law School, is a member of the bars of the state of New Hampshire and the District of Columbia. She is an administrator for Conservation International in Washington, and does not currently practice law. Duncan, a graduate of Evergreen College and Washington Technical Institute, also lives on Lummi Island; he is an automotive mechanic and active in the volunteer fire department. He married Tierra Roughton in the spring of 1994.

Judge was an occasional visitor to the Deanes in St. Louis on his trips to and from Texas. The families visited each other frequently at Pasquaney, Manchester, and Squabetty.

# Grandliden Hotel

*A story like this is what makes the practice of law in New Hampshire interesting.*

The author's client was the owner of the Grandliden Hotel Corporation, which owned a spacious, rambling, three-story white 1880s hotel, complete with verandas and rocking chairs, overlooking the shores of a New Hampshire lake. There was the usual small golf course, tennis courts, shuffleboard courts, horse stable, and plenty of country roads for riding, biking, and walking. Although the resort was elegant in its time, it was showing signs of age: little areas of peeling paint, a few green shutters missing from windows, untrimmed shrubs, a golf course that made one think of a hayfield, and a tennis court that resembled the golf greens.

I had another client who told me, years later, that he used to sell linens, toweling, and sheets to the hotel. The hotel was pretty slow to pay and offered to provide accommodations for credit on the bill, which my client utilized, realizing that a cash payment was extremely unlikely. I found out that the issuance of "due bills" was a common practice in the trade. A due bill—an instrument with limited negotiability in the hotel trade—stated that the maker (the hotel) would provide one double bedroom complete with bath for two nights with two breakfasts and two dinners. This was issued in exchange for credit of a stated amount on the supplier's bill. There was an office in New York City that made a market in due bills. One could sell them for cash, usually at a discount depending on the reputation of the hotel. One could also exchange it for a due bill at another hotel in the Poconos, the Catskills, or most any resort along the East Coast.

Somehow these due bills seemed to be securities exempt from the registration requirements of federal or state law. Apparently, due bills were of dubious value. The holder was admonished to heed the doctrine of caveat emptor. It was not unusual for the holder, upon presentation of the due bill, to find that the best rooms were taken and the only room left was in the unheated detached wood-frame annex for employees. With a number of college-age students working as waitresses, maids, busboys, and caddies living in the outbuilding, it was not always the quietest place on Friday and Saturday nights.

The experienced user of due bills would make his reservations in the usual way, using a credit card and obtaining a confirmed reservation for a specific room. The hotel did not want to create a scene in the lobby at the reservation desk upon his arrival when other guests were arriving too, and therefore had to accommodate the guest in accordance with his confirmed reservation, even though he was paying his bill with the due bill. The food was usually good but the service was something else. The maitre d' would usually seat his guests, whom he had been warned held due bills, in the farthest recesses of the dining room, reserved for "such people." The waitresses knew that "such people" were notoriously poor tippers; "such people" figured that the hotel owed them money, therefore why should they tip generously? Our guests would be served after all other guests had been taken care of.

When I became involved with my client, he had negotiated to sell the hotel real estate together with everything necessary to run the hotel, such as all personal property in the hotel rooms including beds, blankets, sheets, linens, bureaus, chairs, tables, rugs, pictures, radios, televisions, and electric clocks. These had all been carefully inventoried along with the contents of the kitchen, dining room, public rooms, storerooms, maintenance sheds, garages, and other outbuildings and were included in the purchase price. The consumable supplies—including food, cleaning items, laundry soaps, fertilizer for the lawns and golf course, and so forth—had been itemized and priced and were to be paid for separately. All of this had been done a day or two before the closing, and a representative of the buyer remained in residence at the hotel thereafter.

I discovered that my client was an affable middle-aged man, talked a lot about his accomplishments, and seemed to crave approval. I also realized that he stretched the truth a little where it would benefit him, so that I couldn't always rely on what he said and had to do my own checking.

The purchaser was the Society of Jesus, with regional headquarters in Boston. My recollection is that one of their institutions was a college in Fairfield, Connecticut. A portion of its campus was to be taken by new highway construction. The college had decided to acquire property in a location that would not be subject to significant population growth for the next one hundred to two hundred years. It had decided that the Grandliden property met that criterion. The purchase price was something like $200,000. (The time was about 1960.) I learned from my client that the closing would be held in New York City because some mortgages had to be paid off there and discharges obtained.

On the day before the closing, my client and I went to Boston to the society's offices, stark in their simplicity and paucity of decoration or furnishings. This was a new experience for both my client and me. We met the attorney for the society, a Mr. Graham, an elderly gentleman, rather gaunt in appearance. He continually had a glass of milk with him and explained that he had lost a substantial part of his stomach from cancer and needed constant sustenance. We went over the closing documents, then executed the deed, which I sent in escrow to the buyer's attorney in New Hampshire for recording on telephone advice from the closing in New York. I delivered the executed bill of sale in escrow to Mr. Graham. He gave me a society check payable to the Grandliden

Hotel Corporation, certified by the Norfolk County Bank & Trust Company, for $200,000, in escrow with instructions to pay from the purchase price certain mortgages outstanding that were deposited in a New York City bank for collection and to obtain discharges. Mr. Graham, during lulls in our business, made it abundantly clear that he had lots of connections with Cardinal Spellman and the hierarchy of the Catholic Church as well as the Kennedy family. He indicated that young John in the senate was a good friend of his.

The next day my client and I flew to New York City. At the appointed hour we arrived at the appropriate bank, where we met a heavyset, dark-complexioned man dressed in a black suit, dark fedora hat, dark overcoat, and dark glasses—the epitome of the Mafia. Accompanying him was his attorney—tall, slender, a little older than I, laid back, quiet, heavy New York accent, and no hat. This was a time when a felt hat was de rigueur. Later, I learned that the "Mafia" gentleman hailed from Newark and his attorney from Jersey City. We got down to business. The Jersey City attorney gave his client a copy of the Grandliden mortgage and a note with a computation of the amount due, which agreed with my client's figures. I asked where the originals were and was advised that the mortgage had been pledged to the bank as collateral security for a loan by the bank to the "Mafia" gentleman. No problem; we would endorse the check over to the "Mafia" and he would endorse it to the bank. The bank would pay off the mortgage in the agreed amount and pay over the balance of the check to the Grandliden Hotel Corporation, which was still in existence because only the real estate and tangible personal property had been sold. We then went over the plan of action with the appropriate bank official. He looked over the check, front and back, with a fine-tooth comb, and wanted to know who I was. Fortunately, I had a letterhead and business card. He returned the check to me and disappeared for about half an hour, then returned with a more senior gentleman, who introduced himself. He then announced that the bank would not accept the check, although it was bank guaranteed. We were all flabbergasted; I suspect that each party had about five different plans for spending it's particular portion of the check that day. I inquired what the problem was: the Society of Jesus? the Norfolk County Bank & Trust Company? or what? In a very imperturbable manner, the officer informed us that the bank could accept the check only for deposit to the account of the Grandliden Hotel Corporation and could pay out of the account only after the account was properly authorized by vote of the Board of Directors of Grandliden Hotel Corporation and properly certified to by an appropriate official. The bank had no way of knowing whether the endorsement of the check by my client to the "Mafia" was an ultra vires (beyond the legal power of the corporation) act or not. I did some scratching of my head and had to conclude that the bank was justified in its action and that we'd have to find another way to skin the cat. I could see in my mind's eye what Mr. Graham was going to say when I told him that the society's check was no good. I really feared that the shock would do him in. But there was no alternative; he had to be told. On the phone, he yelled, as I had anticipated, that he was going to call Senator Kennedy right away. (Kennedy was chairman of the Banking and Currency Committee.) I tried to calm Graham down and suggest that it was all right to call the senator tomorrow but that I had a plan that might work to close this transaction today. I asked him if the society had an institution in New York City and learned that Fordham University was affiliated with the Society of Jesus and would fill the bill. What if Graham arranged to have the society treasurer in Boston call the Fordham treasurer, explain the predicament, and arrange for me to deliver the Boston check to the Fordham treasurer, who would then issue in exchange a Fordham check payable to the bank. The treasurer would have the check duly certified by an uptown branch of the same bank, deliver the new check to me for delivery to the downtown bank, which could then pay off the mortgages and complete the closing. We agreed that this might work and solve our dilemma. Mr. Graham said he would make the calls and get back to me, which he did in about half an hour. Our contact at Fordham was to be Brother McGrath, the treasurer.

While we waited for the call, we had a cup of coffee together. My client raved about his hotel, what a beautiful place it was, how well he kept it up, and what a good relationship he had with all his creditors in town. The Jersey City lawyer turned to him and said, "What you say, I know." Later, on the subway going way uptown, I sat next to the lawyer, who told me about his client, never mentioned the Mafia, but indicated that his client loaned money to people who needed a lot of money fast and didn't care what it cost—people who had been caught with their hand in the till, caught in bed with another man's wife, or had large gambling debts. He would loan money and expect to get back three times the amount loaned in, say, ninety days. The lawyer would investigate the individual's reputation, assets, et cetera, and tell his boss and make up the papers. He told me he had been to Newport (closest town to the hotel) and talked with my client's many suppliers, employees, and former employees and knew that my client was pretty slow to pay, what waitresses he had tried to take out, and a number of other things about him. He said that when people had to get money in a hurry, it was amazing the stories they would tell. His client was ruthless if his customers didn't live up to their obligations: "He'd take the shirt off your back and your heart out." We talked about our lives, practice, and families on the long ride up and back. He had a son who was starting the practice of law and another son who was just starting in graduate school. He told the lawyer son that he had gotten him through law school but he was going to need his help in getting his brother through school and he would have to contribute money each week to that end. When the brother graduated from school, the father gave his lawyer son a bankbook with all his contributions plus interest and told him he didn't have to use it after all, also that the son never would have saved the money anyway.

In due course, we arrived at Fordham University, met Treasurer McGrath and delivered to him my check from the society in Boston. He made out a new check to the bank. We all then hopped into a taxicab to go to the local branch of the bank to have the check certified.

A horrible thought entered my mind: What if the taxi was hit and all of us were thrown onto the street, unconscious, and the police, news reporters, et cetera tried to reconstruct how we happened to be there in one cab at that time—frocked Brother McGrath with a substantial check in his possession, a "Mafia"-looking man, a New Yorker with an apparent interest in a New Hampshire hotel, a WASP New Hampshire attorney, and a Jewish attorney from Jersey City. What a story for someone! Well, we didn't get hit. The check was certified, we rode back downtown to the bank, and checks were made out to pay off the mortgage notes and the discharges were executed. We called Mr. Graham in Boston and the Registry of Deeds in New Hampshire to record the deed to the society if the title was still clear. It was, and the lawyer released his title opinion. We then distributed the checks and shook hands, signifying that the transaction was closed. After paying off the mortgages and other closing costs, the check to my client for the balance of the purchase price was pretty small, but at least he walked away with the shirt on his back.

# APPENDIX A.4

# Paradise Point

*Paradise Point is a nature preserve on Newfound Lake owned by the Audubon Society of New Hampshire. This is the story of its acquisition by the Spaulding-Potter Charitable Trusts, of which Judge McLane was its first chairman and this author its first executive secretary.*

Paradise Point is a beautiful uninhabited wooded peninsula of several hundred acres that juts into the northerly end of Newfound Lake in the town of Hebron. It forms the westerly side of a bay about a half-mile long and a quarter-mile wide at the southern, or open, end. Camp Mowglis is located on the easterly side of the bay opposite Paradise Point.

About the turn of the century, Elizabeth Holt founded Camp Mowglis for boys who came from affluent East Coast families. Many of them also attended the numerous New England preparatory schools. There are two other camps on the easterly shore of the lake. The oldest is Camp Pasquaney, founded in 1885 for boys; the other is Camp Onaway, started a few years later for girls. These camps continue today (1996), having shifted from a proprietary ownership to a nonprofit educational institution, making possible tax-deductible contributions and ensuring perpetuity. The camps are Protestant oriented and provide physical education in tennis, baseball, boating (canoes, rowboats, sailboats), swimming, diving, camping, and mountain climbing. They also have environmental, art, and drama programs. Many of these camps exhibit a high degree of family and alumni loyalty.

The McLane law firm has represented all three of these camps from time to time. Judge settled the estates of "Mr. Ned" Wilson, founder of Camp Pasquaney; Teddy Jackson, his successor; and Elizabeth Holt.

Colonel Alcott Farer Elwell was engaged to Mrs. Holt's daughter, who tragically died before the wedding. The colonel stayed on with Mrs. Holt, helping her run the camp. Upon her death in 1925, the colonel acquired the camp and ran it until he sold it in the early 1950s. One of the projects the camp undertook was the construction of hiking trails on Mt. Cardigan, many of which bear the Holt or Mowglis name. A number of trails were laid out, cut, signed, and maintained over the years by the campers. During the colonel's ownership, he became interested in Paradise Point and purchased a portion of it to protect Camp Mowglis from unwanted development on the other side of the bay. When he sold the camp and retired to the house he had acquired adjacent to the camp, he retained ownership of Paradise Point.

In the late 1950s, while summering at our family place on Newfound Lake, on several occasions I went paddling early in the morning and found myself pulled to the Paradise Point shore because of its wilderness. It has over 5,000 feet of undeveloped shorefront with many birds and other forms of wildlife. I contemplated what it would be like if it were developed with houses every hundred feet along the shore, and I shuddered. At the time I was a trustee of the Spaulding-Potter Charitable Trusts, so I asked my fellow trustees what they thought about trying to preserve this unique shoreline; their answer: "Go for it." I called on Colonel Elwell and told him of the interest of the trusts to acquire the property for perpetual protection and some limited supervised public use. He was interested in the proposition but indicated no present necessity to dispose of his property. A few years later, he contacted me and wanted to talk about selling because he had concluded he could use the money. We discussed a proposal and agreed on an appraiser to give us an impartial figure; however, the colonel died suddenly before completing the agreement. Fortunately, Mrs. Elwell had been present at our meetings and knew that the colonel wanted to sell the property at a fair price and to preserve its natural state. The transaction was concluded in 1962, when the trust acquired forty-four acres of land with over 3,000 feet of wild shorefront for $50,000.

The Audubon Society of New Hampshire was selected to manage the property, and title was conveyed to it. Subsequently a nature center was built and self-guided trails were cut through the beautiful virgin evergreen woods. The center and trails are open to the public. There is a resident summer manager. The society also conducts an active summer educational program for young people.

# APPENDIX A.5

# Sir Arthur Nicholson
# and Arisaig House

*Sir Arthur Nicholson's son, William, who was killed in World War I, was a close friend of Judge's at Magdalen College, Oxford. Judge and Elisabeth and later other members of the family called on the Nicholsons or the present owners at their beautiful summer home, Arisaig House, on the west coast of the Highlands of Scotland.*

When Judge McLane was a Rhodes scholar at Oxford in 1908 and 1909, he befriended William Nicholson, who was in his class at Magdalen College. Judge's diary refers to "Nicholson" a number of times. In England, students were referred to by their last name rather than their given name. The first reference, on October 18, 1907, states: "Went to Nicholson's room after dinner. He's the best Englishman I've met yet." There were later references to tea, coffee, and dining together. Mr. Nicholson (William's father) and Stewart, a younger brother, joined them several times. There were no references to his two sisters.

In January 1909, Judge, returning after a couple of weeks on the Continent during the Christmas holidays, spent five days—January 12–17—visiting the Nicholsons at their home at Bournemouth on the south coast. Sir Arthur Nicholson was clerk to the House of Commons for forty-five years and was responsible for guiding legislation through that body and supervising its other business. He retired in 1918. The two boys, William and Stewart, were killed during World War I. Mrs. Nicholson, never a robust person, was devastated by their deaths and passed away in 1920. The two girls, Charlotte and Helena, never married; many of the eligible bachelors their age also had been killed in the war. They continued to live with their father, Sir Arthur, spending summers in Scotland and the rest of the year in London with an occasional holiday at Bournemouth.

In 1922, Judge took Elisabeth on their first trip to Scotland as he had promised he would do once the firm received a big fee from the discovery of oil and the sale of Gil Winant's oil well in west Texas. In 1925, they returned. In September Judge wrote, "Had a lovely train ride through the lochs to Fort William and Arisaig to visit Sir Arthur Nicholson at Traigh[1]—most hospitable—beautiful spot on the coast." Judge writes: "He was father of my closest friend at Magdalen, killed early in the War." On September 9, 1925, they gathered shells, drove to Loch Morar, and walked with Sir Arthur, Charlotte, and Helena. Later Judge played a round of golf. The next day, after golf, Judge and Elisabeth and the Nicholsons drove to Arisaig House[2] and Prince Charlie's Cave[3] and had tea with Aunt Connie (Miss Ashley).

In 1932, Judge and Elisabeth took their three older children (this author, Charles, and Elisabeth) on a grand tour of Europe, starting in Scotland and continuing to England, France, and Switzerland. They drove from Fort William, Scotland, through the glens between the high and barren hills to Arisaig House to call on the two Nicholson "girls," Charlotte and Helena, who had inherited the house. Now in their fifties, they continued to summer at Arisaig House after the death of their father. In 1935 Judge and Elisabeth were in London in July. Helena visited them and they all went to the Davis Cup tennis matches.

The next visit to Arisaig House was in 1987, fifty-five years later, when Betsy and I and daughters Gigi and Katie had a wonderful two weeks visiting the Orkneys and the Islands of Harris and Lewis in the Outer Hebrides and Skye in the Inner Hebrides. We took the ferry from the Isle of Skye to Mallaig on the mainland and drove along the only road to civilization from Mallaig through the village of Arisaig. We looked for Arisaig House but did not find it, so we turned back to inquire at a local store. We needed lunch supplies and a bottle of Scotch, so engaged the proprietor in conversation about Arisaig House. Did we know it was now a hotel? No, we didn't, since we knew nothing about it for the past fifty-five years but assumed that all of the Nicholson family had died. The proprietor confirmed that assumption and indicated that on the death of Charlotte, the last of the Nicholsons, the house had passed to a friend, Ms. Beacher, who lived there until 1979, when she sold it. She now lives nearby and would be delighted to meet the McLanes, the store proprietor told us. The proprietor added that his mother used to work for the Nicholsons at Arisaig House.

Our family pushed on slowly about three miles along a beautiful winding, wooded road to a driveway and then headed down about a half mile to Ms. Beacher's house. It was stone, typically Scottish, medium size, with a gravel turnaround by the garage. We rang the doorbell, which started the dogs barking. Soon a distinguished-looking, tall, white-haired lady in her seventies, dressed in slacks, answered the door. I explained that I was from the United States, that my father had attended Oxford with the Nicholson boys in 1908 and had visited the Nicholsons at Arisaig House, and that I had been there in 1932 when my parents had taken some of their children on the grand tour of Great Britain and Europe.

Ms. Beacher was very gracious and invited us in. We were ushered into the living room with its large windows opening to the west to Lock Nan Uamh, the Sound of Arisaig, and the great headland of Ardnamurchan beyond. Madame talked about the Nicholson family history, some of which was familiar, and told of a very serious fire at Arisaig House in 1935 that all but ruined the place. But it had been restored. When Charlotte died in the late 1960s, she had left the house to Ms. Beacher and her brother, who was not interested in it so waived his rights to the property. Apparently their families had known each other for "generations," as she said. She indicated that living in a house built in 1864 with twenty-two rooms was beyond her ability. She sold it to people who converted it into a charming hotel. Thanking her for all the information and hospitality, we continued on our quest.

Just down the main road we came to a grand opening and drive with manicured grass and flowers. There was a handsome, large, simple sign reading ARISAIG HOUSE and in red letters AA with a number of stars, indicating it had the highest rating of the Automobile Association. Down the gravel drive we went, through groves of cedar trees, four to five feet in diameter, rising high above us—a fairyland.[4] In a half mile or less, we came to Arisaig House— stone, three stories high, with a U-shaped courtyard and a crushed stone parking lot with several cars.

Just as we arrived a jeep drove up behind and a white-haired gentleman in his fifties hopped out. John Smithers acknowledged that he was the owner and asked if he could help. I explained who we were, the past family friendship with the Nicholsons, and our recent visit with Ms. Beacher. He was most gracious, wanted us to meet his wife, Ruth, who came in and chatted for a few minutes in the great hall entry, which was graced by a broad staircase. He explained that they were having a staff meeting in five minutes but he would have one of his staff show us around. He offered coffee and apologized for having to leave so abruptly. A Scottish lass came and gave us a tour. The living room (thirty by sixty feet) had a high ceiling and bright lemon walls and occupied an ell with huge windows looking out over the water and distant shores. The paneled dining room, probably larger, had about ten tables seating four each. Then there were two smaller rooms, a morning room and a library, facing the sea to the west and opening onto a large stone terrace looking over lawns and gardens below. Off to one end was the bar and lounge. Upstairs were delightful bedrooms, bright and cheerful— "well appointed," as they say. We went to the third floor with a large high-ceilinged billiard room with table, et cetera. On one side was a great rack with about a dozen oars all marked with the races and the names of the crew. There was a "Nicholson, W." along with other names and "1910-Oxford" on each oar; John Smithers said he had inherited them with the house. There were numerous large paintings of Scotland, some eighteenth and nineteenth century by well-known English landscapists. There were also more contemporary bright-colored works of Scottish life, et cetera.[5]

The McLanes' conclusion: a beautiful place that we wished we'd known about it so that we could have stayed. It was obviously not inexpensive, but if you want to live like a king, go to Arisaig House. We are looking forward to our next trip to Scotland.

## Notes

1. Arisaig and Traigh are small towns on the wild west coast of Scotland looking out over the Sound of Mull to the islands of Rhum with its mountainous

peaks, the flat volcanic mesa top of Eigg, and the low profile of Muck. Farther away one can see the Cuillins of Skye to the north and the volcanic ramparts of Mull to the south. Apparently Sir Arthur owned a house in Traigh, which I have never seen.

2. Arisaig House, built in the mid-nineteenth century, came through Sir Arthur Nicholson's mother's family. At this time (1925) it belonged to his Aunt Connie (Miss Ashley); and after her death, it passed to Sir Arthur Nicholson, whose family owned it in 1932. The house is described in detail later in this section.

3. The House of Stuart provided the kings of Scotland from 1371 to 1603 and from then until 1714 the kings of Scotland and England. James II became king in 1685 and ruled as a dictator, trying to restore the Roman Catholic religion to Protestant England until he was overthrown in 1688. Parliament gave the throne to his daughter Mary and her husband, William of Orange, and thus started the House of Hanover, which still occupies the throne. James II's grandson, Charles Edward Stuart, born in 1720 in exile in Rome, was know as Bonnie Prince Charlie. In 1745, he went to Skye to rally the Highland clans, then, landed at Arisaig and hid in a nearby cave, since known as Bonnie Prince Charlie's Cave, from Skye to lead the gathering of Highland chiefs at Glenfinnan (where the tall monument now stands at the head of Loch Shiel) with a plan to overthrow the Hanoverian German-speaking king of England and restore the throne to the Stuarts. After some initial successes, he was routed at the Battle of Culloden Moor and fled to the Hebrides, where Flora MacDonald helped him cross the Minsch to Skye to escape the British soldiers. He returned to the mainland at Arisaig and was picked up by a French vessel sent to get him and taken to the Continent, where he lived out his life unknown and in poverty. He died in 1788.

4. The west coast of Scotland, although far north of the latitude of the United States, is warmed by the Gulf Stream in its dying course.

5. As the result of my glowing report about Arisaig House, Malcolm and Susan McLane, who had chartered a small powerboat to sail the Sound of Mull and adjacent areas, stopped for a delightful lunch and were equally impressed.

# APPENDIX B
## *The McLane Family*

# APPENDIX B.1

# The Bancroft Family

*The Bancroft family loomed large in Judge's life. Judge married Elisabeth Bancroft. After his marriage, the Bancroft family became an important client. The Bancroft descendants, the Shiverick and McLane families, are held together by their mutual ownership and love for Pasquaney, the Bancroft summer home.*

The McLane family, prominent in Milford and the state, and the Bancroft family, prominent in Concord and the state, were joined by the marriage of Judge McLane and Elisabeth Bancroft on June 12, 1915, at Pasquaney Lodge, the Bancrofts' summer home on Newfound Lake.

Elisabeth's grandfather was Jesse Parker Bancroft. He was born in Gardner, Massachusetts, on April 17, 1815, one of nine children born to Jonathan Bancroft and Betsy Parker. Jesse graduated from Dartmouth College in 1841, Phi Beta Kappa, at the age of twenty-six. He graduated from the Dartmouth Medical School in 1845 (apparently then a four-year school),[1] then he went to St. Johnsbury, Vermont, where he was a physician to the Fairbanks family, whose company made scales that were shipped all over the world. While in St. Johnsbury, Jesse married Elisabeth Speare of Hanover (had they met while he was a medical school student?) and had a son, Charles Parker Bancroft, born on January 11, 1852. They adopted (so Elisabeth Bancroft McLane thought) a girl, Corisand, born in June 1856.

About 1866 Jesse moved to Concord, New Hampshire, to become the superintendent of the new New Hampshire Insane Asylum, where he remained until 1882 when he retired. He was succeeded by his son, Charles. Jesse bought the house in Concord across Pleasant Street from the hospital where he died in 1891 at the age of seventy-six. Charles lived in the same house after his retirement in about 1917.

When he assumed the superintendency, Jesse inherited the results of a national reform movement that in the 1830s and '40s advocated separate medical institutions for the mentally ill and criminals. The New Hampshire Insane Asylum was established in the late 1830s in Concord. Jesse was a lecturer on mental illness at the Dartmouth Medical School from 1878 to 1882 and a professor there after his retirement from 1882 to 1886.

A family story says that shortly after the discovery of gold in California in 1849 and the discovery of silver in Colorado in the early 1850s, a fast-talking stock salesman approached Jesse, painting golden pictures of the West and the

fortunes that lurked in the mountains. These could be acquired only by investing in some of the superior mining stocks that only he was fortunate enough
to be able to offer. The temptation was too much and Jesse invested—how
much or how frequently we do not know. Nothing happened; no dividends
were paid, but encouraging letters came less and less frequently. Then there
were gaps of silence when the stocks were forgotten. However, once in a while,
say every ten years, a letter would announce that the company had been
acquired by another corporation and twice as many shares in the new company
would be forwarded upon receipt of the original shares, all of which did occur.
But there still were no dividends nor was the stock salable. After Jesse died his
stock descended to his two children, Charles and "Aunt Corrie," who had married a psychiatrist who was a friend of her brother's. According to the story,
Aunt Corrie sold her stock and lived modestly on the state salary of her husband, but Charles hung on to his stock. In the early 1900s, the company was
purchased in exchange for a substantial number of shares of Anaconda Copper
stock, then one of the largest and most successful copper companies. Suddenly,
handsome dividends were paid and the money started to roll in. The income
from these investments enabled Dr. Bancroft to educate his three daughters in
prep school and college. In 1909 he was also able to purchase Pasquaney
Lodge on Newfound Lake, which he presented to his wife on the occasion of
their twenty-fifth wedding anniversary. Dividends paid for many additions and
improvements in later years. During his retirement years, Dr. and
Mrs. Bancroft traveled extensively to Alaska and the West. After Dr. Bancroft
died in 1923 at the age of seventy-one, Gaga Bancroft went on an around-the-
world cruise with her sister to visit the former's daughter, Miriam, in China
and Japan. Dr. Bancroft's probate estate in 1923 disclosed stocks and bonds of
over $350,000, including $75,000 of Anaconda Copper stock, and much
smaller amounts of other mining companies: Inspiration Consolidated Copper
Company, Calumet & Hecla Mining Company, Mayflower–Old Colony
Copper Company, Naumkeag Copper Company (his one share was worth
twenty-five cents), Winona Copper Company, Copper Range Company, and
St. Mary's Mineral Range. There was a substantial amount of railroad stocks—
American Locomotive Company (which purchased the Manchester
Locomotive Works in the early 1900s) and Pullman; bank stocks were well
represented along with a few manufacturing and oil stocks. It was an excellent
portfolio and a substantial estate for those days.

As a young boy growing up in Concord at the asylum in the 1860s, when
the great West was the talk of the town, Charles used to climb the hill where
the Brown Building now sits, look out over the flat fields by Clinton Street to
the Dunbarton Hills beyond, and conjure up a hike across the "Great Plains"
to the "Rocky Mountains." About the age of ten, he wrote a delightful journal
of his trips to Turkey Pond, west of Concord, and the building of a cabin on
the shore.[2] Some forty years later, he and his daughter, Elisabeth, attempted to
find the cabin. He was a romantic, loved nature, and was moved by the then-
popular scientific spirit of inquiry. He collected and mounted birds found in

the Concord area. The family still has the original glass case with the birds, which resides on the porch at Pasquaney Lodge in the summers. Included in his collection was a passenger pigeon, now extinct, which was given to the Audubon Society of New Hampshire. When this author was a child, about 1920, "Grampa" used to tell wonderful stories of the activities and conversations of fish in the lake and streams—stories still relished. A couple of examples: The mother and daddy fish would talk to their little fish about where to find food under stones or under the banks of brooks, but they always had to be on the watch for those big bad fish that loved to eat little fish. Sometimes the little boy fish would not be very kind to their little sister fish, and the parents would have to send them behind a big rock to stay quietly until they were ready to be considerate of others. The parents admonished their children always to be wary of a worm wriggling in the water, because it might be on a hook trying to catch the little fish. They should look carefully for a piece of the hook sticking out and also be sure that the worm was alive and moving about on its own and not connected to a string being pulled up and down.

Charles went to Phillips Andover Academy; Harvard College, class of 1874; and Harvard Medical School, class of 1878. He practiced at the Boston City Hospital before taking a job at the New Hampshire Insane Asylum in the early 1880s. It is probable that while he was in Boston, he met Susan Cushing Wood, whom he married on August 6, 1884.

Susan's father, Bartholomew Wood, was born in Newburyport, Massachusetts, in May 1813. Wood graduated from Dartmouth, at age twenty-eight, with Jesse Parker Bancroft in the class of 1841. He was a teacher in the public schools of the Newtons and resided in Newton Center, where he died in November 1888 at the age of seventy-five. Bartholomew's ancestors were French Huguenot sailors (Dubois) who anglicized their name to Wood when they arrived in the United States. Bartholomew married Sarah Burke, with whom he had two children, William and Sarah (Rand). After Sarah Burke's death in 1852, he married her younger sister, Jennette Burke, then thirty-four, by whom he had three children: Moriah (Aunt Minnie), Allen (who died at age nine), and Susan, born in March 1860.

Dr. Bancroft was a relaxed, laid-back humanist with a sense of humor, a love of music (opera), and a desire to help people. His humanistic medical philosophy about the insane asylum was that the human body is a very resilient mechanism about which little is known. When mental problems develop from external pressures, if the patient can be removed from the stress and placed in an environment where the basics of food, shelter, and sympathetic care are provided, there is a 60 to 70 percent chance that the patient will have a voluntary remission. The statistics bear out this theory. Above all, patients were to be treated with respect and compassion. The New Hampshire Insane Asylum became the New Hampshire State Hospital, then the New Hampshire Hospital. It was one of the first New England hospitals to have a school of nursing with a psychiatric specialty.

Two things illustrate Dr. Bancroft's personality. At their home in Concord on the state hospital grounds, a roast chicken dinner on Sunday was the usual fare. Mrs. Bancroft sat at one end of the formal table and the doctor at the other. The three girls were seated on the sides. In the center of the table, there was usually a large vase of flowers from the hospital greenhouse, which obscured Dr. Bancroft from his wife's vision. When the roast chicken was brought in, Dr. Bancroft would stand up, take the knife and the steel sharpener, and with some theatrical motions sharpen the knife to the adoring attention of the three girls. Then he would carefully lay down the sharpener steel and take the knife, hold it in the air, then, turning it over so the blade was pointing away from him, he would plunge the handle into his breast and then flop into the chair as though mortally wounded. The girls would shriek with delight at this familiar routine. Mrs. Bancroft, without any appreciation for the humor, would ask in a stern voice, "Charles, what *are* you doing?"

The other incident involved Elisabeth's close friend Speck Flad (later Deane), a college classmate who frequently visited the Bancrofts at the lake in the summer or in Concord at other times. Speck adored Dr. Bancroft and called him "Dr. Cutie." Their affection for each other was mutual. Speck had pigtails and Dr. Cutie had a goatee. Speck used to correspond from college and signed the envelope of the letter with the letters *OPMPTETPYG*, which Dr. Cutie eventually found out stood for "one pull my pigtail equals two pulls your goatee."

Over time, mental institutions became colossal. Then, fortunately, in the 1960s and '70s pharmaceuticals for the management of psychiatric problems were developed, with remarkable success. Institutions were emptied and the patients were treated locally as outpatients. The New Hampshire Hospital declined from a patient population of over 2,500 in the 1950s to around 500 in the 1980s. Institutionalization is no longer in vogue. Dr. Bancroft wrote extensively for medical journals and was active in medical, particularly psychiatric, organizations in New Hampshire and the rest of New England. He was elected a director of the Mechanics National Bank in Concord in 1907[3] and was a trustee of the New Hampshire Savings Bank and president of the New Hampshire State Board of Charities and Corrections. He was a member of a number of organizations, including the New Hampshire Historical Society and the New Hampshire Society for the Preservation of Forests, of which his grandson Malcolm was president in 1991. After his retirement as superintendent of the New Hampshire State Hospital, in 1921, Dr. Bancroft was appointed Consultant in Mental Hygiene at Dartmouth College, one of the first, if not the first, such position in a college. He greatly enjoyed his work with the students. He was in Hanover on a consultancy in December 1923 when he suffered a stroke from which he died the following day.

In 1889, Charles Bancroft, with a group of men including his brother-in-law, Avery Rand of Boston, and Henry Hollis of Concord,[4] went by train to Plymouth, then by horse-drawn "stage" to North Woodstock, and hiked up the East Branch of the Pemigewasset into what is now known as the Pemi Wilderness, then all virgin forest, to North Fork Junction, as it was later called.

*Dr. Charles P. Bancroft*, in what appears to be a Ford Model T car at the lake about 1910. Credit: Dartmouth College Library.

From there, they bushwhacked up Mt. Carrigain and returned via Carrigain Notch and the Sawyer River to the railroad through Crawford Notch.[5]

In July and August 1897, Dr. and Mrs. Bancroft, ages forty-five and thirty-seven respectively, made a two-week bicycle trip to Mt. Desert, Maine. Dr. Bancroft wrote a delightful journal of the trip. They traveled by train to the coast, then biked the shore route through Portland, Brunswick, Bath, Rockland, Rockport, Camden, Belfast, Castine, Brooklin, Blue Hill, Ellsworth, Bar Harbor, North East and South West Harbors, Bass Harbor, Sommesville, Grindstone Neck, and Sorrento. They had good days, fog, and rain but they averaged about twenty-five miles a day, with no gears. They ate lunches and spent the nights at little inns along the way. They occasionally took boats across rivers and bays. They were exhilarated by the beautiful scenery of the sea, islands, hills, and forests. They found the food good and the people hospitable. I only knew them twenty-five years later when they were in their sixties and seventies. It is hard for me to imagine them making the trip.

In the early 1900s, Dr. and Mrs. Bancroft, usually alone, often went on weekend trips to get away from the state hospital and their children (they lived in the superintendent's quarters in the main administration building). They frequently took the train to Franklin, changing for the short branch run to Bristol, the end of the line, where they had made arrangements for a horse and buggy. Driving around Newfound Lake, along the east side they passed an intriguing house built on a rocky ledge just above the water with a beautiful view northwest up the lake to the town of Hebron and the receding hills beyond. There were two square stone posts at the entrance driveway. If the chain joined them, the Bancrofts knew the owners were not there, so they would hitch old "Dobbin" to the chain and walk down to the porch to enjoy what they considered to be the best view in the mountains. Unbeknownst to his wife, the doctor negotiated with Ms. Elizabeth Wellington of New York. Her father, Aaron, recently deceased, had acquired the property and built the house there about twenty years before. Dr. Bancroft purchased it and presented the deed to Susan Bancroft on their twenty-fifth wedding anniversary in 1909. "Pasquaney Lodge," as it is known, remains in the family and is now loved and enjoyed by the fifth generation.

Judge and Elisabeth were married at Pasquaney Lodge in 1915. One time they went birding when the warblers were in migration in the spring and saw a chestnut-sided warbler. Wishing to impress his father-in-law, Judge looked in the bird book and discovered that the Latin, or scientific name, was *Dendroica pensylvanica*. He then proceeded to describe to the doctor their trip and told about seeing the "*Dendroica pensylvanica*." The doctor responded, without a blink, "Isn't that yellow cap and little streak of brown on the wings of the chestnut-sided warbler beautiful?" Judge never tried to impress his father-in-law again.

Susan Bancroft, or "Gaga" to her grandchildren, was brought up in the Calvinistic Congregational Church in Newton Center, where hard work and worship of the Lord were the motivations of life. She never relinquished these attributes and brought them to Pasquaney. Particularly on Sunday, life was harsh for the young: no funny papers from the Sunday paper—they were frivolous, as was loud, syncopated jazz music on the Sabbath; only hymns were suitable. Judge loved tennis and was very disappointed when he couldn't play on Sunday. We children could row or canoe, but use of the noisy outboard was forbidden. Walking and communing with nature were appropriate, but more violent activities such as climbing a mountain or riding bicycles for pleasure were discouraged. In Gaga's childhood in Massachusetts, the family never celebrated Christmas, because it was a papal holy day and anything to do with the Catholic Church was despised. She had a low opinion of blacks, whom she felt were inferior to whites, and also of the Irish, because they were Catholic. For a people who espoused democracy and equality of opportunity, their personal level of intolerance of race and religion was astonishing.

Susan Bancroft was a doer. She was an ardent and vocal feminist who fought for women's suffrage. She worked for years for the New Hampshire Memorial Hospital for Women and Children in Concord, later merged into the Margaret Pillsbury Hospital. She supported a separate institution for the mentally retarded and was on the original board of trustees of the Laconia State School when it was established in 1900. She served on the Concord School Board for nine years. She was a member of the Stratford Club, which was dedicated to reading aloud the works of William Shakespeare.[6] She was on the boards of a number of social welfare organizations. But she had no aesthetic sense. She was not fond of music or the arts, both of which she considered to be frivolous. Her house was decorated with horrible Victorian framed

*Susan Cushing Bancroft and her three daughters,* about 1900, from left to right, Jennette, Susan, Elisabeth, and Miriam. Credit: Dartmouth College Library.

photographs of ancient places and steel engravings of moralistic biblical scenes. She managed Pasquaney effectively for her daughters Jennette and Elisabeth and their eight children (with frequent guests), who spent most of the summers in the 1920s and 1930s there. Fortunately she had abundant domestic help to run the place. She was always the dominant person, assuming command and issuing rules that included punctuality at meals and neatness around the house.

Charles Parker Bancroft and Susan Cushing Wood had four children. Their first born, Charles Parker, Jr., died in his first year. Then they had three girls: Jennette (Shiverick, Tripp, 1888–1988), Elisabeth (McLane, 1891–1983), and Miriam (Jenkins, 1894–1928). Charles died in December of 1923 at the age of seventy-one; and Susan in May of 1948, aged eighty-seven.

Jennette, known later as "Jane," went to Vassar, class of 1911. She had house parties at Pasquaney and was squired there by Asa Shiverick in 1912 before their wedding. Asa, a successful businessman, was head of the Higbee Company of Cleveland, Ohio, a large and prominent department store. Many years after Asa's death, Jane, in her seventies, married Chester Tripp, a widower of Chicago, a retired businessman who, like Jane, loved to travel and was an art connoisseur. They had a number of happy years before Chester passed away.

On the death of her mother in 1948, Jane acquired an undivided half interest in Pasquaney. Jane and Asa had three children, Jane, Asa, Jr., and Charles. Jane married John Hall, a lawyer in Choate, Hall & Stewart in Boston; they live in Brookline, Massachusetts. Their five children are now all married and scattered but love the lake in the summers. Asa, Jr. married Patricia Coombs of New Canaan, Connecticut; they live in Chagrin Falls, Ohio. They and their five married children are likewise frequent summer visitors to Pasquaney. Charles, while a student at Harvard, was killed in a mountain-climbing accident in the Canadian Rockies.

Elisabeth attended Dana Hall in Massachusetts and graduated from Smith College with the class of 1914. She was wooed at Pasquaney by Judge at the time of Jennette's wedding in 1912. Judge and Elisabeth were married at Pasquaney on June 12, 1915. Elisabeth likewise acquired a half interest in Pasquaney on the death of her mother in 1948. Judge and Elisabeth had five children: John, Jr. (this author), Charles, Elisabeth (Lilla), Malcolm, and Mary.

I graduated from Dartmouth College and Harvard Law School and am a lawyer in the McLane law firm. I live in Manchester. My first wife was Blanche Marshall, with whom I had five children, who produced eleven grandchildren and two great-grandchildren (as of 1996). My second wife, Betsy Deane (Appendix A.2, The H. Towner Deane Family), bore four children, who produced two grandchildren.

Charles, a graduate of Dartmouth College and Columbia University, is now retired from teaching at Dartmouth, where he was a member of the government department, specializing in Russia. He is also an author of books on Maine islands. He married Carol Evarts of New York, the daughter of a classmate of Judge. They had six children. Charles and Carol divide their time between Hanover and Brooklin on the Maine coast.

Elisabeth McLane-Bradley (Lilla) attended Smith College and graduated from the University of Wisconsin, lives in Hanover in a retirement community, having divorced her husband, David Bradley. She has been active in fundraising activities. She has her own cottage on property adjacent to Pasquaney Lodge, which she enjoys with her six grown children.

Malcolm, who graduated from Dartmouth, attended Oxford as a Rhodes scholar, and graduated from Harvard Law School, is an attorney in Concord with the firm of Orr & Reno. He married Susan Neidlinger of Hanover. Both have been active in politics. They have five children and many grandchildren. They usually spend the greater part of July at Pasquaney.

Mary, a Smith College graduate and a teacher turned artist, has spent most of her professional career in the Newton, Massachusetts, area. She also had her own cottage at Pasquaney, adjacent to Lilla's, until she sold it in 1994.

After Judge's death in 1969, Elisabeth, then seventy-eight, continued to live in the house on Union Street. While Judge was alive, she had devoted most of

*Elisabeth*, or "Ibus" to all her
grandchildren, circa 1970.

her time to him, entertaining friends only at home with Judge; she did spend
one night a week in Boston catching up on sleep. However, after his death she
was more active with some of her friends, going to the symphony in Boston or
on short trips. In July 1969, she and Eva Hill drove to Brooklin, Maine, to make
the annual visit with Charles' family. In December, she flew to Geneva with
Kristin and Eben, met Charles, and went to Verbier for ten days of skiing.

In the spring of 1970, Elisabeth traveled to Africa with Lois Booth on a
bird-watching safari, visiting national parks in the Nairobi, Kenya, area. I
remember her describing their stay for a day or so in "Tree Tops," by a water
hole and watching the animals feeding. On the way home, she stopped in
Kensington in London, for a fortnight with Charles and his family. They all
went to Ireland for a week before Elisabeth flew home alone. She and Eva visited Charles in Vermont during the fall and made the annual Christmas trip to
Hanover before Charles and his family left for Garrison, New York, to have
Christmas with the Evarts. Elisabeth invited Harriet Mansfield and others to
the lake a number of times; she had built a little guest house next to the cottage she built for Judge. She went on a Maupintour trip with Ellen Faulkner
of Keene following the Lewis and Clark trail up the Missouri River from St.

Louis to Montana. Part of the trip was by train and bus and part by boat on the Missouri in Montana.

In May 1971, the family celebrated Elisabeth's eightieth birthday at Pasquaney with all of her children and a slew of grandchildren. Her niece Jane Hall and husband, John, also came. One of the highlights was the showing of ski movies of the 1930s, which produced all kinds of laughter from the styles of skiing as well as the clothes. Thanksgiving and Christmas were held in Manchester as usual.

In March 1972, Carol McLane flew with her mother to England a day ahead of Charles and Ibus. They had a spate of theater in London, then drove to Oxford and the Cotswolds and returned to London. In the summer of 1972, Ibus, with granddaughter Tii McLane, accompanied my family on a trip known as "Wagons Ho." The group traveled on the old Smoky Hill trail in west central Kansas, riding about twenty miles a day in covered wagons pulled by mules and horses. We ate meals outdoors cooked on campfires and slept in the wagons. People rotated between walking and riding in the wagons or on horseback. The wagons were pulled into a circle for protection at night; we suffered an "Indian attack" and a plains thunderstorm. In the evenings the wonderful Kansas cowboys and cowgirls provided entertainment with stories, songs, and guitars. Elisabeth celebrated Christmas in Hanover with Lilla and her family.

In February 1973, Charles, Carol, Malcolm, and Susan had dinner with Elisabeth in Manchester at which they read from Judge's diary, specifically his entries about the Portsmouth Russian-Japanese conference in 1905. Later, in March, Elisabeth accompanied Charles and Carol on a motor trip to Mystic, Garrison (Carol's family), Philadelphia, the Wyeth Museum in Chadd's Ford, Williamsburg, Charlottesville, the Skyline Drive (in a snow storm), Gettysburg, and back to Garrison and home. In May, Elisabeth had a birthday party in Hanover—Bobby Emerson (Eva's grandson) drove her. She was rapidly losing her ability to drive and forgot she wasn't supposed to drive. She failed to renew her license on her birthday. We had to hide her keys! By October Bobby was her live-in driver and man about the house. She got pretty upset about her inability to drive and got mad at everyone. Lilla threatened to call the police. Ultimately Elisabeth accepted the restriction. Ibus continued to ski around the fields into her eighties.

In 1974, Charles and Carol organized a series of events for Ibus, which took her to Hanover, with Bobby driving, every month for concerts or other activities, a pattern that continued for several years. Ibus was beginning to be forgetful. Christmas was a bit chaotic; she couldn't wrap presents because she forgot who they were for.

In 1975, Susan McLane, then serving in the legislature, took Ibus with her to the graduation exercises at St. Mary's-in-the-Mountains, where Susan gave the address to the graduating class. On the long drive home, Ibus asked about every ten minutes, "And what was your best bill for this session, Susan?" As Susan says, "She knew the right question to ask, but the answer couldn't stay in her brain."

Elisabeth's life continued on a fairly stable level for several years. With Eva's and Bobby's help, she entertained for lunch, tea, or dinner.[7] I lived with my family on the adjacent property separated by woods and fields. We were frequent visitors for short stops. Ibus had visits at least once a week from other family members. Charles noted in his diary in 1977: "No significant change—just steady deterioration of memory—health good." In 1979 Charles commented that her speech seemed slurred and she spoke in incomplete sentences. In October she fell in the driveway and fractured her hip, which required several days in the hospital after surgery. Nurses were required around the clock for a while after her return, but in a month she was down to one professional nurse, Bobby, and one L.P.N. Eva came most every day to cook and be a friend. Ibus' offspring met and decided to have her stay at home as long as possible. She probably had numerous small strokes that gradually deprived her of her speech and slowed up her ability to get around on her own.

By the fall of 1981, Ibus required professional nurses around the clock and was pretty much confined to the house. A year later, the decision was made to move her to a nursing home where Eva and her favorite nurse, Lynn, could help her. The household furniture and furnishings were divided among the family, and the house and Three Acres were sold after the "last" Thanksgiving. Elisabeth died on April 8, 1983, in her ninety-first year.

Charles and Susan Bancroft's third daughter, Miriam, studied to be a nurse at the Peter Bent Brigham Hospital in Boston. She worked at the Exeter Hospital and in 1922 went to China to work in a missionary hospital. She returned home in the spring of 1924 after the death of her father and went back to China in the fall accompanied by her mother, who arrived back in New Hampshire on December 31, 1924. In the summer of 1926, Miriam was married to Walter Jenkins in Japan in a ceremony that was attended by her mother and her mother's sister, Sarah Rand. Walter Jenkins was a purchaser of wood oil nuts (used in the manufacture of paints before the use of petrochemicals) in the interior of China for the Standard Oil Company. They lived far up the Yangtze River, above the spectacular gorges, in the city of Wahnsien. Miriam and Walter returned to Pasquaney in the summer of 1927, bringing with them a model junk and beautiful Chinese costumes. Miriam loved the life there and the Chinese people. Walter could only stay about a month but Miriam remained until mid-November.

Every so often an event occurs that reminds us how small the world is. When Walter and Miriam lived in Wahnsien, there were very few Westerners. All of them lived in a compound for foreigners on a bluff overlooking the city and the river. There was much political unrest in undeveloped China after World War I. The Yangtze River was declared an international waterway and was patrolled by gunboats of Great Britain, France, and the United States. The infrequent visits of officers and crew from the gunboats were the occasion for social festivities and exchange of information. The naval officers were invited to feasts at the compound, and they reciprocated by providing dinners on their ships. On one such occasion when the gunboat USS *Palos* visited, Miriam sat next to commanding officer Cutts. As was customary, the conversation turned to their respective homes in the States. Miriam said she came from New England, and the captain responded likewise. On further inquiry they discovered they both had lived in New Hampshire, Miriam from Concord and the captain from Milford. Miriam wondered if by any chance he ever knew her brother-in-law, John McLane, also of Milford. "Know him?" responded the captain, practically shouting. "Judge and I grew up together—kindergarten, grade school, and into high school, where we played baseball together. Judge went on to prep school and we both went to Dartmouth for two years when I transferred to the [naval] Academy—what a coincidence!"

Miriam wrote home about witnessing an attack on the city by the Communist boats of Chiang Kai-shek as they descended the river from Chungking in the interior in 1927 to overthrow the government of China. Miriam died in China in 1928 from a viral infection while pregnant. Walter Jenkins returned to Concord with many of Miriam's things and spent Thanksgiving 1928 with Elisabeth and the family in Manchester.

Subsequently Walter married Louise Kimball, daughter of Dr. George Morrill Kimball, a graduate of Phillips Andover, Yale, and Harvard Medical School. Kimball practiced in Concord for thirteen years before becoming involved in banking, insurance, and manufacturing corporations. Louise and Walter lived in the George Kimball mansion on North Main Street in Concord; after their deaths, and upon the death of their daughter, Carolyn, on April 28, 1981, the mansion became the "Kimball-Jenkins House." A charitable trust has preserved the house for the benefit of the public. The stately Victorian structure appears as it was when the Jenkinses lived in it, even to the extent of displaying pictures of China. One picture shows Walter's first wife, Miriam, with her dog, which was buried with her, and objets d'art that Walter brought back from China. When Walter returned to the United States after Miriam's death, he brought back a book of pictures of Miriam and their house and life in China. He assembled the book, intending to give it to his mother-in-law, Mrs. Bancroft. However, he became so emotionally attached to it that he could not bring himself to part with it, so he kept it himself. His daughter, Carolyn, on cleaning the attic nearly fifty years after the death of her parents, found it and presented it to her attorney, Malcolm McLane, Miriam's nephew. She also found all of Miriam's wedding silver, monogrammed with MB, which had been stored in the attic after the marriage of Walter and her mother. She likewise presented the silver to Malcolm. It is now the silverware that the family uses at the lake.

Upon the death of their mother, Susan C. Bancroft, "Aunt Jane" and Elisabeth inherited Pasquaney, which they subsequently gave to their progeny, most of whom have in turn transferred it to the next generation. The property thus continues to be used by many of the family. The spectacular views, the rocky ledges, the delicious water, the tall pines, the abundant wildlife of birds, duck, and mink, the haunting call of the loon, the 1,500 feet of shorefront—all these make it an ideal vacation spot that all look forward to visiting again and again for themselves and future generations.

# Notes

1. For a number of years the Dartmouth Medical School was a two-year school providing a solid basic medical training, particularly in anatomy. The students then went to a metropolitan school of their choice, where more specialties were offered and more patients with a greater variety of problems could be seen in an urban setting. About 1980, the four-year school was revived.

2. Elisabeth McLane had these journals duplicated in the 1960s and distributed copies to his descendants.

3. Jesse Parker Bancroft owned shares of the Mechanics National Bank and received dividend #1 and the following ones; his widow continued to own the shares, which on her death descended to Charles and then to his widow, Susan. This author received those shares as a part of a legacy from her and continues to hold them, now through merger, The Bank of New Hampshire.

4. Appendix B.2, Henry French Hollis.

5. Charles Parker Bancroft, "The Pemigewasset Wilderness in 1889–Log of a Tramp Camping Expedition to the Sources of the South Fork of the East Branch of the Pemigewasset River–1889," *Appalachia* (November 1935), pp. 299–317, published by the Appalachian Mountain Club, Boston, Mass.

6. Gaga invited the Stratford Club for day outings at the lake from time to time.

7. Susan McLane recalls that Ibus' legacy to her was the perfect dinner parties with such memorable dishes as Halibut-à-la-Ritz, cheese soufflé, Capon à la Papa Lebonnard, cream puffs, borscht, hot rolls, huge napkins, and finger bowls. Although Eva cooked in the end, the ideas and the originality were all Ibus'.

# Henry French Hollis

## August 30, 1869–July 7, 1949

*Henry Hollis was a social friend of the Bancrofts, a political opponent of Governor McLane, a U.S. senator, a wine connoisseur, and a friend of Judge and Elisabeth.*

Henry F. Hollis, native of Concord, a U.S. senator and expatriate to France, was a charismatic individual.

His father, Abijah Hollis, a graduate of the Harvard Law School, fought in the Civil War, married the sister of sculptor Daniel Chester French, moved to Concord in 1865, and was engaged for over thirty years in the granite business. He loved the outdoors and forestry. Of his six children, two were prominent lawyers in Concord, namely, Henry F., born in 1869, and Allen, born in 1871.

Allen went to the Concord public schools and Harvard Law School, entered the New Hampshire Bar in 1893, and became a public utilities lawyer, owner, and manager. His son, Franklin, born in 1904, followed in the steps of his father. He was a member of the Sulloway law firm, representing the Public Service Company of New Hampshire for many years, as well as the New England Telephone Company and a number of other utilities.

Henry F. Hollis, after attending Concord schools, graduated magna cum laude from Harvard College in 1892. He studied at Harvard Law School and in Concord law offices and was admitted to the bar in 1893. He later formed the firm of Hollis & Murchie (Robert and Alexander) and won some of the largest plaintiff's verdicts on record. He was much in demand as a public speaker. In the early days of his practice he never liked having a partner because he couldn't just close the office when he wanted to go mountain climbing. The unidentified writer of his obituary in 1949 recalls being on the summit of Mt. Washington in 1909 watching a lone climber with a heavy pack slowly wending his way up to the top where, with a smile, he threw down the pack and greeted the other. The hiker was Henry Hollis, who was off for ten days "afoot in the mountains." In 1889 Henry Hollis joined a trip into the virgin Pemigewasset wilderness to climb Mt. Carrigain with Dr. Charles Bancroft (father of Elisabeth B. McLane, see Appendix B.1, The Bancroft Family) and Dr. Bancroft's brother-in-law, Avery Rand of Newton, Massachusetts.[1] Among his other athletic accomplishments was golf, at which he excelled. Hollis and his brother canoed from Concord to Salisbury, traveling up the Merrimack, Contoocook, and Blackwater Rivers to visit friends.

Hollis was an active Democrat, a warm supporter of William Jennings Bryan in the 1890s, a candidate for Congress in 1900, chair of the state committee in 1902, and an unsuccessful candidate for governor in 1902 and 1904 (against John McLane). In 1905 during Governor McLane's term, Hollis represented the New York Jockey Club, a group of New York financiers who successfully backed legislation to authorize the establishment of Rockingham Racetrack ostensibly only for the purpose of improving the breeding of horses because betting was forbidden. When $1 million of sophisticated gambling equipment arrived from New York, the New Hampshire legislators realized that they had been duped. The true nature of the New York City backers was revealed. The New Hampshire authorities permitted only one race to be run and succeeded in getting the track closed. It reopened twenty years later with the McLane firm playing an important role.

Henry Hollis was finally successful in gaining public office. In 1913 on the forty-third ballot he was elected U.S. senator by the legislature.[2] He held the position for one term until 1919, when he moved to Paris and opened a law practice. He represented General Electric Company and several large utilities. He settled there for the rest of his life.

Hollis was married in 1893 and had two children. So the story goes, in about 1919 he abandoned his wife (reputed to have been a terror) and children, fled to Paris, and there met, as previously arranged, his childhood sweetheart, Anne Hobbs,[3] who, it is said, had faithfully waited for him. Family lore has it that Henry was friendly with the king of Belgium, who assisted in obtaining a Belgian divorce so that Henry and Anne could be married. In New Hampshire legal proceedings, his first wife fought to prevent legal separation. However, Henry, being a good lawyer, never was sure of the validity of his late marriage and therefore never returned to the States.

Henry Hollis was a very charming, urbane, cosmopolitan conversationalist, well informed and read, with many friends from all over the United States as the result of his term in the U.S. Senate. He and Anne loved to entertain. Dinners at their home were events never to be forgotten, according to Judge, who dined there several times with Elisabeth, and according to Charles and Malcolm McLane, who separately were entertained during or immediately after the war. There were interesting guests, stimulating conversation, delicious French food, and exceptional wines. Henry was a true gourmet and traveled throughout the French vineyards at harvest time tasting the wines and buying cases of those he considered to have potential. At dinners, he would serve in small liqueur glasses two or three kinds of wine for each course and would expound on the bouquet, sweetness, or dryness of each wine and the history of each vineyard. It was only natural that many of his guests would ask him to select wines for them and leave a check with him for a couple of hundred dollars to spend as he saw fit for them. One of the secretaries in his law office handled the details. It wasn't so bad to do this for his friends, but then they told their friends about the fabulous Henry Hollis who then wrote asking for the same accommodation. It mushroomed into a big business, and Hollis became businesslike, charging a commission and having labels attached to all bottles reading "Selected By Henry F. Hollis, Paris." I well remember cases of wines in our cellar with that label. (Judge notes in his diary on January 22, 1949, going to Boston: "Got Hollis wine and brought it home.") Hollis' friends naturally ate in the best of restaurants. They persuaded proprietors to send their wine lists for Henry Hollis' comments. They urged restaurant owners to buy quality wines at a good price through Hollis. The fame of Henry Hollis spread far and wide.

On one occasion, as my father told the story, Hollis was invited to an elegant formal dinner at a friend's house in Paris. Sitting down at the table, his dinner partner, previously unknown to him, exclaimed on seeing his place card, "You're not *THE* Mr. Henry Hollis?" Hollis admitted that indeed was his name but disclaimed any implication of being famous. His partner stated she had heard that he knew so much about wines that he could identify a wine from a sip or sometimes simply from the aroma. He responded that if one were quite familiar with wines, such an identification was not beyond the realm of possibility. This seemed utterly unbelievable, his lady friend exclaimed. She asked if he would mind if she requested their hostess to try an experiment by having the five or six wines that they would be having for dinner brought out, covered, and allow Mr. Hollis the opportunity of trying to identify each. That was quite agreeable with both the hostess and Mr. Hollis. Hollis said he probably couldn't pick all the wines correctly, but he ought to come fairly close. So the wine steward brought out the wines carefully wrapped in a napkin, presented them to the hostess for her approval, then poured Hollis a small glass, which he dutifully swirled around to be able to judge its color and density. Then he sniffed and inhaled the aroma, stating that it obviously was a Burgundy or a Bordeaux, that it was from grapes grown on a sunny south slope because of its dryness, that it must be a Château Close or a Château Evigny, et cetera, but he really couldn't tell the vintage year without taking a sip, which he did. "Ah, it's not one of the great vintages; therefore, it was not a 1919 or 1921, nor could it be a 1925 or 1926, which were very dry years." Hollis went on and eliminated several more years, finally concluding, "It is very difficult to do what you have asked me to do, and I'm afraid I'm going to have to guess a little, but I will say that this wine is a Château Close, 1924," whereupon the waiter unwrapped the bottle and showed it around the table. The dinner guests all "oohed" and "aahed" as they saw that Mr. Hollis was exactly correct. He repeated the performance for the other wines. Mr. Hollis, in discussing this with my father at a later date, stated that the story was told frequently in many places as though that were the end of it. Nobody added that Mr. Hollis made a statement at the dinner party at the end of the experiment that the hostess had asked him to select the wines for the dinner!

## Notes

1. Dr. Bancroft wrote a journal of the trip that was subsequently published in *Appalachia*. See Appendix B.1, footnote 5.

2. This was the last election of a U.S. senator by the state legislature; federal legislation subsequently mandated the direct election of senators.

3. A member of the White family for whom White's Park in Concord is named.

# The Treaty of Portsmouth

*Governor McLane was the host of the 1905 conference of Russian and Japanese diplomats that resulted in the Treaty of Portsmouth, which ended the Russo-Japanese War. Now that the McLane law firm has a presence in Portsmouth, the story has a relevance to employees and clients of the firm.*

The Treaty of Portsmouth, which was negotiated by the delegates from Russia and Japan to end the war between them, involved the McLane family. Governor John McLane was the official host of the meeting of the delegates. Judge McLane, then a sophomore at Dartmouth, attended some of the festivities while his father, mother, and the family stayed at the Hotel Wentworth. The treaty is an interesting and sometimes humorous piece of New Hampshire history. It has been said that the Treaty of Portsmouth received far more publicity and is much better known than the war that it ended.

The war between Russia and Japan broke out in 1904 because eastward-moving Russia clashed with westward-moving Japan in Korea and Manchuria.[1] In 1894, Japan defeated the Chinese and continued westerly by ousting them from Korea. Meanwhile, the Russians negotiated with China for permission to build the eastern terminus of its Trans-Siberian Railroad, thus bringing Japan and Russia ever closer together. There was talk of war in each country even as diplomatic ties were maintained between the parties. It is interesting to note that both Baron Komura,[2] the chief negotiator for Japan, and his counterpart for Russia, Sergius Witte, were opposed to war and had urged their respective governments to settle their differences diplomatically. However, the Japanese made a sneak torpedo boat attack off Port Arthur in February 1904. The ensuing war involved the largest number of troops in modern times. The Japanese were victorious on land when 500,000 soldiers were engaged. About 30,000 were killed and wounded. Port Arthur fell on January 1, 1905. In March, Japan won again at Mukden where 750,000 troops fought for two months; Japanese casualties were 50,000, but Russia suffered 30,000 killed, 100,000 wounded, and 50,000 taken prisoner. The crowning blow came when, in a classic maneuver of "crossing the T," the Japanese naval torpedo boats at Tsushima Strait (between Korea and Japan) sunk sixteen vessels of the Imperial Russian Navy, including six battleships and five cruisers, and captured two battleships.[3] The decisive victory, both on land and at sea, of hitherto-unknown Japan over Imperial Russia shocked the entire world.

*Governor John McLane (right of center with his hand holding his formal coat) with the Russian and Japanese peace envoys prior to the conference. To McLane's right are tall Witte and Rosen of Russia; to McLane's left are Komura and Takahira of Japan.*

The Japanese government, on May 30, 1905, secretly asked President Roosevelt to use his initiative to bring the parties together. The Russian tsar secretly let the United States know that he would accept an offer for direct negotiations. President Roosevelt sent a formal invitation, which was accepted by the Japanese on June 10 and by the Russians two days later. When it came to a meeting place, Paris, China, and The Hague were mentioned, but when Russia suggested Washington, Japan quickly agreed. Summer in Washington was then about as unbearable as it is today.

My recollection of my father's story is that Governor John McLane was interested in advertising New Hampshire as a tourist resort state and wanted to get as much publicity as he could. Being of Scottish ancestry, he wanted it either for nothing or at the least possible cost. This was the heyday of the large new hotels served by the railroads both in the mountains and at the seashore. A new highway for the tourist traffic had just been built between Twin Mountain and Franconia Notch along an abandoned logging railroad bed. Governor McLane inquired of President Roosevelt whether he had a meeting place in mind. He told the president that New Hampshire could accommodate the entourage either at the sumptuous Mount Washington Hotel in Bretton Woods or the equally distinguished Hotel Wentworth-by-the-Sea in New Castle.[4] The offer was accepted. The Wentworth Hotel was reserved for headquarters and accommodations, and the Portsmouth Naval Shipyard in Kittery, Maine, was to be the site for the formal meetings. Governor McLane was then embarrassed to find out that the legislative leadership (the legislature was not in session), being their usual penurious selves, were unwilling to endorse payment for the state's share of the expenses. Fortunately, the estate of Frank

Jones[5] (who had very recently died) owned the Wentworth-by-the-Sea and the Rockingham Hotel, both of which stood to gain substantially from the conference. The Jones estate contributed the $25,000 that was needed.

There was a beehive of activity, fixing up meeting rooms in the navy yard, building docks and sidewalks, repairing boats, renting the newfangled automobiles, and hiring horse carriages to transport the dignitaries back and forth between the navy yard and the hotel. The city was decked out with flags and streamers. The press corps, numbering one hundred special journalists, had to be accommodated. Arrangements were made for the admiral's band to play outside the meeting room morning and afternoon. Formal dinners by the governor of the state of New Hampshire, the U.S. secretary of state, the Japanese government, and the Russian Imperial government were arranged, including three truckloads of wine. Although the Japanese spoke English, the Russians spoke only French as a second language, so ten French-speaking waiters were imported from the Waldorf-Astoria in New York City to attend to the Russians' needs.

On July 31, Governor McLane and his family arrived. They stayed at the Hotel Wentworth as official hosts.[6]

On August 5, the Japanese arrived at Sagamore Hill, Roosevelt's home and the summer White House, at Oyster Bay on Long Island. They traveled on the USS *Tacoma* from New York. The Russians arrived on the USS *Chattanooga*. The delegations were introduced to each other on board the presidential yacht *Mayflower* at a stand-up lunch (so there would not be any embarrassment over seating protocol). There were champagne toasts all around. For the trip to Portsmouth, the Japanese were transferred to the USS *Dolphin*, which had Japanese servants. The Russians stayed aboard the *Mayflower*, which had Chinese servants. All was in readiness to cast off for New Hampshire, except that fog settled in and the departure was postponed for twenty-four hours.[7] Sergius Witte, head of the Russian delegation, disliking the sea and getting bored, left and took the train.

One of the vessels—I do not recall which—was scheduled to go to Newport, where the delegation was to be transferred to a special train decorated with banners, flags, and streamers that would then proceed to Portsmouth. The train schedule had been widely disseminated in the papers so that interested citizens could observe its passage. Crowds of people assembled at various stations at the appointed times. The only problem was that the fog persisted, delaying the boat's arrival in Newport by something like six hours, by which time the crowds had long since dispersed. The train passed empty station platforms and arrived in Portsmouth in total darkness late at night. The delegates were transported to their hotels through silent streets.[8]

The Hotel Wentworth flew the Japanese flag, which the Japanese delegation furnished, from one of the two hotel towers. The proprietors, after some delay, found the Russian flag. They discovered when they took it to the flagpole on the other tower that there was no flag halyard to use for a hoist. They quickly dispatched someone to the "rope walk," where rope was made, to obtain a suitable halyard. Lest someone be embarrassed by the presence of the Japanese flag flying without the Russian flag, the Japanese flag was discreetly lowered until both could be flown together.

The delegations were transported to their respective naval vessels, whether they had come by train or by boat, for the start of the conference festivities on August 8. The assistant U.S. secretary of state, Herbert Pierce, led off the procession in his launch. He picked up the Russians leaving the USS *Mayflower* in the admiral's barge, at which time there was a nineteen-gun salute. Then the Japanese fell in line and there were more salutes, seventy-six in all, as the procession meandered through the spectator fleet of tugs, naval vessels, and pleasure craft to the navy yard for a lunch given by Rear Admiral Mead. Apparently the Navy didn't trust the chefs of Portsmouth or the U.S. Navy. Fearing that their food would not grace such an important occasion, the Navy had arranged for the food to be cooked in Boston and transported refrigerated to Portsmouth—a procedure hardly designed to enhance the palatability of the delicacies.[9] After the lunch the delegates were escorted from the navy yard through the streets of Kittery, Maine, to the Piscataqua River Bridge. Neither the governor of Maine nor any representative of the town of Kittery had been invited to participate. On the New Hampshire side of the bridge, an escort parade was waiting. There were five companies of soldiers of the New Hampshire National Guard and several bands followed by the two Russians: Witte—tall, portly, and imperious—and Rosen, in a horse-drawn landau. They were followed immediately by the Japanese: Komura—slight, short, and quiet—and Takahira, in another carriage. All wore tall black silk hats and long formal coats. The procession wound up Market Street through jammed Market Square to State Street and thence to the courthouse (since torn down), where Governor McLane, together with his staff and delegates,[10] similarly accoutered, were waiting in front of the judge's bench to welcome both parties. Following the governor's greeting, the press corps was admitted to take formal pictures of everyone. The procession continued to the Wentworth, where five hundred guests waited for more festivities.[11]

The next day, August 9, the delegations were transported to the navy yard by horse and carriage or by auto[12] (it was too rough to use the boats) to begin the peace conference. The first meeting was designated for the exchange of credentials and the start of the formal proceedings. However, Baron Jutaro Komura, minister of foreign affairs, envoy extraordinary, and minister plenipotentiary of His Imperial Majesty, the Emperor of Japan, and chief of the Mikado's delegation, had left his papers at the hotel, so after meeting for only an hour, the affair was adjourned at noon.

All of the public excitement ended after two days. Then the negotiations began.[13] There was quite a bit of give and take. Each side had to confer by cable dispatches with its government at home, but finally the terms of an agreement were reached in late August, at which time the bells of the city were rung, the first time since the end of the Civil War. At the Wentworth, "Witte was so overcome with emotion, he had difficulty maintaining his composure, while Komura was seen to smile, in fact laugh for the first time."[14] The agreement had to be cast in proper diplomatic language, approved by both governments. It was signed by the parties and witnesses (one of them being Governor McLane) on September 5, after which Witte and Komura shook hands. By prearrangement, one of the secretaries to the Russian mission gave the information to the Marine corporal standing on guard outside the door. The corporal rushed down the stairs and passed on the news to Captain Rowe, who waved a red signal flag to the batteries of waiting guns, which fired their salutes. This was followed by the tolling of church bells in Portsmouth. The champagne bottles were uncorked, but no one had thought to provide glasses, so a motorcar was quickly dispatched to the city to fetch some. There were the customary toasts. And so the Treaty of Portsmouth became history.

A post-conference tour of the White Mountains had been planned, but the delegates were anxious to go home, so the trip was canceled. Before leaving, Komura paid a courtesy visit to Governor McLane and surprised him with a check for $10,000 as a token of his government's appreciation for the hospitality received during the conference. In a note accompanying the gift, the Japanese requested that "you will be good enough to utilize [the donation] for such charitable purposes in the State of New Hampshire as your excellency may deem fit." Three days later the Russians made a similar donation.[15] Thus was created the Russian-Japanese Fund, which invested in the bonds of each country. There was no revenue from the Russian bonds after the 1917 Revolution. In 1963, the New Hampshire legislature dropped the Russian name from the fund. The Japanese bond interest stopped in 1941 with the outbreak of World War II. However, in 1951 the funds were restored, including nine years' interest. This time the funds were invested in U.S. bonds. The fund stood at $40,000 in 1980 and realizes about $3,200 a year.

The Japanese government sent to Governor and Mrs. McLane two Japanese lacquer vases in appreciation of their hospitality during the conference. These vases descended to Judge on the death of his parents. They always sat on either end of the mantelpiece in the living room of their houses, both at 940 Chestnut Street and 1590 Union Street. On the death of Judge's widow, the children placed them on permanent loan with the Hood Museum of Art at Dartmouth College.

If one of the objectives of Governor McLane had been to secure publicity for the state of New Hampshire, he must have succeeded, because newspaper articles and diplomatic dispatches sent by wire during the month of August totaled some 2 million words, said to be the most ever sent in such a short period of time.

The Japanese have continued to maintain an interest in the Treaty of Portsmouth, because it signified the entrance of Japan into the arena of great powers and commemorated for the world to see its military might on land and sea against a major power. Thus it is not surprising that a number of Japanese visitors still come to the Portsmouth Navy Yard wanting to see the Treaty Room where the documents were signed. The Russians, on the other hand, having suffered one of their worst defeats on land and sea, want to forget the whole thing.

# Notes

1. Most of the material for this appendix comes from Peter E. Randall, *There Are No Victors Here.* (Portsmouth, N.H.: Marine Society), Publication 8, 1985.

2. A Harvard Law School graduate.

3. One of the great American naval victories in World War II in the Pacific was at Suriago Strait in the Philippines, where the Japanese were caught sailing single-file (only the forward guns could fire) through the strait and the Americans "crossed the T" and annihilated them (both fore and aft guns fired).

4. Secretary of State John Hay may have talked to Roosevelt about New Hampshire as a possible site since he had a substantial summer home in Newbury that he and his family used (and still do) a great deal, including meetings involving important foreign policy decisions (Squires, *Granite State*, Vol. I, p. 432.) during the Boxer Rebellion in 1900 and the Panama negotiations in 1903. President Roosevelt visited Hay in 1902. Secretary Hay died in Newbury on July 1, 1905.

   Henry Denison, of Lancaster, New Hampshire, legal and financial adviser to the Japanese Department of Foreign Affairs and in the American consulate in Yokahama, may also have promoted New Hampshire as the place for the conference.

5. Frank Jones, a good Democrat most of his life (turned Republican over the gold-silver standard issue), built the Frank Jones Brewery Company in Portsmouth in 1861, at the beginning of the Civil War. The brewery turned out to be a wonderful "cash cow." With the earnings from it, Jones was able to build the Rockingham Hotel in Portsmouth, still an impressive building, and the famous, still-standing Wentworth-by-the-Sea in New Castle. His own lavish estate, Gravelly Ridge, with conservatories, was heated and lighted by his own private steam and electric plants; he didn't trust the utilities. In addition to owning a brewery, he was referred to as a railroad magnate. (Squires, *Granite State*, Vol. II, p. 441.)

6. Judge writes in his diary on July 31, 1905: "People left for the Wentworth." August 1: "Clin and I came to Wentworth via Lowell in rain–disagreeable weather." August 4: "Golf with mamma in morning …" August 5: "Launch ride to Navy Yard & saw Peace Conference room."

7. Judge's diary entry of August 6 reads: "Lots of excitement over Witte's expected arrival."

8. Judge's diary entry of August 7 reads: "Witte came about 11:30 p.m."

9. Witte indicated in his memoirs that he was not happy: He had problems squeezing his bulk into the small bathtub, he had hurt his leg, and he felt that

his rooms were too small. Witte also disliked the food, and in commenting on the luncheons served at the navy yard, he wrote: "Literally dozens of courses were served, but the dishes were mostly cold. It appears that the government had ordered hundreds of luxuriously prepared dishes and stored them in refrigerators to feed us on them. I soon noticed that one must be very careful with this food. Two or three days later I decided to refrain completely from eating it, and for a time I touched nothing but bread and some vegetables. Komura, on the other hand, ate everything with great appetite. … While I left Portsmouth hale and hearty, Komura was taken ill at the end of the Conference and developed an intestinal variety of typhus, so that when I visited him [in New York] before my departure from the United States, I found him sick in bed." Randall, *There Are No Victors Here*, p. 78.

10. Governor McLane appointed state Senator Johann Adam Graf of Manchester, an overseer with the Amoskeag Manufacturing Company and a local politician, as one of his delegates. Mr. Graf was the grandfather of Kenneth F. Graf and great-grandfather of our John Adam Graf. The original Johann Adam Graf emigrated from Bavaria, later a part of Germany, in 1863 at the age of fifteen to escape the political unrest there. He came to Manchester to work as an expert machinist in the mills. He worked his way up the ladder. Over the next twenty-five years, he became an overseer, or foreman, in the mills, was elected an alderman in Manchester, served in the state house of representatives in 1897, and became a state senator in 1905.

11. Judge's diary entry of August 8 reads: "Russian and Jap peace envoys arrived. In town on drag [horse-drawn vehicle] to see parade. Fooled around all evening singing and dancing." August 9: "Mamma's 50th birthday. Doubles in tennis in morning, Bathing. 3rd base for Farragut [hotel] against No. Rye 9-3, 10th Artillery Band."

12. Some of the earliest autos made.

13. Judge's diary entry of August 10 reads: "Clin and I went to lunch with Lieut. Burchfield at the Navy Yard." August 11: "Launch ride with supper." August 12: "Motor boat ride with officers of *Mayflower*." August 13: "Bathing in morning. Party of 14 to *Mayflower* for tea and to Passaconaway Inn for dinner." August 20: "Went sailing on President's yacht *Mayflower* out by Isles of Shoals and Boon Island. Wonderful sail." August 29 [while at Rockland, Maine, sailing with friends]: "Peace reported signed by envoys at Portsmouth." August 30: "Hazel [his sister] and I left Camden & returned to Wentworth. Peace agreed upon." September 1: "Clin and I went to dinner at Pierce's [assistant secretary of state]. Japs were there." Judge does not mention the conference again after returning to Milford.

14. Randall, *There Are No Victors Here*, p. 53.

15. Randall, *There Are No Victors Here*, p. 76.

# APPENDIX B.4

# Huntley N. Spaulding

## 1869–1955

*Huntley Spaulding and Judge McLane served for over thirty years as president and treasurer, respectively, of the New Hampshire Children's Aid Society (later Child & Family Services of New Hampshire). Huntley named Judge as one of the trustees of Charitable Trusts, which Huntley created by an inter vivos trust and by will.*

Huntley N. Spaulding was born in Townsend, Massachusetts, on October 30, 1869. He was educated in the local high schools and Phillips Andover Academy. He entered business with his father's company, Jonas Spaulding & Sons, Inc., manufacturers of fiberboard and shoe counters. The company was first located at Townsend Harbor, Massachusetts, later at Rochester, New Hampshire, then North Rochester, and then Milton, New Hampshire. After World War I, the company acquired a plant at Tonawanda, New York, where there was an ample and inexpensive supply of power and water. The fiberboard product was made with a high percentage of rag fiber and less paper pulp, then impregnated with resins, heated, and compressed. The material was durable; it could be molded into a variety of shapes, drawn into pipes, and machined into shapes such as gears. It had low electrical conductivity, a high resistance to solvents and liquids, and low thermal conductivity. Fiberboard tote boxes for the textile industry, the U.S. Postal Service, and others were popular items.

Jonas Spaulding had three sons—Leon, Huntley, and Rolland. All were active in managing the successful business. The latter two were governors of the state of New Hampshire: Rolland, the younger, in 1915–1917, and Huntley in 1927–1929. Both belonged to the conservative branch of the Republican Party. In addition to his involvement in the family business, Huntley had high visibility in public service.[1] During World War I, national food administrator Herbert Hoover appointed Huntley as the food administrator for New Hampshire. His program of boosting production, conservation, and food preservation increased the supplies of potatoes, corn, and oats by one-third. Immediately after the war, Huntley was the New Hampshire chairman of the committee to approve the adoption of the League of Nations resolution. In 1921, there was an upheaval in the New Hampshire Board of Education. Huntley was asked to come to the rescue as its new chairman. In January 1920, Huntley Spaulding was interested in tackling Senator George

Moses for his U.S. Senate seat and asked Judge to survey his chances in the Republican primary in September. Judge accepted and interrogated about ten politically astute people in the state. Afterward, Judge met with Huntley and his agents to go over the report. (The gist of the report is not disclosed, although I surmise that it was at least mildly favorable.) During the summer, Judge spoke on behalf of Huntley at rallies at Milford, Dublin, Harrisville, Troy, Marlboro, and Exeter. Judge confided to his diary in August that "Spaulding campaign doesn't stir up great excitement." The primaries resulted in a resounding defeat for Huntley, 28,000 to 15,000.

In the 1926 Republican primaries, Huntley Spaulding and Senator George Moses, the conservatives, defeated Winant and Bass, the Progressives, for the nominations for the governorship and U.S. Senate. They easily won in the general election. In the fall of 1928, Spaulding, with his predecessor, Governor Winant, dedicated the new Franconia Notch State Park, which the state had recently acquired with funds appropriated by the state and the donations of 15,000 contributors. In November 1927, there were disastrous floods that ruined many miles of highway and railroad tracks[2] leading Governor Spaulding to call a special session of the legislature to deal with the catastrophe.

For all of his life, Huntley was interested in a variety of charitable organizations to which he devoted substantial amounts of time and his personal fortune. Among them were Lawrence Academy in Groton (which he attended) and Tufts University in Medford, Massachusetts; in New Hampshire, Tilton School, New Hampshire Children's Aid Society (now Child & Family Services of New Hampshire), Golden Rule Farm in Tilton, Daniel Webster Home for Children in Franklin, the New Hampshire TB Association, and the New Hampshire Historical Society.[3]

Sherman Burroughs and Judge McLane, who were law partners, were among the founders of the New Hampshire Children's Aid and Protective Society in January 1914 and were elected president and treasurer, respectively. Upon the death of Congressman Burroughs in 1923, Huntley Spaulding was elected president, a position he held for thirty years until 1953, when he was made president emeritus and Judge McLane was elected president.[4]

Huntley Spaulding was always modest about his own abilities. He acknowledged that his education was meager; therefore, he sought out people who were more knowledgeable than he and relied on their expertise in making his decisions. I do not know whether this story is apocryphal or not, but in the management of Spaulding Fibre Company, Inc., Huntley did have topnotch financial advisers, accountants, attorneys, and engineers as professional consultants. I know that as president of the New Hampshire Children's Aid Society, Huntley also sought top professional qualified staff and relied on the advice of professionals from schools of social work with respect to programs and policy. Huntley Spaulding was a remarkable citizen and benefactor of the state of New Hampshire.

# THE SPAULDING-POTTER CHARITABLE TRUSTS

Harriet Mason Spaulding, wife of Huntley N. Spaulding, died in 1954; Huntley died the next year, and Huntley's sister, Marion Spaulding Potter, died in 1957. Each left similar wills drawn by Norman Bingham, Esq., of Bingham, Dana & Gould in Boston. Each will, after making substantial specific charitable bequests, created a charitable remainder trust. The income was to be distributed annually and the principal was to be distributed 60 percent in New Hampshire and 40 percent in Massachusetts within fifteen years of the death of the survivor of the three. The principal asset of the trusts was stock in Spaulding Fibre Company, Inc., which was subsequently sold. In addition, there was an inter vivos trust of Huntley Spaulding, which was to be distributed in New Hampshire. The testamentary trusts were administered as a single trust, although separate probate accounts were filed for each trust. The New Hampshire trustees named included Judge McLane,[5] who, being the senior member, was elected chairman and served in accordance with the will provision until the end of 1958, at age seventy-two. The other New Hampshire trustees were Dudley Orr of Concord, "Skip" Clow of Rochester, and the Spaulding Fibre Company. Skip resigned when he moved to Tonawanda, New York, the principal headquarters of the company, and was succeeded by probate judge Leonard Hardwick of Rochester, who resigned his judgeship. I served as secretary of the trusts from their inception to the end of 1958, when I was appointed trustee to succeed Judge. Dudley Orr succeeded Judge McLane as chairman, and Eugene Struckhoff, a partner in the law firm of Orr & Reno, became secretary until the termination of the trusts in 1972.[6] The Massachusetts trustees were David Howie of the Fiduciary Trust Company, who retired on his seventy-second birthday and was succeeded by Edward Osgood, also of the Fiduciary Trust Company; John Cushman, of the Old Colony Trust Company; and Gilbert Welsh, of Bingham, Dana & Gould. Fiscal management and custody of assets were maintained by the Fiduciary Trust Company. The aggregate maximum amount of principal assets in the trusts was just under $10.5 million, but over the life of the trusts more than $16 million was distributed. Annual reports of the trusts and a final report were published and disseminated to, among other places, all the libraries of the state.

The grants of the Spaulding-Potter Charitable Trusts over the fifteen-year life of the trusts made a significant impact on the activities of a large number of charitable organizations throughout the state. Generally speaking, grants were not made for annual operating budgets but rather to explore new experimental or expanded programs, to increase efficiency and self-sufficiency, to conduct professional studies, and to fund capital needs. Projects generally were supported for less than three years. Grants were made in the field of social welfare, education, children, the elderly, the arts, humanities, and government.

As the termination of the trusts loomed on the horizon, it became clear that New Hampshire would be the poorer without the innovative support of the Spaulding-Potter Charitable Trusts. Through the initiative and imagination of Eugene Struckhoff, the trust's executive secretary, the concept of a statewide community foundation was explored. Eugene Struckhoff and I attended the Council on Foundations annual conference in St. Paul, Minnesota, and met with a number of people knowledgeable in the community foundation field and received helpful suggestions. Upon returning, Eugene Struckhoff and the Spaulding-Potter trustees organized the New Hampshire Charitable Fund (NHCF) in 1961, with Chief Justice Frank Kenison as chairman, this author from the Spaulding-Potter Charitable Trusts, and three other interested New Hampshire citizens from around the state. The board was a rotating one and started with more enthusiasm than cash. With continuing nourishment from the Spaulding-Potter Charitable Trusts until their termination in 1972 and the gradual spread of knowledge about the charitable fund throughout the state, the NHCF has followed the pattern of growth of other community foundations and now in 1996 has exceeded $100 million in assets.

The concept of a grant-making organization of private citizens to benefit the state's charitable organizations is assured in perpetuity. The benefactions of Huntley Spaulding and his family live on!

# Notes

1. Squires, *Granite State*, Vol. II, p. 641.

2. The flood hit Vermont harder than New Hampshire. In one instance, the *Ambassador*, the high-speed train between Boston and Montreal, was stopped outside Randolph, Vermont, and remained there three months!

3. Annual report, 1955–1956, Spaulding-Potter Charitable Trusts.

4. *The First 50 Years*, New Hampshire Children's Aid Society.

5. Judge never knew of Huntley's testamentary plans and was touched by Huntley naming him a trustee. While they had been president and treasurer of the New Hampshire Children's Aid Society for thirty years, they had been on the opposite sides of the political fence.

6. Annual Report, 1959, Spaulding-Potter Charitable Trusts.

# Matinicus Island

*Over several summers between 1949 and 1961, Judge and Elisabeth spent weeklong vacations on Matinicus Island in a cottage rented from the Bunkers. Judge's children have sailed there and visited the Bunkers and their boys. Other Manchester families, such as the Booths, Kohlses, and Stahles, have vacationed there. It is a unique, wild, and remote fisherman's haven. Many family stories relate to Matinicus Island. One of them is the rescue by Vance Bunker. That story gives one an idea of what is expected of a Maine coast lobsterman.*

Matinicus is the outermost inhabited island off the Maine coast, about twenty miles east of Rockland. It is about one mile long and a half-mile wide, with rocky shores and open fields on either side of a central spine that runs the length of the island, north and south. The spine rises a couple of hundred feet above the sea. The island has a small harbor made safer by breakwaters built in this century. Since the seventeenth century, Matinicus has supported a small population of fishermen who caught cod, haddock, and mackerel. Prior to 1900, the fishermen also ran small farms. With the decline of groundfish and the mysterious disappearance of herring from the Maine coast about 1900, fishing has been almost entirely limited to lobster, which provides a decent living for the twenty or so families who inhabit the island today.

Lobsters were originally caught along the inshore rocky coast until it was discovered that they migrate to and from the deeper waters of the Gulf of Maine. They also inhabit rocky seamounts, which rise several hundred feet above the ocean floor to within fifty to one hundred feet of the surface. The isolated seamounts extend another twenty miles or so out to sea beyond the outer islands such as Matinicus and Monhegan, making for hazardous fishing in inclement weather. During the winter most fishermen leave the island for an extended vacation in a warmer climate. The predominant families on Matinicus are the Philbrooks, Youngs, and Ameses, who have lived there for at least five generations.

Judge and Elisabeth spent many happy weeks there for nine years between 1949 and 1961. They looked for birds, walked around the island, lounged on the beaches, swam in the frigid water, read books, and enjoyed the solitude. Occasionally, they fished for flounder in the harbor and on rare times went out lobstering with Harold Bunker or made the trip to Matinicus Rock to see the colorful puffins.[1] Their friends were lobsterman Harold Bunker and his wife, Rena, who with their son, Vance, and other children, lived in a cozy house surrounded by evergreens that protected them from the sea. It was a short walk from their house through the woods to the harbor. On the other side of the island, the Bunkers owned a small, isolated, and primitive cottage overlooking the sea and adjacent islands, which they rented by the week. Judge and Elisabeth stayed in this cottage.

Bob and Lois Booth (Bob was with the Wadleigh law firm) were about the first people from Manchester to explore Matinicus. They went primarily to see the birds, both the indigenous sea- and shorebirds and the annual migrations of warblers and other species making their long pilgrimage to or from northern Canada and Labrador to South America. At first the Booths rented a cabin, but later acquired their own. They played the part of the Pied Piper and influenced Judge and Elisabeth and others of their age to come to Matinicus. Later, Bob's law partner, Dick Kohls, followed suit. Dick's son, Rick, "turned native" and became a lobsterman; he still resides on the island. Dr. David Stahl and his wife, Barbara, have been longtime summer visitors, too.

In recent years much of the island has been purchased from the departing inhabitants by summer people. To preserve the wildness and beauty of the island, there are no public accommodations, and the one small store has closed. All provisions have to be purchased in Rockland and brought to the island on the twice-a-week ferry or by private boat. There is a generating plant for electricity. Water is supplied by individual wells. Septic tanks buried in the rocky soil provide sewage disposal. There are no publicly maintained roads, only lanes or wagon paths winding over granite outcroppings of ledge or depressions of soil between the ledges, which become quagmires in rain. Most folk have a beat-up old pickup truck to haul supplies, lobster pots, et cetera, from the dock in the one harbor to their homes. The inhabitants refuse to pay any state registration fees since there are no state-maintained roads.

In the late 1940s, my wife, Blanche, and I ended a delightful long day's sail in my brother-in-law's Herreshoff "S" boat (without power). We had sailed from Linekin Bay near Boothbay around Monhegan to Matinicus. As we dropped our "hook" in the tiny harbor filled with lobster boats, we observed a young man cleaning his lobster boat. He proceeded to empty his rifle of bullets by firing into the water. As we rowed past him to the dock, I asked if he used the rifle to shoot sharks. His response in an angry tone was: "I'll get that son-of-a-bitch if it's the last thing I do." We were mystified by his response. We kept on rowing. After tieing up at the dock, we took the shortcut path through the spruce and fir trees festooned with dripping "Spanish moss" to the Harold Bunkers'. We had written them about our possible visit. After catching up on family news, we told them of our experience with the young fisherman firing his rifle. Harold commented with a shrug, "Girl trouble," elaborating that it was a small, tight island, that there were few eligible girls for the hard-working single men, and sometimes ugly incidents occurred. We heard later, whether in connection with this incident or not, I don't remember, that things had gotten pretty bad on the island—feuding and cutting traplines—resulting in a criminal complaint being filed in the Rockland District Court.

The district court judge announced he was going to hold court on the island and wanted everyone to be present. At the hearing in the packed schoolroom, the judge reviewed the evidence that would be offered if the case went to trial and said, in effect: This is a very serious matter. Someone will be badly hurt or killed if this keeps up. There is nothing that I or any government official can do to keep the peace. It is up to you who live here. Your ancestors have lived here on this beautiful island for several hundreds of years, reaping a good life from the sea. Your children and grandchildren will do the same as long as there are fish and lobsters in these waters. I don't ever want to have to return to the island under these circumstances nor do I ever expect to see a Matinicus man in my court on a charge of interference with an individual's right to fish. May you all live in peace. Case dismissed. The court is adjourned. Then the judge left.

There was a rough sort of justice on the island. There is a story of one lobsterman who lost his wife and ultimately married a widow with several children. Over a period of time, he found his young stepdaughter pretty attractive. He built another house, which he furnished, as well as a lobster boat and traps and told his wife she could move out and into her new quarters with boat and traps—and that was that. The islanders look out for each other, in sickness or in health. Each lobsterman has a set of traps marked with his license number and painted a distinctive color. He sets the traps in a place where he thinks he will make a good catch. His boat is equipped with all the modern navigational aids—radar, loran, and fathometers. Although the lobstermen tend to keep information to themselves about where their traps are located and how much they catch in each place, they are aware at least of the general direction in which each person is going when he leaves the harbor in the early hours of the morning. The lobstermen usually go alone, although they might take a friend or a son to teach him how to lobster. The boats start coming back to port in the early afternoon, unload at the lobster "car," then go to their respective moorings. The lobsterman cleans up, making everything shipshape for the next morning or whenever he might be called out unexpectedly. As he works, he instinctively watches the other boats returning and mentally checks them off, and occasionally checks over the empty moorings. If all are accounted for, he'll head for home, but if someone is still out there, he'll get on the radio, listening for traffic from the missing person and maybe try a call. If there is no answer, and nobody in the harbor has information to share on the radio, you will hear the roar of those powerful engines starting up and slowly the little fleet heads out to find the lost boat. Things can happen—engine trouble, collision with a submerged object, fouled propeller, being caught in a fast-running lobster-pot line, or fire. The air will crackle with talk among the boats, and every house ashore will be listening until the problem is resolved.

In the 1980s, we chartered the schooner *Alamar* and visited Matinicus, calling on the Bunkers. We anchored in the harbor for the night. At dawn, we heard the roar of the engines of the lobster boats as the men went out to check their traps and felt the gentle rocking of the boat from their wakes. A couple of hours later, we heard some come back. The engine of one died down close by us. I popped my head up the hatch and saw Harold Bunker swing a gunnysack up onto our deck. "You never saw where those came from, did you?"[2] he said, and with a wave of his hand he shoved off for his mooring. We almost had lobster for breakfast! We certainly had lobster sandwiches for lunch and lobster Newburg or lobster salad for dinner.

## THE RESCUE

After the above was written, we read in the *National Fisherman*, Volume 72, No. 12, April 1992, and the February 1992 issue of *Island News* the story written by Margot Brown McWilliams of the spectacular rescue by Vance Bunker in his *Janellen*. Rick Kohls and Paul Murray were his crewmen. The Coast Guard aided in the rescue.

According to the McWilliams account, the first warning came at 6 P.M. on January 16, 1992, when Clayton Philbrook on Matinicus heard on VHF the tugboat *Harkness* calling the Coast Guard, telling them that it had taken on a foot and a half of water over its stern and was heading for Frenchboro island and its small harbor. The message was intercepted by David Allen, skipper of the *Sunbeam* of the Maine Seacoast Mission, who advised the *Harkness* to head for Matinicus, where there was a better chance of getting help. The skipper of the *Harkness* didn't know anyone lived there. On Matinicus, the wind was blowing forty knots and the temperature was about four degrees below zero. The Coast Guard dispatched a forty-one-foot patrol boat from Rockland as well as the one hundred-forty-foot cutter *Thunder Bay* and a jet from Cape Cod (which was forced to return because of a shattered window). Vance Bunker overheard the conversation between the tug and the mainland and called the tug to find out the tug's trouble. The water was now two feet deep over the stern. Vance responded that he was on his way. Philbrook called Bunker and offered to go along, but Vance had already lined up Rick Kohls and Paul Murray, who can fix anything and might be badly needed on the boat. Vance told Philbrook he'd better stay on standby with the communications and be ready to come if Vance got into trouble. When Bunker steered into the night, he didn't know the exact location of the *Harkness*. According to Philbrook, he started out thinking they were off Northeast Point, at the north end of the island, instead of where they were, which was off Zephyr Ledge.

"Vance had Paul and me watching the loran and telling him which way to steer," Kohls said, "and Paul was writing down the numbers as the *Harkness* was giving them on the radio." They had figured out where they were and were on the way to those coordinates.

Rudi Musetti, the tugboat skipper, had only suspicions about what made the boat start to take on water. Possibly it was the rudder ports or the stuffing box. He had checked everything every two hours and there were no problems. Musetti threw the pump switches and could only hope they worked, because it was too icy on deck to check. "But every time I looked, we were going down and not up."

As the *Harkness* started to sink, Vance Bunker had a new concern. The *Harkness*, which had no tow and was deadheading, had reported that her two five-hundred-foot towropes coiled on the stern had been washed overboard. If the ropes were still fastened to the tug and the ropes became tangled in Vance's propeller and the tug went down, down would go Vance's *Janellen* too. "Things were getting tense," said Vance.

The tug captain indicated that he knew the boat would sink. Then he reported that he was in the wheelhouse with the water up to his chest and he and his crew were going into the water. It was 7:02. Then silence! "When we heard that silence," said Rick Kohls, "I knew I was going to puke. It was a terrible, terrible feeling. Of course the battery might have gone dead, but we knew they were in the water." Just as Vance's boat arrived at the coordinates only two miles off Matinicus, so did the Coast Guard's forty-one-foot patrol boat. The tug was nowhere in sight. The *Janellen* backed off and returned to the last set of coordinates the tug had given. "By then we knew," said Kohls, "there wasn't much of a chance them boys would still be alive. It was jeezly cold, and that sea smoke lay right over the water like a blanket." Kohls and Murray kept at it, looking over the sides of the *Janellen* down into the water. But the sea smoke was impenetrable, and they could see nothing.

For some reason, Kohls looked up instead of down. "I couldn't believe my eyes," he said. "I saw a light shining straight up into the sky above the sea smoke."

It wasn't much of a light, but its effect was huge. "It was like Charlie Brown's Christmas," Kohls said. "We knew at least one of them was out there." Kohls guided Bunker to the light; Bunker couldn't see out his windows because they were caked with ice.

The unlikely, if not the impossible, had happened. A wooden ladder had floated free of the *Harkness* as it went down, and all three men had grabbed onto it.

One of the three, Arthur Stevens, happened to be carrying a flashlight that his daughter had given him for Christmas. "I don't think Arthur was even aware that he still had the flashlight," Musetti said later, "because his hands were too cold to hold onto anything. What had happened was the flashlight had frozen to Arthur's glove."

Then the three men in the water saw the *Janellen* searchlight coming through the sea smoke. "We couldn't see the boat itself," Musetti said, "and it was blowing too hard for us to hear its engine."

Still it was a struggle for the angels to save the men. "We held the gaff out to one of them," said Kohls. "He kind of hooked onto it with his arms, because he had lost the use of his hands. He looked up at us and said, 'Boy, are we glad to see you.' It seemed like a lifetime getting the first two aboard. Paul and I were pulling one of them and Vance got the other aboard himself. Vance is a big boy. He's stronger. Also, fear motivates everyone."

The Coast Guard boat picked up the third man.

When the *Harkness* crew was pulled from the water, the combination of wind and temperature created a windchill factor of fifty-five below zero!

"You have never seen such cold human beings," said Kohls. "They couldn't walk, they couldn't move, except to vibrate like they were coming apart at the seams. We took them down below and had to cut the clothes off them. Luckily Bunker kept a stove going down below." Murray and Kohls stripped off their clothes and gave them to the two men.

It was an incredible rescue. They went into Matinicus, where all recuperated. Apparently there were no long-term injuries, and all recovered. It was fortunate that the boats were equipped with contemporary navigational gear—loran to give accurate coordinates and radios to communicate with one another. It seems strange that the crew of the *Harkness* did not have access (if such was the case) to survival suits and a life raft.

# Notes

1. Judge told the story of two lady ornithologists from New York who came to the island to see the puffins at their southernmost nesting place. They had made arrangements for a house but not for a boat. They inquired around for a boat that would take them out to the "Rock," price not being a consideration, but no one was available. A couple of days later, one of the natives said to Judge, "You tell those women from the city to be at the dock at seven tomorrow morning, if they want to go to the Rock." You can be sure they were there and had a grand visit. They were shocked to find that their money was not acceptable to their skipper.

2. They were all "shorts" that he had cleaned from his traps.

# Family Genealogy of Judge and Elisabeth McLane

*From time to time, there have been references to various relatives of Judge and Elisabeth's that may have been confusing. In an attempt to clarify the family relationships, this genealogy has been prepared, which we hope will be helpful.*

## JUDGE'S PATERNAL GRANDPARENTS

Alexander Maclean, born circa 1820, died 1854.

Born in Scotland, he was a wood engraver in a textile print works in Lennoxtown, Scotland, near Glasgow. He was recruited by an agent for the Amoskeag Manufacturing Company in Manchester, New Hampshire, and emigrated there with his wife and two children in 1854. He accidentally drowned in Black Brook on September 4, 1854, while swimming after work a few weeks after arriving in the United States.

m.  Mary Hay(e) Maclean, born 1819, died circa 1890.

After the death of her husband, Mary went to work in the Amoskeag Manufacturing Company and farmed the children out to a foster family in Dunbarton. Later she married Charles Jondro, and after his death married Thomas Averill, of Milford, brother of her son John's foster father-in-law. Mary is buried in New Boston.

Alexander and Mary had two children, John, Judge's father, and Malcolm (born 1850, died 1901), who became an ironmonger and lived in Massachusetts. He died in Portsmouth and is buried in Dunbarton.

## JUDGE'S MATERNAL GRANDPARENTS

Ebenezar Baker Tuck, born July 1, 1810, in Manchester, Massachusetts, died May 6, 1862.

m. Lydia Smith Frye, born September 8, 1820, in Croyden, New Hampshire, died April 28, 1860; married June 1, 1842. They had two children, Edward Tuck and Ellen Luetta Tuck, Judge's mother.

# JUDGE'S PARENTS

John Maclean, born February 27, 1852, in Lennoxtown, Scotland. (He changed his name in the United States to McLane, so that it would be spoken correctly. The diphthong "ea" in Scotland is pronounced as a broad "a," whereas in the United States it is pronounced as a broad "e.") John McLane lived most of his life in Milford, New Hampshire. He died on April 13, 1911, while visiting in South Carolina. Manufacturer, cabinetmaker, businessman, politician. (See Chapter Six for an extensive history of the McLane family.)

m. Ellen Luetta Tuck, born August 9, 1855, died March 1927.

Ellen's mother died when Ellen was five; her father died two years later. Ellen was brought up by the Clinton Averills of Milford.

John and Ellen were married on March 10, 1880, and had four children: Clinton Averill McLane, Hazel McLane Clark, John R. McLane (Judge), and Malcolm McLane.

# ELISABETH'S PATERNAL GRANDPARENTS

Jesse Parker Bancroft, born April 18, 1815, Dartmouth College AB 1841, Phi Beta Kappa, Dartmouth Medical School MD 1845, died April 30, 1891. Superintendent New Hampshire State Hospital, Concord, New Hampshire.

m. Elizabeth Spear of Hanover, born October 31, 1815.

Jesse and Elizabeth had two children: Charles (Elisabeth's father), born January 11, 1852, died December 23, 1923, and Corisand (adopted), born June 27, 1856, died March 22, 1930.

m. Burnham Roswell Benner, a psychiatrist, and lived in Lowell, Massachusetts.

# ELISABETH'S MATERNAL GRANDPARENTS

Bartholomew Wood, born May 31, 1813, Dartmouth College AB 1841 (same class at Dartmouth as Jesse Parker Bancroft, above), died November 27, 1888. Teacher, Newton Center, Massachusetts,.

m. (1) Sarah Burke, born circa 1815, died October 22, 1844.

They had two children, William and Sarah.

m. (2) Jennette Burke (sister of Sarah Burke, above), born 1819, married November 3, 1853, died 1902.

They had three children: Moriah, Allen (deceased age nine), and Susan, (Elisabeth's mother).

# ELISABETH'S PARENTS

Charles Parker Bancroft, born January 11, 1852, Harvard College AB 1874, Harvard Medical School MD 1878, died December 14, 1923. Superintendent, New Hampshire State Hospital, Concord, New Hampshire.

m.  Susan Cushing Wood, born March 15, 1860, died May 19, 1948.

Charles and Susan were married on August 6, 1884, in Newton Center and had four children: Charles Parker (born circa 1886, died in his first year); Jennette (born 1888), later called Jane; Elisabeth (born May 17, 1891, see below); and Miriam (born 1894, died August 3, 1928 in China). (See Appendix B.1, The Bancroft Family.)

## JUDGE AND ELISABETH MCLANE

John Roy McLane (Judge), born January 7, 1886, St. Paul's School, Dartmouth AB 1907, Magdalen College, Oxford University 1909, Harvard Law School LLB 1912, died April 21, 1969. Attorney, McLane law firm, Manchester, New Hampshire.

m.  June 12, 1915, Elisabeth Bancroft, born May 17, 1891, Dana Hall, Smith College AB 1914, died April 8, 1983. Housewife.

## JUDGE AND ELISABETH'S CHILDREN AND THEIR FAMILIES

An asterisk (*) indicates that the child was born after the death of Judge and Elisabeth. "A" indicates adopted child.

A.  *John Roy McLane, Jr. (this author)*, born February 19, 1916, in Manchester, New Hampshire, St. Paul's School, Dartmouth College AB 1938, Harvard Law School LLB 1941. Attorney, McLane law firm, Manchester, New Hampshire.

m. (1) Blanche B. Marshall, born February 17, 1915, Winsor School, Smith College, ex 1936, divorced 1959, died April 20, 1995.

1.  John R. McLane III (Jock), born September 20, 1935, St. Paul's School, Harvard University AB 1957, University of London, School of Oriental and African Studies PhD 1961. Professor, Northwestern University, Evanston, Illinois.

m. September 7, 1957, Joan Brooks, born August 28, 1935, Putney School, Radcliffe College AB 1957, Erikson Institute, Loyola University MA 1970, Northwestern University PhD 1981. Professor, Erikson Institute, Chicago, Illinois.

a.  Derek McLane, born June 14, 1958, Putney School, Harvard University AB 1980, Yale University, School of Drama MFA 1984. Theater stage designer, New York City.

m. August 10, 1991, Wendy Ettinger, born January 24, 1957, Kent School, William Smith BA 1979. Film producer, New York City.

aa. Cooper Wadsworth Prentice McLane, born April 5, 1993.*

b.  Rebecca McLane, born May 1, 1960, Putney School, Macalester College BA 1982. Battered women's advocate, St. Paul,

Minnesota.

m.  Richard Pemberton, born June 22, 1959, Macalester College AB 1981, University of Minnesota Law School JD 1986, Union Theological School MA 1991. Lawyer, Meacher & Geer, Minneapolis, Minnesota.

aa. Nicholas Duncan McLane Pemberton, born June 27, 1995.*


2.  Andrew Marshall McLane (Sandy), born November 2, 1936, Woodstock Country School, Boston University AB, died December 3, 1984. Builder, pilot, sailor, and adventurer.

m.  Julia Ann Lane, born April 4, 1937, Skidmore, Boston Museum School, Universal Brotherhood Movement BDiv 1988. Artist, spiritual counselor, educator. Divorced 1973.

a.  Tucker McLane, born January 12, 1969, Clarkson University BS 1991. Engineer, Burlington, Vermont.


3.  Lyn McLane, born February 10, 1939, Colorado Rocky Mountain School, Smith College BA 1960, Harvard University MEd 1966. Teacher, Orillia, Ontario, Canada.

m.  February 10, 1973, John Egsgard, born March 20, 1925, St. Michael's School College, University of Toronto BA 1948, MA 1953, ordained RC priest 1953, laicized 1973. Mathematics teacher (ret.), Orillia, Prov. Ontario, Canada.

a.  Jennifer Egsgard, born August 30, 1974, Guelph College (1996).

b.  Erik Egsgard, born March 18, 1976, Queen's University (Class of 1999).

c.  Neil Egsgard, born October 2, 1979.


4.  Blanche Marshall McLane (Bonnie), born December 11, 1943, Antioch College AB 1966, Simmons College MLS 1974. Organizing consultant, Boston, Massachusetts.

m.  August 3, 1969, Adel Foz, born March 24, 1942, Verde Valley School, Harvard BA 1963, School of Design 1968, Massachusetts Institute of Technology, School of Urban Studies MA 1972. Urban planner, Boston, Massachusetts.

a.  Jessica Foz, born July 12, 1971, Harvard College.

b.  Alexander Foz, born June 29, 1974, Eugene Lang College, New York City.

c.  Elizabeth Foz, born July 1, 1978. Brown University, Providence, Rhode Island.


5.  Angus McLane, born December 1, 1947, St. Paul's School, Western Washington State College AB 1972, Gonzaga University MA

1986. Clinical psychologist, Bellingham, Washington.

m. March 27, 1982, Marilyn Ulrich (Rommie), born February 15, 1949, Western Washington State College BS 1977, Washington State University BSN 1985. Nurse, Bellingham, Washington.

    a.  Marie Lauren McLane, born February 15, 1986.*
    b.  Ian Andrew McLane, born January 14, 1990.*

m. (2) December 30, 1960, Elisabeth Towner Deane (Betsy), born June 17, 1926, Ethel Walker's School, Smith College AB 1947. Photographer.

    1.  Towner Deane McLane, born January 5, 1962. Cabinetmaker and builder, Lummi Island, Washington.

m. July 31, 1988, Lynn Hudson, born March 5, 1956, Western Washington State College BA 1978. Restaurateur and horse breeder.

    a.  Kelsey Mae McLane, born February 6, 1989.*

    2.  Virginia Waterston McLane (Gigi), born January 5, 1962, University of New Hampshire AB 1985, MEd 1987. Elementary school-teacher, Monkton, Vermont.

m. June 25, 1988, Scott Moreau, born March 3, 1962, University of New Hampshire BS Forestry, 1985. Forester, Jericho, Vermont.

    a.  Emilie Deane Moreau, born April 29, 1993.*

    3.  Kathryn Elisabeth McLane (Katie), born August 2, 1964, Northfield-Mt. Hermon School, Smith College AB 1987, Washington & Lee Law School JD 1991. Administrator, Conservation International, Washington, D.C.

    4.  Duncan Craig McLane, born November 11, 1965, Cushing Academy, Evergreen College. Mechanic.

m. Tierra Roughton, born August 8, 1971.

B.  *Charles Bancroft McLane*, born March 21, 1919, St. Paul's School, Dartmouth College AB 1941, Columbia University PhD 1954. Professor (ret.) Dartmouth College, author, Hanover, New Hampshire.

m. Carol Evarts, born November 15, 1926, Barnard College AB 1948.

    1.  Kristin McLane, born November 8, 1948, Swarthmore College AB 1970. Psychologist, Kodai Kanal International School, Kodai Kanal, India.

m. (1) Patrick Carlson, born April 29, 1949, died June 1, 1984.

    a.  Mani, born May 24, 1986 (A).*

m. (2) Charles Kehler, born April 23, 1947, University of Maryland AB 1970. Teacher, Kodai Kanal International School, Kodai Kanal, India.

    b.   Devin, born May 27, 1990.*

   2.  Alexander McLane, born December 20, 1950, St. Paul's School, Berklee College of Music AB, University of Illinois, PhD. Music librarian, Youngstown University, Youngstown, Ohio.

   3.  Eben McLane, born August 19, 1953, Harvard AB 1976, University of California at Irvine MA 1991. Student, Syracuse University School of Journalism.
   m.  Cynthia Elaine Garrett, born December 10, 1953, University of California at Irvine PhD 1990. Teacher, Wills College, Aurora, New York.

   4.  Rebecca McLane, born July 19, 1955, Art Institute of Chicago BFA 1979, Erikson Institute MEd 1994. Teacher.
   m.  Paul Andrew Jacobson, born December 14, 1953, Northwestern University BME 1978, Roosevelt College LL, MME 1988. Music teacher, Abraham Lincoln School, Oak Park, Illinois.
      a.   Anna, born April 15, 1983.*
      b.   Evan, born January 22, 1986.*

   5.  Jeremiah McLane (Jerry), born October 23, 1957, University of New Hampshire BA 1981. Musician, East Randolph, Vermont.

   6.  Elisabeth Bancroft McLane (Tii), born January 23, 1960, University of Vermont BA 1984. Forester, South Strafford, Vermont.

C.  *Elisabeth Bancroft McLane-Bradley (Lilla)*, born July 2, 1921, St. Mary's-in-the-Mountains, Smith College, University of Wisconsin AB 1943. Volunteer charitable leader, Hanover, New Hampshire.
   m.  David John Bradley, born February 17, 1915. Dartmouth College AB 1938, Harvard Medical School, MD. Author, teacher. Divorced 1992.

   1.  Kim Bradley, born January 29, 1944. Beloit College BA 1966, University of Puget Sound BS 1971. Occupational therapist; owner, Home for Creative Living, Norway, Maine.
   m.  Wayne Emmons, born March 16, 1940.

   2.  David Bradley (Darby), born April 2, 1945. Dartmouth College BA 1967, University of Washington JD 1972. President, Vermont Land Trust, Montpelier, Vermont.
   m.  Liisa Muukari, born May 7, 1946. Plantswoman. Vermont College AS Nursing 1978.
      a.   Kari, born February 29, 1968. University of Chicago AB 1991.
      m.  Gabrielle Malina.
      b.   Markus, born April 27, 1973. Paul Smith's College AS 1994, University of Vermont AS 1996 (prospective).
      c.   Timo, born April 27, 1973. University of Vermont BA 1996.

3. Josephine Crane Bradley (Wendy), born December 8, 1948. University of California at Berkeley AB 1972, JD 1977. Attorney, Vermont Legal Services, St. Johnsbury, Vermont.

m. Robert Morgan, born June 15, 1944. Dartmouth College AB 1966. Drama teacher and theater designer.
    a. Caitlin, born November 28, 1987.*
    b. Tucker, born October 31, 1989. (A)*
    c. Alex, born June 12, 1990.*
    d. Eli, born August 22, 1993. (A)*

4. Ben Bradley, born October 18, 1952. Proctor Academy. Builder, South Strafford, Vermont.

m. Nicolette Corrao, born July 7, 1954. Secretary, singer.

5. Bronwen Bradley, born June 19, 1954. University of Vermont BA 1977. Psychiatric social worker, Natick, Massachusetts.
    a. Nicholas McLane Bradley, born June 16, 1994.*

6. Steven Rama Bradley, born December 11, 1959. Worker in psychiatric residential community.

m. Jody Willcox, born March 20, 1960. Worker in psychiatric residential community.
    a. Mariah Willcox, born April 28, 1992.*
    b. Kolina Willcox, born February 28, 1995.*

D. *Malcolm McLane*, born October 3, 1924, St. Paul's School, Dartmouth College AB 1946, Magdalen College, Oxford University MA 1950, Harvard Law School JD 1952. Attorney, Orr & Reno, Concord, New Hampshire.

m. Susan Neidlinger, born September 28, 1929, Mount Holyoke ex1951. Former New Hampshire state representative and senator.

1. Susan Bancroft McLane (Robin), born December 17, 1948, Harvard University AB 1971. Educational administrator.

m. Robin Read, born April 10, 1946, divorced 1991.
    a. Marion Read, born November 24, 1982.

2. Donald Walker McLane, born November 22, 1950. Northfield-Mt. Hermon School, Brown University AB 1973. Builder, Twisp, Washington.

m. (1) Joni Messer, born 1950, divorced 1976.
    a. Eric Malcolm McLane, born May 26, 1969.

m. (2) Lois Garland, born April 1, 1959. Restaurateur.
    a. Karissa Garland McLane, born July 27, 1983.*
    b. Abigail Garland McLane, born June 1, 1986.*

3. Deborah McLane, born January 11, 1955. Harvard University AB 1974. Schoolteacher, chair of Norwich School Board.

m. Peter Carter, born September 17, 1947, Milton Academy, Harvard College AB 1969, Vermont Law School JD 1978. Attorney, Norwich, Vermont.

    a. Ashley Bancroft Carter, born July 22, 1982.

    b. Maile McLane Carter, born August 28, 1984.*

    c. Laurel Appleton Carter, born October 29, 1986.*

4. Alan McLane, born July 2, 1954. Construction worker, Jackson, New Hampshire.

m. Alice Nichols, born May 14, 1955. University of New Hampshire RN 1995.

    a. Laura Emily Nichols McLane, born September 19, 1981.

    b. Carrie Nichols McLane, born October 4, 1985.*

5. Ann Lloyd McLane, born September 5, 1956, Dartmouth College AB 1978, Georgetown University Law School JD 1984. Attorney, Rath & Young law firm, Concord, New Hampshire.

m. Bradford W. Kuster, born March 24, 1955, University of Michigan AB 1977, JD 1981. Attorney, Orr & Reno, Concord, New Hampshire.

    a. Zachariah Race Kuster, born July 16, 1988.*

    b. Travis McLane Kuster, born September 17, 1991.*

E. *Mary Craig McLane*, born July 28, 1928, St. Mary's-in-the Mountains, Smith College AB 1949. Teacher, artist, Newton Center, Massachusetts.

# APPENDIX C
## *McLane Law Firm Lore*

# State of Vermont v. State of New Hampshire

### 289 U.S. 593 (1933)

*The boundary line between Vermont and New Hampshire was settled by the United States Supreme Court decision summarized here. The decision was handed down during the time that Ralph Davis, Judge's law partner, was attorney general.*

In 1915, the state of Vermont brought suit against the state of New Hampshire for the determination of the boundary line (the Connecticut River) between the two states. Because it was a dispute between two states, the suit was brought as a matter of original jurisdiction in the U.S. Supreme Court. The question was whether the boundary was the "thread," or midpoint, of the river or the west, or Vermont, side, and if the latter, was it the high-water or low-water mark, was it the "mean" low, the low low, or the high low? The question had more than academic interest; there were a number of hydro-electric dams and generating stations with relatively high value waiting to be taxed, and each state wanted to know how much of the dam was in each state. The case dawdled in the courts through the 1920s and finally was referred to a special master, who, after trial, established the line as the low-water mark on the Vermont shore. The master rejected Vermont's claim to the "thread" of the stream and New Hampshire's claim to the high-water mark. The court defined it as "the point to which the river recedes at its lowest stage without reference to extreme droughts." The report was filed, and the Supreme Court[1] in its opinion went thoroughly into the history of the case, quoting the royal grant in 1674 creating the Province of New York, which extended westerly "from the west side of the Connecticut River." Governor Wentworth, the colonial governor of New Hampshire from 1752 to 1764, created twenty-three towns in New Hampshire along the Connecticut River all beginning at a bound "on the westerly side or bank of the river," a fact that was widely known and not disputed. Vermont, which became a state in 1791, was carved out of the state of New York and therefore took New York's eastern bound, which was the westerly side of the Connecticut River. The U.S. Supreme Court adopted the report of the special master.

Ralph Davis was attorney general (AG) when this case was finally decided. Davis received some credit for its favorable result. Because the firm of Warren,

Howe & Wilson, predecessor to Wiggin & Nourie, had been appointed special counsel to the state and handled the case from 1915 to 1933, the AG's office had only supervisory jurisdiction over the case. I suspect that Judge McLane played some part in the selection of his law school classmate, Charles Evans Hughes, Jr., a New York attorney, son of the chief justice of the U.S. Supreme Court, to argue the case before the Supreme Court.

## Note

1. State of Vermont v. State of New Hampshire, 289 U.S. 593 (1933). C. J. Charles Evans Hughes took no part in the consideration or decision of this case. His son, Charles Evans Hughes, Jr., argued the case for the state of New Hampshire.

# Max Englehart

*Max Englehart was rescued on Mount Washington after being lost in a snowstorm in October 1925. Judge and Elisabeth climbed and skied on the mountain one or more times per year for some fifty years. Max became a client of the firm, which successfully sued the Glen House for negligence in causing Max's injuries.*

Headlines from the *Manchester Union*, Wednesday, October 14, 1925: "Fear Missing Man Dead In Drifts On Mount Washington." "Men On Snowshoes Scour Tuckerman's Ravine For Remains." "Caretaker Englehart left on Friday at Height of Gale."

*Excerpts from*
**The Rescue Of Max Englehart**
by Arthur F. Whitehead
published in the June 1959 issue of *APPALACHIA*, p. 385.

By the 25th of September, 1925, all was quiet around Pinkham Notch. For the convenience of the guests of the Glen House who would make the auto trip to the summit, [of Mount Washington],[1] the Glen House opened the old Stage Office and sent up Max Englehart to serve coffee, sandwiches, and similar food. Max, 58, was a great woodsman and trapper. While mountains were new to him, it was felt that with his experience he could easily adapt himself to life on the summit.

Friday the 9th. About 9 p.m. it started to snow.

Saturday, the 10th. There were 8-9" of snow. About 8 a.m. the temperature suddenly dropped and the wind picked up, before long the temperature was 17 degrees and the wind was terrific. We did not entertain any fears for Englehart on top, however, since he was well supplied with food and firewood, and his building was strong and chained down. By Saturday evening there was no let-up in the storm.

Sunday the 11th the storm lessened. We had about a foot and a half around our place [Pinkham Notch AMC huts] with many deep drifts. The summit and lower peaks were still in the clouds, with the storm raging furiously. Above the Cascades the snow was 2 feet deep and near Hermit Lake it averaged 3-4 feet.

By Monday the 12th the snow was practically gone from the

region around camp, but higher up the storm still continued. Joe [Dodge][2] went to Gorham. On his return he stopped at the Glen House and learned that Englehart was missing from the top! Monday, two Glen House guests reached the top after a terrific battle with the elements. They were to tell Englehart to close up and come down. But no one greeted them. The building was cold, snow had forced in through the walls. They found a note on the table in Englehart's scrawl: "Laf at 12 for Tocmans [Tuckerman's] Arein [Ravine—the shortest and steepest way down] no wood." When the two climbers reached the Glen House again, badly exhausted, shortly before Joe stopped in there, plans for a search party were organized. The search party was to start early the following morning.

By pushing it through the drifts, we managed to get the old Pierce Arrow touring car a little over two miles up the Carriage Road. Joe and I expected to get more help from the search crew at the Halfway House, but the workers there were too intent on getting their house closed that day to be interested in searching—a rather callous reception, Joe and I thought.

We reached the summit at about 11 a.m. In the Stage Office we found on all sides evidences of Englehart's hurried departure—the coffee pot was frozen on the stove, the water in the washboiler was frozen solid. Still there was plenty of food and many pieces of furniture which could have been broken up into firewood. The terrific force of the wind had blown the snow through the walls and built a drift about six feet high extending four feet from the west wall, even partially covering the table. Sharp eyed Joe saw writing on the wall "Je pars, date Oct 11 1925. Poudre de neige; le vent souffle d'une force de 100 miles à l'heure; maisante, temperature tres mugir. Max." The 11th was Sunday; he had now been missing 48 hours!

Our next step would be a search of the cone. We had come to the conclusion that we were searching for a frozen body, we did not see how anyone could live in that terrific storm. We saw many marks which we thought were footprints, but we decided that they were all the work of the wind. Many out-jutting rocks resembled a body. We finally reached the edge of the low scrub on the Alpine Garden, at cloud level. There was nothing in sight to give us hope. We crossed over the head of Huntington Ravine and continued nearly to the road, then headed back for the summit, slabbing the cone. We decided to make another sortie, this time following the general direction of the Tuckerman Trail. The wind was springing up faster. We decided we'd better move down before we got into serious difficulties ourselves, since the weather was increasing in violence.

After supper at the Glen House we discussed the probabilities. If snow shoes could be got hold of, Joe and I would go up the next day and search Tuckerman's, Boot Spur, Lion Head, Huntington's. The others tried to dissuade us from further search, saying it was useless, that Englehart was buried somewhere on the cone, but finally Libby agreed to get us some snowshoes by morning.

The sun was shining bright when we awoke—it was about 10 a.m. wonderful clear day out, warm, the sky a deep blue. At last, about 11:30, a car drove in and Libby stepped out with our snow shoes. At 1:30, one hour after leaving Pinkham we arrived at Hermit Lake Shelter A.

The snow where we now were averaged four to five feet in depth. Suddenly I heard a noise like a railroad whistle far off—but I said nothing. It was a calm, clear day, sound would travel for miles under such conditions, and I thought it was a Crawford Notch train. Then it came again—more like a wail, I looked at Joe, he looked at me. What were we hearing? I asked Joe if he had heard the previous wail—he had. Together we let out a war whoop. Almost on top of the crashing echoes came a yell, strangely near— "HELP"—a long drawn out wail. We could not locate its direction, so we yelled together "stay where you are, we're coming—keep calling."

We had not gone far from the trail when I stopped. I had seen a head low down on the level of the snow. "Do you see him?" asked Joe. I pointed out—and we crashed through, jumping over fallen trees— there he was, crouched in the lee of a boulder, where a brook kept an open spot in the snow. A face lined, cracked, haggard, unshorn, blood shot eyes, no hat, clothes apparently soaked, but still full of life and spirit until we reached him. Then he broke down and cried like a baby. His exact words, at greeting I do not remember, it seems it was a repetition of "Oh my dears!" and an exhortation for us to put on some clothes before we froze. We were still in our steaming undershirts. In a jiffy our snow shoes were off, we laid Max out on them in the sun, took off his wet leather jacket, shirt, and gloves and gave him my green mackinaw shirt, Joe's gloves and toboggan hat. We gave him some coffee with a shot of alcohol and then pressed our bodies to him to give him warmth. Suddenly we were in a shadow; that galvanized us to action. Ways and means of getting him down were the main question. Joe took him on his back for the first carry—but that was disastrous as they sank through the snow. Then we lifted him on an improvised stretcher, but it wouldn't work. The next thought was a drag or travois. When we brought the poles back, Max showed us how to rig it up. He cried only once, then was himself again, a woodsman who did not know the meaning of the word "die." Near the Raymond path we abandoned the drag, we removed the snowshoes and with solid places under our feet we were able to carry Max. On easy stretches, he tried walking with our support—it must have been agony to him.

On the way down Max told us his story: terrific gale, whipping snow. Alone he began to imagine things in the howling gale, rocking cabin and snapping chains were not conducive to clear thought. His wood gone, he broke up chairs. He attempted to go out for more wood but the storm tossed him many feet. The wind took the storm door off its hinges and it went sailing to parts unknown. He did not know how much longer he would be marooned so decided to seek the valley. He fled the office about noon Sunday taking only a few raisins for food. He went straight with the wind. His hat soon blew off. He reached the edge of Tuckerman's but could find no way down, so crawled into a hole in the snow for the night. Next day he wandered but could find no way down and spent a second night on the cone. Tuesday dawned— with hands and feet frozen, he was ready to try anything so approached the Ravine, found the most likely spot and let her go! He had a terrific slide, damaging his shoulder, wrenching his back and hips he rolled over and over in that awful quarter mile ride. He wandered until he found water and slept the third night. He woke, hollered, went to sleep, awoke about one and hollered again when he was heard.

We got him down about 8:00 p.m. in the dark. A doctor arrived, gave him first aid and recommended getting him to the Glen House which was warm. Next morning Joe and I stopped at the Glen House and found Max feeling pretty chipper—feet badly frost bitten, hands and face nipped and a temp of 100 degrees. Max was taken to the Berlin Hospital where it was found necessary to amputate the toes and heel of one foot and later the toes on the other since gangrene had set in. He was at the hospital many weeks. Since, he has had artificial members made to replace the lost ones and manages to get around fairly on them.

Extract from William Lowell Putnam, *Joe Dodge* (Canaan, N.H: 1986), Phoenix Publishing, p. 87 re Max Englehart.

The year before that we had an early season snow storm. It started on a Friday night, October 9th, it was, and when it stopped on Sunday, we had a foot and a half at Pinkham and of course there was more up above. Well, come Monday morning, Elliot Libby was missing one of his men who had been assigned to cook up at the stage house on the Summit. Later on we figured that this guy, Max Englehart, had pan- icked because of the storm and took off down the mountain; he had left a note saying that he was going by way of Tuckerman Ravine. Well, we commenced a search for him, Libby, myself and some others, but it was a funny thing, the people who were working at the Halfway House, their closing crew, they wouldn't help, the only refusal I've ever gotten. We went all over the cone and down the Alpine Garden looking for tracks or clues but we couldn't see any signs and the going was terrible. Everyone was ready to give up, but I decided we'd try once more on Wednesday. So early that morning, Art Whitehead and

I went up on Tuckerman and commenced to holler around. Pretty quick we had an answer and we found the guy, his feet were frozen up a bit, but he was alive and had stayed in a snow cave. So we sort of walked and carried him down to Pinkham, got in there after dark, and he lost only part of one heel and some toes. Four days he was out in the snow, confused and alone. The club elected us life members because of that rescue."

After Max Englehart had recovered from his injuries, he came into the McLane law firm in the spring of 1926 to ascertain his legal rights. Judge and Ralph talked with him and got his story. Then they did their own investigation and interviewed witnesses, including his doctors. They brought suit against the Glen House company for negligently causing his injuries. Ralph took depositions where necessary and negotiated with the Sulloway office in Concord, which represented the defendant. The case was finally settled for $6,000, a sizable sum in 1926. Max was fortunate in not being more seriously injured and lived a good life thereafter.[3]

# Notes

1. The summit of Mount Washington is 6,288 feet above sea level, the highest point in New England. The final 1,500 feet are above tree line, making it one of the most exposed mountain peaks in the world. The world's highest measured wind velocity was recorded there in April 1934 with sustained winds for five minutes of 188 miles per hour and one gust of 231 mph.

2. Then recently appointed head of the Appalachian Mountain Club mountain operations, later father of Ann Dodge, who married Jack B. Middleton, a partner in the McLane law firm.

3. Judge and Elisabeth experienced this same storm returning from Europe. They took a train from Montreal to New Hampshire on Saturday, October 10, "through a heavy blizzard."

# Stan Brown and the
# Little Old Lady

*Lawyers run into all kinds of people, as clients, opponents, or witnesses. Stan Brown had a memorable experience with a rather clever woman. This story was part of the lore of the McLane firm.*

When Stan Brown was in the office as an associate, Miss Mansfield gave him some promissory notes from the estate of Mary McBride[1] to collect.[2] Mrs. McBride was eighty years old when she died. She had been a widow for about fifteen years and lived comfortably in a modest apartment on the first floor of a typical Manchester triple-decker on Green Street. Her husband, Thomas, had a good job with the Amoskeag, Mills as a bookkeeper. He was a good Irishman and had come from the Medford, Massachusetts, area after high school, where he had taken bookkeeping and accounting courses. He had worked his way up the ladder. The McBrides had bought the lot from Amoskeag, which took back a second mortgage for the purchase price. Then the McBrides got a first mortgage, putting up the lot as equity, and constructed their home. They rented out the upper floors, which took care of the mortgage payments, taxes, and most of the insurance. Mary had worked in the mills before the two children were born and again after they were in high school. The result of this was that they were able to put away a nice nest egg, which they had invested conservatively and wisely. They intended to live out their retirement years on the income. Unfortunately, Thomas died suddenly from a heart attack soon after his retirement.

There was nothing unusual about the estate. It contained the real estate and marketable securities for the most part. There were, however, a series of promissory notes payable on demand dated over a ten-year period for amounts of money ranging from $1,000 to $2,500 and totaling about $4,000. Interest and principal payments had apparently been made sporadically. There were no set dates for the payment of either principal or interest. No payments had been made for more than a year. According to some correspondence Stan found, the maker of all the notes was a Katherine Murphy,[3] who lived in Medford, Massachusetts. The children were unable to shed any light on who the person was, although they believed she was some kind of friend of the family. Nor did they know why the loans had been made. Stan dutifully wrote on behalf of the executor making a demand for payment and sent the letter certified mail. It was returned marked "undeliverable, no forwarding address." The telephone line was disconnected. He decided to investigate (there were no paralegals then). He drove to Medford and found the apartment house and her name on the door to her apartment, but there was no response to his knock. Stan tried the other apartments and found a few people at home who said that Mrs. Murphy was rarely there. She occasionally did spend a few days or maybe a week at a time there, but she might be gone for several months. Some thought she went to Florida in the winter. Upon further questioning, Stan found she never appeared with anyone, was always alone, and did not talk much to people. She was perfectly civil but aloof. She was probably in her seventies, short, white haired, well dressed, with a lively step and twinkling eyes. She seemed to be well off.

Stan was running into a blank wall trying to find out anything helpful about this "mystery lady." He decided to try the police department. He was referred by the desk sergeant to the Detective Division upstairs and was assigned to Detective Sullivan, in plainclothes, as most detectives were. Stan introduced himself as a New Hampshire lawyer and indicated he was settling an estate and had a promissory note made by———. The detective interrupted, "Katherine Murphy, I presume."

"That's right. Do you know her?" responded Stan.

"Know her? Do you want to see the file we have on her? Wait a minute. I'll need the paddy wagon to fetch it from the warehouse." The detective leaned back in his wooden captain's chair with his hands behind his neck and roared with laughter. "Good old Katherine has done it again." Stan didn't see anything funny in the situation and inquired, "Well, what's up?"

"Katherine is a real clever Irishwoman—I guess we Irish all are—and there's not much you can do about it. My advice to you, sir, is to forget the whole thing and go back to New Hampshire and carry on your law business there."

"I don't know what she's done or why I can't collect on a perfectly legitimate debt. I can't go back empty-handed."

"Well, I'll tell you the story as well as we can piece it together. You can talk to almost any lawyer in Medford, Reading, Melrose, and Winchester and they will all tell you the same story."

This is the story the detective told. Katherine would read the obituaries in the local papers and mull over the potential of each one.[4] When she found the right one, a man about retirement age without a large family, living in a modest community and preferably of Irish extraction, she would telephone the widow and say how sorry she was to read about the death of, say, Mike, whom she had gone to grade school with about fifty years before. She said she'd like to help out in memory of dear old Mike and suggested that, since she was not doing anything for a few days, she'd be very happy to come over to prepare meals and clean up. She knew there would be a lot of family and friends dropping in over the course of the next week or two and she thought she could be helpful. She didn't want anything for it. She had plenty herself and she just wanted to do it as a friend of Mike. It was an offer the widow, Dolly, could not refuse. Katherine went to the house and did a superb job of helping, cooking, waiting on the table, making the beds, cleaning, and being very pleasant. After the excitement had gone and everyone had left for home, Katherine would take her leave. The poor widow, Dolly, couldn't thank her enough for all she had done and they had really come to know each other like family. Dolly would always say, "If there's anything I can do for you anytime, just let me know."

Well, there was something she could do for Katherine. After a respectable time of six months to a year, the widow would get a newsy letter from Katherine saying how fine she was, but she had just had an expensive minor operation, or an article she had written had been accepted for publication but she wouldn't get paid until the publication date three months hence, or her uncle had died and she should have her legacy by now but the lawyers had written saying there was a glitch and it would be about six months before the court released the funds. She was temporarily strapped since she had to pay her bills, and could Dolly loan her a little money for a while, say $500, and of course she would pay interest. Katherine would say that, just to make it easier for Dolly, she was enclosing a promissory note, all signed for the $500, so all Dolly had to do was to send along her check in the enclosed stamped, self-addressed envelope and, of course, Dolly would comment to herself how thoughtful Katherine always was. Dolly would invariably send the money pronto. Dolly would usually get the interest punctually for the first year or so, then there might be a skip or two, and occasionally there was a principal payment; Katherine might even pay the note off. Sometimes she asked for more or consolidated two or more notes into one, but the total amount owed rarely exceeded $3,000 to $4,000.

"I'm beginning to get the picture," said Stan. "Tell me, did she have any income herself, and how many people did she owe?"

"Oh, yes, she has a modest amount, enough to get along with. She used to work, so she collects her Social Security, and her husband worked for the B&M Railroad, so she gets retirement benefits from the Railroad Fund. Then she sold her house and now rents. Oh, I guess in the last ten years, there have been about fifty people with notes."

"She never seems to be around much. Where does she go and what does she do?"

"Now you're getting hot, Mr. Brown. If you want to know the truth, Katherine plays the horses. She probably knows more tracks, Suffolk Downs, Belmont, Pimlico, Hialeah, up and down the East Coast, more horses, more jockeys, more trainers than anyone. She goes from track to track and wins some and loses some, never in large amounts, and keeps going year in and year out. Everyone apparently knows her. When she runs short, she'll issue some more promissory notes to her friends and recharge her supplies. She always said she wanted to go to the Ascot races in England, but she hasn't made it yet."

"Hell, that woman's a menace to society. Why don't you guys do something about it?"

"Mr. Brown, you're a lawyer. You tell me what we can do. Did she steal anything? No, your client gave her the money; Katherine never took anything. Did she embezzle anything? No, your client gave her ownership and possession of the money. Did Katherine obtain money under false pretenses? She never said what she was going to use the money for, she just said she needed money and gave a note in return and made payments on the note to boot. Where's the criminal intent? Katherine is a very imaginative Irishwoman. We could use her on the force."

"Well, I guess you've got me, and I'm one who doesn't take defeat lightly."

"We can compensate you for that to make you feel better. We'll add your name to the honor roll of distinguished lawyers who are still trying to collect on promissory notes of Katherine Murphy."

"Thanks a bunch," said Stan as he shook the detective's hand and headed for home.

# Notes

1. Fictitious name. Some of the details of the story have been fictionalized.

2. Miss Mansfield always turned over anything that smacked of being adversarial to one of the "boys," or associates. Only the partners were "men."

3. Fictitious name.

4. In our case, Thomas McBride had come from Medford, so the *Union Leader* forwarded the obituary to the local Medford paper, which had printed it.

# Ken Graf and the German Spies

*This is a war story emanating from Ken Graf's tour of duty in the U.S. Army. Although it doesn't have much to do with the McLane law firm, it was a familiar story that was told originally by Ken Graf and repeated by him and others to the newcomers in the office. The story improved with age and the number of storytellers. It is too good not to include in this history.*

## INTRODUCTION

Kenneth F. Graf, a partner in the McLane law firm, served in the U.S. Army, Office of the Judge Advocate General (JAG), in 1944. He was stationed at the Port of Embarkation in New York City. He participated on the prosecution team headed by Mr. Justice Tom Clark (appointed after the war), which tried and convicted two German spies. They had landed from a German submarine off the coast of Maine in November 1944 and were apprehended in New York City within a month. After the war and upon returning to Manchester, Ken told the law firm office the story, which was retold many times by different members of the firm and thus became part of the "Lore" of the office. The names of the spies in the "Lore" version were Hans Colepaugh and Max Gimbel. Forty years later, in the late 1980s, when I started to write this history of the law firm, I decided to include, as an appendix, Ken Graf's spy story. This was after his death in December 1991, so I was unable to consult with Ken about his recollections. I wrote the story as well as I could remember it, with a few "assumed" added facts and a little dramatization. Ken's son, John Graf, read it and confirmed the general tenor as being in line with what he remembered of Ken's story. A year or so later, John Graf said that he found a brown file folder in his father's papers with a great deal of material about the spy story. He knew that I would be interested, but the file was temporarily mislaid. Before John Graf could find the missing file, he died prematurely from cancer. His widow, Ann Graf, in going through some of John's papers, found the missing folder and turned it over to me in the spring of 1994. The file contained much of the investigation by the FBI, including summaries of the interrogation of the principal defendants and persons with whom they came in contact; the summaries had formed the basis for the trial testimony. The true names of the spies were William Colepaugh and Erich Gimpel. The folder did not include the transcript of the trial. What follows is the true story derived from the record. The "Lore" story is printed below in italics, because for many years it is what the office believed, plus it adds some dramatization to the story. In a few events it is different from the factual story, which follows.

# THE SPY STORY
## Lore

*It was in the wee hours of the morning in the fall of 1944 during World War II at the 46th Street police precinct headquarters in midtown Manhattan, an area of cheap hotels and gay bars. The sergeant on duty was experiencing a quiet night enjoying a dime novel to pass away the time. The heavy outside door to the massive, fortresslike Victorian brick building opened with a creak and the sergeant heard footsteps coming up the noisy, dusty old wooden stair treads. A medium-height man with blondish hair in his twenties neatly attired in a trench coat stood at attention in front of the counter, waiting for the sergeant to speak.*

*"What do you want?" growled the sergeant, not really looking up from his book.*

*"Sir, I want to report that I am a German spy," the man stated in a clear voice without any indication of a foreign accent.*

*The sergeant looked up at the man, detected the odor of alcohol on his breath, and concluded he had too much to drink. There were plenty of queer people at this station anytime of the day or night. "I can't do anything about that now. You'll have to come back in the morning and tell it to the lieutenant. He'll take care of you then."*

*"But I can't leave now. They will get me."*

*"Who's going to get you?" The sergeant noted that the man spoke clearly without any slurring or sign of drunkenness, nor did he sway on his feet.*

*"The other German that I've been with since we landed."*

*"Landed? What do you mean?"*

*"We came over to the States in a sub and landed up on the Maine coast about two weeks ago and came to New York."*

*The sergeant said to himself, Boy, I'd look pretty stupid if I let this guy go and he did turn out to be a spy. Matter of fact, he does look kind of German, doesn't he? I'd better let the boss know. He called his superior at the main headquarters and told him what had happened.*

*The boss said he wanted to talk to the gentleman. He found out that the man, whose name was Hans Colepaugh, had come to the United States with an accomplice in a German sub that had worked its way up into Frenchman's Bay near Mt. Desert, on the coast of Maine, on November 29 and landed the two from a rubber lifeboat on Hancock Point. With a couple of suitcases apiece, they found the road, walked to Ellsworth, and spent the night in a motel. The next day they took the* State of Maine Express *to New York City.*

*The lieutenant instructed the sergeant to book Hans and lock him up for the night; in the morning they would decide how to proceed. The lieutenant contacted the Maine State Police to verify the story. The police knew of no German submarine but searched their records and called back to the lieutenant in New York City to say that on the day mentioned, there had been a local police report from a Boy Scout stating that as he was walking along the Hancock Point Road, he observed two pairs of men's boot tracks in the snow coming up from a small beach and no tracks going down toward the water and that looked suspicious. There also had been a separate report made the same day that there were two odd-looking men in trench coats carrying suitcases on the Hancock Point Road walking toward Ellsworth early in the morning. By the time anyone could investigate these two low-priority incidents in a somewhat remote area, the footprints had been obliterated and no such men were found. Hans, however, certainly seemed to know what he was talking about.*

*In the morning, the New York City police concluded that this was out of their jurisdiction and that it belonged to the U.S. Army, New York Port of Embarkation command, to which Kenneth F. Graf was assigned by the Office of the Judge Advocate General (JAG). The military police van picked Hans up and transported him to the Battery, then via the ferry to Governor's Island, the headquarters of the New York Port of Embarkation. He was incarcerated in the military prison on Governors Island. The JAG assumed control of the investigation and prosecution of the case.*

# Factual

On September 24, 1944, William Curtis Colepaugh, a U.S. citizen using the name of William Charles Caldwell for his espionage mission to the United States, boarded German submarine U-1230 in Kiel, Germany, with Erich Gimpel, a German citizen, with the name of Edward George Green for this mission. Two SS officers (a special part of the German army, not under the high command but under Heinrich Himmler, who was in charge of political affairs, security, and intelligence) were at Kiel with them and supplied them with $60,000 in American bills and forged identification papers from selective service boards, including registration and classification cards, birth certificates, driver's licenses, and discharge papers from the U.S. Naval Reserve. There also were blank sheets of paper with forged signatures and official seals to be filled out in case of need. They also had several rolls of film with microdots that could be read under a microscope, which provided information for radio communication such as call signs, frequencies, times of transmission, and code instructions. They had two bottles of secret ink and a list of American prisoners of war in Germany to whom they were to write innocuous messages in plain language (but embedded in the paper was the message with the secret ink). The letters would be intercepted by the Germans and the secret message decoded. They had previously been provided with American-made Colt .32 revolvers and a Leica camera. Their mission was to obtain information from newspapers on the progress of the war; the attitude of the Americans toward the Germans, British, and Russians; and particularly technical developments in manufacturing and defense work, names and activities of groups and organizations opposed to the war, and statistical information on production, the economy, et cetera.

They departed and laid off Kiel for two days awaiting a convoy. They traveled with it part time, reporting that when they were detached from the convoy and were traveling submerged, they heard depth charges daily about a mile or two away. They proceeded to Norway, where they spent six days undergoing final tests. This was an old sub that had been outfitted with the new Schnorkelmasts so that the sub, with its diesel engines, could cruise just under the surface taking in and discharging air through the Schnorkel. The sub could cruise at about seven knots on diesel power but only two knots on its electric batteries. They proceeded to Kristiansand, Norway, for final fueling and provisioning and departed on October 6 for the trip across the Atlantic, passing just south of Iceland and taking fifty-four days.

About a week and a half at sea, the intake valve of the Schnorkel failed, permitting water to enter and shut off the diesel engines. This flooded the sub with dangerous fumes, which could not be exhausted through the Schnorkel. Fortunately, someone turned on the electric motors so the sub could surface, open the hatches, purge the boat of the fumes, and also let the crew go topside for fresh air. The Schnorkel valves gave the Germans much grief. Shortly after this incident, they were depth bombed, but they escaped by descending to a deeper level. About seven days before landing, a message was received that another sub with an espionage agent bound for the United States had been sunk about November 22 off the New England coast. While at Kristiansand, Colepaugh learned that the British had bombed and sunk a sub off Norway with several agents bound for the United States.

After entering the Gulf of Maine, they stayed near Mt. Desert Rock for about a week observing the relatively few boats, mostly fishermen. On November 29, they proceeded, submerged, into Frenchman's Bay, passing Egg Rock Light and hauling up off Crabtree Point opposite Hancock Point. Colepaugh and Gimpel changed to civilian clothes, took their bags and got into the rubber dinghy to row ashore. There was supposed to be a long painter attached so the dinghy could be pulled back to the sub, but it broke on launching, so two sailors jumped in and rowed them ashore, about three hundred yards, just before midnight with a full moon and a light dusting of snow. The sailors gave a "Heil Hitler" salute and pushed off for the sub while Colepaugh and Gimpel took their bags and made their way through the woods several hundred yards to a dirt road. They started walking toward Ellsworth. About 12:30 A.M., two cars passed them going in the opposite direction. A car going in their direction stopped; it turned out to be a taxi, which gave them a ride to Ellsworth. They really wanted to get to Bangor, so they negotiated the trip there and arrived about 1:30 A.M. in time to make a 2 A.M. train for Portland. They arrived there at 6 A.M., caught the 7A.M. train for Boston, and arrived at 10 A.M., they bought two hats, registered at the Essex Hotel, and slept.

## Lore

*They took the train to New York City, and found a small, inexpensive apartment-hotel midtown on the East Side near Third Avenue and set about doing their work. Hans spent a lot of time doing research at the main New York City library at Fifth Avenue and 42nd Street checking out organizations and the* New York Times. *It was pretty dull and uninspiring work, which set his mind to thinking. He had been promised more education and stimulating work to challenge his creative mind. True, he had had some more education, but no stimulating work. The thought came to him, "Maybe they are taking advantage of me; maybe they never did intend to carry out their promises; maybe all they wanted was my command of the English language. What's in it for me? More promises of money, fame, and jobs if the Nazis win. What if they don't? I'm in a pickle, a spy behind the enemy lines in wartime." He started to wonder if the Germans could win. In Germany, the Nazis seemed invincible, but over here, military production was just getting rolling. The Allies had already landed in Africa and jumped over to Sicily and Italy. In the Pacific, in spite of Pearl Harbor, the Allies were beginning to score naval victories against the Japanese and had gained a foothold on Guadalcanal and the Solomon Islands. The idea began to gnaw at him; it kept coming back to him, day after day, that he was a fool. What could he do about it? That took a lot of thought. Probably it would be smart to get out of the United States; then if he were caught, he might avoid any spy charge. He'd been to Montreal, Canada, when he was at MIT, and liked it, although it was about 100 percent French, for whom he didn't care. If he went farther west, he would find more Anglo-Saxons, which would be better. He'd never been to South America or to the Caribbean and felt uncomfortable thinking about it. He knew there were many Germans there in the underground. So after a couple of more days mulling over his options, his mind firmed up on a plan that made sense. He would go to Montreal and then head west to a city where he could get a job as a machinist or an engineer, either civil or mechanical. With his forged documents, he should have no problems. Now all he needed was some of the money that Max kept in the apartment in the spare suitcase. Hans would leave for work as he usually did before Max, watch from across the street until Max had gone, then return to the room, pick up his things and the money and go directly to Grand Central Station. He waited a couple of days so Max wouldn't detect any mood changes, then put the plan into action. Everything worked out beautifully.*

*At Grand Central Station, it was at about 10 in the morning, he went to the ticket counter, bought his ticket, and found that the next train for Montreal left about five o'clock and arrived the following morning, so Hans had some time to kill. It would be best to lay low and not be seen, so he decided to go to the movies—there were several nearby. He also decided that he didn't want to carry the heavy bag around, so he checked it in one of the checkrooms, after putting the ticket in the suitcase. The attendant asked how long he was going to be, because the place was sort of full. Hans responded that it would be only for a few hours, so the attendant put the bag along the wall near the front of the checkroom and gave Hans his receipt. Hans took in a couple of movies, had some lunch, trying to be as inconspicuous as possible, then returned to Grand Central about three o'clock, entering from the north side at the Park Avenue upper-level entrance.*

*Grand Central Station is a monumental piece of architecture: The main room is about two hundred feet square, six stories high, with skylights in the roof and large glass windows on all sides through which the sunlight streams; the floor of the main hall is about two stories below the upper entry level. The two levels are connected by a grand marble staircase that rises from the main floor one story to a broad landing and then splits in two and rises at right angles ascending to the upper level. Here there is a broad walkway with shops on the outer side and a balustrade on the inner side overlooking the main floor below. At nine in the morning and at five in the evening, when all the commuter trains are loading or unloading, there are probably 2,000 to 3,000 people at any one time scurrying across the main floor to and from the trains.*

*Hans entered Grand Central at the upper level, crossed the walkway to the balustrade, and looked down on the main floor. To his right the handsome spacious stairs descended to the main floor. Beyond the foot of the stairs Hans could see the counter of the checkroom where he had left his suitcase. He gave a gasp; the pit of his stomach sank and his knees caved in. He grabbed the balustrade for support. There in front of the checkroom was Max, seemingly in a hurry, taking Hans' bag and then hurrying off in the direction of the trains. There went all of Hans' worldly possessions, all the money, and his ticket to Montreal. What should he do now? Slowly, the realization came that he was in big trouble. He decided he needed a drink, so he wandered over to a gay bar he knew on 46th Street and had a beer. He met a "friend," a somewhat older man who seemed a sympathetic individual. They had a beer, then supper together, and retired to his apartment a block or two away. There Hans poured out his story and sought advice. His friend quickly concluded that Hans could do only one thing, namely, turn himself in, be cooperative, and hope that the authorities would recommend something less than the death penalty. His life would never be safe from the German "apparatus" and, at some point, he would undoubtedly be caught by the Allies and his identity revealed. In fact, his friend pointed out, in all likelihood, Max had already anonymously reported his existence in New York City to the authorities. Hans readily agreed that his friend was right, so in the wee small hours of the morning he said good-bye, walked over to the fortresslike brick 46th Street precinct station, pulled open the huge heavy door, walked up the creaky wooden stairs to the reception area, and addressed the sergeant on duty.*

## Factual

On December 1, William and Erich took an early train to New York, arriving about 1:30 P.M. They left one bag at the Grand Central Station parcel checkroom and the other (with the money) at Pennsylvania Station. Gimpel kept the key and the tickets for that bag. They each had about $4,000 cash on them, enough to pay expenses for several weeks. At the Kenmore Hall Hotel they registered as Caldwell and Green and stayed until December 9, going off each morning and returning at night to give the impression they had regular jobs. Gimpel didn't want to let Colepaugh out of his sight, although at night Colepaugh got loose to socialize. They didn't do much, attending movies and killing time. They said nothing about visiting libraries, reading newspapers, or collecting intelligence. They did pore over papers to find a place to rent in a wooden building, without steel girders, which would permit shortwave radio transmission and receiving. They looked over many possibilities, finally found a satisfactory apartment at 39 Beekman Place, and signed up for two months, paying in advance. Between December 9 and 20, they bought some electronic testing equipment and materials so Gimpel could make a shortwave radio.

Colepaugh had idealistically admired the German army and went to Germany to enlist, having received encouragement from the German consul in Boston. However, the SS sent him back to the United States on an espionage mission. This was not what he had been promised, and he felt jilted. On the sub he decided to defect and get in touch with the American authorities as soon as he arrived in the United States. There was no opportunity to do this until December 22.

On December 13, Gimpel retrieved the bag with the money from Penn Station and brought it to the apartment. At about the same time, both Gimpel and Colepaugh had ordered new suits from different stores. On Thursday, December 21, in the afternoon, they went to Rockefeller Center to pick up the suits. Colepaugh obtained his first at the Roger Kent store and had it in a box with the store name prominently displayed. Then they went to the Robert Reed store to pick up Gimpel's purchase. Colepaugh said he would be embarrassed to go into the store with a Roger Kent package, that he would wait outside, listen to the Christmas carols, and watch the skating in the sunken plaza of Rockefeller Center. As soon as he thought Gimpel could not observe him in the crowd, Colepaugh grabbed a cab, went to the Beekman Place apartment and told the cabdriver to wait while he got his bags and then they would go to Grand Central Station, where he had to catch a train. Colepaugh retrieved the two bags they brought with them (including the one with the money). Passing the landlord in the hall, he said he was going to Connecticut for Christmas with relatives and would be back. He got in the cab for Grand Central, where he checked the two bags at 6 P.M. in the west parcel room on the main floor. He had about $4,000 cash with him and did not need more money, so he never did go back to Grand Central to recover the bags.

He took the Lexington Avenue subway uptown to 57th Street, registered at the St. Moritz Hotel until the twenty-sixth, and thought about his next course of action. He had been interrogated by the FBI in Philadelphia several years before about a violation of the draft law when he was in the merchant marine. He remembered the agent's name but decided he was too far away and probably wasn't there anymore. He then recalled his classmate, Ed Mulcahey, at the Admiral Farragut Academy in New Jersey and remembered he had been in the army so would know what to do.[1] On December 23 about 11 A.M., he took the train to Jamaica and found Mulcahey's house, which he had visited once. Mulcahey's mother remembered him and informed him that Ed was working at a Thom McAn shoe store not far away. Colepaugh called him and made a date for lunch at 2 p.m. and later agreed to meet that evening after Ed finished work. Ed's mother left to spend Christmas with friends in Philadelphia, so was gone for the next few days. That evening Colepaugh poured out his whole story until early in the morning and asked for help. Mulcahey knew an FBI agent, William Oakley, whom he could contact. On the twenty-fourth, Colepaugh went in town for a social engagement and returned to Mulcahey's in the afternoon. On Christmas Eve they went to several gay bars in Greenwich Village. Mulcahey acknowledged that he was gay and propositioned Colepaugh, who refused. Colepaugh had had a number of encounters with females, some picked up at bars and others arranged for; some were paid—he appears to have been a confirmed heterosexual. Each went a separate way late Christmas Eve. Colepaugh returned about 9 A.M. on Christmas and slept all day. In the evening, they went to dinner with a Mr. Gaylord, whom Mulcahey had brought home the previous night. After Gaylord left, they talked about contacting FBI agent Oakley or someone in the FBI. Mulcahey went to work on December 26. Colepaugh went in town, bought a bag, checked out of the hotel, and brought his things to Mulcahey's.

Colepaugh met Mulcahey at his work place at 5 P.M., had a bite to eat and returned home. At 6 P.M. Mulcahey called the FBI and asked that an agent come to the house as soon as possible, that it was very important but he could not talk about it on the phone. At 7:30 P.M. agent McCue arrived and was introduced to Colepaugh, who told his story and turned over to the agent all of his possessions. McCue called for backup; other agents arrived and further interrogated Colepaugh, who was appropriately warned of his legal rights and that whatever he said could be used against him. At about 11:30 P.M., Colepaugh, with the agents and Mulcahey, went to the FBI headquarters in New York, where he was booked. The FBI were interested in knowing everything about Gimpel in order to try to apprehend him.

Colepaugh had turned over to the FBI the baggage receipts for the bags checked on December 21. At 3:30 A.M. on December 27, two agents went to the baggage checkroom at Grand Central Station, which is open twenty-four hours, to reclaim the bags. They were advised that on December 22, at 12:25 A.M. (about six hours after they were checked), they were released to a Mr. Green, who had arrived stating he had lost his claim checks. In accordance with standard procedure, the gentleman was permitted entry to identify his bags. The attendant opened the bags with the key furnished by Green, who correctly identified articles in the bag, including a Leica camera. Upon signing a receipt, he was given the bags—a not uncommon occurrence. The attendant, Adam, who had given Gimpel his bags, was not on duty at the time so arrangements were made to interview him the next day while on duty.

When the FBI interrogated Colepaugh on the early morning of the twenty-seventh, they asked a lot of questions about Gimpel: his appearance, places he frequented, where he might go, idiosyncracies, and any clues that might help to find him. In the course of this, Colepaugh said that Gimpel did not carry a wallet but kept his larger bills in a roll in his pant pocket and had a habit of stuffing smaller bills in the breast pocket of his suit coat. He frequented the better steak houses and, because he spoke Spanish fluently and lived in Peru, he patronized Spanish restaurants, where he might find friends. He also liked to read Peruvian newspapers and often went to the bookshop and out-of-town newspaper stand located at the foot of the subway stairs of the Times building in Times Square. The FBI established surveillance of the place the next day and had two agents present at all times the store was open. The FBI had samples of Gimpel's handwriting and began checking practically all hotels in New York City, as well as contacting ticket agents for trains and planes to watch for registration in the name of Gimpel or Edward Green. On the twenty-seventh, when checking the George Washington Hotel, at Lexington and 23rd Street, the agent found that Edward Green had registered there on December 22 at 4:02 P.M. without baggage (this was the afternoon of the day he recovered the bags at Grand Central Station), paid in advance, and left the next day.

On December 30, agents Gillies and Nelson were on duty at the newsstand. At 8:55 P.M. a man answering Green's description entered (the agents signaled each other and paid close attention to his activities), began examining foreign newspapers, then bought the paperback Penguin edition of *Russia* and proceeded to the cashier to pay. He reached beneath his overcoat and took a bill out of his breast coat pocket and gave it to the cashier. When he started to depart, on signal, agent Nelson preceded him and Gillies followed close behind to the stairway landing outside the entrance to the store. The agents stopped Green, identified themselves, and asked him his name. When he hesitated, they told him it was a routine check, and he responded "Green." He was then told to step inside the store and was led into a back room, not observable by the public, where he produced his forged identification papers, was notified he was being detained, and then was handcuffed to agent Nelson. The New York office was notified, and at 9:35 P.M. three additional agents arrived. Gimpel told them he had been staying at the Pennsylvania Hotel since December 22, where he had registered under the name of Collins. Gimpel was told of his right not to talk and that anything he said would be used against him. Gimpel said he had intended to check out of the hotel about Monday, January 1, 1945, and had thought of going back to Lima, Peru, where his wife and two children were, but getting to South America was difficult. They got in an FBI car and, with Gimpel's permission, checked him out of his room at the Pennsylvania Hotel, and took his bags and everything to the FBI headquarters.

Upon the apprehension of Colepaugh on December 26, it was determined that proper jurisdiction lay with the military authorities. He was transferred to the U.S. Army, Office of the Judge Advocate General, New York Port of Embarkation, headquartered at Governors Island, New York City. Gimpel was likewise turned over to the military after his apprehension.

In preparation for the trial, the FBI conducted a thorough investigation that included lengthy statements made by the very cooperative prisoners and interviews with hotel personnel—desk clerks, bellboys, chambermaids, et cetera—of all places at which they stayed; clerks in stores where they made purchases; the taxicab driver in Ellsworth, Maine; and people whom they met at bars or other places.

Erich Gimpel was born on March 25, 1910, in Germany. He was employed in South America from 1935 to 1942 by Telefunken, the German Radio

Corporation. He was stationed mostly in Lima, Peru, but traveled around extensively until the outbreak of war in 1942, when he was interned, brought to the United States in July, and repatriated to Germany. He arrived on August 1, 1942. He was employed by the German Foreign Office as a courier to Madrid, because he spoke Spanish fluently. He also designed and built shortwave transmitters and spent a year and a half studying radio high frequencies. He could not enter the German army because of the provisions of the agreement between the United States and Germany regulating the exchange of internees. He translated technical books and news articles obtained from foreign countries, mostly aeronautical research. Under the supervision of the SS, he also investigated repatriated Germans and other assigned matters. According to Colepaugh, he investigated a German countess who had made derogatory remarks about the government and who was executed the day after his report was filed. The same thing happened to a German who had been in England and returned to Germany and was suspected of being a spy.

Gimpel was approached by the SS forces, which operated under Himmler independent of the German Military High Command, to go to the United States to find out about the political situation. Gimpel didn't want to go unless he could stay in the United States. The SS officer wasn't happy about Gimpel's attitude and said that if he were in the army he could be compelled to go, but because he was a repatriate and couldn't serve in the army, he would have to go voluntarily. Gimpel felt he had no choice but to do what they wanted. In July 1944 he was sent to an espionage school in The Hague, where he first met Colepaugh. Gimpel sought Colepaugh's help with his English, which was not good. All of the students and the instructors were given new assumed names. The school taught espionage activities—politics, explosives, firearms, photography, microphotography, and investigation. Gimpel thought Colepaugh would be a desirable companion because of his fluent English. Colepaugh wasn't exactly happy about the assignment but felt trapped with no options.

William Curtis Colepaugh was born on March 25, 1918, in Niantic, Connecticut to William Colepaugh, a plumber, who died in 1927, and Havel Lina Colepaugh (née Schmidt), born at sea en route to the United States. Her parents were German. Colepaugh attended schools in Niantic and New London, then attended the Admiral Farragut Academy (a maritime training school) in New Jersey. He graduated in 1938, then entered Massachusetts Institute of Technology, from which he withdrew in 1940 because of scholastic difficulties.

While at MIT, he met at the Hofbrau House on Stanhope Street the captain and chief officer of the *Pauline Frederick*, a German tanker interned in Boston. He visited the ship and got a job working on her as a deckhand in the summer of 1940. He also met the secretary to the German consulate, visited the consulate on a number of occasions, and met Dr. Scholz, the German consul. Dr. Scholz, having become well acquainted with Colepaugh, in May 1941 asked him to ship on the *Reynolds*, a British ship bound from Halifax to Scotland. Colepaugh was to observe the convoys and the ships protecting the convoys and report to him on his return to Boston. Colepaugh attempted to do this, but the consulate had been closed and Dr. Scholz returned to Germany.

During 1941 and 1942, Colepaugh worked on various ships as deckhand, motorman, oiler, wiper, and mess boy. These trips were to Buenos Aires, South America, from New York City, Venezuela, and Philadelphia. While in Buenos Aires, he visited the German consulate and asked to go to Germany, but the consul said he had no way to arrange such a trip. In August 1942, he was picked up by the FBI for draft delinquency (failing to report a change of address) and, for lack of bail, spent several weeks in jail. He was told that he had to join the military. He joined the Navy and spent four months at the Great Lakes Training Center. He was honorably discharged in early 1943 when German propaganda was found at his home in Niantic. He worked for the Waltham Watch Company in Massachusetts as a designer, engineer, and draftsman until June 1943, when he went into the poultry business. At the end of the year, he joined the crew of the *Gripsholm*, sailing for Lisbon; there he jumped ship in the latter part of February 1944. During his school days and thereafter, Colepaugh had become dissatisfied with conditions in the United States and developed a great admiration for the German army as a military machine. He had no interest in the Nazis. He planned to go to Germany, join the German army, remain in Germany after the war, and engage in private business as a shipbuilder.

Colepaugh went to the German consulate in Lisbon, and told the consul he wanted to go to Germany and join the German army, which the German consul in Boston had said was all right. He was advised to return in a couple of days. He was sent with a group of Germans being repatriated by train to Biarritz, France, just over the border, where he was met by a Dr. Lange, a go-between between the army and the SS. Next, he went to Saarbruecken, arriving on March 4. He stayed until March 20. He was in the charge of a member of the Gestapo and was put on the train for Berlin. There he was met by Dr. Lange, who turned him over to Sergeant Denker, a noncom in the SS, who stayed with him for the next three months interrogating him about his attitude toward the United States and Germany, about conditions in the United States and other matters. At the end of June, Colepaugh was interviewed by a colonel in the SS who told him, through an interpreter, that he was going into the SS, but he did not mention leaving the country. Then he was sent to the spy school at Den Haag in Holland for eight weeks of training. He was told that it might be necessary to go out of the country and that he might have to go behind enemy lines. His hope of joining the German army was apparently gone. Here he first met Erich Gimpel. Colepaugh was given the name of William Collier and furnished identification papers with his picture. Colepaugh and Gimpel wound up in Berlin, where they had a week and a half of training with a Leica camera, developing and printing, and then to Dresden to study microphotography and microdots—espionage tools. Colepaugh accompanied Gimpel to his home in Halle for a social visit and then they had training in the use of secret ink. On September 22, 1944, Colepaugh and Gimpel, accompanied by two SS officers, went to Kiel; on the twenty-fourth they boarded U-1230 with forged identification papers, money, clothes, and instructions and departed for Norway.

# Lore

*The trial was before a military court-martial and was held at the New York Port of Embarkation headquarters on Governors Island in New York harbor in 1944. The charge was espionage by persons of a belligerent nationality during time of war. The verdict was guilty. The sentence against Hans was only twenty years in prison, because of his cooperation with the investigative and prosecution personnel. The sentence against Max was capital punishment by hanging in accordance with the provisions of the U.S. Code. The presiding officer, after announcing the verdict and sentence, asked Max if he had anything to say. Max indicated that the trial had been eminently fair and that he had no complaints about his treatment. In fact he said that when he had been arrested in Times Square some months before, he never thought that he would see the light of the next day. Certainly he would not have, if this had occurred in Germany. He said that he had one request to make. The presiding officer asked what it was. Max responded, "I am an officer of the German army and in my country when an officer is to suffer capital punishment, he is shot. I, therefore, request that I be shot, rather than hanged." The presiding officer responded, "I am sorry to advise you that in this country, the military code of justice, which has been duly adopted by our legislative branch of government, provides that all capital punishment shall be carried out by hanging. Your request is denied. Is there anything else?" "No, sir," Max responded with a click of his heels. The trial was ended.*

*On the day appointed for the execution, which was scheduled for seven in the morning, Max was awakened about four by a visit from the chaplain, who inquired whether there was anything he could do. Max left some letters to be mailed to his wife and family in Germany after the war ended. Then they discussed burial arrangements, and the chaplain left. A breakfast of his choice was served in his cell. He showered, shaved, dressed in clean clothes, and waited. An orderly came to explain the procedure that would be followed. Then he waited again. Finally, he heard the escort squad marching up the corridor to his cell. The sergeant in charge said, "Your time has come." Max responded, "I am ready." The little group marched down corridors to the main portal; its massive doors were open onto the small paved square on Governors Island with the New York skyscrapers towering in the background. Max could see the light color of the raw wood of the recently erected platform and hear the muffled roll of military drums. The heavy army boots of the marching squad made a dull thump, thump as the group descended the granite steps and crossed the cobblestone square to the waiting gallows.*

# Factual

According to General Orders No. 52 issued by the War Department in Washington by order of the secretary of war, G. C. Marshall, chief of staff, and signed by Norman B. Nussbaum, adjutant general, dated 7 July 1945, a military commission was convened at Governors Island, New York, from February 6 to 14, inclusive, 1945. Colonel Clinton J. Harrold was president.

William Curtis Colepaugh and Erich Gimpel were arraigned and tried on three charges relating to espionage, to which they pleaded "Not Guilty." The findings of all Charges and Specifications was "Guilty" and the Sentence, as to each accused, "To be hanged by the neck until dead." The sentences were adjudged on 14 February 1945.

> The sentences having been approved by the Convening Authority and record of trial forwarded for action by the President, under Article 501/2 the following are his orders thereon:
> In the foregoing case of William Curtis Colepaugh, an American citizen, and Erich Gimpel, a German, the sentence as to each is confirmed, but the sentence as to the accused Colepaugh is commuted to confinement at hard labor for the term of his natural life. As thus modified the sentence as to each accused will be carried into execution. The sentence as to the accused Gimpel will be carried into execution under the direction of and at a time and place to be designated by the Commanding General, Second Service Command, Army Service Forces.
> Harry S Truman
> The White House
> May 15, 1945

Upon further consideration the president amended the foregoing orders as follows:

> In the foregoing case of Erich Gimpel the sentence to death hereto confirmed is hereby commuted to confinement at hard labor for the term of his natural life. As thus modified the sentence will be carried into execution.
> Harry S Truman
> The White House
> June 13, 1945

> The United States Penitentiary, Leavenworth, Kansas, is designated as the place of confinement for each accused.

The following was sent on a McLane law firm letterhead.

> July 22, 1994
> Office of the Clerk of Court
> US Army Legal Services Agency
> 5611 Columbia Pike
> Falls Church, VA, 22041-5013
> ATTN. Mary Dennis

Re: *William Curtis Colepaugh and Erich Gimpel*

Dear Ms. Dennis:

In 1944, my senior law partner, Kenneth F. Graf (now deceased), served in the Office of the Judge Advocate General and was stationed at the New York Port of Embarkation, Governors Island, New York City. While there, he participated in the trial team, headed by Mr. Justice Tom Clark (later appointed to the Court) which tried two spies, whose names appear above, who landed from a German submarine off the coast of Maine in late November 1944 and were apprehended within a month in New York City. They were tried by a military court in February 1945, found guilty on all counts and were sentenced to be hanged by the neck until dead. However President Truman, on May 15th, commuted the sentence of Colepaugh, an American citizen, to confinement at hard labor for the term of his natural life and on June 13th similarly commuted the sentence of Erich Gimpel. The United States Penitentiary, Leavenworth, Kansas, was designated as the place of confinement.

My interest in this matter derives from a history I am writing of this Law Firm which was founded in 1919 by my father. I am including in the history as an appendix an account of the "Spy Case" in which Ken Graf participated. My story now ends with the commutation of the sentences by President Truman. I would like to write an ending — What happened to the two spies? Are they dead or alive? Did they serve out their sentences? Were they pardoned and, if so, by whom and for what reason? Is their present whereabouts known?

Any information you can furnish would be greatly appreciated. If you are unable to answer my question, can you direct me to where I might be able to obtain the answers. Many thanks for your assistance.

Very truly yours
John R. McLane, Jr.


Department of the Army
United States Army Judiciary
Falls Church, VA
September 14, 1994


Dear Mr. McLane:

This replies to your letter concerning the trial by military commission of William Colepaugh and Erich Gimpel, U.S. Army Judiciary Docket Number CM 276026. . . .

According to the Archives Office at the Bureau of Prisons, Colepaugh served part of his sentence at Leavenworth, Kansas, and was transferred to Lewisburg, Pennsylvania. He ultimately served fifteen years and was released on parole May 10, 1960. Gimpel was confined at Alcatraz, then at Atlanta, served a total of ten years and was paroled to deportation and transferred to Immigration Naturalization Service in 1955. . . .

Also, it may be of assistance to you in your research to know that a copy of this record was recently purchased by Mason Philip Smith, who is doing research on this topic. His address is. . . . Cape Elizabeth, Maine. . . .

Finally, I am told that Gimpel wrote a book which was published in German. The English translation of the title might be "I Was a Spy for Germany."

I wish you luck with your research. If this office can be of further assistance, please do not hesitate to contact me. . . .

Sincerely,
Mary B. Dennis
Deputy Clerk of Court

Mason Philip Smith, of Cape Elizabeth, Maine, was contacted by telephone and affirmed that as of early 1994 Colepaugh was living in the United States and Gimpel was living in Germany. Gimpel's book in German contained many inaccuracies and did not add anything to the record, according to Mr. Smith. Mr. Smith is writing a book on the spies and hopes to have it published in about a year.

# Note

1. Mulcahey had received an honorable discharge from the Army for medical reasons—psychopathic personality (read homosexual).

# INDEX